Access® 95

UNLEASHED

Dwayne Gifford et al

SAMS
PUBLISHING

201 West 103rd Street
Indianapolis, IN 46290

To my wife and kids—Iris, Kevin, Monica, and Jason—to my mother and father, and to my mother-in-law. Also, to two people who were very important to me—my father-in-law and my very good friend Marc Neima. They gave me the courage to strive to be better, and both are dearly missed by me and their coworkers. This one's for you.

Copyright © 1996 by Sams Publishing

Trademarks

Publisher and President	Richard K. Swadley
Acquisitions Manager	Greg Wiegand
Development Manager	Dean Miller
Managing Editor	Cindy Morrow
Marketing Manager	Gregg Bushyeager

Acquisitions Editor
Kim Spilker

Development Editor
Michael Watson

Software Development Specialist
Steve Straiger

Production Editor
Gayle L. Johnson

Copy Editors
Cheri Clark, Ryan Rader,
Angie Trzepacz, Joe Williams

Technical Reviewers
Robert Bogue, Chris
Capossela, Mark Dunning,
Angela Murdock, Berry Rogers

Editorial Coordinator
Bill Whitmer

Technical Edit Coordinator
Lynette Quinn

Formatter
Frank Sinclair

Editorial Assistants
Sharon Cox, Andi Richter,
Rhonda Tinch-Mize

Cover Designer
Jason Grisham

Book Designer
Alyssa Yesh

Production Team Supervisor
Brad Chinn

Production
Mary Ann Abramson, Terrie
Deemer, Mike Dietsch, Jason
Hand, George Hanlin, Sonja
Hart, Mike Henry, Louisa
Klucznik, Clint Lahnen,
Kevin Laseau, Paula Lowell,
Laura Robbins, Bobbi
Satterfield, Craig Small,
Laura Smith, SA Springer,
Andrew Stone, Tim Taylor,
Mark Walchle, Susan Van
Ness, Todd Wente

Indexer
Gina Brown

Contents

Part III Queries and SQL

Part IV Access Forms

Part VII Programming in Access

Part X Connectivity

Acknowledgments

It is impossible for only one person to write this type of book. If not for teamwork, this book would have been even more difficult to finish. Many good people helped write this book. I would like to thank my friends for coming together to make this book a success. Those people are Merrill Mayer, James Bettone, Michael Murphy, Rob Newman, Ricardo Birmele, and Ted Williamson.

I would also like to thank my wife, Iris, and my three children, Kevin, Michelle, and Jason, for putting up with me through the completion of this book.

I would also like to thank the team at Sams—Kim, Michael, Gayle, Cheri, Angie, Joe, and Ryan—for being patient and very helpful in the writing of this book.

Special thanks to Labatt Breweries of Canada, especially Eric Borrows, Bill Gipps, Karen Alajica, and fellow workers.

About the Authors

Alison Balter is the president of Marina Consulting Group, a firm based in Thousand Oaks, California. She is an experienced independent trainer and consultant, specializing in Windows applications training and development. During her 12 years in the computer industry, she has trained and consulted with many corporations and government agencies. Balter is a Microsoft Solution Provider and Certified Professional. Recently, she became one of the first professionals in the computer industry to become a Microsoft Certified Solutions Developer. She is the author of more than 50 internationally marketed computer training videos for Keystone Learning Systems, including seven Access 2.0 videos, 10 Access 95 videos, six Visual Basic for Applications videos, and seven Visual FoxPro videos. She travels throughout North America giving training seminars in Microsoft Access, Visual Basic, and Visual FoxPro. Balter is a regular contributing columnist for the *Advisor* magazines as well as other computer publications. She is also a regular on the Access and Visual Basic national speaker circuit. She can be reached via CompuServe at 70372,3707.

Ryan Edward Bailey is a Microsoft Certified Trainer based in Nashville, Tennessee. He develops Access applications for small businesses. In addition to developing customized business solutions, he stays actively involved as a contract instructor for the Athena Computer Learning Center in Nashville, where he teaches the Microsoft Access certification courses. Currently, Bailey is developing applications full-time, along with launching JTR Productions into an Internet project. Bailey can be reached at rebelnet@aol.com or http://www.jtr.com/rebelnet.html.

Chris and Debbie Barnes are programmer/analysts for two Fortune 500 companies—Eli Lilly & Co. and Electronic Data Systems. They have a combined 12 years of experience writing business applications in the areas of finance, engineering, and pharmaceuticals. They also teach about various Windows applications, including Access, at an adult career center.

James Bettone is a software developer for BEST Consulting in Kirkland, Washington. He has been working with Microsoft Visual Basic and Access since their initial releases and has been developing a variety of PC applications for almost 10 years. He is currently developing information systems for Microsoft's Information Technology Group.

Ricardo Birmele is a widely published author of computer books on subjects ranging from desktop publishing and programming languages to applications. His articles reviewing software and hardware have appeared in *BYTE, PC,* and *PC World* magazines. He has also edited a number of computer books on multimedia, database programming, and simple applications.

Craig Eddy is employed by Pipestream Technologies, Inc. as Senior Developer for Contact-Builder, a customer information management and sales force automation tool that runs in either a client/server or desktop environment. He has been involved in computer programming for more than 15 years and has concentrated on Visual Basic, Microsoft Access, and SQL Server applications for the past three years.

Richard Freeman is a freelance technical writer who has designed, written, and edited user manuals, online help systems, and technical documentation for major companies such as Microsoft, Weyerhaeuser, Windmere Real Estate, and the Trane Company. Working under contract for Excell Data Corporation of Bellevue, Washington, Freeman created user documentation and online help for the Microsoft Access Solutions Pack. He also wrote a guide to software asset management for the Microsoft Select program that was distributed to Microsoft's top corporate clients.

Dwayne R. Gifford is employed by Excell Data Corporation as a Systems Analyst for Microsoft. Before that he worked for Labatt Breweries of Canada, where he was a professional trainer in Access, Excel, Visual Basic, and Microsoft Project. He can be reached at a-dwayg@microsoft.com.

Ewan Grantham has been involved with microcomputers since the days of the Apple II and the TRS-80. He now runs an independent consulting firm that specializes in the design and creation of electronic documentation and multimedia presentations. In addition to his programming and writing, he teaches classes on related subjects and publishes an "almost monthly" electronic magazine called *RADIUS*. He can be reached on CompuServe at 74123,2232.

Michael Harding is cofounder and managing partner of VisualAccess Corporation in Charlotte, North Carolina. His firm specializes in building Microsoft Access database systems that integrate with the Microsoft Office suite as well as Windows and Windows NT. He is also the chief developer for the Eclipse Accounting Kit for Access. He is a coauthor of *Inside Microsoft Office Professional* and *Inside Microsoft Access 2.0,* Third Edition, both published by New Riders Publishing. Harding is also a contributing author for *The Visual Guide to Microsoft Access 2.0* from Ventana Press. He has written for several industry magazines and newsletters, including *Access Advisor, Windows Outlook,* and *KeyNotes.* He serves as a judge for the Charlotte Chamber of Commerce Blue Diamond Awards, an annual banquet held to recognize local and regional technological achievements and contributions. Harding is also an organizer of the Piedmont Computer Guild, the Microsoft Access Users Group, the Microsoft Windows Users Group, the Microsoft Office Users Group, and the Microsoft Windows NT Users Group. In addition, he speaks nationally at seminars, trade shows, and training sessions.

Matt Kinney works for Integra Technology International in Bellevue, Washington. He is a graduate of Louisiana State University in Shreveport with a B.S. in computer science. Kinney has been programming computers since 1978, when he began using the original Commodore PET. He specializes in online application development and marketing. He has developed successful applications for Prodigy, America Online, CompuServe, GEnie, and the Internet.

Carmen Knowles has been working with computers for more than 10 years. She is a university graduate in sciences and is now pursuing post-graduate studies, and her main interests lie in the computer world. She is a member of ClubWin, a select group of Windows user support volunteers that is active at various online services. She is interested in helping small businesses and institutions computerize and run their equipment at a minimum cost.

Merrill M. Mayer is a software developer for BEST Consulting in Kirkland, Washington. She has been working with Microsoft Visual Basic and Access for several years, developing a variety of business applications. She is currently a consultant/developer for Microsoft's Information Technology Group.

Alan McConnell is an independent software developer and trainer who specializes in providing business solutions using database programs. He has been working with database languages for more than 12 years and has used Access since it first came out. He has developed numerous applications, vertical market programs, and library routines with Access. His articles regularly appear in Access/Visual Basic *Advisor* magazine. He speaks at user groups and conferences. McConnell can be reached through CompuServe at 71572,131 or through the Internet at acmcconn@ix.netcom.com.

Jude G. Mullaney entered the computer industry in 1989, holding positions in administration, hardware and software technical support, sales, and training. Her software training includes Microsoft products such as Windows, Windows for Workgroups, Windows NT, Access 1.1 and 2.0, Word, Excel, Project, PowerPoint, Publisher, Mail, and Schedule+, as well as Lotus Ami Pro, CorelDRAW!, and GeoWorks Ensemble. In 1994 she founded VisualAccess Corporation, a Microsoft Solutions Provider that defines companies' software needs and develops software for future technologies. VisualAccess's clients include NationsBank, WIX Corporation, First Union National Bank, and Michelin North America, Inc. Mullaney has been the newsletter editor of the Clarion User Group in Charlotte since 1989. She is currently the Vice President and Newsletter Editor for both the Charlotte Area Access Users Group and the Windows User Group in Charlotte. She is a contributing author for *Inside Microsoft Office Professional* from New Riders Publishing and *The Visual Guide to Microsoft Access 2.0* from Ventana Press. She is also a lead author on *Inside Microsoft Access 2.0* from New Riders Publishing.

Michael Murphy has been employed at Microsoft for the past three years and is currently the Production Manager for Licensing and Sales Programs. He has produced tools that are used worldwide by Microsoft customers and employees in support of the licensing business. The applications he has written and supported utilize the full suite of Microsoft products, including Visual Basic, Access, and SQL Server.

Rob Newman has more than 10 years of experience in creating desktop applications. Using languages such as xBASE, PAL, Visual Basic, and Access on the desktop, and RDBMSs such as Informix, SQL Server, and Oracle, he has delivered many successful applications for a wide variety of customers, including the military, health care, banking, and Fortune 500 companies. Currently, Newman is working as a contract consultant developing client/server applications using Access and Visual Basic. He is excited about employing some of Microsoft's new technologies such as RDO (remote data objects) to enhance the current two-tiered design trend.

James J. Townsend is president of Information Strategies, a Microsoft Solution Provider in Washington, D.C. He is certified in Microsoft Access, and he specializes in analysis, systems integration, custom database design and implementation, and training. He has written more than 40 books and articles, including *Introduction to Databases* and *Using Paradox for Windows,* both from Que. He is also a contributor to computer journals, including *Data Based Advisor, Smart Access, The Quick Answer,* and *Dialogue.*

Ted Williamson is a Senior Solutions Architect with Redmond Technology Partners. Although he is new to writing, he has extensive experience in client/server application development.

Introduction

Access 95 is the first 32-bit version of the popular database from Microsoft. Here are some of its many new features:

- Improved data filters
- Enhanced Control Wizards
- Better file exporting
- A new Database window that offers flexibility
- Briefcase replication, which takes advantage of the functionality of the Windows 95 Briefcase
- Performance Analyzer, which optimizes the objects in a database
- Table Analyzer, which shows you how to store related data more efficiently
- New and improved query functions
- New Form and Report Wizards, which let you create a multitable form or report without having to create a query beforehand

Access 95 Unleashed will take you from advanced beginner to expert level as you master this professional database tool. Filled with tips, tricks, and shortcuts, this book reveals the secrets of unleashing the full power of Access 95.

Who Should Read This Book?

This book is designed for users and developers who have worked with Microsoft Access in the past and who have upgraded or are considering upgrading to Access 95. This book quickly covers the basics and new features of Access 95, and then it moves into intermediate and advanced topics such as replication and the Jet engine.

Conventions Used in This Book

This book uses the following conventions:

- Notes, Tips, Cautions, and Warnings appear in gray boxes.
- Menu names are separated from menu options by a vertical bar (|). For example, "File | Open" means "Select the File menu and then choose the Open option."
- All code appears in a monospace font.
- New terms appear in *italic*.

- Placeholders (words that stand for what you actually type) in regular text appear in *italic*.
- Placeholders in code appear in `italic monospace`.
- When a line of code is too long to fit on only one line of this book, it is broken at a convenient place and continued to the next line. The continuation of the line is preceded by a code continuation character (➥). You should type such a line of code as one long line without breaking it.

An Overview of Access 95

PART

Getting Started

1

by Matt Kinney

Positioning Access 95 in the Database Market

A database is an integrated repository of data that can be shared among users. Databases serve two primary purposes: to provide information to users and to capture data about entities and relationships. Access 95 is Microsoft's fantastically successful desktop database product. Every database has software called the Database Management System (DBMS) that controls the storage and retrieval of the data contained in the database. Access 95 uses the relational model in its database management system software. The relational model views all data as groups of tables or relations that consist of a fixed number of columns and rows. Relational Database Management Systems (RDBMSs) are one of the largest segments of the database market, because RDBMSs comprise everything from client/server to database front-ends and desktop RDBMS databases.

The big question is, where does Access 95 fit into the database market? The rage in today's market is the client/server model. Client/server databases use a distributed computing model, in which the database resides on a server or servers and the front-end, which sends high-level requests to be processed by the server, resides on the client system. Access 95 certainly has aspects of the client/server model, such as its single-file approach and inclusion of user permissions to retrieve, edit, and add data to the database. Access 95 can also function as a front-end for other databases through attaching tables from other RDBMSs or importing them into Access 95's proprietary structure. Once they're imported or attached, creating forms, reports, and queries is the same for the attached tables as for Access 95's native format. You can also buy the Access Developer's Toolkit and have a royalty-free runtime version of the Access 95 engine with which to distribute your applications. Because Access 95 presents a nice blend of the features of the three RDBMS models, and because it supports the new functionality that is afforded by the Windows 95 operating system, it certainly deserves consideration as your database development platform.

What's New in Access 95

With the introduction of Windows 95, Microsoft provides an unprecedented upgrade to what is arguably the most popular desktop environment ever. In conjunction with this introduction, Microsoft also released an upgrade to its Microsoft Office suite, which included major enhancements to Access 95. These major enhancements and features are directed toward end users and developers alike. The first noticeable new feature is the new Windows 95-compliant interface. The features of the interface that encompass the Windows 95 look and feel are not covered here, except where they introduce a new feature due to the Windows 95 functionality. The following sections describe features that apply to the end user and developer; however, the majority of new features are aimed toward developers, so that is where the focus lies.

32-Bit Implementation

One of the features that might not be immediately apparent to users is the fact that Access 95 has a 32-bit engine—at least it might not be apparent to the users until they experience the speed that 32-bit Access provides. Also included is a 32-bit Open Database Connectivity driver (ODBC) that enables developers to use the Access 95 engine via ODBC. An especially beneficial element of this implementation is that future versions of Visual Basic, starting with version 4, will be able to use the 32-bit Access engine, thus giving developers a marked speed improvement over the 16-bit version of the same application.

The Database Window

The familiar Database window, which is what many users first work with in Access, has been greatly enhanced to provide more flexibility and functionality. You can now hide objects you don't want others to see, automatically create a shortcut to a database object, and drag and drop data to Microsoft Excel or Microsoft Word. You can also display icons for database objects in three different views—List, Details, and Large or Small Icons—to see more information about an object, such as its creation date or a description. Figure 1.1 shows the Database window in Details view.

FIGURE 1.1.

The maximized Database window in Details view.

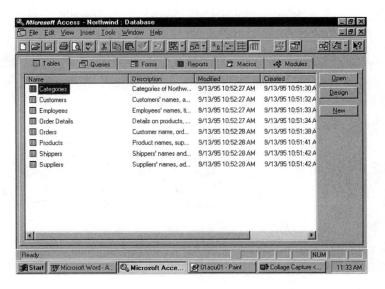

Briefcase Replication

One of the most significant new features in Access 95 is the briefcase replication functionality. Briefcase replication enables the creation of replicas, or "special copies" of a database to distribute to users in different locations so that they can work on their copy of the database independently of other users. Replicas allow for data synchronization so that all the replicas can be put together into a single entity, incorporating all the changes that have been introduced in the individual user's copies.

Briefcase replication requires that Briefcase be installed on your computer. Briefcase is installed as part of the Typical setup option in Access 95. Synchronization with another replica is as simple as selecting the database file in Briefcase and then selecting Briefcase | Update Selection in Windows 95. Note, however, that once you convert a nonreplicable database into a replicable database, there is no going back—you can't convert it back to a nonreplicable database.

Performance Analyzer

The Performance Analyzer is a feature that assists not only the developer, but the end user as well. Performance Analyzer optimizes any or all of the objects in a database. When the analysis is complete, three kinds of performance suggestions (such as query optimizations or form control changes) are displayed: Recommendations, Suggestions, and Ideas. When you click an item in this list, information about the optimization is presented below the list. Access 95 can perform Recommended and Suggested optimizations for you, but Idea optimizations must be performed manually. Idea optimizations, however, present a list of instructions to follow in the Analysis Notes section, similar to a cue card (see Figure 1.2). Performance Analyzer does not provide suggestions on how to improve the system you are running Access 95 on or how to improve Access performance itself.

FIGURE 1.2.

The Performance Analyzer results dialog box.

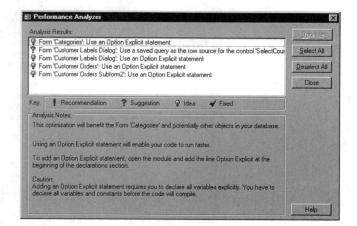

The Database Splitter

The Database Splitter Wizard splits a database into two files—one that contains the tables, or the back-end component, and one that contains the queries, reports, forms, and other Access objects, or the front-end component. This enables an administrator to distribute the front-end files to users while keeping a single source of data on the network. This results in less overhead and traffic on the network, because the network is used only to retrieve or modify data rather than respond to a user's request to go to another form or report. This results in a significant performance increase in a multiuser environment. Another big advantage for the Access 95 developer is the fact that splitting the database allows for continuous development of forms, reports, and other front-end objects while not disturbing the data in the back-end component.

The Table Analyzer

The Table Analyzer, shown in Figure 1.3, is used to analyze the table objects in the database and normalize the data. Normalization is the process of taking duplicate information in one or more fields and splitting it into related tables to store the data more efficiently. Normalization is defined by a set of five rules, the first three of which were defined by Dr. E. F. Cobb and which are used to design relational databases. Access 95 can either normalize the tables you specify or normalize your table automatically. The Table Analyzer is especially useful if you're importing a large flat-file database into Access 95, because normalizing the database enables you to take advantage of relational database features. Also included in the Table Analyzer is the ability to create a query to view the information from the split tables in a single datasheet. This saves the user or developer from having to create this query after normalization and should make it easier to convert any reports or forms to use the new normalized tables.

FIGURE 1.3.

The Table Analyzer Wizard.

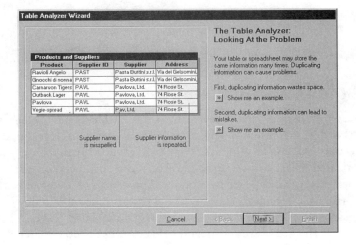

Table Design

Table design is greatly enhanced under Access 95, with new features that make designing tables easier and much more powerful. A table can now be created by entering data in a blank datasheet. When the datasheet is saved, Access 95 evaluates the data entered and creates what it thinks are the correct field types and formats. It also deletes any unused columns. You can also rename the fields (columns) you will be using by double-clicking the column and typing in a name for the column. Note that all column names must follow Access 95 object-naming rules. The data entered should be of a consistent format to enable Access 95 to create an appropriate data type and display format. You can then go to the Design view and customize the table definition further, as well as define validation rules.

Another significant enhancement to table design is the Lookup Wizard, shown in Figure 1.4. The Lookup Wizard creates a field that displays a list of values that are looked up from another table. The Lookup Wizard can also be used to create a list of user-defined values. A major benefit of this approach is that the field created by the Lookup Wizard is automatically added to any query that includes the field. In other words, a field created with the Lookup Wizard needs to be created only once, whereas other combo box or list box fields must be created repeatedly.

FIGURE 1.4.

The Lookup Wizard.

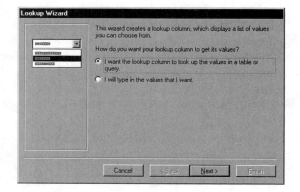

Data Manipulation

Access 95 includes many new features that enable the user to put data from the database into other documents more easily, as well as spell checking, error correcting, and new ways to filter records. Because of Windows 95's drag-and-drop functionality, you can now select data from a datasheet and drag it into an Excel or Word document, or save it as a rich-text format document that can be opened by most word processors or used to create a Windows Help file. (See Chapter 2, "Components of Access 95," for more on Windows Help files.) This allows for easier presentation and analysis of data by the end user. Access 95 has the ability to automatically spell-check text and memo fields, because it now shares the spell-checking engine of Microsoft Office 95. Therefore, any changes made or words added to the spell-check dictionary in Access 95 will also show up in all Microsoft Office 95 applications. It also capitalizes words such as days of the week automatically. Although this feature results in extra overhead as far as resource usage, it's well worth it to have your data free of typographical errors.

Two new record filtering techniques have also been introduced in Access 95. Filtering is the process of specifying parameters so that only a subset of the entire recordset is displayed. You can now filter by selection and filter by form. Once a filter is created using these methods, you can elect to save the filter as a query, thus bypassing the query design process altogether. Access 95 also enables you to do new things with filters, such as base a new form or report on filtered data, save a filter with a report, form, or table, save a filter sort order, apply filters automatically, and apply a filter to a subform. Note that a saved filter does not appear as a separate object in the Database window unless it is saved as a query.

With Filter By Selection, you specify which records you want to work with by highlighting or selecting them directly on the form or datasheet. Once a subset is selected, you can create another subset of the subset to narrow the scope of records even further. This is by far the easiest way for an end user to create a filter with the least amount of effort and hassle.

Filter By Form enables users to enter the value or values for the records they're searching for. The value can be typed in or chosen from a list in the fields. This method is more similar to the query design grid and is probably more familiar to experienced Access users.

Query Features

Access 95 includes several new features that make querying easier and more efficient. The new Simple Query Wizard enables you to create a Select query (a query that returns data based on specified parameters) for one or more tables. It also allows for the creation of calculations such as sums, counts, totals, and averages on a table or tables. The filter characteristics discussed earlier can now equally apply to a query's Datasheet view to narrow the focus even further in the query's results. Also, you can now sort a query's records on demand from the datasheet in ascending or descending order. In previous versions of Access, you could specify a sort order only in the Query Design window.

In Access 2.0, Microsoft introduced the feature of enforcing referential and domain integrity at the table level, so the developer no longer had to write code to enforce these rules for every update performed on the data. Access would automatically create joins (relationships between a field in one table or query to a field in another table or query) in Query Design view if the fields had the same name and data type and a relationship wasn't already defined between the fields. A join tells Access how the data is related. In Access 95, this feature, called AutoJoin, can be turned off, so automatic joining does not occur; however, you can still create joins yourself. Figure 1.5 shows the Table/Queries Options dialog with Enable AutoJoin turned on.

FIGURE 1.5.

The Tables/Queries
Options dialog with
Enable AutoJoin checked.

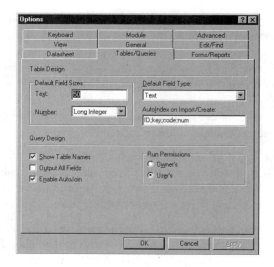

Form and Report Design

It's now easier than ever to create great-looking forms and reports in Access 95. The new Form
and Report Wizards are greatly enhanced, and a new Subform/Subreport Wizard has been added.
You can also create a report or form based on a query you've already filtered so that the new
form or report inherits the filter from the query. The appearance of a form or report can be
greatly enhanced with the new AutoFormatting capability, the addition of background pictures, and the new Formatting toolbar. The creation and formatting of controls, special effects, and screen tips also make the creation of top-quality forms a breeze. New drag-and-drop
object support, as well as support for the new OCX custom controls, is also added.

The new Form and Report Wizards enable you to create a multiple-table form or report without having to create a query beforehand. The Form Wizard, shown in Figure 1.6, enables you
to effortlessly create a form linked to another form, a form with a subform, or a form with two
subforms. Access 95 presents a list of options based on the data you specify for the form. The
Report Wizard, shown in Figure 1.7, can just as easily create reports that summarize, group, or
total data. If you have difficulty linking a subform to its main form, or a subreport to its main
report, simply use the Subform/Subreport Field Linker function of the new Subform/Subreport
Wizard. As with all Access Wizards, tell it what you want to do, and the Wizard will magically
do your bidding.

Form and report appearance have been enhanced as well. If you don't like the way your report
or form looks, simply use the AutoFormat function to change the look of your entire report or
selected aspects of it. Access 95 also provides a selection of predefined form and report formats
and templates that you can use as is or customize. You can also create your own predefined

formats for future use or distribution. You can now have a background picture or logo on your form or report by simply entering the picture's filename for the `Picture` property of the form or report. To add special effects or color, you can use the new Formatting toolbar, which makes many formatting tasks available.

FIGURE 1.6.

The Form Wizard—field selection.

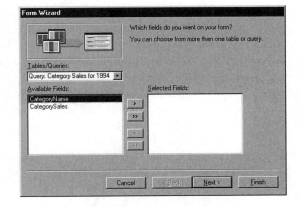

FIGURE 1.7.

The Report Wizard—grouping selection.

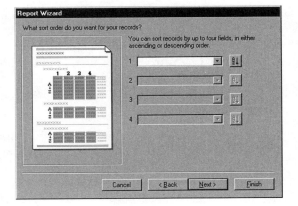

Control creation and appearance can also enhance the appearance and feel of your forms and reports. Access can now create a default control for the field you drag from the field list in the Field List window. If you use the Form or Report Wizard, Access 95 automatically creates the correct control for you on the form or report. You can now also copy a format from one control to another using the Format Painter. New special effects have been added so that you can create etched, shadowed, and chiseled effects as well as the other special effects of flat, raised, and sunken. Your Access 95 forms and reports can now have the screen tips functionality as well. Simply enter the message you want to display in the `ControlTip` property. When the user moves the mouse pointer over the control, your tip appears!

System Requirements for Access 95

First and foremost, Access 95 requires Windows 95 or Windows NT 3.51 build 1057 or later. It won't run on any version Windows 3.x, even if the Windows 32s extensions are installed, nor will it run on OS/2. Therefore, you should meet all the requirements necessary to run Windows 95 or Windows NT 3.51. Access 95 also requires 6 MB of RAM, but with just that amount, performance will be quite unsatisfactory at best and unacceptable at worst. 8 MB of RAM is a bare minimum for a practical recommendation, but 16 MB is more appropriate, especially if you're going to do serious development or use large applications that are OLE- and multimedia-intensive. The amount of disk space required varies by what you have installed with the Access 95 system, such as Wizards, builders, and add-ins, but a minimum of 30 to 40 MB should be sufficient, because a typical developer's setup takes 39 MB. Developers should definitely consider as much RAM and hard drive space as they can afford, as well as a large monitor (17 inches or larger). The larger monitor is especially useful for working at higher resolutions, because you can see the maximum number of tables and their relationships.

The Workgroup Concept

The modern work environment necessitates working with other people, either in your own company or with your customers. A common way to accomplish this in the information age is the network. Networks are built for two main purposes: sharing resources and sharing information. A workgroup is a way of grouping users on a network to make the exchange of information among these users easier by having the networked computers take care of some of the details. For example, the computers can keep track of a workgroup's schedule, send and receive e-mail, and share files or printers.

Databases have become a common way to store and share information over a network. That's because all the users access the data stored in the database from a single data source, and changes can be propagated to everyone else using the database. A complete database system should include features to make this propagation easy, as well as administer access to data and data security features.

Access 95 is designed to be used effectively in a workgroup environment and includes many features to make the implementation of the sharing of files among users a painless process. Some of these features were discussed earlier, such as Briefcase Replication and the Database Splitter Wizard. Access 95 also includes features to maintain the balance between the user's demand for speed and ready access to data, as well as ease of administration for the database administrator. The administrator can combine the security features of Access 95 with those of the network operating system to maintain control over who has access to your Access 95 application and what they are allowed to do to the data stored in it.

The workgroup security process can be a major concern for the database administrator, and Access 95 has several tools to make this process easier. Access 95 has two ways to secure a database—with a database password and with user-level security. The simplest manner of security is using a password for a database. The password is required to open the database and is encrypted in the database file. To password-protect a database file, select Tools | Security | Set Database Password.

> **NOTE**
>
> Do not use a database password if the database is being replicated, because replicas can't be synchronized if they have a password.

A more comprehensive method of security is user- and group-level security. With this option, the administrator can set permissions and access to certain objects in the database for a certain user or group of users. For example, a user can have read-only privileges on a table but full rights on another. Permissions affect how a user or group of users can interact with objects in the database. The easiest way to implement user-level security is with the Security Wizard, which you can access by selecting Tools | Security.

Summary

This chapter provided some insight as to where Microsoft is positioning Access 95 in the database market and gave reasons for this positioning. Although it's impossible to say how successful this positioning has been, sales of earlier versions of Access give an overwhelming indication that it has been a successful stance for Microsoft. This chapter also introduced many of the new features of Access 95 and discussed several of the improvements to existing features. Improvements to existing features alone should give you a reason to upgrade, not to mention the new features that make Access 95 one of the most compelling upgrades or new product purchases you can make.

Components of Access 95

2

by Matt Kinney

IN THIS CHAPTER

What's New

A major component of Access 95 is the new Windows 95-compliant interface. Because this is such a major part of Access 95, it would be wise to examine a few key features of Windows 95 to better understand all the benefits it provides to the Access 95 user. The most immediate changes you will notice are the absence of the Program Manager and an appearance similar to Macintosh and OS/2, which provides for a very friendly user interface. One of the main methods of interaction is the Task Bar, which contains the Start button, where many of your Windows 95 experiences begin (see Figure 2.1). The Start button reveals a set of cascading menus whose selections represent the programs previously available in program groups. This simple set of menus completely replaces the Program Manager and is very intuitive from the start.

FIGURE 2.1.

The Windows 95 desktop.

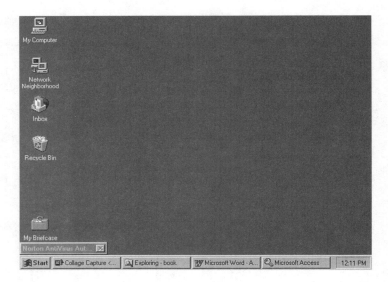

A major change in Windows 95 is the change from the directory to a folder metaphor. Windows 95 no longer uses the concept of a directory; it now uses the notion of folders. Folders are containers that can hold other folders, files, or applications. Folders can be displayed in different views—Large Icons, Small Icons, Details, or List, depending on which option you select. The folder metaphor is also used to represent your system. After installation, three folders are used to represent your system: My Computer, Network Neighborhood, and Microsoft Exchange if you install it. You can explore these folders just as you would any other folder. These folders can contain not only other folders, files, and applications, but also the devices available, such as CD-ROM drives. Therefore, working with any of the available resources on your computer is a matter of manipulating folders and the icons they contain.

Another way in which Windows 95 distances itself from the directory concept is through the use of shortcuts. Shortcuts are represented by specialized icons that serve as aliases or shortcuts to files and applications. Shortcuts provide a way to build links to folders, applications, files, and documents. For example, you could create a shortcut to your Access 95 database and have it directly on your desktop, thus enabling you to click the shortcut icon and have Access 95 automatically start and load your database. The benefit of this approach is that you no longer have to think about which application to open, but only which documents you need to use. Windows 95 takes care of the details of managing the application links to the documents for you.

As you explore further, you will find that the use of the mouse has also changed. You will be double-clicking much less in Windows 95, because the Start menu eliminates most of the need for double-clicking. Anything you used to do with a double-click can now be done with a series of single-clicks in most cases. Another feature that is now standard in Windows 95 is the use of the right mouse button. If you right-click a screen object such as an icon, a floating menu appears with a list of choices. Not all screen objects have an associated menu, but most icons and shortcuts do. The user can also customize these choices using the Registry Editor; however, I don't recommend that you do so until you're familiar with Windows 95 and the System Registry. In a mail-enabled environment, one of the greatest features of the right-click is the capability to Send To automatically. This means that you can right-click an icon or shortcut and e-mail it to a colleague or friend, saving you the trouble of attaching objects to an e-mail message.

Another new concept in Windows 95 is the Explorer. The Explorer replaces the File Manager from Windows 3.x. It provides a tree-style view of your computer (including network paths and drives) and the files and resources it can use, as shown in Figure 2.2. This view provides several advantages over the File Manager: it provides access to every file storage device on your system, and it provides access to all icons on the desktop, which is the highest-level folder in the system. The Explorer is not only a file management system but also a complete control center for your computer. The Explorer can manipulate and control any resource that is represented by a folder or icon in the Windows 95 system. The Explorer is discussed in greater detail later in this chapter.

Also included in Windows 95 is Microsoft Exchange. Exchange is the Windows 95 mail, fax, and messaging center component. It can even control all your online mail, such as Internet, CompuServe, and Microsoft Network. You can directly receive messages in your Microsoft Exchange mailbox from these sources or a standard network e-mail connection from within your company or organization. Exchange provides Inbox, Outbox, Sent Items, and Deleted Items folders, as shown in Figure 2.3, all of which are extensible and can be customized. The Microsoft fax software also resides in Exchange, thus keeping track of addresses, phone numbers, and other details that At Work Fax previously did.

Windows 95 includes a major overhaul of the Help System. The Help system has new features, a new model that makes it easier for users to find help, and more focus on "how" rather than "what" or "why." These major changes and others in the Windows Help concept are discussed in the next section.

FIGURE 2.2.

The Explorer.

FIGURE 2.3.

Microsoft Exchange.

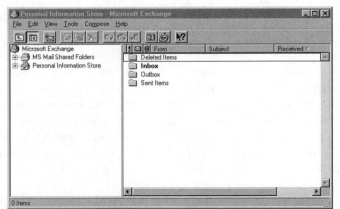

Getting Help

Getting help in Access 95 couldn't be easier or more intuitive for the user and developer alike. No longer do you have to dig and search for answers in a help system that is tedious and frustrating. Access 95 provides the standard Access Help topics, as well as the new Answer Wizard, which enables you to ask how to do something in plain language. You can also get help from the Help system by clicking the Help button on the tool bar, which changes the mouse pointer to an arrow with a question mark, or by positioning the mouse pointer over an object and clicking. The Access 95 Help system is based on the new Windows 95 Help system, which is explored in detail next.

The Windows 95 Help System

Windows 95 adopts a much more simple and direct approach to online Help. The entire Help system follows a new model that has the following new features:

- Help is always available to the user via the Start menu.
- Cue cards keep a procedure or list of instructions visible until you close it.
- Context sensitivity has been improved. Help for an individual field is for that field and not the entire dialog box.
- Help topics are short and focused on procedures. The text is more direct and focused on the completion of the task for which you need help. Shortcuts can be embedded in Help to take you directly to the screen that will complete the task at hand.
- Pop-up topics appear when the user right-clicks a program object.
- More keywords are provided for indexing topics, while cross-referencing is kept to a minimum to reduce complexity.

The Help system is now task-centric, meaning that the Help focuses on how to complete a task or how to get the user to his goal rather than giving a broad description of the topic.

The Contents page of the Help Topics dialog box, shown in Figure 2.4, is very similar to a library. All the major topics are grouped in a "book" that can be opened into further "chapters." These chapters can, in turn, contain other chapters or topics related to that chapter. A book can merely contain a single topic and no chapters at all. A topic is generally a document that the user can read or a procedure list that can be used to complete a certain task.

FIGURE 2.4.

The Contents page of the Help Topics dialog box.

The Index page of the Help Topics dialog box, shown in Figure 2.5, is a vastly improved version of the Search dialog box from Windows 3.1 Help. You can more efficiently scroll through keywords to locate information, and the indexing of topics is more thorough due to the inclusion of more keywords.

FIGURE 2.5.

The Index page of the Help Topics dialog box.

The Find page of the Help Topics dialog box, shown in Figure 2.6, provides an even better way to search for a Help topic. You can enter a word or group of words, and Help searches the Find database for words that match what you typed. You can then click a word or phrase in the list to narrow your search even further and finally select the topic in the lower window and read it.

FIGURE 2.6.

The Find page of the Help Topics dialog box.

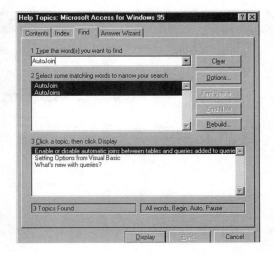

Access Help

Access 95's Help system is very complete and thorough. Everything is logically organized and easy to find—a good side benefit of Access 95's following the new 95 Help system standard. One of the features of Access 95 that is not standard to the Windows 95 Help System is the Answer Wizard. You enter a task in the Answer Wizard, and it returns a list of topics for you to peruse. In Figure 2.7, I wanted to know how to print more than one copy at a time. The Answer Wizard searched the topics and returned topics that were relevant to the inquiry.

FIGURE 2.7.

The Answer Wizard page of the Help Topics window.

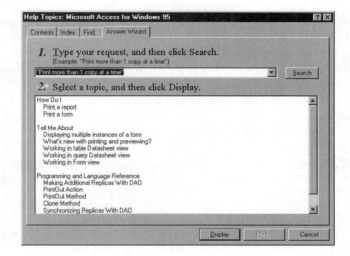

The Answer Wizard provides several types of help. The first section it returns is called "How Do I," which contains topics that are procedure lists to accomplish a specific task. These topics provide step-by-step solutions to a problem that relates to the searched-for item. The next section is titled "Tell Me About," which contains explanations and visual answers related to the topic searched for. "Tell Me About" is generally broader in scope and deals more with the conceptual level than the procedural or how-to level. The last level is "Programming and Language Reference," which contains programming information related to Access and Visual Basic for Applications (VBA). This section is invaluable to the developer, because it is a veritable online programming manual. Not every topic contains all of these types of help; only the valid types are shown.

Other ways to get help in Access 95 include the ToolTips, which are the boxes that pop up when you place the mouse pointer over a screen object, and context-sensitive Help. To access context-sensitive Help, when a field has focus in a dialog box or screen, press F1, and Help regarding that particular object comes up, instructing you what to do in that particular field instead of for the entire dialog box. One component of Access 95 Help is the Microsoft Network. On the Help menu is an option for the Microsoft Network (MSN). If you're a member of MSN, it automatically logs you on and searches for help on Access 95. This option is very exciting and useful, because you can get up-to-the-minute help, the latest knowledge bases, and assistance from fellow Access 95 users on MSN, all while you're sitting at your desk scratching your head for ideas.

Visual Basic Help

Access 95 now includes the Visual Basic for Applications language, which is the standard language for the Microsoft Office suite. The online Help is extensive and includes answers to VBA questions and keywords. While you're working in a VBA module, you can click a keyword in a line of code for a function, statement, method, property, or object and press F1. The Object Browser, shown in Figure 2.8, is another easy way to get help for VBA. You can use the Object Browser to see a list of an object's properties and methods. The Object Browser can be used to view and navigate between the objects available not only to Access 95 but to other applications that support VBA and their controls, methods, and properties.

FIGURE 2.8.

The Object Browser.

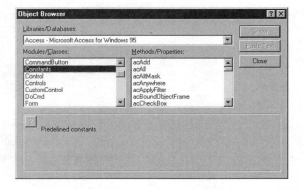

The previously discussed Answer Wizard is another good place to look for help. Simply type in your query and look under the "Programming and Language Reference" section in the Answer Wizard for topics with reference information about the Visual Basic programming language.

In the standard Help system for Access 95, click the Contents tab to go to the Contents page. From here, double-click the Microsoft Access Programming Language Reference book to see the topics of reference information on various actions, functions, methods, and so forth. In the Index page, you can type in the first few letters of the programming topic you're searching for, click the index entry you want in the second box, and then click Display. The Find page enables you to type words or phrases, which might be a more beneficial manner in which to search, because you can probably narrow topics down faster.

NOTE

When you set up Access 95, if you chose the Typical Setup, the language reference was not installed for components shared between Access 95 and other applications. To install all language reference topics, run Setup again and select Help Topics, click Change Option, and select Language Reference. This ensures that you have installed the complete VBA Help system.

Data Access Object Help

Access 95 contains extensive help on the Microsoft Data Access Objects (DAOs) that are included in Access 95. The main source of help is the Data Access and Collections Reference topic, which contains all the DAO objects and collections grouped by category or listed alphabetically. The DAO is used by programs such as Visual Basic or for OLE automation. It's not quite the same as Access 95 Database objects, because it allows for much finer programmatic control of the Access 95 engine. Although database objects such as forms and reports are included, they are called collections because they contain many objects, including a form and a report object. The DAO is generally used only by programmers, so a general user would probably not directly use the Data Access Object. Each object and collection is explained thoroughly, as are its methods and properties and various code tips and tricks related to the object's behavior.

Navigating with the Explorer

The Explorer is simply an application that lets you browse system devices, folders, and resources. Being able to navigate within it is a key skill in order to fully grasp the capabilities of Windows 95. You can use several methods to navigate and move files in Explorer. I'll touch on each one briefly.

Navigating with Explorer is similar to the File Manager in Windows 3.1, except that you can do much more with Explorer. File Manager was just a file manager, whereas Explorer manages your files, devices, and other system resources. To move through these items, you simply navigate through folders. The top-level folder is the Desktop—it contains all the other folders. To open other folders, simply click them with the mouse pointer and you will see all the folders and files contained in the folder you just opened. To open folders on the left side of the window, simply click on the icon. Its contents will appear on the right side of the Explorer window. For folders on the right side of the Explorer window, all you need to do is double-click on them to view their contents. You use the same methodology to navigate the devices on your system or in your Network Neighborhood. (A sample Explorer window is shown in Figure 2.9.)

FIGURE 2.9.

The Explorer window showing the Msoffice folder and its contents.

The first method of moving files is to use drag-and-drop functionality instead of menus. To do so, all you need to do is locate the file or folder you want to work with, make sure the place you want to drag the file or folder to is visible, and then drag the file or folder to the destination. Another method that is more familiar to the Windows user is the concept of cutting and pasting. You're probably quite comfortable cutting and pasting information to and from a document; now you can treat files and folders the same way. In Explorer, select the file or folder you wish to move, select Edit | Cut or Edit | Copy, open the folder where you want to put the file, and select Edit | Paste. You can select more than one file at a time by holding down the Ctrl key and clicking the items you want.

Find and Advanced Find

Windows 95 includes a sophisticated set of Find functions. You can access the Find functionality from the Start menu or the Tools menu in Explorer. Windows 95 enables you to find not only files and folders but also information on the Microsoft Network and other computers. The simple Find enables you to type in a name, including wildcard characters, and specify where to start looking for that named entity, as well as whether to include subfolders in the search (see Figure 2.10).

Advanced Find is more sophisticated and takes a little more time, because it enables you to search based on a broader set of characteristics. It enables you to search for a specified object type that contains certain text, as shown in Figure 2.11. It also includes the option to specify a size maximum or minimum. This is a powerful feature, because this is the function you would use if you forgot your database name and wanted to search for it based on the characteristics or statistics of the database.

FIGURE 2.10.
The Find dialog box.

FIGURE 2.11.
The Advanced Find dialog box.

You could also search for the database based on a custom-defined characteristic that is defined in the Database Properties dialog box, as shown in Figure 2.12. To access this dialog, start Access 95, open a database, and select File | Database Properties. To define a custom property, click the Custom tab in the Database Properties dialog.

FIGURE 2.12.
The Custom Database Properties dialog box.

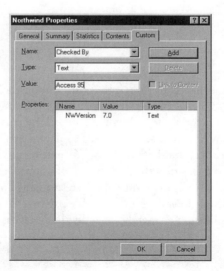

The Access 95 Interface

The Access 95 interface includes several features that make it fast and easy to accomplish tasks in Access. Because it is Windows 95-compliant, it offers all the benefits and advances provided by the Windows 95 operating system. You now can customize just about any feature you can think of to make your life easier in Access. This includes not only the customizable interface, but also options such as the startup window in Access 95, always keeping hidden objects hidden, colors, and other effects you use routinely.

The Windows 95-compliant interface of Access 95 offers many advantages, which we've discussed. Besides the new visual appeal of Access 95, the integrated Help system and right-click QuickMenus are very valuable. You can automatically have your forms and reports designed with the 3D effects that are standard in Windows 95, as well as the Large and Small Icon, List, and Details views in the Database window (see Figure 2.13). The ability to define custom characteristics for your databases and search on those characteristics is a distinct advantage if you work on many different databases at one time.

FIGURE 2.13.

Access 95 with Large Icon view.

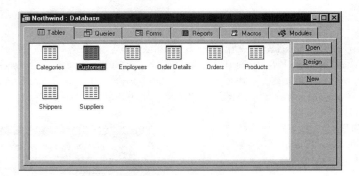

One of the most handy features is the customizable toolbars and menus. You can now customize the Access 95 environment to your liking or to the type of development you're currently doing. A new Button Editor, shown in Figure 2.14, enables you to edit an existing button image or design a new one from scratch. The Format Painter lets you copy formatting characteristics from one control to another. The new Formatting toolbar in the form and report Design view enables you to customize the appearance of your forms and reports. The formatting choices previously available through the palette are available on this toolbar. You can also have buttons that include drop-down lists and portable palettes. Your custom toolbars can be for the entire Access 95 application or merely for individual databases.

NOTE

To prevent other users from customizing your toolbars, you can disable the shortcut menu on the toolbar.

FIGURE 2.14.

The Button Editor.

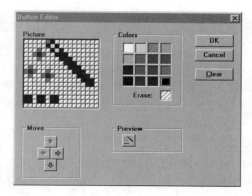

The ability to add a custom menu bar, complete with your custom commands, is a very helpful feature in Access 95. Custom menu bars are created using the Menu Builder, or you can create one by using macros. The Menu Builder is by far the easiest manner in which to create custom menus. The creation of custom commands is somewhat more involved, because you must edit the macros that the Menu Builder creates or create the macros from scratch. Your menu bars can be specific to a particular view, such as Design view, or global, enabling you to control tasks that others can perform in your database or application.

If you often choose the same set of tasks repeatedly, you can customize the Access 95 environment to those settings so that they are used by default. Select Tools | Options. You'll see the Options dialog box, shown in Figure 2.15, which has several tabs in it. Select the tab for the options you want to set, and then select the options you want to use. You can click Apply if you want to see the settings immediately without closing the dialog box; otherwise, click OK to apply the settings and close the dialog box.

FIGURE 2.15.

The Options dialog box.

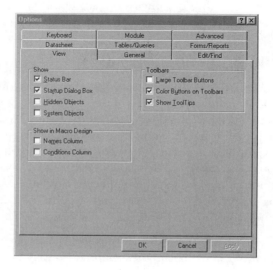

> **NOTE**
>
> If you change the environment settings in Access 95, Access saves the option settings in your workgroup information file, not in your user database. Because these changes are global, they apply to any database and anyone in your group who uses the same workgroup information file. This also applies to stand-alone users, because changes to the Access 95 environment settings apply to any database opened on the stand-alone system.

> **TIP**
>
> One of the first things you might want to do is to show (or hide) the Access Startup dialog box by default. To do this, select Tools | Options and then click the View tab. Under Show, select (or unselect) the Startup Dialog Box check box (see Figure 2.15). Click OK to apply the settings and close the window.

Changes Between Access 2 and Access 95

As you probably know if you have read this far, there are significant changes and new features in Access 95 that were not in Access 2. Some of the menus have changed, such as the File and Tools menus. New functionality has been added, such as replication (see Chapter 1, "Getting Started"), and old functionality has been expanded, such as the Options dialog box and customization features. The Database window has undergone several changes, such as the new views it is capable of. We've discussed many of these features, so we will focus on some of the menu changes to help your transition from Access 2 to Access 95.

The File and Tools Menus

The File and Tools menus have changed the most (Tools is new), with commands being grouped more logically from the File menu to the Tools menu. When no database is open, the Tools menu becomes more of a database utilities menu. Database management functions and workgroup administration are now under the Tools menu, as are Security, Replication, and Custom Control registration. When a database is open, the Tools menu now houses the Add-ins option, as well as several new options such as spell checking. The Tools menu (instead of the View menu) now has the Options menu selection. Security is now an option on the Tools menu instead of having its own separate menu listing. This new command structure is much more intuitive than the old structure under Access 2.

Figures 2.16 and 2.17 show the new Access 95 Tools menu as it appears with a database open and without a database open. The Compact, Convert, and Repair functions now reside under the Database Utilities option on the Tools menu with no database open instead of on the old File menu.

FIGURE 2.16.

The Tools menu with a database open.

FIGURE 2.17.

The Tools menu with no database open.

Figures 2.18 and 2.19 show the restructured Access 95 File menu as it appears with a database open and without a database open. Much of the functionality of the File menu has been properly regrouped under the Tools menu, providing for a more logical menu structure.

FIGURE 2.18.

The File menu with a database open.

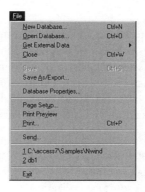

FIGURE 2.19.

The File menu with no database open.

Other Menu Changes

Every menu in Access 95 has undergone some change or deletion from the menu items in Access 2. The Security menu no longer exists; Security is grouped under the Tools menu as an option. The previously discussed Tools menu is new, as is the Insert menu in Access 95. I'll touch on each of the menus and their changes briefly.

The Edit menu has undergone a few changes as well. The Rename option is now on the Edit menu instead of the File menu, and the Relationships option is now on the Tools menu (see Figure 2.16). A new option has been added—Create Shortcut—which, as its name suggests, creates a shortcut. (Shortcuts were discussed earlier in this chapter.) With this command, you can create a shortcut to a specific object or table, thus maintaining Windows 95's new document-centric approach.

The View menu has had some functionality added to it and has had some of its options regrouped. In Access 95 you now select Database Objects and are then presented with a cascading menu of the objects, such as forms, reports, and tables, instead of having all the objects directly listed under the View menu. The new Database window view functionality is controlled here, so you can change the type of view in the Database window to the following: Large Icons, Small Icons, List, and Details. Because the Database window is icon-based, the functionality to arrange icons by various parameters and line up icons has been included here. The Properties selection has been added here so that you can view the properties of an individual database object. The Options selection, which has been greatly expanded, is now located on the Tools menu.

Another menu new to Access 95 is the Insert menu. It contains options to create new database objects such as forms, tables, and reports. This provides you with another way to create a new object. You can still select the object type tab in the Database window and click New, but this new approach is much more direct. Options for AutoForm and AutoReport are also included in this menu. AutoForm and AutoReport, as their names suggest, automatically create a form or report that shows all the fields from a selected table or query.

I discussed the Tools menu earlier, but a few new options are worth noting. The Spelling option enables you to spell-check the text and memo fields in your tables, which is similar to the AutoCorrect option (also on the Tools menu), except that AutoCorrect automatically corrects the spelling, as well as some capitalization errors. OfficeLinks is a new feature that enables you to outline and analyze a database object with Microsoft Excel or publish it as an .RTF file with Microsoft Word. The Analyze option is a cascading menu that contains options for the Table and Performance Analyzers, as well as the Database Documentor. The startup properties sheet for the database that is open is also located on the Tools menu in the Startup option. This enables you to specify things such as what is to be opened first and what your application's icon will be.

The remaining two menus, Window and Help, have only minor changes. The Window menu now has the capability to arrange icons, due to the new icon metaphor of the Database window. The Help menu now contains an option for the new Answer Wizard. The Help menu has also been shortened, so that getting help involves merely selecting a single option and then selecting the tab in the Help system. The Contents, Search, and Index options are no longer on the Help menu in Access 95.

The Database Container

The Database Container is just what it sounds like—a container for database objects. A database is simply a collection of these objects; these objects define and comprise the database. These objects and a brief description of each follow:

- Table: Tables are the fundamental structure of the database. They store data as records (rows) and fields (columns).

- Query: Queries are used to change, view, and analyze data. The Form and Report objects often use a Query object as their record source.

- Report: Reports are a way to present your data in printed form in the manner you specify. Reports are fully customizable, or you can use predefined Report objects that come with Access 95.

- Form: Forms are used for several purposes and do not necessarily have to present data from a Table or Query object. You can use a form to present data, as a data entry vehicle, or as a dialog box to get user input, such as a Switchboard.

- Macro: Macros are ways to automate common tasks. They often contain a series of statements to accomplish a task, such as showing a form or report.

- Module: A module is a collection of VBA procedures, functions, declarations, and constants that are used to control an Access 95 database. They can often be used to provide greater control and functionality over a macro object.

Within each of the preceding objects can be collections of other objects. For example, in the Table object there is a Fields collection. The Database Container and the Data Access Object are discussed in more detail later in this book; however, the basics outlined here should provide you with a good jumping-off point. The Data Access Object (DAO), which includes the Database Container, is a fundamental component of Access and should be fully understood as you move further into Access and Visual Basic development.

Summary

This chapter highlighted many of the new features of Access 95. Some of these new features, such as the new Help System, Exchange, and Briefcase Replication, occur as a result of using the enhanced functionality of the Windows 95 interface. Others, such as the Button Editor and Database Custom Properties, are new to Access 95. Access 95's menu structure is better organized and more logically grouped for users and administrators alike.

PART

IN THIS PART

Data, Databases, and Tables

Databases

3

by Matt Kinney

What's New

One of the significant new features of Access 95 is the Database Wizard, shown in Figure 3.1. It creates all the tables, forms, and reports for the predefined database you specify in one operation. The predefined database types vary from contact management to a video collection database. Each predefined database type has its own characteristics and advantages unique to the type of application it's supposed to be building. A blank database type is also included, which, as its name specifies, creates a blank database that you need to add the tables, forms, and reports to.

FIGURE 3.1.

The Database Wizard.

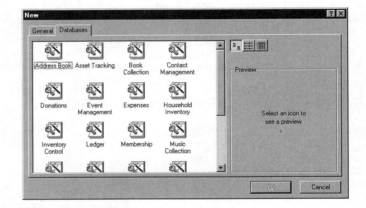

Access 95 now enables you to change, view, and define database properties, as well as define your own database properties to identify characteristics of a database. You can even search on these characteristics to get a list of databases that meet your criteria. Some of the statistics include author, title, and subject of the database, as well as statistics on the database, such as creation date and time and the last user to access the database. You can also obtain a list of all the objects in the database. To see the Database Properties dialog box, shown in Figure 3.2, select File | Database Properties.

The new Startup properties enable you to create customized applications that specify different options. Some of these options include toolbar customization, status bar and Database window display, and what form is displayed when a database is opened. They also enable you to set whether the user can view the code after an error occurs or whether the Access 95 special keys—such as Show Database Window, Pause Execution, and Display Code Window—are active. To see the Startup dialog box, shown in Figure 3.3, select Tools | Startup.

FIGURE 3.2.

The Database Properties dialog box.

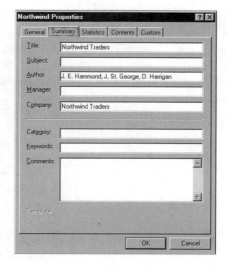

FIGURE 3.3.

The Startup dialog box.

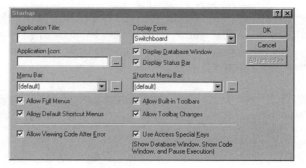

Creating a Database

Access 95 has two convenient methods for creating databases. The more user-friendly approach is to use the Database Wizard, which creates all the tables, forms, and reports for the database type you choose. The other, more work-intensive method is to create a blank database and add the tables, forms, and reports separately. This method leads to more flexibility for the developer; however, it means that each element must be defined separately. At any rate, you can extend and modify your database definition any time after it has been created.

Creating a Database Using the Database Wizard

First we'll examine the simplest method of creating a database—using the Database Wizard. When Access 95 first starts, a dialog box is displayed that enables you to open an existing database or create a new one (see Figure 3.4). From this dialog box, select Database Wizard and click OK. If you have already been working in Access 95, you can click the New Database button on the main toolbar—if you haven't customized it.

FIGURE 3.4.

*The opening selection
dialog box.*

From here, select from the list the type of database you wish to create. If the exact type you want is not in the list, either create a blank database or select the type that is the closest match to the type you want, and you can modify it later. For this example, we will create a Wine List database (see Figure 3.5).

FIGURE 3.5.

*The Database Wizard with
the Wine List database
selected.*

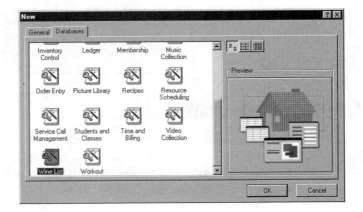

You then must specify a name and location for the database. Note that Access 95 uses the Windows 95 common file dialog box, shown in Figure 3.6, so you don't have to specify an extension. Access 95 databases are registered in the Registry, so Windows 95 knows to add the .MDB extension.

FIGURE 3.6.

The File New Database dialog box.

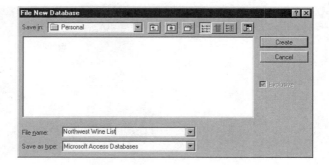

When you click Create to define your database, Access 95 begins to create your database. You are first shown some summary information about what kinds of data your selected database will store. Click Next to move forward. You are then prompted as to whether you would like to include any extra fields or include sample data to help you learn to use the database (see Figure 3.7). If this is your first experience with Access, including the sample data is a good idea to help you learn the various features of the database you created.

FIGURE 3.7.

Prompting for additional fields and sample data.

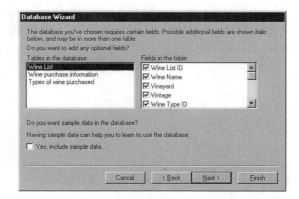

The Database Wizard then prompts you for what type of screen display you wish to use, as shown in Figure 3.8. There are several types to choose from, but the Windows 95 look and feel is probably the most beneficial.

After you choose a screen display type, you are asked to choose a report type, as shown in Figure 3.9. You can see what each report type looks like in the preview window before you decide which type you want to use.

FIGURE 3.8.

Prompting for the screen display type.

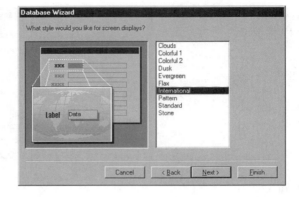

FIGURE 3.9.

Prompting for the report type.

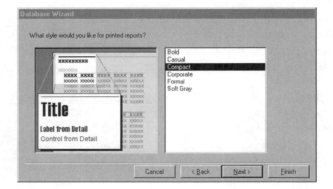

You are then prompted as to what the title of your database will be, as shown in Figure 3.10. Enter a title or just use the default title. You can also add a picture in the background of the forms and reports on-screen. Do this by clicking the checkbox with the caption "Yes, I'd like to include a picture.", clicking the Picture button, and locating the picture you wish to use, or by providing the filename for the picture.

FIGURE 3.10.

The title and picture dialog box.

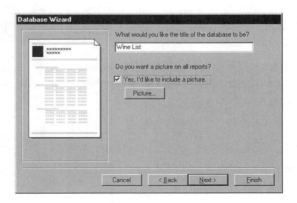

After you've clicked the Next or Finish buttons, the Database Wizard creates the database based on the parameters you have provided. Depending on what kind of system you have, the RAM it contains, and so forth, this could take a few minutes. When the Database Wizard is finished, your new database is shown in the Database window (see Figure 3.11). Congratulations! You have just created an Access 95 database application!

FIGURE 3.11.

The Wine List Database window.

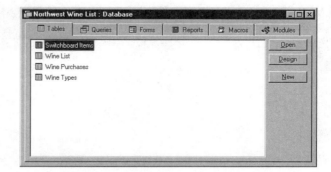

Creating a Database Without Using the Database Wizard

If you're just starting Access 95, you're presented with options to create a new database or open an existing one. See Figure 3.4 for an example of this dialog box. To create a database manually, select Blank Database and then click OK.

If you have been working in Access 95 and wish to create a new database, click the New Database button on the main toolbar and select the Blank Database icon in the New Database dialog box, shown in Figure 3.12.

FIGURE 3.12.

The New Database dialog box with the blank database selected.

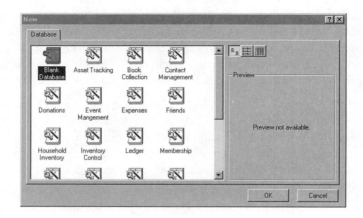

You then see the Database window with your blank database in it, as shown in Figure 3.13. The blank database is similar to an empty container waiting for you to put something into it. You need to add objects such as tables, forms, and reports to the database. Doing this is the subject of other chapters in this book, so we will continue our discussion of databases and some database management features of Access 95.

FIGURE 3.13.

The Database window with a blank database.

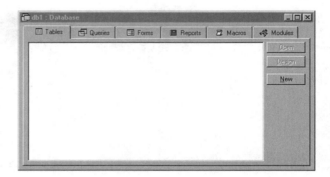

Maintaining Databases from the Tools Menu

You can do most, if not all, database maintenance from the Tools menu when you don't have any databases open. The options of particular note for maintenance are Database Utilities, Security, and Custom Controls. Two other options are Macros and Options, but they aren't as important in database maintenance as the previously mentioned options.

The first menu option is Database Utilities, which contains several useful options. The Convert Database option takes an Access 1.x or 2 database and converts it to Access 95, thus enabling it to take advantage of the new features of Access 95. The Compact Database option enables you to compact the database so that it uses disk space more efficiently; this should aid performance if you haven't compacted the database for some time. The Repair Database option attempts to repair a damaged database. Access 95 usually detects damaged databases; however, you can attempt to repair any database you think might be damaged.

The next option is Security, which contains options to maintain user and group accounts, as well as the ability to encrypt or decrypt a database. The User and Group Accounts option enables you to administer workgroup accounts by adding, deleting, and modifying various users and group accounts. The Encrypt/Decrypt option either encrypts a database so that it can't be read by a general utility program or word processor or decrypts the database and removes the previously applied encryption.

A new option in Access 95 is replication. This option, which is available only if a database is currently open, has an option that enables you to convert a database into a replica. This is necessary if you wish to utilize Access 95's new Briefcase Replication feature. Replication is a powerful feature and should definitely be considered if you have multiple users in different locations working on the same database.

The Custom Controls option enables you to register or unregister custom controls. Access 95 and Windows 95 use OLE custom controls (commonly called OCX controls for the file extension they are named with), which are an upgrade to the immensely popular VBX control. OLE custom controls provide several advantages over VBX controls, the least of which is that they are designed from the ground up, meaning that they are not dependent on the Visual Basic environment and that they are extensible. The more you develop in Access 95, the more apparent the advantages of OLE custom controls will become.

Converting an Access 95 Database

As you probably know by now, Access 95 has many new features that you can take advantage of—that's probably one of the reasons you bought it! In Access 95 you can work with databases from older versions of Access. However, you can't change the design of the objects in the older database or take advantage of all the new features until you convert the database to Access 95. This also means that you can't add new objects to the older database under Access 95. Note, however, that the conversion is a one-way ticket: once you convert the database to Access 95, it can't be opened by an older version of Access, and it can't be converted back to the older version.

With all these benefits, is there a reason you shouldn't convert a database to Access 95? A primary reason you shouldn't convert your Access database from a previous version to Access 95 is if you have users who can't or haven't upgraded to Windows 95. Users who aren't using Windows 95 or Windows NT 3.51 build 1057 or later can't open an Access 95 database and thus can't use your application. Also, if a database was created or is being used in Visual Basic 2 or 3, you shouldn't convert the database. Visual Basic 2 and 3 can't open or use Access 95 databases. Visual Basic 4, however, should be able to use an Access 95 database, so you should wait to convert the database until your VB application can be upgraded to Visual Basic version 4.

Converting a database is straightforward and easy. The first step you should take is to back up the database you're going to convert so that you can still use your old database until you're comfortable using Access 95. You should also ensure that any linked tables or databases are still in the directory where your database refers to them. You should then close the database you're going to convert; if the database is located on a server or is shared, make sure no other users have it open. If you're using a secure workgroup, make sure you have Modify Design or Administer permissions on all tables in the database before you proceed, or you will be unable to convert the database. If you have successfully completed the preceding steps and have the proper permissions, you're ready to convert the database.

Select Tools | Database Utilities, and then select Convert Database. From here, select the database you wish to convert, as shown in Figure 3.14.

FIGURE 3.14.

Selecting the database to convert.

You are then prompted for the name of the file you would like to save the converted database in, as shown in Figure 3.15. To keep the same name, change to another directory. Otherwise, type in a new name without the .MDB extension and click Save. Access 95 then converts the database. Depending on the size of your database, this could take several minutes. Note that, depending on the size of your forms, reports, and modules, this conversion could be as much as double the size of your original database due to the size of storing Visual Basic for Applications as opposed to Access Basic. All Access Basic objects, and the objects they refer to, are converted to Visual Basic for Applications. You should also be aware that any 16-bit API calls will have to be converted to their 32-bit counterparts manually, because the conversion process does *not* do this. Otherwise, a runtime error will occur.

FIGURE 3.15.

Selecting the database to convert to.

> **NOTE**
>
> If your database uses linked tables, you also have to convert the database that the linked tables reside in.

> **NOTE**
>
> Access 95 is generally compatible with version 1.x databases; however, Access 95 might change the behavior of some database objects.

Compacting an Access 95 Database

As time goes by and you delete tables and records, your database file becomes fragmented on the disk, thus using disk space inefficiently and causing performance degradation. Compacting the database makes a copy of the database, removing the fragmentation so that the database uses disk space better. To compact the database, you must have Modify Design or Administer permission for all the tables in the database if you are in a secure workgroup. To compact the database, you should close it on your system; if the database is shared or on a server, make sure no other users are in it; otherwise, you will be unable to compact the database. If you have successfully closed the database and you have the proper permissions, you are ready to compact the database.

> **WARNING**
>
> If you're compacting an Access 1.x database and an object in it has the backquote character (') in its name, you must go into Access 1.x and rename the object. You then have to change all references to the old object to the new object name in the forms, queries, reports, macros, and code. If you fail to do this, you will be unable to compact the database.

Select Tools | Database Utilities and then select Compact Database. From here, select the database you wish to compact, as shown in Figure 3.16.

You are then prompted for the name of the file you would like to save the compacted database in, as shown in Figure 3.17. To keep the same name, change to another directory. Otherwise, type in a new name without the .MDB extension and click Save. Access 95 then compacts the database. Depending on the size of your database, this could take several minutes.

FIGURE 3.16.

Selecting the database to compact.

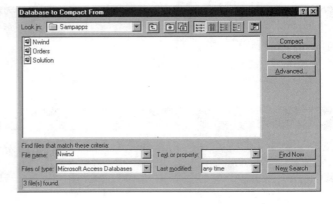

FIGURE 3.17.

Selecting the database to compact to.

Repairing an Access 95 Database

On rare occasions, your Access 95 database might become damaged or corrupted. In most cases, Access detects that the database is damaged and gives you the option to repair it. However, there are times when Access can't detect database damage, and you must repair the database. Another case when you might have to repair the database is if your database is behaving unpredictably. A good first step is to try repairing the database and see if that remedies the problem. To repair the database, you should close it on your system; if the database is shared or on a server, make sure no other users are in it. Otherwise, you will be unable to repair the database. If you have successfully closed the database, and you think a repair is warranted or Access prompts you to repair, you're ready to repair the database. The following procedure is for manually repairing the database. If Access prompts you to repair the database, it handles the procedure automatically.

Select Tools | Database Utilities and then select Repair Database. From here, select the database you wish to repair, as shown in Figure 3.18.

FIGURE 3.18.

Selecting the database to repair.

After you select the file, click Repair. Access 95 attempts to repair the database. Depending on the size of your database, this could take several minutes. Note that not all databases can be repaired if the damage is severe enough.

Administering Users and Groups

In a workgroup environment, the concept of permissions and who has what type of permission is critical. There are two types of permissions: explicit and implicit. Permissions can be granted either to a single user (a user account) or to a group of users (a group account). Granting permission to a user account is called *explicit permission;* granting permission to a group account is called *implicit permission.* If a user is a member of a group, he has that group's permissions. Therefore, by adding or removing users from a group, you can change permissions for a user (or group of users). The topics of assigning and removing permissions for a database and database objects, as well as the types of permissions available, are discussed later in this book in further detail.

Encrypting and Decrypting Databases

There are times when you want your database to be read only by Access. The encrypt function accomplishes this so that your database can't be read by any other program except Access. As part of the encryption process, Access compacts the database as well. To compact a database without encrypting it, see "Compacting an Access 95 Database" earlier in this chapter.

Whereas the encryption process makes your database indecipherable to a word processor or utility program, the decryption process removes the encryption and reverses its effects. Encryption and decryption, and their advantages and disadvantages, are discussed in further detail later in this book.

Creating an Access 95 Database

One of the new features of Access 95, as mentioned earlier, is replication. Replication enables multiple users to work on their own copies of the database, and you can take all the various changes and incorporate them into a single database file. To do this, you must create a replica before you distribute the database for the users to begin making changes to. The concept of replication is very powerful in database management and is discussed in its own chapter because it is deemed so important.

Custom Controls

The Windows 95 version of the venerable VBX control is called the *OLE custom control.* Access 95 includes the functionality to utilize OLE controls and is much the better for it. OLE custom controls are a very powerful item in the move toward component software and reusability. This means that you can buy a control that does something unique. For example, the control could create an outline of your data. You could drop the control on your form or report and have it do the data outline for you. You don't have to write that functionality yourself every time. The Custom Controls option enables you to register OLE controls in the Windows 95 Registry. Controls that aren't included in Access 95 (or if you didn't check the register controls option during setup) need to be registered so that Access 95, as well as your other applications that can use OLE controls, can utilize the functionality of the control.

Summary

This chapter discussed several new features of Access 95 databases. Significant improvements were made in database creation with the advent of the Database Wizard and the predefined databases. Some of the functions from previous versions of Access are still present but are now easier to use, such as compacting and repairing a database. New functions, such as replication, have been added to make Access 95 a truly robust relational database management system.

Tables

4

by Craig Eddy

In a relational database system such as Access, tables are the basic building blocks. An individual table is similar to an Excel spreadsheet: it can be thought of in terms of rows and columns. In database terminology, the rows of data stored in a table are called *records*. The columns that make up a table are called *fields*.

When Access is first started, you have the option of opening an existing database or creating a new database, either from scratch (a blank database) or by using the Database Wizard. If you choose to use the Database Wizard, a database structure is created for you, tables and all. You can even have Access 95 load the database with some sample data. This data can help you learn how the tables work both by themselves and in relation to each other. If you choose to create a blank database, however, you create your own tables. Fortunately, you're in the right place for doing just that—this chapter covers the creation and modification of tables in depth.

The Access Database window includes several tabs for the different kinds of database objects stored inside an Access database: tables, queries, forms, reports, macros, and modules. This chapter focuses on the Tables tab. Access 95 provides many ways to create a new table. These are all covered in this chapter and include the following:

- Datasheet view: Creates the table structure based on data entered (and a little nudging on your part).
- Design view: Creates a table in design mode, where fields are added and all properties are specified.
- Table Wizard: The Wizard guides you through creating a table based on built-in templates.
- Import Table Wizard: Adds a table to the database by importing its structure from an external file such as another database, a spreadsheet, or a delimited text file.
- Link Table Wizard: Adds a link to a table in another database on your computer (or across the world).

TIP

When you create an application using Access, it's often best to actually create two .MDB files: one to hold just the data tables (which are discussed in this chapter) and another to hold the queries, reports, modules, forms, and macros. This second file has the data file's tables attached (attaching tables is the subject of the section "Using the Link Table Wizard"). Using this method, you can modify application-specific information using test data and then merely distribute the application .MDB file when your changes are completed.

Creating a Table Manually

There are basically two ways to create a new table in Microsoft Access: manually and by using the Table Wizards that come with Access.

NOTE

If you didn't install the Wizards when Access was installed, you should probably do so now. Otherwise, you won't be able to follow the examples presented later in this chapter. You install the Wizards using the Access 95 setup program. Running the setup program after Access 95 has been installed brings you to the installation maintenance dialog box. This dialog has an Add/Remove button, which is where you can add components such as the Wizards if they weren't installed originally.

Each of these methods has several different ways of physically creating the tables. This section discusses manual table creation. To create a table manually, you can use either Table Datasheet view (see Figure 4.1) or Table Design view (see Figure 4.2).

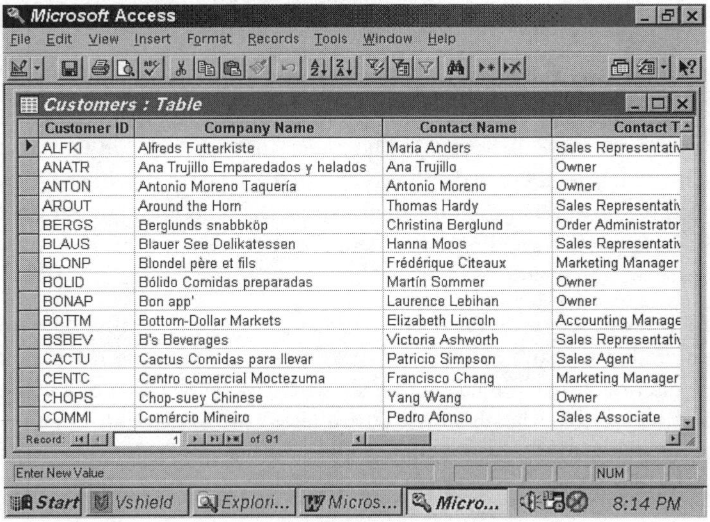

FIGURE 4.1.

The Northwind database's Customer table in Table Datasheet view.

Using Table Datasheet view makes it easier to create simple tables. Data is entered into the table in a process similar to entering data into a spreadsheet. Access then determines field types and formats based on the data provided. Access can also create a primary key field (a field that serves as the unique identifier for each row of data, analogous to a row number in a spreadsheet) if you choose.

In most cases, however, creating tables using Table Datasheet view doesn't provide enough detail for a working database. Table Design view provides control over all available field properties, including validation rules and default values.

FIGURE 4.2.

The Northwind database's Customer table in Table Design view.

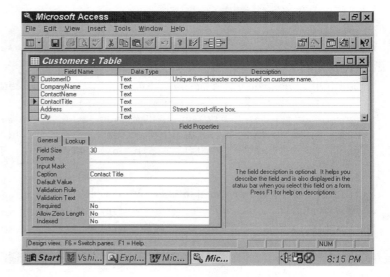

Using Table Datasheet View

Creating a table using Table Datasheet view lets you kill two birds with one stone: the basic table structure is created and is populated with data at the same time. In most real-world applications, however, much of the data entered when the table is created is test data. Most databases aren't designed to merely store existing data, but to provide a mechanism for future data entry and analysis.

As you can see in Figure 4.1, using Datasheet view is much like using Microsoft Excel: data is entered in row and column format. Each row represents a single record of data (a *record* is a set of data fields, each relating to a single entity). For instance, each customer in the Northwind Trader database has his own customer record. Each column (or field) in a row represents a property of the entity being described in that row.

When you open an existing database or create a new blank database, the first window you come to is the Database window, shown in Figure 4.3. (Of course, if you open an existing database, this window will most likely contain the names of existing tables.) This window provides quick access to all the objects that can reside in a database. This chapter focuses on tables, so we'll stay on the Tables tab.

Chapter 4

FIGURE 4.3.

The Database window of a blank database.

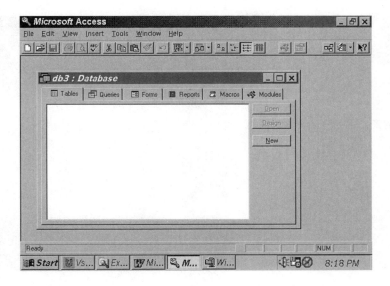

To create a new table, click the New button. The New Table window, shown in Figure 4.4, appears. This window enables you to select the method to be used to create the new table. If you click each of the provided options in the list box on the right, the picture and description on the left change to provide a brief description of the currently selected method.

FIGURE 4.4.

The New Table window.

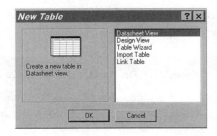

Select Datasheet view in the list box and click the OK button. A blank Table Datasheet view window appears, as shown in Figure 4.5.

The cursor is now in the first column of the first row. Access wants some data, but you need to do a little preparation first. Table Datasheet view provides a spreadsheet with 20 columns and 30 rows (you can add more if necessary).

Each column has a *column header* (also known as the *column selector*) at the top of the column. The column header displays the name of the field that the column represents. The default field names are Field1, Field2, and so on. As you will see in Chapter 7, "Database Fundamentals," field names should describe the property that will be stored in the field (LastName, Address, Phone, and so on). Obviously, the name Field5 doesn't describe much of anything.

FIGURE 4.5.

The blank Table Datasheet view.

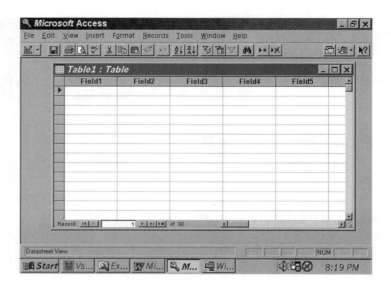

To change a field's name, move the cursor over the column selector. The cursor changes to a black downward-facing arrow. Double-click the left mouse button. An edit box appears, enabling you to modify the field name. Be sure the name you specify obeys Access's object-naming rules (see the Access Help file for more details). Repeat this for all the fields that will be created for this table. You can also choose Format | Rename Column to rename the field. In addition, you can right-click over the column header to display a shortcut menu with a Rename Column choice.

> **TIP**
>
> Although you can use spaces in table and field names, it isn't advisable to do so. If these fields are referred to in any expressions or any Visual Basic for Applications code, the names must be surrounded by square brackets ([]). This requirement can be annoying, but you can easily avoid it. Also, some database systems (such as dBase) don't allow the use of spaces in field names. If you're going to link to an Access table from such a DBMS, don't use spaces!
>
> You should also avoid names that are excessive in length. Access allows for a 64-character field name. Good luck remembering a name this long! Also, if the field is referred to in code or an expression, the name takes up a lot of space (if you can remember it without using the Expression Builder).

If you need more than 20 columns, you can easily insert new columns. To insert a column using the mouse, follow these steps:

1. Move the cursor to the column selector of the column just to the right of where you want the new column to be inserted.

2. When the downward-facing arrow appears, click the left mouse button. The column is now selected (highlighted).

3. With the column highlighted, click the right mouse button and select Insert Column from the shortcut menu.

4. The new column appears in place and has the default name Field*x*. Rename the field to something meaningful.

You can also select Insert | Column to insert a new column.

The same processes enable you to insert a *lookup* column—a special type of column that is used to retrieve column values from another table. These values are then stored in the new table either as a literal value or as an identifier pointing to the desired value in the other table. This type of column can be used, for example, in a scheduler database to display a contact's name along with the scheduled item. The name itself isn't stored in the scheduler table. Instead, a pointer is stored that represents the contact in the contact table. This is a very useful feature of Access because it hides the details of the link between tables. Instead of displaying a ContactID, which isn't meaningful, the lookup column would always display the contact's name. The steps involved in inserting a lookup column are described in the next section. The theory behind lookup tables is described in Chapter 7.

If you need to rearrange the columns, you use a process similar to inserting columns with the mouse. First, select the column to be moved by clicking the left mouse button while the cursor is over the column selector. The column is selected (the entire column is highlighted). With the cursor over the column selector, click and hold the left mouse button. While holding the button, drag the column left or right to move it to its new position. A vertical line moves as the mouse is moved. This line is the left edge of the column being moved. When the vertical line has reached its desired destination, drop the column in place by releasing the mouse button. Repeat this process with any other columns you would like to move.

> **NOTE**
>
> Although it helps from a data entry standpoint to have columns in a logical sequence, it makes no difference to Access. Most often the fields are referred to by name rather than by ordinal position (the numbering of the columns). Therefore, fields can be assigned in any desired order.

Now that you've given the fields some sensible names and arranged the columns in a logical order, it's time to enter the data. It's not necessary to enter all the data at this time, but you should enter data for at least one record into each column. You don't have to fill an entire row with data; empty fields in a record are okay as long as any empty columns aren't later marked as Required in Design view. Also, any columns left completely empty are deleted when you save the table.

> **TIP**
>
> Access considers an empty field to have a special value known as NULL. This value can be tested for in code or an expression to find records with that field empty. The NULL value is independent of the data type the field represents, so an empty date field and an empty numeric field both evaluate to NULL, making testing for emptiness easier.

If you find that the data being entered exceeds the default column widths, Access provides several ways to expand the columns. All of these actions take place with the cursor in the column header of the column. The first method is the manual method. Move the cursor between the column to be sized and either adjacent column. The cursor changes shape—it now has arrows pointing left and right. Click the mouse and drag the column to size it. The last two methods adjust the column to the "best fit" for the data present. Move the cursor between the column header of the column to be resized and the column header of the column immediately to the right. When the cursor changes, double-click, and the column will be resized to best fit. Finally, best fit can also be accomplished by right-clicking over the column header. When the shortcut menu appears, select Column Width. A dialog box will appear, from which you can manually enter a column width, choose the standard width, or choose best fit.

It's important to enter dates, times, and numbers in a consistent format throughout a column. Access uses this formatting to set the field's format property. Also, if you want to store zip codes, Social Security numbers, or any other alphanumeric data in text fields, be sure to include hyphens or other nonnumeric characters. Otherwise, Access assumes that this is a numeric field and assigns it the data type Number. You can change this in Table Design view, but you can easily avoid this extra step.

> **TIP**
>
> Data consistency can also be enforced in the table's design. As you'll see later, Access 95 provides field properties such as `InputMask` and `Validation Rules`. These allow you to force a consistent look and operation for the data.

> **CAUTION**
>
> For text fields entered in Table Datasheet view, Access assumes a character length of 50 characters (unless you've typed more than 50 into a field). Although Access doesn't

waste space by using all 50 characters if only 10 are stored in the field, it's not good design practice to greatly overestimate the field sizes. Be sure to use Table Design view to fix any text field lengths.

There is no need to manually save each row as you enter data. Access automatically validates and saves a record when you move to a new row.

When you're satisfied with the data, click the Save button (it looks like a floppy disk) or choose File | Save Layout to save the new table. The Save As dialog appears, prompting you to enter a table name. Although the default, Table1, is a valid table name, it's not very descriptive. Provide a meaningful name, taking into account the suggestions I mentioned in the discussion of field names.

When you click the OK button, Access displays a message box like the one shown in Figure 4.6. Don't be alarmed! This is supposed to happen. Access is informing you that the newly created table doesn't have a primary key—the mechanism used to uniquely identify a record in the database. Access is graciously asking if you would like one created automatically. If you have no fields (or group of fields) that can serve as the primary key (see Chapter 7 for a thorough explanation of primary keys), you should click Yes. Access adds a new field to the table, assigns it the Autonumber data type, and sets it as the primary key. If you click No, the table is saved just as you defined it. You need to use Table Design view to define the primary key. If you click Cancel, you're taken back to Table Datasheet view, and the new table isn't saved. Click Help to see more information on table relationships and primary keys.

FIGURE 4.6.

The Create Primary Key message box.

Having saved the table, it's now time to switch to Table Design view to refine the field properties. You do this either by clicking the Table View button of the Table Datasheet toolbar (if you haven't customized your toolbars, it is the leftmost button on the Table Datasheet toolbar) or by selecting View | Table Design. The next section discusses creating a table in Table Design view and refining field properties. Several properties can't be defined in Table Datasheet view. Among them are `Validation Rules`, `Default Values`, `Field Captions`, and `Lookup Properties`. Because these can be important properties, you should visit Table Design view to set them up where needed.

Using Table Design View

Unlike Table Datasheet view, Table Design view doesn't let you enter data as you create the table. It does have several features that make its use unavoidable, however.

To create a new table using Table Design view, select the Tables tab of the Database window. Click the New button to bring up the New Table window (see Figure 4.4). Select Design View from the list and click OK. An empty Table Design view window appears, as shown in Figure 4.7. The top portion of the window shows the field definition. The field properties defined here are field name, field data type, and a description of the field. The bottom portion is used to further define field properties. The items shown in the bottom portion of the window change depending on the data type assigned to the field.

FIGURE 4.7.

An empty Table Design view window.

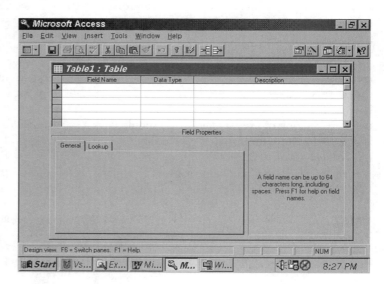

Defining Fields

The top portion of the window is used for basic field definition. To add a field to the new table, start in the first column of the first row of Table Design view. Enter a field name here. (Review the preceding section for information and tips on naming fields.)

> **TIP**
>
> While the cursor is in the Field Name column, clicking the Builder button of the toolbar (which looks like a magic wand) causes the Field Builder to appear. You can choose from many different predefined fields to help create a new table.

Press the Tab key, and the cursor moves to the Data Type column. This column has a drop-down list of all the available data types. The default data type is Text, but it's a simple matter to choose another data type. Click the button on the right side of the column to drop down the list of choices. Select the data type that describes the field. The available field data types are as follows:

- Text: A string of characters (up to 255 characters or the length set by the `FieldSize` property, whichever is less) used to store alphanumeric data. Numbers that won't be used in calculations, such as Social Security numbers or telephone numbers, should also have a Text data type since they often contain nonnumeric characters as well as numeric characters.

- Memo: Used to store long text fields. No maximum is specified by the user, but Access imposes a limit of 64,000 characters.

- Number: Used to store numeric data in the form of integers, long integers, and single-precision and double-precision floating point numbers.

- Date/Time: Used to store dates and times.

- Currency: A special numeric data type that is used for monetary values because it prevents rounding off of numbers during calculations.

- Autonumber: A special numeric data type that can be used for primary key fields (defined later). Fields of this data type are always read-only because Access automatically inserts either the next number in the sequence or a random number when a data record is created.

- Yes/No: Used to store Boolean data, which can contain only one of two values, such as On/Off, Yes/No, or True/False.

- OLE Object: A special type of object or component that is provided by a Windows OLE server (Excel spreadsheets or Word documents can be OLE objects). The data in the field is either linked to or embedded in the Access table.

- Lookup Wizard: Enables you to define a field in which the user selects a value from either another table or a predefined list of values. This is discussed later.

CAUTION

If the Number or Currency data types are chosen, Access places the value 0 in the `Default` property for the field. In some instances, this causes problems, particularly when the field is used to store lookup table ID values. These ID values will probably never be zero, so you get a validation error if you try to save the record and haven't modified this value. Also, if you wanted to count the number of records that have data entered into the field in question, having Access default a value into the field would cause an erroneous count. Even records that haven't had the field's value modified would be included, since they *do* have a value.

After you choose a data type, press Tab again to move to the Description column. Although field descriptions are optional, they are highly recommended. The description can store a definition of the field and the data it contains or valid data for the field, for instance. The description has no bearing on the operation of the table, so enter anything you like. Bear in mind, however, that someday another person will probably need to peek into your database definition. A good description will go a long way toward documenting the purpose of the field.

Refining Field Properties

This section discusses the many properties of a field that can be set using the bottom portion of the Table Design view window. The properties that can be set here vary, depending on the field's data type.

Many basic properties are common to all field data types. I'll discuss these first, and then we'll move on to properties that apply only to specific data types. The table in Figure 4.8 shows the different data types and the properties that apply to them. Although Lookup Wizard is included in the list of data types, it actually isn't a data type. Selecting Lookup Wizard from the list will invoke the Lookup Wizard (described in detail later). The field's actual data type will depend on the information you supply to the Wizard.

FIGURE 4.8.

A spreadsheet showing the properties that apply to specific data types.

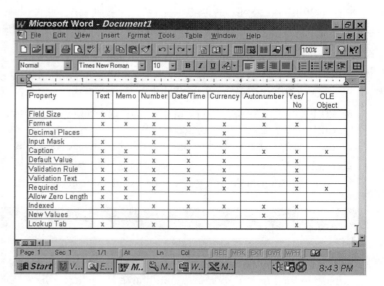

Property	Text	Memo	Number	Date/Time	Currency	Autonumber	Yes/No	OLE Object
Field Size	x		x			x		
Format	x	x	x	x	x	x	x	
Decimal Places			x		x			
Input Mask	x		x	x	x			
Caption	x	x	x	x	x	x	x	x
Default Value	x	x	x	x	x		x	
Validation Rule	x	x	x	x	x		x	
Validation Text	x	x	x	x	x		x	
Required	x	x	x	x	x		x	x
Allow Zero Length	x	x						
Indexed	x		x	x	x	x	x	
New Values						x		
Lookup Tab	x		x				x	

> **NOTE**
>
> Access 2 veterans are probably wondering what happened to the Counter data type. It's been replaced by Autonumber, an enhanced version of the counter. You can use it to assign random numbers to the field by setting the New Values property to Random.

Besides the Boolean-style properties (Required, Allow Zero Length, and Indexed), the only properties that are required to have a value are the Field Size property (for Text, Number, and Autonumber fields) and the New Values property (for Autonumber fields). All other properties are optional. For the required fields, Access picks a default value. If you don't want to accept the default, simply modify the property. If a data type has an X in the Lookup Tab property, you can specify how that field appears on forms and Table Datasheet view and where it obtains valid values. The field properties are as follows:

- Field Size: Specifies the type of number or length of text that can be stored in the field. For Numbers, possible values are Byte, Integer, Long Integer, Single, Double, and Replication ID. (This is used in synchronizing databases that have replication enabled. See Chapter 39, "Replication," for more details.)

- Format: Specifies how data is displayed and printed. There are different predefined formats for each data type. To see the list of available formats, click the button to the right of the property's text box. You can also specify your own format. The setting doesn't affect how data is stored in the field.

- Decimal Places: Controls the number of decimal places appearing after the decimal point. The property value Auto indicates that the Format set for the field determines the number of decimal places.

- Input Mask: Similar to the Format property, but controls how data is input into a field. Can be used to force the user to enter only numbers or only letters. A phone number field could use an input mask to aid the user in entering the number properly. The Input Mask Wizard greatly simplifies creating input masks and lets you try out the mask before you apply it. Click the button to the right of the property's text box to access the Wizard.

- Caption: Defines the label that is used on reports or forms on which the field is placed. This will also be the column heading for Table Datasheet view. Note that if the Caption property is left blank, Access will use the field's name anywhere it would have used the Caption property's value.

- Default Value: The value that is assigned to the field when a new record is inserted. This value can also be an expression. Click the button to the right of the property's text box to bring up the Expression Builder.

- Validation Rule: An expression that is used to check values entered into the field. This can be used if a field should be restricted to certain values or to ensure that a date is after a certain date, for example. This property also uses the Expression Builder.

- Validation Text: The text that is displayed when data is entered that violates the Validation Rule property.

- Required: Specifies whether data is required to be entered into this field before the record can be saved.

- **Allow Zero Length:** Indicates whether zero-length strings are allowed in Text and Memo fields. The Help file explains in great detail the use of this property and how it interacts with the Required property.

- **Indexed:** Specifies whether the field should be indexed. There are three possible values: Yes (No Duplicates) means that the field is indexed and the value stored in this field must be unique; Yes (Duplicates Allowed) means that the field is indexed and doesn't have to be unique; No means that the field isn't indexed.

- **New Values:** Specific to the Autonumber field, this property specifies how Access generates numbers to be stored in the field. The two choices are Increment and Random.

- **Lookup Tab:** Data types with the Lookup Tab property allow you to specify how data is input and whether the valid data should be taken from a list, a query, or freeform text.

> **TIP**
>
> The default properties that Access chooses for field data type and Text and Number field sizes are specified in the Options dialog box. Select Tools | Options and then move to the Tables/Queries tab.
>
> You can also specify fields that should be automatically marked as being indexed. In the AutoIndex on Create/Import text box, enter either the beginning or ending characters of field names you want automatically indexed. For example, if you enter ID;unit, fields named ContactID and UnitPrice are indexed by default.

The properties marked as using the Lookup tab in Figure 4.8 are Text, Number, and Yes/No. The Lookup tab in the lower portion of Table Design view enables you to specify how the field appears and how possible field values are retrieved. Figure 4.9 shows the Lookup Tab for a text field. The Display Control property is set to Combo Box to show all available properties.

The first property on this tab, Display Control, controls how the field is displayed. The values chosen here also determine what other lookup properties are available. For fields with a Text or Number data type, the Display Control property can be set to Text Box, Combo Box, or List Box. For fields with a Yes/No data type, the Display Control property can be set to Text Box, Combo Box, or Check Box. The Display Control is set automatically if you selected Lookup Wizard as the data type.

If you choose Text Box, no other properties need to be set; the field appears as a simple data entry text box. The Combo Box and List Box settings enable you to specify lists of data from which the user can choose when data is being entered. This data can come from predefined lists, from queries based on data in other tables, or even from a list of fields in a table.

A detailed discussion of the Lookup tab would encompass a chapter in itself. The easiest way to learn about the Lookup tab is to use the Lookup Wizard (described next) by selecting Lookup

Wizard as the field's data type. Then you can see how the various Lookup tab properties are used to define the lookup field.

FIGURE 4.9.

The Lookup Tab.

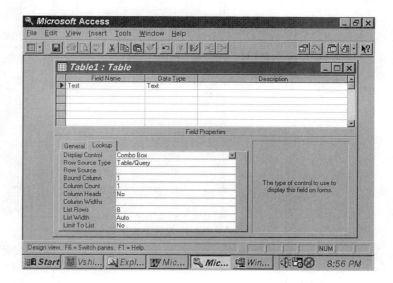

Using the Lookup Wizard

The Lookup Wizard can be used to define how a field retrieves and displays valid or suggested values. The values can be retrieved from other tables, from a query, or from a list of values that are manually entered at design time.

In order to understand the use of the Lookup Wizard, you will add a new CustomerNotes table to the Northwind Traders database included with Access. You use the Lookup Wizard to retrieve which customer the note applies to and to specify a list of possible note types. If you want to work along with the text, make sure you've installed the Lookup Wizard and the sample database.

Figure 4.10 shows the layout of the new table. Keep all field properties at their default values. The NoteID field is the table's primary key.

After you've added the CustomerNotes table to the Northwind Traders database, follow the next steps to define a lookup into the Customers table.

CAUTION

If you have the Customers table open in either Datasheet or Table Design view, you won't be able to complete the Wizards. Close the view before starting the Wizard.

FIGURE 4.10.

The Table Design view for the CustomerNotes table.

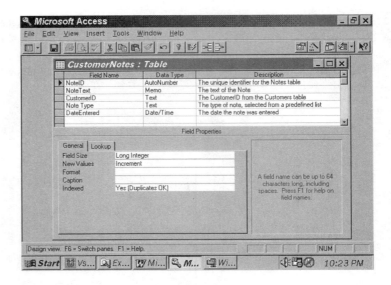

1. Select the CustomerID field and move to the Data Type column.
2. Select Lookup Wizard from the list of data types. The Lookup Wizard appears, as shown in Figure 4.11.

FIGURE 4.11.

The initial dialog of the Lookup Wizard.

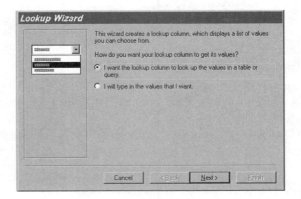

3. Choose how the lookup column gets its values. For the CustomerID field, choose "I want the lookup column to look up the values in a table or query" and click the Next button. The next dialog lets you select which table or query provides the values.
4. Select the Customers table from the list and click Next. This dialog lets you define which columns from the chosen table will be used for the lookup column.

5. Select CompanyName and CustomerID (in that order) from the list box on the left. These two fields move to the Selected Fields box, as shown in Figure 4.12.

FIGURE 4.12.

The field selection dialog of the Lookup Wizard.

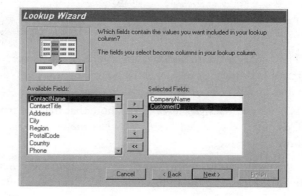

6. Click Next. The dialog box shown in Figure 4.13 appears. Although you chose two column names in the preceding step, only one appears in the grid. The check box labeled "Hide key column (recommended)" is checked. Access has correctly assumed that CustomerID will be the key, or linking, column between the two tables. If you uncheck this box, the CustomerID column will appear. For this example, we'll leave it checked.

FIGURE 4.13.

The column layout dialog of the Lookup Wizard.

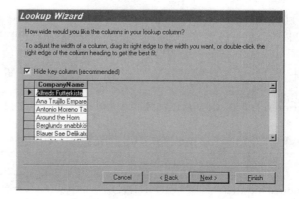

7. Adjust the CompanyName column's width to a reasonable width by dragging the right edge of the column. You also can double-click the right edge of the column to autosize the column to fit the longest company name stored in the table.

8. Click Next to come to the final dialog. Here you enter a label for the lookup column. Change the default text ("CustomerID") to "Customer" and click Finish.

NOTE

If you had left the "Hide key column" check box unchecked in step 6, you would first see a dialog asking you to specify the key column.

9. The Lookup Wizard will save the modified CustomerNotes table and establish referential integrity relationships between CustomerNotes and Customers (see Chapter 6, "Relationships").

10. When Table Design view returns, note that the Caption property now has a value of Customer, as specified in step 8. Select the Lookup tab. The properties on this tab now have values.

To see the results of this work, switch to Table Datasheet view. Select the Customer column and click the button to the right of the field. The list of customers stored in the Customers table is displayed. Selecting one causes the name to be displayed in the field. However, the CustomerID is what is actually stored in the Notes table. That way, if the CompanyName field changes, the Notes table will display the updated name without having to manually change each note applicable to the customer. Press the Esc key to restore the record to the empty state.

Next, you define a list of values that can be stored in the NoteType field:

1. Return to Table Design view and select the NoteType field's data type column.

2. Select Lookup Wizard as the data type.

3. This time, select "I will type in the values that I want" and click Next. The dialog that appears enables you to specify the number of columns to be displayed and the values in the list for each column.

4. Enter 2 in the Number of Columns text box. The display changes to show two columns.

5. Enter data as shown in Table 4.1 and click Next when finished.

Table 4.1. Values for the NoteType lookup column.

Col1	Col2
Product Inquiry	PRODINQ
Product Comment	PRODCOM
Complaint	COMPLNT
Order Inquiry	ORDRINQ
Misc. Note	MSCNOTE

6. In this dialog, you define which field from the chosen table has its value stored in the lookup column.

7. You will be storing the data entered in Col2, so select Col2 in the list and click Next. The final dialog asks for a field label.

8. Change the default to add a space between Note and Type and click Finish.

9. Again, switch to the Lookup tab for the NoteType field and enter 1.5;0 in the Column Widths property. Make sure the List Width property is 1.5 or greater.

10. Save the table, switch to Table Datasheet view, and check out the NoteType column.

The Lookup Wizard is a powerful addition to Microsoft Access. It enables you to easily take advantage of the relational database features of Access.

Defining the Primary Key and Other Indexes

A primary key is a field or group of fields that uniquely identifies each record stored in a table. Although primary keys aren't required, they are highly recommended because they allow Access to quickly relate data among different tables. Primary keys are also automatically indexed, which speeds the lookup of records in the database.

Primary key fields must contain unique data throughout the table. For this reason, an Autonumber field should be added to each table and used as the primary key for the table. Fields such as Social Security number or employee ID, which should be unique, can also be used as primary keys.

To specify the primary key for a table, go to Table Design view for the table. Select the field (or fields) to be used and either click the Primary Key button on the toolbar (it resembles a key) or select Edit | Primary Key.

> **NOTE**
>
> To select multiple fields, move the cursor to the leftmost column of the Table Design view grid. The cursor changes to an arrow pointing to the right. Click the left mouse button. To select another field, hold down the Ctrl key and repeat the process for that field. Continue until the needed fields have been selected.

Notice that when you assign a field to the primary key, the Indexed property for the field changes to Yes (No Duplicates). This means that Access indexes this field and duplicates aren't allowed in the field. The Required property should also be set to Yes because a table can't have NULL values in its primary key fields.

If fields in the table will often be used in searches or in sorting the data, they should be indexed. To create a single field index, select the field in Table Design view and set its `Indexed` property to either Yes (No Duplicates) or Yes (Duplicates Allowed).

To create an index consisting of multiple fields, do the following:

1. Click the Indexes button on the toolbar (directly to the right of the Primary Key button). The Indexes window for the table appears, as shown in Figure 4.14. Note that the NoteID and CustomerID fields already appear in the list of indexes. This is because Access 95 has an AutoIndex on Import/Create option. This option specifies the beginning or ending characters of field names that will automatically be indexed when a table is created or imported. The default value for the option is `ID;key;code;num`. Since NoteID and CustomerID both end in ID, they are automatically indexed.

FIGURE 4.14.

The Indexes window for the CustomerNotes table.

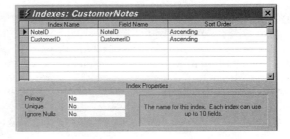

2. In the CustomerNotes table, you'll want to sort on CustomerID and NoteType, so you'll create a multiple field index based on these fields.

3. Place the cursor in the Field Name column of the row below the CustomerID row and select NoteType. Leave Sort Order as Ascending for both fields in the index. If you want a field to be sorted in descending order, simply change its Sort Order column to Descending.

4. Move the cursor back to the Index Name column on the first row (the row for NoteID). Notice the three properties in the lower-left corner of the window. These properties let you specify if this index is the primary key, whether the combination of values stored in the fields must be unique, and whether Access includes records containing NULL values when the index is created. For example, if you wanted to make sure each customer had only one note of a specific type, you would set the `Unique` property for this index to Yes.

5. Change the value for Primary to Yes. This specifies that NoteID is the primary key for this table. Note that the value for Unique changes to Yes as well. The window should now look like Figure 4.15.

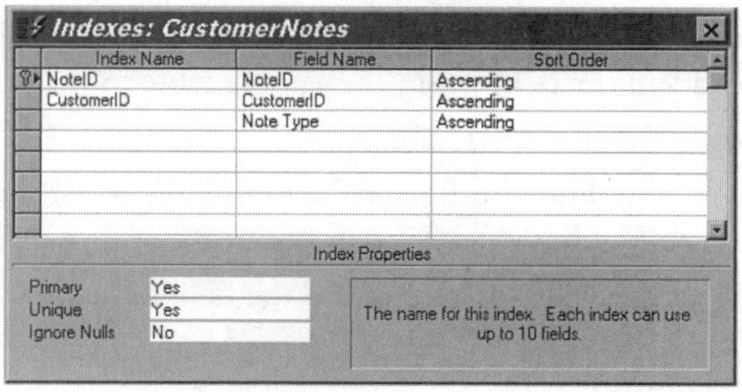

FIGURE 4.15.

The completed Indexes window for the CustomerNotes table.

Creating a Table Using the Access Wizards

So far this chapter has discussed creating tables the hard way. The next several sections describe creating tables using Access's various table creation Wizards.

Creating a Table Using the Table Wizard

The first of these Wizards is called, simply, the Table Wizard. This Wizard creates a table that is based on any one of a predefined set of tables. This Wizard enables you to select a table to use as a model, select which fields from the table to use, rename the fields, specify a table name, allow Access to set a primary key, and set up relationships between the new table and any existing tables. The steps are described as follows:

1. Create a new table by clicking the New button in the Tables tab of the Database window (see Figure 4.3).

2. In the New Table dialog box, select Table Wizard and click OK (see Figure 4.4).

3. The first dialog of the Wizard, shown in Figure 4.16, shows the sample tables and their fields in either the Business or the Personal category.

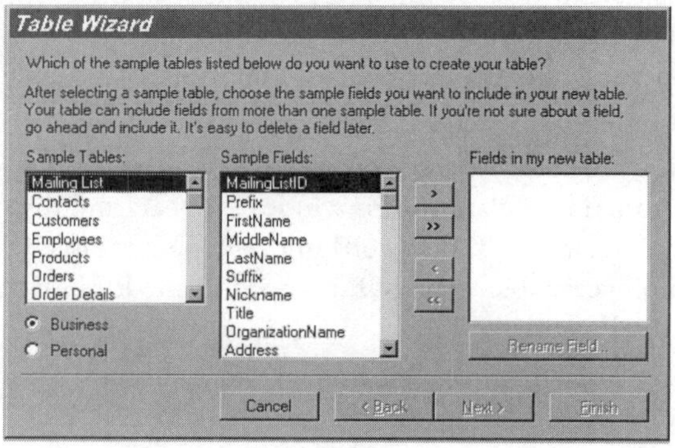

FIGURE 4.16.

The first dialog of the Table Wizard.

If you select a table in the leftmost list, the list of sample fields changes.

To add all the fields from the sample table to the new table, click the >> button.

To add fields individually, click the > button.

If you would like to change a field's name, select the name in the rightmost list, click Rename Field, and enter a new name.

Once you've chosen a table and the fields you want to base your new table on, click Next.

You will add an Expenses table to the Northwind database.

4. Find Expenses in the Business list of tables and select it.

5. Move all fields to the rightmost list. The dialog should look like Figure 4.17. Click Next.

FIGURE 4.17.

The completed first dialog of the Table Wizard.

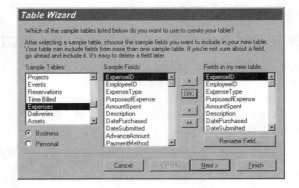

6. The next dialog enables you to rename the table and specify whether you want Access to set a primary key. Leave the defaults as they are.

7. Click Next to move on. The next dialog appears only if there are other tables in the database. This dialog is where relationships between tables are established. The Expenses table will be related to the Employees table, and Access has already assumed this (see Figure 4.18).

8. Select the item Related to Employees in the list box and click the Relationships button. The Relationships window appears and displays three choices: "The tables aren't related"; "One record in the Expenses table will match many records in the Employees table"; and "One record in the Employees table will match many records in the Expenses table."

9. Because each employee can incur many expenses, leave the third option selected and click OK.

FIGURE 4.18.

The relationships dialog of the Table Wizard.

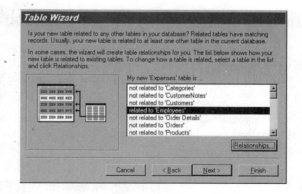

10. This is the only relationship you have, so click Next to move to the last dialog of the Wizard. This dialog enables you to specify where you will go once the new table is created (see Figure 4.19).

FIGURE 4.19.

The final dialog of the Table Wizard.

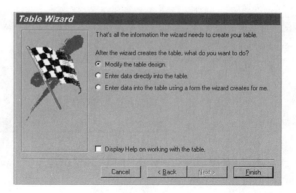

11. For this example, choose the first option, "Modify the table design," and click Finish.

Once you're in Table Design view for the Calls table, you can modify properties as necessary. You should also use the Lookup Wizard (described earlier) to set the EmployeeID field to be a lookup column into the Employees table.

This method is obviously easier and more efficient for users new to Access to create tables than creating them from scratch. However, once you've created enough tables, you will find it much quicker to start with Table Design view.

Creating a Table Using the Import Table Wizard

The Import Table Wizard allows data and objects to be imported from external sources. These include Excel spreadsheets, dBASE database tables, any ODBC data sources defined on your system, other Access databases, and many other sources. The Wizard proceeds differently depending on which source is chosen. This section covers two of the most common examples.

To begin an import, click the New button in the Tables tab of the Database window. In the New Table dialog box, select Import Table Wizard and click OK. The Import dialog box appears, as shown in Figure 4.20.

FIGURE 4.20.

The Import dialog box.

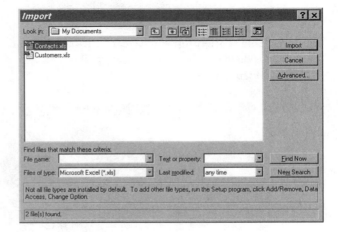

Although this is a very busy-looking dialog box, there are really two main components. This is a standard Microsoft Office File Find dialog box. It enables you to search for files on your hard drive or network using a variety of criteria. For now, we'll just cover the important parts. To choose which type of file to use as the source for the import, select it from the Files of Type list box in the lower-left corner. The top left side is used for directory navigation and enables you to manually locate a file on your hard drive or network.

Importing an Excel Spreadsheet

To import an Excel spreadsheet into a new table of the database, follow these steps:

1. Select Microsoft Excel (*.xls) in the Files of Type list box.

    The top portion of the dialog box changes to show only Excel spreadsheet files. For this section, we import a spreadsheet that contains a list of contacts and some information about them. (This file, CONTACTS.XLS, is included on the CD that comes with this book.) After you select the file using the Import dialog box, the first Import Spreadsheet Wizard dialog appears, as shown in Figure 4.21. This dialog enables you to specify which row to start importing from (in case some rows contain header information, for example) and whether the first row of data contains the column names.

FIGURE 4.21.

The initial dialog of the Import Spreadsheet Wizard.

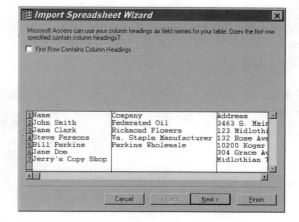

2. For this example, use row 1 as the starting row. The first row contains the field names to use, so check the First Row Contains Column Headings check box. The grid at the bottom changes to show that the first row is the field names.

3. Click Next. This dialog enables you to specify field names and whether the field is indexed. Also, you can choose not to import a column by checking the Don't import field (Skip) check box. This dialog also shows the data type Access uses for the field when it creates the new table, as shown in Figure 4.22.

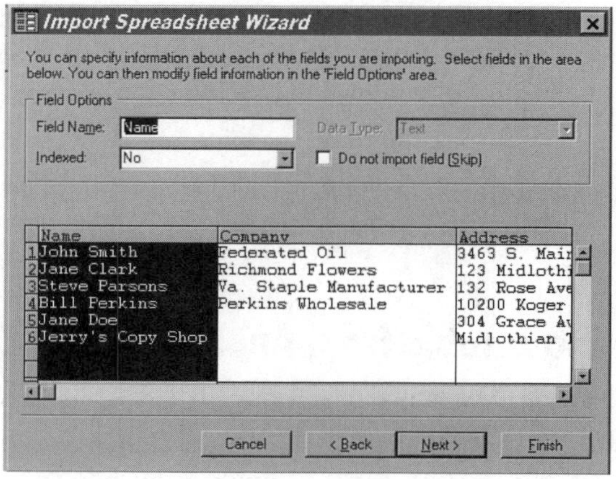

FIGURE 4.22.

The Field Options dialog of the Import Spreadsheet Wizard.

4. To make changes here, click the column to be modified and change as necessary. When you're satisfied, click Next. This dialog, shown in Figure 4.23, enables you to specify how the primary key field is created. The first option, Let Access add Primary Key, adds a field named ID. This field contains sequential numbers for each record imported. This is the recommended method. The second option, Choose my own Primary Key, enables you to specify a field from the imported data to serve as the primary key. The third choice, No Primary Key, leaves the primary key undefined (this is highly discouraged).

FIGURE 4.23.

The Primary Key dialog of the Import Spreadsheet Wizard.

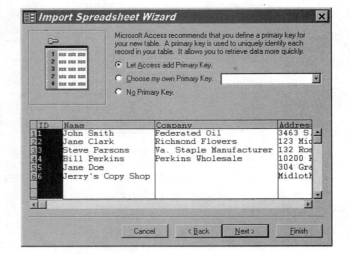

5. Clicking Next takes you to the final dialog of the Wizard.
6. This is where you name the table. Give it a meaningful name that obeys the naming rules. You can also have Access invoke the Table Analyzer Wizard by checking the check box in the window. This Wizard analyzes the new table's relational structure.
7. Click Finish to create the new table.

The new table is shown in Table Datasheet view in Figure 4.24.

Importing a Table from Another Access Database

The Table Import Wizard can also be used to copy both data and structure from an existing Access table. The beginning steps are identical to importing a spreadsheet, except that an Access database file is selected in the Import dialog box.

The Import Objects dialog box, shown in Figure 4.25, displays all the objects stored in the selected database. These include not only tables, but also queries, forms, reports, macros, and modules. For now, just stay in the Tables tab. You can select more than one table by simply clicking the tables to be imported. After the tables have been selected, click the OK button. The table and its data are copied into the current database.

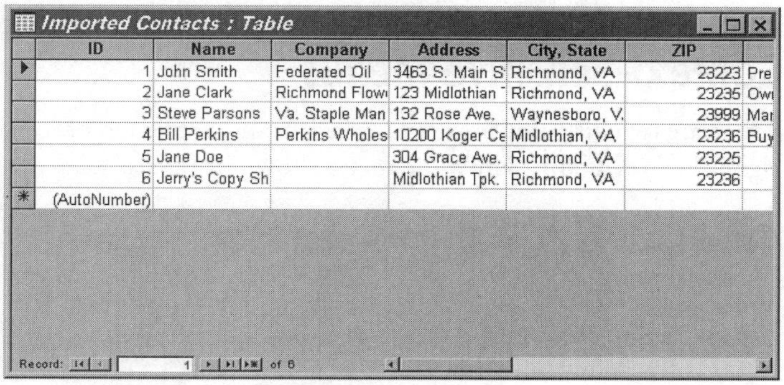

FIGURE 4.24.

The imported table in Table Datasheet view.

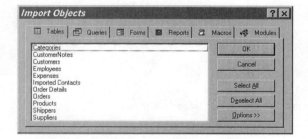

FIGURE 4.25.

The Import Objects dialog box.

Using the Link Table Wizard

The Link Table Wizard creates links between the current database and tables in an external file. Select the Link Table Wizard in the New Table dialog box and click OK. The Link dialog box appears. It's identical in form and function to the Import dialog box. After the file containing the table to be linked to is selected, the Link Tables dialog box appears. Select the tables to be linked and click OK. These tables are now linked to the current database.

You can view and modify the data in linked tables, join data in your database to them, and modify certain properties of them. If you delete the linked table from the current database, only the link is removed. The table isn't deleted from the source database.

This feature is useful for linking a test database to production data or accessing data contained in an ODBC database, such as SQL Server.

Using the Database Window's Tables Tab

The Database window is packed with features that assist you in maintaining your Access database. A few of these are highlighted here. However, experience is the best teacher. I recommend that you open an existing database such as one of the samples included with Access and experiment with the Database window.

Context-Sensitive Menus

There are two different shortcut menus for the Tables tab of the Database window. When you right-click on a table name, the menu shown in Figure 4.26 appears.

FIGURE 4.26.

The pop-up menu for a selected table in the Database window.

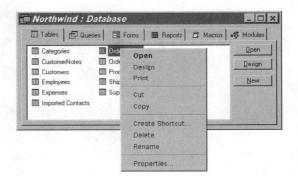

The items on this menu are as follows:

- Open: Opens the selected table in Table Datasheet view.
- Design: Opens the selected table in Table Design view.
- Print: Prints the data stored in the table to the default printer.
- Cut: Deletes the current table and makes a copy available on the clipboard.
- Copy: Copies the current table to the clipboard.
- Create Shortcut: Creates a Windows shortcut (in the location specified) to the table. Double-clicking the shortcut opens Access and loads the table in Table Datasheet view.
- Delete: Deletes the table and all its data from the database.
- Rename: Enables the name of the table to be changed.
- Properties: Displays the property sheet for the selected table. This is where a description of the table can be entered and system information about the table is displayed.

The shortcut menu that appears when you right-click in the List view but not on a table name enables you to change the way the table names are viewed (similar to the Windows Explorer) and the way the list of table names is sorted. If a table is saved on the clipboard, this menu has a Paste option. It also provides a quick means to access the Import and Link Tables Wizards as well as the Relationships window.

Using OfficeLinks

The OfficeLinks menu item is available on the Tools menu. This menu item provides a quick way of using other Microsoft Office products to publish or analyze the data in a table.

You can merge data in the table with a Microsoft Word document. Select Tools | OfficeLinks | Merge It. The Microsoft Word Mail Merge menu appears. You can either merge the data with an existing document or create a new document and then merge the data. This is a quick way of creating address labels or form letters based on data in the table.

You can create a spreadsheet containing the data in a table by selecting Analyze It With MS Excel. This copies the data into a new Excel spreadsheet.

Finally, you can create a Word document that contains the data in tabular form by selecting Publish It With MS Word.

Establishing Table Relationships

Relationships are the building blocks used to establish a relational database. Chapter 6 discusses relationships and how they are created. Here we discuss the basics of creating the relationships contained in a database.

There is a window devoted to table relationships. You access it by selecting Tools | Relationships or by selecting the Relationships item from the shortcut menu that appears when you right-click with no table selected in the Database window's Tables tab. The Relationships window for the Northwind database is shown in Figure 4.27.

The Relationships window is a graphical design tool. Relationships between tables are established by dragging and dropping common fields between tables. The properties of the relationship (such as join type and how to enforce referential integrity) are changed to meet the needs of the database design (see Chapter 7).

Modifying an Existing Table

Once a table is created, it is by no means set in concrete. It might become necessary to add a field or modify some properties of a field (text length, validation rules, and so on). You might also discover that a field is unnecessary and should be deleted.

Changes to a table are made in Table Design view for the table. To open Table Design view, select the table in the Database window and click the Design button.

FIGURE 4.27.

The Relationships window.

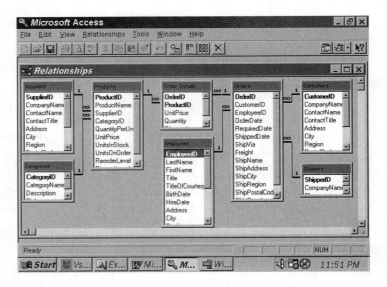

Changing a Field

You modify a field's properties using the same method used to assign the properties. Select the field to be modified, select the property, and enter the new value in the property box. For example, to change the caption associated with a field, select the field, place the cursor in the text box next to Caption, and edit any existing caption.

You should be careful when changing some properties, however. For instance, if you change a Text field's `Field Size` property to a smaller value, you could lose some data if the value entered is smaller than the longest piece of text in that field. Also, changing validation rules requires Access to validate any existing data for compliance with the new rule. If data is found that doesn't follow the validation rule, Access asks you how to handle the situation.

> **NOTE**
>
> If you change a field's data type, Access checks the new data type against any data contained in the field when you save the table design. If there is data that isn't valid for the new data type, Access will prompt you about how it should be handled. You can either delete the offending data and continue, or cancel the save operation. You must then fix the data type to match the data or fix the data to match the desired data type.

Adding a Field

To add a field to the table, select the row where you want the new field to appear. Do this by clicking in the leftmost column of the grid on Table Design view. Then either press the Insert key or select Insert | Field. A blank row is added to the grid. Create the new field following the instructions in the section "Using Table Design View."

You can also add a row by placing the cursor in any column on the row of the grid where you want the field to be inserted, right-clicking, and selecting Insert Field from the shortcut menu.

Deleting a Field

To delete a field, select its row in the grid on the left side of the Table Design view window. Select Edit | Delete or Edit | Delete Row. When Access displays a confirmation dialog box, click Yes to permanently delete the field.

You can also delete a row by placing the cursor in any column of the row to be deleted, right-clicking, and selecting Delete Field from the shortcut menu.

Summary

This chapter discussed the many ways of creating tables in an Access database. The hard ways (Table Design view and Table Datasheet view) were discussed first. I then moved on to explain how to use the built-in Wizards to create tables or link to external tables. I discussed a few of the many features of the Database window, as well as the Relationships window. Finally, you learned that modifying a table is just as easy as creating one. This chapter has prepared you to create a working database with a minimum of effort. Future chapters discuss how to optimize the database's design to get the maximum benefit of relational databases.

The final database, including all examples from this chapter, is included on the CD that comes with this book. It's called Modified Northwind.mdb.

Importing and Exporting Data

5

by Dwayne Gifford

In today's business world, most database applications rely on giving data to or getting data from other applications. In order for an application to have access to this data, the data must be made available to it. One of the ways for data to be made available is to export the data from the other application and import it into the current application. If the application needs to share its data, it needs to export the data in a format that other applications can import. The goal of this chapter is to explain how to import and export data to and from Access. This chapter uses the Graphical User Interface (GUI) tools that Access makes available.

The Import and Export Interfaces

Access supplies many GUI tools to help you import and export data in many different formats. These tools have many similarities, so none of them should seem too unfamiliar.

The Import Interface

To get to the Import tool, you can either select File | Get External Data | Import or right-click in the Database window. When you click Import, the dialog box shown in Figure 5.1 appears. This is where you select the appropriate file to import.

FIGURE 5.1.

Selecting a file for import.

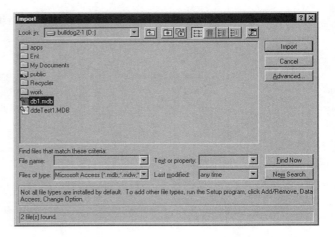

The Import dialog box enables you to navigate your way through the file folders until you locate the file you wish to import. First, select the type of file you wish to import; the Import dialog box limits the file list to the type selected. You select the type of file from the Files of type list box. After selecting the type, you need to navigate your way to the correct folder. To change drives, click the Look in list box. To change to a folder other than the current one, you need to click the Up One Level button, which has an arrow pointing up inside a folder. After you select the file you wish to import, click the OK button.

Depending on the format you've chosen, you're presented with appropriate dialog boxes and selections.

The Export Interface

Access gives you the flexibility to export all database objects. However, you must remember some rules when exporting any of the objects:

- When exporting a table or a query, you can save the object to a new file or database or a new table or query within the current database.

- When exporting a form or a report, you're limited to Access, Excel versions 5 through 7, text files, and rich text format. In all cases except the Access format, the data that makes up the form or report is exported. Access actually exports the form or report, not the data.

- When you're exporting a macro, you're limited to an external file or database, a Visual Basic module, or a new macro within the current database.

- When you're exporting a module, you can export into Access and text files.

After deciding what to export, select File | Save As/Export to start the export process. You're presented with a dialog box that asks if you want to save within the current database or to an external file or database. If you select an external file or database, the export dialog box, shown in Figure 5.2, appears.

FIGURE 5.2.

Using the Export Interface to export data.

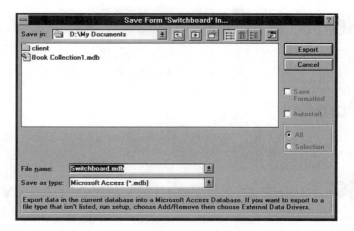

This dialog box enables you to navigate your way through the file folders until you locate the file you want to export. First, select the type of file you want to export so that only that type of file appears in the list. Do this using the Save as type list box. Once the type has been selected, you need to navigate your way to the correct folder. To change drives, click the Save in list box.

To change to a folder other than the current folder, click the Up One Level button, which has an arrow pointing up inside a folder. After you select the file you want to export, click OK or press Enter.

Depending on the format you choose, you're presented with different interfaces. These different interfaces are covered in the following sections.

Standard File Formats

Access has more than 10 different formats available for export and more than eight formats available for import. Import has fewer formats because the available Text Import Wizards grouped all text files as one format. In export, the text files are separated into the following groups: delimited and fixed-width, rich text format, and Word mail merge format. Rich text format is the only file format that can't be imported into Access.

Microsoft FoxPro

Versions 2.x and 3.0 of Microsoft FoxPro file formats are available to you for importing or exporting. When exporting to any of these formats, you're prompted for the location and filename. When importing, you need to locate the file, highlight it, and click OK. If the file is imported successfully, a prompt is displayed, giving you the table name. These files usually have an extension of .DBF.

dBASE

dBASE III, IV, and 5 are all supported. These files usually have a .DBF extension, the same as Microsoft FoxPro. The Import and Export tools work the same as they do for FoxPro.

Paradox

Versions 3.x, 4.x, and 5.0 of Paradox are all supported. These files usually have a .DB extension. The Import and Export tools work the same as for FoxPro.

SQL Tables and Databases Supported by ODBC

In order for Access to import or export a table from or to Microsoft SQL Server, Sybase SQL Server, Oracle Server, and other formats, you need to have an installed ODBC driver. Click Save as type and choose ODBC Databases. A SQL Data Source dialog box appears, prompting you to select the data source from the list. When you're exporting, a prompt for the table or query name appears before the SQL Data Source dialog box. If your data source is in the list, select it and then click OK. If it's not in the list, you can create a new source by clicking the New button.

> **WARNING**
>
> If you select ODBC Database and you receive the error message `Unable to locate ODBC32.DLL`, you need to either reinstall Access or add the option Microsoft SQL Server ODBC Driver, which is located under Data Access. When reinstalling, you will need to select the custom installation option and make sure that the option Microsoft SQL Server ODBC Driver is selected.

Follow these steps to create a new data source for a SQL Server database:

1. Choose the type of ODBC driver that the source will be based on.

2. Set up the DataSource Name (DSN), Description, Server (the name of the host machine), Network Address, and Network Library.

   If you wish to set up further options, click the Options button. This enables you to set up the database name, the language, an option to have the stored procedures generated for prepared statements, and an option to convert OEM to ANSI characters or click Select and choose another available translation type. After you've entered all the information, click the OK button. If you have any questions regarding this section, click the Help button.

> **NOTE**
>
> If you select an installed ODBC driver other than SQL Server, you will be prompted for the DSN and the description. After that, each of the available drivers has different requirements.

3. You're returned to the DataSource window with your new entry as the active item. To use this new source, click OK.

4. You're asked to sign into the source. DataSource is defaulted to the DSN you selected in the previous window. Login ID is blank, or if you're using Windows NT, it defaults to the name you used to sign into Windows NT. The password is left blank.

   If you click the Options button, you're presented with four new choices. The first is a drop-down list of Database names; it defaults to the database name that was typed in the database option field in the previous window. If it was blank there, it is blank now. The next choice you have is Language, and the last two choices are Application Name and Workstation ID. Both of these fields are filled in with the appropriate information. The Application Name is Microsoft Access, the owner of software name is the name that you would enter in the Name and Information Dialog when Setup is run, and the Workstation ID is the name used to identify your computer.

> **NOTE**
>
> If an invalid username and/or password is entered, you will receive an ODBC error when you try to click the Database list box or the Language list box.

5. If you're exporting, you're returned to the Database window unless there was a problem with the export. If you're importing, you have a few more steps.

6. After you've typed in a valid username and password (if required), the Import Objects dialog box, shown in Figure 5.3, appears. This dialog box includes a list of available tables that can be imported.

FIGURE 5.3.

The Import Objects dialog box.

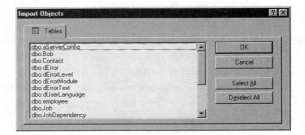

7. With the new Import engine, you can import one table or multiple tables. To select all the tables, click the Select All button. To select multiple tables, either Shift-click or Ctrl-click on the tables you want to select. Shift-click will select all the tables between the first and last one that you highlight, and Ctrl-click will select the table you click on. If you want to start the selection process over, click the Deselect All button. When you're satisfied with your selection, click OK. The dialog box shown in Figure 5.4 appears, giving you an import status. If there were no problems with the import, you're returned to the Database window.

FIGURE 5.4.

Clicking the Options button to import objects to Access.

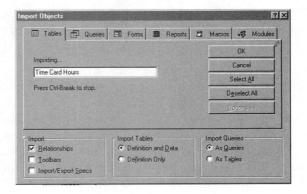

Microsoft Excel

Versions 2.0 through 7.0 of Excel are supported by Access 95. When you select a spreadsheet file from the Import Objects dialog box, shown in Figure 5.3, or the Export dialog box, you're presented with the Import Spreadsheet Wizard or the Export Spreadsheet Wizard. These Wizards are fully covered in the section "Text and Spreadsheet Data."

Lotus 1-2-3 Spreadsheets

Three formats are supported by Lotus 1-2-3: WKS, WK1, and WK3. When you select any of these formats, you are walked through the Import Spreadsheet Wizard or Export Spreadsheet Wizard just like you are in Excel. These Wizards are fully covered in the "Text and Spreadsheet Data" section of this chapter.

Text Files

After selecting Text file from the Files of Type list box in the Import or Export dialog box and locating your file, click OK. You're presented with the Text Import Wizard dialog box or the Text Export Wizard dialog box. The Text Wizards help you import or export the text file. These dialog boxes are covered in the section "Text and Spreadsheet Data."

Access

Selecting an Access .MDB file to import or export is much like importing or exporting from an SQL Server source. When you select an .MDB file for import and click OK, you see the dialog box shown in Figure 5.5. Instead of just the Tables tab, it also has tabs for queries, forms, reports, macros, and modules. Inside this dialog box you can select multiple items in each of the tabs. You also can click Select All to select all entries for the current tab. If you click Deselect All, the items that are selected for the current tab are deselected.

FIGURE 5.5.

The Import Objects dialog box.

After selecting the items you want to import, click OK. You see the dialog box change from the one shown in Figure 5.5 to the one shown in Figure 5.4. You can watch it go through the items that were selected. Upon completion of the import, you're returned to the Database window.

When you select an .MDB file for export, you can export only one table at a time. Your only options are Definition and Data, and Definition Only.

Text and Spreadsheet Data

Access has three Wizards available to help you import and export data—the Import Text Wizard, the Export Text Wizard, and the Import Spreadsheet Wizard. When you select one of these formats, the corresponding Wizard starts up and helps you import or export the data.

The Import Text Wizard and the Import Spreadsheet Wizard

Because these two Wizards have the same last steps, I'll cover the unique steps from each Wizard before covering the common steps. The Import Text Wizard asks whether the file is delimited or fixed-width.

As you change between the two options, you see the sample window change to the new choice. When you click the Advanced button, the dialog shown in Figure 5.6 appears. Here you can change the file specifications for import. The options here are File Format, File Origin, Date Order, Date Delimiter, Time Delimiter, Four Digit Years, Leading Zeros in Dates, and Decimal Symbol. You also can change the size of the column by adjusting the Field Information. If you've already set up your own import specifications, you can load them by clicking the Specs button. If you like these specifications and want to use them again, you can click Save As and give them a name to be used later.

FIGURE 5.6.

The Customers Import Specification dialog.

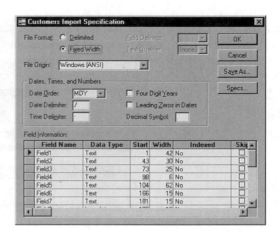

If you select Fixed Width, you're prompted to tell the Wizard where the breaks occur. A break is where you think one column of information stops and a new column starts. The default for Fixed Width is best guess, meaning that it tries to decide for you. If you select Delimited, you need to tell the Wizard what type of delimiter it is and whether the first row contains the header information. The default for delimited files is best guess; if it isn't one of the common delimiters, it is still best guess from the common delimiters. If you're importing a file that isn't using a common delimiter, don't click Finish before you've completed this step.

Now that you've told the Wizard how to divide the text into columns, it needs to know if it should append the text to an existing table or place it in a new table. The default is a new table.

The Import Spreadsheet Wizard, shown in Figure 5.7, gives you two options. The first option is to show worksheets, and the second option is to show named ranges. Depending on which item is selected, you're given a list of available items. By default, the first item in the list is selected. This list item tells the sample data window what to display. As you change between items in the window, the sample data is changed to the correct data.

FIGURE 5.7.

The initial Import Spreadsheet Wizard dialog.

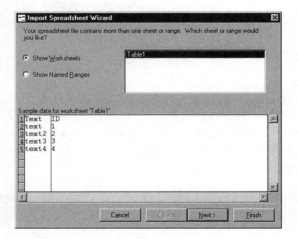

If you select a worksheet in the initial window, the Wizard asks which line to start the import from and whether the first line contains the header information. If you select a named range, the Wizard asks only whether the first line contains the header information. The default is to start with line 1 and leave the Include Field Names option unchecked.

The following information is the same for the Import Text Wizard and the Import Spreadsheet Wizard.

If you choose to append to an existing table from the Import Text Wizard, you skip the next prompt. Otherwise, both Wizards ask whether each column has an index. If you're running the Import Text Wizard, it also lets you change the data type. Figure 5.8 shows the Text Import Wizard. Here you can set the data type for each column. It does a best guess for all columns. After you've checked each column and verified that the column is the way you want it, click the Next button. The default is no index for all columns and best guess on the data type.

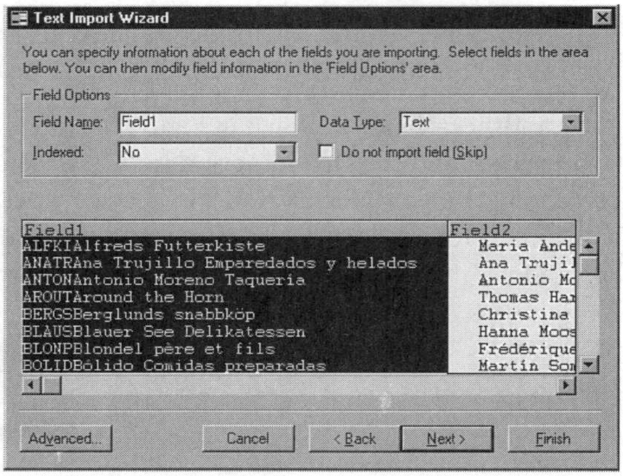

FIGURE 5.8.

The Text Import Wizard with Data Type enabled.

If you choose to append to an existing table from the Import Text Wizard, the next step is bypassed. You have three options: allow Access to add an index, identify the index from the columns that are being added, or import the file as is. Figure 5.9 shows this dialog with the Let Access add Primary Key option selected. Notice that Access has added a new column called ID to the sample window.

FIGURE 5.9.

The Text Import Wizard with Primary Key selected.

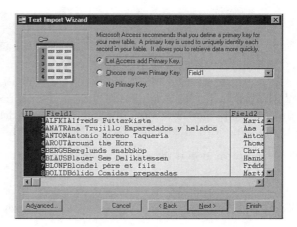

It's recommended that all data being added have an index. By default, Access assumes that you want it to add an index for you.

The last step for the Import Wizards is to type in a name for the new table and choose whether you would like to have Access analyze the structure after the table has been imported. The defaults are table1 for the name and No for the Analyze my table after the import is over option. If you haven't clicked Analyze table, you see the Import Success dialog box when the table has been imported. This is only if no errors were encountered in the import.

If you select Analyze Table After Import, you're presented with the Import Spreadsheet Wizard message box, shown in Figure 5.10. It tells you that the import was successful and asks if you want the Wizard to analyze the table. If you click Yes, you will be placed in the Table Analyzer Wizard (covered in Chapter 7, "Database Fundamentals").

FIGURE 5.10.

The Import Spreadsheet Wizard message box.

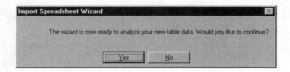

At any time during the Import Text Wizard or Import Spreadsheet Wizard process, you can click the Finish button, and the Wizard supplies the default answers for the remaining questions and imports the data. After it has imported the data, you're presented with the Import Wizard Success dialog box.

The Export Text Wizard

When you're exporting a table to a Text-formatted file, Access saves the name of the table and the type of Text extension.

Throughout the Export Text Wizard, you can click the Advanced button. You can then change the file specifications for export. Figure 5.11 shows the options that are available. The options here are File Origin, Date Order, Date Delimiter, Time Delimiter, Four Digit Years, Leading Zeros in Dates, and Decimal Symbol. You also can change the size of the column by adjusting the Field Information. If you've already set up your own export specs, you can load them by clicking the Specs button. If you like these specs and wish to use them again, click Save As and give the specs a name to be loaded later.

You also can choose whether the file is delimited or fixed-width. As you switch between the two options, you see the sample window reflect the new choice.

If you select Fixed Width, you must tell the Wizard where the breaks occur. The default for Fixed Width is best guess. If you select Delimited File, the Wizard needs to know what type of delimiter to use and whether the first row should be used for the header information.

The last step for the Wizard is to name the file. The default is the current directory and the table name as a filename plus a .TXT extension. If all goes well, you see a success dialog stating that the file has been created.

FIGURE 5.11.

The Customers Export Specification dialog.

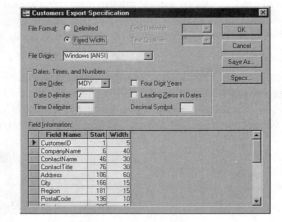

Legacy Data

Legacy data refers to existing business data. It's often in a format that is native to an obsolete, midrange, or mainframe system. Usually it would come from DB2, Oracle, Ingres, or other RDBMSs. The file formats of these types of systems differ from Access 95's native file format.

When this type of data is imported into Access, you should use a fixed-width text file. When Access imports the data, it sets the field length to the size of the fixed width you defined when saving the data to the file. This guarantees that the field length is set to the same as in the original system, making future imports possible without field-length problems. This format is generally the fastest, most reliable, and easiest to support and maintain. Delimited-width file formats aren't typically used because Access defaults the field lengths to the maximum current field length in the delimited file. This wastes disk space by allocating it to field lengths that won't be completely filled.

Summary

Access tries to give you the easiest way to get at data, no matter what its format. Access also tries to make sure that this data comes across without errors. This is why Access gives you so many Wizards to help you through difficult tasks and why Access has so many default formats available.

Relationships

6

by Craig Eddy

IN THIS CHAPTER

Microsoft Access is what is known as a relational database management system (RDBMS). The word "relational" is the key to the power of Microsoft Access and all other RDBMSs. It is the ability to create and act on relationships between tables that is the real power of relational databases.

Relational databases use fields called *key fields,* which are common among one or more tables, to establish these relationships. Records having the same value in the key field or fields that relate the tables they belong to can be "joined" to produce a new pseudo-table. This pseudo-table more than likely won't physically exist in the database. Its purpose is to gather data from the tables that were joined so that it can be acted on by the front-end application.

Three types of relationships can be created. However, for all practical and academic purposes, one of these types is not allowed in a relational database. The three types are

- One-to-one: For every record in one of the tables, there is one corresponding record in the other table.
- One-to-many: For each record in a table, there may be many corresponding records in the related table.
- Many-to-many: For each record in table A, there may be many records in table B. Likewise, for each record in table B, there may be many records in table A. Many-to-many relationships should not exist in a well-designed database. (See Chapter 7, "Database Fundamentals," for more details.)

This chapter discusses the basics of establishing relationships between tables in an Access database. The details of database design are left for the next chapter because they are unnecessary for the discussion at hand.

Creating Relationships While Creating Tables

Relationships can be defined either while the table is being created or afterwards. In order to define a relationship, both tables must exist in the database. This section describes creating relationships between tables while a new table is being created. There are two useful methods for doing this. The first is part of the Table Wizard. This wizard can be used to create a new table based on table templates included with Microsoft Access. The second method is to define Lookup Columns while a table is being created or edited in either Table Design view or Table Datasheet view.

Using the Table Wizard

The Table Wizard is a handy way to create a new table that will be based on a predefined template. You will first use the Table Wizard to create a table to store customers and a table to store orders, as well as to create the relationship between the customers and orders tables. To create the customers table, follow these steps:

1. Start Access with a blank database. Name the database Relationship Example.

2. Click the New button on the Tables tab of the Database window. Select Table Wizard from the list that appears and click OK.

3. On the first dialog of the wizard, select Customers from the Sample Tables list box. Then move all the fields in the Sample Fields list box to the Fields in the new table list box by clicking the >> button. The dialog should appear identical to the one shown in Figure 6.1. Click Next.

FIGURE 6.1.

The initial dialog of the Table Wizard for creating the new Customers table.

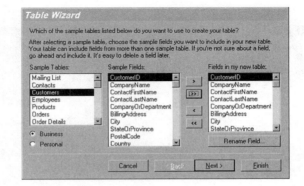

4. Accept the defaults on the next dialog by clicking Next. Finally, accept the defaults on the last dialog and click Finish. When the Customers Table Datasheet view appears, close the window to return to the Database window.

Now you add the Orders table in a similar manner. However, because an existing table is in the database, the Table Wizard provides an additional dialog allowing you to establish a relationship between the Orders table being created and the existing Customers table. Follow these steps to create the Orders table and establish the relationship:

1. With the Tables tab active in the Database window, click New. Select Table Wizard from the list and click OK.

2. Select the Orders table from the Sample Tables list. Select all fields from the Sample Fields list by using the >> button. The dialog should be identical to the one shown in Figure 6.2. Click Next.

3. Accept the defaults in the next dialog. Click Next.

4. The dialog shown in Figure 6.3 appears. As you can see, Access has already assumed that there is a relationship between the Customers and Orders tables, thanks to the CustomerID field that appears in both tables.

FIGURE 6.2.

The initial dialog of the Table Wizard for creating the new Orders table.

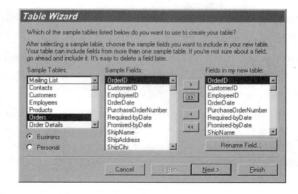

FIGURE 6.3.

The Relationships dialog of the Table Wizard for the new Orders table.

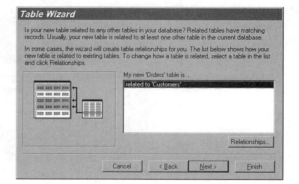

5. To view or modify the type of relationship that is established, click the Relationships button. The Table Relationships dialog, shown in Figure 6.4, is displayed with three options: The tables aren't related, One record in the Orders table will match many records in the Customers table, and One record in the Customers table will match many records in the Orders table. Because each customer will (hopefully) have many orders, leave the default option as is and click OK.

FIGURE 6.4.

The Table Relationships dialog of the Table Wizard for the Orders and Customers tables.

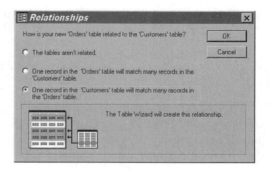

6. Click Next. On the final dialog, click Finish. Once again, when Table Datasheet view appears, close the window to return to the Database window.

The relationship established when using the Table Wizard is a true relationship from the database design standpoint. You can open the Relationships window by selecting Tools | Relationships and see the relationship you've just established. (See the section "Setting Up Relationships for Existing Tables" for more details.) Lookup Columns, the subject of the next section, do not create such relationships.

Using Lookup Columns

Access has a mechanism for creating lookup columns, known as the Lookup Wizard. You access the Lookup Wizard in Table Datasheet view by inserting a lookup column (select Insert | Insert Lookup Column) and in the Table Design view by selecting Lookup Wizard in the field's data type column. Chapter 4, "Tables," covers the Lookup Wizard in depth.

Lookup columns are fields in a table that retrieve their values from another table. An example of a good situation to use this in is the CustomerID field in the Orders table created earlier. If the field is defined as a lookup column, it can be linked to the CompanyName field of the Customers table. Whenever an order record is displayed or edited, the CustomerID field displays the company name of the Customer record that is associated with the given order. The field provides a drop-down list box containing all of the company names available in the Customers table. The value that is stored in the field for a given contact record is the identifier for the customer that was chosen. However, the company name for the specific customer chosen for that order record is displayed. Figure 6.5 shows the Orders table in Table Datasheet view. Notice that the Customer field (the CustomerID field has Customer stored in its `Label` property) displays company names. The Customer drop-down list has been activated in the second row, showing the available customer company names.

FIGURE 6.5.

The Orders table showing the CustomerID field being used as a lookup column.

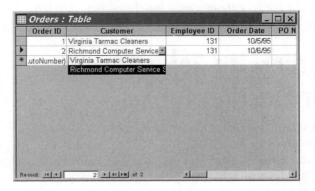

Defining a Lookup Column to retrieve a field's displayed value also creates a relationship between the two tables. Whenever the field that was defined as a lookup column is displayed (in a Query Datasheet, on a form, or in a report), the value displayed is the value from the associated field in the lookup table. This produces the same effect as creating the relationship. But it doesn't require manually inserting the lookup table into the query or form while it's being created. Access automatically retrieves the values from the lookup table whenever a lookup column field is displayed.

To view the lookup properties of a lookup column field, open the table in Table Design view. Select the field in the grid at the top of the Table Design view window. Then, in the properties section at the bottom of the window, select the Lookup tab. This will allow you to view and modify the properties that define how the lookup column operates.

When you know that your database will include many lookup tables (such as ContactTypes and SaleTypes), it's often easier to create the lookup tables first. Then you can create any "base" tables (tables that will use lookup tables for several fields) and define the foreign key fields' Lookup Columns using the matching lookup table as the table source in the Lookup Wizard. If you create the base tables first, you won't be able to use the Lookup Wizard to establish these lookup properties until after the lookup tables have been created.

Types of Relationships Created

Both of these methods create a relationship between the two tables. If both of the related fields are part of the primary key for its table, the relationship will be one-to-one. In most cases, however, the field from the base table (the Orders table, in this example) will be a foreign key. The field from the other table (the lookup table) will be that table's primary key. This causes Access to create a one-to-many relationship between the tables. The lookup table will be the table on the "one" side of the relationship, while the base table will be on the "many" side (one customer can have many orders, but a given order has only one customer).

Also, Access 95 leaves referential integrity enforcement disabled on newly created relationships. To modify the properties of the relationships established, open the Relationships window (by selecting Tools | Relationships) and double-click the line connecting the fields involved in the relationship you want to modify.

Setting Up Relationships for Existing Tables

Relationships don't have to be defined while tables are being created. As a matter of fact, the easiest way to create a relationship is by using the Relationships tool. However, any tables that will participate in the relationships to be created must already exist in the database. It's also possible to create relationships between tables that were actually created within the current database and tables that reside in external databases linked (or *attached*) to the current database. However, referential integrity can be enforced only between tables from databases that are in Microsoft Access format.

Opening the Relationships Window

To open the Relationships window, either select Tools | Relationships or click the relationships button on the toolbar (on the standard Database toolbar, it's the third button from the right).

> **WARNING**
>
> You should close any open Table Datasheet or Design windows before modifying any of the relationships in the Relationships window. The `Enforce Referential Integrity` property can't be modified while a table involved in the relationship is open in either Table Datasheet view or Table Design view.

If this is the first time the Relationships window has been opened for this database, or if these relationships haven't been saved yet in previous usages, a blank Relationships window will appear, along with the Show Table dialog box, as shown in Figure 6.6. If there is a previously stored relationship layout, that layout populates the window, and the Show Table dialog box won't appear.

FIGURE 6.6.

The Relationships window displayed for the first time.

The Relationships window displays tables and the relationships that have been defined between those tables. The relationships are shown by solid lines connecting the key fields of the tables participating in the relationship.

To add a table or query to the layout, either double-click its name in the Show Table dialog box or choose its name in the list and click the Add button. This places the table or query into the layout and shows any relationships that have already been established with it.

There is a quick way to see all the relationships that have been established for a specific table:

1. Add the table to the layout using the Show Table dialog box.
2. Close the Show Table dialog box.
3. Select Relationships | Show Direct.

Access will add all related tables to the layout and show the relationships that exist. Figure 6.7 shows the relationship between the Customers and the Orders table.

FIGURE 6.7.

The Relationships window for the Customers and Orders relationship.

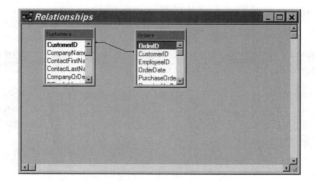

To view all the relationships that have been established between all of the tables in the database, select Relationships | Show All. Any table that participates in a relationship will be added to the Relationships window and all relationships will be displayed.

To remove a table from the layout but not delete any of its relationships, select the table by clicking on one of its field names. Then select Relationships | Hide Table. Selecting Edit | Delete will accomplish the same task (make sure a table is selected, not a relationship).

To remove all tables from the layout but not delete any relationships, select Edit | Clear Layout and click Yes on the confirmation dialog box that appears. This will clean the slate, so to speak, and provide a clean place to work. This feature comes in handy when there are a large number of related tables. In this case, you would probably want to view only a single "base" table (such as the Contacts table) and its related tables. If too many tables are shown in the layout, the relationship lines can become quite a tangled web.

You can also access a table's design from the Relationships window. Select the table in the Relationships window. Right-click and select Design Table from the pop-up menu that appears. When you've finished with the table, be sure to close the Table Design view window (or the Table Datasheet view window, which you can switch to from the Table Design view window).

Establishing Relationships

Now that you know how to add and remove tables from the Relationships window, it's time to learn how to establish a new relationship between two tables. As you'll see in Chapter 7, a many-to-many relationship is best handled as a relationship between three tables. However, each *individual* relationship is still a relationship between two and only two tables.

For this section, you'll add an Employees table to the database. Here are the steps to create the table:

1. In the Database window, activate the Tables tab and click New.

2. In the New Table dialog box, select Design View and click OK.

3. Add the EmployeeID field, giving it a data type of AutoNumber. Add the LastName and FirstName fields as Text data types with a field size of 25. Add HireDate as a Date/Time field and Active as a Yes/No field. Finally, add a ReportsTo field as a Number with Long Integer size. The table should look like Figure 6.8.

FIGURE 6.8.

The Employees table.

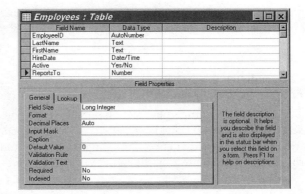

4. Save the table by selecting File | Save. When Access prompts you to create a primary key, click Yes to allow Access to assign the primary key for you (the EmployeeID field will be correctly chosen as the primary key).

5. Close the Table Design view window.

Now you can establish a relationship between the new Employees table and the Orders table. To do so, follow these steps:

1. Open the Relationships window if necessary (by selecting Tools | Relationships). The first step in creating a relationship is to make sure that both tables are in the layout. To do so, open the Show Table dialog box by selecting Relationships | Show Table.

2. Select the Employees table and click the Add button. (If you need to add more than one table to the layout, you can select each table and click Add for each, or you can select all needed tables by Ctrl-clicking or Shift-clicking (hold down the Ctrl or Shift key and click on the next table) and then clicking Add. Shift-clicking extends the selection from the previously selected table to the current table. Ctrl-clicking on a table adds the table to the selection if it wasn't previously selected or removes it from the selection if it was previously selected.)

3. Once the necessary tables are in the layout, click the Close button of the Show Table dialog box. The Relationships dialog box should look like Figure 6.9.

FIGURE 6.9.

The Relationships dialog box with the Employees table added.

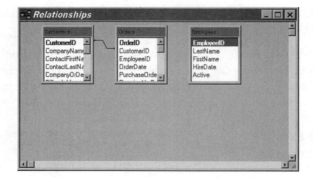

4. Click and drag the EmployeeID field in the Employees table. Drop it over the EmployeeID field in the Orders table.

5. The Relationship properties dialog box, shown in Figure 6.10, appears. For now, accept the defaults by clicking Create. You are returned to the Relationships window, where the relationship between the Employees table and the Orders table is now shown by a line connecting the EmployeeID fields of the two tables.

FIGURE 6.10.

The Relationships properties dialog box.

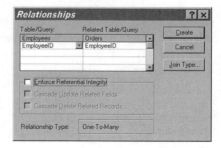

In most cases, you will drag the primary key (displayed in bold) from one table to the matching field, called the *foreign key,* in the other table. The related fields must have the same data type. The exception is that AutoNumber fields having NewValue set to Increment and Long Integer Number fields can be linked. In addition, if the fields have the Number data type, they must have the same FieldSize property.

Relationship Properties

The dialog box shown in Figure 6.10 is where basic relationship properties are set. If you must add more fields in order to define the relationship, you can do so using the empty rows below the EmployeeID fields. To add a field, select an empty row in the grid. A drop-down button appears at the right side of the column. Either type the first few letters of the name of the field to be added to the relationship (Access will fill in the rest as you type) or select it using the drop-down list box. If you add a field, you must have a matching field from the other table. You can't leave one column blank.

If you need to change a field to a different field in the table, select the incorrect field. Then either type the first few letters of the correct field's name (Access will fill in the rest as you type) or select the correct field from the drop-down list box.

From this dialog, you can also set the default join type that Access will use when you create a query involving these two tables. You set this by clicking the Join Type button. Join types will be discussed in the next section.

Finally, you can specify that Access should enforce referential integrity. You do this by checking the Enforce Referential Integrity box. This ensures that if you have assigned a customer to an order, that customer will always exist in the Customers table. Referential integrity is discussed in more detail in the section titled "Referential Integrity" later in this chapter.

Join Types

A relationship's join type doesn't affect the relationship itself. The join type simply specifies the type of join that Access will use when creating queries based on the related tables. The join type specified in the Relationships window can be overridden when defining a query. The default join type is "Only include rows where the joined fields from both tables are equal," which is known as an *inner join.*

The three main types of joins are inner joins, outer joins, and self-joins. The outer join is further specified as being either a left outer join or a right outer join, but both accomplish the same thing.

An inner join will combine two tables and add a new row to the query results only if the fields specified in the relationship have the same value in both tables. This type of join is useful when the related fields are required to have values in both tables or when you want to view only the records that have data in the related fields. Inner joins are commonly referred to as *equi-joins.*

An outer join is the opposite of an inner join. An *outer join* lets Access add a row to the query results for one table even if there is no corresponding record in the joined table. For instance, suppose you wanted to view all contacts and their ratings. If you wanted to view the contacts regardless of whether a rating had been assigned, you would use an outer join. If you wanted to view only contacts that had a rating assigned, you would use an inner join. The difference between a left outer join and a right outer join is merely a matter of semantics. A left outer join (or left join) specifies that you want to include all of the records from the table on the left side of the join statement and only the matching records from the right side. The right outer join (or right join) specifies that you want to include all the records from the table on the right side of the join statement and only the matching records from the table on the left side of the statement. Therefore, a right join statement could be rewritten to a left join by simply swapping the order of the table names and changing "right" to "left."

A *self-join* is a join between two copies of the same table. You create it by joining two fields of the same table. For example, if you wanted to create a report listing the employees stored in the Employees table along with the name of their supervisor, you would use a self-join. The Employees table contains a ReportsTo field. This field is populated with the EmployeeID of the current employee's supervisor. The self-join would match a given employee's ReportsTo field with another employee's EmployeeID field to determine which record contains the first employee's supervisor. Inner joins are discussed in more detail in Chapter 7.

To specify the type of join to use as the default when creating queries, click the Join Type button. Three options will appear, as shown in Figure 6.11.

FIGURE 6.11.

The Join Properties dialog box.

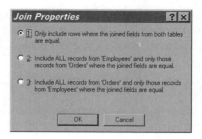

The first option will cause Access to create an inner join. The second option will create a left outer join. The third option will create a right outer join. Choose the join type that will be used most often in your queries. For the Orders/Employees relationship, choose the right outer join, because you'll typically want to see all orders, even if they don't have an employee assigned. Click OK to set the join property.

Finally, you want to enforce referential integrity (discussed later), so check the Enforce Referential Integrity check box. Then click Create to establish the relationship. The window should appear as shown in Figure 6.12.

FIGURE 6.12.

The Relationships window showing the Orders/ Employees relationship.

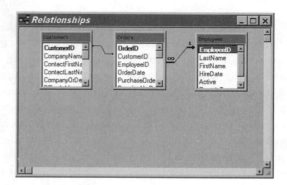

Figure 6.12 shows a one-to-many relationship between the Orders table and the Employees table. This is depicted by the 1 next to the EmployeeID field in the Employees table and the infinity symbol (∞) next to the EmployeeID field in the Orders table. The line between the two tables is called the *relationship line*. The arrow pointing to the Employees table signifies the join type you selected. All records from Orders will be included in a query, but only the matching records from Employees will be included. If you had chosen the inner join, the line would have had dots at either end.

Referential Integrity

Referential integrity is basically a set of rules that ensures that the relationships between tables within a database are all valid. For our EmployeeID field, for instance, referential integrity ensures that if there is a value in the EmployeeID field in the Orders table, there is a corresponding value in the Employees table. Otherwise, the order record would have an "orphaned" employee; it would have a value in the Orders table that had no corresponding (parent) value in the related table (Employees). If referential integrity had been enforced, you wouldn't have been able to enter an orphaned employee in the Orders table. Likewise, you wouldn't be able to delete an employee from the Employees table if the employee to be deleted had been assigned to any of the orders in the Orders table.

If you attempt to insert or modify a record and the data validates referential integrity—for instance, if you attempt to change the EmployeeID to a number that doesn't have a corresponding employee—Access displays an error dialog box similar to the one shown in Figure 6.13. You are then returned to the record you were editing. You must correct the problem before the record can be saved. Note that Access has also told you which tables you must use valid values from. Click the Help button to receive some specific information as to why the error occurred.

FIGURE 6.13.

The error dialog that is displayed by Access when referential integrity is violated.

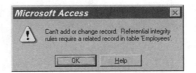

If you attempt to delete an employee who has been assigned to an Orders record, Access displays a similar error dialog, shown in Figure 6.14. Note that this dialog even specifies which related tables are causing the referential integrity error.

FIGURE 6.14.

The error dialog that Access displays when referential integrity is violated by deleting a record.

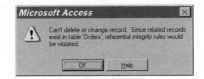

If you specify that you want referential integrity enforced (by checking the Enforce Referential Integrity box), you can also tell Access that you want to cascade any delete and update operations that involve related records. If these options are set, Access cascades the changes to the related tables to preserve the database's referential integrity. This is discussed in the following two sections.

Cascading Updates

This option lets Access update the related table's foreign key to the new value of a primary key in all related records. This way, if you change an employee's ID in the Employees table, the Employee field in the Orders table is automatically updated for every order assigned to that employee. This occurs without any message to the user.

Although this feature is certainly handy to have around, it violates good database design practices. As you'll see in the next chapter, the field chosen to be a table's primary key field should be read-only. In other words, you should never have a situation in which you would need to modify the value of the primary key for a record after that record is created. However, because Access allows you to cascade updates, the situation isn't so bleak, as long as referential integrity is being enforced. Aside from that, however, if you have related tables that are in a different database system (SQL Server, for example), Access can't cascade the updates to those tables. If you had the Employees table linked to a table on a SQL Server database via the EmployeeID and you modified the local EmployeeID, the referential integrity between the two tables would be lost. You would leave invalid records on the SQL Server database. If you're linking to external tables, it's a good idea to not allow updating of the key fields.

Cascading Deletes

Cascade Delete works much like Cascade Update. If you delete a record in the primary table, Access automatically deletes any related records in the related tables. For example, if you delete a contact, all of the contact's notes are automatically deleted from the Notes table. When you delete records while on a form or in Table Datasheet view and the Cascade Delete option is set, Access warns you that related records might also be deleted. When you delete records using a Delete query, Access deletes the related records without displaying a message.

Modifying Existing Relationships

Sometimes it will be necessary to modify some existing relationships. You do so in the Relationships window using steps similar to those for creating relationships.

WARNING

If you have several relationships already defined in your database, it's a good idea to make a copy of the database file (using Windows Explorer, for example) before modifying relationships. That way, if you incorrectly modify or delete many relationships, you can use the backup copy of the database to go back to where you started.

To change a relationship, open the Relationships window by selecting Tools | Relationships. If the tables in the relationship to be modified don't appear in the window, add them using the Show Table dialog box (select Relationships | Show Table). Find the relationship line that represents the relationship to be modified (the line that connects the key fields of the two tables).

To modify the relationship's properties, double-click on this line. Access displays the Relationships dialog shown in Figure 6.10 (discussed in the section "Relationship Properties"). To delete the relationship, click on the line and press the Delete key.

Summary

This chapter discussed the creation of relationships between tables. A table's relationships can be created when the table is created or any time thereafter. Each relationship has a number of properties that affect how Access will operate on the records in the tables and what actions can be taken on them. The ability to enforce referential integrity is one of the most useful features of Microsoft Access and helps distinguish it from many other desktop database systems.

Database Fundamentals

7

by James J. Townsend

Even though Access is arguably one of the easiest Windows databases to use, first-time database designers still have many things to learn; a database is quite different from a word processing document or a spreadsheet. This chapter provides an introduction to relational database theory. It distills the fundamentals you need to know to create a successful database application.

Relational theory isn't an arcane, obscure science. It is quite practical, and it defines the rules every business application must follow.

Planning for Success

To build a database, you need a plan called a data model. The data model is a list of all the things you will track (called entities), the characteristics that describe these entities (attributes), and the relationships among the entities. The entities end up as tables in your database, and the attributes show up as fields.

To be more specific, you want to create the following items in your data model:

- A list of all the entities you're tracking.
- The field or fields that will be used as the primary key for each entity, including field type and field length.
- A list of all the fields you need to contain the attributes describing each entity, including field type and field length.
- A list of the relationships and relationship type for each link among the tables. This can be depicted visually in the Access Relationships window.
- Rules for referential integrity among the entities (as you just learned in Chapter 6, "Relationships").

Data modeling is a purely analytical exercise. You don't need Access or even a computer to create a data model. Many excellent data models have begun as lines and boxes drawn on a cocktail napkin.

> **WARNING**
>
> The best time to plan your data model is before you create queries, forms, and reports based on your tables. If you postpone your data modeling until after you start writing queries, forms, and reports, you might have to redo quite a bit of work.

Relational Basics

In a relational database, all data is stored and manipulated in two-dimensional arrays called relations. Relations, commonly called tables, are depicted as rows and columns, like this:

First Name	Last Name	Address	Phone
Nicholas	Andrews	43 East 87th St.	212-782-4502
Louise	Smith	1501 Polk Street	415-395-9822
Madeline	Carter	6508 Maple Lane	617-729-0038
Charles	Johnson	770 Avenue B	703-403-2842

Each row (or record) is a single instance of the thing being tracked. This representation is a snapshot of the data in the table. In a relation, however, the order of the rows and columns isn't meaningful. Indeed, one of the main differences between relational and nonrelational databases (such as hierarchical and network databases) is that a row can be found only by the values in its fields, and not by its location. Similarly, a column is referenced by its name, not by its relative location in a table.

When you run a query or view data in a form, Access shows record numbers at the bottom of the window. These numbers, however, don't represent an absolute record number or show the order in which the records are stored in a disk file. Instead, they're relative numbers for the records in a dynaset, a relation that Access creates at runtime, retrieving data according to selection criteria and sorting specifications. If the same query is run an hour later, the record numbers might be different due to additions and deletions made by other users. Similarly, changing the filter for a form might change the number associated with a given record.

Relational database management systems separate the logic of the data from its underlying physical storage. A database user or programmer doesn't need to know which disk sector or block contains certain information. Indeed, these physical details are hidden from the developer so that they can't be referenced.

Relational databases offer several advantages over nonrelational database management systems. They are flexible, and they lend themselves to ad hoc queries. Most relational databases share a common language, Structured Query Language (SQL), the language used in Access.

The Concept of Uniqueness

Because data in a relational database is retrieved based on the contents of the fields, not on their physical locations, duplicate records are anathema to the database administrator. What would happen if you entered a customer twice in the customer table? It would be difficult to determine which record was accurate and up-to-date. And, for example, reports that counted the number of customers would be inaccurate. Duplicate records waste millions of dollars each year for business, as a glance at the addresses on your junk mail reveals.

When a new record is entered in a table (directly or via a form or query), Access checks the value in the primary key against all the existing records. If another record is found with the same key value, the record is rejected, and an error message is displayed for the user.

To proceed with data modeling, you need to know when a record is a duplicate record. Each record in a table needs to be unique; that is, the table should have no two records that are the same. The fields that determine whether two records are duplicates are called *key fields* or *primary keys*. When you define a table, Access expects you to assign one or more of the fields in the table as a primary key by clicking the key icon in the toolbar.

Ideally, a primary key is a meaningful field that can be determined by examining or interrogating the object you're tracking. A universal product code (UPC) is a good primary key for products, because it's written on the product label. A Social Security number is a good primary key for employees, because U.S. law requires that employees report their Social Security number for tax purposes. The order number and product number together are a good primary key for order details, because you wouldn't want to enter the same line item twice for the same invoice.

Candidate Keys

Sometimes you have several viable options when choosing a primary key. Each of these potential keys is called a candidate key. In an employees table, you might use the Social Security number, the employee identification number, or a combination of employee first name and employee last name.

How do you choose among candidate keys? First, the primary key can never be null, so you should be sure that it will contain a value for every record. Therefore, a middle name field shouldn't be part of the primary key, because many people don't have a middle name. If two candidates are non-null, choose the shortest field. The shorter the field, the more quickly Access can read the index and check for duplicates when records are inserted or updated.

Surrogate Keys

Sometimes the database designer opts to use an artificial primary key to boost performance or simplify data entry. In the Northwind sample database, the primary key of the Customers table is a five-character text field called Company ID. This field isn't meaningful, in the sense that customers probably don't know their own Customer ID, and, unlike a Social Security number, it isn't assigned by an outside agency and isn't inherently unique.

The Customer ID is a surrogate key, taking the place of a longer, meaningful key. It's used to link the Customers table to other tables. The surrogate key can speed data entry by enabling users to enter only five characters to identify a customer.

AutoNumber fields (known as Counter fields in earlier versions of Access) are excellent surrogate keys. They're assigned by Access when a record is inserted and are inherently unique. Be aware that an AutoNumber field as a primary key does nothing to prevent duplicate entries in a table. For instance, you might use an AutoNumber field called Customer Number as the primary key for a Customers table. You could then enter `Acme Industries` two or more times, because each time you entered a new record it would be assigned a different customer number. You should create a unique index on another field in the table to prevent duplicates.

The Art of Normalizing Databases

Relational database theorists have developed structured, logical methods for organization data. Through the process of *normalization*, the optimum database structure is achieved. After you learn the rules of normalization, you will know the questions to ask to build a data model for any database.

Simply stated, the goal of normalization is to reduce data to its simplest structure with a minimum of redundancy. The aesthetics of the database designer are similar to those of an aircraft builder—strip away all unnecessary elements to reveal the barest structure that will fly. Less is more in database design.

Fortunately, normalization follows common sense. Start with the golden rule of normalization: Enter the minimum data necessary to represent what you're modeling. Unnecessary redundancy is to be avoided at all costs. Redundant data wastes storage space, potentially forces users to enter information more than once, and, most important, leads to data inconsistencies.

Normalization Goals

Before you embark on normalization, you should bear in mind the goals you are trying to achieve:

- Eliminate redundancy
- Avoid anomalies in updating
- Accurately represent what is being modeled
- Simplify database maintenance and retrieval of information

The penalty for failing to heed the rules of normalization is severe. An unnormalized database puts data integrity at risk and performs poorly. It's more difficult to maintain, and some types of reporting are nearly impossible.

Fortunately, Access not only enables you to obey the rules of normalization, but it also provides you with facilities to make it easier to build normalized database applications. Access offers powerful query tools to combine data from multiple tables for data entry, analysis, and reporting. Access 95 is the first database management system to provide a wizard to check a table for normalization errors.

Normal Forms

To approach the peak of relational perfection, you must pass through several stages, called normal forms. You can think of normal forms as tests your database design must pass to receive the relational seal of approval. Each normal form adds new restrictions your design must meet. The higher the normal form, the more stringent the test. By definition, a relation in a higher normal form is also in all the lower normal forms.

A database that conforms with third normal form is considered normalized. For most business applications, this is as far as you have to go.

First Normal Form

The most common normalization error of beginners is to repeat fields within a table. To achieve first normal form (1NF), you must eliminate repeating fields so that each record represents a single instance of the thing you're tracking.

For instance, you might be tracking wedding plans, as shown in tables 1 and 2.

Table 1: Unnormalized Wedding Plans

Wedding Code	Wedding Date	Wedding Name	Bridal Party
191	2/3/96	Montgomery/O'Neill	Samuel Jones, Sarah McGregor
192	10/7/95	Wilson/Valdez	Hanna Moos
193	4/27/96	Carlisle/Rivera	Mario Pontes
194	9/2/97	Ronan/Thomas	David Schlarbaum, Elizabeth Lincoln
195	6/7/96	Washington/Lewis	Marcus Saavedra, Francisco Chang

Table 2: Unnormalized Wedding Plans

Wedding Code	Wedding Date	Wedding Name	Party Member1	Party Member2
191	2/3/96	Montgomery/O'Neill	Samuel Jones	Sarah McGregor
192	10/7/95	Wilson/Valdez	Hanna Moos	
193	4/27/96	Carlisle/Rivera	Mario Pontes	
194	9/2/97	Ronan/Thomas	David Schlarbaum	Elizabeth Lincoln
195	6/7/96	Washington/Lewis	Marcus Saavedra	Francisco Chang

Obviously, this table doesn't contain atomic values because the bridal party contains more than one value. The problem wouldn't be solved by creating more fields such as Bridal Party2, Bridal Party3, and so on. It doesn't matter whether the repeating values are stored in a single field or multiple fields; the values are interchangeable, and therefore they constitute repeating fields.

Repeating fields are taboo for many reasons:

- You can't enforce uniqueness with a primary key. There is nothing to prevent you from entering the same person's name twice as a member of the bridal party.

- You must search more than one field to find all records with a specified value. You couldn't be sure in which position the value was entered, so you would have to search in more than one place.

- Queries to calculate totals are much more difficult. Queries would have to look in more than one field, and the number of members in the party couldn't be determined by looking at the number of records in this table.

- Repeating fields waste space by using fields that are often left blank. If you create 10 fields to allow entry of a bridal party with up to 10 members, many of those fields will be blank for most entries.

- You must add new fields if the record exceeds the capacity of the table. If someone plans a wedding with 20 people in the wedding party, the table structure must be changed to allow all the names to be entered.

- Building indexes is inefficient because multiple indexes would be needed. Indexes would be needed on all repeating fields to speed searches in the fields, using more disk space and computing resources to maintain them.

To cure the problem, you need to create a table to store weddings and a table to store the wedding party members, as in tables 3 and 4.

Table 3: Weddings

Wedding Code	Wedding Date	Wedding Name
191	2/3/96	Montgomery/O'Neill
192	10/7/95	Wilson/Valdez
193	4/27/96	Carlisle/Rivera
194	9/2/97	Ronan/Thomas
195	6/7/96	Washington/Lewis

Table 4: Wedding Parties	
Wedding Code	**Party Member**
191	Samuel Jones
191	Sarah McGregor
192	Hanna Moos
192	Hanna Moos
193	Mario Pontes
193	Mario Pontes
194	David Schlarbaum
194	Elizabeth Lincoln
195	Marcus Saavedra
195	Francisco Chang

In the improved table structure, you can enter zero or an infinite number of members for each wedding. Queries based on a person's name are simplified because there is now only one field to search. By making Wedding ID and Child the primary key for the Wedding Parties table, you can ensure that no duplicate records are allowed and both fields are required.

Repeating fields can arrive in clever disguises. For instance, a seasoned spreadsheet user might build an Access table that would contain data like that shown in table 5.

Table 5: Unnormalized Monthly Sales												
Rep/Mo.	**Jan**	**Feb**	**Mar**	**Apr**	**May**	**Jun**	**Jul**	**Aug**	**Sep**	**Oct**	**Nov**	**Dec**
Guziak, Chris	55	78	66	54	101	103	69	98	79	102	85	120
Pino, Daniel	85	103	54	103	64	81	82	101	85	103	63	85
McHenry, Bill	64	79	102	103	79	77	64	52	103	85	101	74

Although the values in the sales fields for each month aren't interchangeable, they are repeating fields, and they violate 1NF. Follow the prescription outlined earlier to convert this table to 1NF.

Second Normal Form

Now that you have achieved first normal form, you can eliminate additional redundancy and ambiguity by obeying the law of second normal form (2NF). In plain English, second normal form requires you to eliminate any fields that don't directly describe the thing you're tracking. Fields that describe other entities are moved to the tables where they do describe the primary key.

For instance, table 6 contains information on computer users.

Table 6: Unnormalized Computer Users							
Employee ID	**Name**	**Department**	**Room**	**Ext**	**Serial Number**	**Make**	**Model**
123	Montgomery, Scott	Engineering	522	3341	T501C	Compaq	Deskpro 486
345	Wilson, Chris	Accounting	524	4375	53NY	Dell	425
541	Carlisle, Chris	Engineering	522	3343	672933	Gateway	4DX2-66V
541	Carlisle, Chris	Engineering	522	3343	42201	IBM	ThinkPad
653	Irven, Gary	Production	525	6712	922830010	Dell	NL25

This table is in first normal form, because there are no repeating fields and each record represents only one instance of the item tracked. The problem with this table is that it forces the user to reenter the employee information for each computer assigned to a person. This work is unnecessary and risks entry errors. What would happen, for instance, if a different department or phone extension were entered for the same person in two different records? How would personnel transfers be handled?

The solution is to break this table into two separate tables and keep the fields with the entities they describe, as shown in tables 7 and 8.

Table 7: Computers			
Serial Number	**Make**	**Model**	**Assigned to Employee**
T501C	Compaq	Deskpro 486	123
53NY	Dell	425	345
672933	Gateway	4DX2-66V	541
42201	IBM	ThinkPad	541
922830010	Dell	NL25	653

Table 8: Employees				
Employee ID	**Name**	**Department**	**Room**	**Ext**
123	Montgomery, Scott	Engineering	522	3341
345	Wilson, Chris	Accounting	524	4375
541	Carlisle, Chris	Engineering	522	3343
541	Carlisle, Chris	Engineering	522	3343
653	Irven, Gary	Production	525	6712

Now all information describing the employee is in the Employees table, and all information describing the computer is in the Computers table. If an employee's department or phone number changes, it must be changed only once. The only redundant information is the employee ID, which exists in both tables. This redundancy is necessary, however, to link the computer to the employee. Note that some fields have the same data, such as the same room number for several people, but the data here isn't redundant.

Third Normal Form

The next level of normalization is third normal form (3NF). This level of normalization eliminates fields you can derive from existing fields in the database. The goal is to have independent attributes. Independence means that the attribute doesn't describe or depend on another attribute. One test for independence is to determine whether changing one attribute forces changes in other attributes.

Say that you're building a membership database for an association. Each member is assigned to a region based on the state in which he lives. Table 9 shows the membership table, with some fields omitted.

Table 9: Membership						
Member ID	**Member Name**	**Address**	**City**	**State**	**ZIP**	**Region**
522	Montgomery, Scott	5501 Great Bear Run	Tampa	FL	33511	South
524	Wilson, Chris	6522 Old El Paso Way	Dallas	TX	75209	Midwest
522	Carlisle, Chris	3701 P Street, NW	Washington	DC	20057	East
525	Snyder, Joel	44 Chipotle Terrace	Tucson	AZ	85716	West

The problem here is that the user is required to enter the region even though it could easily be determined from the State field. This means that the region is dependent on the state and should therefore be moved to another table (table 10), and the Region field should be removed from the Membership table.

Table 10: States	
State	**Region**
FL	South
TX	Midwest
DC	East
AZ	West

On closer examination, you can see that the table contains additional dependent values that could be broken out to a separate table. The City and State fields both depend on the ZIP field. By creating a table containing all ZIP codes along with the city and state they represent, you could eliminate this source of errors. The only problem with having the user enter the ZIP and deriving the city and state is that this method fails to account for cases in which a member furnishes his city and state but not the ZIP. In such a case, the user would have to look up the ZIP code.

Higher Normal Forms

Third normal form is usually sufficient for business applications, but higher normal forms exist. Chief among these are Boyce-Codd normal form, a more rigorous version of third normal form, as well as fourth normal form and fifth normal form.

Getting Normal

Unfortunately, the world isn't laid out in a normalized way. A single business form, for instance, might contain data that should be stored in half a dozen different tables. When you meet with users, they're likely to assume that a single form translates into a single table. Your job is like that of a sculptor, to chip away the excess material and free the underlying data structure.

Normalization consists of two main activities: integration and decomposition. Decomposition is the process of breaking a single table into two or more tables without losing the meaning of the fields. Integration involves combining two or more tables into a single table.

Integration

Integrating data is like organizing your closet; the first step is to group similar things. In your closet, you might want to store all shirts in one place, all trousers in another place, and all jackets in yet another place. You might create groups of clothing with similar functions, hanging belts and suspenders together, or consolidating neckwear (ties, bow ties, and mufflers).

In the database, the process is similar but more abstract. Take a look at all the things you will track, and group them into tables. You can group things in many ways, some of them not obvious. In a banking application, for instance, you would probably want to put all deposits together in a group, because they contain the same fields (account number, date, amount), and you might want to store all checking account debits in another table, with fields such as date, amount, account number, and check number. On the other hand, you could consolidate the two into a single table, Transactions, which includes all the fields in both tables. A positive dollar amount would be used for deposits, and a negative amount would be used for checks and other debits. You would simply add a new field to denote the type of transaction (deposit, check, automated teller machine withdrawal, fee). Combining these items into a single table would mean you could write all your reports on account balance from a single table.

A common normalization error is to maintain separate tables for things that are fundamentally the same. For instance, you could run a business with multiple locations, using a separate table for customers from each location. This would create several problems for database users. They wouldn't know which table to open to enter a change of address. Some customers might be duplicated if they buy from more than one store location. The solution is to integrate the tables and add a field to the Orders table to indicate the store location.

One of the best ways to check for duplicate tables is to compare key fields. If the key field is the same, the tables probably should be integrated. For instance, separate tables for mailing lists would likely contain the same key field—the person's name. This method risks storing duplicate information if a person is in more than one mailing list, and makes it more difficult to process a change-of-address form because there are several places to look for a person. These tables should be consolidated into one table, and another related table should be added to show which lists the person belongs to.

Now that all the entities have been integrated, it's time to reach for the chisel and take the normalization process further.

Decomposition

Although the word *decomposition* conjures up images of rotting leaves or worse, it isn't an unpleasant process in the context of relational database design. By following the well-trodden path of normalization, a file structure can be broken down into its most basic elements.

Analyze the tables using the rules for first through third normal form as outlined earlier. Systematically eliminate repeating values, creating additional tables as necessary to show these one-to-many relationships. Move fields to the table where they describe the key. Delete fields that can be derived from calculations (from fields in their own table, or from another table).

After the normalization process is complete, you can use queries and forms to make data easier to use and understand. You can join tables in a query and then build a form on top of the query to simulate a business form. The user doesn't need to know that the data is actually stored in four tables rather than one.

For one-to-many relationships, take advantage of the powerful subform features offered by Access, such as those offered by the Form Wizard. Again, users will perceive that data is coming from a single source because they will be viewing it from a single form.

Tradeoffs

Although normalization is essential work in database design, it isn't a panacea. Data modeling involves tradeoffs.

One apparent disadvantage of normalization is that the data is no longer stored in one table. This means that you won't be able to view all the information by looking at a single record. Access minimizes this effect, however, by allowing several tables to appear (to the user) as one by joining them in a query. Through subforms, data can be entered into several tables from one form. Therefore, fear of multiple tables is no reason not to normalize.

The real tradeoff of normalization is performance. Despite its evils, duplication of data can make operations such as searching, sorting, and especially aggregation faster. For instance, storing the total amount of an order in the Orders table would make it much faster to calculate total sales, because you wouldn't have to join Orders with Order Details and multiply the quantity by the unit price for each line item. On my 486-75 PC with 20 MB of memory, Access takes about five seconds to calculate the order totals by joining Orders and Order Details. If the total amount is stored in the Orders table, the query that produces the same results takes about one second to run. Five seconds isn't a long time to wait for a query, but the speed difference would be more important when the database is being run on a network, on a slower workstation, or, most realistically, with thousands rather than hundreds of records.

Archiving Strategies

One of the simplest ways to boost database performance is to reduce the number of records that are actively searched, sorted, or joined. All other things being equal, searching for a customer from 100 records is faster than searching for the customer from 1,000,000 records.

Archiving records that are no longer needed can provide dramatic performance improvements. For instance, you might want to transfer completed invoices to a table separate from the one containing active invoices. This means that the active invoices table contains only outstanding orders. Similarly, you might want to archive inactive customers after a certain period.

The most accessible place to put your data is in another table in your database. You can use the Archive Query Wizard to transfer data from one Access table to another. If you don't need to have ready access to the data, you could archive data by exporting it to another file, making your Access database smaller.

Summary Data

An earlier section discussed why data that could be derived shouldn't be stored. Similarly, you wouldn't want a table to store monthly totals for each salesperson, but rather would want it to calculate the monthly totals by joining the orders, line items, and invoice tables and summarizing based on the salesperson assigned to each account.

Unfortunately, although this approach obeys relational rules, it can result in poor performance, especially if you do extensive analysis on aggregate figures. If you need to generate 10 graphs based on monthly sales figures, each of the graphs will run the underlying queries that return the required rows. If 5,000 line items are sold per month, and 20 salespeople are involved, the queries would process 50,000 rows.

On the other hand, if you created a table to store the monthly totals by salesperson, queries would have to pass through only 20 records per month.

The easiest way to create a summary table is with a Make Table query. Start by building a query that groups your data and calculates the totals you need. Change the query from a Select query, as shown in Figures 7.1 and 7.2, to a Make Table query.

FIGURE 7.1.

A sample summary table query from Northwind.

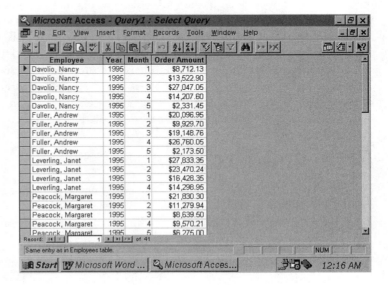

FIGURE 7.2.

A sample summary table query from Northwind in Design view.

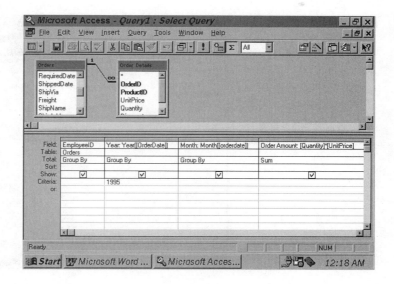

Remember that you're duplicating data and that your totals won't be automatically synchronized with the tables that track orders. If an order is added, modified, or deleted, it won't show up in the monthly totals until the summary table is updated.

Union Queries

Union queries are used to combine data from two or more tables into a single view. For instance, you might want to send a change-of-address notice to all your suppliers and customers. You could write two queries, one for each table, but the Union query enables you to run both at one fell swoop. Note that a Union query can't be shown in the Access Query window. You must write the query in the SQL window, shown in Figure 7.3.

A Union query is quite different from a join. When two tables are joined, the resulting rows consist of fields from both tables that share a common field. These tables are related to one another. In a Union query, the records aren't related to one another. The fields in the two tables of a Union query should be the same type and length for best results, but they don't have to have the same field name.

FIGURE 7.3.

A Union query.

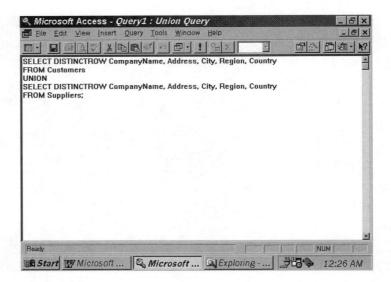

The Table Analyzer Wizard

The most exciting new Access feature for data modeling is the Table Analyzer Wizard. The Table Analyzer is your virtual assistant for normalizing your data. It starts by examining a selected table and checking it for repeated data. Next, it suggests an improved data structure, proposing new tables and relationships as necessary. If you accept these suggestions, the Table Analyzer creates the new tables and the relationships, copies the data from the old table to the new tables, and renames the old table. Finally, it creates a query to join the data back together in a view that closely resembles the original table.

Many times you end up with data that was created in another database, or even in another kind of program, such as a spreadsheet. You might be converting an application to Access or downloading information from the corporate mainframe. The Table Analyzer simplifies the process of fixing the table structure.

Now take a closer look at how the Table Analyzer runs. Figure 7.4 shows a table in need of normalization help.

To run the Table Analyzer, select the table you want to analyze in the Database window. Choose Tools | Analyze | Table. Figure 7.5 shows the dialog box that appears.

This dialog box explains the purpose of the Table Analyzer and enables you to view additional help to explain the benefits of good data modeling. Click Next > to proceed to the second dialog box, shown in Figure 7.6.

FIGURE 7.4.
A table to be analyzed.

OrderDate	CustomerID	CompanyName	Address	ProductName	Quantity	UnitPrice
8/13/93	LILAS	LILA-Supermercad	Carrera 52 con A	Genen Shouyu	20	$12.40
10/4/93	KOENE	Königlich Essen	Maubelstr. 90	Genen Shouyu	5	$12.40
4/6/94	LAMAI	La maison d'Asie	1 rue Alsace-Lorr	Genen Shouyu	12	$15.50
6/22/94	LETSS	Let's Stop N Shop	87 Polk St.	Genen Shouyu	10	$15.50
7/5/94	LEHMS	Lehmanns Marktst	Magazinweg 7	Genen Shouyu	25	$15.50
9/1/94	SAVEA	Save-a-lot Markets	187 Suffolk Ln.	Genen Shouyu	50	$15.50
7/9/93	RICSU	Richter Supermark	Grenzacherweg 2	Pavlova	35	$13.90
7/20/93	ERNSH	Ernst Handel	Kirchgasse 6	Pavlova	60	$13.90
8/19/93	RICAR	Ricardo Adocicado	Av. Copacabana,	Pavlova	40	$13.90
8/31/93	LILAS	LILA-Supermercad	Carrera 52 con A	Pavlova	30	$13.90
9/17/93	THEBI	The Big Cheese	89 Jefferson Way	Pavlova	10	$13.90
10/5/93	SAVEA	Save-a-lot Markets	187 Suffolk Ln.	Pavlova	21	$13.90
11/18/93	SEVES	Seven Seas Import	90 Wadhurst Rd.	Pavlova	56	$13.90
12/31/93	ERNSH	Ernst Handel	Kirchgasse 6	Pavlova	21	$13.90
2/4/94	MEREP	Mère Paillarde	43 rue St. Lauren	Pavlova	16	$13.90
2/7/94	SAVEA	Save-a-lot Markets	187 Suffolk Ln.	Pavlova	49	$13.90
2/18/94	LAMAI	La maison d'Asie	1 rue Alsace-Lorr	Pavlova	20	$13.90
3/7/94	WHITC	White Clover Mark	305 - 14th Ave. S	Pavlova	35	$13.90
3/25/94	PICCO	Piccolo und mehr	Geislweg 14	Pavlova	18	$13.90
4/20/94	QUICK	QUICK-Stop	Taucherstraße 1C	Pavlova	50	$17.45

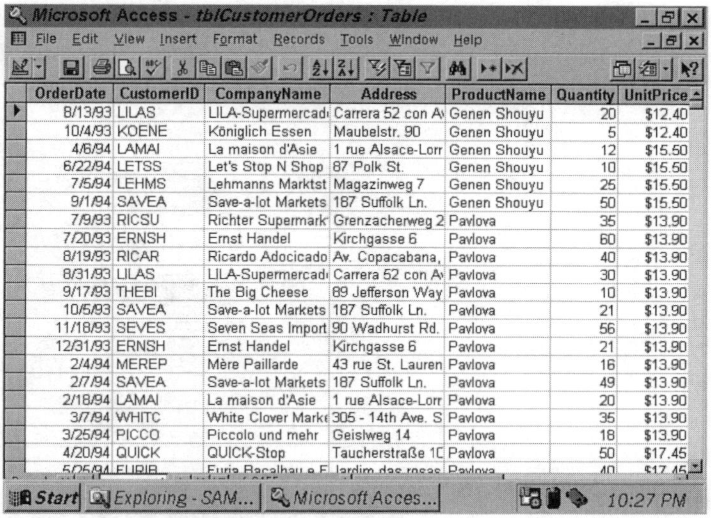

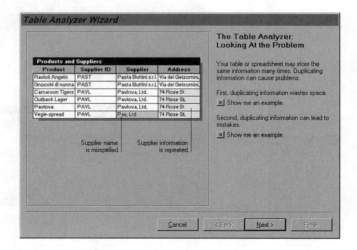

FIGURE 7.5.
The first step in analysis.

This screen tells how the Table Analyzer will solve the data modeling problems. Again, you can click to view additional examples. Click Next > to continue. The dialog box shown in Figure 7.7 appears, enabling you to choose the table to analyze.

If you already selected the table before running the Table Analyzer, click Next > again. In the dialog box shown in Figure 7.8, you can choose whether to have Access recommend changes to you or change the data model on your own.

FIGURE 7.6.

The wizard before it splits the table.

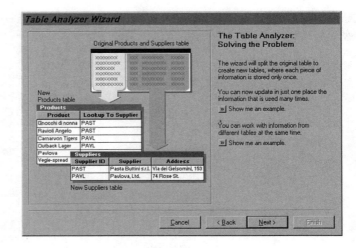

FIGURE 7.7.

Selecting the repeated fields.

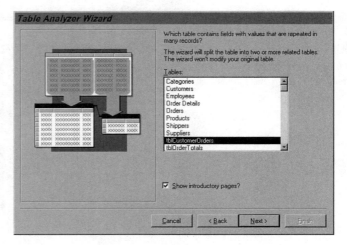

For this example, choose Yes, let the wizard decide. Now you get the screen you've been waiting for. Figure 7.9 shows the suggested data model for the table.

Access is recommending that the original table be broken into three tables. It has created the tables and named them Table1, Table2, and Table3. Access correctly determined that you were tracking information on three entities in one table: Orders, Customers, and Products.

At this point, you can correct any errors in the data model. You should rename the tables, using meaningful names that describe the entities you're tracking. To rename a table, click the Rename Table tool in the upper section of the dialog box, or double-click the title of the table in the data model and enter the new name in the dialog box that appears. You can also drag fields from one table to another, or even drag them into an empty space on the data model to create a new table. For additional tips, click the Tips icon. Figure 7.10 shows how the data model looks after editing.

FIGURE 7.8.

Picking a method of assigning fields to tables.

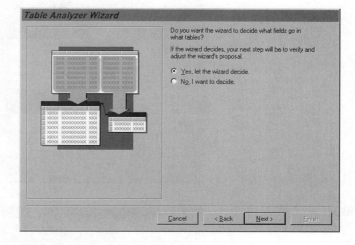

FIGURE 7.9.

The suggested data model.

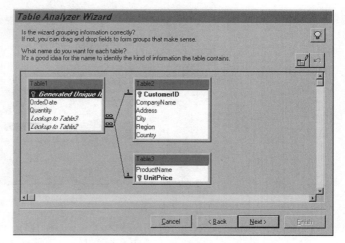

Click Next > to proceed. Now you get to determine the primary keys of the tables. As shown in Figure 7.11, you can change the field that is the key or have Access create an AutoNumber key for you.

FIGURE 7.10.

The completed data model.

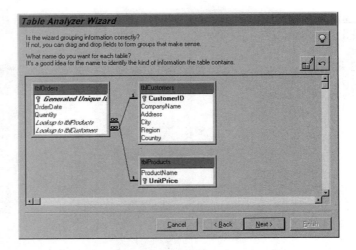

FIGURE 7.11.

Choosing primary keys.

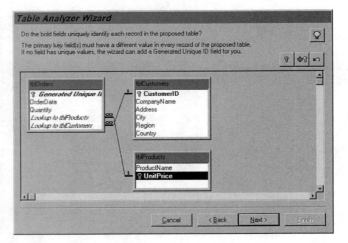

In this example, Access correctly identified the Customer ID as the primary key for the Customers table and created a sequenced key for Orders. Unfortunately, the Table Analyzer was incorrect in making the Unit Price the primary key for the Products table. You could use the product name as the primary key, but an AutoNumber field would be shorter and hence more efficient. Click the Add Generated Unique Key button to add the new key, as shown in Figure 7.12.

FIGURE 7.12.

After adding the primary key for the Products table.

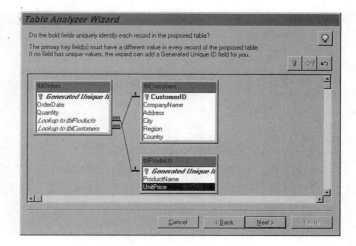

After splitting the tables, Access checks the spelling of the entries to find duplicates and near duplicates. You can then correct the entries in the next Wizard screen, shown in Figure 7.13.

FIGURE 7.13.

Correcting typographical errors.

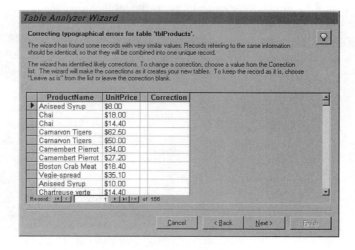

Click Next > when you're finished with spelling corrections. The final dialog box, shown in Figure 7.14, asks you whether it should create a query to rejoin the tables.

FIGURE 7.14.

The final step of the Table Analyzer.

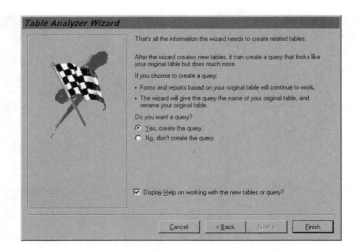

Click Finish to complete the analysis of the table.

Access displays the new query it has created. The table is renamed, and the query, shown in Figure 7.15, is given the same name as the table.

FIGURE 7.15.

The query in Datasheet view.

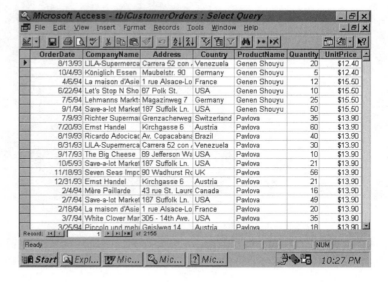

If you switch to Design view, as shown in Figure 7.16, you can see that the query is now joining three tables: tblOrders, tblCustomers, and tblProducts.

FIGURE 7.16.

The query in Design view.

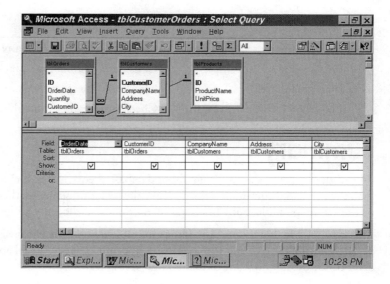

Here are some tips to get the most out of the Table Analyzer:

- Be sure to run the Table Analyzer Wizard on a table with data in it. The data provides valuable clues to Access on which fields contain repeating values and where each field belongs.

- Remember that the Table Analyzer doesn't get the data model right every time. Use the principles you've learned here to make corrections to the data model. The Table Analyzer has an especially difficult time when it's working with only a few fields or a few records.

- If you're unhappy with the results of the Table Analyzer, you might be better off to run it again on the original table (which it preserves for you) than to fix the resulting tables by hand.

- Be sure to check the field types when you're finished restructuring your table, especially if you have imported data from a text file. You might need to change the field types or lengths to protect against invalid entries.

Warning Signs of Poor Normalization

Unfortunately, not even Access (at least not yet) can ensure that you're following normalization. Creating a poor table structure doesn't result in error messages flashing on-screen or harsh dialog boxes chastising you. The database might even work, but it will never perform as well as if you had followed edicts of relational design. Fortunately, there are warning signs that might indicate a normalization problem:

Symptom	Possible Solution
Many-to-many relationships	Convert to two one-to-many relationships.
One-to-one relationships	Consider consolidating tables.
Many blank fields	Check for repeating fields.
Duplicate records in system	Check primary keys and check for repeating fields.

Summary

One of the most reassuring things about database theory is that it changes much more slowly than the mercurial computer industry. Like the logic and semantic theory on which is it based, relational design philosophy has a special usefulness and beauty all its own.

This chapter has shown sound methods for table design, the elimination of data redundancy through normalization, and the creation of appropriate keys. The Table Analyzer Wizard was detailed for those who want to use its time-saving features.

PART

III

Queries and SQL

Querying Data:
The QBE Grid
and Select Queries

Queries enable you to extract specific information from a database. That information could be from one table or from multiple tables. There are two ways to query data in Access. The first is through the Query module of the Access database container, and the second is as an SQL statement for the record source of a form or a report. The ability to query information is considered the brain of a relational database system. You could enter information all day long, but if that information couldn't be queried, it might as well be kept in a flat file.

New Query Features

The Query module of Access 95 has several new features. These new features make it easier to manage, locate, and share information. This enables people who extract data from Access 95 databases to make more informed decisions quickly. Here are a few of the major features:

- Filter by Form/Datasheet: This enables the end user to type information needed to formulate a query, and Access builds the underlying query. The data is then placed in Form view for the end user.

- QuickSort Queries: The Ascending and Descending Sort buttons have appeared in the toolbar in previous versions. In Access 95, the Sort Ascending and Sort Descending buttons appear on queries when they're viewed in Datasheet view. In previous versions, this feature was available only for tables.

- Simple Query Wizard: This new feature enables the user to select information from different tables. The Simple Query Wizard handles the inclusion of the related tables and establishes relations between the necessary tables with intelligent joining technology. The end result is the information that the user picked.

- Pivot Table Wizard: This Wizard enables the user to create a Microsoft Excel Pivot Table based on an Access table or query. The advantage is that the Excel Pivot Table can give users the ability to change the criteria of a pivot table on-the-fly.

- Improved Relationships Dialog: In previous versions of Access, if you had two tables and dragged one field from the table on the left to the table on the right, your join would be different than if you dragged one field from the table on the right to the table on the left. Now, you can drag a field from either side of a one-to-many relationship and Access executes the join intelligently.

- Background Joins between Wizards: Intelligent joining technology is an option that can be turned on or off (the default is On). It automatically figures out the joins between tables in a query, based on field names and field types.

- Top Values: This enables the user to select the top numbers or percentages for a given field in the query.

- Enhanced Properties: Properties for queries in the past were limited. With Access 95, the user has enhanced properties not only on the query itself but on each individual field in the grid.

■ New Object: Eight objects are available—Auto Form, Auto Report, New Table, New Query, New Form, New Report, New Macro, and New Module. All can be summoned from a Query window.

Using the QBE Grid

In Access, data is stored in tables. Simple queries involve sorting all the records in one table by one field. More complex queries sort all the records in one table by two or more fields. Relational databases enable the user to sort records in two or more tables by two or more fields. Queries are used to view, change, and analyze data in different ways. Query data can also be used as the source for forms and reports.

Access makes the querying process simple by placing all the tables with the necessary information in a query and drawing lines to show the relationship between the tables. Whether a query is accessed from the Query module of the database container or through the Query Builder on the record source of a form or a report, the QBE grid looks and functions the same way. The Access QBE grid is shown in Figure 8.1.

FIGURE 8.1.

The Access Query window is divided into two sections: the table pane and the query grid.

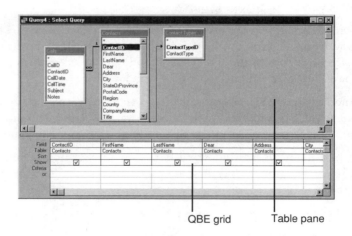

QBE grid   Table pane

The upper half of the Query window shows the relationship between the tables being queried. This is called the table pane. The lower half of the window shows the fields from the tables and the criteria by which the data is to be queried. This is called the query grid or the QBE grid. The Access method of QBE (Query By Example) is arguably the best and easiest method of querying data available. However, it does have limitations. The following list shows some of the limits for Access queries:

■ The maximum number of tables in one query is 32.

■ The maximum number of fields in a recordset is 255.

■ The maximum size of a recordset is 1 gigabyte.

- The maximum number of sorted fields in a query is 10.
- The maximum number of nested queries is 50.
- The maximum number of characters in a cell in the QBE grid is 1024.
- The maximum number of ANDs in a WHERE or HAVING clause is 40.
- The maximum number of characters in an SQL statement is approximately 64,000.
- The maximum number of characters for a parameter in a parameter query is 255.

A query can be viewed in its Design view, Datasheet view, or SQL view. The query's Design view is just a means for the user to come up with the criteria needed for a particular form or report. Access takes the query generated by the user and builds an SQL statement. This SQL statement performs the work of the query.

Adding to the Query Window

Adding to the Query window can be divided into two segments. The first is adding tables or other queries during the creation of the query itself. The second segment is adding tables or other queries to an existing query.

During the creation of a blank query, all the tables and queries are listed in a Show Table window. By highlighting the desired tables or queries and clicking the Add button, those items are placed in the table pane of the Query window. You can perform the same function by double-clicking each item in the Show Table window.

Another way to add tables or queries to an existing query is from the menu. Select Query | Show Table to add a new table or query to the query. Microsoft has provided a Show Table button that serves as a shortcut to adding tables to an existing query.

To add to the Query window, click the Add Table button. It pulls up a Show Table window. This window gives the user the option of viewing just the tables for that database, just the queries, or both.

Follow these steps for yet another way to add tables or queries to a query:

1. Position the current query so that it takes up half your screen.
2. Press the F11 key to bring up the database container.
3. Position the database container so that it takes up the other half of your screen.
4. Click the Tables or Queries module that contains the items to be placed in the query.
5. Click the desired table or query to highlight it and, while holding down the mouse button, drag the item into the table pane of the Query window.
6. When the mouse pointer is over the table pane of the Query window, you see a small, white box with a plus sign attached to the pointer. Release the mouse button to drop the desired table or query onto the table pane.

CAUTION

If there are two or more objects in the table pane of a query, there must be a relationship between those objects. Otherwise, the output of the query is a Cartesian product. (Cartesian products are discussed more in Chapter 11, "Understanding the Jet Engine," in the section "Avoiding Design Mistakes.")

Just adding tables or queries to the query is only the first step in producing a query. To produce a query, you must have at least one table or query and one field in the query grid. A query is a compilation of data. This data can be subject to different criteria. The output of a query is the data it produces. A query can't run unless it has at least one output field. Output fields are obtained by placing fields from the objects in the table pane of the query into the query grid. To make an output field, click a desired field needed for the query output and drag it to the query grid.

If you want all the fields in a table or query to be dragged to the query grid, double-click the title bar that appears at the top of every table and query. This highlights all the fields for the table. Click and hold any of the highlighted fields and drag them to the query grid. When the mouse button is released, all the fields appear in the query grid.

Another method of bringing all the fields in a table or query to the query grid is to click the asterisk that appears at the top of the table or query. This asterisk brings all the fields to the query grid. It acts like the asterisk wildcard that you use when you're trying to find a file using the Explorer. For example, to find all the files that start with ACC, you would enter ACC* in the Named line of the Find All Files dialog box.

When you drag just the asterisk to the query grid, even though all the fields are present in the Datasheet view, only the asterisk appears in the query grid. If you need to set criteria for a particular field, that field needs to be visible, so it must be dragged to the query grid individually.

The click-and-drag method of moving fields from the table pane to the query grid can be expedited by double-clicking each desired field. If you need all the fields from a table to be moved to the grid, double-clicking the asterisk can achieve that result.

TIP

Multiple fields can be added to the query grid at one time. If the fields are consecutive, you can highlight the first field, hold down the Shift key, and click the last field. All the fields in between are highlighted. If the fields are scattered throughout the table, hold down the Ctrl key while clicking the desired fields.

Setting Query Properties

Every object has properties. That also goes for objects in the database container. Setting query properties can be done to the query object as a whole, or on the individual objects within the query. This section covers setting properties to the query object as a whole, followed by information on setting properties to the individual tables and fields within a query.

When the Queries tab of the Database window is active, a list of all the queries is visible. In Access 95, every individual query object can have properties assigned to it. Highlight a query and click the Properties button on the toolbar to see its properties.

For every object, the user can assign a description. Each description can be 255 characters long. The Properties dialog box shows when the object was created, when it was modified, and who owns it. At the bottom of the dialog box are two check boxes that pertain to the attributes of the object. When the Hidden check box is checked and applied, the object is no longer visible in the Database Container window. This enables you to set security on an object-by-object basis in the database. The second check box deals with the ability to make this individual object replicable. (Replication is covered in greater detail in Chapter 39.)

> **NOTE**
>
> If you put the letters USYS in front of an object name, that object doesn't appear in the Database Container window. USYS means User System objects. The object can be unhidden by viewing the system objects.

To view objects that are hidden, select Tools | Options. Click the View tab and check Hidden Objects. This unhides all the objects that were hidden in the properties sheet. Notice that there is also a check box for System Objects. This unhides any objects with a prefix of USYS or MSYS.

> **CAUTION**
>
> USYS objects are objects created by the developer and hidden from the end user by the prefix USYS. MSYS objects are objects created by Microsoft and hidden from the developer with the prefix of MSYS. Giving users access to any system objects isn't recommended. They could inadvertently corrupt the database.

Everything discussed about setting properties so far has dealt with the whole query as an object. Within each query, there are also objects. Every object, including tables, fields, and joins, has properties. To access the properties for an object, highlight the object and select View | Properties. You can also highlight the object and click the Properties button on the toolbar. Another way to get to the properties for an object is to highlight the object and click the right mouse button. A different way to get to the properties of some of the objects is to double-click the joins or the table pane itself in the Query window and get to that object's properties. If you double-click the table, all the fields in that table are highlighted. If you double-click a field in a table, that field is automatically placed in the query grid.

Bring up the table pane's property sheet by double-clicking the table pane or right-clicking the table pane and choosing Properties from the shortcut menu. The properties for the table pane can be seen in Figure 8.2. This is a detailed property sheet for the query. The Description line has the same information as the Description line from the Property dialog box accessed from the database container.

FIGURE 8.2.

Detailed query properties can be viewed.

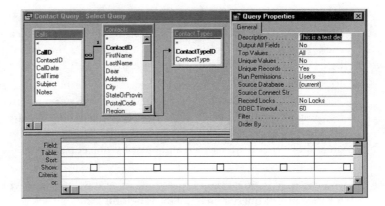

Several items can be manipulated for a query. The following lists all the items available on the query property sheet:

- ■ Description: If a description line was entered in the Property dialog box of the query through the database container, it's visible here. If not, the user can enter up to 255 characters for a description of a query.

- ■ Output All Fields: The fields placed on the QBE grid produce values when the query is run. Setting this feature to Yes means that every field on the QBE grid is visible when the query runs. This is the same as placing a check mark in every Show box in the QBE grid.

- ■ Top Values: This enables the user to query the top 5, 25, 100, 5 percent, or 25 percent of the records in the query. It's actually calculating the top number or top percentage on the left-most sorted field. For example, there are 27 records in the query. The third field from the left contains Last Names. The Last Names field has a Descending sort. The top 5 percent would be based on the Last Names field. If no fields in the query grid have any sorting attributes, Access 95 gives the top 5 percent of the 27 records as they appear when the query is executed without any top value impositions. It's important to mention that the values that are automatically offered by Access 95 aren't the only ones available to you. You can enter any number or percentage, and the query will return the value you asked for. These incremental values—5, 25, 100, 5%, and 25%—are just the most commonly used ones.

■ Unique Values: Unique Values enables you to return only records that are unique. An example of where to use this is a contact management database. The user needs to know how many different countries are represented in the database. A Contact table in the query has only one field in the QBE grid: Country. If there are thousands and thousands of records in the database, when the query is executed the recordset shows all the records. If Unique Values is set to Yes, there might be only three records in the set—Canada, Mexico, and United States.

■ Unique Records: Unique Records is similar to Unique Values. The major difference is that with Unique Values, the user is getting the unique values for the fields listed in the QBE grid. With Unique Records, the user gets the unique records based on all the fields in the underlying datasource, not just those fields present in the QBE grid.

■ Run Permissions: This option enables you to give an end user authorization to perform an action that he or she would otherwise not be allowed to execute. An end user might have Read Only authorization, but if you gave him Owner's authorization on a query, he might be able to append to this query. This enables you to turn security on and off for an end user on an object-by-object basis.

■ Source Database: The default for the Source Database is (current). With this property, you can specify, in a string expression, an external database where the tables or queries for the current query remain. This is helpful for databases that are created in applications that don't use attached tables.

■ Source Connect String: This works in conjunction with the Source Database item. This is the name of the application the external database was created in.

■ Record Locks: This feature is used for multiuser systems. It determines how the records are locked while the query is being executed by a user. There are only three options for this item—No Locks, All Records, and Edited Record. No Locks means just that. In a multiuser system, two or more users can access the same record at the same time. They might all edit that same record at the same time. He who saves first wins. The other users who try to save the record are prompted that the record has been changed. They can reject the changes they have made, overwrite the saved changes, or copy their changes to the clipboard and view the saved record. When the All Records option is selected, all the records are locked so that if one user is working with record in a table, the entire table is locked from the other users. Consequently, if that table is being used in a query and a record in that query is being used, the entire query is locked. This means that if there are many tables in the query and a user is working with one record in one table that appears in that query, all the tables in the query are locked—even if another user wants to access a record that has nothing to do with the record being accessed by the first user. The Edited Record option means that if one user is working with a record, that page of records is locked until she moves to another record. A page of records is usually 2 KB, and the actual number of records around the record being edited can vary, depending on the size of each record.

■ ODBC Timeout: This item is important only when the database is networked. It refers to how long this workstation checks a network connection for a response before the workstation lets the user know that the network station is no longer connected to the network. The default is 60 seconds. You might ask why that time isn't shorter. Wouldn't the user want to check for a response every five seconds? Maybe. However, if the user runs a query on data located on the server, the workstation waits for a response from the server. If that response doesn't come in five seconds, the workstation assumes that the network connection has been dropped, and the user gets an error. If network traffic is heavy when the query is run, the response might also be slower than expected. If there is no response in five seconds, the workstation still gets a message stating that the connection has been dropped. The timeout shouldn't be so long (10 minutes) that the user has time to do several operations before realizing that the network connection has been dropped.

> **NOTE**
>
> The time range for the ODBC Timeout is entered in seconds, starting at one second. Zero can be entered as a timeout, but the effect isn't what you would expect. If a zero is entered, the workstation doesn't continuously check for connection. Zero is a special number to the ODBC Timeout. Entering a zero is like turning the ODBC Timeout feature off, and no timeout errors occur.

■ Filter: This is a great novice developer's tool. It functions similarly to the Criteria section of the QBE grid. This line is automatically filled in for you after specifications have been made to the query during a run (see Figure 8.3). When the query is run, all the records are shown. On the toolbar, the user has access to the filtering buttons. When the Filter by Form button is selected, the Query view changes.

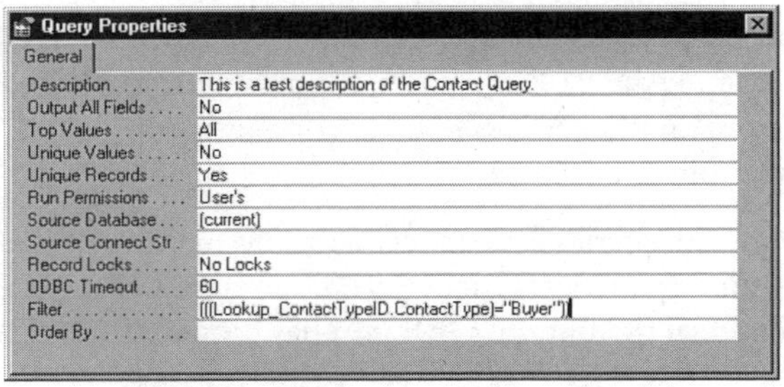

FIGURE 8.3.

The Filter line of the properties of the query is automatically filled in.

Query Properties	
General	
Description	This is a test description of the Contact Query.
Output All Fields	No
Top Values	All
Unique Values	No
Unique Records	Yes
Run Permissions	User's
Source Database	[current]
Source Connect Str	
Record Locks	No Locks
ODBC Timeout	60
Filter	[[(Lookup_ContactTypeID.ContactType]="Buyer")]
Order By	

■ Order By: This is another novice developer's tool. It functions similarly to the Sort section of the QBE grid. This line is filled in by Access for you when the query is run and specifications have been made. When the query is run, all the records are shown. On the toolbar, you or the user have access to the Sort Ascending and Sort Descending buttons. The user selects a column of data and sorts that data ascendingly or descendingly. The Sort column is automatically entered into the Order By text box of the query's properties, as shown in Figure 8.4.

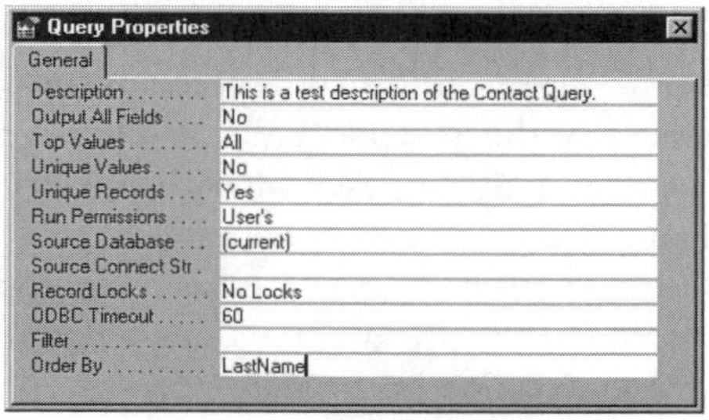

FIGURE 8.4.

The Order By line is automatically filled in.

So far, properties concerning the query as a whole object have been covered. Each query object contains several objects. Those objects are tables, other queries, and fields. You can observe the properties for each object by clicking the desired object and selecting View | Properties in Design view.

The two properties for tables are Alias and Source.

Alias enables the user to give a name to a table. Normally, this isn't important, but there are situations in which this might be helpful. If there are two copies of the same table in one query, this feature is helpful. For example, a user needs a query on employees and supervisors. The Employee table contains a list of all the employees and their supervisors. Supervisors are also employees, so the user needs two copies of the Employees table. As the tables are added, the first table is called Employee. The second table is called Employee_1. The user has the option of using the Alias feature to rename the second table to Supervisors. It's easier to make a distinction between two tables with different names than two tables with similar names.

The other property for the tables in a query is called Source. This line shows where the table is coming from. If the table is coming from the current database, this line is blank. If the table is coming from another Access database or another back-end database like Oracle, the property reflects the source of the table.

The purpose of queries is to extract data and make it available to the user. Data is made available by running queries. Queries can't run unless there is at least one field in the QBE grid. Each individual field in the QBE grid has properties, which can be seen in Figure 8.5.

FIGURE 8.5.

The properties for a field in the QBE grid.

Input Mask Wizard
Builder button

The Properties dialog box for a field has two tabs. The first tab is the General tab, which has four attributes. The Lookup tab has one attribute. The following are the five attributes found for field properties:

- Description: This feature functions exactly like the Description feature found in the Design view of a table. It enables the user to enter up to 255 characters for a description, which appears in the status bar when a form is created. If the field isn't from a table in the current database, the description is automatically filled in by Access with the connection information used for the field.

- Format: Format enables the user to customize the way datatypes are displayed and printed. Usually, either the Format or Input Mask of a field is filled out when the user wants to control the display of a field. If both are filled out at the same time for the same field, the Format line takes precedence.

- Input Mask: Input Mask is similar to Format in that it controls the way you want to display data. In fact, a Wizard is available that builds the code in correct syntax based on the type of output you selected. The Wizard button is visible in Figure 8.5. The Input Mask Wizard itself is shown in Figure 8.6.

FIGURE 8.6.

The Input Mask gives the developer several commonly used input masks to choose from.

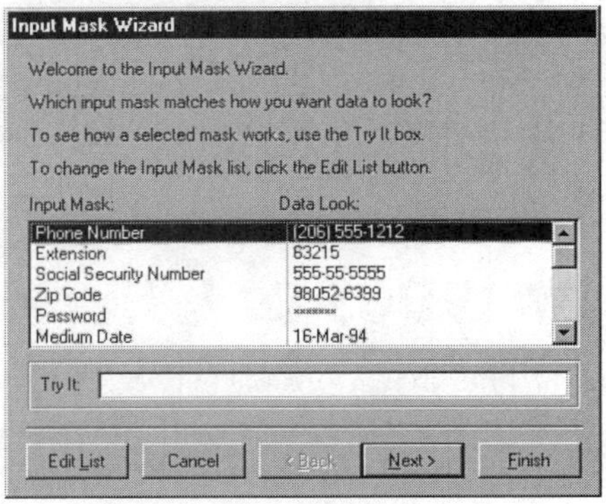

NOTE

The difference between Format and Input Mask is that the Input Mask can control how the data is entered. You can use certain symbols in a mask that make the field a mandatory field. If a form is created based on a query that has a mandatory field, the user must enter information that conforms to the input mask. For example, you could set the Input Mask of the Postal Code field to 00000. When a form is built based on this query, the user can't enter only three digits in the Postal Code field. The user must enter a five-digit postal code.

■ Caption: Caption functions the same way as it does in the Design view of a table. The caption is the text that appears in the label of a field. Even though a caption can be 2,048 characters long, if there isn't enough room for the caption to appear, it is truncated.

■ Display Control: The Display Control is found on the Lookup tab of the properties for a field in the QBE grid. Three types of controls are available—a text box, a list box, and a combo box. Each control has its own attributes, which become visible when the control is selected. When a form is based on a query where a lookup control has been set, all the configurations for that control stay with the field. When that field is pulled from the Field List onto a form, the lookup control with all the appropriate properties remains with the field. For example, the customer type field is set to combo box. When a form is based on this query, as you pull the customer type field onto the form, it appears as a combo box with all the properties already set.

NOTE

All the field properties found in a query can be found in a table. If you set a single field's properties to perform an action in the table and have a query based on that table, the properties for that single field don't follow through to the query. You can have different properties for the same field in several different queries. The attributes for a field in a form are based on the record source of the form. If the form is based on a table, the attributes for the field are the same as they are in the table. If the form is based on a query, the attributes for the field are the same as they are in the query.

Different Types of Query Joins

Query joins are the lines that are visible between two or more tables. They relate the tables and queries in the table pane of the grid to each other. These lines can be created manually or automatically. To create a join line, simply click one field in one table and drag it to a field in another table. Actually, there is more to a query than dragging any field to another field, but the join line itself is produced by dragging a field from one table to another table.

Microsoft Access can automatically create join lines between tables if the AutoJoin option is turned on. Access uses one of two sources of information that you might have already provided. The first way Access can automatically create a join line is based on a relationship that already exists. If you've already created a relationship, Access uses the relationship schema when automatically creating a join between two or more tables or queries. The other way that Access automatically creates joins is based on the naming conventions used to create the fields in a table. If two tables have the exact same name and comparable datatypes, Access automatically joins the two tables by the fields that have the same name.

> **NOTE**
>
> Whether the join line is automatically drawn when two or more tables or queries are placed in the table pane of the query or you draw the line by dragging one field in one table to the matching field in the other table, the line can have symbols attached to it. Only two types of symbols can exist—either a 1 or an infinity symbol (∞). There are only three relationship types: one-to-one, one-to-many (signified by the infinity symbol), and many-to-one.

You can access the Join Options dialog box in several ways. You can double-click an existing join line. You can highlight an existing join line and right-click to show the Join Properties line item. You can highlight an existing join line and select View | Join Properties. Finally, if no join line is available, you can create one by dragging a field from one table to the field of another table. With the line created, you can perform one of the previously mentioned methods of accessing the Joins Options dialog box. This is the same way joins are created and classified in the Relationships window, which is available by bringing up the database container and selecting Tools | Relationships.

There are only three types of joins in an Access query:

- INNER JOIN is the first option. This is usually the default join. This join selects records from the two tables where the values of the joined field are equal in both tables. The join doesn't have an arrow on either end of the line.

- LEFT JOIN is the second option. A LEFT JOIN is also commonly known as a LEFT OUTER JOIN, which is a reserved word in Microsoft Access. LEFT OUTER JOINs include all the records from the table on the left side of the join even if there are no matching record values in the table on the right side of the join. Records from the right table are combined with records from the left table only when they match.

- RIGHT JOIN is the third option. A RIGHT JOIN is also commonly known as a RIGHT OUTER JOIN, which is a reserved Microsoft Access word. This join includes all the records from the table on the right and all the records that have a matching value from the table on the left. Records from the left table are combined with the records from the right table only when they match.

As stated earlier, when two or more tables are added to a query, joins are automatically drawn based on a relationship that already exists, or on fields with the same name if the AutoJoin feature is turned on. If lines aren't automatically drawn, you or the user can draw them by clicking one field in a table and dragging it to another field in another table. Properties for the join are set when you click the join line and bring up the join's properties. If you select option #1, the join becomes an INNER JOIN and includes only the records from both tables where the fields by which they are joined have the same value. If you select option #2, the join becomes a LEFT OUTER JOIN; if you select option #3, the join becomes a RIGHT OUTER JOIN. In Figure 8.7, it appears as if both queries are LEFT OUTER JOIN queries, but they are not. Only the one on the left is a LEFT OUTER JOIN query.

FIGURE 8.7.

Both queries only appear to be LEFT OUTER JOIN queries.

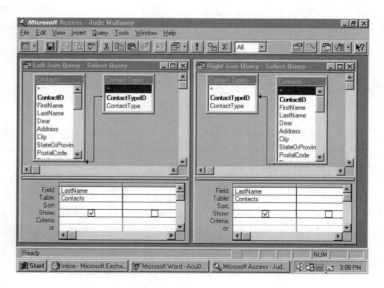

Even though both queries have an arrow pointing to the left, they aren't both LEFT OUTER JOIN queries. Remember, once a join is established, the tables can be moved around the table pane. This changes which way the arrow points. The important thing to remember in creating a join is where the join line originates from. A LEFT OUTER JOIN originates from the left-most table, and the arrow points right. Conversely, a RIGHT OUTER JOIN originates from the right-most table, and the arrow points to the left. Only the query on the left side of Figure 8.7 is a LEFT OUTER JOIN query. When these queries are run, they don't produce the same results, as shown in Figure 8.8.

FIGURE 8.8.

Just because both queries have the same tables and have arrows pointing to the left doesn't mean they produce the same results.

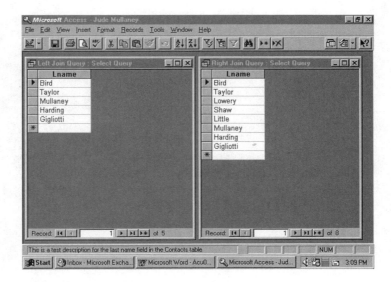

Just looking at which way an arrow is pointing isn't a reliable source when trying to find out if a join is a LEFT OUTER JOIN or a RIGHT OUTER JOIN. Sometimes it's hard to remember which option means left and which means right. One of the best ways to find out if the query is using a LEFT or RIGHT OUTER JOIN is to view the query in its SQL form. Select View | SQL. As shown in Figure 8.9, even though both queries looked similar in Design view, they're different in SQL view. In a LEFT OUTER JOIN, all the records in the table on the left side of the LEFT join appear in queries even when there are no matching records in the table on the right side. Conversely, in a RIGHT OUTER JOIN, all the records in the table on the right side of the RIGHT join appear in queries even when there are no matching records in the table on the left side.

NOTE

It's helpful if the joined field names are the same, but they don't have to be. Even though the fields don't have to have the same name, they must be of the same datatype or comparable datatype. Each field must also have the same kind of data. For example, there are two tables, and each table has a field called Field*X*. Field*X* in Table 1 is a Text datatype. Field*X* in Table 2 is a Date/Time datatype. Only a LEFT OUTER JOIN works in this scenario. An INNER JOIN or a RIGHT OUTER JOIN doesn't work because of the datatype conflict. A date/time value can go into a text field, but a text value can't go into a date/time field.

So far, the discussion has been of the three different types of joins. Knowing the different types of joins is only half the battle. When to use each join is the other half. Figure 8.10 shows the three types of joins—LEFT OUTER JOIN, INNER JOIN, and RIGHT OUTER JOIN. Each query contains the same two tables: Contacts and Contact Types. Each query is joined by the same field: Contact Type ID. Each query has only one output field: Last Name.

FIGURE 8.9.

By looking at queries in SQL view, it's easy to determine whether the query contains a LEFT OUTER JOIN or a RIGHT OUTER JOIN.

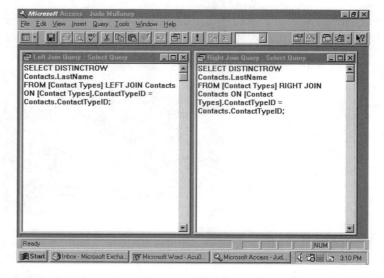

FIGURE 8.10.

LEFT OUTER JOIN, INNER JOIN, and RIGHT OUTER JOIN queries in Design view.

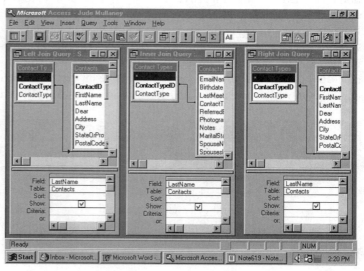

Each query is using the same data tables joined by the same fields, yet they are joined differently. The SQL view of each query is shown in Figure 8.11. The type of join is defined by the words LEFT, INNER, and RIGHT.

FIGURE 8.11.

It's easy to determine whether the query contains a LEFT OUTER JOIN, INNER JOIN, or RIGHT OUTER JOIN in SQL view.

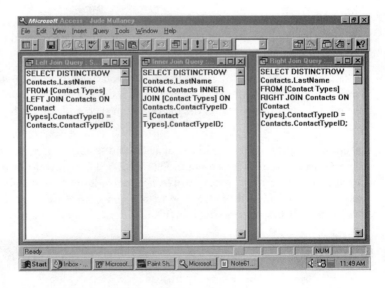

Even though all three queries have the same tables, joined by the same fields, and have the same field in the QBE grid, the output is different. Figure 8.12 shows the data output for each query.

FIGURE 8.12.

The queries might look the same, but the joins result in different outcomes.

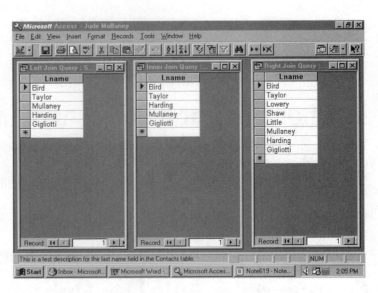

A LEFT OUTER JOIN is usually illustrated by a join line arrow that goes from the left table to the right table. This visual representation of a LEFT OUTER JOIN query is necessary to the description of the effect of the join. In Figure 8.10, the LEFT OUTER JOIN actually has an arrow that points to the right. Where the arrow points isn't important, but where it originates is. All the records from the left side of the join are added to the query's results even if there are no matching records from the table on the right. However, if the table on the right has records that match the join field, they are added to the results.

An INNER JOIN is depicted by a line drawn between two tables without an arrow on either end, as shown in Figure 8.10. As stated earlier, this is usually the default join between objects in the table pane of the query. It takes the records from each table only when they match the joining field.

A RIGHT OUTER JOIN is a mirror image of a LEFT OUTER JOIN in that the join line arrow goes from the right table to the left, as shown in Figure 8.10. The arrow originates from the right, which is what makes this a RIGHT OUTER JOIN. All the records on the right side of the join are added to the query's results even if there are no matching records from the table on the left. Yet, if the table on the left has records that match the join field, they are added to the results.

> **NOTE**
>
> It's important to note that a LEFT OUTER JOIN and a RIGHT OUTER JOIN can appear the same because the arrows can point to either the left or the right. Once the join is established, you can move the objects in the table pane of the query anywhere you want to. The way to tell if the join is left or right is to either double-click the join line to pull up the Join Properties box and see which option is selected or view the query's SQL statement and see if the join is left or right. In the Join Properties box, if option #2 is selected, the join is a LEFT OUTER JOIN. If option #3 is selected, the join is a RIGHT OUTER JOIN.

Relationships and Referential Integrity

When establishing relationships between tables, it's important to understand that they aren't created in the Query module of the database container. The relationship isn't a query even though it looks similar to a query. It is actually created from the database container and affects the database as a whole.

It's possible to create relationships based on queries, but referential integrity isn't enforced. Referential integrity ensures that relationships between records in related tables are valid. This prevents the user from accidentally deleting or changing related data.

Changing the AutoJoin Option

Relationships are logical joins, or lines drawn between tables for the database as a whole. Joins in a query are the lines drawn between tables and pertain only to the query itself. Once the query is closed, the joins are no longer relevant.

An option called AutoJoin is available to the developer. You can access AutoJoin by selecting Tools | Options. When the option is enabled, Access automatically creates an inner join between two tables on two conditions. The first condition is that the fields have the same name. The second condition is that one of the fields must be a primary key.

It's also possible to create a join between two tables if the AutoJoin feature isn't activated, but you must create the join manually by clicking one field in the first table and dragging it to another field in the second table. If the AutoJoin feature is turned on, more than one join can be created between the same two tables. If the join created by the AutoJoin isn't desired for the current query, you must delete it by highlighting the join line and pressing the Delete key. If the join that is created by the AutoJoin is desired and a second join is required, you just need to create the second join by dragging one field from the first table to another field in the second table.

Because the join created by the AutoJoin option is an inner join, you can change the join at any time. Highlight the join line and click the right mouse button to bring up the Join Properties dialog box. Select the desired join, either #2, LEFT OUTER JOIN, or #3, RIGHT OUTER JOIN, and click OK to save.

Analyzing Query Performance with Analyzer

Often you develop a query but aren't satisfied with it. The query might be sluggish or not performing to your satisfaction. What is a developer to do? Access 95 has come up with a way to analyze the query and all the objects within that database to give suggestions to the developer. It's called the Analyzer.

You can access the Analyzer by selecting Tools | Analyze from the database container and clicking Performance. Once the Performance Analyzer has been launched, a dialog box like the one in Figure 8.13 appears. You then have the ability to choose one object in the database or all the objects in the database.

FIGURE 8.13.

The Performance Analyzer enables the developer to choose objects in the database.

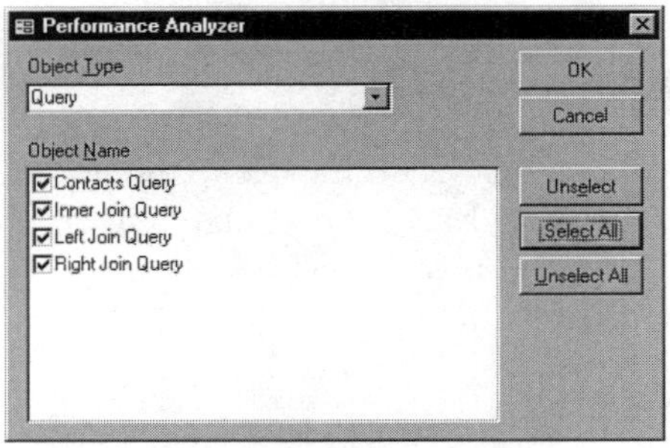

You can select an individual object type from the drop-down list or select all objects from the drop-down list. By selecting All, you can see every object that was created for this database. All the objects appear in the Object Name list. You can pick and choose the individual objects to be analyzed by checking the box associated with the object. If you want the entire database analyzed, you can click Select All, and the whole database can be analyzed.

Depending on the size of the database and the complexity of its objects, the analyze process can take several minutes. Once the process has finished, Access displays a dialog box like the one shown in Figure 8.14.

FIGURE 8.14.

The Analyzer offers advice on how to increase the speed of an object within a database or the entire database itself.

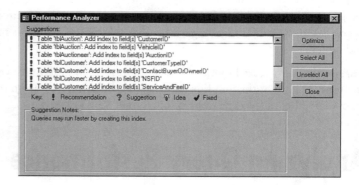

When the Performance Analyzer is finished grinding away, it returns advice to you. This advice is broken down into three categories: Recommendations, Suggestions, and Ideas. Recommendations have a red exclamation point for an icon. Suggestions have a green question mark, and Ideas have a yellow light bulb. The suggestion list shows the icon, the object module, the name of the object in question, and a brief suggestion of how to improve it.

If you click a Recommendation or Suggestion, Access gives a proposal on how to increase its performance. When the item is highlighted, the Optimize button is enabled. Access can make the changes to the database automatically. All the hints with a light bulb icon are Ideas, and Access can't optimize the object if the advice is only an idea. Developers must perform the Idea optimizations themselves.

CAUTION

The Performance Analyzer can make some changes automatically, but be careful. Some recommendations and suggestions might not be what you intend for the database.

Optimizing Queries

A developer can take several actions on his own to increase the speed of his queries, including the following:

■ Index the join fields in both tables. This includes tables joined from different sources. If there are multiple index fields to be queried, the query's speed increases if you use the indexed fields in the order they appear in the table's Index window. If fields are not or cannot be indexed, use sorts on those fields only when absolutely necessary.

■ Choose the appropriate datatype size for each field, especially the join fields. If you always choose a Long Integer as a datatype, you might not be utilizing the database to its best ability.

■ In the QBE Grid, choose only those fields that need to be shown. Showing all the fields slows down the display of the datasheet. Depending on the size or complexity of the query, this slowdown time could be a few minutes.

■ Nested queries shouldn't have calculated fields. If it's necessary to have calculated fields in nested queries, try to have the calculation performed in the top level of the query or have a control on the form that performs the calculation.

■ Group Bys also slow down queries, so try to keep them to a minimum. If they are needed, the placement of Group Bys is important. Calculate aggregates on the same table as the field that is to be totaled. If the number of Group Bys is reduced, the speed is increased. At times Group Bys are necessary for extracting data from the database in the format needed. First and Last Functions might be more appropriate than Group Bys.

■ Total queries that have joins might be faster if the single query is made into two queries. The first query performs the join then adds that query to a new query to calculate the totals.

■ Restrictive query criteria might perform faster depending on which side of the join the criteria is placed on. Criteria on one field might perform differently if the criteria is set on the One side rather than the Many side.

■ Make Table queries can be used to create tables if the data being used doesn't change often. Any form or report runs faster when it's based on a table as opposed to a query.

■ Crosstab queries utilizing fixed column headings run faster than nonfixed column headings.

Using Each of the Standard Query Types

A finite number of queries are available. Queries are like colors. Even though several thousand different colors are available, each color is derived from the three primary colors—red, blue, and yellow. Although there may be several different variations of queries, there are only two types of queries—queries that are acted on and queries that are viewed. These are called Action queries and Select queries. The following sections describe the different types of Action and Select queries and when to use them.

Action Queries

Action queries are queries where the data resulting from the query is acted upon. Changes are made to the records in one operation. There are four types of Action queries: Make Table, Delete, Append, and Update.

> **TIP**
>
> Access can't perform an AutoForm or AutoReport operation on any of the Action queries. They aren't considered valid queries for the basis of an AutoForm or AutoReport.

Make Table Queries

Make Table queries do exactly what the name implies. They make tables based on one or more other tables that utilize part or all the data from each table. What is the purpose of making a new table when the old ones work just fine? Developers use Make Table queries for several reasons. One reason is that you need to send information from the Employee table to another database, and the Employee table contains sensitive information. You would make a table with just the name and address and be able to export that make table to another database.

Developers use the Make Table query to create a query of history information. The make table retains all the information on a table or group of tables up to a specific date. The make table retains the information and could be considered a backup table. Make tables created for the purpose of holding history information have a two-pronged benefit. First, they enable you to retain all the information in smaller groups—say yearly. Any information needed can be quickly generated based on a yearly make table. Second, with a make table containing the history information of years gone by, those records could actually be deleted from the real tables, thus increasing the speed of any forms or reports based on those tables. You don't move old records as you think of a move with the Explorer. You simply copy the older records to another table and delete the older records from the main table.

If you had several forms or reports based on the same two or more tables, you could increase the speed of the forms and reports by creating a make table. The key phrase in the previous statement is "several forms or reports." If only one table or report was based on a multitable query, it wouldn't be any faster because the query still has to run. If the form or report is used only periodically, a query running to generate a dynaset or a query running to generate a make table takes the same amount of time. However, if there were several different forms or reports, it would make sense to have a Make Table query. The first time the query is run, speed doesn't increase, but each time a form or report is run after the query has generated the make table, the speed does increase. The speed increases because forms and reports run faster when based on tables than when based on queries.

To create a Make Table query, create a new, blank query with the desired tables. Pull the fields into the QBE grid and set the criteria, if any. Select Query | Make Table or click the Query Type button on the query's design toolbar and select Make Table. A Make Table dialog box appears. Type the name of the new table you're creating, as shown in Figure 8.15.

FIGURE 8.15.

When creating a Make Table query, type the name of the new table here.

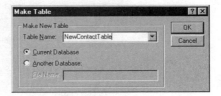

A different database can be accessed from here. Before the Make Table query is created, click the Datasheet view of the query to make sure the results of this query are the ones needed. The make table is created when the query is actually run. After the query is run, check the Tables module of the database container. The new table should be there. Open the new table to see the records. As new records are added to the original table, they don't appear in the make table unless the Make Table query is run again. If the Make Table query is run again, new records that match the criteria set by the query are added to the new table.

> **NOTE**
>
> Any field properties from the tables used in the Make Table query don't follow through. If you have default values or input masks set, those properties aren't duplicated in the new table.

Append Queries

The Append query does exactly what it says it does—it adds. Suppose you need to combine the Contact table with a Customers table. The two tables are similar in fields except the

Contact table has more fields than the Customer table. The Append query takes the records from one table and matches the fields in the other table. All records are appended to the table, and those fields that don't match are ignored.

To create an Append query, create a new, blank query with the table whose records will be appended to another table. In Design view, select Query | Append or click the Query Type button on the toolbar. The Append dialog box appears. Type the table name that these records are to be appended to. A different database can even be accessed from here. Drag the fields from the table onto the QBE grid. Specifications can be set in the QBE grid. Notice in Figure 8.16 that there is an extra line in the QBE grid of an Append query. It is the Append To line. Here is where the matching field name in the other table is entered.

FIGURE 8.16.

An Append query has an extra line in the QBE grid where the matching field name is entered.

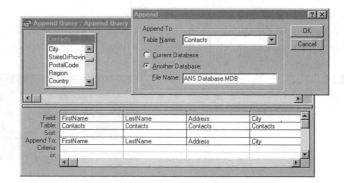

TIP

If a primary key field is placed on the QBE grid for appending, the corresponding field in the table the records are being appended to must have an equivalent datatype field. For example, if the Contacts ID field is to be appended, the corresponding field must be a Long Integer datatype.

Once the Append query is run, the records are added to the other table. If seven records match the criteria, seven new records appear in the other table. In this case, the seven records were added to another database. If new records are added to the table in the current database, the changes aren't reflected in the other database until the Append query is run again. Then the new records are added to the other database.

WARNING

Access automatically renumbers any record that is appended if the AutoNumber field isn't placed on the QBE grid. If the original AutoNumber field is needed to remain with the record, place the AutoNumber field on the QBE grid. Any duplicate AutoNumber values aren't appended.

Update Queries

Update queries give you the ability to change data on a global scale. For example, if all the employees get an annual raise of 5 percent, their salaries are increased by 5 percent through an Update query. If all the customers' area codes in the Charlotte area changed to 701, the change could be made through an Update query.

To create an Update query, open a new, blank query and add the tables needed to make the change. In Design view, select all the criteria that is needed for the update. If all the contacts that were categorized as Buyers became Sellers, the field that needs to be changed is ContactTypeID. First, set the criteria to read only those records where the ContactTypeID is 1 (in the ContactType table, Buyer = 1). Look at the query in Datasheet view to make sure the right records are being changed.

Next, select Query | Update or click the Query Type button on the toolbar. Only when the query is run does the update take place. If the view is changed to Datasheet, the same information appears as before the query was changed to Update. Notice in Figure 8.17 that an Update To line is added to the QBE grid. To change all the Buyers to Sellers, the ContactTypeID number for Sellers (2) must be added to the grid. If the words Buyer and Seller are used instead of 1 and 2, an error occurs. This error occurs because the field pulled down is the ContactTypeID, not ContactType. Access is looking for a number, not a string.

The changes are made to the data only when the query is run. In Figure 8.17, three records are changed from Buyer to Seller. New records can be added to the table, and their ContactTypeID can reflect that the contact is either a Buyer or a Seller. Only when the Update query is run again do all the Buyers become Sellers.

FIGURE 8.17.

When the Update query is selected, an Update To line is added to the QBE grid.

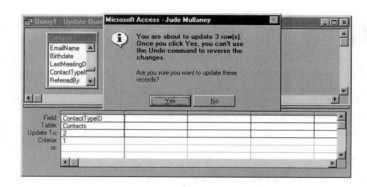

Delete Queries

The Delete query gives you the ability to delete records from one or more tables in a single action. As helpful as this can be, it can also be very dangerous. If the Delete query is based on one table, when the query is run, the records that match the criteria are deleted. If the Delete query is based on more than one table, two Delete queries must be run. A Delete query can delete records from only one table at a time. For example, if all the contacts in North Carolina need to be deleted, two Delete queries need to be run—one on the calls associated with the North Carolina contacts and one on the North Carolina contacts themselves.

To create a single-table Delete query, open a new, blank query with the table containing the records to be deleted. Pull down the asterisk field that represents all the fields in the table and place it in the first column of the QBE grid. In the other columns, pull down additional fields to set the criteria. Set the criteria for the query to reflect the records that need to be deleted. View the query in Datasheet view before running the Delete query. If the Datasheet view doesn't reflect the records that need to be deleted, return to Design view and check the criteria until the results of the datasheet equal the records that need to be deleted.

Select Query | Delete Query or click the Query Type button on the toolbar and select Delete. Click the Run icon (the exclamation point) to activate the delete. Access tells you how many records are affected by the Delete query and gives you the option canceling the delete. Remember, once the delete has taken place, nothing can undo the delete. The only way to retrieve the records that are deleted from a Delete query would be to restore them from a backup of the database.

Select Queries

The first type of query discussed was the Action query; the second type of query is the Select query. Select queries are queries where the data resulting from the query is viewed. There are two types of Select queries—Simple Select queries and Crosstab queries.

Simple Select Queries

Simple Select queries are the most common of all the queries. They enable you to extract data from different tables and view it. Limited manipulations can be made with Select queries. Select queries are so common that a Select Query Wizard is available. The Wizard lists all the existing tables and queries and asks for the fields that should appear in the query. From that information, the Wizard creates the Select query.

To create a Simple Select query without the Wizard, open a new, blank query and add the tables desired for the query. A relationship must exist between two or more tables in a query. If a relationship isn't automatically established when the tables are entered into the table pane of the query, it is because either the table fields don't adhere to a standard naming convention or no relationship was established in the Relationships window of the database. You can establish a relationship for this query by dragging a field from one table to a related field in the other table. This kind of relationship appears only in this query.

By dragging fields from the tables to the QBE grid, a Simple Select query is built, as shown in Figure 8.18. Criteria can be set on Select queries. Select queries can calculate sums, averages, counts, and other types of totals on one or more tables.

FIGURE 8.18.

A Simple Select query.

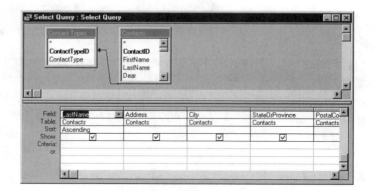

Crosstab Queries

The second type of Select queries is Crosstab queries. They're somewhat like Simple Select queries in that they can calculate sums, averages, counts, and other types of totals on one or more tables. They differ from Simple Select queries in that Crosstab queries display information not only down the left column of the datasheet (like a Simple Select query), but also across the top. Crosstab queries are similar in appearance to Pivot Tables. Crosstab queries have row headings as well as column headings. Simple Select queries can produce the same information as Crosstab queries, but the Crosstab queries give a more concise datasheet.

To create a Crosstab query without the help of a Wizard, open a new, blank query and add the tables needed for the desired result. Add the fields from the tables into the QBE grid. Select Query | Crosstab or click the Query Type button on the design toolbar, as shown in Figure 8.19.

FIGURE 8.19.

You can create a Crosstab query by selecting Crosstab from the Query Type button.

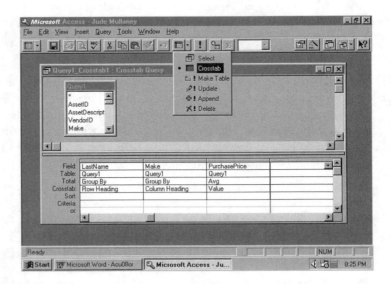

> When you're creating a Crosstab query, there must be at least three output fields. One field must be a Row Heading, one field must be a Column Heading, and one field must be a Value.

When the Crosstab query is selected, Access automatically adds a Total row and a Crosstab row to the QBE grid. There must be at least three output fields in a Crosstab query—one for the column heading, one for the row heading, and one for a value, as shown in Figure 8.19.

There might be occasions where data is missing or data that has been appended to the table or query in the Crosstab and fields might be missing. This missing data might be data in the row or column headings of your Crosstab query. When data for headings is missing, Access returns a < > sign, which means that this field is null. You can prevent a null sign from appearing in a heading by typing Is Not Null in the Criteria cell in the design grid for that field. This means that any time a heading comes across a null field, that record isn't considered for the Crosstab query. However, if you need to know that there are records that should be visible in the query even if there is a null heading field, you can use the Nz function. This function is an expression that is placed in the Criteria cell of the heading field and returns a string Unknown instead of a null.

> **NOTE**
>
> Data in Crosstab queries can't be edited.

You can't create an AutoForm or AutoReport based on an Action query or a Crosstab query. However, you can display Crosstab data on a form or report without creating a separate query in the database. This is achieved by adding a PivotTable control on the form or report. With the Excel Pivot Table, row and column headings can be changed on-the-fly, enabling users to analyze the data in different ways.

Summary

Access 95 includes several new features that make querying more efficient. This chapter covered the new query features available, such as the Filter by Form button. It also covered the design and new properties of a basic query. The differences between relationships and joins were discussed, as well as the different types of joins. The AutoJoin option was described, and the six standard query types were covered—Make Table, Append, Update, Delete, Simple Select, and Crosstab. The Performance Analyzer was examined and illustrated. The following chapters expound on the Action queries. They also discuss some of the nonstandard query types.

Specialized Queries

9

by Mike Harding

IN THIS CHAPTER

Crosstab Queries

Crosstab queries were discussed briefly in the preceding chapter. This chapter will take our discussion of Crosstab queries to the next level.

The purpose of a Crosstab query is to perform a consolidation process on sections of data that intersect and to give summary information on that data. The data appears in a two-dimensional array or matrix, and mathematical operations are performed at each intersection. The word *Crosstab* comes from the phrase *cross tabulation,* which is the action executed by the Crosstab query.

In the past, Crosstab queries were difficult for a novice user to understand and execute. Today, the Crosstab Query Wizard gives the novice the ability to create Crosstab queries, but it's still the experienced developer who can actually make these queries produce valuable results. By the end of this section, Crosstab queries shouldn't pose any problems for the developer who wants to create Crosstabs without the guidance of the wizard.

To really understand Crosstab queries, it's necessary to create one without using the Crosstab Query Wizard. Let's say a user has requested a way to list the payments made by his customers. Our mission is to give the user the total payment information for every customer, referenced by state. This sounds like a job for a Crosstab query!

For the following example, let's create a Customer table and a Payment table using the table wizards. Select all the suggested fields when asked which to include in your new tables. Create a new, blank query and add the two tables to the query. All new, blank queries automatically default to a Select query, as shown in Figure 9.1. Accept the default join between the tables. The fields needed for the Crosstab query, based on the mission statement mentioned earlier, are the PaymentAmount field, the ContactLastName field and the StateOrProvince fields. Either drag and drop the fields from each table into the query grid or simply double-click the fields. Remember that the order in which you double-click is the order in which the fields will be added to the grid.

> **NOTE**
>
> Only one table or query can be accessed from the Crosstab Query Wizard. If two or more tables are needed for a Crosstab query, you have two options. First, you can cancel the wizard and create a query based on the number of tables needed for a Crosstab and then run the wizard again and base it on the newly created query. Or you can go directly into a blank query and create the Crosstab from there.

In our example we have entered a few records in each table manually. The Select query simply pulls all of the records in the exact order that they were entered into the tables. Figure 9.2 is a Datasheet view of the query that appears in Figure 9.1. Notice that all of the records appear and aren't sorted by last name in ascending order. Even though all the information needed to complete the mission is available in this Select query, it isn't presented in a concise manner.

FIGURE 9.1.

All new, blank queries automatically default to a Select query.

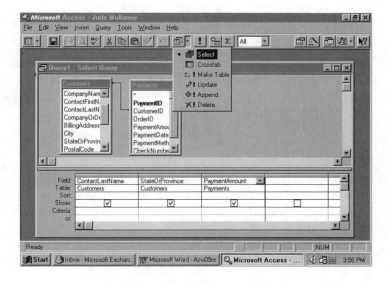

FIGURE 9.2.

The result of a Select query before it becomes a Crosstab query.

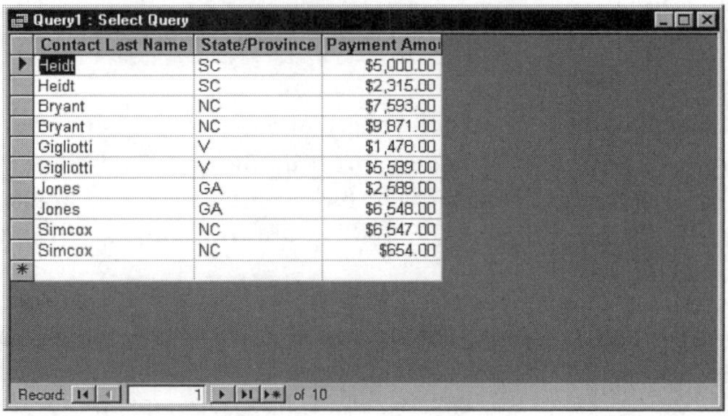

Crosstab queries are similar to Total queries in that a Total line is added to the query grid. In Figure 9.3, the Totals button is clicked and the Total line is added to the query grid. When the Total row is added to the query grid, a drop-down box appears for each field in that grid. Automatically, Access fills in the Group By option for each Totals cell. In Figure 9.3, the PaymentAmount fields' Total cell has been changed to Sum. It was originally the Group By option, but it was changed to Sum because the mission of the query is to produce a total payment for every customer.

FIGURE 9.3.

The Total row in the query grid makes a Select query similar to a Crosstab query.

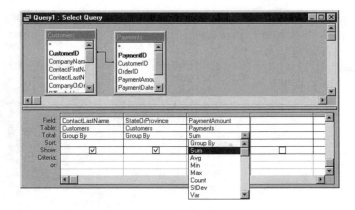

A Totals query is closer to obtaining the information requested by the user. Figure 9.4 shows the result of the Totals query. This query is more concise than the Select query in Figure 9.2, yet it isn't exactly what the user is looking for. It's the developer's job to try to give the users exactly what they want.

FIGURE 9.4.

The result of the Totals query is similar to a Crosstab query.

Contact Last Name	State/Province	SumOfPaymentAmount
Bryant	NC	$17,464.00
Gigliotti	V	$7,067.00
Heidt	SC	$7,315.00
Jones	GA	$9,137.00
Simcox	NC	$7,201.00

Whether the query is a Totals query or a Crosstab query, the Totals row will appear in the query grid. To change the query, bring up the query in Design view. Change the query from a Select query to a Crosstab query by selecting Query | Crosstab. You can achieve the same objective by clicking the Query Type button and selecting Crosstab, which is visible in Figure 9.5.

> **NOTE**
>
> Notice that if the Totals button is deactivated, the Totals row will disappear from the query grid. If you select Query | Crosstab, not only is the Crosstab row added to the query grid, but so is the Totals line.

In Figure 9.5, Access has added the Crosstab row to the query grid. Certain requirements must be met before a Crosstab query can be executed:

- At least one output field must be a row heading.
- One output field must be a column heading.
- One output field must be a value field. This field is usually a number field where calculations are performed at each column/row intersection.

FIGURE 9.5.
The Crosstab query adds the Crosstab and Total rows to the query grid.

TIP

If more than one output field is listed as a row heading, they should appear in the grid the same way they are to appear in the datasheet. For example, there are three row headings, listed from left to right, in the query grid: Country, State, City. The Datasheet view of that Crosstab query would list all of the countries in the left-most column of the array. Within each country category, all of the states would be listed. Within each state category, all of the cities would be listed.

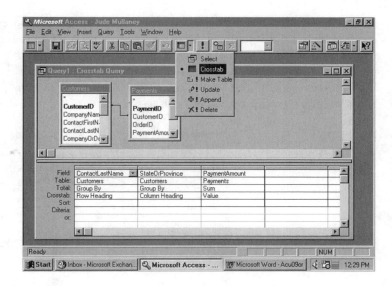

It's important to remember that with every Crosstab query there must be at least three output fields. The maximum number of output fields is five. Users are allowed up to three output fields for row headings, one field for a column heading, and one field for a value. Notice in Figure 9.5 that there are only three output fields—one Row heading, one Column heading, and one Value heading. In Figure 9.6, the results of the Crosstab query are visible. They are similar to the Totals query results seen in Figure 9.4, yet more condensed.

FIGURE 9.6.
The results of the Crosstab query.

Contact Last Name	GA	NC	SC	V
Bryant		$17,464.00		
Gigliotti				$7,067.00
Heidt			$7,315.00	
Jones	$9,137.00			
Simcox		$7,201.00		

The main difference between Figure 9.6 and 9.4 is that the Totals query (Figure 9.4) allows for repeating states, whereas the Crosstab query (Figure 9.6) groups those states under one column heading. This presents the data that the user requested in a more compact manner.

You might ask, "What really makes a Crosstab query work?" To answer that question, it's necessary to look at the SQL statement that is created during a Crosstab query. Figure 9.7 shows two views of the SQL statement for the query. The view on the left is the SQL statement for the Totals query. The view on the right is the SQL statement for the Crosstab query. Both have the same tables joined by the same field with the same output. The major difference between the two views are the words TRANSFORM and PIVOT.

FIGURE 9.7.

The major differences between the Totals query and the Crosstab query can be seen in the SQL statement.

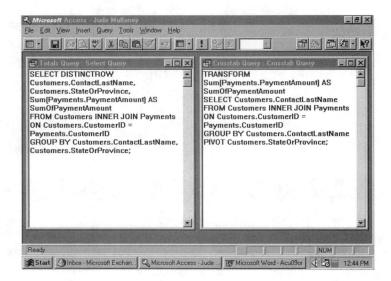

Let's look at and dissect the SQL statement for a Crosstab query. A Crosstab query has several distinct parts. The Crosstab query's SQL statement is shown in Listing 9.1.

Listing 9.1. The Crosstab query SQL statement.

```
TRANSFORM Sum(Payments.PaymentAmount) AS SumOfPaymentAmount
SELECT Customers.ContactLastName
FROM Customers INNER JOIN Payments ON Customers.CustomerID =_ Payments.CustomerID
GROUP BY Customers.ContactLastName
PIVOT Customers.StateOrProvince;
```

The first word, TRANSFORM, actually creates the Crosstab query. It's followed by the aggregate function. The aggregate function is the meat of the Crosstab query. In the Crosstab query's Design view, the aggregate function would be the field where the word Value appears in the Crosstab row of the query grid. In Listing 9.1, the aggregate function is Sum, followed by a reference to a field and its table—in this case, the PaymentAmount field from the Payments table. There are several different aggregate functions, and they are listed in Table 9.1.

Table 9.1. SQL aggregate functions available for Crosstab queries.

Function	Description
SUM	Returns the result of adding a set of values contained in a specified field.
AVG	Returns the result of the sum of all of the values contained in a specified field which is divided by the total number of values contained in that specified field.
MIN	Returns the minimum value contained in a specified field.
MAX	Returns the maximum value contained in a specified field.
COUNT	Returns the number of records in a query—in this case, a Crosstab query. Null records won't be counted.
STDEV	Refers to the standard deviation for a population sample that is represented as a set of values within a specified field. In statistics, standard deviation indicates how a set of figures is spread about its arithmetic mean. It's used to measure the dispersion of a set of data from the average value or mean.
STDEVP	Refers to the standard deviation for a population that is represented as a set of values within a specified field. The difference between STDEV and STDEVP is the word "sample." Only a portion of a population is used in the STDEV, whereas the entire population is used when figuring the STDEVP. This function can't be selected from the QBE grid. It can only be used directly in SQL statements.
VAR	Returns a variance for a sample of the population represented by a set of values within a specified field. Mathematically speaking, it is the square of the standard deviation.
VARP	Returns a variance for the entire population represented by a set of values within a specified field. The difference between VAR and VARP is the fact that VAR deals with only a portion of the population, whereas VARP deals with the entire population. This function can't be selected from the QBE grid. It can only be used directly in SQL statements.
FIRST	Returns the first value from the table or query.
LAST	Returns the last value from the table or query.

NOTE

If the underlying query contains only two or fewer records, the STDEV, STDEVP, VAR, and VARP functions can't be calculated and will return a null.

The first part of a Crosstab query is the word TRANSFORM, which actually creates the Crosstab followed by the SQL aggregate function. The aggregate function is followed by the SELECT statement. The SELECT statement utilizes the Microsoft Jet engine to return a set of records from the database table.

In Select queries, a SELECT statement can have predicates restricting the number of records being returned. Predicates are ALL, DISTINCT, DISTINCTROW, and TOP. These parts of the SELECT statement are described in Table 9.2.

Table 9.2. SELECT statement predicates.

Predicate	Description
ALL	If a predicate isn't defined, Access selects all of the records that meet the conditions as dictated by the SQL statement.
DISTINCT	Omits all of the records that contain duplicate data for a field. For example, DISTINCT Country FROM Customers would show a list of all of the countries that have at least one customer associated with it, yet the list returned would show only one occurrence of a country, even if there were 5,000 customers from the same country.
DISTINCTROW	Functions similarly to DISTINCT with the exception that DISTINCTROW is based on omitting entire records that have duplicate data, as opposed to DISTINCT, which performs omissions based on fields.
TOP	Can be generated by the Top Values button on the design toolbar. It specifies a number of records that are in the top range. It can be reversed to show the bottom values if the ORDER BY field is shown in descending order.

TIP

Crosstab queries don't allow the use of the Top Values property. You can simulate this by basing your Crosstab query on a Select query where the Top Values property has already been set.

> **NOTE**
>
> If the top five values of yearly sales are 100, 99, 98, 97, and 96, any record whose value is equal to one of those values will be returned by the query. Even though there are five top values, seven records may meet that predicate condition. TOP predicates don't choose between equal values.

The SELECT statement is a powerful tool in Access. In the SQL statement in Listing 9.1, the SELECT statement is followed by the field names and their associated tables. The word SELECT constitutes the beginning of the statement. In Listing 9.2, the SELECT statement has been extracted to give you a better understanding.

Listing 9.2. Extraction of the SELECT statement.

```
SELECT Customers.ContactLastName
FROM Customers INNER JOIN Payments ON Customers.CustomerID =_ Payments.CustomerID
```

The SELECT statement is taking the ContactLastName field from the Customers table. The Customer table is joined to another table called Payments. The field that relates the two tables is the CustomerID field, and that join is an INNER JOIN.

> **NOTE**
>
> INNER JOINs select only the records in which the join fields from both tables are equal.

As mentioned earlier, the SELECT statement can be a powerful tool for developers. Several different clauses enhance the gathering of information. They have a specific order of appearance. Any variation of the order may result in a syntax error. The following is a schema of the correct order of appearance of clauses in a SELECT statement. All of the clauses aren't mandatory; in fact, a SELECT statement really just needs to contain SELECT *fields* FROM *table* to meet the minimum syntax requirements.

```
SELECT tablename.field1, tablename.field2 FROM tablename WHERE condition GROUP BY
➥tablename.field1 ORDER BY tablename.field1
```

Table 9.3 lists the clauses that may appear in a SELECT statement.

Table 9.3. Clauses that make up a SELECT statement.

Clause	*Description*
FROM	States the tables or queries that embody the fields listed in the SELECT statement.
IN	Used only when accessing external databases that are compatible with the Microsoft Jet engine. Don't confuse this with the word In, which appears after the pivot field in the Crosstab query's SQL statement. The word In specifies a sort order for a column heading field.
WHERE	Works in conjunction with the FROM clause and specifies the records from the tables. This clause is used in Select Update and Select Delete statements (queries). The WHERE clause is similar to the HAVING clause in that the HAVING clause determines which records are displayed and the WHERE clause determines which records are selected. The WHERE clause is used to eliminate records that are not to be displayed by a GROUP BY clause. If no WHERE clause is specified, all rows from the tables will be considered.
GROUP BY	Combines records with identical values. These records are then displayed as one record, even though they don't affect the actual data. For example, sales can be grouped by country. There would be only one record where the country equals USA, and the sum of all of the sales for USA would be listed.
HAVING	Works in conjunction with the GROUP BY clause. It specifies which group of records is displayed.
ORDER BY	Works on the resulting records of a query. It isn't an obligatory clause, but it is still present even if you don't state an ORDER BY.
WITH OWNERSACCESS OPTION	Deals with the security of each object within a database container.

Access Security is always on. This technique can be used to give you field-level security on a database. This declaration is used with a query to give the user the same permissions as the query's owner.

So far, our discussion of the SQL statement has covered TRANSFORM, the aggregate functions, and SELECT. The next part of a Crosstab query's SQL statement is the PIVOT. Webster's defines a pivot as a pin or shaft on which a wheel or other body turns. Mechanically speaking, that is correct. Applied to database software, a pivot is a field on which a table is calculated. However, just because a field is calculated doesn't mean that the query is a Crosstab. There must be at least two other fields (for a minimum total of three fields) to create a Crosstab query.

To appreciate the results of a Crosstab query, it's necessary to view a Select query that has the same output fields as a Crosstab query. In Figure 9.8, the Crosstab query has been changed to a Select query by clicking Select from the Query Types button. The same can be achieved by choosing Query | Select. Notice that in the first column, the fields ContactLastName and ContactFirstName have been aliased as ContactName.

FIGURE 9.8.

A view of a Crosstab query that has been changed to a Select query.

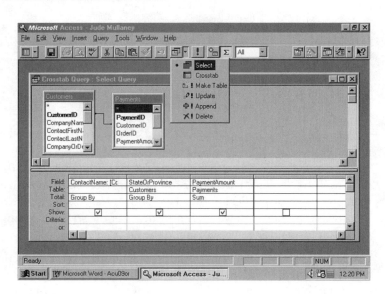

The result of such a query can be seen in Figure 9.9. Notice that all of the data appears in rows and columns but the data isn't really grouped in any kind of fashion. It's safe to say that the ContactName is the X axis in a one-dimensional query.

FIGURE 9.9.

A view of a Select query's results before being changed to a Crosstab query.

ContactName	State/Province	SumOfPaymentAmount
Bryant, Chris	NC	$17,464.00
Gigliotti, Steph	VA	$7,067.00
Heidt, Karen	SC	$7,315.00
Jones, Ann	SC	$9,137.00
Jones, Jeanine	GA	$9,137.00
Simcox, Mary	NC	$7,201.00

Now, return to the query and change it back to a Crosstab query by selecting Crosstab from the Query Type button or by selecting Query | Crosstab. In Figure 9.10, the Crosstab row has been added to the query grid. If the Totals row weren't already present, it would be added to the query grid too. Both rows are needed in the grid to display a Design view of a Crosstab query.

FIGURE 9.10.

A Crosstab query has the Total and the Crosstab rows added to the query grid.

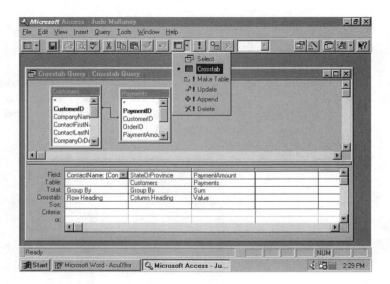

There must be at least one row heading field, one column heading field, and one value field in the Crosstab cells. The default for a row heading is GROUP BY in the Totals row. If there is more than one row heading field in the query grid, at least one of the fields must have GROUP BY in the Totals cell. A drop-down list is provided, but the selection of any other aggregate function will result in an error when moving to the Datasheet view.

Criteria can be set for the Row Heading field, but the placement of the criteria depends on the outcome desired. If you need the criteria to take place *before the calculation is performed,* the expression is entered into the Criteria row for the Row Heading field.

If you need to limit the records *before the row headings are grouped and before they are cross-tabulated,* add the field needed to perform the limitation to the query to the design grid. Set the Total cell for that field to WHERE. Leave the Crosstab cell blank. Enter the desired expression into the Criteria row. The criteria will be acted upon when the query is run, even though this field won't be visible.

The column heading has a default of GROUP BY in the Totals row. Even though a drop-down list is associated with the Totals row for a Column Heading, GROUP BY is the only option allowed. If another option is chosen, you can't view the query's results. There can be only one column heading field per Crosstab query.

Column headings can be sorted in a different order or even limit the headings to be displayed. You can do this by entering in the criteria for the column headings in the query's Properties sheet in the Column Headings field. To get to the Properties sheet for the entire query, click in the table pane of a query (not on a table or join line) and select View | Properties. Right-clicking in the table pane will bring up a shortcut to the query's properties too.

The Value field is the field that actually performs the cross-tabulation. There can be only one Value field. Its Totals row must perform some aggregate function, such as SUM, AVG, or COUNT.

Just looking at the results of the query, which can be seen in Figure 9.11, you might think that the PIVOT field in the figure is the PaymentAmount field because it performs a calculation at every column and row intersection. This is a natural assumption, but an incorrect one.

FIGURE 9.11.

The Crosstab query results.

ContactName	GA	NC	SC	VA
Bryant, Chris		$17,464.00		
Gigliotti, Steph				$7,067.00
Heidt, Karen			$7,315.00	
Jones, Ann			$999,999.00	
Jones, Jeanine	$9,137.00			
Simcox, Mary		$7,201.00		

Regular Select queries display rows of records. Even though there are titles on the columns for each record, those titles are the names of the individual fields for each record. A Crosstab query differs from a Select query in that the columns that appear are actually based on only one field, whereas a Select query's columns are made up of different fields. Therefore, the actual pivot field is the column heading. This can be proven by looking at the code in Listing 9.3.

Listing 9.3. The pivot field is the StateOrProvince field.

```
TRANSFORM Sum(Payments.PaymentAmount) AS SumOfPaymentAmount
SELECT Customers.ContactLastName
FROM Customers INNER JOIN Payments ON Customers.CustomerID =_ Payments.CustomerID
GROUP BY Customers.ContactLastName
PIVOT Customers.StateOrProvince;
```

The word PIVOT is followed by the name of the pivot field. Some may ask if it's possible to change the Row Heading field to Column Heading and the Column Heading field to Row Heading. The answer is yes, and the results can be seen in Figure 9.12.

FIGURE 9.12.

The Crosstab query's column and row headings can be interchanged.

State/	Bryant, Chris	Gigliotti, Steph	Heidt, Karen	Jones, Ann	Jones, Jeanine	Simcox, Mary
GA					$9,137.00	
NC	$17,464.00					$7,201.00
SC			$7,315.00	$999,999.00		
VA		$7,067.00				

The Column Heading field is usually sorted in alphabetical order. That sort order can be changed in SQL view by following the pivot field with the word IN and the sort-order criteria. When you aren't sure of the correct syntax, let Access create the syntax automatically. In Figure 9.13, a sort order has been specified for the Column Heading field through the query's Properties dialog box.

FIGURE 9.13.

Column headings can have a specific sort order.

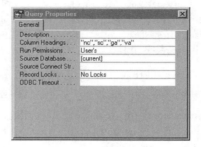

The result is that the column headings will appear in the order stated in Figure 9.13. This can be helpful when the Column Heading field is Months. Normally, that field would be displayed in alphabetical order. The developer can go in and make the columns appear in chronological order. In Figure 9.14, the order specified in the Column Heading field from the query's Properties dialog box can be seen in its SQL view.

FIGURE 9.14.

The column headings' order of appearance can be seen at the end of the SQL statement preceded by the word IN.

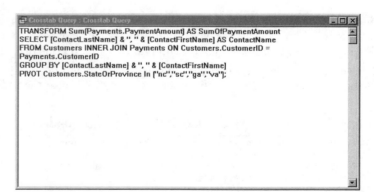

```
TRANSFORM Sum(Payments.PaymentAmount) AS SumOfPaymentAmount
SELECT [ContactLastName] & ", " & [ContactFirstName] AS ContactName
FROM Customers INNER JOIN Payments ON Customers.CustomerID =
Payments.CustomerID
GROUP BY [ContactLastName] & ", " & [ContactFirstName]
PIVOT Customers.StateOrProvince In ("nc","sc","ga","va");
```

Before ending the discussion on Crosstab queries, it's important to answer questions on blank values. Sometimes data on a record is incomplete. In Figure 9.15, a name wasn't entered into a record. That record is still a valid record, even though there isn't a customer name. If a row is missing data, that record will appear at the top of the Crosstab query.

FIGURE 9.15.

Records that are missing row data appear at the top of the Crosstab query.

ContactName	nc	sc	ga	va
,				$7,067.00
Bryant, Chris	$17,464.00			
Heidt, Karen		$7,315.00		
Jones, Ann		$999,999.00		
Jones, Jeanine			$9,137.00	
Simcox, Mary	$7,201.00			

However, if the data missing from a record is data that would be found in the column heading, a different result will occur. In Figure 9.16, a state field is missing from a record. Column heading fields that have null values appear in the left-most column of the Crosstab query. Since there is no column heading name, Access displays the Boolean symbol for not equal to, which is < >.

FIGURE 9.16.

Column headings that have null values are signified by a < > symbol.

ContactName	<>	GA	NC	SC
Bryant, Chris			$17,464.00	
Gigliotti, Steph	$7,067.00			
Heidt, Karen				$7,315.00
Jones, Ann				$999,999.00
Jones, Jeanine		$9,137.00		
Simcox, Mary			$7,201.00	

This problem can be rectified by two methods. The first method is to perform the calculation without the records that are null. To view the records where the column heading is < >, return to Design view. In the criteria cell of the Column Heading field, enter `Is Null`.

NOTE

When searching for null values, you type the word `Null` into the criteria cell of the desired field. When searching for zero-length strings, you should type `""` (two double quotation marks without a space) into the criteria cell of the desired field.

When the criteria is run, only the records that have a null value in the StateOrProvince field will be returned. This is how many records will be left out of the cross-tabulation. Now, to remove those records from the calculation, remove the `Is Null` function and replace it with `Is Not Null`. This function will remove all of the records where the value in the StateOrProvince field is empty, as shown in Figure 9.17.

FIGURE 9.17.

Column headings that have null values can be removed from the query.

ContactName	GA	NC	SC
Bryant, Chris		$17,464.00	
Heidt, Karen			$7,315.00
Jones, Ann			$999,999.00
Jones, Jeanine	$9,137.00		
Simcox, Mary		$7,201.00	

However, if the records need to be calculated in the Crosstab query even though there may be a null value in the StateOrProvince field, it can't be done through the Null function. So, the object here is to perform a cross-tabulation and identify those records that have null values in the Column Heading fields. The best way to tackle this problem is through the `Immediate If` function (`IIF`). First, remove the `Is Not Null` function from the criteria cell of the Column Heading field.

The objective of the `Immediate If` function is to return one of two parts—either the truepart or the falsepart. Currently, the StateOrProvince field name is in the field cell. The `Immediate If` function will need to be placed in the field cell that now contains StateOrProvince, so highlight StateOrProvince and press the Delete key.

> **NOTE**
>
> When removing a field name from a field cell on the query grid, it isn't necessary to highlight the entire row and press Delete. Simply highlight the name and press Delete. This preserves all of the Totals and Crosstab information that will be used later.

With the Field cell empty, type in the following code:

```
IIf(IsNull([StateOrProvince]),"No State",[StateOrProvince])
```

Once the focus is moved off the field cell (either by clicking on another cell or pressing the Enter key), the field should look like the one shown in Figure 9.18. To expand the width of the cell so that the entire line of code is visible, click on the right sideline of the column selector and drag to the right.

FIGURE 9.18.

Design view of an `Immediate If` *function in the Column Heading field.*

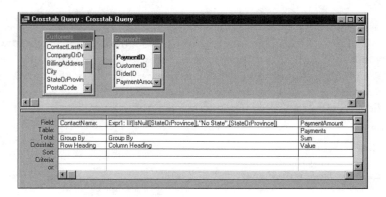

Notice that when the Enter key was pressed, the characters `Expr1:` appeared at the beginning of the code. `Expr1:` indicates that an expression has been created. The expression can be named by replacing the Expr1 with the desired name of the expression. Rename the expression to State so that your code line looks like this:

```
State: IIf(IsNull([StateOrProvince]),"No State",[StateOrProvince])
```

> **TIP**
>
> The reason for renaming expressions is to identify the expression more easily. When using code to make references to queries, Expr1 can be confused with another query's Expr1.

The breakdown of the preceding expression is as follows:

State	Refers to the name of the expression.
IIf	States the beginning of an Immediate If function.
(IsNull([StateOrProvince])	The expression to be evaluated. It's checking to see if the StateOrProvince field is null. The comma at the end shows separation between the expression to be evaluated and the rest of the function.
"No State"	The truepart of the Immediate If function. In English it would read "If the StateOrProvince field is empty, make it say No State." The comma at the end shows a separation between the truepart and the rest of the function.
[StateOrProvince])	The falsepart of the Immediate If function. In English it would read "If the StateOrProvince field is empty, make it say No State, or else show the name of the state."

With the code in place, the results of the Crosstab query with the new expression should look like the one shown in Figure 9.19.

FIGURE 9.19.

The results of an expression to handle null column values.

ContactName	GA	NC	No State	SC
Bryant, Chris		$17,464.00		
Gigliotti, Steph			$7,067.00	
Heidt, Karen				$7,315.00
Jones, Ann				$999,999.00
Jones, Jeanine	$9,137.00			
Simcox, Mary		$7,201.00		

Notice that the column headings are in alphabetical order. Remember, that can be changed through the properties on the query itself by selecting View | Properties. You can also right-click in the Table pane (the upper portion of a Query window) to launch the context menu. Choose Properties from the pop-up menu. In Figure 9.20, the sort order of the column headings has moved the null values of a column field to the far right.

The Column Heading field has the names of the columns exactly as they appear in the Datasheet view. The column headings specified for the Column Heading property must exactly match the data *values* in the Column Heading field in the Query Design grid. The value being returned from a null column heading is No State, hence the reason that No State appears in the Column Heading property field. The result of the query is shown in Figure 9.21.

FIGURE 9.20.

Changing the order of appearance for null-value column records.

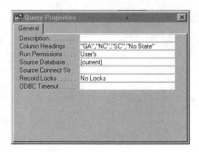

FIGURE 9.21.

The order of appearance for the null-value column is to the far right.

ContactName	GA	NC	SC	No State
Bryant, Chris		$17,464.00		
Gigliotti, Steph				$7,067.00
Heidt, Karen			$7,315.00	
Jones, Ann			$999,999.00	
Jones, Jeanine	$9,137.00			
Simcox, Mary		$7,201.00		

> **NOTE**
>
> The AutoForm Wizard and AutoReport Wizard can't use a Crosstab query as their record source. Data returned by a Crosstab query can't be modified.

Crosstab queries are similar to pivot tables in Microsoft Excel. Pivot tables are discussed in greater detail later in this book.

Action Queries

Action queries are queries that move or change data. Through Access action queries, you can make bulk changes to tables of data. The unique facet of an action query is that it makes these bulk changes in one operation. There are only four types of action queries: the Make Table query, the Update query, the Append query, and the Delete query. In some circles, an SQL Pass-Through query can also be considered an action query. It's important to remember that the AutoForm and AutoReport wizards can't be based on an action query.

The Make Table Query

The first of the action queries to be covered here is the Make Table query. The action performed by the Make Table query can be described in one sentence: It creates a new table from the recordset of an existing query. That existing query can be based on one table or many tables.

There are several reasons why a developer would use the Make Table query. Make Table queries are perfect for creating tables to export data to other Access databases. With the creation of a Make Table query, you can control exactly what can be exported. For example, a department might need to send a mailing to all of its employees. The mailing information is contained in the Employee table along with other information that is considered confidential. Instead of exporting the entire Employee table, you can create a Make Table query that only transfers the information needed for a mailing to the department.

Make Table queries can be used for creating a backup copy of a table. Granted, the table resulting from a Make Table query isn't very helpful if the hard drive crashes, but that isn't its intended purpose. A backup copy of data is very useful to developers who are working with existing data and need to tinker with other queries. This allows the existing data to remain intact while you fine-tune different queries, forms, and reports based on a Make Table query or table.

Make Table queries allow you to freeze time, programmatically speaking. For example, accounting information for a company can be broken into quarters. Reports generated for the end of the first quarter are usually generated at the end of March. By the end of the year, those figures on those reports generated for the first quarter may be different due to accounting adjustments. If a company were to generate new first-quarter reports in December, any adjustments made to the first three months of the year would be reflected in those new reports. However, if that company wanted the information on those reports to reflect the information that was available at the end of March, it would be difficult. Access creates a way to utilize the information available to a company at a given time through the Make Table query. The Make Table query produces a new table based on the information available at a certain point in time. This doesn't affect the current data at all. It simply takes a snapshot of the data available at the time of the Make Table creation and preserves it. You would base new queries and reports on the Make Table to retrieve the preserved data, as opposed to using a new query that extracts the most current data.

Make Table queries can actually increase the speed of existing queries. For example, currently a Catalog query tracks all of the inventory items for a company. If the company has been in business for a couple of years or the inventory changes drastically from year to year, there may be many records in the Catalog table. If the company is like a computer company, inventory items get outdated and are no longer relevant to current Catalog reports. The company no longer needs to see all of the information concerning 8088 machines. The table created from a Make Table query can archive that old data. With the old data archived in a Make Table query, you are free to remove the old data from the existing tables. Because the number of inventory records is reduced, current queries, forms, and reports run faster. The data isn't permanently deleted; it is segmented and archived.

Make Table queries can accelerate the performance of forms and reports that are based on multitable queries. Suppose a number of forms and reports are based on the same three tables, and those forms and reports include totals. By creating a Make Table query, all of the information and totals needed are retrieved and stored in one table. The query isn't rerun for each form or report. Speed isn't increased the first time the Make Table query is run; however, forms or reports based on the table resulting from a Make Table query will be faster than the original three-table query. All the data for the form or report is now in one table, and all the form or report has to do is read it.

To create a Make Table query, open a new, blank query and select the tables desired. Bring down the fields from the table objects that will be used for the new Make Table. Select Query | Make Table or click the Query Type button and select Make Table.

The first field in the Make Table dialog box is the Table Name. Enter the name of the Make Table that is about to be created. Notice that near the bottom of the dialog box are two radio buttons. The first is for the Current Database, and the second is Another Database. The Current Database is the default. Where is the new table that is about to be created going to reside? If it is to reside in the current database, click the OK button. If the Make Table is to appear in another database, check the Another Database button. If the other database is an Access database, type in the name of the database. It may be necessary to type in the entire path of that database. If the database isn't an Access database, follow the name of the database with name of the database in quotes—for example, `C:\MyDocuments\db1"Paradox;"`. After the name of the other database has been entered, click OK.

It appears as though nothing has happened. If the database container were up, this new table wouldn't appear in the Tables module. The reason is the query hasn't been executed yet. To execute the query, select Query | Run or click the Run button (the red exclamation mark) on the toolbar.

CAUTION

Check Make Table queries before they are executed by viewing the datasheet of the query. The Datasheet view of a query lets you look *before* a commitment is made. If the output is correct, run the query. If it isn't correct, return to Design view and make modifications.

When the query is executed, Access brings up a dialog box for confirmation of the change to the table. This is your absolute last chance to prevent the table from being created. Once the table is created, the Undo command won't reverse the creation.

After the table is created, bring up the Tables module of the database container. The new table will be present. As new data is added to the database, the data in the table that the Make Table query made won't be affected. In Figure 9.22, the table on the left reflects changes made to the database. The table on the right is the table that the Make Table created, and it holds the same data as the day it was created.

Listing 9.4 shows the SQL statement used in creating the Make Table query shown in Figure 9.22. The SELECT DISTINCTROW statement makes the outcome of the query so that identical records are listed only once. In this case, it is the StateOrProvince field from the Customers table. If there were 500 records from the state of North Carolina, NC would appear only once on the datasheet. The next section of the SQL statement for the Make Table query follows the comma. It takes the sum of the PaymentAmount field from the Payments table and places it in the SumOfPaymentAmount column on the datasheet. This section of code, shown in Listing 9.4, comes from the Totals cell in the PaymentAmount field on the query grid.

FIGURE 9.22.

The data in the Make Table isn't affected by changes and additions made to the real data.

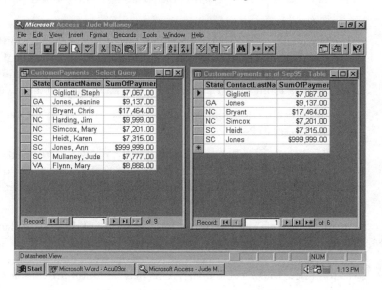

Listing 9.4. The SQL statement of the Make Table query shown in Figure 9.22.

```
SELECT DISTINCTROW Customers.StateOrProvince, Customers.ContactLastName,
➡Sum(Payments.PaymentAmount) AS SumOfPaymentAmount INTO [CustomerPayments
➡as of Sep95]
FROM Customers INNER JOIN Payments ON Customers.CustomerID = Payments.CustomerID
GROUP BY Customers.StateOrProvince, Customers.ContactLastName HAVING
➡(((Payments.PaymentDate)<#10/1/95#));
```

The Make Table query is actually created from the INTO word. INTO works in conjunction with the SELECT portion of the SQL. It's taking all of the records acquired by the SELECT statement and placing them INTO a new table called Customer Payments as of Sep95. If this table is already in existence, a trappable error will occur allowing the user to either write over the old table or not create the table at all.

The section starting with the word FROM deals with the tables in the Make Table query and how they are linked. In English, it reads "From the Customers table inner joined with the Payments table on the CustomerID field."

The last section of the SQL Statement deals with the display of the output of the query. The output is first GROUPED BY the state field and then GROUPED BY the last name field.

> **NOTE**
>
> When you're creating a Make Table query, only the field size of the original table(s) will follow into the new table—properties such as field size and data type. Anything else pertaining to the properties of the table(s) won't follow through to the new table.

To update a table of a Make Table query to reflect the changes in the data, simply reexecute the query. You can reexecute the query by opening it from the Database Container window or by selecting Query | Run. When this happens, Access will display a message stating that a Make Table query is about to be run and that the data in the current table will be modified.

Access displays a message offering a last chance to preserve the data in the first Make Table. The default is set to No.

If you choose to create the Make Table anyway, the data in the Make Table will reflect what is available at the time of the re-creation. In Figure 9.23, the actual data is visible on the right, and the Make Table data is visible on the left. This figure shows that the data is identical in the original and the newly created table.

Remember, Make Table queries are just a snapshot of the data available at the time of creation. The data in that table can be edited without affecting the real data. It's even possible to create a Make Table query on an existing Crosstab query. To do this, use the Crosstab query as the basis for a new Make Table query. This may be useful for complex reports. If a Make Table query is the source for a form or a report, it may be wise to create an AutoNumber field for the new table, because one isn't generated at the time of creation.

The Update Query

The next action query to be covered is the Update query. The Update query allows you to make bulk changes with the click of a button. It's different from the Make Table query in that the Update query actually makes changes to the real data, whereas the Make Table query makes a copy of the data and creates a new table based on that data.

FIGURE 9.23.

When a Make Table is re-created, the data will reflect exactly what is available at the time of re-creation.

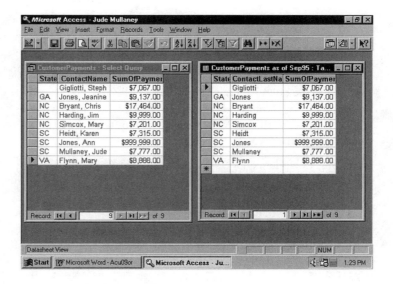

Why would one use an Update query? The answer is simple: to make bulk changes to data at one time. Suppose that all of the customers for a company received a discount of 10 percent on their payment amount. If there are only a few customers, this discount could be figured individually within a short amount of time. However, if there are many customers, this task could take hours or even days. With an Update query, it can be done in seconds.

To create an Update query, open a blank, new query and pull in the table(s) desired. In the example, a 10 percent discount is given to all of the customers. To update the payment amount, the PaymentAmount field is added to the query grid.

To make this an Update query, select Query | Update or click the Query Type button and select Update. In the query grid, the Update To row is added, as shown in Figure 9.24.

FIGURE 9.24.

The Update To row is added to the query grid for an Update query.

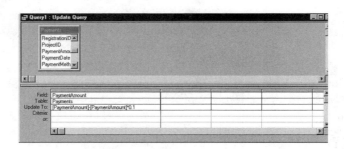

In the Update To cell, type in the criteria for that field to be updated to. In this case, a discount of 10 percent is to be given to all customers. The actual expression is shown next. It takes the PaymentAmount field and subtracts it from the PaymentAmount field times 10 percent:

```
[PaymentAmount]-[PaymentAmount]*.1
```

After this is typed into the Update To cell in the query grid, the query is ready to run. An Update query can't really be viewed. It's possible to press the Datasheet View button, but only the field in the grid would show, and the criteria entered in the Update To cell of the query grid hasn't taken place yet, so there's really nothing to see. Update queries don't return results.

To execute the query, select Query | Run or click the Run button (the red exclamation mark) on the toolbar. Once an Update query is run, Access displays a message stating how many records will be affected by this update. The only two options are to either proceed by selecting Yes or cancel by selecting No.

Executing an Update query is uneventful. The records being changed don't fly past the screen. No meter or gas gauge shows that an action has taken place. Nothing happens. The only way to tell if the update took place is to open the table where the data was being updated. In Figure 9.25, you can tell that an Update query has taken place. The table on the left contains the actual data. The table on the right is a table created by the Make Table that was created earlier. It is provided so that you can see the difference.

FIGURE 9.25.

The table on the left shows that the data has been updated. The table on the right is a Make Table of the data before it was updated.

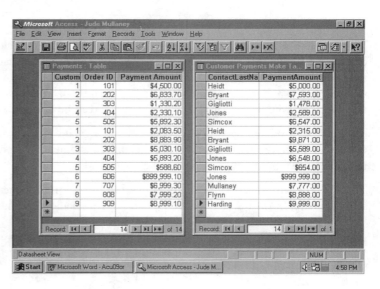

The SQL statement that built the Update query in Figure 9.25 is shown forthwith. The word UPDATE actually creates the Update query. DISTINCTROW is a predicate that is generated by the query. Payments refers to the table where the field being updated (in this case, PaymentAmount) originates. SET is the word that precedes the field that will have a new value. The PaymentAmount field will be set to equal a new value. The equal sign (=) is followed by the expression that was entered into the Update To row of the query grid.

```
UPDATE DISTINCTROW Payments SET Payments.PaymentAmount = [paymentAmount]-
➥[PaymentAmount]*0.1;
```

Many different expressions can be entered into an Update query. They don't even have to pertain to numeric or currency data type fields, as shown in the preceding code example. Table 9.4 shows some of the most common expressions. Use expressions in the Update To cell in the query-design grid for the field you want to update.

Table 9.4. Common Update query expressions.

Desired Result	Expression to Enter in the Update To Cell
Need a field to read Completed	`"Completed"`
Need to change the date to Dec. 31, 1995	`#12-31-95#`
Need to change all the No fields to Yes fields	`Yes`
Need the first name and last name to appear as one field	`[ContactFirstName] & " " & [ContactLastName]`
Need to calculate Total Price from two different fields	`[OrderDetail].[UnitPrice]* [OrderDetail].[Quantity]`
Need to increase salaries by 5 percent	`[Salary]*1.05`
Need to keep only the first eight characters	`Left([FieldName], 8)`

It's important to remember that there are certain limitations to Update queries. Certain situations occur and Access returns error messages that prevent the Update query from firing. Table 9.5 shows some of the errors that Access can return.

Table 9.5. Some Access errors.

Error	Description
Query Not Updatable	This error occurs when executing an Update query on another query that contains totals. Queries that contain totals usually can't be updated.
Key Violations	The Update query can't be executed because of referential integrity rules that are already established.
Lock Violations	Lock violations will occur on fields or records that have been locked by the developer (on a form) or by another user (in a multiuser environment).
Validation Rule Violation	This error occurs when the Update query is trying to put data into a field where the validation rule has been set back at the table level for that field.

continues

Table 9.5. continued

Error	Description
Type Mismatch Error	Type Mismatch refers to the data type established for a field. If the Update query tries to put text in a date/time field, this error will occur.

Usually, Update queries based on one table are updatable. If the Update query contains two tables with a one-to-one relationship, it will usually execute. If the Update query is based on three or more tables having a one-to-many relationship, it won't work. The reason may be that the Cascading Updates option has been checked. As a rule, queries containing three or more tables aren't updatable. Likewise, Crosstab queries, Pass-Through queries, and Union queries can't be updated.

You might want to consider using criteria for the Update query to control which records are updated. This allows you to update only data that meets specific criteria.

The Append Query

The third action query is the Append query. It adds a group of records from one or more tables to the end of one or more tables. The benefit of an Append query is that it saves the user time. Instead of the user typing in each new record (and there could be hundreds), the developer can create an Append query. The Append query simply takes the new records and adds them to the end of an existing table.

Before you create an Append query, you must find out three things:

1. What field is to be appended (source)?
2. Where is the table that the field is going to be appended to?
3. What is the name of the field(s) that it is being appended to (destination)?

After the three questions have been answered, create a new, blank query and place the table(s) in that query. The source table is the Contacts table, and the source field is the ContactLastName field. ContactLastName is the field to be appended.

Make the query an Append query by selecting Query | Append. Access will display a dialog box like the one shown in Figure 9.26. In this box, the answer to question #2 will be entered.

FIGURE 9.26.

The Append Query dialog box.

The first field, Table Name, needs the name of the destination table that the field(s) in the query grid will be appended to. If the destination table isn't located in the current database, the name of the database will have to be entered into the File Name field.

> **NOTE**
>
> It may be necessary to enter the entire path of the database that contains the destination table—for example, `D:\MyDocuments\db1.MDB`.

Notice that a new line is added to the query grid after the Append Query dialog box has been filled. This line will contain the answer to #3. In this example, the answer is ContactLastName.

When the Append query is run, all of the ContactLastNames in the current database will be appended to the ContactLastName field in the CustomerPayments as of Sep95 table in the C:\MyDocuments\DB1.MDB database. Access displays a message letting you know that nine records are about to be appended. The only way to prevent the records from being appended is to select No.

> **NOTE**
>
> The field matched in an Append query must be the same data type. Otherwise, a type mismatch error will occur. Match text to text fields, number to number fields, and so on.

How do you know if an Append query has executed? Check the destination table to see if the records have been appended to the bottom of the list.

Now let's look at the SQL statement of the Append query. It doesn't start with the familiar SELECT statement as do the other queries covered to this point. INSERT INTO is the beginning statement of all Append queries. The information immediately following the INSERT INTO statement defines the destination. The statement is inserted into the ContactLastName field in the table called CustomerPayments as of Sep95. That table happens to be located in the db1 database.

```
INSERT INTO [CustomerPayments as of Sep95] ( ContactLastName ) IN 'db1.mdb'
SELECT DISTINCTROW Customers.ContactLastName
FROM Customers;
```

The SELECT portion of the SQL follows the INSERT INTO statement. DISTINCTROW is the predicate that groups all of the same last names together. In layman's terms, the SQL would read "Place all the records from the contact last-name field of the Customers table into the contact last-name field of the table called 'Customer Payments as of Sep95' in the db1 database."

What if you want to append more than one field? You can do this by dragging the fields from the source table onto the query grid. If the fields in the destination table have the same name,

Access will fill in the Append To row of the query grid. If the field names don't match, you will need to bring down each field from the source table and assign it to the desired destination table field name.

Another concern is if you append all of the records from one table to another table and have included the AutoNumber field in the Append query grid. If the destination table has an AutoNumber field and it's the primary key for that table, any duplicate AutoNumber records won't be appended.

Access will renumber the AutoNumber fields from the source table if you don't bring the AutoNumber field into the Append query grid. It isn't recommended that you include the AutoNumber field in the query grid when creating the Append query.

The Delete Query

The fourth action query we will cover is the Delete query. It does exactly what it says. It deletes records. Sure, it's easy to delete records one at a time without using a query, but if hundreds and hundreds of records need to be removed, it would be easier to perform that action through a Delete query.

Don't be intimidated by Delete queries. They're easier than you might think. To create a Delete query, open a new, blank query. Bring in the table containing the fields that will be used for the Delete query. Select Query | Delete, or select Delete from the Query Type button on the toolbar. Access automatically adds a Delete row to the query grid, which is visible in Figure 9.27.

The Delete row of the query grid gives you only two options: FROM and WHERE. These clauses work in conjunction with each other. The entire table (*) is brought down to the grid. A single asterisk (*) denotes "all fields." This is the FROM part of the Delete query. The individual field, StateOrProvince, is the WHERE part of the Delete query. It is here that criteria is entered for the

Delete query. In this example, the user is allowed to enter the state where all of the customers will be deleted. Allowing the user to enter the criteria makes a query more flexible.

FIGURE 9.27.

The Delete query in Design view.

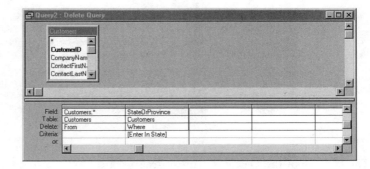

Make sure that the Delete query is always checked in Datasheet view *before* it's executed. The records that appear in the Datasheet view of a delete query are the same records that will be deleted. Figure 9.28 shows the parameter expression that was entered into the criteria field for StateOrProvince.

FIGURE 9.28.

An expression in the criteria field gives the delete query more flexibility.

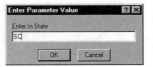

Only three records meet the criteria of SC. These are the desired records to be deleted. Select Query | Run or click the Run button (the red exclamation mark) on the design toolbar. This will execute the query, and the records that were returned in the Datasheet view will be removed from the Customer table. When the query is executed, Access will display a message informing you that *x* number of records will be deleted. This is your last chance to cancel the Delete query. Once the Delete query has been executed, the Undo command won't be available.

Check the table to make sure that the query has been executed. In Figure 9.29, the names that appeared in the Datasheet view of the delete query are no longer present in the Customers table.

Following is the SQL statement that actually performs a Delete query. The word DELETE is the creation of the Delete query. DISTINCTROW is the predicate followed by the name of the table where records are being deleted from, Customers*. The field where the criteria will be entered follows the name of the table. In this case, it is the StateOrProvince field from the Customers table.

```
DELETE DISTINCTROW Customers.*, Customers.StateOrProvince
FROM Customers
WHERE (((Customers.StateOrProvince)=[Enter In State]));
```

FIGURE 9.29.

Records have been deleted by the Delete query.

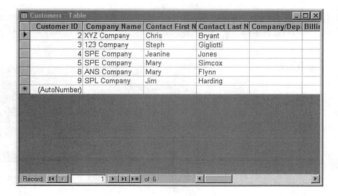

The last line of the Delete statement deals with the criteria specified by the developer. The WHERE clause works in conjunction with the FROM clause, and in this example, users are allowed to type in the criteria themselves.

Some restrictions in creating Delete queries need to be mentioned here. Deleting records from one table isn't hard; however, when dealing with two tables, you must look at the relationship between those tables. One-to-many relationships must have the Cascading Delete option turned on for a query to work. All of the records in the table on the "many" side will be deleted when the "one" side's corresponding record is deleted. Also remember, Delete queries remove the entire record from the database, not just the specified fields.

Parameter Queries

Parameter queries are queries that give the user more flexibility at the time a query runs. When a parameter query is run, Access displays a dialog box prompting the user for more information. In the previous Delete query, a parameter was used. It required the user to "Enter In State." The parameter declaration in SQL view appears at the end of the WHERE statement:

```
WHERE ((Customers.StateOrProvince)=[Enter In State]));
```

The section that is in brackets is the parameter.

Parameters can be set on just about all queries, including action and Select queries. These parameter queries can be used for the record source for forms and reports. In Figure 9.30, a regular Select query involving two tables has been set. In the OrderDate field, a parameter has been set. The parameter is looking for all of the orders that are older than the date being entered by the user.

FIGURE 9.30.

Parameters being used in a Select query.

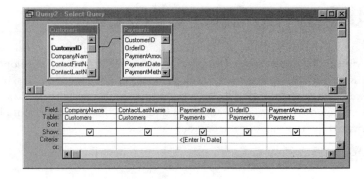

Nesting Queries

It's a fact that a query can be based on another query. This process can be several levels deep. When one query is based on the existence of another query, it's called a *nested query*. Why would a developer have a nested query? Nested queries are more manageable. Instead of having 10 different tables in one query, it's easier to break the one big query into several smaller, more manageable queries. Another benefit to having nested queries as opposed to one big query involves the SQL statement. A SQL statement can hold only about 64,000 characters. Once a SQL statement has reached its limit, Access displays an error message stating that the SQL statement is too large. At that point, Access attempts to fix the SQL statement by removing sections from the end of the statement, but you aren't informed of this attempt. Not until you examine the statement will you notice that sections of the SQL have been removed. With nested queries, there are fewer characters in the SQL to perform the same action. Here is an SQL statement for a query:

```
SELECT DISTINCTROW Customers.StateOrProvince, [ContactLastName] & ", " &
➥[ContactFirstName] AS ContactName, Sum(Payments.PaymentAmount) AS
➥SumOfPaymentAmount
FROM Customers INNER JOIN Payments ON Customers.CustomerID = Payments.CustomerID
GROUP BY Customers.StateOrProvince, [ContactLastName] & ", " & [ContactFirstName];
```

If this query were used in another query, instead of entering this statement, the SQL would just have `CustomerPaymentQuery`. It performs the same function and takes up fewer characters.

The trade-off of having several nested queries is speed. Nested queries are slower than one giant query because Access must run both the nested query and the main query.

Nested queries have been compared to subqueries, but they aren't the same. An example of a subquery is when you take the SQL statement from one query and place it in the criteria cell of a field in another query. This is slower than a nested query, because each field criteria cell has to be run before the query itself can run.

Using the Query Wizards

One of the trademarks of the Access database is its ability to create common objects through wizards. Microsoft spent a lot of time getting feedback from developers. The company noticed that many developers were creating the exact same types of queries, repeating the same required steps. So Microsoft developed wizards that built queries based on information given by the developer. By answering a couple of questions, the developer could have Access create sophisticated queries in a minimal amount of time.

Access 95 has four query wizards. Table 9.6 describes them.

Table 9.6. Access's query wizards.

Wizard	Description
Simple Query Wizard	Constructs a Select query based on the fields chosen by the developer. The fields can be from multiple tables and existing queries. The wizard will group data and perform summary calculations. If the database has had relationships established and the AutoJoin property is turned on, links between two or more tables will automatically be created.
Crosstab Query Wizard	Builds a query that displays its results in a spreadsheet-type format. By processing user input about row headings, column headings, and values, Access creates a Crosstab query.
Duplicate Query Wizard	Finds the duplicate values for a group of fields in a single table or query. After processing the answers to three or four questions, Access displays the duplicate values. This is helpful for identifying customers that may have been added twice to the same database.
Unmatched Query Wizard	Finds records in one table that have no related records in another. After processing the answers to three questions, Access creates a query that can locate the unmatched records.

Union Queries

Union queries are queries that combine the results of two or more independent tables or queries. There is a catch to creating a Union query: The entire query must be written in code. It can't be done from the Design view of a query.

To create a Union query, open a new, blank query. When the Show Table box appears, don't select any objects to be placed in the query. Simply close the Show Table box. Place the query in SQL view. The only word in the SQL statement is SELECT. This constitutes the beginning of a query.

In a Union query, all of the fields being unioned must have the same name. It works like a common denominator. There can be several different tables, but if the field that is being unioned doesn't have the same name from table to table, the union will fail. The following is an example of a Union query:

```
SELECT LastName, Address, City, Region, PostalCode FROM Customers UNION SELECT
➥LastName, Address, City, Region, PostalCode FROM Vendors.
```

Notice that the field names of LastName, Address, City, Region, and PostalCode are exactly the same. One side of the union must exactly match the other side of the union, with the exception of the table names. There may be more than one UNION statement in a Union query. It's possible to union the Customer table, the Vendor table, the Employee table, and so on, as long as the field names remain exactly the same.

Even though there must be the same number of fields having the same name in the Union query, those fields don't have to be of the same size or data type. Duplicate records are usually not returned by a Union query. If they do need to be returned, use the ALL predicate in the statement. The Group By clause, the Where clause, the Having clause, and the Order By clause can all be applied to the Union query to establish criteria for the returning data. The Order By clause can appear only at the end of the last query argument.

Summary

This chapter covered many types of specialized queries. Crosstab queries were discussed in great detail. The design and construction of the SQL that creates the Crosstab was dissected and explained. All of the different action queries were categorized and covered: Make Table, Update, Append, and Delete. The different parameters that can be applied to queries were discussed and illustrated. This chapter also covered Union queries, nesting queries, and query wizards. The following chapter contains information on expressions and functions that are used in queries.

Using Expressions and Functions

10

by Mike Harding

Expressions Defined

Expressions are tools that are utilized by the developer to give power to applications. They are a combination of operators, constants, literal values, and functions that evaluate to a single value. Expressions can be found in queries, forms, reports, and controls on forms and reports.

Expressions are used not only in queries but also can be used in all of the modules in the database container. Expressions can be entered into the properties of fields in a table. When the following expression is entered into the `Default` property of a Date/Time field in a table, the data that is stored pertains to a period from now until one year from today:

```
=Now() + 365
```

> **NOTE**
>
> You might encounter some problems using this expression. Leap years will throw off the result.

Because the `Default` property appears for just about all fields in tables, forms, and reports, this expression could be entered anywhere. Depending on the location, the expression would be executed on the opening of that table, form, or report. Expressions can also be located in the Criteria line of a field in a query. With a slight modification to the preceding code, the following expression, when entered in the Criteria cell of a Date/Time field in a query, will return all of the records with a date earlier than now:

```
<Now()
```

Because expressions are pieces of code that contain a combination of operators, constants, and variables, expressions can appear in macros and modules too. In essence, expressions can appear in all six objects of the database container: tables, queries, forms, reports, macros and modules. They can be used to calculate fields, set criteria, or as a validation rule.

Parts of an Expression

Expressions can be summed up as a kind of mathematical sentence. Many different parts can be combined to make up this sentence. The parts of this mathematical sentence have to be presented in such a way as that they make logical sense. The result of this mathematical sentence is that it returns a value.

There are different parts to expressions. These parts can stand either alone or in combination with each other. Like real sentences, one word or several words can make up the sentence. Real sentences are made up of parts called subjects, verbs, adverbs, adjectives, and so on. Expressions have parts too. They can be used individually or in a combination. They are described as follows:

- Operators: Symbols that are prevalent in Boolean algebra, as well as other symbols
- Constants: A numeric or string value that doesn't change
- Literal values: Exact representations, such as numbers, strings, and dates
- Functions: A procedure that returns a value; for example, Now returns the current date
- Field names: Usually surrounded by brackets

Most expressions perform calculations that return a value. Usually calculations are performed with operators. Operators play a big part in expressions. There are many different operators, but all can usually fall under one of the following four groups.

Arithmetic Operators

The first of the four groups of operators is the arithmetic group. These operators are used to execute mathematical calculations between two or more numbers. These symbols are as follows:

^	Raises one number to the power of another number.
*	Multiplies one number by another number.
/	Divides and returns a floating-point result.
\	Divides and returns an integer result.
MOD	Stands for *modulus*; it returns the remainder of two divided numbers.
+	Adds one number to another number.
-	Subtracts one number from another.

Concatenation Operators

The second group of operators is the concatenation group. These operators are used to bring strings together. There are only two symbols in this group:

&	Brings two string fields together as one field.
+	Brings two variable number fields together and sums them. It can also be used to bring two text strings together; however, it won't sum these text strings.

Comparison Operators

Comparison operators are the third group of operators. They are used to perform comparisons between two or more fields and/or expressions. They utilize Boolean symbols and are as follows:

=	One field is equal to another field.
<>	One field is not equal to another field.

<	One field is less than another field.
>	One field is greater than another field.
<=	One field is less than or equal to another field.
>=	One field is greater than or equal to another field.
Like	Pattern-matching similar to the Find feature; Like abc* finds all records that start with abc.
Is	Object-reference comparison that checks if two object references refer to the same object.

Logical Operators

The final group of operators is the logical operators. They perform logical actions; the logical symbols are listed forthwith:

Not	Negation between two fields or expressions.
And	Conjunction between two fields or expressions.
Or	Disjunction between two fields or expressions.
Between	Midsection between two fields or expressions.
Xor	Exclusion between two fields or expressions.
Eqv	Equivalence between two fields or expressions.
Imp	Implication between two fields or expressions.

Order of Operations

There may be times when several different operations need to take place during an expression. Operations must be performed in a predetermined order as designated by Access. When operations from the same group appear in an expression, the predetermined order takes place. Within each group above, the operators are listed in that predetermined order. If two or more groups are involved in an expression, these groups also are performed in a predetermined order. The four groups of operators described earlier appear in the predetermined order. The arithmetic operators are first, followed by the concatenation, comparison, and logical operators. This is called *operator precedence*.

If it's necessary to perform a certain operation before the preordained order, place that operation in parentheses. Parentheses override Access's operator precedence. However, if more than one operation is enclosed in parentheses, operator precedence again is maintained.

Constants

Operators aren't the only pieces used in an expression. Constants can be used in expressions too. Constants are somewhat like Access reserved words in that the numeric or string value doesn't change during program execution. Constants can be divided into three groups: predefined access basic constants, intrinsic constants, and system-defined constants.

Predefined Constants

Predefined constants are constants that the developer creates, usually in modules. A predefined constant begins with the letters CONST. For example:

`CONST C = 186,000`	Speed of light
`CONST Dearth = 7926.68`	Diameter of the Earth
`CONST Pi = 3.14159`	Pi is 3.14159

These things hold true no matter the circumstances. After constants are loaded, they can be used anywhere.

Intrinsic Constants

Intrinsic constants are constants that are supplied by Visual Basic and don't have to be loaded or declared separately. VbString and VarType are examples of intrinsic constants. Intrinsic constants can be divided into five categories: data access constants, macro action constants, security constants, variant constants, and miscellaneous constants. Because these can't be disabled, other constants can't use the same name. Intrinsic constants can be used only in modules.

System-Defined Constants

There are only five system-defined constants—Yes, No, On, Off, and Null. They can be used in every object of the database container except modules.

Literal Values

Literal values are another component that can make up an expression. Literal values are just that; they use the exact representation of numbers and strings in an expression.

Functions

Functions can constitute an expression. Functions operate similarly to operators; however, they aren't represented by symbols. For example, the + operator and the SUM function perform the same action. They add. The difference between the two is that the operator can add only two items at a time, whereas the SUM function can total all of the items. Of course, you could have *one item + another item + another item* and so on, but it may be easier to SUM all of the items. Functions return values such as totals. You can see some of the different functions in the query grid by adding the Totals row to the grid. In each Totals cell is a drop-down box that shows some of the different functions available. Altogether, Access provides more than 160 different functions.

Field and Variable Names

Field names and variable names are another part of expressions. Field names are usually surrounded by brackets. Field names are names given to fields in a table. Variable names aren't found in tables. They are alternative names you give fields or expressions to create a shorter reference. For example, LastName and FirstName fields can be combined into a field called Name. It is like a memory placeholder.

An Example of an Expression

Earlier, expressions were summed up to be a mathematical sentence that makes logical sense. The parts of an expression must be combined in such a manner that they make sense when Access tries to execute the expression. The following is an example of an expression.

```
TotalCost: [delivery charge] + (([quantity]*[price]) +
(([quantity]*[price])*[tax]))
```

In order to explain the preceding expression, it's necessary to assign each item a value. For this example, assign the following values to the items.

Total Cost is the field name of the expression

Delivery charge is $35

Quantity for the first record is 100

Price for the first record is $50

Tax is 6 percent

The symbols such as * and + are operators. TotalCost is a variable name. Delivery Charge, Quantity, Price, and Tax are field names. These are the parts of the preceding expression.

Which answer is returned by Access for the preceding expression: 405.00 or 5335.00? The correct answer is 5335.00. Expressions are read from left to right; however, any part of the operation that is contained in parentheses is performed first. The correct way to read the preceding expression is

([quantity]*[price]) = 5000

([quantity]*[price])*[tax]) = 300

(([quantity]*[price]) + (([quantity]*[price])*[tax])) = 5300.00

[delivery charge] + 5300.00 = 5335.00

TotalCost = 5335.00

In Figure 10.1, the expression is entered into the Field cell of a query grid. If only the expression were typed into the cell, the word TotalCost wouldn't appear; Expr1 would. The expression can be given a name to avoid confusion throughout the database. Expr1 is an alias field name for the calculated field. The colon is used to create a new field name. The text that appears to the left of the colon is the name of the field—whether Expr1 or TotalCost.

FIGURE 10.1.

Expressions can be entered into field cells to produce a new field.

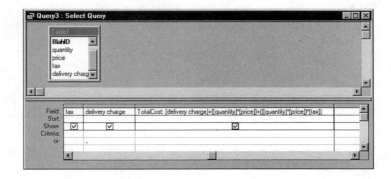

The results of the expression are calculated for all of the records in the table. The results can be seen in Figure 10.2.

FIGURE 10.2.

Expressions can appear on the datasheet.

quantity	price	tax	delivery charg	TotalCost
100	$50.00	$0.06	$35.00	$5,335.00
250	$25.00	$0.06	$20.00	$6,645.00
10	$1,000.00	$0.06	$15.00	$10,615.00
0	$0.00	$0.00	$0.00	

Notice that all of the numbers in the TotalCost column are in currency format. How can that be, when the field wasn't established in the table as a currency data type, nor was it established in the expression as a currency format? Logically, when a currency is calculated by another number, currency is assumed to be the common denominator and the results are passed in currency format. Type the following expression into a blank Field cell in the query grid:

```
[Price]+10
```

The value returned is shown in Figure 10.3. Also notice that since the expression wasn't named, Access created a name for it: Expr1.

FIGURE 10.3.

The new expression is named Expr1.

quantity	price	tax	delivery charg	TotalCost	Expr1
100	$50.00	$0.06	$35.00	$5,335.00	$60.00
250	$25.00	$0.06	$20.00	$6,645.00	$35.00
10	$1,000.00	$0.06	$15.00	$10,615.00	$1,010.00
0	$0.00	$0.00	$0.00		

Expressions can be entered into the Field cell on a query grid. They can also be entered in the Criteria cell of an existing field. In Figure 10.4, the expression entered into the Price field is >25.

FIGURE 10.4.

Expressions can also appear in the Criteria cell of the query grid.

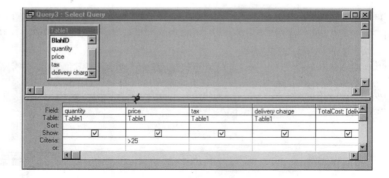

The result of the expression is to return all of the records where the price is greater than $25.00. The dollar sign ($) isn't used in the equation because the data being stored doesn't contain a dollar sign. The dollar sign is part of the display format for that field, yet it isn't stored.

Locating Expressions

Placing expressions in different locations of the database produces different results. In Figure 10.5, two expressions are taking place. The first expression appears in the first column of the query grid. It's using the concatenation operator &. It not only joins the LastName and FirstName fields, but it also adds a comma and space between the two fields.

FIGURE 10.5.

Two expressions in one query.

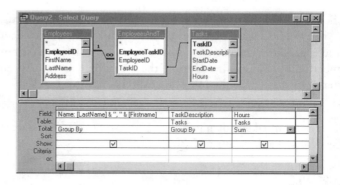

The second expression doesn't contain an operator, yet still contains one of the parts of an expression. The part of the expression that it contains is called a function. The SUM function sums all of the hours needed to complete a task for each employee. The results of this expression and the concatenation expression are shown in Figure 10.6.

When entering expressions in the query grid, you may type an expression into a cell. Depending on the location of the expression, the results will vary. If an expression is typed into the Field cell, a new field is available to be displayed on the datasheet. If an expression is typed into the Criteria cell or Totals cell, limitations and calculations are evaluated on that field. When you type an expression into the grid and press Enter, Access parses the expression. Any errors will cause Access to alert you. A dialog box will appear with Access's best guess as to what is causing the error and some advice on how to correct it. Errors must be corrected before the query is run.

FIGURE 10.6.

The results of a query that contains two expressions.

Name	Task Description	SumOfHours
Bryant, Chris	Billing	2
Bryant, Chris	Mailing	3
Doyle, Steph	Billing	2
Doyle, Steph	Mailing	3
Heidt, Karen	Mailing	3
Heidt, Karen	Programming	5
Jones, Jeanine	Billing	2
Jones, Jeanine	Selling	1
Simcox, Mary	Programming	5
Simcox, Mary	Selling	1

NOTE

When Access parses an expression, it's checking for syntactical correctness. If there is an error in the expression, Access alerts you to the probable syntax error and directs you to the section of the equation that isn't "grammatically correct." You can't run the query until the problem has been corrected or eliminated.

Expressions entered without any operators are automatically assumed by Access to be employing an equal sign (=). It's possible to use field names in the expressions only if the field is present in the table pane of the query or is obtained through a subquery or the DLookup function. However, the field that is being referenced in the expression doesn't need to appear in the query grid.

The Expression Builder

Access provides an Expression Builder button to help developers build expressions. You can access this by selecting the Criteria cell or the Conditions cell of the desired field and clicking the right mouse button. This will bring up a shortcut menu where Build is available. (The Expression Builder button is discussed in detail later in this chapter.)

Entering Expressions in Forms and Reports

Expressions are the building blocks of many of the Access operations. With expressions, you can calculate, specify criteria, control macro execution, and create Access Basic Function and Sub procedures. The only limits to what can be done exist within the developer. So far, this discussion has covered expressions in tables and queries. The next logical step is to show expressions in forms and reports. Expressions are most commonly used on fields—either on existing fields or to create new fields.

Creating Forms with Expressions

Expressions can also be used to create forms. To demonstrate this, create a blank new form. Pull up the properties for the form by clicking on the box in the upper-left corner of the form itself, where the horizontal and vertical rulers meet. Click the Properties button on the toolbar or select View | Properties.

Specifying the Record Source

In Figure 10.7, there isn't a record source for this form. There are two ways to get a Record Source for a form. One way is to select an existing table or query from the drop-down list denoted by the arrow pointing down to the right of the record source.

FIGURE 10.7.

The Build button helps developers create expressions for the record source of a form or report.

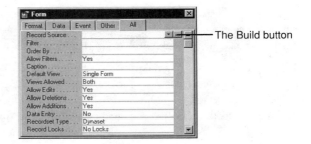

The Build button

Building an Expression

To build an expression for the record source, click the Build button that is to the right of the Record Source field in the Properties box. This button, which has an ellipsis (…), can be seen in Figure 10.7.

When you click the Build button, Access brings up a screen that is exactly the same as a Design view of a query (see Figure 10.8). Three tables are added to the table pane of the query. Expressions can be performed just as if this were a real query created from the query module of the database container. All of the tools available in a query are available in the Expression Builder of a record source for a form.

There is a Build button to assist you in creating the record source for a form or report. To further assist you in creating expressions within the query, Access offers the Expression Builder. Right-click on a desired field in the Criteria cell or Condition cell to bring up the Expression Builder, shown in Figure 10.9.

FIGURE 10.8.

The Expression Builder for a record source appears to be exactly the same as a query in Design view.

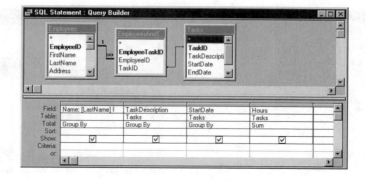

FIGURE 10.9.

The Expression Builder is launched from the Build shortcut.

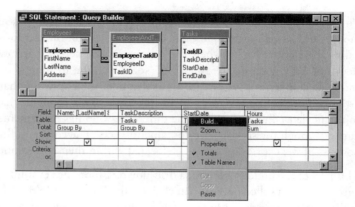

> **NOTE**
>
> It's possible to create different kinds of queries in the Expression Builder, just like in a real query. However, some of the queries can't be used as record sources. Those queries are Action queries. If you tried to use the AutoForm or AutoReport Wizard on a Crosstab query, an error would occur. A Crosstab query isn't a valid query for the record source of a form or report. It still can be created through the Expression Builder of the record source of a form, yet the only fields available in the Field list are the row and column headings.

If the Expression Builder is launched from a field within a query grid, that field is assumed in the expression. There is no need to restate the field name in the expression. If an expression existed in the cell before the Expression Builder was launched, the value in the cell is brought into the Expression Builder. Once the OK button is clicked, the new expression will replace the old expression. The Expression Builder is shown in Figure 10.10.

FIGURE 10.10.

The Expression Builder.

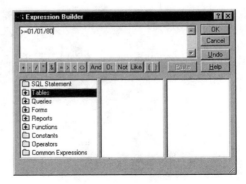

The Expression Builder is a modal form, meaning that nothing else can be done in Access until the OK or Cancel buttons are clicked. The Expression Builder form is sectioned off into two halves. The upper half is where the expression is entered. The lower half contains all of the elements that can create an expression. Notice that the arithmetic, concatenation, comparison, and logical operators buttons are available under the Expression half of the builder form. The lower half of the Expression Builder form contains the elements that constitute an expression. In the far-left column are all of the different groupings of elements. Field Names can be obtained through the six database container objects. The constant, function, and operator components of the expression can all be located within their corresponding groups.

This part of the builder works in a drill-down fashion. For example, a developer needs to work with a function called Date. If you click on the Functions folder, all of the different functions available are exposed within the far-left column. Click on the Built-In Functions supplied by Access. In the center column, all of the different groups of functions are presented. (There are about 16 groups.) Clicking on the Date/Time group exposes all the different functions that pertain to Date/Time. In the far-right column, the Date function is presented. Approximately 165 different functions are built into Access. Double-clicking the Date function brings the function into the Expression half of the Expression Builder form.

Complex Expressions

Using only the mouse, it's possible to enter a complex expression by clicking on expression elements and operators. If a field in an existing table were drilled down to and placed in the Expression half of the Builder, all of the correct identifiers would automatically be entered. To refer to the start date field, the builder would return [Tasks]![StartDate]. As elements are pasted into the Expression half, the builder may insert <<Expr>> into the expression. If elements are pasted into the expression and they require other elements, Access will insert the <<Expr>> where the missing element should be placed. Simply highlight the <<Expr>> and replace it with the desired element.

NOTE

There may be times when the Expression Builder doesn't list all of the objects or functions in the leftmost column of the form. Where the Builder was launched will determine the different objects and functions available. For example, when the Expression Builder is launched from the `ValidationRule` property of a field in a table, reference to other tables, queries, forms and/or reports isn't logical.

In Figure 10.11, the Expression Builder has been used to create an expression. The Expression Builder was launched from the StartDate field from the Tasks table in the query grid. Because it was launched from this field, the Expression Builder assumes that this is the field that will be in the expression; therefore, it's not necessary to restate the field name.

FIGURE 10.11.

The Expression Builder in action.

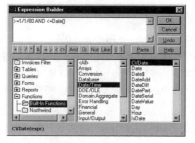

This expression is bringing in all of the records where the start date is greater than Jan. 1, 1980 and less than today:

```
>=1/1/80 AND <=Date()
```

The expression starts off with two comparison operators—the greater-than sign and the equal sign. The operators, in this case, are followed by a literal: `01/01/80`. `AND` is the comparison operator. Two other comparison operators are next and followed by a function: `Date()`. In English, the expression reads "Show all of the records where the start date is greater than or equal to Jan. 1, 1980, but less than today."

TIP

It's possible to use the `Between...And` function in place of the greater-than/less-than operators.

Using the Expression Builder helps you create expressions in a logical order. Once the expression is finished, click the OK button to place it into the cell on the query grid. When the focus is moved off the expression, Access immediately checks the syntax. If there are any syntax errors, Access alerts you and suggests the cause of the error.

Notice that when the focus is moved off the expression, as in Figure 10.12, Access automatically places pound signs (#) around the literal date. During the parsing process, Access noted that the literal was a date and automatically placed the pound signs around the literal, making the statement syntactically correct. If you don't see the # sign, check to make sure that your field is a date/time datatype field.

FIGURE 10.12.

Access parses the expression and automatically adds the pound signs.

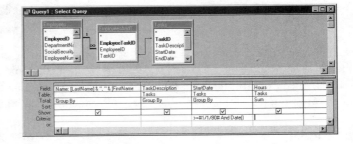

Three expressions are visible in Figure 10.12. The first is the concatenation of the first and last name in the leftmost column of the query grid. The second expression is the start-date criteria. The third is the SUM function of the Hours field. The fourth, for the top 25 values, is visible on the toolbar. It brings up the top 25 records when the query is run.

Once the desired statement is entered into the query, close the query. Access will display a message box like the one shown in Figure 10.13. Every time you make changes to the record source expression, this message box will appear. This is the last chance to undo all of the changes made to the record source.

FIGURE 10.13.

Access warns of changes to the record source.

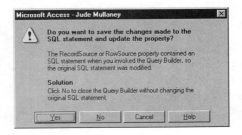

The Query as an SQL Statement

The entire SQL statement that was used to create the query for the record source now appears on the Record Source field in the Properties section of the form. Figure 10.14 shows this SQL statement. The same statement now sits on the Record Source field property. You can see it by pressing Shift-F2. Shift-F2 places the entire field into a zoom box so that the information is more easily read.

FIGURE 10.14.

The SQL statement that generated the query is now sitting on the Record Source field of the Form Properties section.

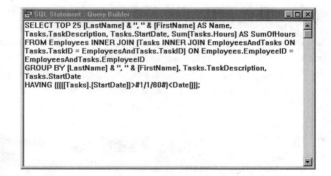

Now that the record source for the form has been established, the form is ready to have fields placed on it. Click the Field List button to display the fields available or select View | Field List. In Figure 10.15, only four fields are available for this form. These fields are directly derived from the SQL statement on the Record Source field in the form's Properties section. To add more fields to the field list, you should return to the Builder that created the SQL statement and make the modifications in Query Design view to assure correct syntax.

FIGURE 10.15.

The field list is derived from the SQL statement that sits on the Record Source field of the form's Properties section.

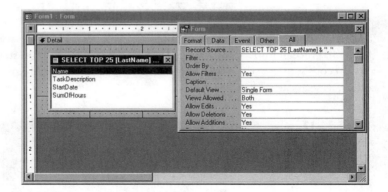

A form has 74 properties. Of those 74 properties, 33 of them have the Expression Builder on them. That is before any fields are added to the form. Each field has approximately 58 properties, of which 23 have the Expression Builder on them. Just about every object that can be placed on a form has properties that have the Expression Builder available. This gives you the ability to create sophisticated forms without extensive knowledge of expressions. You only have to know that certain functions, constants, and operators exist. You can combine these functions, constants, and operators through the Expression Builder.

Creating Reports with Expressions

Just as forms can utilize expressions, so can reports. To demonstrate expressions in reports, it's necessary to create a new, blank report. Pull up the properties for that form by clicking on the box in the upper-left corner of the form where the horizontal and vertical rulers meet. Click the Properties button or select View | Properties. To the right of the Record Source property is the Build button, which is visible in Figure 10.16.

FIGURE 10.16.

The Record Source for a report has the Build button associated with it.

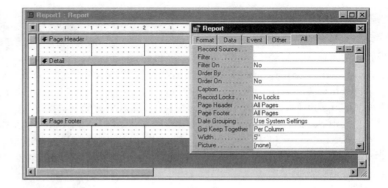

The Expression Builder is activated by pressing the Build button. In Figure 10.17, the Build button has brought up a query that assists you in creating the SQL statement that can be used as the record source of the report. It looks and functions exactly like the one on a form's record source, as seen earlier.

FIGURE 10.17.

The Build button for a report is the same as the Build button for a form.

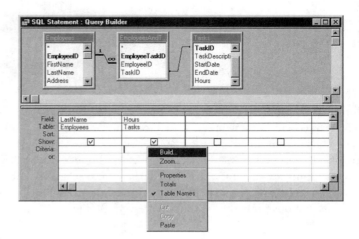

You launch the Expression Builder the same way, by right-clicking in the Criteria or Conditions cell of an existing field or by pressing the Build button on the toolbar. In Figure 10.18, you enter elements into the expression by clicking on the available elements in the lower half of the Expression Builder screen and typing any additional information needed for the SQL statement to return the desired record source for the report.

FIGURE 10.18.

The Expression Builder works the same whether launched from a form or a report.

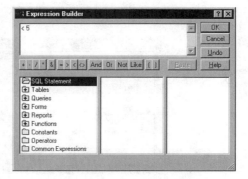

Options for Reports

Reports are similar to forms in that they gather data. They differ from each other in that reports produce hard copies of that gathered data. Because they are different, different options are available to reports that aren't found on forms—for example, grouping. In Figure 10.19, the sorting and grouping is activated by selecting View | Sorting/Grouping. It can also be activated by clicking the Sorting and Grouping button on the toolbar.

FIGURE 10.19.

In reports, groups and sorts can have expressions.

Most of the options that were available to fields in forms are available to fields in reports. Of course, the Event properties are fewer than the Event properties on a form because data isn't entered in reports. There are fewer occurrences where the Expression Builder is available than in forms because reports are usually read-only. Because the user isn't permitted to cause many events to take place during a report, the Expression Builder isn't as available as it is in forms.

There are instances where an expression may be used when the Builder isn't available. In Figure 10.20, a Grouping action is being performed on a report. An expression is entered into the Field/Expression cell. Usually, the only type of expressions performed here are string-type expressions. `Left Function`, `Right Function`, `Mid Function`, and `Len Function` are all types of string expressions that can be performed in a grouping and sorting action on a report.

FIGURE 10.20.

Places where expressions can be entered aren't always accompanied by the Expression Builder.

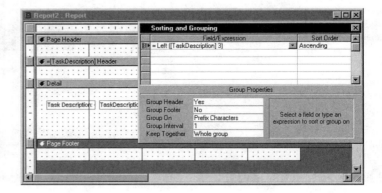

Using Concatenation

The word "concatenation" actually means to unite or bring things together. In Access, concatenation refers to a family of operators found in expressions. The Access concatenation operators are used to unite or bring strings together. There are two types of concatenation symbols—the ampersand (&) and the plus sign (+).

The & concatenation operator forces two string expressions together. The correct syntax for the & operator is as follows:

```
MyResult = expression1 & expression2
```

The & operator can be used in queries, forms, reports, macros, and modules. One of the most useful actions that the & operator performs can be seen in the report shown in Figure 10.21. This is a report where the FirstName and LastName fields were pulled down from the Field list. These fields were placed near the top of the form. Under these fields, a text box was added. On the Control Source field of the Properties section of the text box, the following expression was added:

```
=[LastName] & ", " & [FirstName]
```

The code concatenates not only the two fields, FirstName and LastName, but also places a comma and space between the LastName field and FirstName field. Concatenations can contain field names as well as other literal characters and spaces. Figure 10.22 shows the result of the concatenation. If a last name were longer than the length of the field, the end of the last name would be cut off or truncated. This can be seen on the third name. The last name is a long, hyphenated last name. When the regular field size is too small for the output, the name is cut off. In the case of a concatenation, the entire field is used, no matter the size of either field. The same thing will happen if you use a field that isn't concatenated. If the space provided for the data is too short, the field won't display all the data.

FIGURE 10.21.

The use of the & operator in a concatenation of two fields.

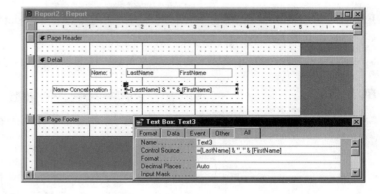

FIGURE 10.22.

The result of using the & operator in a concatenation of two fields.

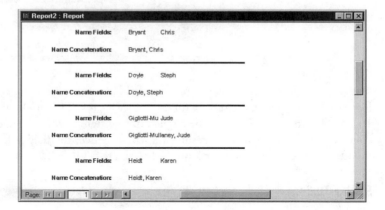

The other concatenation operator is the + symbol. It's used to sum two number expressions. The correct syntax for the + concatenation operator is as follows:

```
MyResult = Expression1 + Expression2
```

The + operator can be used to concatenate two string expressions but may prove to be confusing in a code module. The + operator actually adds the results of two variant or numeric expressions. If a date field is involved, the + operator should be used instead of the & operator. During the execution of a concatenation using the + operator, the result (addition or concatenation) depends on the fields being concatenated.

> **NOTE**
>
> If the expressions being concatenated are null, the result is null. If they are both empty, the result will be an integer. If one of the expressions is empty, it's treated as a zero-length string, and the other expression is returned.

In Figure 10.23, the + operator is used to add 90 days to the start date. The Review Date is a text box, and its record source contains the following code:

```
=[StartDate]+ 90
```

FIGURE 10.23.

Using the + operator in a concatenation of a field and a literal.

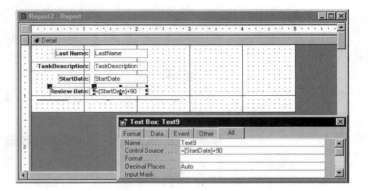

The result of the + operator isn't a numeric field but rather a date string. The result is shown in Figure 10.24. When you re-create this example, the results won't look like the results in Figure 10.24. The StartDate field will be aligned on the right because it's a date field. However, the concatenated field returns the result of a string; hence, the field is left-aligned. To make the report aesthetically pleasing, click on the StartDate field and click the left-align format button.

FIGURE 10.24.

The result of using the operator to concatenate two fields.

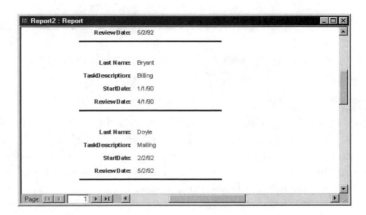

Working with Dates and Times

Expressions can contain dates and times. A date expression is any expression or part of an expression that can be interpreted by Access as a date. The date expression can be a literal date, numbers and strings that look like dates, or dates returned by functions. The range represented can be any date from January 1, 100, to December 31, 9999, inclusive. A time expression works in conjunction with a date expression. A time expression can't exist without a date expression. Dates and times are stored as real numbers. This real number is broken down into two half values separated by a decimal. The value that appears to the left of the decimal represents the date. The value that appears to the right of the decimal represents the time. Time is represented in increments between 0:00:00 and 23:59:59, inclusive.

> **NOTE**
>
> Date/time values can appear as negative numbers. Negative values represent dates prior to December 30, 1899. The left side is the number of whole days that have expired since December 30, 1899. Midnight is represented by 0, and midday is represented by .5. So if today were January 1, 1900, at noon, the number stored would be 0.5. A full day has not been completed; only exactly one half of a day has been completed. The time is .5, and the day is still 0. At the second before midnight on January 1, 1900, the time stored would look like 0.9999999999. At the stroke of midnight, the time stored would look like 1.0. Even though the time is stored like that, it's displayed according to the time format as set on the computer (either 12-hour or 24-hour format).

Dates are stored as 64-bit floating-point numbers. When a date/time string is entered into an expression, Access recognizes the literal format of a date/time during its parse and places the pound sign (#) on either side of the date/time. Access converts January 1, 1995, to #1 Jan 95#.

Dates and Times in Expressions

When using dates and times in expressions, you have access to the date/time functions. Access has approximately 22 different date/time functions. Figure 10.25 shows the expression entered in the Criteria cell of the DateHired field. The words Between and And are reserved operator words.

The result of the Between. . . And operator with a date/time field is that it returns all of the records where the hire date is greater than Jan. 1, 1987, and less than Jan. 1, 1989, inclusive. The results are shown in Figure 10.26.

FIGURE 10.25.

The use of the Between...And *operator in an expression with a date/time field.*

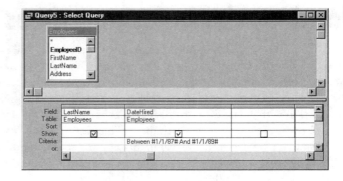

FIGURE 10.26.

The results of the Between...And *operator with a date/time field.*

	First Name	Last Name	Date Hired
▶	Mary	Simcox	1/1/87
	Jeanine	Jones	1/1/88
	Steph	Doyle	1/1/89
*			

Earlier in this chapter, the greater-than (>) and less-than (<) operators were used in an expression working with a date/time field. Also earlier in this chapter, a date/time field was used in an expression with a literal number that added 90 days to a date (=[DateHired] + 90). The preceding example worked with a date/time field and the Between...And operator. In the following example, a new field is created that states the quarter in which the date hired falls. In Figure 10.27, the following code is entered into a new Field cell on the query grid:

```
Quarter: Format([DateHired],"q")
```

FIGURE 10.27.

A new expression using a custom date/time expression.

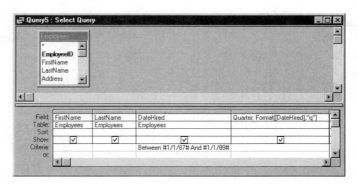

The name of the new field created by the expression is Quarter. A year is divided into four quarters. This expression takes the DateHired and computes which quarter it falls into. The value returned is either 1, 2, 3, or 4, depending on the date. The piece of the expression that actually returns the value is the letter q. This is known as a custom setting on a date/time format. The results of the new expression can be seen in Figure 10.28.

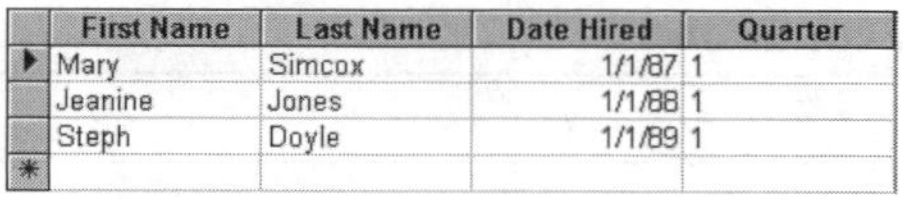

FIGURE 10.28.

The results of the custom date/time expression.

First Name	Last Name	Date Hired	Quarter
▶ Mary	Simcox	1/1/87	1
Jeanine	Jones	1/1/88	1
Steph	Doyle	1/1/89	1
＊			

Date and Time Formats

The date/time data has several predefined display formats. These formats usually appear in forms and reports and datasheets. They can appear in tables; however, the data is stored in a 64-bit floating-point number. Table 10.1 lists the predefined formats that are visible in the date/time datatype of a field in a table.

Table 10.1. Predefined date/time formats provided by Access.

Format	Display
General	01/01/95 12:00:00 AM
Short Date	01/01/95
Medium Date	1-Jan-95
Long Date	Sunday, January 1, 1995
Short Time	00:00:00 (Midnight)
Medium Time	12:00 AM
Long Time	12:00:00 AM

> **TIP**
>
> If the numbers being returned don't coincide with the preceding chart, check the machine's Control Panel for the predefined number and date/time formats. They can be found under the Regional Settings in the Date and Time tab.

Through expressions, it's possible to customize the displays of the date/time formats. Table 10.2 shows the different formats that can be used to customize the display of date/time formats.

Table 10.2. Custom date/time formats.

Format	Display
d	Day of the month between 1 and 31
dd	Day of the month between 01 and 31

continues

Table 10.2. continued

Format	Display
ddd	Day of the month between SUN and SAT (displays only three letters)
dddd	Day of the month between Sunday and Saturday (displays the whole word)
w	Day of the week between 1 and 7
ww	Week of the year between 1 and 52
m	Month of the year between 1 and 12
mm	Month of the year between 01 and 12
mmm	Month of the year between JAN and DEC (displays only three letters)
mmmm	Month of the year between January and December (displays the whole word)
q	Quarter of the year between 1 and 4
y	Number of the day in the year between 1 and 365
yy	Number of the year between 00 and 99
yyyy	Number of the year between 0100 and 9999
h	Number of the hour between 1 and 23
hh	Number of the hour between 01 and 23
n	Number of the minute between 1 and 59
nn	Number of the minute between 01 and 59
s	Number of the second between 1 and 59
ss	Number of the second between 01 and 59
AM/PM	Uppercase AM/PM on a 12-hour clock
am/pm	Lowercase am/pm on a 12-hour clock
A/P	Uppercase A/P on a 12-hour clock

A slash (/) is used as a date separator. This may vary according to the time separator established in the Regional Settings of Control Panel.

A colon (:) is used as a time separator. This may vary according to the time separator established in the Regional Settings of Control Panel.

By using these custom formats, it's possible to create expressions that return values such as the following:

```
Day of Hire was Saturday.
```

To get the preceding value, type the following in a new Field cell in the query grid:

```
Day: "Day Hired" & Format([DateHired ],"dddd")
```

`Day:` is the name of the expression and appears at the top of the column. `"Day Hired"` is the literal string that appears before the name of the day. The string is concatenated with the date format. `Format` is a reserved word in Access that begins the custom formatting of a date. `[DateHired]` is the name of the field from which the day is being extracted. `"dddd"` can be found on the preceding chart; it extracts the name of the day the person was hired on.

> **NOTE**
>
> If the information being returned is inaccurate, check the date and time on the computer itself. All of the dates and times that are being entered are based on that time. (You can check it through Control Panel under Date/Time.) If the date or time is changed, all existing records will still have the inaccurate date and time; however, any new records will be stamped with the changed date and time.

> **TIP**
>
> The `Date()` function returns the current date as specified by the computer's date. The `Now()` function returns the current date and time as specified by the computer's clock. There is a difference between the two. If you used the `Date()` function to stamp each new record, all of the records entered today would have the same information. If you used the `Now()` function, all of the records entered today could be chronologically listed by the times that they were entered. The greater-than (>) operator can show all of the records entered today before noon.

Using the *IIF* Function

The `IIF` statement is a function that helps control the program flow of a database. It can be found in the Expression Builder under the Built-In Functions in a grouping called Program Flow. In the following example, it is a statement that is executed on every record in a query. This statement has two parts—a truepart and a falsepart. Here is the syntax:

```
Status: IIF([StateOrProvince]="NC","VAC Employee","XYZ Employee")
```

The beginning of the statement starts with `IIF`. `Status:` is the name of the new field on the query grid in Figure 10.29. The expression follows the `IIF`. The expression is `[StateOrProvince]` `= "NC"`. The truepart and the falsepart of the `IIF` statement are all separated by commas. The truepart is `"VAC Employee"`. The falsepart of the statement is `"XYZ Employee"`.

FIGURE 10.29.

Using the IIF *function to create a new field in a query.*

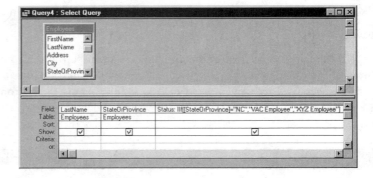

This IIF function will evaluate every record in the query. If the record's StateOrProvince field equals NC (true), the value in the new field called Status will be VAC Employee. If the record's StateOrProvince field doesn't equal NC (false), the value in the new field called Status will be XYZ Employee. The results of the query are shown in Figure 10.30.

FIGURE 10.30.

The results of an IIF *function.*

Last Name	State/Province	Status
▶ Bryant	NC	VAC Employee
Heidt	NC	VAC Employee
Simcox	SC	XYZ Employee
Jones	GA	XYZ Employee
Doyle	V.A	XYZ Employee
Gigliotti-Mullane	NC	VAC Employee
*		

IIF functions can have only one of two answers. The expression equals either true or false. There are no maybes. Both parts of the expression are evaluated for every record. Be careful when using the IIF function on numbers. If the falsepart of an IIF statement results in a division-by-zero error, an error occurs even if the expression is True.

Making Calculations

The reason for calculations in queries, forms, and reports is to return values that are useful to the user. Calculations can't be discussed without mentioning data types. The precision of the results from a calculation depend a lot on the number data type of the field in the expression. There are six different types of data concerning numbers, and they are listed in Table 10.3.

Table 10.3. The number data types.

Data Type	What It Stores
Byte	Can handle 0 to 255
Integer	Can handle –32,768 to 32,767
Long	Can handle –2,147,483,648 to 2,147,483,647

Data Type	What It Stores
Single	Can handle −3.402823E38 to −1.401298E-45 and 1.401298E-45 to 3.402823E38
Double	Can handle −4.94065645841247E-324 to −1.79769313486232E308 and 1.79769313486232E308 to 4.94065645841247E324
Replication ID	Global Unique Identifier
Currency	Can handle −922,337,203,685,477.5808 to 922,337,203,685,477.5807

Remember, the precision of the data resulting from the calculations that are performed depends on the number data type. The more precise the data type, the more precise the result.

Creating Calculations

The equal sign (=) constitutes the beginning of a calculation. When the calculation expression has been entered into the field, Access converts the field to an alias name, such as Expr1. Calculations can sum, average, count, or total all of the records in a query. You can access this by clicking the Totals button on a query to expose the Totals row in the query grid. In Figure 10.31, a simple calculation is performed with the Salary and BillingRate fields.

```
=[Salary]/[BillingRate]
```

FIGURE 10.31.

A simple calculation in a query.

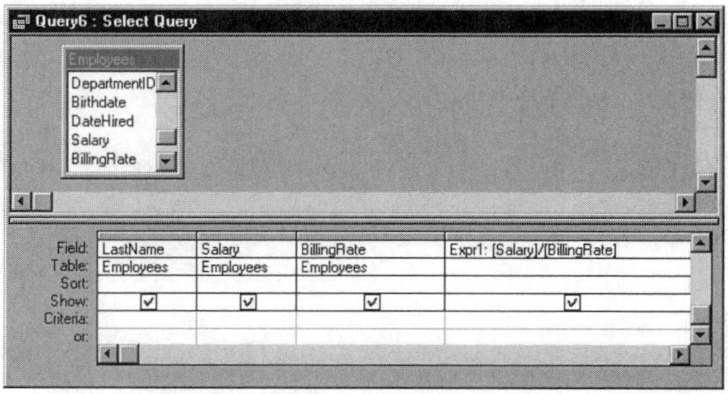

The calculation takes the Salary field for each record and divides it by the BillingRate field. The result is how many hours each employee must bill in order to cover the cost of his or her salary. When this calculation is entered into a new Field cell of a query grid, the equal sign is replaced by Exp1:. This can be renamed Must Bill: so that Datasheet view will make more sense. The results of the calculation are shown in Figure 10.32.

FIGURE 10.32.

The results of the calculation.

Last Name	Salary	Billing Rate	Hours Must Bill
Bryant	$30,000.00	$20.00	1500
Heidt	$29,000.00	$10.00	2900
Simcox	$28,000.00	$25.00	1120
Jones	$27,000.00	$10.00	2700
Doyle	$26,000.00	$20.00	1300
Gigliotti-Mullaney	$35,000.00	$25.00	1400

You can perform simple calculations by using the Totals button on the toolbar of a query. When this button is clicked, the Totals row is added to the query grid. Each Totals cell has a drop-down box associated with it. This box displays some off the most common calculation functions used. In Figure 10.33, the SUM calculation will be performed on the Hours field.

FIGURE 10.33.

The common calculation functions are in the drop-down box.

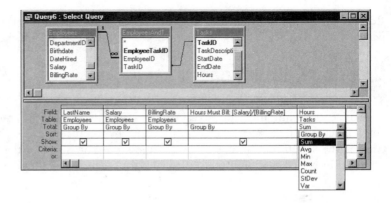

The result is that all of the hours for each record will be added together. Without the SUM function, all of the hours for each employee would be listed, not added. Figure 10.34 shows the results of the SUM calculation.

FIGURE 10.34.

The results of the SUM calculation.

Last Name	Salary	Billing Rate	Hours Must Bill	SumOfHours
Bryant	$30,000.00	$20.00	1500	5
Doyle	$26,000.00	$20.00	1300	5
Heidt	$29,000.00	$10.00	2900	8
Jones	$27,000.00	$10.00	2700	3
Simcox	$28,000.00	$25.00	1120	6

The different types of aggregate functions found in the drop-down box are as follows:

SUM: Returns the sum of a set of values contained in a field on a query.

AVG: Returns the arithmetic mean of a set of values contained in a field on a query.

MIN: Returns the minimum set of values contained in a field on a query.

MAX: Returns the maximum set of values contained in a field on a query.

COUNT: Returns the number of records returned by a query.

STDEV: Return estimates of the standard deviation for a population or a population sample (STDEVP) represented as a set of values contained in a field on a query.

VAR: Return estimates of the variance for a population or a population sample (VARP) represented as a set of values contained in a field on a query.

Notice that when an aggregate function is performed on one field, that field is renamed on the datasheet with a combination of the name of the function performed, the word "Of," and the name of the field—for example, SumOfHours. These fields can be renamed in the SQL view of the query. The name of the field follows the word AS in the statement. Replace the name of the field with the desired name and test Datasheet view.

NOTE

Because calculations return results, the results aren't actually stored in the underlying table. Hence, information can't be manipulated manually in Datasheet view.

Custom calculations can be performed on numeric, text, and date calculations. Several aggregate functions can be performed using information from one or more fields in a query. These custom calculations need to be created in a new Field cell entered as an expression. Through the logical combination of several literals, field names, functions, and operators, complex calculations can be performed.

TIP

For long, complex calculations, it's necessary to view the entire expression. You can change the size of the cell by clicking on the right line between the two column selectors and dragging it to the right. If the expression is really long, press Shift-F2 to get the zoom box of the cell.

Summary

This chapter covered expressions. The different parts of an expression were identified and described. Expressions can contain operators, constants, literal values, functions, field names, and variable names.

Operators are the symbols used in an expression. There are four groups of operators: arithmetic, comparison, concatenation, and logic.

Developers can get assistance in building expressions through the Expression Builder. The Expression Builder allows you to point and click on different elements that make up an expression. Access assembles the expression, and if the expression is syntactically correct, Access accepts the expression. If the expression is logically correct, a value is returned in the Datasheet view of the query.

Expressions can be used in tables, queries, forms, reports, and macros. Expressions can be used to set the value of properties and to calculate fields and conditions in queries. They can also be used as record sources for forms and reports.

Understanding the Jet Engine

11

by Ted Williamson

IN THIS CHAPTER

Understanding how the Jet Engine processes queries will enable database developers to achieve superior speed of execution in their applications. Some basic principles of design will result in a many-fold increase in the speed of executing queries. This chapter outlines the essential aspects of the Jet Engine's operation to enable designers to structure their queries so that they will provide the desired performance.

Although the purpose of the Query Engine is to execute queries efficiently (no matter how poorly they are structured), simpler queries typically execute faster than complex ones. The primary rules for performance remain: Use the simplest SQL statements that will perform the desired task, and follow accepted database design principles.

How the Jet Engine Processes Queries

The Access Jet Engine processes queries in three distinct stages: compilation, optimization, and execution. Each stage or step must be completed successfully before the Jet Engine proceeds to the next stage. If a problem occurs at any stage along the way, the process is halted and an error message is returned to the calling application. Most of these error messages are displayed for the user. In addition, the developer can trap for these errors and display a custom error message.

The Definition of the Query

Before a query can be processed by the Jet Engine, it must be created using one of the many tools provided by Microsoft Access. The Query By Example (QBE) interface, the Access SQL language, or Data Access Objects (DAO) can all be used to create queries that are submitted to the Jet Engine. These queries are then passed to the Jet Query Engine in the form of a SQL Select statement.

Compilation

The Jet Engine's first step in compilation is to check the syntax of the SQL query and return an error if any problems exist. The next step is to parse the query. The names referenced in the query are bound to the corresponding columns in the associated tables. Finally, the SQL string is compiled into an internal query-object definition format by replacing names used in the query string with unique tokens generated by the Jet.

Once the query is in the internal format, it goes through a series of "preoptimization" processors that try to rearrange the query to produce an updateable result set, or dynaset, and increase the likelihood that the optimizer will be able to improve the query's structure. In this stage, the query is basically torn apart into fundamental elements and reformatted into simple element groupings, thus reducing the overall complexity of the query while maintaining the original request in a manner that is most likely to result in optimum performance.

Optimization

The Jet Engine's Query Optimizer is probably the most complex component of the Query Engine. The optimizer is responsible for choosing the optimum query-execution strategy for the previously compiled query object. The Jet Query Engine is a cost-based optimizer that uses statistics from the table being queried to determine the most efficient way to execute a query. (For more detailed information, see the section "Table Statistics" later in this chapter.) Because the algorithms used by the optimizer are dependent on accurate statistics for the table being queried, it's important that these table statistics be current. (See the section "The Importance of Compacting the Database" later in this chapter for details.)

> **TIP**
>
> In a cost-based optimizer, the "cost" is the time that will be spent in executing the query. The optimizer chooses query-execution strategies that result in the lowest "time cost."

This cost-based optimizer scans through the query and creates task lists of potential execution strategies. It then evaluates each task in the lists and chooses the "least costly" list of tasks that will generate the desired result set. The longer a task takes to perform, the more costly or expensive it is. The two tasks that are most significant in their effect on the performance of the query and which therefore must be evaluated are the reading of base tables and the execution of joins.

The Jet Query Optimizer can choose from three different base table access plans: index range, Rushmore restriction, and table scan. The choice depends on the size of the table, the presence of indexes, and the presence of any criteria and how restrictive they are. For more detailed information, see the section "Base-Table Access Strategies" later in this chapter.

The Jet Query Optimizer can choose from five different join strategies when more than one table is involved: nested iteration, index, lookup, merge, and index-merge. For more detailed information, see the section "Join Strategies" later in this chapter.

Execution

Once the optimum query-execution plan has been determined, the Query Engine executes each step in the final query plan and returns the result set. If the query involves an ODBC source, the Jet Engine tries to create a pass-through query by sending as much of the query as possible to the back-end for processing by the server. The compiled query is then translated to a new, more efficient data-execution structure where the join strategy, chosen by the optimizer, is executed to return the desired result set.

Improving the Performance of the Jet Engine

To minimize the speed of process execution using a Microsoft Jet Database Engine, the database designer should understand how the Microsoft Jet Query Engine optimizes queries, when Rushmore technology helps, and what performance tricks to use in query design to achieve superior performance.

Because the purpose of most database applications is to extract information from data stored in tables, queries are used more than any other object in a database. Understanding how queries are handled by the Jet Engine can help the database developer create more efficient queries.

The Microsoft Jet Query-Engine Optimizer

As mentioned earlier, the Microsoft Jet Query-Engine Optimizer uses table statistics to determine which join strategy to use in the query. This section of the chapter takes a closer look at how these table statistics—and the base-table access methods themselves—affect the selection of join strategies.

The optimizer first stores an estimate of the number of records used in the expected result set and the time cost of reading those records from the associated table for each of the base-table access strategies. Next, the optimizer creates a list of the table joins, with the time cost of the associated join strategy. Finally, the optimizer locates those combinations of base-table access strategy and join strategy that produce the most efficient query plan.

Base-Table Access Strategies

The Microsoft Jet can choose from three base-table access strategies:

- Table scan: Because during a sequential table scan all data pages are read, this is typically the slowest means of accessing a table. While all the single-table restrictions are checked for each row in the table, no base-table page is read more than once. This method is most useful for small, unindexed tables.

- Index range: This method is employed when one of the single-table restrictions falls on one of the table's indexes. The indexed records are checked against all remaining restrictions. Although these base-table pages may be read more than once, there are fewer to read, thus reducing the process time, particularly on larger tables.

- Rushmore restriction: When there are restrictions on multiple-indexed columns, the Rushmore restriction is employed. The use of multiple indexes to solve a query drastically reduces the number of base-table pages that need to be read. (See the section "When Rushmore Helps" later in this chapter for complete details.)

Table Statistics

The optimizer must check the statistics of both the base tables and the nonbase tables when determining which join strategy to employ. For every base table in the query, the optimizer checks the following:

■ Base-table record count and data page count: Both of these statistics help the optimizer determine which join strategy to use. In general, the higher the record and page counts, the more costly the query.

■ Table indexes: Consideration is given to the indexes: selectivity, index page count, and the occurrence of duplicates and nulls. Selectivity refers to the number of rows that are returned with a single index value. The fewer values returned, the better. A unique index is considered to have the highest selectivity, because every value is distinct. As with data pages, the higher the index page count, the more costly the query. Nulls in an index might prohibit the use of an index-merge join. Duplicates in an index affect its selectivity.

■ Table location: If the table resides on a remote server, a remote query is created and set to the ODBC source, which can help lessen the query cost.

For every nonbase table (input query) in the query, the optimizer checks the following:

■ Record count: As with base tables, the record count of the input query determines which join strategy is chosen.

■ Input query cost: Input query execution costs are added to the total query cost.

■ Ordered input queries: An ordered input query may be a nominee for a lookup join.

■ Input query location: If the input query resides on a remote server, a remote query is created and set to the ODBC source, which can help lessen the query cost.

Join Strategies

Join strategies are chosen by the Microsoft Jet Query-Engine Optimizer, employing the statistics described earlier. Because the optimizer uses a cost-based algorithm, every possible join strategy is examined to determine the most economical query-execution plan.

The optimizer can choose from five join strategies: nested iteration, index, lookup, merge, and index-merge. Join strategies range in complexity from "brute force" table scans to more complex execution plans. Each join strategy is ideally suited to solve specific query circumstances.

■ Nested iteration join: The nested iteration join is a "brute force" method that is used by default to perform a join when no better means can be found. A nested iteration is usually performed on tables with few records and no indexes.

■ Index join: Index joins are used when the inner table has an index over the joined column. The index join tends to be used when the inner table is small or data doesn't have to be retrieved from the inner table. An index join may also be used if the outer table is small or highly restricted. Index joins are often used for dynasets.

- Lookup join: A lookup join is very similar to an index join. The only difference is that the lookup join performs a projection and a sort on the inner table before performing the join. Projection reduces the set of columns in the inner relation and therefore reduces its size. A lookup join is often used for static queries and ordered dynasets.

- Merge join: Merge joins tend to be performed when the inputs are both close to the same magnitude and large. Merge joins also tend to be used in cases where ordering the output of a join can save resorting.

- Index-merge join: An index-merge join may be used when each input is a table in native Microsoft Jet database format. Each input must have an index over its join column, and at least one of the indexes must not allow nulls if there is more than one join column.

When Rushmore Helps

Rushmore query-optimization technology provides dramatically increased query execution. Basically, Rushmore query optimization involves the use of indexes to increase the efficiency of locating records for a result set. Rushmore query optimization is used on queries involving multiple-column, indexed restrictions. Index intersection alone is the most straightforward and obvious Rushmore feature, but Rushmore encompasses several other ideas. Index union and index minus are also possible.

- Index intersection: Used when the column restrictions that are involved must be intersected on multiple indexes in order to select the desired records. (For example, `column1 = <exp> AND column2 = <exp>`.) A result set is created for each indexed restriction, and the result sets from each of the indexes are intersected to find the records that match both criteria.

- Index union: Used when the column restrictions that are involved require a union on multiple indexes in order to select the desired records. (For example, `column1 = <exp> OR column2 = <exp>`.) A result set is created for each indexed restriction, and the result sets from each of the indexes are unioned to find the records that match both criteria.

- Index minus: Used when the column restrictions that are involved must be intersected on multiple indexes in order to select the desired records. (For example, `column1 = <exp> AND column2 <> <exp>`.) A result set is created for each indexed restriction, and the result set from the `column2` index is then removed or subtracted from the `column1` result set to find the records that match both criteria.

Avoiding Design Mistakes

Many common mistakes can cause unnecessary bottlenecks when Jet Access executes queries. The following is a list of common design mistakes that reduce the efficiency of a query:

- Redundant tables: Although the Microsoft Access QBE tool lets you create queries easily, sometimes the same table is added to a query without the table's being joined to anything. This causes a Cartesian product to occur. A Cartesian product is one in which every row in one table is joined to every row in another table or tables. Not only does this slow down the query, but it can result in unwanted records appearing in the query result.

- Expressions in query output: Microsoft Jet can't optimize a query when expressions such as IIf are placed on the output column of a query. This can be even more troublesome if the offending query is used as the input to another query. The more appropriate place for expressions is in a control on a form or report, where they operate only on the final output.

- GROUP BY on too many columns: When creating a "totals" query, use the GROUP BY clause on as few columns as possible. The more columns in the GROUP BY, the longer the query takes to execute. Be sure that you don't include extraneous columns.

- GROUP BY in the same query as a join: Whenever possible, place GROUP BY clauses on tables and *then* join them to another table rather than performing the GROUP BY in the same query as the join.

- Indexing the join column from only one table: When joining tables, always index the fields on both sides of a join. This can speed query execution by allowing more sophisticated join strategies, such as the index and index-merge joins. The use of indexes also provides better statistics.

- Under-indexing fields: When the frequency of updating the database is low, indexes should be placed on all columns used in a join or restriction. With the use of Rushmore query optimization, Microsoft Jet can take advantage of multiple indexes on a single table. This makes indexing many columns quite advantageous.

- Use COUNT(*): When you must determine the number of records, you should use COUNT(*) rather than COUNT(*ColumnName*). This is because of Rushmore optimizations that allow COUNT(*) to be executed much faster than COUNT(*ColumnName*).

The Importance of Compacting the Database

If you've been using computers for a while, you're probably familiar with the benefits of disk-defragmentation software. The purpose of a defragmenter is to improve the overall performance of the system by realigning the files on the disk so that the files are in order (sorted), all parts of each single file are together on the disk (defragmented), and all the free space on the disk is collected together (contiguous). The performance increase depends on how thorough a job the defragmenter does. Compacting a database performs some of the same functions as defragmentation.

Because database systems are really just sophisticated/specialized filing systems, they suffer from the same sorts of problems. The tables and other database objects become fragmented as they're used. In Access, as objects and records are deleted from the database, the unused space becomes deallocated but remains in the database. This results in an increase in the size of the database file and a decrease in performance as processes must identify and skip past these deallocated spaces. The only means of reclaiming this unused space is to compact the database. As with disk defragmenters, Access's Compact command will remove the wasted space from the database and realign all the database objects in a contiguous manner.

The following things are accomplished when an Access database is compacted: Table records are resorted, unused space is reclaimed, counter fields are reset, and table statistics are recalculated.

- The table's records are placed on adjoining database pages in the order of the table's primary key. As a result, the performance of sequential record scans of database tables will improve, because the number of database pages that are read in order to retrieve all of a table's records will be minimized.

- Table statistics are recalculated. Table statistics, which become dated as the database is used, have the greatest effect on the performance of querydefs whose query plan was created and optimized with the older statistics. Out-of-date statistics are most often caused by rolling back transactions. But because statistics are cached in memory, they can become dated as the result of the computer's crashing, being reset, or getting turned off before the database is closed and the statistics are written to disk.

- Unused space, the result of deleting objects and records, is removed from the database. Although deletions of database objects and records mark the newly freed space as available, the size of the database doesn't shrink unless the database is compacted.

- Counter fields are reset to the maximum Counter record in the table. The next value generated will be one greater than the current maximum.

The most important things accomplished by compacting the database are the reordering of the table's records and the updating of the table's statistics. Both of these provide the greatest increase in query performance, which is possibly the most important reason that databases are used in the first place.

Summary

This chapter detailed the internal compilation, optimization, and execution processes of the Jet Engine, which helps the developer design efficient queries. The Jet Engine's internal methods and strategies can be matched to design characteristics that the developer chooses. This chapter also listed some common design mistakes and optimization tips and detailed the benefits of compacting.

PART

IN THIS PART

Access Forms

Creating and Using Simple Forms

This chapter includes a basic overview of forms, along with a discussion of why forms are used and how to use them. One section details the design and customization of forms, giving a deeper definition of the capabilities of forms. These capabilities aren't utilized in the AutoForm or Form Wizards. Finally, the advanced section details other form controls.

An Introduction to Forms

Access forms can give databases a professional image in a relatively short time. Splash screens and Main menus are just a few examples of items that appear in mass-distributed professional software products. Forms give flexibility to databases by being either very simple or very complex. A developer can control the end user through different properties such as defaults, input masks, and modals. There are more than 70 properties just on the form itself. That number doesn't include any fields or controls on the form. Each field or control can have as many as 58 additional properties, and other controls, such as option buttons, can have an extra 38 properties. Understanding form properties and how they work and when they are executed is the crux of creating complex and sophisticated databases. The form properties are discussed in greater detail later in this chapter.

Record Sources for Forms

Record sources for forms, as well as reports, provide the location where the data is being stored. Not all forms, however, must have record sources. Forms can be used for purposes other than data entry. They can be used as splashes, Main menus, and date rangers, just to name a few. These forms are detailed later in this chapter.

Forms are primarily used for data entry. The record source for the form can be found in the form's properties. In Figure 12.1, the record source for the form is a table called Vendors. To pull up the properties for the form, click the Form Selector button, which appears in the upper-left corner of the form. Or you can click the form's selector button and choose View | Properties. The Properties button on the toolbar can be used to bring up the form's properties.

> **NOTE**
>
> No matter where the focus is on the form, if you select the Properties button or select View | Properties, the properties sheet appears. To ensure that the focus is on the entire form, make sure that the form's selector button has a small black square in its center. This square means that the focus is on the entire form and the properties box pertains to the entire form. By clicking anywhere in the form, you can then set the focus to that piece of the form and not the entire form. The record source for the form can't be viewed unless the properties box for the entire form is selected.

FIGURE 12.1.

You can find a form's record source by clicking the form selector and viewing its properties.

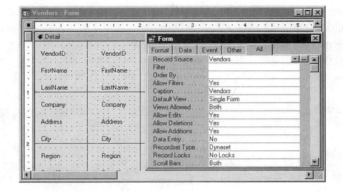

The record source of a form is the table, query, or SQL statement on which the form is based. Notice that the `RecordSource` property has two small controls to the right of the field. The first control is a drop-down list denoted by the arrow pointing down. This list, when clicked, displays all the tables and queries currently in the database. When you click any of the tables or queries, the record source changes to the item you clicked. If a form exists with fields on it and you change the record source, all the fields that are no longer present in the record source display an error to the end user. This error is shown in Figure 12.2. The record source was changed from the Vendors table to the Vendors Query, which doesn't contain the Company name field. All the other fields from the Vendors table, however, were present in the Vendors Query query. The error appears as `#Name?` in the Company Name field. The reason for the error is that the Company Name field doesn't appear in the query grid of the Vendors Query upon which the form is now based.

FIGURE 12.2.

When an existing record source for a form is changed, any fields that aren't in the new record source display an error to the end user.

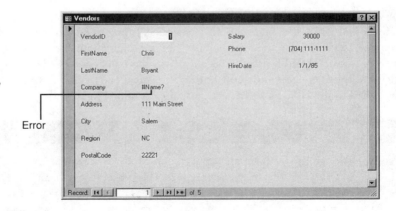

This error problem can be rectified in one of two ways. The first way is to remove the Company field from the form. The second is to go into the query and add the Company field to the query grid. You can do this by clicking the ellipse button (...) that appears to the right of the drop-down box. This action launches the SQL Builder, shown in Figure 12.3. Because the query called Vendor Query was already present on the RecordSource property, Access brings up the query itself. This is the same as pressing the F11 key to bring up the database container, clicking the Query tab, and opening the Vendor Query in Design view. Notice that it looks exactly like a query. Any modifications made here will be reflected in the actual query.

FIGURE 12.3.

The builder looks exactly like a query in Design view.

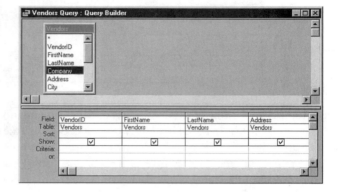

TIP

If, and only if, a query appears on the RecordSource property when the Builder button is invoked, the query itself will appear. Modifications made from here can be seen in the actual query.

When a table name appears on the RecordSource property of a form and the builder is invoked, a form that looks like and functions like a query is presented. For all intents and purposes, the builder uses a query to help you "build" an SQL statement for the form. The table that appeared on the record source line is already in the table pane of the query. You can then add fields to the query grid and apply criteria or expressions if needed. Other tables or queries can be added to the table pane the same way they're added in any other query.

NOTE

Even though the SQL Builder appears to be like a query, it is not. Due to certain factors, query options might or might not be available. For example, when a blank SQL Builder (one that isn't based on another table or query) is being invoked, the capability to create an Action query or create a new object isn't available.

If the RecordSource property is blank and you click the builder (...), the same process starts as if you were starting a new, blank query. Figure 12.4 depicts the screen as it appears when the Builder button is clicked and no information is on the RecordSource property.

FIGURE 12.4.

What appears to be a blank query is generated when the Builder button is pressed and no other table or query information appears on the RecordSource *property of a form.*

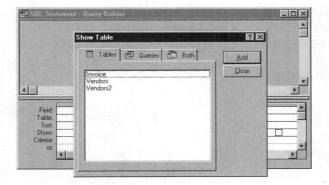

TIP

At times, you might not be able to remember whether you're working with a real query or with a record source builder. You can tell whether the query on-screen is a real query in two distinct ways. The first method is to look at the title bar for the query. If it reads "SQL Statement: Query Builder," the query on-screen is being generated from the RecordSource property of a form. The second method is to try closing the query in question. If changes have been made, Access displays a message box stating that the SQL statement for the form has been changed and asking whether the changes to the query should be saved.

When you're working with an SQL Statement Query Builder, most of the features available to a query are available. In future references, the SQL Statement Query Builder will be referred to as the SQL Builder. For detailed information concerning queries and their properties, refer to Chapter 8, "Querying Data: The QBE Grid and Select Queries," Chapter 9, "Specialized Queries," and Chapter 10, "Using Expressions and Functions." The SQL Builder, like a query, enables you to set properties. When you right-click in the table pane, the properties for the SQL Builder are displayed, as shown in Figure 12.5. Each property is described in greater detail in Part III, "Queries and SQL."

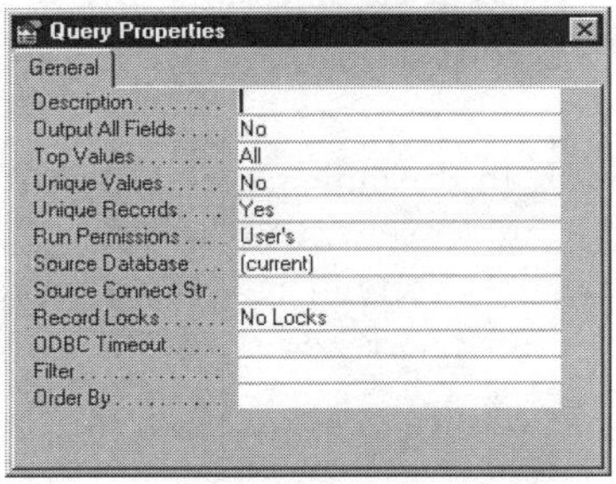

FIGURE 12.5.

SQL Statement Query Builders also have properties.

Fields that appear in the QBE grid are the same fields that will appear in the form's field list. If a field that is needed doesn't appear in the field list, this is where you would need to go to rectify that situation. The SQL Builder's fields can also have properties, just as in a query. Each field can have its own set of properties. The field properties are shown in Figure 12.6. Each property is detailed in Part III.

FIGURE 12.6.

SQL Statement Query Builders' fields have properties.

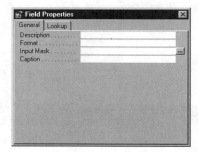

> **NOTE**
>
> The `Input Mask` property is visible on all the field properties; however, it's available only on text fields or date fields. If you try to run an input mask on a numeric field, Access displays a box reminding you that this option is available only on text or date fields.

To add other tables or queries to the SQL Builder, select Query | Show Table. Or you can click the Show Table button on the toolbar. Access brings up the Show Table dialog box (see Figure 12.4).

> **NOTE**
>
> When two objects appear in the table pane of the SQL Statement Query Builder window (such as two tables, two queries, or one table and one query), a join line must appear between the two. If a relationship already exists between the objects and the AutoJoin feature is turned on, Access automatically relates the two objects.

Several objects can be in the table pane of the SQL Builder; however, if no fields are in the QBE grid, the SQL Builder statement will fail. At least one field must be in the query grid for the SQL statement to be accepted as a record source for the form. After placing fields on the grid, you can create expressions and set criteria.

As mentioned earlier, some features appear in the SQL Builder yet aren't accessible due to the nature of the "query." There are two types of queries: Action and Select. Only Select type queries can be used as a basis for a form's record source. In fact, the Action queries—Make Table, Update, Append, and Delete—aren't available even when the drop-down list is invoked. Developers don't get access to those types of queries from the Query Type button or the Query menu.

Which is faster: a form based on a query or a form based on an SQL statement? The correct answer is a form based on a query. The reason is that the SQL statement must be passed to the query optimizer, which interprets the statement and then runs the statement. The stored query is faster because Access has already interpreted it; all that is left to do is run it. By reducing the optimizer step, the form based on a stored query is faster. The key word in the preceding sentence is *stored*. You must, however, consider certain trade-offs. Yes, stored query-based forms are faster, but because they're stored in the query module, they are actually objects in that module. Each object takes up space in the application. The more objects in a database, the larger the database gets. A good rule of thumb is that the more complex queries should be stored queries. Simple queries should be SQL statements.

Creating Simple Forms with AutoForm

The AutoForm feature in Access enables you to create quick-and-dirty data entry forms in the blink of an eye (depending on the speed of the computer). AutoForms are fast and ask no questions of the developer. AutoForms are performed only on existing tables or queries. The AutoForm Wizard can be accessed from either the Tables module or the Queries module of the database container. It can also be accessed from the Forms module, but only when a new form is created. When you access the AutoForm Wizard from either the Tables or the Queries module, the record source for the new form will be the object that was highlighted when you clicked AutoForm. You can also, however, invoke the AutoForm Wizard from the Forms module by creating a new form, selecting the table or query on which the form is to be based, and clicking the AutoForm Wizard option. In Figure 12.7, the AutoForm Wizard is being invoked on the Vendor Invoice query.

To understand how the AutoForm places its fields, you must look at the query (or table, as the case may be) on which the AutoForm is being based. In Figure 12.8, the Vendor Invoice query is shown in Design view.

The forms produced from the AutoForm Wizard aren't much to look at. Background pictures are assigned to them, and they usually appear in a single-column format, unless the base table or query contains many fields. The forms have a label for each field, and the label usually appears to the left of the field, as shown in Figure 12.9. All the fields that are on the form were present in the query. Their order of appearance on the form also follows their order of appearance on the query. The same goes for a table-based AutoForm.

FIGURE 12.7.

The AutoForm Wizard will create a form on the Vendor Invoice query.

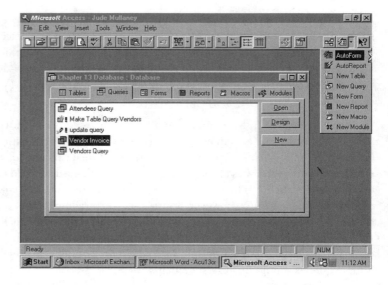

FIGURE 12.8.

A peek at the query on which the AutoForm Wizard is being based.

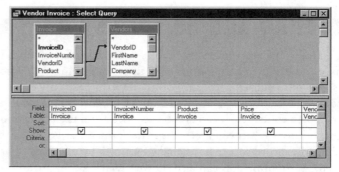

FIGURE 12.9.

AutoForm produces quick forms using all the fields in the table or query on which the AutoForm was based.

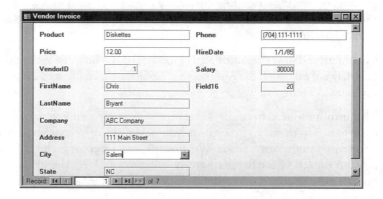

There is another special note to make about AutoForms. In this case, the query on which the AutoForm was based contained a table that had a field for which the `DefaultControl` property was changed from Text Box to Combo Box. This feature was inherited by the AutoForm, and the field was placed on the form as a Combo Box. Also, in Figure 12.9, the AutoForm Wizard used the caption property of the Region field. The label for that field now reads "State."

> **TIP**
>
> If fields in a table have their `DefaultControl` property changed, the AutoForm Wizard uses the `DefaultControl` property when creating the form. In addition, any of the caption properties follow through to the AutoForm.

Notice that the form generated by the AutoForm already has background and font specifications to the labels and colors assigned to them. You can change all of these items so that every time the AutoForm Wizard is used, a specific background is used and certain colors and fonts and pitches are used. You can achieve this effect by opening the form in Design view and making the desired changes to the labels and fields. The form then becomes the template for the changes to the AutoFormat Wizard. Then choose Format | AutoFormat. Figure 12.10 shows the AutoFormat dialog box.

FIGURE 12.10.

The AutoFormat Wizard template can be changed.

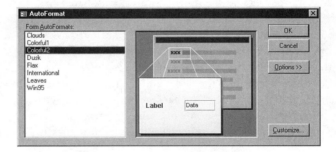

Click the Customize button in the lower-right corner of the dialog box. The Customize button enables you to perform one of three actions, as shown in Figure 12.11:

- Create a new AutoFormat template based on the current form and background
- Change the current AutoFormat template based on the current form and background
- Delete the current AutoFormat template

After selecting the background and the font, style, and color changes, click OK. The AutoFormat creates all new forms using the new template. You can change this option as many times as desired. Each time you change the template, the new forms created will use the new template. Any old forms won't be automatically updated but will retain their existing backgrounds and colors.

FIGURE 12.11.

The AutoFormat Wizard Customize button enables you to create a new template, change the existing template, or delete the current template.

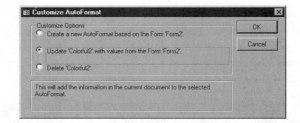

> **NOTE**
>
> When you're basing an AutoForm on a query, the query must be a Select query, not an Action query. Only two queries fall into the Select query category: the Select query and the Crosstab query. The AutoForm Wizard doesn't work on an Action query.

Creating Simple Forms with the Form Wizard

Form Wizards, such as the Form Wizard, the Chart Wizard, and the PivotTable Wizard, are different from AutoForm Wizards, such as the AutoForm Columnar Wizard, the AutoForm Tabular Wizard, and the AutoForm Datasheet Wizard. The AutoForm Wizards don't allow for any developer interaction during the creation of the form—the interaction comes only after the form has been created. Form Wizards differ in that they ask questions of the developer. The questions pertain to the tables and queries to be used for the form, which fields from each can be used, the sort orders, the backgrounds, and the like. In Access 2.0, when a Form Wizard was used, you could choose only one table or query. In Access 95, this feature has been changed. You can now choose certain fields from different tables and queries.

> **NOTE**
>
> When you're using multiple tables and queries, it's necessary to have the relationships between those tables and queries established. When the relationships are established, the joins (whether they be INNER, OUTER LEFT, or OUTER RIGHT) will be used in the creation of the SQL statement needed for the RecordSource property of the form.

The only way to access the Form Wizards is by clicking the New button in the Forms module of the database container. The first dialog box that appears is shown in Figure 12.12. This dialog box is a modal form, meaning that you must click OK or Cancel to proceed in Access.

FIGURE 12.12.

From this screen, you can choose from multiple wizards or create one from scratch.

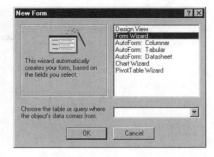

NOTE

After a modal form is on-screen, you must answer the question being posed by the modal before you can proceed in that piece of software. All hot keys, such as the Esc key and the F11 key, are turned off.

TIP

If the wizard being used isn't an AutoForm type wizard, you need not select a table or query on which to base the form here.

After you have selected an option, in this case the Form Wizard option, you must click OK to proceed. The next screen enables you to choose the fields that are to appear on the new form. Access 95 enables you to choose multiple fields from multiple tables or queries. This feature is a major enhancement over the 2.0 version. This part of the wizard determines the SQL statement that will appear on the RecordSource property of the new form. In Access 2.0, you were allowed to choose only one table or query.

In the dialog box shown in Figure 12.13, you select tables and queries from the Tables/Queries drop-down box. The fields associated with the highlighted table or query are displayed under it, in the Available Fields list box on the left. Any field that appears in the box on the right side is considered a "selected field" and will appear on the new form. To move fields from the left box to the right box, click the greater-than keys between the two boxes.

NOTE

All the tables are available, and only the Select type queries will appear in the drop-down list. Remember, Action type queries can't have forms or reports based on them.

FIGURE 12.13.

The Form Wizard enables you to choose fields from more than one table or query.

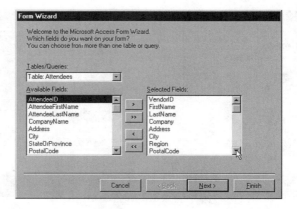

What happens if fields are selected from two or more objects? Those objects must have an existing relationship before the wizard will continue. Access displays a message box stating that one or more objects aren't connected. You then choose whether to go into the Relationships window of the database and rectify the situation or return to the wizard and remove the fields that are causing this error.

NOTE

If you choose to modify the relationships of the database, the wizard is canceled.

The next step in the Form Wizard process concerns the layout of the fields. Your three choices are Columnar, Tabular, and Datasheet. This screen is shown in Figure 12.14. Remember, the fields will appear in the order you chose previously.

FIGURE 12.14.

You can choose the layout of the fields.

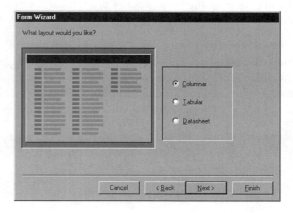

After the layout has been decided, the background style is next. Eight different formats ship with Access 95. If you have modified any of the formats or added and deleted formats, those changes are reflected here. The background style screen is shown in Figure 12.15.

FIGURE 12.15.

Eight different background styles ship with Access.

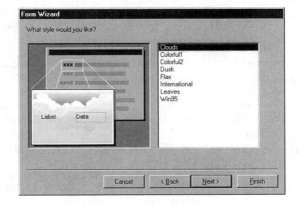

The fourth and last step in the wizard enables you to modify the name of the form. The suggested title is based on the name of the table or query on which the form is being based. As shown in Figure 12.16, you can choose to go into the form and begin entering data or to go into the Design view of the form to make modifications. The Access Help files can also be displayed.

FIGURE 12.16.

The last screen in the wizard lets you choose the name of the new form and decide whether to go directly into the data entry mode or the Design view.

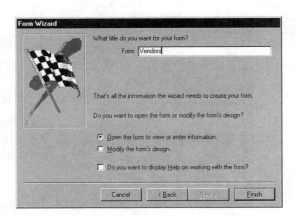

This is the end of the Form Wizard. You can create a sophisticated and professional data entry form in a fraction of the time it would take to create the form from scratch. A Form Wizard isn't as fast as an AutoForm Wizard, but it does allow more flexibility in the customization.

Opening and Using a Form

Forms can be opened in a number of different ways. The most common way is through the Database Container window in the Forms module. End users, however, might get confused with the Database Container window. To shield this from the end user, developers can launch forms from buttons on other forms, from a macro, or from Access Basic Code (ABC). Forms can even be opened from the database container without the Open button being clicked. Drag the desired form from the database container to the application background. Access automatically opens the form. The pointer changes to reflect the fact that an object is being dragged.

Forms should always be used rather than tables or query datasheets. Through forms, developers can control what the user enters, how it is entered, and what is required before the user can move to the next record. Direct access to tables or query datasheets enables the user to modify and delete existing data as well as add data. This capability could be hazardous if the user is a novice to Access or Windows.

When forms are opened from other forms, a button usually launches them. A common example of one form being used to launch other forms would be a Main menu. Main menus might have several different buttons that launch several different forms. Figure 12.17 shows a blank form. In the toolbox is a button called the command button. This tool, when coupled with the wizard, helps developers through the process needed to have a button launch another form.

FIGURE 12.17.

The command button creates an object for the user to click to launch a form.

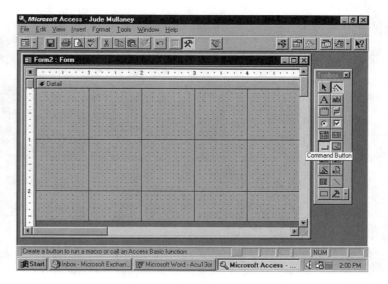

TIP

The Wizard button, which is shown in the upper-right corner of the toolbox in Figure 12.17, must be activated for the Command Button Wizard to run. Click the Wizard button first, and then create the command button.

On the form, click and drag a small square about the size of the desired button. When the box is drawn, the wizard is launched. A button on a form can perform several actions, as shown in Figure 12.18. Because this example deals with the opening of a form, the operation to be performed is a Form Operation, and the action is the Open Form action.

FIGURE 12.18.

The wizard lists the different options available to a command button.

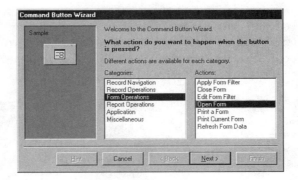

The next screen in the wizard asks for the name of the form that is to be opened when the button is clicked. In Figure 12.19, the Vendors form is the form that is to be opened.

FIGURE 12.19.

The Vendors form is the form that is to be launched when the button is clicked.

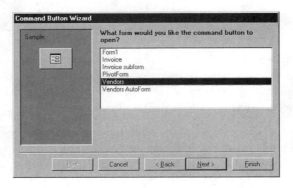

The following screen deals with how the form being launched is to be opened. It can display specific data that can be linked to the form the button is sitting on. It can also just open and display all the records in the form. Figure 12.20 shows these two options.

FIGURE 12.20.

The opening of the form has two options.

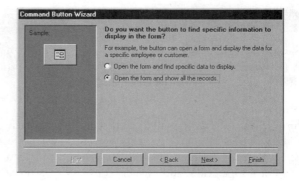

Only two screens are left in the Command Button Wizard. After choosing how the form should open, you must choose how the button appears. The button can display either a line of text or a picture. You can use one of the more than 220 button pictures that ship with Access, or you can choose a custom picture through the Browse button. In the example shown in Figure 12.21, the button will sport a picture of a toilet.

FIGURE 12.21.

Each button can have either a line of text or a picture on it.

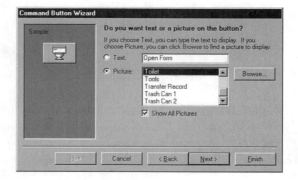

The final screen in the Command Button Wizard is shown in Figure 12.22. This is where you give the button a name. A suggestion from Access is usually pretty generic, such as Command2. You would be wise to rename the button to reflect what the button does when clicked—such as Vendors, because it opens the Vendors form.

Forms don't have to be opened from a button. They can be opened through a macro. Macros function like small bits of Access Basic code. Look at the macro shown in Figure 12.23. The action being performed is the OpenForm action.

FIGURE 12.22.

The name of the button should reflect the action it performs.

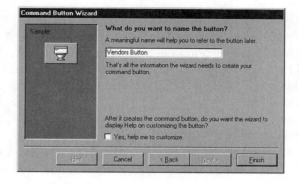

FIGURE 12.23.

The Vendors form will be opened by this macro action.

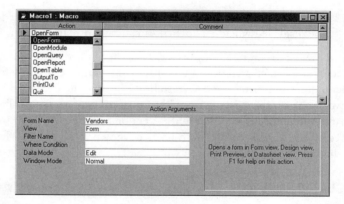

TIP

Notice that the word *OpenForm* appears without a space separating the two words. This is because the action code is SQL-compatible. SQL doesn't accept spaces or special characters, such as @, #, $, %, &, or *, in the code.

The lower half of the macro contains the Action Arguments information. These arguments must be filled out before the macro will work:

- The Form Name argument determines the form to be opened. The name comes from the drop-down list—in this case, the Vendors form.
- The View argument can determine how the form is opened. It can be Form, Design, Print Preview, or Datasheet view.

■ The Filter Name argument is either a query or a sort order for the records. This isn't a required field.

■ The Where Condition argument refers to the Where clause in an SQL statement. This is not a required field, and Access opens the form regardless of whether or not this field is filled out. If the form being opened already has a Where Condition, Access uses the Where Condition on the form. However, if a Where Condition is not imposed on the form, you can add one here. The builder button can help developers build the Where Condition.

■ The Data Mode argument indicates how the form will be opened for the user. It determines whether they will be allowed to Add, Edit, or Read-Only the records in the form.

■ The Window Mode argument refers to the size of the window in which the form will be displayed when it's opened. It can be Normal, Hidden, Icon, or Dialog.

Now that all the argument information has been filled out, close and save the macro. After the macro has been created, it can be called from a form. Open any form in Design view. Pull up the toolbox and turn off the Wizard button. Click the Command Button tool, and then draw a small box on the form. A blank button appears on the form. Pull up the properties box for that command button. Choose the Vendor Form macro from the drop-down list on the On Enter event for this command button, as shown in Figure 12.24. The macro code will be attached to the command button without the help of the wizard.

FIGURE 12.24.

Macro code is attached to an event on a command button that appears on a form.

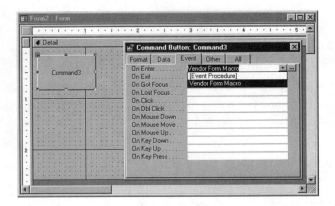

Developers should ask themselves, "What action will the end user want to do to bring up the form?" The action they decide on is called an event. On the command button's property sheet, click the Event tab to display all the events that pertain to the button. There are 12 actions or events that the end user could do to the command button. Usually, users Click or Enter on the button. This is the action that the macro will be attached to. From the On Enter property, click the drop-down list to display all the macros available, as shown in Figure 12.24. Select the desired macro, and the code behind the button is finished. The only thing left to do is change the caption that appears on the button to reflect what action it takes. The end user doesn't know that "Command3" means "Open the Vendors form." The caption for the button can be found under the Format tab of the button's property sheet.

> **TIP**
>
> The `DefaultView` and the `ViewsAllowed` properties of a form can be overridden by the `View` argument of the macro.

A form can be opened in one other way—through Visual Basic for Applications (VBA) code called the `OpenForm` method. This differs from the `OpenForm` action that appears in a macro. VBA changed the syntax of the code. In Access 2.0, `DoCmd` was an action. In Access 95, it is an object.

```
DoCmd.OpenForm formname [,view] [,filtername] [,wherecondition] [,datamode]
➥[,windowmode] [,openargs]
```

The syntax can actually be reduced to the following:

```
DoCmd.OpenForm formname
```

When the syntax is reduced, Access accepts the defaults for each of the arguments that are preceded by commas. The *view* argument is defaulted to `Normal`. The *filtername* is left blank. The *wherecondition* is also left blank. The *datamode* is defaulted to `Edit`, and the *windowmode* is defaulted to `Normal`. The difference between the `OpenForm` action that appears in macros and the `OpenForm` method that is available in code is the *openargs* argument. This argument allows for Visual Basic arguments and expressions to be entered.

In Access 95, each argument is a named argument. This is a wonderful new feature, because the arguments need not be position-specific as they were in Access 2.0. Each named argument is followed by a colon and an equals sign:

```
DoCmd.OpenForm FormName:=Vendor, Datamode:=acReadOnly
```

This code opens the Vendor form in read-only mode. `DoCmd` is the object and `OpenForm` is the method of that object. Remember that all objects are followed by a period. `FormName` is the named argument, which is followed by a colon and an equals sign. The `ReadOnly` value is an intrinsic constant. Because the intrinsic constant is Access-specific, it is preceded by `ac`. As long as you have the correct named argument followed by a colon, an equals sign, and the value, you can place the named arguments in any order. With this feature, you don't have to remember that the `OpenArgs` argument has six commas in front of it.

TIP

The *wherecondition* argument in the macro's OpenForm action allows up to 256 characters. The OpenForm method's *wherecondition* argument increases the number of characters to 32,768.

No matter how forms are opened—whether from the database container, through buttons on other forms, from a macro, or through code—the forms can switch among the three views. You can access these views—Form view, Design view, and Datasheet view—from the View menu or through the View button in the upper-left corner of the form.

Navigation in a Form

Navigation in a form refers not just to the fields that appear on the form but also to the records within the form. When a user is working on a form, she can navigate around the form by using several different methods. The first method is to use the Enter key. The Enter key accepts the data that the user entered into the field and moves the focus to the next field. The Tab key performs the same action, but the user doesn't need to enter any data. If hot keys are associated with buttons on the form, the user can hold down the Ctrl key and press the corresponding underlined letter.

NOTE

The Tab Order of the form can affect the way the Tab key and the Enter key move the user around the form. To change the Tab Order, select View | Tab Order when the form is in Design view.

Users can move from record to record by moving to the last field on the current form and pressing Enter. This action brings them to the first field on the next record. The same isn't true of the Tab key. If the user is on the last field on the form and presses the Tab key, the focus is moved back to the first field on the same record. The Tab loops the user around all the fields on the same record. Users can also use the Page Up and Page Down keys to move them to the next sequential record.

TIP

Users can move to the first record in the form by pressing Ctrl-Home. They can also move to the last record in the set by pressing Ctrl-End.

You can choose to turn on the navigation buttons on a form. The navigation buttons are a property that appears on the form's property sheet, as shown in Figure 12.25.

FIGURE 12.25.

The navigation buttons are a property of the form.

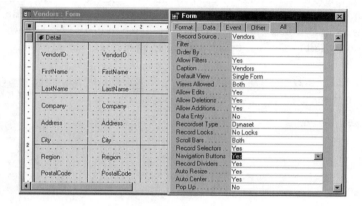

These buttons give the user a graphical way of moving around the records. When this feature is turned on, the navigation buttons appear in the lower-left corner of the form. These buttons appear in Figure 12.26. The buttons show which record is currently on-screen. The triangle pointing to the left enables the user to move back one record. The triangle pointing to the right enables the user to move forward one record. The other two triangles that are pointing to vertical lines enable the user to move to the first record or to the last record. The other button in the navigation button area is the triangle pointing to an asterisk. When this button is clicked, it brings the end user to the next blank record, which is ready for data entry.

FIGURE 12.26.

When the navigation buttons are turned on, they appear in the lower-left corner of the form.

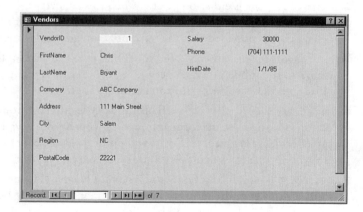

Navigation through a form can be done either by using the keyboard or through mouse clicks on the navigation buttons. The user can pilot through each field on a record or from record to record.

Editing Data on a Form

Editing data on a form actually means that the user can add, edit, or delete information in individual fields or information on entire records. Developers can actually control what the user can do when a form is opened. As shown in Figure 12.27, several new properties give you more flexibility when it comes to enabling end users to edit data.

FIGURE 12.27.

A few new properties give you more control over the editing of data.

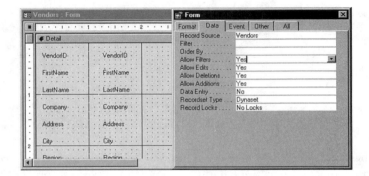

Six properties pertain to the editing of data. These properties are Allow Edits, Allow Deletions, Allow Additions, Data Entry, Recordset Type, and Record Locks:

- Allow Edits is either on or off. This property enables the user to save records when using the form. When turned off (No), it prevents the changing of any data displayed by the form.

- Allow Deletions is either on or off. When this property is set to No, the user can view and edit existing data but can't delete any records. When it's set to Yes, the user can delete records provided that the referential integrity rules aren't broken.

- Allow Additions is either Yes or No. When this is turned on (Yes), the user can add a record to the form. When it's set to No, the user can't add records. The Add Record button on the Navigation Button group isn't activated.

- Data Entry is either Yes or No. This property is different from Allow Additions in that when it's turned on, the form automatically opens to a new, blank record. The user can't view existing records. Errors will occur if Allow Additions is set to No and Data Entry is set to Yes. When this feature is set to Yes, the form must have a record source.

- Recordset Type can be set only to Dynaset, Dynaset (Inconsistent Updates), or Snapshot. It deals with the multiple tables and their fields being bound to controls on the form. The bound controls can be edited if the Recordset Type is set to Dynaset. Snapshot removes the ability of the user to edit the bound controls. This property is similar to the AllowUpdating property in Access 2.0.

- `Record Locks` deals with the multiuser application environment. It can be set only to No Locks, All Records, or Edited Records. No Locks means that two or more people can edit the same record. He who saves first, wins. All others get a message stating that the record has been changed. The only option from there is to dump the changes, overwrite the changes of the person who saved the record first, or copy a version of the changes to the Clipboard and view the saved changes. The Edited Records option enables the user to edit a record while locking out the other users. Depending on the size of the record, Access might also lock down other records stored around the edited record. This action prevents other users from editing records that aren't being used by any other user. The All Records option locks all the records in the form and their underlying tables. Only one person at a time is allowed to edit any records on the form.

Saving the Form

When it comes to forms, you can save data in several ways. Selecting File | Save is one way. Another way is to close the form. Any changes made to the design of the form will send up a flag in Access and cause the display of a message box stating that changes have been made since the last save of the form. You can then save the new changes over the old form, dump the new changes, or cancel the close process and return to the form.

Figure 12.28 shows the Vendors form. The record shown has been changed. Developers and users can tell that the record has been changed by looking at the Record Selector that appears to the left of the record. Notice the little pencil above the mouse pointer. This image indicates that the current record is in the process of being modified. The user can press Tab or Enter, and the record still shows the little pencil. Only when the focus is moved to the next record or when the form itself is closed are the changes written.

FIGURE 12.28.

The record has been changed since its last save.

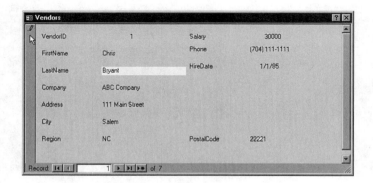

The user can save the record in the following ways:

- By using the navigation buttons at the bottom of the form
- By pressing Enter until the focus is moved to the next record
- By pressing the Page Down key (or Page Up if the record is the last in its set)
- By pressing Ctrl-End (or Ctrl-Home)
- By pressing Shift-Enter
- By closing the form
- By pressing the Record Selector button
- By pressing the Save button (if the developer has placed a Save button on the form)

Creating a Sample Form

This section covers four simple sample forms that can give any application a sophisticated look. The first form is a Splash form. This form will appear when the application is first executed.

Create a new, blank form. On that form, place an image and a label stating the name of the application. In Figure 12.29, a splash screen has been created. The logo was placed on the form using the Image button in the toolbox. The title "Vendor Software" is a label. The font and pitch have been changed. The foreground color is black; the background color and the line color have been turned transparent. This was done so that there are no lines on the splash screen. The properties for the form show that there is no record source. Turn off the Record Selectors and the navigation buttons. Make sure that the `AutoResize` and `AutoCenter` properties are set to Yes.

FIGURE 12.29.

The splash screen in Design view.

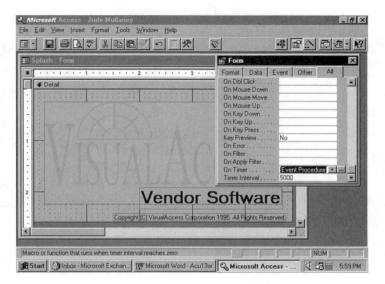

To make this perform like a real splash screen, you should set the Timer property to 5000 cycles (1 second = 1,000 cycles). After the 5 seconds have passed, the On Timer event will be fired. Now comes the VBA code that was discussed earlier. On the On Timer event, click the ellipse button (…) to activate the Code Builder. The object of the splash is to bring up the form for a few seconds and then make it go away. Enter the following code into the code section shown in Figure 12.30. The first line of code closes the splash screen, and the second line opens the Main menu form, which has yet to be created.

```
DoCmd.Close
DoCmd.OpenForm "MainMenu"
```

FIGURE 12.30.

The On Timer *event code should look like this.*

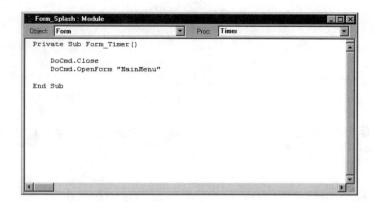

Close the form and save it as Splash.

Now for the creation of the Main menu form. Create another new, blank form. On that form, use the Label tool to create the name of the software and the Main Menu label. Use the Command Button tool to create a button that launches the Vendors form. The form should look like the one shown in Figure 12.31.

On the form's properties, notice that there is no record source. The Record Selectors and navigation buttons have also been turned off. Make sure that the AutoResize and AutoCenter properties are set to Yes. An Exit button was added that takes the user entirely out of the software. When the Vendors button is clicked, the Vendors form launches. Close the form and save it as MainMenu. Make sure that if you used a space between the two words in the preceding code, you stay consistent.

Now, to tie it all together. From the database container, open a new, blank macro. The only action to be performed in this macro is the OpenForm action. In the Action Arguments section of the OpenForm action, choose Splash from the drop-down list on the Form Name argument, as shown in Figure 12.32.

FIGURE 12.31.

The Main menu form in its raw state.

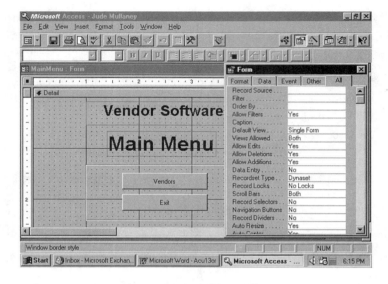

FIGURE 12.32.

The macro ties it all together.

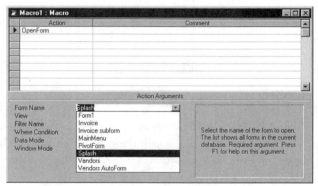

Close the macro and save it as AutoExec. AutoExec is a special, reserved word in Access, and it's the first macro launched when the software is opened. Anything in the AutoExec macro runs without the end user having to do anything until the MainMenu form appears on-screen.

Test the database by closing and reopening it. The splash screen should open first, followed by the Main menu screen. Try it.

Summary

This chapter covered the new features of the Access 95 Forms module, of which there are more than 25. It also reviewed the basics of forms. It covered the types of record sources on which forms could be based and discussed the options of not using any record source for forms. In the Auto Wizard and Form Wizard department, the many new features added to Access 95 were detailed. Opening, navigating, editing, and saving forms were also discussed. Finally, everything was pulled together through the section on sample forms, which opened a splash form, closed it, and then opened the MainMenu form. From there, an end user could immediately open the Vendors form for data entry. The following chapters delve deeper into the art of creating and customizing forms and give advanced details about controls.

Designing and Customizing Forms

by

IN THIS CHAPTER

Forms are the driving force behind an Access application. Forms enable the user to enter and view data and navigate through the application. Forms are created using the various tools that Access provides. As with all other areas of database design and implementation, Access makes the job of creating and modifying forms quick and easy. A few of the tools that Access provides are

- form wizards
- AutoForms
- form templates
- spell checking

A form can be used for data entry, data retrieval, or both. Also, all applications require some forms that are merely navigational in nature. (The Main Switchboard form in the Northwind Traders database is an example.) These allow the user to specify what step to take next, what function to perform, and so on. This type of form always requires some amount of code in order to perform its actions. Data-entry and data-retrieval forms, however, can often be built with no code modules, using the built-in functionality that Access provides.

Creating a Form and a Subform

The steps to creating a form are identical to the steps for creating a report, a table, or a query. The starting point is the Forms tab of the Database window, shown in Figure 13.1. This tab provides the same user interface as the other tabs on the Database window. A new form is created by clicking the New button. The Open button will open the form in data mode. The Design button will open the Form Design view to allow modification of the form.

FIGURE 13.1.

The Forms tab of the Database window.

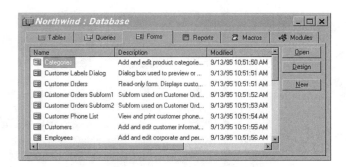

While on the Forms tab, you can right-click over a form name to use the context-sensitive pop-up menu. Here are the items on the menu when a form is selected:

- Open: Opens the form in data mode. This allows the viewing or modification of data in the underlying tables or queries.

- Design: Opens the form in Design view.
- Print: Prints the form to the default printer.
- Cut: Makes a copy of the form on the clipboard and removes it from the current database.
- Copy: Makes a copy of the form on the clipboard.
- Save as Report: Creates a report that is basically a copy of the selected form but won't allow entry of data.
- Create Shortcut: Allows you to create a Windows shortcut that, when activated, will start Access, open the current database, and open the form in data mode. The dialog that is presented when you're creating the shortcut allows you to specify a location other than the default location (the Desktop).
- Delete: Removes the selected form from the database.
- Rename: Renames the table.
- Properties: Activates the property sheet for the selected form.

As with most Windows 95 applications, a given task can be accomplished in several different ways. For instance, double-clicking a form's name opens the form in data mode. You can also change the name of a form by selecting the form's name and clicking the name again (being careful not to double-click).

The list box containing the form names can be viewed as large icons, small icons, list, or details. The form property sheet provides information on when the form was created, when it was last modified, who the owner of the form is, and whether or not the form is hidden. The property sheet also has a text box for entering a description of the form. The description and other property-sheet information is displayed when the Forms tab is in Detail view.

Subforms

A subform is a form that is displayed on another form. A form/subform combination can be thought of as a master/detail form or a parent/child form. An example of a form/subform is shown in Figure 13.2. The subform in Figure 13.2 is the grid near the bottom of the form. It has columns for Product, Unit Price, Quantity, Discount, and Extended Price. Note that subforms are often viewed in Datasheet mode, but that's not a requirement. However, the main form can't be viewed in Datasheet mode when a subform is present.

A subform is in fact a completely separate form that is embedded into another form. A subform is added to a form using the Subform/Subreport control. The subform can also be created by dragging the name of the subform from the Forms tab of the Database window onto the main form. The two forms are "linked" using the LinkChildFields and LinkMasterFields properties. The field names that are used to relate these two forms are placed in these properties. Creating and refining subforms will be covered in more detail in the next chapter.

FIGURE 13.2.

A form/subform example.

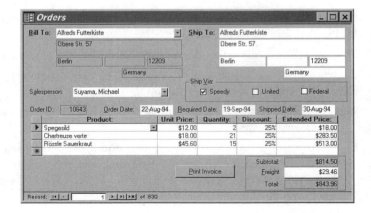

Subforms are especially effective at showing data from tables or queries participating in one-to-many relationships. For example, you could create a form with a subform to show data from an orders table and a line-items table. The main form would contain order detail information, such as customer name and address, ship-to address, shipping method, and so on. The subform would contain the items that were purchased on the order displayed in the parent form. It would contain fields such as stock number, item description, item cost, quantity, and so on.

Form Templates

As in Microsoft Word, Access uses templates when creating forms and reports without the use of a wizard. The template specifies which sections will be present and what their dimensions will be. It also specifies default property settings and controls.

Access uses the Normal template as the default. This can be changed to any existing form using the Forms/Reports tab of the Options dialog. (Choose Tools | Options.) Type the name of the form to be used as the template in the text box provided. The template information is stored in Access's workgroup information file, so the new template setting will apply to any database you open or create. You must also export or copy the template to any database you want to use them in, however. If the template form isn't present in the newly opened database, Access will fall back to using the Normal template. The template name you specified will still appear in the Options dialog even though the actual form is inaccessible.

The Form Wizard Revisited

Like tables, reports, and queries, a new form is easily created using one of the form wizards provided with Access. In the examples given in this chapter, we will use the Northwind Traders database that is provided with Microsoft Access as a sample database. If you want to follow along exactly, make sure the Northwind database is installed. (It should be in the Access\Samples directory.) However, the examples to be provided will be general enough that the steps can be applied to any database.

> ### WARNING
>
> If you intend to follow along with the examples in this chapter, you should make a backup copy of the database before proceeding.

To begin using one of the form wizards, select the Forms tab of the Database window and click the New button. The New Form dialog box, shown in Figure 13.3, is displayed.

FIGURE 13.3.

The New Form dialog box.

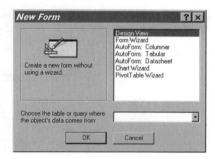

In the New Form dialog, select the Form Wizard entry in the list box. Next, select the table or query that will supply the data for the new form in the drop-down list box at the bottom of the dialog. In this example, you'll choose Products, which is a table defined in the Northwind database. After you've chosen the Products table, click OK.

> ### NOTE
>
> Although the drop-down list box can be left empty, the first screen of the Form Wizard requires the selection of a table or query to proceed. Entering it here allows the wizard to load the fields of the selected table or query and will speed navigation through the first screen of the wizard. The Wizard automatically selects the first table (alphabetically) in the database if you don't specify a table in the New Form dialog box's table/query drop-down list box.

The first dialog box of the Form Wizard is where the data fields to be used on the form are specified. Move the desired fields from the list box on the left (Available Fields) to the Selected Fields list box. This is done be either double-clicking on the field name or selecting the field and clicking the > button. You can select all the fields by clicking the >> button. If you select another table in the Tables/Queries drop-down list box, fields from another table or query can also be included on the form. This will cause the next dialog box of the wizard to prompt for information about how the data should be viewed based on the common fields chosen.

You can remove fields from the Select Fields list box in a similar manner: by double-clicking or using the < or << buttons.

For this example, we'll select the ProductName, QuantityPerUnit, UnitPrice, UnitsInStock, and UnitsOnOrder fields. The completed screen appears in Figure 13.4. Click the Next button to move on.

FIGURE 13.4.

The completed field selection.

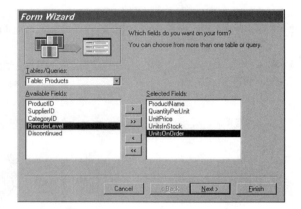

As an aside, if you selected fields from multiple tables or queries, the next dialog would prompt you for information about the structure of the form. Depending on the relationships that have been established between the tables and/or queries being used on the form being created, the wizard prompts for different information. Basically, the wizard is asking which table/query should be considered the "main" table/query (the table/query selected in the list box on the left side of the dialog box) and how the other table or query's fields should be linked to the main table/query. (See Figure 13.5.)

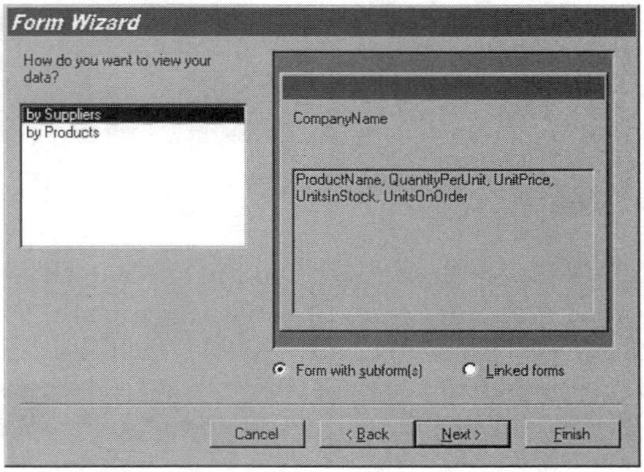

FIGURE 13.5.

The Form/Subform wizard dialog box.

The layout process is next. This dialog box of the wizard allows you to specify how the data will be presented: Columnar, Tabular, or Datasheet. By selecting each radio button, you can view a preview of the layout in the left side of the dialog box. We'll choose Tabular for our example. (See Figure 13.6.)

FIGURE 13.6.

The completed form layout.

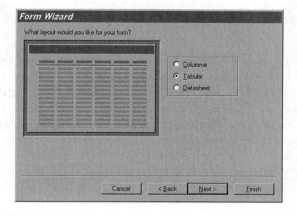

Click the Next button to proceed to style selection. Here we can choose from several predefined styles, complete with background graphics. As with the layout selection, selecting an item in the list box will display a preview of the style on the left side of the dialog box. For our example, we'll choose Colorful 2, as shown in Figure 13.7.

FIGURE 13.7.

The completed form style.

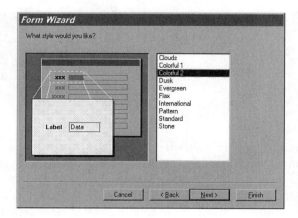

TIP

The items in the list of styles can be modified. To customize the list or change one of the styles, open a form in Design view, select Format | AutoFormat, select a format, and click the Customize button. This will enable you to delete the selected format, redefine it based on the current form, or add a new format based on the current form.

Click the Next button to move to the last dialog box of the Form Wizard, shown in Figure 13.8. Here we give a title to our new form and specify the action to be taken after the form is created. The form title defaults to the table or query name that supplies the data and will also be used as the name that appears in the Database window. However, if the default title would produce a duplicate form name, Access will append a number to the table/query name to make it unique. Change the title to Product Listing. After selecting whether you want to open the form in data mode or modify the form's design, click the Finish button to generate the new form. We'll leave the default action (Open the form to view or enter information) selected and click Finish.

FIGURE 13.8.

The final Form Wizard step.

The finished product is shown in Figure 13.9. As you can see, this form probably needs to have its column widths modified so that all of the caption text appears. This type of modification will be covered in a subsequent section of this chapter. For now, just poke around the form we've created to get a feel for how forms work. Better yet, run through the Form Wizard again, selecting different layouts or styles to see how these affect the final form.

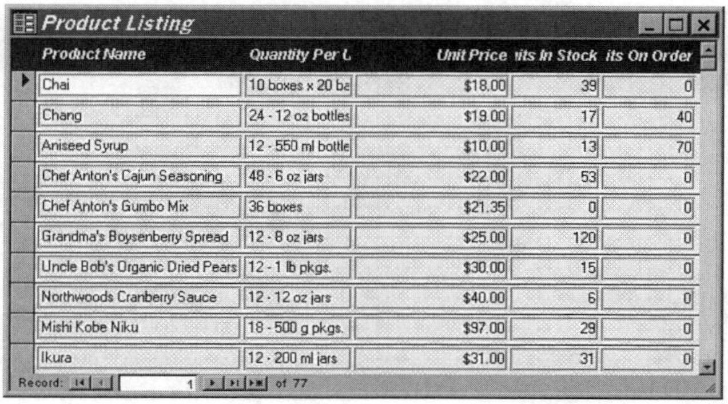

FIGURE 13.9.

The finished Product Listing form.

Using the AutoForms

Another quick way to create a new form is to use one of the AutoForms provided by Access. As shown in Figure 13.3, three different AutoForms are available:

- Columnar: This form will display data in a single column with the field names to the left of the data. A record selector is placed at the bottom of the form to allow scrolling through the records in the table or query. Figure 13.10 shows a Columnar AutoForm created by specifying the Customers table in the New Form dialog box.

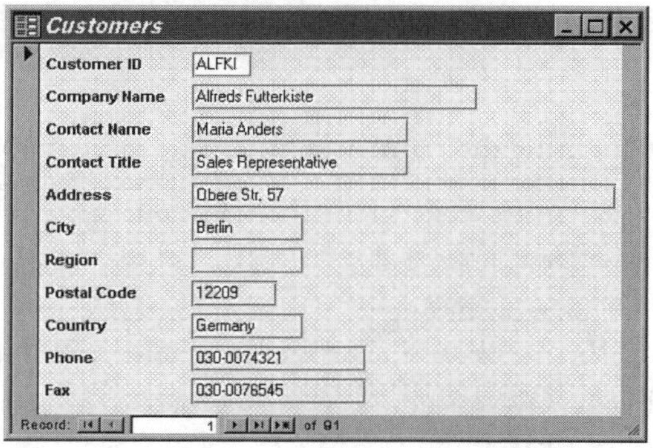

FIGURE 13.10.

A form created using the Columnar AutoForm.

- Tabular: This form will display each field in its own column and each record in its own row, as shown in Figure 13.11.
- Datasheet: This form displays all fields in the table or query in a Datasheet view, as shown in Figure 13.12.

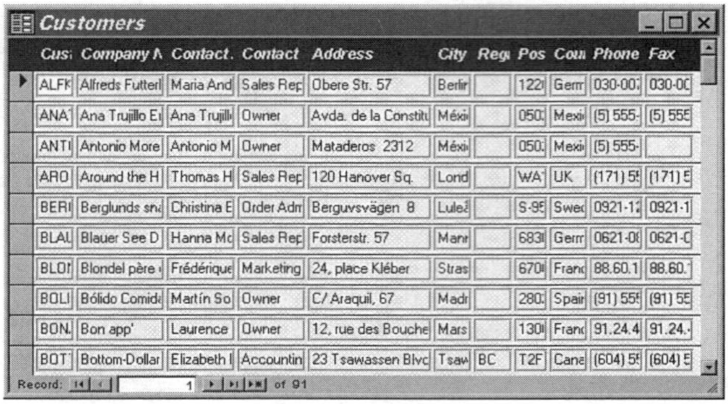

FIGURE 13.11.

A form created using the Tabular AutoForm.

FIGURE 13.12.

A form created using the Datasheet AutoForm.

The steps for using the AutoForm feature are quite simple:

1. On the Forms tab, click the New button.
2. On the New Form dialog, select one of the AutoForms.
3. Select the table or query to be used for the form. One must be selected to continue using the AutoForms. The form generated will be based on this table only.
4. Click the OK button. Access will generate the form and display it in Form view. (See Figures 13.10 through 13.12.)
5. The form can now be modified in Design view if desired.
6. The form hasn't yet been saved. Click the Save toolbar button if you wish to save the form. Otherwise, simply close the form and answer No when Access prompts you about saving the form.

About the Toolbox

Every item appearing on a form is a control of some sort. Controls are added to a form in Design view using the Toolbox. Figure 13.13 shows the Toolbox and lists the function of each button. To display or hide the Toolbox, select View | Toolbox or click the Toolbox button on the toolbar (it's the one with the hammer and wrench). Access can display a tooltip giving the type of control or setting each button represents. To view the tooltip for a button on the toolbox, let the mouse rest over the button for a few seconds.

FIGURE 13.13.

The Form Design Toolbox explained.

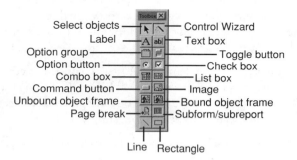

Most of the buttons on the Toolbox represent controls that can be added to a form. The top two items, however, are special. You can restore the selection arrow by clicking the button with the arrow on the top left. Restoring the selection arrow is necessary if you have selected a control and then decided not to place it on the form. The Control Wizard is turned on and off using the Control Wizard button on the top right. (Control wizards will be discussed later.)

Adding Controls to a Form

To add a control to a form, click the Toolbox button for the desired control. The button will change to its pressed state and the cursor will change to resemble the button you just pressed. Move the mouse onto the form, press the left mouse button where you want the control located, then drag the mouse to size the control. To cancel this operation, press the Esc key either before you press the mouse button or before you release it. You can also add a control simply by clicking on the form. The control will be added using a default size.

If you want to add several controls of the same type to a form, you can "lock down" the Toolbox button by double-clicking it. This will allow you to add several labels to the form without having to reselect the label tool each time. To release the lock, either click the button again, press the Esc key, or select a different tool (other than the Control Wizard) from the toolbox.

If the Control Wizard is active, adding a control with an associated Control Wizard will cause that wizard to be activated.

To make a copy of a selected control (or group of selected controls), select Edit | Duplicate. Access will create a duplicate of the selected control(s) directly below the selected control(s). You can also use the Edit | Copy (Ctrl-C) and Edit | Paste (Ctrl-V) menu options. This is handy if you prefer to use the keyboard instead of the mouse to access the menu. Most of the properties, including the all-important Control Source, will be copied to the new control. The name will be changed, however, because Access doesn't allow for duplicate control names on a form.

There are several ways to select a group of controls. The first is to "lasso" the desired controls. To do this, press and hold the left mouse button in an unused portion of the form. Drag the cursor in any direction. A rectangle is shown with one corner where you pressed the button and the other corner at the current location of the cursor. Use this method to surround the controls you want to select. When the controls are selected, release the mouse button.

The second method complements the first. To use this method, position the cursor over a control and Shift-click (hold down the Shift key while clicking the left mouse button). This toggles the selection state of the control. If you have previously selected a control with the lasso technique and don't want it to be selected, simply Shift-click to deselect it.

Sometimes you'll need to cancel a selection action. To do so, simply click an empty area of the form. Now there are no controls selected.

> **WARNING**
>
> The Control Wizard won't be activated when you're creating a duplicate. Also, any code associated with a control won't be copied to the new control.

Types of Controls

An Access form can contain one of three types of controls: bound, unbound, and calculated. The differences between these types will be discussed in this section.

Unbound Controls

An unbound control is used to convey information to the user or to receive input from the user that won't be stored in the database. Here are some examples of using unbound controls:

■ A label for a text box is used to describe what the text box represents.

■ Text boxes or drop-down list boxes can be used to select different scenarios on a what-if form.

■ A line can be placed on a form to separate different sections of the form.

■ A company logo can be placed on the form to add graphical effects.

When a control is added using the Toolbox and no Control Wizard is activated, the control will automatically be unbound.

Bound Controls

Bound controls are used to display and edit data from the database. The term "bound" refers to the fact that the control is tied to a field of a table, query, or SQL SELECT statement. The most common type of bound control is the text box, but nearly any control can be a bound control (with the exception of lines, rectangles, page breaks, command buttons, image frames, and labels).

When a bound control is added to a form, it will default to the control specified in the DisplayControl property for the field to which it's bound. This can be changed after the control is added by using the Change To feature, discussed in the section titled "Changing a Control to Another Type."

A bound control will inherit many of the formatting and text properties defined for the field to which it's bound (Caption, Description, Input Mask). These properties can be changed on the form using the control's property sheet.

To add a bound control to the form, the Field List must be visible. You can turn the Field List on and off using View | Field List (or using the Field List toolbar button, which is to the left of the Toolbox button and looks like a single piece of lined paper). The steps are as follows:

1. Select a single field, a group of fields (using Ctrl-Shift-click), or all fields (by double-clicking the title bar of the Field List window).

2. Drag the mouse from the Field List to the form. The cursor will change to a small box (or group of boxes if more than one field is selected). Place the upper-left corner of the box where the upper-left corner of the first bound control should be placed.

3. The control(s) will be placed on the form and a label will be placed to the left of each control. The text of the label will be the Caption property for the field to which the control is bound.

You can also change an unbound control to a bound control using the control's ControlSource property. Doing so, however, won't cause the control to inherit many of the field's properties (except for ValidationRule, ValidationText, and DefaultValue, which are always enforced for the field).

Calculated Controls

Calculated controls use expressions to derive their data. Expressions are combinations of operators, fields, control names, functions, and constants. Although text boxes are the most common form of calculated control, any control having the ControlSource property can be a calculated control. For example, a calculated control can be used to compute sales tax on an order entry form.

All expressions must begin with an equals sign. A sample expression is

```
=[OrderForm]![SalesTaxRate]*[OrderForm]![OrderTotal]
```

The `[OrderForm]![SalesTaxRate]` part refers to a control named SalesTaxRate on the form named OrderForm. `[OrderForm]![OrderTotal]` refers to the control named OrderTotal on the same form. A control with this expression in its `ControlSource` property will display the value of the order total multiplied by the applicable sales tax.

To create a calculated control while in Design view, follow these steps:

1. Select the type of control to be used from the Toolbox and position the control on the form. (See the section titled "Adding Controls to a Form" earlier in this chapter.)

2. Enter the expression using one of the following methods:

   ■ If the control is a text box, the expression can be entered directly into the control. Click inside the text-box portion until the blinking edit cursor is visible. Type the expression into the edit box.

   ■ If the control isn't a text box or if you don't want to enter the expression directly, double-click the control to open its property sheet. Move to the `ControlSource` property. Here you can enter the expression as text or use the Expression Builder. (Click the Build button to the right of the ControlSource text box.) The Expression Builder, shown in Figure 13.14, is an extremely useful tool for creating expressions because it allows you to browse all the objects in the database, including controls from other forms, fields from queries, and built-in functions.

FIGURE 13.14.

The Expression Builder in action.

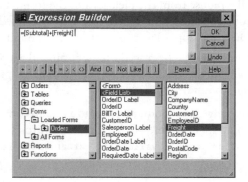

TIP

If you're typing in the `ControlSource` property and need a larger text box, Access provides a Zoom box that you can activate by pressing Shift-F2.

Of Combo Boxes, List Boxes, and Option Groups

Combo boxes, list boxes, and option groups make up a group of controls which make the use of the Control Wizard extremely helpful. If the Control Wizard feature is enabled (the Control Wizard button of the Toolbox is depressed), adding one of these controls to a form will cause the Control Wizard to activate. The wizards for the combo box and list box are very similar and will be dealt with together.

To follow along with the forthcoming examples, create a new form by selecting Design view and the Orders table on the New Form dialog.

The Combo Box and List Box Wizards

These wizards allow you to easily bind a combo box or list box to another table or query in the database. The steps followed in the wizard are similar to the steps followed when using the Lookup Wizard for a table field. In this example, we'll create a new customer-name field on a form based on the Orders table of the Northwind database.

In the Forms tab of the Database window, click the New button. Select Orders from the drop-down list box of the New Form dialog. Leave Design View selected in the list box at the top and click OK.

Make sure that the Toolbox is visible and that the Control Wizard feature is enabled (the rightmost button in the top row of the Toolbox should be depressed). Click the combo box button on the Toolbox (see Figure 13.13) and place a combo box on a blank form. The Combo Box Wizard activates, as shown in Figure 13.15.

FIGURE 13.15.

The initial dialog box of the Combo Box Wizard.

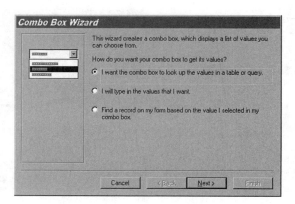

The three options will determine how the combo box relates to the Orders table. Since we're adding a combo box that will allow the user to select a customer name, we'll choose the first option ("I want the combo box to look up the values in a table or query"). If we were adding a control to allow the user to select an order from all of the orders currently in the database, we'd choose the third option. If we wanted to enter a predefined set of values from which the user could choose, we would choose the second option. Leave the first option selected and click the Next button.

As shown in Figure 13.16, this dialog box of the wizard is where we'll choose the data source. The data source will be the table or query that provides the list of data to be displayed in the combo box. Choose Customers and click Next.

FIGURE 13.16.

The table/query selection.

The next dialog box is where we'll choose which fields should be included in our combo box. Because we'll be using the combo box to pick a CustomerID for an Orders record, we need to choose not only the CompanyName field but also the CustomerID field. The completed dialog box is shown in Figure 13.17. Select the fields shown and click Next.

FIGURE 13.17.

The field-selection step.

The next dialog box, shown in Figure 13.18, enables us to define how the columns will look in the combo box. Note the Hide key column check box. Because we chose the Customers table and the CustomerID field, and because the Orders and Customers tables are related via this field, the wizard is smart enough to assume we want to use this field as the key field for the combo box. Unchecking the AutoLookup combo box will cause the CustomerID column to be displayed as well. We'll leave Hide key column enabled. We'll also leave the column width as is and click Next.

FIGURE 13.18.

The column format step.

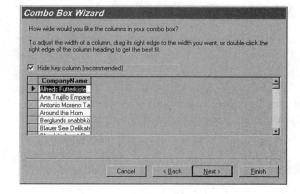

In the next dialog, we'll specify how the data that the user enters is stored. As shown in Figure 13.19, Access can either remember the value for later use or store that value in this field. Because the combo box in this example specifies a customer for an order record, we'll select the second option. In the drop-down list box, select the CustomerID field. Click Next.

FIGURE 13.19.

Specifying what to do with the combo box value.

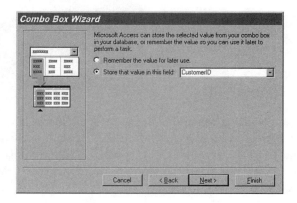

The final dialog box lets us specify the label text for the label to be placed next to the new combo box. Replace the default text with Customer. Click Finish to close the wizard and create the control.

Finally, switch to Form view and cycle through the records using the record selector at the bottom of the form. The text in the combo box will change. You can change the customer associated with an order by using the drop-down of the new combo box and selecting a new customer. Because of the way this control was created, if you enter text into the edit box that isn't a valid CompanyName, you'll get a validation message stating that you must choose an item that is in the list. This way a customer must appear in the Customers table before it can have an Orders record.

The Options Group Wizard

To create an example for the Options Group Wizard, we need to add a field to the Orders table. This field will specify an order type. Close the form created earlier (don't worry about saving it; we can just use a new form for this example). Open the Orders table in Design view. Add a field to the bottom of the field list called OrderType. Make it a Number field with a field size of Integer. Leave all other properties at the default values. Close the Table Design window and click Yes when Access prompts you about saving the modified table.

Create a new form, again using Design view and the Orders table on the New Form dialog. Make sure that the Toolbox is visible and that the Control Wizard feature is enabled. Click the option group button on the Toolbox (see Figure 13.13) and place an option group on the form. The Option Group Wizard activates, as shown in Figure 13.20.

FIGURE 13.20.

The initial dialog box of Option Group Wizard.

In the initial dialog box of the wizard, we'll specify the labels to be used in the option group. We'll track two types of orders: wholesale and retail. Although only one row is shown in the grid initially, another will be added when you begin typing in the top row. Enter Wholesale on the top row. Press the Tab key to move to the second row. Enter Retail. Click the Next button.

The next dialog allows us to specify whether we want a default and, if so, which option item to use. We'll choose Retail as our default and click Next.

The next dialog, shown in Figure 13.21, is where values are stored in the table. The wizard chooses the default values as integers, but we can enter whatever values make sense here (as long as they're valid for the data type of the field to which this option group will be linked). We'll leave the default values intact. Click the Next button.

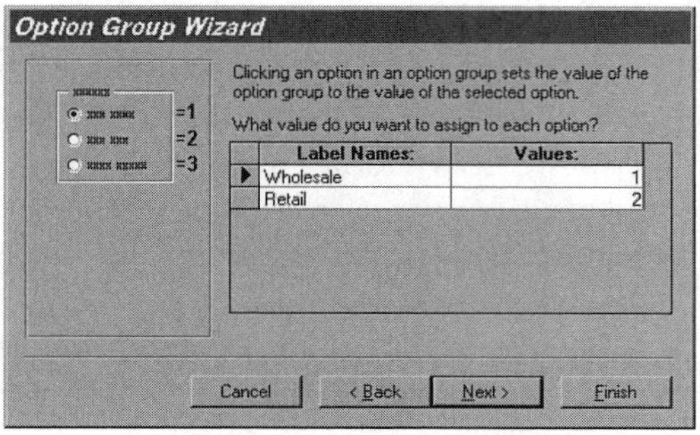

FIGURE 13.21.

The values selection.

This dialog box, shown in Figure 13.22, is where we specify if we want to tie the option-group value to a table field, and if so, which field. We're doing an order-type option group, so we'll choose the OrderType field and click Next.

FIGURE 13.22.

The option-group value selection.

The next dialog box is where we set the type of control to be used for the user interface, as well as the style to display the option group with. Selecting different options will change the preview shown on the left side of the dialog box, enabling you to see the effect of the different options. We'll leave the defaults as they are, and click Next.

Finally we've reached the last screen. Enter a caption (such as Order Type) for the option-groups frame and click Finish. Switch to Form view and play with the option group, and navigate the orders record using the record selector at the bottom of the form.

Inheriting and Overriding Table Properties

As mentioned in the section covering bound controls, many of the properties of a field are carried over into a form control to which the field is bound (as long as the control was created by dragging from the Field List window). An example of this is the InputMask property. When a field has its InputMask property set, any bound text box created using the field will have an identical InputMask property. Table 13.1 illustrates the various inherited properties for different control types.

The control properties can be modified once the bound control is created. You do this using the control's property sheet. Changing these inherited properties on a form won't affect the field's properties. Likewise, changing the field's properties won't affect those inherited properties on any previously created forms. It's best to set the properties on the fields before creating forms. This will make it easier to create a consistent look and feel throughout the forms—not to mention the time savings gained by having all those properties set automatically.

Table 13.1. Inherited properties for various bound control types.

Bound Control	Properties Inherited
Text box	Format, DecimalPlaces, InputMask, StatusBarText (field's description property)
Combo box, list box	All field properties from the Lookup Tab in the Table Design view, StatusBarText (field's description property)
Check box, option button, option group, toggle button, bound object frame	StatusBarText (field's description property)

Modifying Default Properties

Every control has a default control style. The default control style specifies the default properties for new controls added to a form. For instance, the TextAlign property has a default value of General. It's possible to change this default to a different setting by modifying the default control style. This feature can save hours of work when designing forms, because you can decide on the look to be presented, modify the default control style so that the control properties reflect that look, and then add controls to the form. This saves having to modify each control's properties to match the desired look.

Follow these steps to modify the default control style for a control:

1. In the Form Design view, click the button on the Toolbox for the control you wish to modify.
2. Open the property sheet by using the property-sheet toolbar button or by selecting View | Properties. The Property Sheet window's caption should read "Default *x*," where *x* is the type of control whose default properties are being modified.
3. Modify the properties to match your desired set of defaults.

These changes will affect only new controls added to the form, not existing controls.

Formatting Data in Controls

Data presented on a form can be formatted in a multitude of ways. The Format property is one of the properties that a bound control inherits from the field to which it's bound. However, the formatting information can be modified on the control's property sheet.

The *Format* Property

The main formatting property is the Format property. Access has many built-in formats that you can access by using the drop-down list of the Format property's text box. The list will show valid formats for the data type of the field to which a control is bound or all formats for an unbound control. The built-in formats are as follows:

- General Number: Displays a number as entered.
- Currency: Displays a number using the currency symbol, the thousands separator, and parentheses for negative numbers. The DecimalPlaces property is set to 2.
- Fixed: Displays at least one digit. The DecimalPlaces property is set to 2.
- Standard: Use the thousand separator. The DecimalPlaces property is set to 2.
- Percent: Displays the value multiplied by 100. Displays a percent sign. The DecimalPlaces property is set to 2.
- Scientific: Displays a number using standard scientific notation.
- General Date: This setting is a combination of the Short Date and the Long Time settings.
- Long Date: Same as the Long Date setting in the Regional Settings section of the Windows Control Panel.
- Medium Date: Displays as *dd-mmm-yy,* where *dd* is the day of the month, *mmm* is a three-letter abbreviation for the month, and *yy* is the year (without the century).
- Short Date: Same as the Short Date setting in the Regional Settings section of the Windows Control Panel.
- Long Time: Same as the Time setting in the Regional Settings section of the Windows Control Panel.
- Medium Time: Displays the time as *hh:mm AM/PM.*
- Short Time: Displays the time in 24-hour format.
- Yes/No data types: These can be displayed as Yes/No, True/False, or On/Off.

In addition to these built-in formats, you can also specify a custom format using a variety of formatting characters. The Format property for text and memo fields can contain three sections, separated by a semicolon. The first section is used for fields with text, the second for fields with a zero-length string, and the third for strings with null values. This third section is useful if you want to have some default text when nothing is entered in the field. Likewise, for numeric data, the Format property can have four sections: the first for positive numbers, the second for negative, the third for fields with a value of zero, and the fourth for fields with null values.

As an example, let's look at a text box that is tied to the Freight field of the Orders table. We'll use the following for the Format property: `$#,##0.00;;"(n/c)";"(n/c)"`. The first section is the standard currency format and is for values greater than zero. The second section isn't specified, but we'll assume that there is no possibility for a negative freight charge. The last two sections specify that if the value is zero or if no data is entered, `(n/c)` should be displayed in the text box. If you also added a calculated control that used the Freight control as part of its expression, the text displayed wouldn't affect the outcome of the expression: the value of 0 or NULL would still be used in the calculation.

The *DecimalPlaces* Property

This property specifies the number of digits to appear to the right of the decimal point for numeric fields. The default setting is Auto, which means that the number appears as specified in the Format property. The property can also be set to an integer value from 0 to 15. Note that the property has no effect if the Format property is set to General Number. Also, if the Format property is blank, Access uses the General Number format.

The *InputMask* Property

The InputMask property allows you to specify how data is input into a control. Use the InputMask property to display literal characters in the field with blanks to fill in. For example, you could create an input mask for a Phone Number field that specifies exactly how to enter a new number: *(000) 000-0000*. This would specify that digits 0 through 9 must be entered at the places indicated by the *0*. The *(,)*, and *-* characters are literals that will be placed in the field to aid in entry.

If you define both a display format and an input mask for a field, Access uses the input mask when you're adding or editing data, and the Format setting determines how the data is displayed when the record is saved. When using both the Format and InputMask properties, be careful that their results don't conflict with each other.

The InputMask property has a wizard to assist in creating an input mask. The wizard allows you to test out the mask before applying the mask to the control.

Aligning and Sizing Controls and Control Placement

Access provides a treasure chest of tools to align and size controls in Form Design view. After controls are added to a form, it's necessary to align and size them to present a readable, usable form for both data display and entry. Access provides several tools to help the form designer lay out the controls in such a manner.

Control Alignment and Placement

The most obvious tool is the alignment grid. This is a grid that is displayed as dots when the form is in Design view. You can turn the grid on and off using View | Grid. To change the grid's spacing, change the form's GridX and GridY properties by double-clicking the form selector in the upper-left corner of the form to access the form's property sheet.

One way the grid is useful when adding controls to a form is evident when you use the Snap To Grid feature. This causes Access to place controls on the nearest grid point when one is placed on the form. Also, when moving or sizing controls, Access will snap to the nearest grid point. This feature is enabled or disabled using Format | Snap To Grid (in Design view).

If some controls aren't aligned to the grid, they can be placed at the nearest grid point. To accomplish this, select a control and then select Format | Align | To Grid. This will move the control to the nearest grid point.

In addition to using the grid for alignment, Access also allows you to align a group of controls using a common side. For example, a group of controls can have their left sides all on the same vertical line. To do this, select a group of controls (by lassoing them or by individually selecting them by Shift-clicking on each control to be included in the group), and then select Format | Align | Left, Right, Top, or Bottom (depending on which side you would like aligned).

> **NOTE**
>
> If any of the selected controls would overlap after being aligned, Access won't overlap them. Instead, the controls will be placed with their edges next to each other.

You can change the horizontal or vertical spacing among a group of controls by using Format | Horizontal Spacing and Format | Vertical Spacing. These items are available only when a group of controls is selected. Select at least three controls. To make the distance between the tops and bottoms of these controls evenly spaced, select Format | Vertical Spacing | Make Equal. The middle controls will move to make the spacing even. The top and bottom controls will stay in their original positions. To increase or decrease the vertical distance between each of the controls, select Format | Vertical Spacing | Increase or Format | Vertical Spacing | Decrease. The Horizontal Spacing menu options work in the same way but affect the distances between the left and right edges of controls.

Sizing Controls

The Format menu also contains a Size submenu, which aids in sizing controls. The first item on the Size submenu, To Fit, sizes a control or group of controls so that all the data in the control is visible. This is useful for a label if you increase the length of the label's caption. The second item, To Grid, is similar to the Align To Grid menu discussed earlier. When used, this menu item causes Access to size the selected control or group of controls with the nearest grid points.

The next four items on the Size submenu are active only when multiple controls are selected. The first item, To Tallest, sizes all the controls to be as tall as the tallest selected control. The next item, To Shortest, sizes all the controls to be as short as the shortest selected control. Next, To Widest sizes all the controls to be as wide as the widest selected control. Finally, To Narrowest makes the controls as narrow as the narrowest selected control.

Using the AutoFormat Feature

Access comes with some predefined form styles that enable you to modify the look of an existing form. You can also create one of the AutoFormats from any existing forms, allowing you to maintain the same look and feel throughout the database. AutoFormat can be used to change the look of your whole form or just selected controls.

To modify a form, select Format | AutoFormat. Selecting this item opens the AutoFormat dialog, shown in Figure 13.23.

FIGURE 13.23.

The AutoFormat dialog.

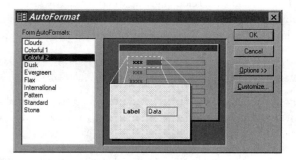

The list box on the left side of the dialog box displays all available formats. As an item is selected, the preview box on the right side changes to show what the form will look like if that format is selected. Select an AutoFormat and click OK to apply it to the current form. To cancel the AutoFormat, click the Cancel button.

The Styles To Apply check boxes at the bottom of the dialog are accessed using the Options button. These will affect which properties are modified when the format is applied to the form. Select only those styles that you want to be modified.

To add a new AutoFormat, modify the selected AutoFormat, or delete the selected AutoFormat, click the Customize button. The Customize AutoFormat dialog box appears. The dialog allows three choices: create a new AutoFormat based on the current form, update the selected

AutoFormat with values from the current form, or delete the selected AutoFormat. Note that if you create a new AutoFormat or modify the selected AutoFormat, only those properties belonging to the selected Styles To Apply check boxes will be used. Select one of the options and click OK or Cancel to cancel the dialog.

Alignment, Colors, Borders, and Effects

Access provides control properties that affect virtually every characteristic of how data in the control is displayed. The following sections discuss some of these properties in detail. One of the keys to designing a readable form is using graphical properties consistently. This section will discuss text alignment, colors, borders, and graphical effects.

Alignment

The TextAlign property of a control affects how the text (whether it is characters or numbers) is aligned in the control. Although there is no real guideline stating that all form labels must be left-aligned and all text boxes must be right-aligned, it's important to keep all the forms within a database consistent.

There are four choices for the TextAlign property:

- General: Text is aligned left. Numeric data and dates align to the right.
- Left: Text aligns to the left.
- Center: Text is centered.
- Right: Text aligns to the right.

To change the TextAlign property, select the control to be modified and double-click to bring up the property sheet. The TextAlign property is on the Format tab. You can also use the alignment buttons of the Formatting toolbar (discussed later) to quickly change the TextAlign property. The default setting is General (unless the default has been modified).

Colors

Colors used on a form make the form easier to understand and read. One good use of color on a data entry form is to distinguish fields that require values to be entered before a record can be saved. Typically, either the data-entry control itself will have its BackColor property modified or the label attached to the control will have a different ForeColor property than the rest of the labels on the form. The default colors match those of the system colors (unless the default control style has been modified).

Access provides a Color Builder dialog box that you can use when you're modifying the color properties (see Figure 13.24). This dialog enables you to choose the value by viewing colored boxes. If you were to use the text box for a color property on the property sheet, you'd need to know the long integer representation of the color you wanted. To use this dialog, click the builder button to the right of a color property's text box on a control's property sheet. On the Color Builder dialog, select the color to be used and click OK. You can also create custom colors by using the Define Custom Colors button.

FIGURE 13.24.

The Color Builder dialog.

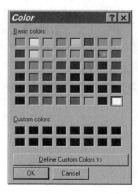

The following properties are provided to control how color is used on a form:

- BackColor: Specifies the color for the interior of a control or form section.
- ForeColor: Specifies the color for the text of a control.
- BorderColor: Specifies the color of a control's border.

Borders

Several properties affect the borders of controls and forms. These are BorderStyle, BorderWidth, and BorderColor (discussed earlier).

The BorderStyle property sets the type of border to be used for a control. For a form, this property sets the type of border and border elements (title bar, Control menu, Minimize and Maximize buttons) to use for the form. The BorderStyle property as it relates to forms will be discussed in the following chapter.

For controls, the BorderStyle property has the following settings:

- Transparent: The border is transparent.
- Solid: A solid line.
- Dashes: A dashed line.
- Short Dashes: A dashed line with short dashes.
- Dots: A dotted line.
- Sparse Dots: A dotted line with widely spaced dots.
- Dash Dot: A line with a dash-dot combination.
- Dash Dot Dot: A line with a dash-dot-dot combination.

The `BorderWidth` property is an integer property that specifies the width of a control's border. The settings range from 0 to 6. A setting of zero specifies the narrowest possible border. The `SpecialEffect` property (discussed forthwith) must be set to Flat or Shadowed, and the `BorderStyle` must be set to something other than Transparent in order for this property to have any effect.

Effects

The `SpecialEffect` property for a control or form section enables you to specify how the control or section appears. Setting this property will affect the `BorderStyle`, `BorderColor`, and `BorderWidth` properties. (For instance, if the property is set to Raised, the settings of the `BorderStyle`, `BorderColor`, and `BorderWidth` properties are ignored.)

Here are the available settings for the `SpecialEffect` property:

- Flat: This is the default setting. Controls appear flat and use the system colors or any colors specified by the color properties.
- Raised: The control has a highlight on the top and left and a shadow on the bottom and right.
- Sunken: The control has a shadow on the top and left and a highlight on the bottom and right.
- Etched: A sunken line surrounds the control.
- Shadow: The control has a shadow on its bottom and right sides.
- Chiseled: The control has a sunken line below it.

Changing Text Fonts and Sizes

Another set of properties that need to remain consistent throughout the database are the font properties. Also, special fields or labels can be denoted by different font sizes or by the use of italics, for example. Typically, form headers have larger font sizes than the data fields.

The font properties are `FontName`, `FontSize`, `FontWeight`, `FontItalic`, and `FontUnderline`. These properties are set either using a control's property sheet or the Formatting toolbar.

The `FontName` property lets you set the font used to display text to any font installed on your system. If the `FontName` property is set to a font that isn't on the system, Windows will substitute a similar font. If you choose a TrueType font, the text will appear the same on screen and when printed.

The `FontSize` property specifies the point size of the font. For all controls except command buttons, the default `FontSize` is 8. Command buttons have a default `FontSize` of 10. The `FontSize` property text box has a drop-down that allows you to choose values from the list. However, you can also type into the text box to set a `FontSize` to a value not on the list. Be careful when setting `FontSize` to make sure the text will display properly on all possible screen resolutions. If you are using a font that isn't a TrueType font and you modify the value to be less than the minimum size for the font, it will still display using the minimum size. Also, using such a font might not produce the easiest-to-read output on all possible devices, especially if you modify the `FontSize` property.

The `FontWeight` property enables you to specify the thickness of the characters that Windows uses to display the text. The possible values are Thin, Extra Light, Light, Normal, Medium, Semi-bold, Bold, Extra bold, and Heavy. The text may appear different between the screen and its printed version, depending on the display and printer being used.

The last two properties, `FontItalic` and `FontUnderline`, are Boolean properties (that is, they have values of Yes or No). To make the text appear in italics, set `FontItalic` to Yes. To underline the text, set `FontUnderline` to Yes.

If you change any of the font properties and wish to resize the control to fit the new settings, select Format | Size | To Fit.

About the Formatting Toolbar

In addition to letting you set control properties with the property sheet, Access provides a very useful Formatting toolbar. The Formatting toolbar gives you easy point-and-click access to most of the format properties for a control. Figure 13.25 shows the standard Formatting toolbar and its various components. The buttons appearing on the toolbar can be modified using the Customize Toolbars feature. You can remove a button from the toolbar by simply dragging it off of the toolbar onto the Access main window.

FIGURE 13.25.

The standard Formatting toolbar.

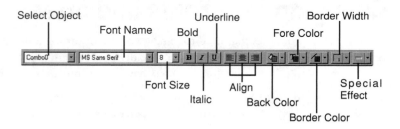

Moving from left to right, the components of the standard Formatting toolbar are as follows:

- Select Object: This drop-down allows you to select a control or section by picking its name from the list of controls and form sections.
- Font Name: This drop-down contains a list of possible fonts. To change the font assigned to a control, simply select another font from the drop-down list.
- Font Size: Changes the `FontSize` property of the selected control.

- Bold, Italic, and Underline buttons: You set the font to the respective style by pressing the button. The button stays pressed until it's pressed again. The Bold button changes the control's FontWeight property to Bold.

- Text Alignment Buttons: Sets the TextAlign property to (from left to right) Left, Center, or Right.

- Back Color drop-down: Use the small color dialog displayed when clicking the drop-down arrow to set the control's BackColor property.

- Fore Color drop-down: Same as the Back Color drop-down, except it sets the ForeColor property.

- Border Color drop-down: Same as Back Color drop-down, except it sets the BorderColor property.

- Border Width drop-down: The drop-down graphically displays the possible BorderWidth settings. Click on the desired width to set the control's BorderWidth property.

- Special Effect drop-down: The drop-down shows the possible settings for the SpecialEffect property. Click on the desired effect to set the control's SpecialEffect property.

Copying Formatting Properties Between Controls

Access provides a handy feature called the Format Painter, which allows you to copy formatting properties from one control to another. The Format Painter button is on the standard toolbar between the Paste and Undo buttons. Its icon is a paintbrush.

To copy the formatting information from a selected control to another control, click the Format Painter button. Then click the control to which you want to copy the information. If you want to copy the same formatting information to many controls, double-click the Format Painter icon. It will stay pressed, and Access will continue to copy formatting information to any control clicked until you click the button again or press the Esc key.

The following properties will be copied if they're valid for both the source and destination controls:

BackColor	FontName	LabelX
BackStyle	FontSize	LabelY
BorderColor	FontUnderline	LineSlant
BorderStyle	FontWeight	SpecialEffect
BorderWidth	ForeColor	TextAlign
DisplayWhen	LabelAlign	Visible
FontItalic		

Changing a Control to Another Type

As you're designing forms, it's often necessary to change a control to another type. For instance, suppose you have a text box on a form but you realize a drop-down list box would better serve the user. The drop-down list would contain commonly used values, for instance. You could delete the text box, add a combo box, and then go through all the trouble of setting the new control's properties to match the look of the form. However, Access has a more efficient method.

If you need to change a control to another type, you don't need to delete the control and start over. Select the control you want to change and then select Format | Change To. Select the type of control you want to change it to. Access copies the appropriate properties from one control to the other.

Adding Shapes and Lines to Forms

Forms don't have to contain only data and labels. You can make forms more readable by breaking up sections using shapes and lines. To add a shape or line to a form, select the desired control on the Toolbox and draw it onto the form.

The Line control has the following format properties affecting its display (these were discussed earlier): SpecialEffect, BorderStyle, BorderColor, and BorderWidth.

The Rectangle control has the same formatting properties as the line control. It also has the BackColor property, which specifies the color with which the rectangle is filled.

Adding Graphics to a Form

Graphics are another means of creating an impact or drawing attention to a form. Access supports two methods for adding graphics to a form.

The first method is to add a background picture to the form. To add a background picture, follow these steps:

1. In Form Design view, open the form's property sheet either by selecting the form on the Select Object drop-down of the Formatting toolbar or by double-clicking the form selector (the small etched box to the left of the ruler at the top of the Form Design view window).

2. Select the Picture property and use the Picture Builder to open a picture file. (The Picture Builder is accessed using the button to the right of the Picture property's text box.)

3. Use the PictureAlignment property to specify the location of the picture on the form.

4. Set the PictureTiling property to determine whether the picture is repeated across the form.

5. Set the `SizeMode` property according on how you want the picture to be proportioned. Here are the possible settings:

- Clip: The picture is actual size. If the picture is larger than the form, the image is cut off.

- Stretch: The picture is sized to fit within the form and may be distorted.

- Zoom: The whole picture is displayed after it's sized to fit either the height or width of the form. The picture won't be distorted.

The other method of adding a graphic to a form is to use the image control. This method allows you to place many graphics on the form and position them wherever you desire. Add the image control from the Toolbox or choose Insert | Picture, and Access will pop up the Picture Builder dialog. The other picture properties are identical to those described earlier.

To remove the picture from either the form background or an image control, select the `Picture` property on the appropriate property sheet, highlight the text in the edit box, and press the Delete key. The text should change to "(none)," and the picture will be blank.

Adding Charts to a Form

As with most aspects of form design, Access provides a Chart Wizard to assist in adding charts to a form. Charts display data in a graphical format. They often make visualizing the impact of a set of data easier for the user. As we'll see in the following steps, the most difficult part about adding a chart to a form is designing the query that will provide the data. Access uses the Microsoft Chart OLE server as its charting and graphing engine, so make sure this is installed on your system before continuing. Figure 13.26 shows the form we'll create in this section. (Many of the steps required to create this form are beyond the scope of this chapter, however, and won't be discussed in detail.)

FIGURE 13.26.

The Completed Chart form.

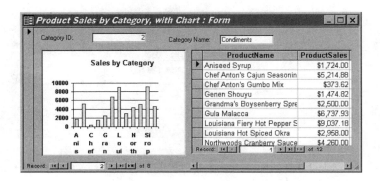

Figure 13.26 shows a form with a Sales by Category chart and a subform listing products and product sales. The chart and the subform display the same data. The subform is used to present precise information to the person who is viewing the form.

To create the form shown in Figure 13.26, follow these steps:

1. In the Forms tab of the Database window, click New. Select Categories in the drop-down list at the bottom of the dialog. Leave Design View selected in the list box at the top of the dialog. Click OK.

2. Display the Field List if it isn't displayed. Add bound text boxes for CategoryID and CategoryName by dragging these fields from the Field List window into the Form Design window. Position them next to each other near the top of the window.

3. Make sure that the Control Wizard button on the Toolbox is depressed. Add a subform/subreport box to the form near the right edge. The Subform/Subreport Wizard will activate. If it doesn't, you can activate it by right-clicking over the Subform/Subreport control and selecting Control Wizard from the shortcut menu.

4. In the first dialog, select the Table/Query option button. Click Next.

5. In this dialog, select Query: Sales by Category from the drop-down list box at the top of the dialog. Double-click on ProductName, ProductSales, and CategoryID (in that order) in the Available Fields list. You can now click Finish because the default answers are sufficient for the remainder of the wizard dialogs.

6. Stretch the subform control to make it taller. You can also delete the label that was placed above the subform.

7. Select Insert | Chart. The cursor will change to show a small cross and a chart. Position the chart on the left side of the form. After the chart is placed and you release the mouse button, the Chart Wizard will activate, as shown in Figure 13.27.

FIGURE 13.27.

The initial dialog of the Chart Wizard.

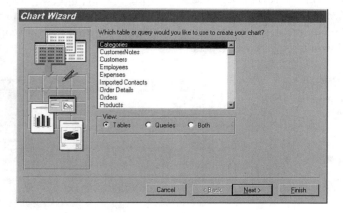

8. Select the Queries option button. Select Sales by Category from the list box at the top of the dialog. Click Next.

9. In this dialog you will select which fields to use for the chart. Double-click ProductName and ProductSales in the Available Fields list box. The field names will move to the Fields For Chart list box. Click Next.

10. This dialog is where you select the type of chart to be created. If you click on different chart types, the description at the right side of the dialog will change to describe the selected chart. Leave Column Chart selected and click Next.

11. This dialog allows you to specify where the selected fields should be placed on the chart, how the numeric field should be summarized, and which field should serve as a legend if multiple types of data are being displayed. The defaults that Access has assigned are perfect for this example, so click Next.

12. This dialog is where you specify the links between the chart and the form. Because you want the chart to change when a new category is selected, leave the defaults as they are. The CategoryID field is present in both the query and the form's record source (the Categories table). Click Next.

13. This is the final dialog of the wizard. The default title is sufficient. However, because only a single type of data is displayed, you won't need a legend. Select the No, don't display a legend option button. Click Finish to return to the Form Design window.

14. The chart control will display a sample chart while in Design view. If necessary, adjust the height of the chart control so that the entire sample chart is visible (including the data captions along the horizontal axis of the chart).

15. Switch to Form view. As you can see from Figure 13.26, the product name doesn't display very well on the chart. That's one reason you added the subform. Right-click the ProductSales column heading in the subform and select Column Width from the shortcut menu. Click the Best Fit button in the Column Width dialog box. The ProductSales column will be adjusted so that you can read the sales data.

16. Select another category by using the record selector at the bottom of the form. The chart and subforms should change accordingly.

17. Save the form if you wish.

Linking OLE Documents to a Form

You can add objects created in other Windows applications to an Access form. For example, you can add a picture created with Microsoft Paint, a worksheet created with Microsoft Excel, or a Word document created with Microsoft Word.

The type of control used to display the OLE document depends on whether you want the object to be bound or unbound. A bound object is stored in a field of the table. As you change records, the object displayed in the form changes to match the data stored in the field. For example, the Northwind database stores a picture of each employee in the company. This field would be displayed using a bound OLE control. Unbound objects are stored in the design of the form. Changing records has no effect on the object. For example, you might want to add a logo that you created with Microsoft Paint.

Both controls have an important property called SizeMode that affects how the data in the object is displayed within the control. The operation of the SizeMode property is identical to the SizeMode property for an image control. This was discussed in the section titled "Adding Graphics to a Form."

Unbound Objects

Unbound objects are added to the form using the Unbound Object Frame control. Unbound objects can be either embedded into the form or linked to the original file. The difference is that an embedded object won't change if the source file changes. It's stored in the form and will always be available. A linked object will be updated when the source file changes, because the data for the object isn't stored in the form—it's stored only in the source file. Therefore, the source file must be available to Access in order to display the contents of the object.

To add an unbound object to a form in Design view, click the Unbound Object control in the Toolbox. Click on the form where you want the object to be placed, or select Insert | Object.

If you want to create a new object, select the Create New radio button (it's selected by default) and then select the object type from the list box. This list box displays all of the available OLE objects on your system. On the form, you can display either the contents of the object or an icon representing the object. The object will be activated when the icon is double-clicked. To show the object as an icon, check the Display As Icon check box. When you click the OK button, the OLE server for the object you selected will open and enable you to create the new object. After the object has been created, exit the server application and you'll be returned to Access with the object shown on the form. This object is embedded by default, because it was created within the Design view.

To embed or link an object from an existing file, follow the same steps to get to the Insert Object dialog. Select the Create From File radio button. The list box disappears and is replaced by a text box and a Browse button. You can enter the filename in the text box directly, or use the Browse button to locate the file on your system. To link the object to the source file, check the Link check box. Again, you can select Display As Icon to display the object as an icon instead of its contents.

Bound Objects

To create an OLE object that is bound to a field whose data type is OLE Object, bring up the Field List in Design view. (The form's RecordSource property must be set to a table or query that has an OLE Object field.) Select the OLE Object field and drag it to the form. Position the drag box where you want the object frame to be displayed. A bound object frame is created on the form. You can now size and position the frame to fit on the form as well as set necessary properties.

To add data to a bound OLE control, open the form containing the control in Form view. Right-click the control and select Insert Object from the shortcut menu. The standard Windows Insert Object dialog box activates. Here you can select whether to create a new object or create the object's data from an existing file. The types of objects in the list box (when Create New is selected) depend on which OLE server applications are registered on your system. Selecting an object type and clicking OK launches the object's server application and allows you to enter data as you normally would in that application. If you select Create from File, you can specify the file that contains the data to be placed in the control. Again, the server application that created the file must be registered on your system in order to use the data. Also, if you've copied data to the Windows clipboard from an OLE server application, you can insert it into the control by right-clicking and choosing Paste. This is often the quickest way to add data to an OLE control.

Summary

This chapter showed you the basics of creating a form in Microsoft Access. By now you should know how to

- create a new form using the Form Wizard
- add controls to a form and manipulate some basic properties
- format the data displayed in the controls
- add a chart to a form
- add OLE containers to a form

As with most of Access, good form design is best learned in the line of fire. Experimenting with forms and controls is the best way to learn how they work and interact with each other.

The next chapter goes into form design on a more advanced level.

Building Advanced Forms

14

by Ted Williamson

No discussion of Access forms creation would be complete without a treatment of some of the finer details of creating professional forms. Some of these features you no doubt will have discovered for yourself while building forms in the preceding two chapters. However, we will examine all available form properties to ensure detailed coverage.

When you're done reading this chapter, you will be able to set the overall properties of a form to make its behavior suit the requirements of your application. We will also discuss topics that are essential for the creation of professional Access forms. In addition, you will learn to create the different types of forms available in Access that allow you to tailor your application to your clients' needs.

Although it's my intent to give a brief description of each topic, the definitive source remains the Help file and the manuals. Each of the properties described in this section has its own entry in the Microsoft Access Help file.

Defining a Form's Behavior with Properties

Four areas of a form's behavior can be adjusted with form properties:

- Format
- Data
- Events
- Other

Each of these groups of properties gives you the ability to shape a different area of the form's attributes. Format deals with the presentational aspects of the form—the things the user sees. Data properties control the means by which the form handles the data it displays. Events are actions that happen in response to a user's input. Other properties are those not covered in the other three areas but that still affect the behavior of the entire form. We will discuss all these aspects of forms except for the Events properties, which are described more in Chapter 27, "Programming in Reports."

To set the properties of a form, you must display the Properties sheet. To do this, right-click on the form selector—the black box in the upper-left corner of the form (see Figure 14.1). This will display a pop-up menu that contains a Properties menu item. Selecting this menu item will display the Properties sheet. Double-clicking on the form selector also will make the Properties sheet appear, as will selecting View | Properties or clicking the Properties button on the toolbar.

FIGURE 14.1.

The location of the form selector and its pop-up menu.

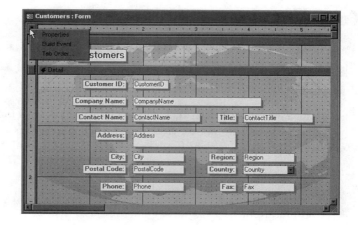

Setting the Format Properties

Each of the items in the Format tab of the Properties sheet changes an aspect of the form that is visible to the user. Because it's important to use a consistent format when presenting data, most designers select one form style or format to use for most of their data presentations in lieu of the alternatives. We will explore each of the effects that these properties have on the overall form presentation to enable you to better choose the proper style for your project. The Format properties are found on the first tab on the Properties sheet, as shown in Figure 14.2.

FIGURE 14.2.

The Format properties on the Form Properties sheet.

Controlling Views

Two aspects of a form's view can be adjusted from the Format tab:

- `DefaultView`
- `ViewsAllowed`

The `DefaultView` property determines which of the three types of form views is the default view. The default view is automatically displayed when the form is opened in view mode. The `ViewsAllowed` property sets which of the available views can be displayed.

Three different views are allowed to be the default view:

- Single form
- Continuous form
- Datasheet

Single forms are those that display only one record at a time. Continuous forms allow multiple records to be displayed at one time within the same window. This is accomplished by appending copies of the detail section of the form one after another, which then display a different record in each copy of the detail section. Datasheet view consists of rows and columns like a grid. It's the same type of view that is used by the Access QBE tool or an Excel spreadsheet. The default view is Single Form view.

The `ViewsAllowed` property allows three modes:

- Form
- Datasheet
- Both Form and Datasheet

The Form setting limits the display to either of the form views (Single or Continuous), while the Datasheet setting restricts the display to only the Datasheet mode. And, of course, the Both setting allows the display of both types of views. This is the default setting.

The `DefaultView` and `ViewsAllowed` properties also interact to produce *transition effects*. These effects can be used to restrict how the user views the data at certain points in a process or transaction. For example, if the form's `DefaultView` is set to Form and `ViewsAllowed` is set to Datasheet, the transition is set to switch from Form view to Datasheet view but not back to Form view. A complete list of the different conditions that the combinations of these controls create is given in the Access Help file under the heading "DefaultView, ViewsAllowed Properties."

The *RecordSelectors* and *DividingLines* Properties

The `RecordSelectors` and `DividingLines` properties are most useful when used on Continuous forms. Together they help make Continuous forms easier to view.

The `RecordSelectors` property enables and disables a bar on the left side of the form in Form view. (This bar is always displayed in Datasheet view.) Record selectors indicate the status of the current recordset record. Four statuses are displayed: Current, Editing, Locked, and New. Current simply indicates the current record. Editing indicates that the current record has been edited but not saved. Locked indicates that the record is locked by another user. New indicates the new record row on the form. This row doesn't actually exist in the database until it's edited and saved. The Record selectors are enabled by default.

The `DividingLines` property enables and disables horizontal lines that separate each record detail section from the others in Continuous Form view. Dividing lines are enabled by default.

The *NavigationControls* and *ScrollBars* Properties

Access provides two methods by which a user can traverse the records in a recordset: navigation controls and scroll bars. These are enabled and disabled by setting the `NavigationControls` and `ScrollBars` properties, respectively.

The `NavigationControls` property toggles the display of the recordset navigation controls in the bottom-left corner of the form for both Form and Datasheet views. These controls give the user an easy method of traversing the records in the recordset. Buttons are included that move to the first, last, previous, next, and new records in the recordset. The record number box indicates the number of the currently selected record, and a record count is provided as well. By default, the navigation controls are enabled.

The `ScrollBars` property allows the application's designer to display the standard horizontal and vertical scroll bars on the right and bottom sides of the form window. These scroll bars may be enabled separately or one at a time. The default setting enables both scroll bars.

The *AutoResize* and *AutoCenter* Properties

These two properties provide a means by which the designer can adjust the overall size and position of the form. The `AutoResize` property, when enabled, ensures that the form will always display at least one entire record on the form. If this property is disabled, the form can be sized in Design view and saved so that when the form is opened it defaults to the set size. The `AutoCenter` property works to ensure that the form is automatically centered in the application window when the form is first opened. The defaults are `AutoResize` on and `AutoCenter` off.

Title Bar Buttons

The following four properties, each enabling a different control, enable the buttons on the form's title bar. (The appearance of each of these controls is modified by the `BorderStyle` property.)

- `ControlBox` enables the control menu in the upper-left corner of the form. The control menu contains the usual entries: Restore, Move, Size, Minimize, Maximize, Close, and Next. Setting the `ControlBox` property to No disables not only the control menu but also the Minimize, Maximize, and Close buttons.

> ### TIP
>
> Unless the `MinMaxButtons` property is also disabled, you can maximize the form by double-clicking on the form's title bar.

- `CloseButton` enables the Close button in the upper-right corner of the form. Clicking this button closes the form. The control menu entry is also disabled.

- `MinMaxButtons` enables the Maximize and Minimize buttons in the upper-right corner of the form. As you might expect, the Maximize button expands the form so that it fills Access's parent window. The Minimize button reduces the form to an icon at the bottom of Access's parent window. The control menu entry is also disabled.

- `WhatsThisButton` enables the What's This button in the upper-right corner of the form. Clicking the What's This button changes the mouse pointer to the Help-select pointer, which allows you to access the Help topic referenced by a control's `HelpContextID` property.

> ### WARNING
>
> The Minimize and Maximize buttons can't be enabled if the What's This button is enabled, and vice versa. Further, if the Minimize and Maximize buttons are enabled, the Close button can't be disabled.

The *BorderStyle* Property

The `BorderStyle` property enables the application designer to set or change the style of the form's border. Each of these styles is generally used to border a particular type of form:

- None: No border or related border elements. Most often used for start-up splash screens.

- Thin: A thin border with most border elements, except that sizing is disabled. This style is most often used for pop-up forms.

- Sizable: The default border for Access forms. It can include any of the border elements. This style is used for standard Access forms.

- Dialog: A thick border with only a title bar and a control menu. The form can't be maximized, minimized, or resized. (The related items are disabled on the control menu.) It is most often used for custom dialog boxes.

Setting the Data Properties

This section describes the properties of a form that affect the handling of data. Each of the items in the Data tab of the Properties sheet changes the way data will be used on the form. We will explore each of the effects that these properties have on data manipulation so that you can better control what the user can or cannot do with the data. The Data properties are found on the second tab of the Properties sheet, as shown in Figure 14.3.

FIGURE 14.3.

Data properties on the
Form Properties sheet.

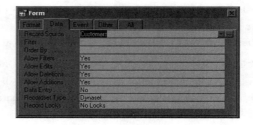

The *Filter, OrderBy,* and *AllowFilters* Properties

The `Filter`, `OrderBy`, and `AllowFilters` properties give the database designer more control over the data that is displayed on a form. These properties, individually or used in combination, give the designer the ability to limit and/or sort the data that is displayed to the user.

- `Filter` contains the SQL `where` clause that defines the subset of records to be displayed when a filter is applied to the recordset associated with a form.

- `OrderBy` contains the names of the field(s) that the recordset is to be sorted by.

- `AllowFilters` determines whether the `Filter` property is applied to the recordset to limit the data that will be visible to the user.

Filters are most commonly used to view a subset of the records in a recordset. When a filter is applied, only the records that meet specific criteria are displayed. This gives the designer the ability to restrict access or protect certain records from being viewed or edited.

The *AllowEdits, AllowDeletions, AllowAdditions,* and *DataEntry* Properties

The following properties control the user's ability to change the data displayed on a form. These properties can be used in combination to give the designer a wide range of control over the user's manipulation of the data.

- `AllowEdits` enables changes to the saved records that are displayed by a form.

- `AllowAdditions` enables the addition of records to a form.

- `AllowDeletions` enables the deletion of records that are displayed by a form.

- `DataEntry` enables the entry of new records onto the form by opening the form for data-entry only.

To set the recordset to read-only status, all of these `Allow` properties must be set to False. If the form is to be used for data entry, the `DataEntry` property must be set to True.

The *RecordsetType* Property

The `RecordsetType` property lets the database designer determine which type of recordsets to use for the bound controls on the form. There are three types of recordsets to choose from. Each of these types has a different effect on the user's ability to edit and view the data in the recordset.

- `Dynaset` allows the editing of a single table or tables in a one-to-one relationship. (The join field on the "one" side of a one-to-many relationship can't be edited unless Cascade Update is enabled between the tables.)
- `Dynaset (Inconsistent Updates)` enables fields in all tables to be edited.
- `Snapshot` prevents the fields in any table from being edited.

Dynasets and Snapshots

The result set returned from the execution of a query is either a dynaset or a snapshot. One of the main differences between a dynaset and a snapshot is updatability. Dynasets can be edited, and snapshots cannot. Additionally, the result sets for dynasets and snapshots are populated in different ways. The overall effect is that snapshots are better suited for small, uneditable queries and dynasets are better suited for queries where the result set is large or where editing is required.

Populating Result Sets

Initially, dynasets and snapshots are populated with the same data, enough for the first screen or two. After the initial records in the result set are retrieved, the snapshot continues to populate the recordset with the rows from the query, while the dynaset only fetches and caches the primary key values. The remaining values in the result set are retrieved as follows:

- As a result of user actions: Snapshots fetch the data in all the columns up to the current record; dynasets fetch only primary keys up to that point and then fetch a small amount of data surrounding the current record.
- During Access idle time: Snapshots fetch and store all queried columns; dynasets fetch and store primary keys, as well as a 100-row data window, during this idle time.

In either case, the dynaset has to perform a second query, which employs the cached primary keys, to retrieve the remaining columns in the records surrounding the current record. Snapshots, in contrast, continue to fetch the entire result set, row by row.

Part of the reason for the dynaset only caching the primary keys is to ensure that the data that is fetched is always the most current, thus giving dynasets a greater "liveliness" to the data. A snapshot, in contrast, caches the entire result set, and it is not refreshed except by complete re-execution of the query.

Performance Issues

Because of their behavior differences in retrieving and caching data, snapshots and dynasets provide different performance characteristics and thus are better suited to distinct tasks:

- For small result sets, snapshots are faster to open and scroll through. Also, if you don't need to update data or see changes made by other users, use a snapshot.

- For larger result sets, dynasets are faster and more efficient. Moving to the end of a snapshot requires the entire result set to be downloaded to the client. In contrast, a dynaset downloads only the primary key columns and then retrieves the last screen of data that is referenced by those keys.

- Dynaset open time and scrolling speed are affected most negatively by the number of columns you select and the number of the query's tables that are output. Select only the columns you need; outputting all columns using Table.* is more convenient but slower. Sometimes joins are used simply as restrictions and don't need to be output at all.

Setting the Other Properties

The remaining properties are used to control aspects of the form that aren't covered by the property sets described earlier. These properties touch on both the data and the format of the form, as well as some of the events associated with the form. See Figure 14.4.

FIGURE 14.4.

Other properties on the Form Properties sheet.

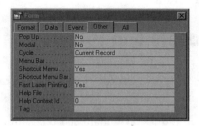

The *Modal* and *PopUp* Properties

These two properties combine to help create different types of form behavior. They are used in conjunction with the BorderStyle property to create common dialog boxes.

- The `Modal` property determines whether the form opens in modal form. This means that the user must finish with this form before doing anything else in the application, such as setting focus to a control on another form. The default is nonmodal (no).

- The `PopUp` property determines if the form is to remain on top of all other forms in the Access window. The is useful for creating floating toolbars and menu bars. The default is non-pop-up (no).

The *Cycle* Property

The `Cycle` property specifies how the cursor behaves if the Tab key is pressed when the last control on a bound form has the focus. You can choose from the following three settings:

- All Records moves the focus to the first field in the next record in the underlying source of data.

- Current Record moves the focus to the first control in the tab order on the form in the same record.

- Current Page moves the focus back to the first control in the tab order on the same form page.

The `Cycle` property is affected by the tab order. To determine which control is first in the tab order, the `TabIndex` property for the control that is to be first must be set to 0. (See the section "Setting the Tab Order" for a complete discussion of tab order.)

Other Form Settings

The topics discussed in this section have an overall affect on the way a form behaves. They are included here because of their importance in form design and because they don't really belong under any other heading.

Form Headers and Footers

One of the more useful features of the Access form is its ability to display headers and footers. These areas on the form are most useful for displaying the column names and column sums on continuous forms.

Both the header and footer remain stationary during the scrolling of continuous forms and thus are the most useful places to display command buttons or other input or selection controls that need to remain fixed in place.

Setting the Tab Order

Tab order refers to the sequence in which the cursor traverses the fields and controls on a form. The cursor simply follows the sequence of the Tab Index property of those controls that have their tab stop enabled. Setting the tab order of the controls is simply a matter of changing the number in the `TabIndex` property of each control that the designer of the form wishes to be in the tab order. This can be a tedious task at best. Fortunately, Access provides a handy little tool that enables the database designer to set the order in which the cursor traverses the fields on a form: the Tab Order dialog (see Figure 14.5). To display it, right-click on the form selector and select Tab Order from the pop-up menu.

FIGURE 14.5.

The Tab Order dialog.

The form appears, with the section defaulting to Detail (Header and Footer sections are also available) and the Custom Order list box indicating the current tab order on the form. The designer may rearrange the items in the list into the desired tab order and click the OK button to apply the settings to the form.

In case the form contains many controls, the Auto Order button is provided to automatically align the controls on the form from left to right and from top to bottom. Even after the Auto Order button has been used, changes may be made to the order of the controls on the form so that the tab order may be customized to the user's needs.

Printing Forms

Although it's true that reports are most often used for printing information contained in Access databases, now and then there is a need to print what is displayed on a form. There are a number of things to consider when designing forms that are to be printed. Access gives the application designer a great deal of control over many aspects of the form's format.

The designer can control what appears on certain parts of forms when printing and other parts when displaying on-screen. The `DisplayWhen` property of controls and subforms determines this.

`LayoutForPrint` enables you to choose which type of font to use when printing to the printer or screen. If the form is to be printed, the printer fonts are the best choice, because they leave a crisp, clear image.

Creating Sample Forms

Now that we've reviewed all the key properties of Access forms, we're ready to create some sample forms. This section is an overview of some of the most commonly used forms in database design.

Continuous Forms

Continuous forms are most commonly seen, because they are used in reports. There are, however, many times when the editing or viewing of data would better take place on a repeating, continuous form. For example, a mailing list might need to be reviewed and edited before being printed. This allows the user a larger overview of the data before printing.

To create a continuous form, simply change the `DefaultView` property to Continuous and set the `RecordSelectors` and `DividingLines` properties as needed.

Let's take a look at the Customer Phone list form in the Northwind database that ships with Access 95, shown in Figure 14.6.

FIGURE 14.6.

The Customer Phone List form in Design view.

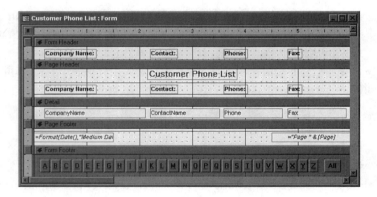

Look at it in Single Form view by changing the `DefaultView` property to Single Form. (See Figure 14.7.) Notice that only one name is listed. A directory is much more useful when a list of names is displayed instead of just one.

Now let's change the appropriate properties to make this form show a list of phone numbers (see Figure 14.8). Set the `DefaultView` property to Continuous and set `DividingLines` to Yes.

Much more useful if you're using it as a directory, don't you think?

FIGURE 14.7.

The Customer Phone List form in Single Form view.

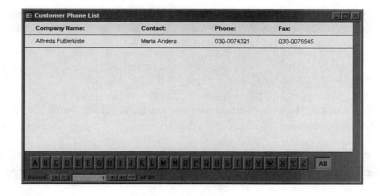

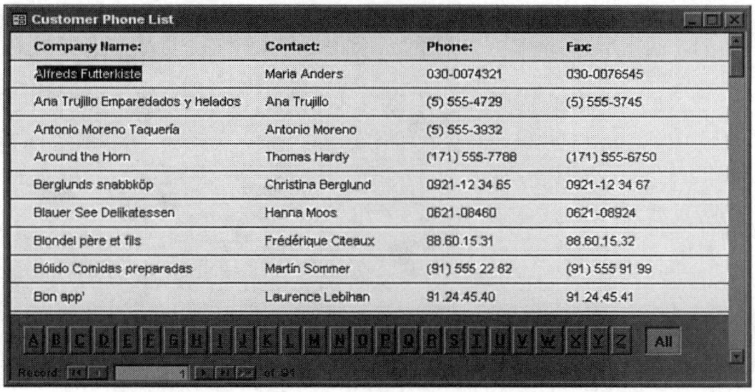

FIGURE 14.8.

The Customer Phone List form in Continuous Form view.

Adding Subforms

Another of the more commonly used forms in an Access database is the subform, which was introduced in Chapter 13, "Designing and Customizing Forms." Subforms are most often used to display dependent records in a one-to-many relationship. Quarterly Orders in the Northwind database is an example of this type of form (see Figure 14.9).

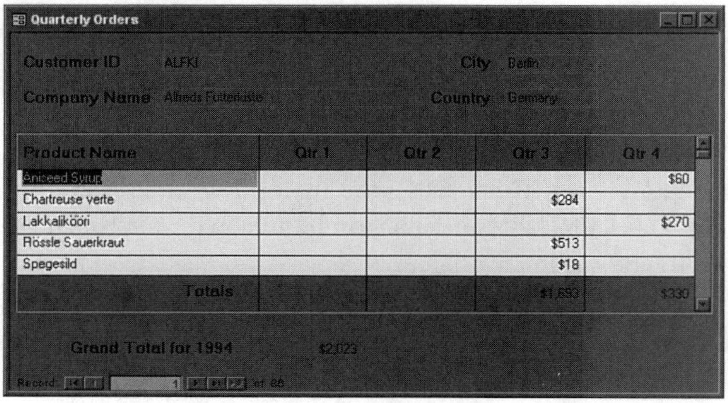

FIGURE 14.9.

The Quarterly Orders form in Form view.

NOTE

We will concentrate here on the things that make the master form and subform work together. The creation of these types of forms was discussed earlier in this book.

Let's look at how the master form was made. We'll start with the basic header design, which is already complete. The header section of the form contains information about the "one" side in the one-to-many relation (see Figure 14.10).

FIGURE 14.10.

The Quarterly Orders form in Design view and without the subform.

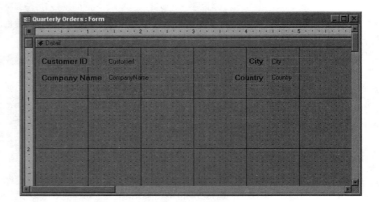

Before we add the subform, let's look at how the subform was made. Notice that this form has a header and a footer that display the column names and column sums (see Figure 14.11). This form uses a query as the datasource. The subform contains information about the "many" side in the one-to-many relation.

FIGURE 14.11.

The Quarterly Orders subform form in Design view.

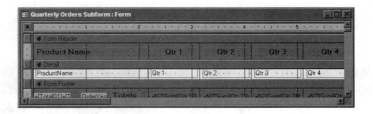

Now we will add the subform to the master form. There are two methods of adding a subform to a master form. The first uses the Subform Wizard to add the subform to the master form. Simply click the Subform/Subreport button on the toolbar and follow the instructions to pick and bind the form.

The second and more direct method is to simply drag and drop the subform from the Database window onto the master form (see Figure 14.12). Place and size the form as needed and then establish a connection between the master form and subform by setting the `LinkChildFields` and `LinkMasterFields` properties of the subform. (See the section "Subform Properties" later in this chapter.) Now, as the database is navigated, the subform's data will change in sync with the master form's header.

FIGURE 14.12.

The Quarterly Orders form with the subform in Design view.

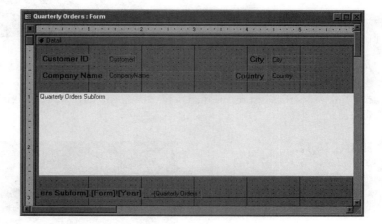

Although this is one of the more common uses for subforms, this is still a simple application. One of the more advanced uses of subforms involves the use of VBA code to change the subform while the application is running. (See the section "Switching Out Subforms" in Chapter 28, "Putting It All Together," for a more in-depth treatment of subforms.)

Subform Properties

Many of the properties that are associated with subforms are common to other controls. As with other controls, there are certain properties that affect the format, some that affect the data, and others that affect the events and miscellaneous aspects of the subform. We will discuss only those properties that are unique to the subform or whose use with the subform is unique. The most important are the properties that are used to establish the data relationship between the subform and the master form: the `LinkChildFields` and `LinkMasterFields` properties.

To display the property sheet for the subform, shown in Figure 14.13, right-click on the subform control on the master form and select Properties from the pop-up menu.

The `LinkChildFields` and `LinkMasterFields` properties specify how the master form and the subform are to be linked. These properties contain the names of the fields that are used to connect the two forms in a one-to-many relation. While typically the fields that are named represent the same fields in different tables, it's possible to use different named fields as long as the same datatype is used.

FIGURE 14.13.

The Subform property sheet for the Quarterly Orders subform.

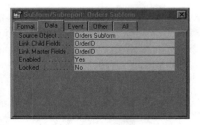

An alternative method of linking master forms and subforms is to use the Subform Field Linker dialog, shown in Figure 14.14. To see it, double-click the ... button at the end of either of the two link properties just mentioned. This dialog will have suggested fields to use to link the two forms.

FIGURE 14.14.

The Subform Field Linker dialog and the Suggest Link Fields dialog.

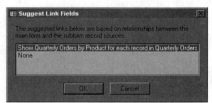

Dialog Forms

In Access, a form creation is often just the result of setting certain form properties in a certain manner to achieve the desired effect. The dialog box is no exception. All that is really required is a single-mode form and some property adjustments.

To create this type of form, let's start with a basic form and change the required properties. The following settings are required in order to create a true dialog box from a default form:

Property	Setting
Views Allowed	Form
Border Style	Dialog
Modal	Yes

It's optional to set the following properties. They may be useful on some dialogs:

Property	Setting
Auto Center	Yes
Pop-Up	Yes
Record Selectors	No
Navigation Buttons	No
Dividing Lines	No

Another item that might be useful on a dialog box is the What's This button, which can only be displayed when the Maximize and Minimize buttons are disabled, no matter what the Border Style is set to.

Multipage Wizard-Style Forms

The multipage form is very useful when the user needs to be led through a sequence of events. One of the most common types of multipage forms is the wizard-style form. This type of form can also be useful for step-by-step instructions, questionnaires, or simple messages.

To make a multipage form, start with a simple form. Enlarge it vertically so that it is large enough to hold the different pages to be displayed. (See Figure 14.15.)

FIGURE 14.15.

A multipage form in Design view.

The pages are placed in the Detail section of the form. On this sample, each page has a single-line message contained in a label control. A page may contain as many controls and subforms as can be displayed on-screen.

Each page is separated by a PageBreak control. The page breaks are represented by the little dots next to the 1 and 2 marks along the left ruler.

The footer contains the control buttons for moving through the pages. These could just as easily be placed in the header. Both the header and the footer can contain any instructions or controls that need to remain for the entire form.

The following code is required in this form:

In the General Declarations section:

```
Dim curpage As Integer
```

In the Form Open event:

```
Private Sub Form_Open(Cancel As Integer)
curpage = 1
End Sub
```

In the Prev Page button:

```
Private Sub PrevPage_Click()
    curpage = curpage - 1
    If curpage < 1 Then curpage = 1
    DoCmd.GoToPage curpage
End Sub
```

In the Next Page button:

```
Private Sub NextPage_Click()
    curpage = curpage + 1
    If curpage > 6 Then curpage = 6
    DoCmd.GoToPage curpage
End Sub
```

Both the code and the form are included on the CD that comes with this book.

Summary

You should now have a clearer understanding of the various aspects of creating professional forms for your applications. We reviewed how format, data, and other properties affect form customization, and you saw some examples. We also explored various types of forms and their applications in actual programs.

Using OLE Custom Controls

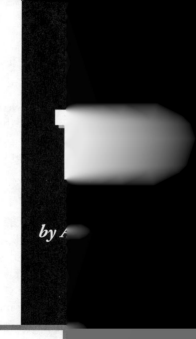

by A

One of the powers of Access 95 is that it's extensible. In addition to the controls that are available as part of the product, you can incorporate OLE custom controls on your forms. This means that you aren't limited by what Access provides. Instead, you're limited only by the imaginations of the third-party developers who design OLE controls.

What Are OLE Custom Controls?

OLE controls support the OLE 2.0 custom control architecture and provide support for 32-bit operating systems. They contain their own code, methods, events, and properties. An OLE custom control's functionality is stored in a file that has an .OCX extension. A calendar OCX ships as part of Microsoft Access. Additional OCX controls are included in the Microsoft Access Developer's Toolkit and are available from third-party vendors such as Crescent, Sheridan, Far Point, and many others.

Two types of OLE controls are available. The first type is visible at both design time and runtime. After being placed on a form, it provides a front-end interface that allows the user to directly manipulate the object in some way. One example is the calendar control that ships with Access 95. The second type of OLE control is visible at design time but not at runtime. An example of such a control is a control that gives you access to all of Windows' common dialog controls, such as Open, Print, and so on. The control itself is invisible to the user, but its functionality is available to the user at runtime. Another example is a timer control. This control operates within the application, triggering event code to run, but it's invisible to the user.

Why Should You Use OLE Custom Controls?

OLE controls let you easily incorporate additional functionality into your applications. For example, if you need to include a calendar on your form, you don't need to worry about how to build your own. Instead, you can include a custom calendar control on the form. You can modify the calendar's behavior by changing its properties and executing its methods.

How to Use OLE Custom Controls

To incorporate an OLE custom control in your application, you must follow these steps:

1. Install the custom control.
2. Register the control.
3. Add the control to a form.

When you purchase a custom control, it generally includes an installation program. Usually the installation program copies the OCX file (the OLE control) to your Windows System folder.

The path or name of this folder can vary, depending on whether you're running Windows 95 or Windows NT and what you named your Windows directory during the installation of your operating system.

Registering a Custom Control

After you've properly installed the control, you're ready to register it with Access. You use the Custom Controls dialog box, shown in Figure 15.1, to accomplish this task. You open this dialog box by selecting Tools | Custom Controls.

FIGURE 15.1.

*The Custom Controls
dialog box.*

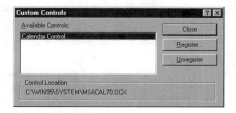

The Custom Controls dialog box contains a list box showing all the custom controls that are currently registered within Access. To add a custom control to the list, click the Register button. The Add Custom Control dialog box, shown in Figure 15.2, will appear.

FIGURE 15.2.

*The Add Custom Control
dialog box.*

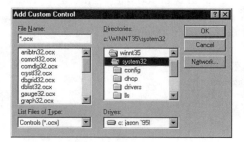

Make sure that the directory containing the OCX file that you want to register is highlighted. The control that you're registering must already be installed. If it hasn't been installed, it won't appear in the list. Select the OCX file that you want to register and click OK. You are returned to the Custom Controls dialog box, and the custom control that you selected will now appear in the list of registered controls. You are now ready to include the control on a form.

Adding a Custom Control to a Form

You can add a custom control to a form in one of two ways:

1. Add the custom control to a toolbar or the toolbox.
2. Select Insert | Custom Control when in Form or Report Design view.

If you will be using the custom control on a regular basis, you will want to add it to a toolbar or the toolbox. To do so, right-click anywhere over the toolbox or over any toolbar, and then select Customize from the pop-up menu. The Customize Toolbars dialog box, shown in Figure 15.3, will appear. If you scroll down through the list of categories, you will find a category named Custom Controls. If you click on that category, all of the registered custom controls will appear.

FIGURE 15.3.

The Customize Toolbars dialog box.

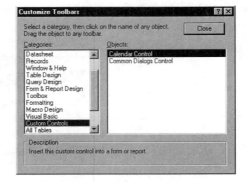

To add a custom control to a toolbar or the toolbox, click and drag the object to place it anywhere on the toolbar or the toolbox. Close the Customize Toolbars dialog box. The tool now appears on the toolbox or toolbar. Figure 15.4 shows the toolbox with the calendar control added. When you have added the custom control to a toolbar or the toolbox, you can add it to a form just like any other control.

FIGURE 15.4.

The Toolbox with the calendar control added.

If you aren't planning to use the custom control on a regular basis, you can select Insert | Custom Control. The Insert OLE Custom Controls dialog box appears. After you select a control from the Select a Custom Control list box, the control is placed on the form. You can move the control around the form and size it as needed.

After you've placed a custom control on a form, it's ready to operate in its default format. If you insert the calendar control in a form and then run the form, it will look like Figure 15.5.

FIGURE 15.5.

A calendar control with no properties explicitly set.

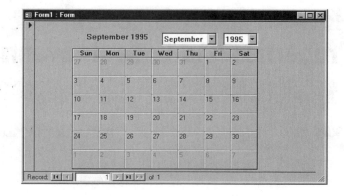

In the case of your calendar control, it knows how to display all of the months of the year, along with the corresponding days of each month. You haven't yet set any properties for the calendar, nor have you written code to respond to any calendar events.

What Are a Custom Control's Methods, Events, and Properties?

The methods, events, and properties associated with each custom control differ. They are specific to that control and are determined by the author of the control. They are used to manipulate the control's appearance and behavior. Each control's methods, events, and properties are contained in a separate OCX file.

Why Do I Need to Modify a Control's Properties and Code Its Events?

If you don't modify a control's properties, it will function only with its default appearance and behavior. Much of the richness of third-party controls comes from the ability to customize them by changing their properties during design and at runtime. Furthermore, the ability to respond to a custom control's events allows you to respond to the user's interaction with the control. Finally, the ability to execute the control's methods enables you to manipulate the control.

> **TIP**
>
> Some controls support data binding, which enables you to store or display data in a control from an underlying field in a table.

How to Modify a Control's Properties and Code Its Events

Figure 15.6 shows some of the calendar control's many properties. As with any control, most of the calendar control's properties can be set during design and modified or read at runtime.

FIGURE 15.6.

The calendar control property sheet.

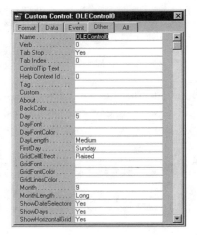

Another way to set properties for a control is to set them graphically. You can do this by selecting Custom from the object's property sheet. For example, if you select Custom from the calendar control's property sheet, the dialog box shown in Figure 15.7 appears. It lets you modify many important attributes for the calendar, including what should be the first day of the week, whether you want the days of the week to show, and the colors and fonts for the calendar. The properties shown in this dialog box will vary for each control.

FIGURE 15.7.

The Calendar Control Properties dialog box.

Just as the control's properties can be set or evaluated at runtime, the control's events can be coded. To obtain a list of all the events associated with a custom control, open the Proc box in the Module window. Make sure that the control name for your custom control is listed in the Object box. When viewing the events of the calendar control, you might notice that there is an event called `AfterUpdate` and another called `AfterUpdateObject`. Often there is an overlap between the name of an event in Access and the name of an event of the custom control. In this case, Access appends the word Object to the name of the Access event. For example, if the control supports an `AfterUpdate` event, it will appear as `AfterUpdateObject` in the Object box. This is the event that you should code if you want to execute code after the custom control is updated.

The `AfterUpdateObject` event of your calendar control is triggered when the user selects a date from the calendar. The following code changes the value of a text box named `txtSelectedDate` to the value property of the `OLECalendar` control. This code is placed in the `AfterUpdateObject` event of the calendar control, so that it executes whenever the user selects a date on the calendar.

```
Private Sub OLECalendar_AfterUpdateObject()
    txtSelectedDate.Value = OLECalendar.Value
End Sub
```

Let's look at a couple of examples. The form pictured in Figure 15.8 contains three custom controls—two spin controls and one calendar control. This form is called `frmCalendar`. The spin control is included in the Access Developer's Toolkit. One of your spin controls contains event code that will move the calendar forward or backward a month at a time. The other spin control contains event code that moves the calendar forward or backward a year at a time.

FIGURE 15.8.

The calendar control with spin controls for month and year movement.

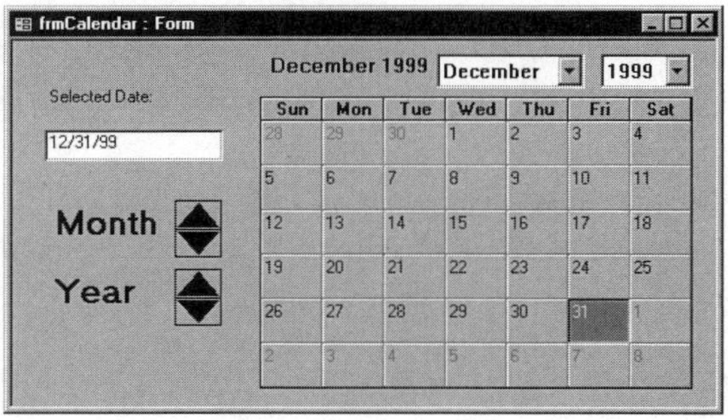

The following is the code that makes it all work properly. A spin control has a `SpinDown` event and a `SpinUp` event. Here's the code behind each:

```
Private Sub OLESpinMonth_SpinDown()
    OLECalendar.PreviousMonth
End Sub

Private Sub OLESpinMonth_SpinUp()
    OLECalendar.NextMonth
End Sub
```

```
Private Sub OLESpinYear_SpinDown()
    OLECalendar.PreviousYear
End Sub

Private Sub OLESpinYear_SpinUp()
    OLECalendar.NextYear
End Sub
```

These routines utilize four methods of the calendar control: `PreviousMonth`, `NextMonth`, `PreviousYear`, and `NextYear`. These methods cause the calendar to move back one month, forward one month, back one year, or forward one year, respectively. As seen in `OLECalendar_AfterUpdateObject`, the calendar itself is responsible for synchronizing the text box named `txtSelectedDate` with the currently selected calendar date.

Let's look at one more example. The form called `cmdCommonDialog` uses an OLE control that comes with the Access Developer's Toolkit. This tool is the Common Dialog Control. It's used to display the standard Windows File Open, File Save As, Font, Color, and Print common dialog boxes. Figure 15.9 illustrates your form.

FIGURE 15.9.

frmCommonDialog lets you display the common dialog boxes.

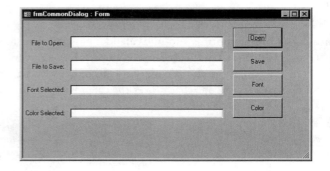

Each command button on the form calls a different common dialog box. Properties on the form are then set based on the choices selected in the common dialog box. The code for File Open looks like this:

```
Private Sub cmdOpen_Click()
    dlgCommon.Filter = "All Files (*.*)¦*.*¦Database Files (*.MDB)¦*.MDB"
    dlgCommon.Action = 1
    txtFileOpen.Value = dlgCommon.FileName
End Sub
```

Your common dialog control is named `dlgCommon`. The preceding code sets the `Filter` property for the common dialog. This determines what will be listed in the List Files of Type dropdown. The `Action` property of the common dialog control is then set to 1. This invokes the Open common dialog. After the Open common dialog is closed, the code proceeds with the line `txtFileOpen.Value = dlgCommon.FileName`. This code reads the `FileName` property of the common dialog control and sets the value of the `txtFileOpen` text box to whatever file was selected from the Open dialog box, shown in Figure 15.10.

FIGURE 15.10.

The Open common dialog box.

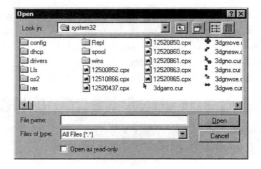

The Save As dialog box works very much like the File Open dialog box. The code looks like this:

```
Private Sub cmdSaveAs_Click()
    dlgCommon.Action = 2
    txtFileSaveAs.Value = dlgCommon.FileName
End Sub
```

This code sets the `Action` property of the common dialog control to 2, thus invoking the Save As common dialog. After a filename is specified in the Save As dialog box and the dialog box is closed, the value of `txtFileSaveAs` is set equal to the filename that was entered in the Save As dialog box.

The Font dialog allows the user to select a font name, style, and size. After you've selected these attributes, you can use the properties of the common dialog control to set the font of various objects on your form. The code looks like this:

```
Private Sub cmdFont_Click()
    Const CF_BOTH = &H3&
    dlgCommon.Flags = CF_BOTH
    dlgCommon.Action = 4
    txtFont.FontName = dlgCommon.FontName
    txtFont.Value = dlgCommon.FontName
End Sub
```

The constant `CF_BOTH` is used to set the `Flags` property of the common dialog control. By setting the `Flags` property to `CF_BOTH`, you indicate that you want to display both screen and printer fonts in your common dialog control. Setting the action property of the common dialog control to 4 invokes the Font common dialog. After exiting the dialog box, set the `FontName` property of the text box `txtFont` to the `FontName` selected from the common dialog. You also set the `value` property of `txtFont` to the value returned from the common dialog.

The last command button on your form invokes the Color common dialog box. The code looks like this:

```
Private Sub cmdColor_Click()
    dlgCommon.Action = 3
    txtColor.Value = dlgCommon.Color
    Me.Detail.BackColor = dlgCommon.Color
End Sub
```

This code sets the action property of the common dialog control to 3. After the Color common dialog is closed, the value of the text box txtColor is set equal to the color selected from the common dialog. The BackColor property of the detail section of the form is then set equal to the color selected within the common dialog.

Licensing Issues Regarding Custom Controls

Some OLE controls can be distributed freely, and others contain various levels of restrictions. The licensing policies for a particular OLE control are determined by its vendor and are usually detailed in the control's documentation.

The licensing rules that are in effect for an OLE control are enforceable by law. This means that improper distribution of the control is a crime. Distributing an OLE control without proper licensing is just like copying a software product illegally.

If you have any questions about the licensing of a third-party control, you need to consult the vendor who authored the control. Sometimes a one-time fee is required so that you can freely distribute the OCX file of the control. Other times, a royalty might be required for each copy of the control that is distributed. If you aren't sure whether you want to purchase a third-party control, you might want to contact the vendor of the control. Many vendors allow potential customers to try out their products for a limited period of time. In fact, many demo versions are available online or directly from the vendor.

A Custom Control Example

Start by selecting Tools | Custom Controls. Verify that the calendar control is registered. Open a new form in Design view. Base this form on the Orders table that is part of the Northwind database that is included with Access 95. Add three bound controls to the form: CustomerID, OrderID, and ShipVIA. Next, select Insert | Custom Control. Select the calendar control. Move and size the calendar control on your form as desired. Name the control oleOrderDate. Now set the ControlSource property of the calendar control to the OrderDate field. View your form and move from record to record. Notice that the selected date on the calendar changes to reflect the date that is stored in the OrderDate field of each record.

Now let's add two command buttons to the form. Call the first one cmdPreviousMonth and the second one cmdNextMonth. Place this code in the Click event of the cmdPreviousMonth button:

```
Private Sub cmdPreviousMonth_Click()
    oleOrderDate.PreviousMonth
End Sub
```

and place this code in the Click event of the cmdNextMonth button:

```
Private Sub cmdNextMonth_Click()
    oleOrderDate.NextMonth
End Sub
```

View your form and test your new command buttons. Be aware that because the calendar is bound to the OrderDate field, you're modifying the value contained in the field as you click the Previous Month and Next Month command buttons. Your completed form should look like Figure 15.11.

FIGURE 15.11.

The completed form using an OLE calendar control bound to the OrderDate field.

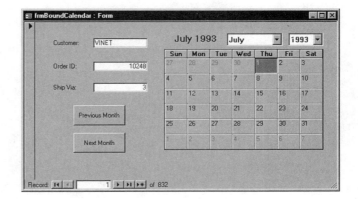

Summary

OLE controls are easy to use and extremely powerful. Each one contains its own properties, events, and methods. OLE controls greatly extend the capabilities of Access 95 and let you incorporate additional functionality into your applications. By modifying properties, reacting to events, and executing methods, you can access the rich features contained within each OCX. The licensing of OCX controls varies, so it's important to understand the licensing aspects of your particular controls in order to know whether you can distribute them to your users.

PART

V

Access Reports

Creating and Using Simple Reports

by

IN THIS CHAPTER

Reports are the method by which data can be presented in a meaningful and easily understood way. Reports can be viewed, printed, or exported to another format. Access lets you create reports easily. The design can then be modified to best present the data to the user.

A report is similar to a form. Reports can only display data, however—they can't be used to input data. Reports can contain most of the same elements and layouts as forms, with the exception of controls that require user interaction (combo boxes, for example).

The data source for a report is a table, a query, or an SQL statement. The information displayed changes automatically as the underlying data tables are changed. The format of the report, however, is stored in the report design and changes only when the report design is modified.

This chapter serves as a brief introduction to reporting. It covers creating a simple report and what can be done with that report. The next chapter, "Designing and Customizing Reports," goes into great detail about reporting in Access. The Northwind database included with Access is used as the source of the examples in this chapter.

How to Create a Simple Report

Access provides many different mechanisms for creating reports. No single method is better than any other. This section introduces most of the available methods. I go into detail on a few of the easier ones but save the others for the next chapter.

Using the New Report Dialog Box

The standard method of creating a new report is to select New from the Reports tab of the Database window. This opens the New Report dialog box shown in Figure 16.1. This dialog box provides methods for creating a new report in a list box on the right side of the window. As a method is selected from the list box, the description on the left side of the window changes.

FIGURE 16.1.

The New Report dialog box.

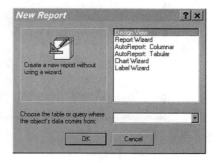

At the bottom of the New Report dialog box is a drop-down combo box. This combo box is used to select the table or query that will serve as the data source for the report. It isn't necessary to select a table or query at this time if Design view or Report Wizard is used to create the report, but doing so saves some steps later in the process. If any of the other methods are used, a table or query must be selected before you can continue.

The available new report creation methods are as follows:

- Design view: The new report is created by hand.
- Report Wizard: An Access Wizard guides the report creation process.
- AutoReport: Columnar: A report is created that displays the fields from a table in a single column.
- AutoReport: Tabular: A report is created that displays the data in a tabular format similar to a spreadsheet.
- Chart Wizard: A Wizard guides the process of inserting a chart into a report.
- Label Wizard: A Wizard guides the process of creating a report formatted for printing on labels.

We won't go into detail on all of these methods. That is left for the next chapter. The following sections give you a feel for how easy it is to create reports in Access.

Design View

The use of Report Design view is beyond the scope of this chapter. This is the method used when creating a report from scratch. It enables tweaking of all the report properties, as well as any code that may be necessary for the report. We will visit this window later in this chapter.

Report Wizard

The Report Wizard guides you through the process of creating a report. It is an in-depth method of easily creating a report. This section describes each window of the Wizard. Several of the dialogs have a long list of possible options. Each of these options is explained only briefly, because they are usually variations of other options.

To create a report using the Report Wizard, follow these steps:

1. To start the Report Wizard, select Report Wizard in the New Report dialog box.
2. Select a table or query to be used as the source of data for the report. The first dialog of the Wizard is shown in Figure 16.2. The Employees table was selected as the data source. You can modify this choice using the Tables/Queries list box in this dialog box.

FIGURE 16.2.

The initial dialog of the Report Wizard.

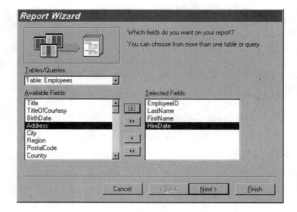

3. Select the fields to be displayed in the report from the Available Fields list box. Use the > button to move a single field to the Selected Fields list box. Use the >> button to move all the available fields. You can select fields from another table or query as well. Simply select the table or query in the Tables/Queries list box and select the needed fields.

TIP

In some cases it may be easier to move all fields to the Selected Fields list box and then remove the fields not needed in the report individually using the < button.

4. For this example, select the EmployeeID, LastName, FirstName, and HireDate fields from the Employees table, and click Next.

5. The next dialog box enables you to set grouping options for the report. You want to group the employees by the first letter of their last name. Select the LastName field in the list box and click the > button. The dialog changes to the view seen in Figure 16.3.

6. Because you want to group on the first letter of an employee's last name, you need to click the Grouping Options button. A Grouping Intervals dialog appears. It lists all the fields selected in the preceding step (in this case, only the LastName field) and a list box for each one. This list box is used to select the grouping interval. The default is Normal, which means that the grouping changes whenever the LastName field changes. You want to group on the first character of the last name.

7. Select 1st Letter from the list and then click OK. Click the Next button.

8. The next dialog of the Wizard helps you set a sort order for your report. The fields to be used when sorting the report's detail section are specified using the list boxes on the right side of the dialog box shown in Figure 16.4. Sort by LastName and then FirstName.

FIGURE 16.3.

The grouping setup dialog box of the Report Wizard.

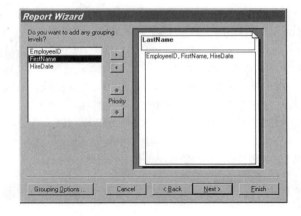

FIGURE 16.4.

The sort order dialog box of the Report Wizard.

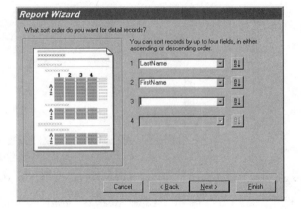

9. You can change the sort order for each field by clicking the button to the right of the field's list box. You are sorting in ascending order for both fields, so leave the default setting.

10. If you had chosen to include some numerical fields in your report, this dialog would also contain a Summary Options button. The Summary Options button enables you to specify if any of the Number fields in the report should have summary values calculated for them. Summary values can be sums, averages, minimum values, or maximum values. The Summary Options dialog also enables you to specify where summary values should be displayed. Because this report doesn't include any summarized fields, the Summary Options button is hidden.

11. Click the Next button after the LastName and FirstName fields are chosen.

12. The next dialog enables you to set a layout for the report. Choose one that presents the data in the clearest way. The preview on the left of the dialog will change as you

select different layouts. Also, choose the page orientation that best fits the report. The check box at the bottom of the dialog forces Access to adjust the width of fields so that they all fit on the report. Click Next to move on to the Style dialog box.

13. Select a style that is appropriate. Click Next to move to the last dialog of the Wizard.

14. Enter a name for the report. If you want to see how the report looks with data, click the Preview the Report option button. If you want to see the Report Design view for the newly created report, click the Modify the Report's Design option button.

15. To preview the report for this example, click Finish to create the report and open the preview window, shown in Figure 16.5.

FIGURE 16.5.

The final report in preview mode.

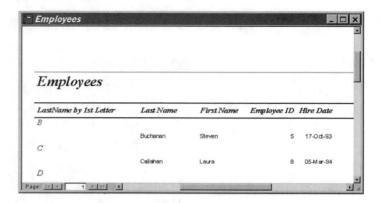

As you can see, the report could use some tweaking. To modify the report, follow these steps:

1. The field LastName by 1st Letter can be omitted from the report entirely. Select View | Report Design. The Report Design view shown in Figure 16.6 replaces the preview window.

FIGURE 16.6.

The final (unmodified) report in Report Design view.

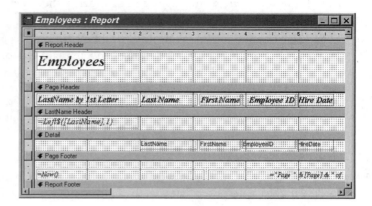

2. Select the box with the text LastName by 1st Letter inside it and press the Delete key. This removes this label from the report.

3. Select the box with the text =Left$([LastName],1) and press the Delete key.

4. Next, select each field on the report by Shift-clicking on the fields. Do this for the labels in the Page Header section and the fields in the Detail section. After the fields have been selected, move the cursor over the LastName field in the Detail section. When the cursor changes to a small hand, click the left button and drag the fields to the left.

5. The window should now appear similar to Figure 16.7.

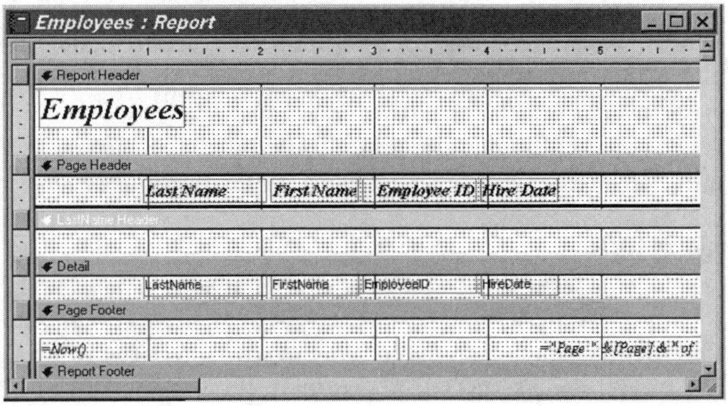

FIGURE 16.7.

The modified report in Report Design view.

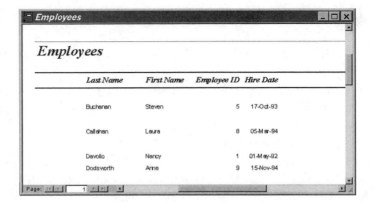

6. Select View | Print Preview to see how the report looks now. It should look similar to Figure 16.8.

FIGURE 16.8.

The modified report in Print Preview mode.

Columnar and Tabular AutoReports

AutoReport creates a report that displays all fields and records in the selected table or query. AutoReports allow you to create a report quickly and painlessly. The report can then be modified to match your requirements.

In a columnar AutoReport, each field appears on a separate line with a label to its left. In a tabular AutoReport, each field appears in its own column, with each record of the table occupying a separate line. AutoReports create reports quickly, but they usually must be modified in Report Design view to make them usable. To format the report, Access uses the last autoformat you used on the report. If you haven't created a report with a wizard before or haven't used the AutoFormat command on the Format menu, the Win95 autoformat is used.

To create an AutoReport, bring up the New Report dialog box. Select either AutoReport: Columnar or AutoReport: Tabular from the list box. Select a table or query to use as the source. Click OK, and the new report is created and displayed in Print Preview mode. It is assigned a default name that should be changed when the report is saved. You can modify the report using the Report Design view, just like with the previous report.

Chart Wizard

The Chart Wizard aids in creating a report that has a chart embedded in it. This Wizard requires the MS Graph 5 applet in order to work properly. If MS Graph 5 wasn't installed when Access was installed, run the Access setup program and add MS Graph 5 to the installation. This Wizard is used to create reports that would be enhanced by a graphical representation of data stored in a table. The Chart Wizard is perfect for placing a chart on the report and binding it to data in a table or query. However, the chart object usually requires a fair amount of tweaking using the MS Chart applet in order to get the chart to look just right.

To create a report using the Chart Wizard, follow these steps:

1. Select Chart Wizard in the New Report dialog box and select a table or query from the list box at the bottom. Use the query Category Sales for 1994 as an example. Click OK.

2. The first dialog of the Wizard, shown in Figure 16.9, asks you to specify which fields are used in the chart. For this example, choose both fields and click the Next button.

3. The next window enables you to specify the graph type for the chart. Keep the default (Column Chart) and click Next.

4. The next dialog of the Wizard, shown in Figure 16.10, lets you choose how data is displayed in the chart. Because you chose only two fields for the report, Access has correctly assumed that you want to graph the sum of the sales for each category.

5. Double-click the SumOfCategorySales button to invoke the Summarize dialog box, which enables you to change how the field is summarized. Leave it as Sum for now.

FIGURE 16.9.

The field selection dialog box of the Chart Wizard.

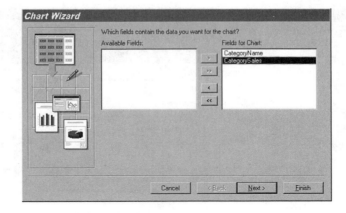

FIGURE 16.10.

The data layout dialog box of the Chart Wizard.

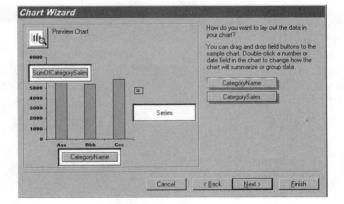

6. Click the Preview Chart button in the upper-left corner to see a preview. Click Next to move on.

7. Enter a title for the chart, specify whether you want the chart to display legends, and specify what to do when the chart is created.

8. Finally, click Finish to create the chart. The chart shown in Figure 16.11 is the final result (after a fair amount of tweaking of the MS Graph object).

Label Wizard

The last of the Wizards is the Label Wizard. This wizard is used to create standard mailing labels or other types of labels, typically by choosing a style of Avery label. Once this Wizard is started, the first item of business is selecting the type of label that the data is printed on. You can select from a list of existing styles or define your own using the Customize button (see Figure 16.12). Select the style to be used and click Next.

FIGURE 16.11.

The chart created using the Chart Wizard.

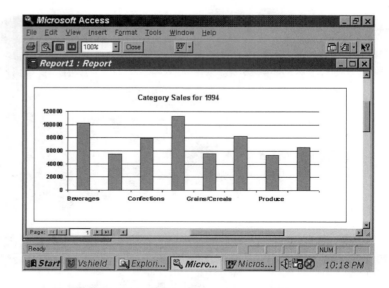

FIGURE 16.12.

The initial dialog of the Label Wizard.

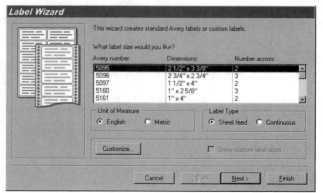

The dialog box that follows sets up the font to be used when printing the labels. Set the properties as desired and click Next. The next dialog box enables you to lay out your label using the fields from the selected table and any text you care to add (see Figure 16.13). After the label is set up, click Next.

This dialog box lets you specify how the labels are sorted. Select a field (or group of fields) to sort by and click Next. This brings you to the last window, where you define a name for the report and tell Access what to do after the report is created. Set the properties as desired and click Finish. The new label report is created and displayed.

FIGURE 16.13.

The layout dialog of the Label Wizard.

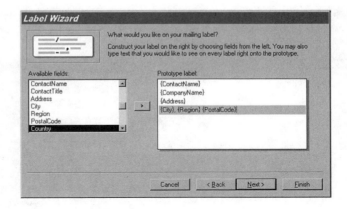

Saving a Form as a Report

If existing forms are already created in the database, you can make a copy of them saved as a report. This assumes that the form is of a suitable style to also serve as a report. In the sample database, the Customer Labels dialog box can't serve as the source of a report because it isn't a form that contains data, but rather a form that is used for navigating the Northwind application.

To create a report from an existing form, follow these steps:

1. In the Forms tab of the Database window, select the form to be saved as a report. Select the form named Suppliers for this example.

2. Right-click and select Save As Report from the pop-up menu.

3. Enter a name for the report in the Save Form As Report dialog box. You can also leave the default intact. Change the name to Supplier List. Click OK when the name is satisfactory.

4. The report is created and placed in the Reports tab of the Database window, shown in Figure 16.14.

FIGURE 16.14.

The Reports tab of the Database window.

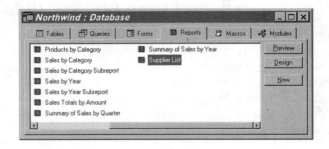

5. Preview the new report by selecting it from the list and clicking Preview. The output for this example is shown in Figure 16.15.

FIGURE 16.15.

The report created from the Suppliers form.

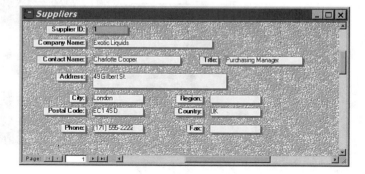

As you can see from Figure 16.15, a form's data fields aren't all that gets carried over to the report. The `Picture` property of the form and any field formatting are carried over as well. For forms that will be printed, however, it might be necessary to remove some of the graphical elements (such as the assigned picture and shading). To do so, open the report in Report Design view by selecting the report in the Database window and clicking Design.

> **CAUTION**
>
> Code associated with a form is also copied into the report. Often this can cause problems if the code is used for data validation or navigation of records in a table. It's best to review the code (select View | Code while in Report Design view) to make sure that it applies to the report.

Saving forms as reports is an effective way to leverage the effort required to create a form by also using the form as a report.

Importing a Report from Another Database

Using methods similar to importing tables from an external file (which is covered in Chapter 4, "Tables"), reports can also be imported. Although this might seem like an attractive method of copying a report from one database to another, it has some drawbacks and requires precautions. First and foremost, the tables or queries accessed in a report must be available in the database into which the report is imported. After you import a report, use Report Design view to check a report for valid structure in the target database. If necessary, import any queries from the source database in addition to the report.

Follow these steps to import a report from an external Access database:

1. With the Reports tab of the Database window selected, select File | Get External Data | Import.
2. The Import dialog box appears. Select the database that contains the report to be imported and click Import.
3. The Import Objects dialog box appears with the Reports tab selected, as shown in Figure 16.16. It shows all the reports in the selected database.

FIGURE 16.16.

The Import Objects dialog box for importing reports.

4. Select the reports you would like to import (you can also switch tabs and import tables or queries that might be necessary for the report) and click OK.
5. Access copies the report into the current database. If the report name in the source database is the same as a report name in the current database, Access creates a unique name by appending a number to the end of the name.
6. You can now work with the report as if it were created from scratch.

You should use Report Design view to preview the imported report. Make sure that the report accesses valid fields and queries for the current database. Also, check any code in the report for messages or validation rules that don't apply to, or should be modified for, the current database.

How to Use Simple Reports

You have now created many different reports. However, all you have done is looked at the reports in the Print Preview window. There are several other ways of displaying or distributing reports. These are described next.

Page Setup

You can control how a report looks when printed by modifying the Page Setup. Choose a report and then select File | Page Setup. The Page Setup window has three tabs: Margins, Page, and Layout. The Margins tab, shown in Figure 16.17, enables you to modify page margins.

This can be helpful when you want to put more data onto a page and aren't concerned with wide margins. The Page tab sets the orientation (Portrait or Landscape), the Paper Size and Source, and which printer to use for the report—either the default printer or a specific printer. The Layout tab enables you to specify various field layout properties for a report.

FIGURE 16.17.

The Page Setup dialog box.

Printing a Report

To send a report to the printer, select the report in the Database window and select File | Print. This displays the Print dialog box, allowing you to change printers (if there are multiple printers on your system) and change the properties of the selected printer. You can also specify a page print range for multipage printouts, the number of copies to be printed, and whether to collate the copies. After you've set all the desired properties, click the Print button to start the print job.

Another method for printing a report is available on the Reports tab of the Database window. The shortcut menu for a report (accessed by right-clicking on the desired report's name) contains a Print item. Using this menu bypasses the Print dialog box discussed earlier. It sends output directly to the default printer (or to the printer specified in the Page Setup window).

To print from the Print Preview window, click the Print button in the toolbar (it has a picture of a printer). This sends the report to the default printer (or to the printer specified in the Page

Setup window) without showing the Print dialog box. You can't choose which printer to send the report to if you use this method.

If you're printing a label report on a dot matrix or tractor-feed printer, make sure that the printer is set up properly. This includes setting the printer as the Windows default printer and making sure that the paper size matches the label's size.

Using OfficeLinks to Publish a Report

If you use the other applications in the Microsoft Office suite, you can take advantage of Access 95's built-in OfficeLinks. These tools enable you to export the data and formatting from your reports to either Word or Excel. The report can be sent to Microsoft Word to be published as a Word document. You can also send the data of a report to Excel to analyze it using the spreadsheet tools. This feature basically enables you to export a report to Excel or Word for use in those applications.

Mailing a Report Using Microsoft Mail or Exchange

If you're using a MAPI-compliant e-mail system such as Microsoft Mail or Microsoft Exchange, you can mail a report to another user's mailbox. To do so, select the report to be mailed and then select File | Send. A Send dialog box appears, asking you to select a file format (Microsoft Excel, Rich Text Format, or MS-DOS Text) to be used when the report is mailed. The report will be converted to a file of the type you select. This file will then be attached to the mail message you'll create. Select the desired format, click OK, and follow the prompts to log in to your mail system (if necessary) and create a new message.

Exporting a Report

This option enables you to save the report into a separate Access database or other external file (such as Excel or a text document). To do this, select a report in the Database window. Select File | Save As/Export. When the Save As dialog box appears, select To an external File or Database and click OK. The Export dialog box appears. Select a file type (Microsoft Access, Microsoft Excel versions 5 to 7, Text Files, or Rich-Text Format) in the Save As Type list box. Use the dialog box as you would use the standard Save As dialog box to store the file in the desired folder with the desired name.

Troubleshooting Simple Reports

As this chapter has demonstrated, Access 95 has many features that enable you to quickly create a usable report. However, there will come a time when you can't rely solely on the Report Wizard to create a report. Or, perhaps the report you will create with the Report Wizard is close but not quite right. This section covers several possible problems with reports and how to solve them.

To illustrate these troubleshooting techniques, create a simple report based on the Customers table in the Northwind database using these steps:

1. In the Reports tab of the Database window, click New.

2. In the New Report dialog box, select Customers from the table/query list box at the bottom of the dialog. Make sure that Design View is selected in the list at the top of the dialog and click OK.

3. When the Report Design view appears, make the Field List visible (if it's not already) by selecting View | Field List. The list should contain all of the fields from the Customers table.

4. Drag the Country field onto the report. Drag the CompanyName field onto the report and place it directly to the right of the Country field. Delete the field labels for both fields (the field label is the transparent box placed to the left of the field).

5. The report should look similar to Figure 16.18. Preview the report by selecting View | Print Preview. This report obviously has some problems. You'll correct them in the following sections.

FIGURE 16.18.

The report created for troubleshooting.

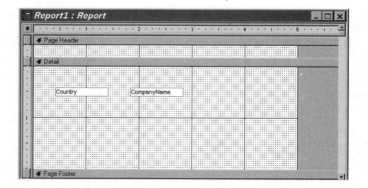

Troubleshooting Data Problems

Several possibilities for problems exist with the data shown in a report. Most are easily overcome; others require careful scrutiny of the report design to correct. This section discusses how data in a report is sorted, how to hide duplicate values, and what to do if the report prompts you for unexpected parameters.

Sorting Data in Reports

One of the first problems you usually notice when you preview a report is that the data is sorted in an unexpected way. Usually, there seems to be no rhyme or reason for the order. Fortunately, fixing the sort order for a report is an easy task.

For this report, you want to sort the list of customers by their country. Access 95 provides several methods of defining the order in which the records of a report will be sorted. All of these methods involve specifying fields from the table or query to determine the sort order. Note that the fields used to sort the data aren't required to appear in the report.

One method is to use the `OrderBy` property of the report. In Report Design view, display the Properties window by selecting View | Properties. View the properties of the report by clicking the report selector box (the small square on top of the vertical ruler). Switch to the Data tab of the Properties window. In the Order By text box, type `Country`. This specifies that you want to sort by the customer's country name. The `OrderBy` property defaults to an ascending order (A to Z). To sort in a descending order, add the keyword `DESC` after the field name. If you wanted to specify multiple fields to sort by, you would separate them with a comma. Preview the report to verify that the data is now sorted by country. Clear the `OrderBy` property for the report before continuing to the next paragraph.

Another method that provides more features is the Sorting and Grouping window (see Figure 16.19). View this window by selecting View | Sorting and Grouping. In this window, you select the fields to use for sorting and grouping using the list box in the Field/Expression column of the window's grid. To accomplish the same sort order used earlier, select the Country field from the list. You can specify Ascending or Descending for each field by using the column labeled Sort Order. It has a list box that lets you pick the desired setting. This window also allows you to specify whether and how you want to group the data based on the fields selected. You can add header and footer sections that will appear whenever the grouping changes (in this example, when the country changes). You can specify a grouping interval (in this example, a value of 1 indicates that the grouping will change when the first character of the country field changes) and force Access to keep the group together on one page.

FIGURE 16.19.

The Sorting and Grouping window of Report Design view.

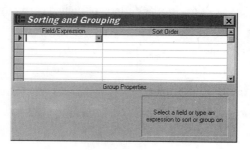

After you've played with the sorting and grouping properties and previewed the results, clear this window by deleting any entries you've made.

The third method for defining the sort order involves modifying the record source for the report. As you'll recall, you simply specified the Customers table when this report was created. To illustrate the third method of sorting records, bring up the report's Property window once again. Select the `RecordSource` property on the Data tab. Highlight the existing text (Customers) and type `select * from Customers Order by Country` into the property's text box. Preview the report to verify that the sorting is identical to the two previous methods. Although this might seem to be an obscure method (because you can simply use either step discussed earlier), it illustrates the fact that the sort order can also be specified in the report's underlying query or record source. If the report were based on one of the queries defined for the database, that query could contain an ORDER BY clause, which would cause the report to be sorted. Create a report based on the query Customers and Suppliers by City to verify this behavior.

Hiding Duplicate Values

You probably noticed in the previous examples that many of the country names were repeated (Argentina appears three times, for example). To remove duplicate data from within a group, Access 95 provides a HideDuplicates property for data controls such as text boxes, list boxes, and option buttons. To hide duplicate country names in the report, follow these steps:

1. Select the Country field in Report Design view.
2. Right-click over the field and select Properties from the shortcut menu.
3. Select the Format tab of the Properties window and change the value of Hide Duplicates to Yes.
4. Preview the report (by selecting View | Print Preview) to verify that duplicate country names are no longer displayed.

If You're Prompted for Unexpected Parameters

If, when previewing or printing a report, Access 95 prompts you for an unexpected parameter, a spelling error probably exists in the report design. Ensure that all field names used in the following areas of the report's design are spelled correctly and match field names in the underlying table or query:

- ControlSource property of controls bound to the table or query
- Text in the Field/Expression column in the Sorting and Grouping window
- Expressions in controls or in the Sorting and Grouping window

Also, make sure that if any aggregate functions are in the report, they use field names from the underlying table or query and not any control names.

Troubleshooting the Report Layout

More prevalent than data problems are layout problems. This is particularly true when you actually try to print your reports on different types of printers. The most common problems involve white space and margins, which are discussed in the following sections.

Too Much White Space

White space is a term used to describe blank areas on a report. Having too much white space not only wastes paper, but it also makes your reports harder to read and follow. The report shown in Figure 16.18 obviously has a tremendous amount of white space.

One way to reduce the amount of white space in a report is to decrease the overall height and/ or width of the report or of the sections in the report. To do so, move the cursor to the right or bottom edge of a section. The cursor changes to a double-headed arrow. If you're at the right edge of a section, drag the cursor left or right to change the width of the section. If you're at the bottom edge of a section, drag the cursor up or down to change the height of the section. To change both height and width at the same time, place the cursor in the lower-right corner of the section. Drag it diagonally in any direction to change the size of the section.

Another way to reduce white space is to move controls closer together. This reduces the spacing between data when the report is previewed. You can also use the `CanShrink` and `CanGrow` properties of text boxes and report sections to allow the text box and section to be dynamically sized based on the length of the data to be printed.

Problems with Page Margins

Page setup is perhaps the most prevalent place that reports get into trouble. Having an incorrect page setup can cause blank pages, chopped-off data, and other problems.

If you get a blank page only at the end of a report, make sure that the `Height` property is set to zero for the report footer. If data spills over onto the next page when you want it all on one page, make sure that the total height of all of the sections in the report, plus the top margin and the bottom margin, doesn't exceed the height of the paper specified in the Page Setup dialog box.

If every other page of the report is blank, adjust the margins so that the total width of the report plus the widths of the left and right margins don't exceed the paper size that is specified in the Page Setup dialog box.

To correct these problems, either adjust the width and height of the report and its sections until the report prints correctly, adjust the margins (within the printable region for the specified printer) using the Margins tab in the Page Setup dialog, or change the paper orientation on the Paper tab. Often, if a report is too wide to fit using portrait orientation, simply changing the orientation to landscape will fix the problem.

Summary

This chapter served as an introduction to creating and using simple reports. By now you should be able to generate a simple report using any of the wizards and print, export, or e-mail the report. The next chapter goes into greater detail about designing and customizing reports.

Designing and Customizing Reports

Printing a report from Access is often the final result of the database effort. No matter how great a user interface is, printed output is more comprehensible to most people. Even though reports can be simply rows and columns of text displayed in the Courier font, people have high expectations for how a report will look. In the days of DOS, people didn't question a report that rivaled a teletype printout, but now reports have to be not only functionally correct but cleverly formatted as well. This chapter focuses on creating the back-end data structures that make up a good report, along with the powerful formatting tools included in Access 95.

Access is an excellent tool for data publishing, which is the database equivalent of desktop publishing. Many people use Access just as a publishing tool, publishing data that has been downloaded from their company mainframe or an existing database. Reports in Access are now created much like laying out newsletters in PageMaker or Quark. The tools in Access, known as *controls,* are used to draw lines, words, fields, and pictures. You can use knowledge gained from creating the company newsletter to create company reports. Microsoft has included functional similarities between desktop publishing applications and Access. For instance, holding down the Shift key while drawing with the line tool lets you draw a straight line.

What's New in Access 95

Access 95 has tremendous new functionality compared to the previous version of Access. In the reporting area, no revolutionary changes have been made in this release. Some bells and whistles have been added to make the work easier, such as the new Print Preview, which mimics Microsoft Word's Print Preview, or the ability to attach a report to an e-mail message. Word users will feel right at home with the similarities between generating an Access report and formatting a Word document. The advances made with reporting in Access follow a general trend with all the new Windows 95 products: tighter integration and standardization within the Microsoft Office applications. Access now looks and feels even more like Word and Excel, sometimes to the point that it's easy to forget which program you're using.

Here are some of the new features provided in Access 95:

- More intuitive Report Wizards: There is no need to guess what a Groups and Totals report is, because a sample is created in the Wizard window.
- The Report Wizard can now create a multitable query. The Wizard can be instructed to pull fields from multiple tables, and Access generates a query. Access doesn't require a query first for multitable reports. See Figure 17.1 for an example.
- Improved Print Preview: Users can now preview many pages at once and pick the Zoom level desired, just like in Microsoft Word (see Figure 17.2).
- Improved Formatting toolbar: Formatting tools from Word and Excel are now included on the Access toolbar. Useful tools such as the format painter make the task of reformatting a control simple.

FIGURE 17.1.

The new and improved Report Wizards can now create queries that pull from more than one table.

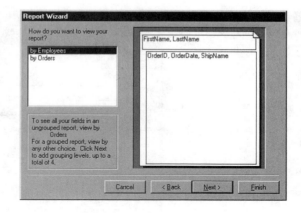

FIGURE 17.2.

The Print Preview is now like Microsoft Word's Print Preview, where multiple pages can be displayed.

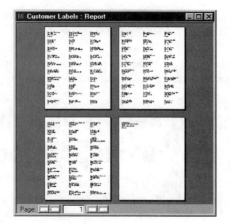

■ Control morphing: Remember the drudgery of having to delete a text box control and re-create it as an identical label or combo box? Now a new formatting feature called control morphing is available. Select Format | Change To, which can convert a text box to a label, for example.

■ Improved Help: In accordance with the Windows 95 Help engine, Access now has more ways to answer your questions.

■ Tabbed dialog boxes: The Property Sheet and Print Setup now have tabs that are consistent with Windows 95.

■ Insert menu: Access now has an Insert menu for easy insertion of pictures, objects, and the report expressions of date, time, and page numbers.

■ Sending a report in e-mail: The sought-after feature of including a report in an e-mail message is now available (see Figure 17.3).

FIGURE 17.3.

Reports can now be output to an e-mail document.

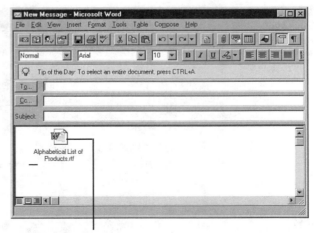

Report embedded in e-mail message

■ Background pictures: One of the new report properties, the Picture property, lets the report have a background image or watermark.

Creating a Report Instantly Using the AutoReport Tool

Access has the tools and flexibility to let beginners see results quickly and lets advanced developers generate complex documents. Microsoft's answer for "I want it now!" managers is a feature called the AutoReport, which is similar to the AutoForm feature for form creation. AutoReport takes a chosen table or query and generates a report with a click of the mouse. This is an excellent way to get a jump-start on report creation.

The steps for creating an instant report using AutoReport are as follows:

1. In the Database window, click either a table or query to select it.

TIP

Selecting a table sets the source of records for the report.

---

2. Click the drop-down box of the New Object tool on the far right of the Database toolbar.
3. Choose AutoReport. Within moments, the report is generated for you and displayed in Print Preview. See Figure 17.4.

FIGURE 17.4.

An AutoReport made from the Categories table in Northwind.

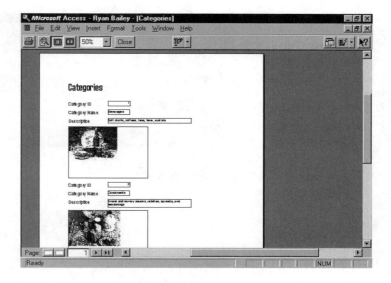

AutoReport displays the completed work in Print Preview. Exploring Print Preview reveals how to display the report in different ways and change the printing properties. To make report modifications, click the Close button to enter Design view.

The Architecture of Access Reports

When creating reports, don't forget that the foundation of a report begins as a recordset, such as a table or query. Either the developer creates the recordset or an Access Wizard generates the recordset. After the report is given records to display, it's up to the developer to arrange the data controls on the report to make it display as needed. An understanding of how Access manipulates the different bands or layers of a report is important. The sample database Northwind has some excellent examples.

How Reports Are Structured

When Access is instructed to run a report, it works with the controls that either the developer or the Wizard has inserted into its sections to format a page of information. Note the report sections the Wizard generated in the report shown in Figure 17.5.

FIGURE 17.5.

Design view of a columnar Access report.

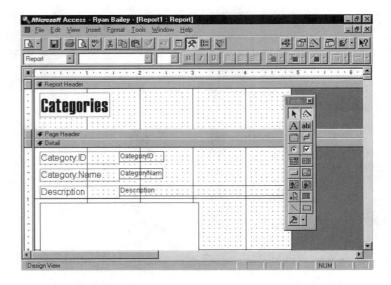

Notice that the sections begin with the Report Header and end with the Report Footer. The following diagram represents this sectional construction:

Report Header

Page Header

Group Header

Detail Section

Group Footer

Page Footer

Report Footer

Compare the report in Design view to Print Preview. Note that the controls are printed in their corresponding sections:

- Report Header: The label named Categories is in this section. It appears only at the top of the first page of the report.

- Page Header: The page header is of zero height, which means that no header is displayed on page 2. The Page Header appears at the top of every page, unlike the Report Header, which appears only as the first part of the report.

- Detail: This section is where the individual records get printed. The Detail section can also be thought of as where the records get cycled. Note the bound control Title, which displays data from the underlying table.

- Page Footer: In the Page Footer of the report design, note the text box expressions =Now() and ="Page " & Page & " Of " & Pages. These expressions display the date and time, and the page numbering, respectively.

- Report Footer: The final section to all reports is the report footer. Here the Report Footer is of zero height, so it doesn't display anything.

NOTE

A control is an element placed on forms and reports. Examples include labels, text boxes, OLE picture controls, lines, and rectangles. All controls have properties that can be set in the Property Sheet.

Types of Reports

There is only one basic report—the type with sections that have controls that get displayed on-screen and, ultimately, on paper. However, by manipulating a report section's height and width, its properties, and page setup, you can display it in various ways. After learning the fundamentals of reporting, you have control over the data. Until then, Microsoft has created Wizards that break the report creation process into five major report categories:

- Columnar reports: One record on each page, displayed vertically.

- Tabular reports: Rows of records going across like a spreadsheet, displayed horizontally. A multicolumn report that snakes the text flow in columns is a type of tabular report.

- Grouping reports: Grouping of data with totals.

- Label reports: Columns of data spaced out in groups, such as mailing labels.

- Chart reports: A report that has only a graph.

NOTE

An excellent way to learn about reporting is to examine the work of others. The sample application Northwind contains sample reports that are worthy of investigation.

Establishing the Datasource for a Report

An Access report needs a recordset as its underlying source. This recordset can be either a table or a query. If report information comes from more than one table, a query has to be built first, or the Report Wizard has to be used. Forms and reports are identical in how they are tied to tables and queries.

> **TIP**
>
> The Report Wizard in Access 95 creates a query if the fields are chosen from two different tables. However, if the report is extremely complex and pulls records from multiple tables, I recommend creating and saving a query first; then base the report on the new query.

> **NOTE**
>
> An Access report receives records from a recordsource. This source can be either a table or a query, which results in rows and columns of data. A report doesn't care if its recordsource is a table or a query—it treats them both the same.

> **NOTE**
>
> Treat forms and reports as nearly identical twins. Much of the knowledge you gain from building forms can be used in building reports. Substantial similarities exist in the controls and properties of both. For example, they are both based on either a single table or query, and they both have a layering type of structure like headers and footers. Think of forms as the parts of Access that a user views on the monitor and reports as the parts that come out of the printer. Because reports are usually confined to an 8 1/2×11 inch page, certain properties and structures make them different from forms.

Report Creation from the Bottom Up

When you create a report, begin with the end in mind. In other words, acquire an existing example or sketch of what the report should look like when it's completed. With a blueprint in hand, begin to ask questions: What tables does this data live in? What elements are part of groups? What type of totaling does each group require? Is this report so complex that it needs subreports?

Preliminary Foundations

The first step is to question what fields are involved in this report. Do all the fields for this report reside in a single table, or does a query need to be created to bring these fields into one recordset? If the fields come from more than one table, can the Report Wizard handle the task, or is this situation so complex that it requires query creation? Does this report need subreports?

> **NOTE**
>
> If the report is so complex that it is based on two or more unrelated queries, a subreport might be required.

The second step in the creation of any report is to begin with the finished product in mind. A few minutes of sketching on paper will provide a blueprint from which to work and save considerable time in the long run.

The next step is to create and test the query that underlies the upcoming report. Most reports are based on queries. Access 95 has the new feature of creating the query for you inside the report generator. Experience will help you determine whether to build a query first or let the Report Wizard generate the query.

Initiating the Report Generation Process

To start a new report, follow these steps:

1. Click the report tab of the Database window.
2. Click the New button on the right side of the Database window.
3. In the New Report dialog box, choose a table or query on which to base the report.

> **NOTE**
>
> A quick way to create any Access object is to use the New Object tool, which is on the right end of most toolbars.

You have several choices of how to perform the next step:

- Design view: Start from scratch with a blank report.
- Report Wizard: Answer a series of questions that results in a report.
- AutoReport: Create an instant columnar or tabular report.
- Chart Wizard: Construct a chart using Microsoft Graph.
- Label Wizard: Build mailing labels.

Building a Single-Table Report Using the Report Wizard

The only way to really learn reporting is to do it. The following is a step-by-step creation of a popular report style, the Grouping Report. This report answers the request "Show me all the employees of Northwind Traders, grouped by title, and display their names, cities, and phone numbers, sorted by last name and then first name."

> **NOTE**
>
> Keep in mind that Wizards don't have to be used to create reports. Their only purpose is to save developers time in the report creation process. Wizards can be used only with a new report—they can't be reinvoked after the report is finished.

The following steps show you how to use the Report Wizard. Refer to Chapter 16, "Creating and Using Simple Reports," for more discussion of Report Wizards.

1. To select the record source, click the New button while in the Report tab of the Database window. Single-click the Report Wizard and choose the Employees table, which is the underlying source of data for this report. Click OK.

2. From the Employees table, select the fields you need to display. For this report, select Title, FirstName, LastName, City, and HomePhone. After each step, click the Next button.

3. This step is the trickiest. Question which single field will define the grouping. In this example, many people share the same title, so double-click the field Title to declare it as the grouping field. Each Title could have many Employees, as shown in Figure 17.6.

FIGURE 17.6.

Which table will define the grouping?

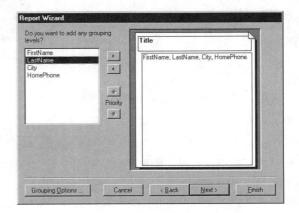

4. By default, the grouping field (Title, in this case) is sorted alphabetically. This step asks which fields determine the sort order within the grouping. Specify further sorting by double-clicking on the fields Last Name and First Name. This report will sort by the Grouping field Title, and within each group the records will be sorted by last name and then first name.

5. Next, you will choose a look for the report. Click on the various layout choices. Depending on the choice, not only do you see a preview of the layout, but Access will set numerous report options as well. If no options are chosen, the default layout is used.

6. From the drop-down box, choose the font style that is appropriate for this report. Will this report need to fit lots of information on a page? If so, 8-point Times New Roman will work. Will this report need to be displayed in large letters to be quickly understood? If so, 12-point Arial should suffice. Beware of using fonts in your Access database that might not exist on the end user's computer. For example, if the font Impact is used in a report, and the database is used on a computer that doesn't have Impact, Windows will find the most similar type style. To be safe, use Times New Roman or Arial for all your reports.

NOTE

Remember that all the settings that the Wizard generates can be modified after the report is finished.

7. Type an appropriate title for this report and click the Finish button.

8. Save this report as "Employees by Title," because it is used later in this chapter for customization.

Print Preview Unleashed

The Print Preview feature has been completely rebuilt for Access 95. This new utility is almost indistinguishable from the Microsoft Word Print Preview.

The Many Ways to View a Report

When the report is displayed on-screen, the following options are available for final approval before the report is sent to the printer:

- The mouse is a magnifying glass that zooms in and out when you click it in the report.
- The toolbar has the One Page and Two Page tools, as well as a Zoom Control drop-down list box.
- The View menu has Zoom and Pages choices (see Figure 17.7).

FIGURE 17.7.

*Choosing View | Pages
shows several pages at once.*

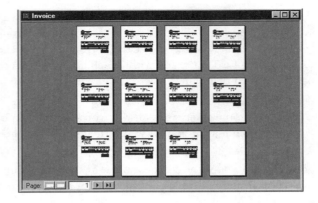

- Right-click anywhere on the report to display the shortcut menu, which has Zoom and Pages options.

How Grouping Works in Reporting

Select View | Sorting and Grouping to display the Sorting and Grouping dialog box, shown in Figure 17.8. Examining the previously created Employees by Title report gives you clues to what the Wizard did. Note that Title is the first entry in the dialog box, and its Group Header property is set to Yes. Setting the Group Header property to Yes establishes another section in the report called Title Header. After the grouping section is established, place field controls in this section to be displayed at the top of every grouping. If the LastName field's Group Header property is set to Yes, another section appears. From a sorting aspect, LastName and FirstName were chosen, and the sort order is ascending (A to Z).

FIGURE 17.8.

*The Sorting and Grouping
dialog box defines the
report's structure.*

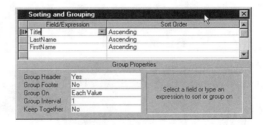

Building a Multitable Report Using the Report Wizard

In previous versions of Access, if the report was based on more than one table, a query had to be created. In this version, multitable reports can be built using the Report Wizard. Access generates an SQL statement as fields are selected from different tables. The Wizard then displays previews of the various models of chosen data. This Wizard is identical to the one in previous versions except in one instance—if a table or query isn't chosen in Step 1, an added feature is brought up. The Wizard gives you the ability to choose fields from multiple tables.

To take advantage of the new feature of building a multitable query using the Report Wizard, follow these steps:

1. In the Report tab of the Database window, click New.

2. Select the Report Wizard and click OK. Don't choose a table or query as a record-source. By purposely leaving the field blank, you invoke another step in the Wizard.

3. From the Tables\Categories drop-down box, choose a table or query and then double-click on the available fields that you need from this recordsource.

4. From the Tables\Categories drop-down box, choose a related recordsource and the fields you need.

5. Repeat step 4 until all the needed fields are chosen, and then click Next.

6. Access interpolates the fields and tables and provides different ways of displaying the information. Click on the different recordsource in the upper-left corner. For example, it might say By Category and By Products. When you choose either one, the Wizard redraws the structure of the result on-screen. Click Next.

7. Access intelligently groups the data as they are chosen from the field list. The Priority buttons, shown in Figure 17.9, let you move fields higher or lower in the grouping chain. Choose a field and click Next to create more groupings in the report.

FIGURE 17.9.

Numerous fields used to group by.

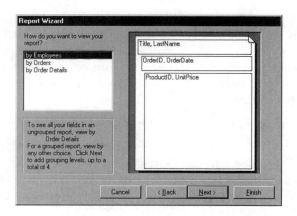

8. The report will automatically sort by the Grouping field. In this step, you will specify which fields within each group will be used to sort by. From the drop-down boxes, choose the fields to sort by within each group, if any, and click Next.

9. Keep choosing options until the Wizard creates a layout that you like, and then click Next.

10. Styles determine which fonts and font sizes will be used. Remember that you can change the font choices, along with all choices, in the report's Design view. Choose a style from the list and click Next.

11. In the final step, you define the report title that appears in the report header. Type in a new name for the report if needed.

12. Click Finish.

When the process is complete, investigate the Recordsource property for this report. You will discover that an SQL statement has been generated that pulls from the tables requested. Clicking the Recordsource Builder button shows you that the query is laid out in Query Design view. This Report Wizard finds all the linking tables necessary and includes them in the query. In order for this step to be successful, the tables must be related.

> **CAUTION**
>
> If Access finds that the tables chosen in the Wizard do not have a relationship, it asks you to establish one or choose other fields.

Multitable Reports and Relational Databases

Creating simple reports requires the ability to manipulate controls. Creating complex multitable reports can require a tight knowledge of the relational model of the databases and the actual data in the database. The preceding method gives you insight into the background needed for complex reports. However, complex reporting isn't possible unless proper relational rules have been followed and relationships thought out. Consider the following points before you begin the report definition process:

- Are the tables normalized for minimal redundancy?
- Are relationships established between tables and queries?
- Do you need to base the reports query on other queries for complex calculations? This chain of queries can go many layers deep and include calculations. Reports based on chains of queries can often be an answer to complex reporting problems and a way to speed up a slow-to-display report.
- Is a subreport necessary?
- Should special functions be written that will be executed in the underlying query?

Customizing Reports

Forms and reports are very similar in how they manipulate controls, sections, and properties. The tricks and techniques in form and report design could fill an entire book themselves. This section covers the foundations of customizing, which should be the base needed to drive creativity. Refer to Chapter 13, "Designing and Customizing Forms," for more information.

Many developers who rush into report creation and assume that customizing is just as intuitive as the Wizards are often left frustrated. They feel tricked when 90 percent of the report is built in a few minutes and the last 10 percent takes several hours. By studying the techniques covered next, you can cut that last 10 percent of the building process drastically. The techniques discussed here are best learned through hands-on experimentation.

Toggling Between Design View and Print Preview

Reports have only two views: Design view and Print Preview. Previewing is split up into the actual Print Preview or a formatted sample of records, the Layout Preview. The View menu shows all views; it appears in both Print Preview and Design view.

Shortcuts for toggling the view are as follows: In Print Preview, click the Close button to enter Design view; in Design view, the toolbar choices are Layout Preview and Print Preview.

> **TIP**
>
> In the Database window, hold down Ctrl and double-click on a report to enter Design view, or right-click on a report and choose Design from the shortcut menu.

The Layout Preview displays a quick formatted sample of records, giving an instant example of the formatting. Print Preview shows the actual formatting of all the records

Manipulating Controls

This section discusses some power features that accelerate the design process.

Moving and Sizing Controls

Move a control and its label together by placing the cursor on the border of a selected control, as shown in Figure 17.10. You can also press Ctrl-arrow keys to move the control.

Move a control independently of its label by placing the cursor on the large black square of a selected control. The "index finger" will be visible only over the large black square in the upper-left corner of a selected control, as shown in Figure 17.11.

FIGURE 17.10.

Moving the control and label together with the flat hand.

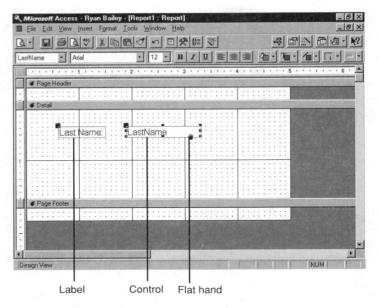

Label　　Control　Flat hand

FIGURE 17.11.

Moving the control independently of its label with the index finger.

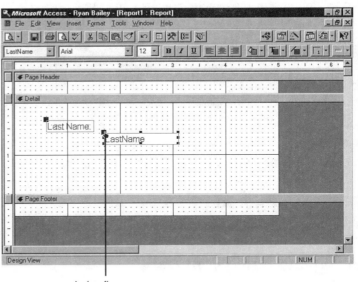

Index finger

TIP

To have the control not snap to grid, hold down the Ctrl key while moving it.

You can size a control by placing the cursor on one of its handlebars and dragging, as shown in Figure 17.12. You can also press Shift-arrow keys to size the control.

FIGURE 17.12.

Sizing a control.

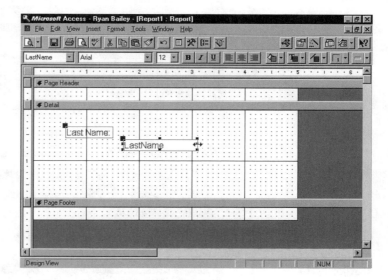

TIP

To size a control automatically, hold the cursor over a sizing handle until the double-headed arrow appears, and then double-click.

The Four Methods of Selecting Controls

When more than one control is selected, they can be manipulated as a group and moved, sized, or deleted. Here are the four methods of selecting controls:

- Hold down the Shift key while clicking separate controls.
- Select View | Select All.
- Click the report's background and drag a square around one or more controls to capture a group, as shown in Figure 17.13.
- Click in one of the rulers at the top or left edges of the report to "shoot" across the reports design, which selects every control in its path, as shown in Figure 17.14.

FIGURE 17.13.
Dragging around a group to select controls.

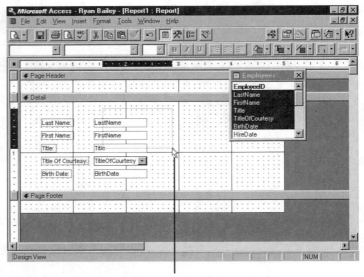

Dragging around a group to select controls

FIGURE 17.14.
Shooting the controls by clicking in the ruler.

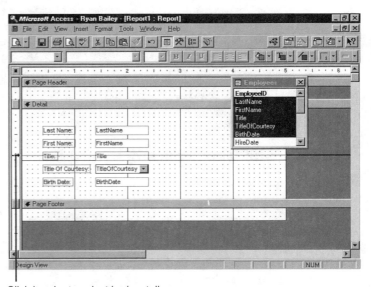

Click in ruler to select horizontally

Deleting and Reestablishing Controls

To delete a control, simply select it and press the Delete key. To reestablish a control, display the report's field list by selecting View | Field List. Then drag the fields off the list and onto the report. (Hold down Ctrl to select more than one field.)

> **NOTE**
>
> The field list displays the fields in the underlying table or query.

Creating Controls with the Toolbox

You can display the toolbox by selecting View | Toolbox or clicking the wrench and hammer icon on the toolbar. The toolbox is just what it sounds like—a construction kit for controls.

To create any type of control, follow these steps:

1. Display the toolbox by selecting View | Toolbox.
2. Click a tool—the line tool, for example.
3. Drag and draw a line in one of the report's sections.

> **NOTE**
>
> The toolbox in Report design is identical to the one in Form design. Chapter 13 discusses the use of each tool in the toolbox.

Changing Control Properties

Changing control properties is the final step in manipulating the report. Everything in Access has properties. The report has properties, each control has properties, and each report section has properties. Changing a property to Yes or No can change the entire structure of the report.

Here are four methods of displaying the Property Sheet:

- Select View | Properties.
- Click the Properties tool on the toolbar.
- Right-click a control and choose Properties.
- Double-click any control or section.

The most crucial report property is the Record Source property. If the developer deletes the contents of this property, the report no longer has data to display. If you activate the drop-down list box of the Record Source property, as shown in Figure 17.15, you can redirect the data source to another table or query.

FIGURE 17.15.

The Record Source property defines the report's underlying record set.

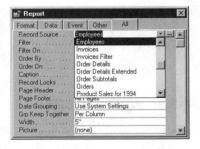

TIP

To see the Help screen for any property, press F1 while the cursor is inside the property.

TIP

Once the Property Sheet is open, click any element of the report to show its properties. To see the overall report properties, click the square in upper-left corner of the Report window where the two rulers meet.

Modifying a Report to Display One Grouping Per Page

Often a page break is needed in an Access report. You create this by setting the section property called Force New Page, as shown in Figure 17.16.

FIGURE 17.16.

Forcing a page break with the Property Sheet.

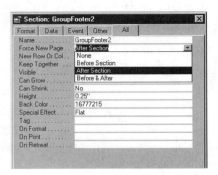

To place different groupings on separate pages of the report, follow these steps:

1. Open the Northwind sample database.
2. Double-click the report called Summary of Sales by Year.
3. Notice that each year gets repeated one after the other. The task is to put each year on a separate page.
4. Select View | Report Design.
5. Once in the Design view, click the View menu again and display the properties.
6. Click the background area of the second ShippedDate footer to display its properties.
7. Choose the All tab in the Property box.
8. Change the property Force New Page to After Section. This forces a page break after this section is formatted on the report.
9. Use Print Preview on the report to see that each group (or year) is on a separate page.

Making Massive Changes with the Format Menu

The new features that show up under the Format menu in this version of Access are AutoFormat, Control Morphing, and some new sizing tools.

Formatting with AutoFormat

Identical in functionality to AutoFormat in Word and Excel, the Access AutoFormat can be very useful. If a report has been built from scratch or modified and needs a new look, AutoFormat reformats every control, as shown in Figure 17.17.

FIGURE 17.17.

AutoFormatting a report.

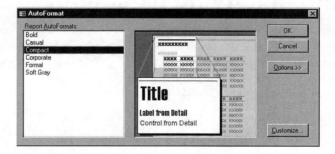

Aligning and Sizing Multiple Controls

The Format menu changes depending on the report element chosen. If several controls are selected, you have the option of aligning or sizing them.

TIP

Right-clicking a selected control brings up the option to align. This is very useful if many controls are selected.

NOTE

Because labels and controls are linked to each other, aligning columns can be frustrating. Try selecting only the labels, aligning them in the opposite direction. Then move one label to where the group should align. Finally, realign them to desired position.

Redefining the Default for Controls

When controls are created from the tools in the toolbox or dragged off the field list, they assume the default size and fonts. The developer has the ability to change these defaults. With this technique, report development time can be radically decreased.

To redefine a text box control's default properties, set the size, font, and other properties to those desired, and then Select Format | Change Default. All new text boxes for this report now assume the new default set.

Building a Report from Scratch and Modifying Its Controls

Creating a report from scratch is an excellent way to learn what the Report Wizards do and how to harness that power. An example of when not to use the Report Wizards is when a report looks the same as an existing business report. In contrast, an insurance policy, for example, has many lines and boxes with lots of fine print. In this case, creating the report from scratch is the only choice. The following steps initiate a blank report:

1. In the Database window, choose the Report tab. Click New and then click OK. A blank report based on no record set is generated.

TIP

To change the Normal template for blank reports, choose Tools | Options | Forms/Reports. In the Report Template dialog box, type the name of a report in the current database.

2. Set the Record Source. Choose View | Properties. Click in the square box to the left of the horizontal ruler to display the report properties. Set the `Record Source` property to Table Categories.

3. Place the fields. Choose View | Field List to display the field list. Drag each field needed on the form into the Detail section. To drag more than one field at a time, hold down Ctrl and click the fields.

4. Arrange the fields. Using the customizing techniques discussed earlier in this chapter, move, size, and change the fields inside the Detail section. Don't forget that by selecting individual controls you can change their properties of font, border, alignment, and size.

> **TIP**
>
> Pressing Ctrl-arrow key moves controls in fine increments; pressing Shift-arrow key sizes them. The Format menu also contains useful design tools.

5. Display one record per page. Double-click the background of the Details section to show its properties. Set the `Force New Page` property to After Section.

6. Use Print Preview on the report and fine-tune.

At the end of this chapter are some power user tricks for customizing reports. Here are some other excellent sources of inspiration:

- The Microsoft Access Knowledge Base
- The expressions generated by the Report Wizard, such as `=Count(ProductID)`
- Expressions used in forms and queries
- Studying the report examples of other developers

Working with Subreports

A subreport is one report inserted into another. Subreports are a very useful way of showing information from two or more tables that have a relationship, although a relationship isn't required in certain circumstances. One example of a main report\subreport is the same as for a main form\subform. In the database are two tables with a one-to-many relationship, also known as a parent-child relationship. A subreport displays the children of the parent report, as shown in Figure 17.18. Although this can be accomplished with a grouping report, some situations require the use of a subreport. Subreports are particularly useful for displaying the parent record and multiple child records from unrelated tables. Note that a relationship isn't required to use subreports. Figure 17.18 shows the underlying one-to-many relationship for the proposed subreport.

FIGURE 17.18.

Main reports and subreports are based on one-to-many relationships.

Relationship

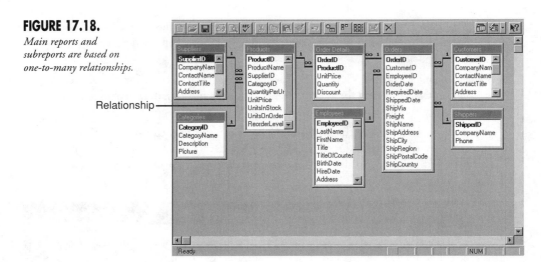

Figure 17.19 shows the use of a subreport in a report. Using a subreport is similar to having a groups and totals report. The advantage of using a subreport is that more than one grouping can be displayed for a single group.

FIGURE 17.19.

A subreport showing the children of the main report.

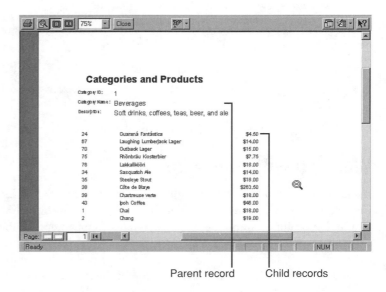

Parent record   Child records

Creating Subreports

Subreporting can be accomplished through the Subreport Wizard or by manual construction. Use of the Wizard is recommended for beginners because the concept of subreports is often confusing. To invoke the Subreport Wizard, turn on the Wizard tool in the toolbox, click the Subreport tool, and draw a box on the report. At this point, the Subreport Wizard initiates.

TIP

The topic of subreports can be a complex one. Online Help is an excellent resource.

Creating a Subreport Without the Wizard

Usually, when a report needs a subreport, the task is very specialized and requires manual intervention. The Wizards can be useful, but they are limited. This section shows you how to create a subreport and embed it into a report. The process of building a main report or subreport has several steps:

1. Ensure that the two tables have a one-to-many relationship. Take note of the field that links the two tables.
2. Compose and save a report based on the parent table. This will be the main report.
3. Create and save a report based on the child table. This will be the subreport. Be sure to include the linking field in the soon-to-be subreport. Subreports are usually of the tabular style.
4. Open the Main report in Design view. Using the Subreport tool in the toolbox, with the Wizard tool off, draw a rectangle where the subreport will go.
5. Display the subreport's properties and set the `Source Object` property to the name of the saved subreport.
6. Examine the subreport properties `Link Child Fields` and `Link Master Fields`. If the linking fields have the same Field Name, Access fills in this property automatically. If Access doesn't populate these properties, the field names need to be typed in manually.

If all goes well, you should have created a working main report\subreport. To edit the subreport, double-click on the subreport in Design view. Some common problems with subreports occur with the sizing of controls and having proper linking.

CAUTION

The architecture of subreports that display related tables hinges on the properties `Link Child Fields` and `Link Master Fields`. If these properties are left blank, the subreport won't work. Keep in mind that subreports don't need to be linked in order to be useful. For example, a subreport could display an address block that needs to be next to every record.

Building a Subreport with the Subreport Wizard

If the concept of subreports is new to you, using the Wizards will be a helpful training device. The Subreport Wizard is a new feature. To bring it up, follow these steps:

1. Click the Wizard tool in the report toolbox.
2. Click the Subreport tool.
3. Draw a rectangle on the report.
4. Answer the Wizard's questions.

The Subreport Wizard builds and embeds a subreport into your report. You can edit the embedded report by double-clicking on it in Design view.

NOTE

The main report doesn't have to be based on records. For example, the parent record could come from a reference to a form, a global variable, a parameter query, or a field in another section of the report. The creative use of subreports can greatly extend reporting in Access.

The Many Ways to Publish a Report

Keeping with the current trend of integrating software and hardware, Microsoft has enhanced some features of Access 95 to allow reports to be transported to different systems. Access gives you numerous ways to publish your reports.

Publishing on Paper

Although publishing on paper is an obvious choice for reports, it's not the only choice. By changing Page Setup, you can make the report take the form of a label, envelope, or postcard.

Publishing to E-Mail

Reports can now be embedded into a MAPI-compliant mail package such as Microsoft Exchange. While viewing the report in Print Preview, select File | Send. Three choices of formatting come up: formatted text (.rtf), spreadsheet (.xls), and text-only (.txt). Next you see the Microsoft Exchange E-Mail dialog box, complete with the report displayed as an embedded icon ready to ship.

Exporting in Another Format

If the report needs to be viewed by someone who doesn't have Access but has a word processor or a spreadsheet, you need to export the report in a common file format. To do this, choose File | Save As/Export | To an External File. This invokes the Save As dialog box. At the bottom of this dialog box, choose the format to export and click OK.

Publishing to Word or Excel Through Office Links

Using the Office Links tool in the middle of the toolbar, you can publish a report to Word or Excel. Access opens the chosen program and then transports the data to that program.

Using the Office Links feature of Access, you can take a report in Print Preview and turn it into a Microsoft Word document or a Microsoft Excel spreadsheet. If you click the Office Links drop-down list box and then choose Publish It with MS Word, Access opens Word and transfers the formatted text. The same is true of Microsoft Excel.

NOTE

This export feature can be performed programmatically through the macro action `OutputTo`.

NOTE

Subreports are now transferred to Microsoft Word when you use the Office Links feature. This was a major limitation of previous versions of Access. However, in Access 95, some report elements, such as rectangles and lines, occasionally don't get transferred from Access to Word.

TIP

To stretch the concepts of what a report is capable of, investigate the catalog report in Northwind.

Ten Great Ways to Customize Reports with Expressions and Code

The key role of a good report is displaying data in an understandable fashion. When table data is simply placed on a form, it can be confusing for the user. For example, it's easier to understand the combination of the first and last names than it is to display them separately (*Jill Smith* as compared to *Jill   Smith*). You can do much of this fine-tuning through clever expressions written in a text box control. This section covers 10 examples of common report expressions:

- Concatenating fields for a text box
- Turning a Yes/No field into text
- Using If...Then statements with the IIF function
- Turning the display off for a field if the value is Null
- Creating and calling an If...Then function in the report
- Retrieving records through Dlookup statements
- Combining text fields for an address block
- Referencing an open form on the report
- Adding report data using the Sum function
- Writing a Select Case function for a text box

Concatenating Fields for a Text Box

The text box shown in Figure 17.20 combines the values of the following three elements: First Name, a space, and Last Name. This is known as a calculated control. This control was created with the Text Box tool. Inside the control or in the Control Source property, write the calculated expression. Calculated fields always start with an equal sign (=). Here are some rules to observe:

- Field names must have square brackets around them if they have spaces: [Order ID]
- Text values must have quotation marks around them: "Title"
- Date values must have pound signs on both sides: #12/22/65#

Turning a Yes/No Field into Text

The properties of Yes/No fields are divided into three parts. The first part is not used, the second part is for True values (–1), and the third part is for False values (0). These are separated by semicolons. The example shown in Figure 17.21 was created by placing an unbound text box on the report, setting its Control Source property to the field Discount, and typing the expression in the Format property. This expression changes a –1 value to read "Discount" and a 0 value to "No Discount." Refer to the online Help for more details.

FIGURE 17.20.

The concatenation of text fields.

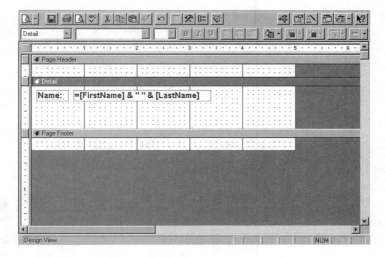

FIGURE 17.21.

Format property expression to change display.

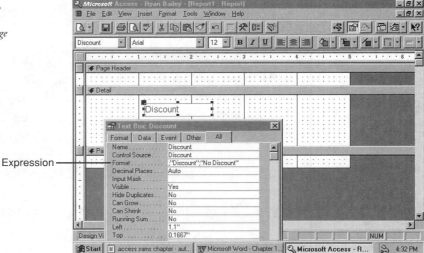

Using *If...Then* Statements with the *IIF* Function

The IIF, or immediate if, function performs a simple If...Then test. The arguments for this function have three parts: the Test, True value, and False value. In the Test portion, write a test against a field value. If that test passes, it displays the contents of True; otherwise, it displays the contents of False. These True and False values can be text values surrounded by quotation marks, such as "PAID"; field values enclosed in brackets, such as [Order Amount]; or calculations, such as Date()–30.

Figure 17.22 shows an IIF statement in action. This simple expression displays No Discount if there was a value in the field Discount = 0. If the value of Discount was not equal to zero, it displays the actual value. To recreate this example, follow these steps:

1. Create a blank report in Northwind based on the OrdersDetails table.
2. Using the toolbox, choose the Text Box tool and draw an unbound control on the report.
3. Type in the Name property CheckDiscount. If the actual field named Discount is placed in the Name property, it is likely to produce an #Error value.
4. Type the expression into the Control Source property, as shown in Figure 17.22.

FIGURE 17.22.

The IIF function is a simple If... Then test.

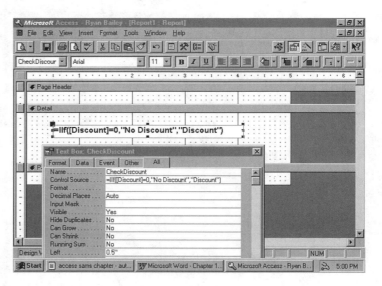

Turning the Display Off a Field If the Value Is Null

If a customer on an invoice report doesn't get a discount, you don't display the control for Discount or its label. The IsNull function, like the IIF function, is a built-in Access function. In the preceding example, the IIF function performs a test. The IsNull function tests whether a field is null. If the field is null, it displays " ". (Two quotation marks print as nothing.) If it isn't null, it prints the value of the field.

Note that the example in Figure 17.23 is identical in structure to the one shown in Figure 17.22. The only difference is in the Control Source expression. To re-create this example, follow the steps outlined in the preceding example, but change the expression.

FIGURE 17.23.

Combining the IsNull and IIF functions.

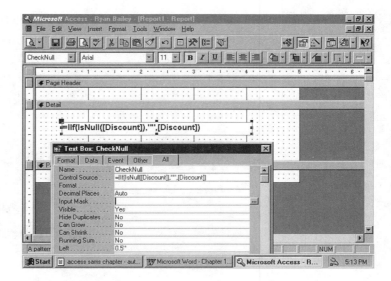

Creating and Calling an *If...Then* Function in the Report

The previous IIF function is useful for single-level tests. Some developers feel that they have more control by creating If...Then functions and then calling them in the OnFormat property of the Detail section. This is one method of calling functions in reports. An exercise in calling functions in reports is outlined next. Begin with an equal sign (=), followed by the function name, and end with parentheses ( ). Place this function call in the OnFormat property of the section the control is in. An unbound text box named DisplayDisc is placed in the Detail section (see Figure 17.24). The properties of the Detail section are displayed. Type the function name =SampleIF() into the OnFormat property of the Detail section. When the report is run, and the Detail section is formatted one record at a time, the function evaluates the test and sets the DisplayDisc field accordingly.

1. Inside the Northwind database, create a blank report based on the OrderDetails table.

2. Place an unbound text box on the report.

3. In the Name property, name the control DisplayDisc.

4. Save the report as OrderDetailsRPT.

5. Select View | Code to open the Code module for this report.

6. Create the following function:

```
Private Function SampleIF()
    'Sample function to test If...Then statements in reports
If Discount = 0 Then
      Reports!OrderDetailsRPT!DisplayDisc = "No Discount"
Else
        Reports!OrderDetailsRPT!DisplayDisc = "Discount Given"
End If
End Function
```

7. Close the Code module.

8. Display the Property Sheet for the Detail section of the report.

9. Type the function name into the OnFormat property, preceded by an equal sign (for example, =SampleIF()).

10. If you typed everything correctly, the Report Preview will display what the function instructed it to do.

FIGURE 17.24.

Calling a function in a text box control.

OnFormat property

Retrieving Records Through *Dlookup* Statements

When the report requires a record from a foreign table, and a subreport is not justified, the Dlookup statement is a solution. The Dlookup function is syntactically identical to the other domain functions: Dcount, Dmax, Dfirst, and so on. The example in Figure 17.25 looks up the value of the field named Discount in the table named Orders, where the OrderID is equal to the OrderID on the open form called MyForm. (The online Help provides additional information.) The Dlookup syntax can be dissected as Look up what?, Where?, and When?, each enclosed in quotation marks and separated by commas.

Combining Text Fields for an Address Block

Address blocks are common in reports and can be frustrating. For an address block, use regular text concatenation in a text box with the ASCII character codes CHR$(13) and CHR$(10). These

ASCII codes are the line feed and carriage return codes that drop down a line. To have the address block confirm the existence of a second address, insert the following code:

```
=IIf(IsNull([Address2]),[Address],[Address] & Chr$(13) & Chr$(10) & [Address2])
```

FIGURE 17.25.

Using the Dlookup. *function.*

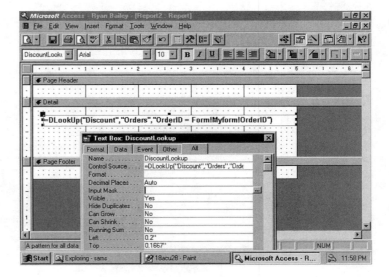

Figure 17.26 delivers the address with each part concatenated and placed on its proper line.

FIGURE 17.26.

Combining fields for an address block.

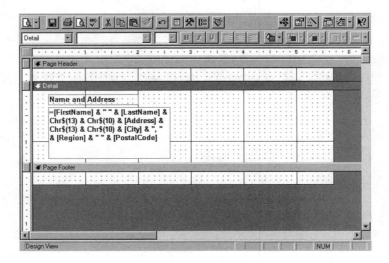

Referencing an Open Form on the Report

Sometimes a report is run from a button the user presses on a form. The data on that form can be used in the report without queries or Dlookups. The expression can be typed into the Control Source property of a text box; however, it's much easier to use the Expression Builder. To invoke the Expression Builder, display the Property Sheet for a new text box control and click the Control Source property (see Figure 17.27). Click the Builder button on its right, which invokes the Expression Builder. Begin drilling down into the form's objects to find the field in question.

FIGURE 17.27.

Referencing a form from the report.

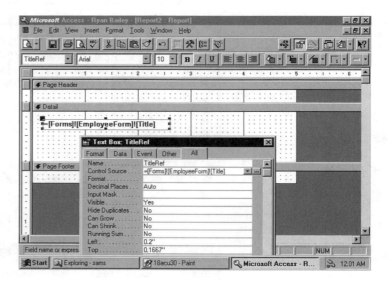

Adding Up Report Data with the *Sum* Function

You can use a Wizard to insert the Sum function into the Report Footer automatically, as shown in Figure 17.28. The Sum function sums up the field specified in the Detail section.

> **CAUTION**
>
> Functions such as Sum and Count will work properly only when placed in Group Footers or Report Footers. If these expressions are placed in the Page Footer, they will display #Error.

FIGURE 17.28.

Using the Sum *function in a Report Footer.*

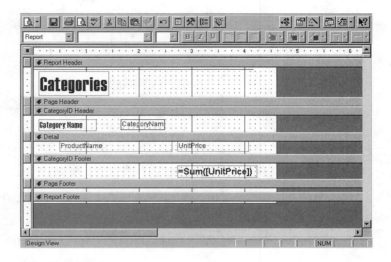

Writing a *Select Case* Function for a Text Box

When an expression needs to evaluate numerous conditions and an If...Then statement isn't appropriate, a Select Case statement is a good option:

```
Private Function CheckTarif()

    'Determine the tariff by checking ShipCountry field
Dim shipcountry As String
    Select Case Reports![Report1]![shipcountry]
    Case "USA"
        CheckTarif = "No Tarif"
    Case "Japan"
        CheckTarif = "15%"
    Case Else
        CheckTarif = "10%"

    End Select

End Function
```

When the choices of If...Then statements are numerous, the Select Case statement helps you manage the multiple conditions. This function is called differently than the If...Then statement in the earlier example. The previous function was called in the OnFormat property, whereas the Select Case function shown in Figure 17.29 was placed in the Control Source property of a text box. Both methods are shown here to demonstrate ways to call functions on reports. Depending on the nature of the function, it can be called from the Control Source property, OnFormat, OnPrint, OnRetreat, or others. Each method has its own merits.

FIGURE 17.29.

A text box calling a `Select Case` *function.*

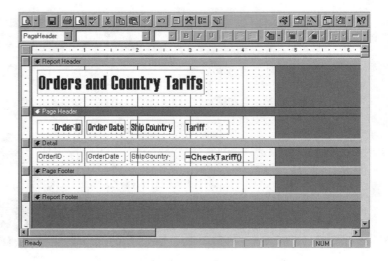

Power Areas to Focus on in Reporting

This chapter has covered the creation and customization of reports. Over a period of time, certain report power tricks have risen to the surface:

- Use Ctrl or Shift with the arrow keys to move and size controls.
- Double-click selected handlebars of controls to autofit.
- Use the Format menu to change a control's default.
- Use the Format menu to align and adjust controls.
- Right-click to bring up the shortcut menu.
- Use subreports whenever possible.
- Do as many calculations as possible at the query level instead of in the report.
- Use the Expression Builder to write complex expressions.

Summary

Typically, it takes an average of three hours to complete each report of a database project. This is due to the placement of the controls and lines, formation of queries, creation of subreports, and numerous other unaccounted-for database housekeeping chores. This three-hour estimate is only a working figure, depending on the developer's experience and the complexity of the report. You'll find that during report creation, flaws in the underlying database design emerge. This redesign time results in extra project hours. To avoid this common pitfall, begin the project with a sketch of all the reports, and test the database design by working backwards.

Studying the techniques and examples in this chapter will greatly decrease your report creation time. The tools available in Access 95 offer an incredible amount of creativity. With the new freedom found in reporting, you'll also find new frustrations. Because you can do so much, things can become even more confusing. Complex reporting will be easy after you study the literature, read the Help screens, investigate examples, and get plenty of practical experience. As with most elements of Access 95, nothing is more beneficial than hands-on experience.

Producing Mailings

18

by Jude
Mullaney

IN THIS CHAPTER

Comparing Forms and Reports

One of the benefits of a database is reports. Reports are tangible results of data entered. Data usually is entered into an Access database via forms. Forms and reports are alike in that the data being entered into a database is the same data that will be printed. Forms and reports both can use tables and queries as records. Both can have fields, criteria can be set on each object itself, and both can contain expressions. They are also the same in that each gives you a blank section to work on. As you drag fields from the Field list, the form and report start to take shape.

Forms and reports differ in that additional records can be added to forms, whereas reports don't allow for user intervention in the addition of records. Reports can have groupings associated with them because they use the existing data. Forms, on the other hand, don't have groupings associated with them because the data is in the process of being entered.

A large percentage of databases contain some kind of table that tracks people information—Name, Address, City, State, ZIP. With this information, you can create mailings. Access offers several report wizards that create sophisticated reports by having you answer a few questions. This chapter shows you how to create mailings with and without wizards, how to produce labels, how to export to Word, and much more.

Creating Mailing Labels with the Label Wizard

To create mailing labels, whether with a wizard or without, it's highly recommended that you use an existing source of records that contain the information found on mailing labels. In fact, if a wizard is used to create anything other than a table, a record source must be stated before the wizard will execute. The examples in this chapter are based on a table called Vendors. This table contains the following fields:

VendorID: AutoNumber field
FirstName: Text field
LastName: Text field
Company: Text field
Address: Text field
City: Text field
StateOrProvince: Text field
PostalCode: Text field
Country: Text field

You can use data from other databases when creating mailing labels in Access. The only requirement that Access has when creating mailing labels is that the data must exist in a table or query. If you have data in another application such as Excel, dBASE, FoxPro, or Paradox, simply import that data into an Access table or query.

To create a mailing label using the wizard, you must click the Reports tab in the Database window and then click the New button. In Figure 18.1, the Label Wizard is selected. The Vendors table is selected to be the data source for the wizard.

FIGURE 18.1.

The Vendors table is selected for the Label Wizard.

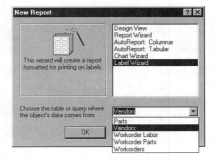

> **NOTE**
>
> A wizard, whether a Form or Report wizard, can't be executed without a data source. The data source for each wizard can be found in the drop-down list box in the New Form or New Report dialog box.

After selecting a data source for the wizard, click OK to continue. The great thing about wizards is that they do the bulk of the work concerning the operation being performed. In this case, the Label Wizard is sizing and centering a label and entering all the measurements concerning the labels being used. Figure 18.2 shows the next step in the Label Wizard process.

FIGURE 18.2.

Selecting the label format is the next step in the Label Wizard.

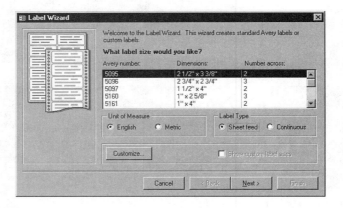

Notice that the different label options utilize the Avery label formats. Avery labels are one of the most common labels available today. They can be found in most office supply stores. There are 66 Avery label formats to choose from. These labels are broken down into two categories: sheet and continuous. There are 25 Avery sheet label formats and 41 Avery continuous label formats. Select the type of label to be used—Sheet feed or Continuous. By using the scroll bar found at the side of the label combo box, you can view all the label formats. Click the desired Avery format number, and then click the Next > button.

NOTE

A Customize button is available in the dialog box shown in Figure 18.2. This button is used to create a new custom label. A custom label is any label that doesn't appear in the Avery label listing in the wizard. This means the label can be from a company other than Avery. This subject is covered later in this chapter.

The next dialog box of the Label Wizard, shown in Figure 18.3, deals with the font and color of the text that will appear on the labels. At this point, a developer can choose from different fonts. Depending on the font chosen, you can also choose the font size, more commonly referred to as the pitch.

FIGURE 18.3.

Selecting the text format for the label.

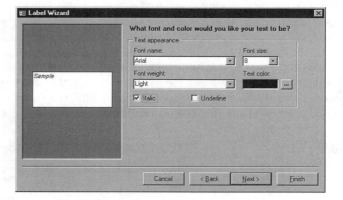

CAUTION

Even though the font-size option can be as large as 72 points (there are 72 points in 1 inch), the smaller font sizes are recommended. Common sense dictates that a mailing label that is 2 inches tall can't have three lines of text that are each 1 inch tall.

Font weight, along with text color, can also be selected. The Access Label Wizard gives you the option of making the text appear italicized, underlined, or both. To select these options, click in the box that appears next to the desired option.

The left side of the dialog box contains a simulated label. As changes are made to the text options, these changes are reflected on the simulated label. In Figure 18.3, the Italic option is on, and the word "Sample" on the simulated label appears italicized. Remember, this simulation contains only one line. When you're choosing the font and size, you should keep in mind that more than one line will need to appear on the label.

Click the Next > button to move to the third dialog box in the Label Wizard. In this step, Access is asking you how the label is to be filled out. In Figure 18.4, different fields appear on the label. You can add these fields to the prototype label by highlighting the desired field and pressing the > button or by double-clicking the field. You can also choose the punctuation that is to appear on every label. For example, a comma should appear after the name of a city and before the name of a state on a mailing label. Carriage returns, spaces, punctuation marks, and literal words are entered onto the prototype. As they appear on the prototype, they will appear on every label.

FIGURE 18.4.

The prototype represents how each label will appear.

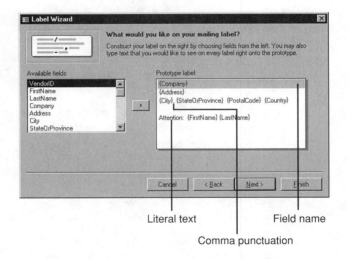

Literal text

Comma punctuation

Field name

The prototype shown in Figure 18.4 includes four carriage returns (pressing Enter brings the focus down to the next line). You can also use the mouse to click the next line down, or, if you prefer, you can use the arrow keys to move between the lines. The City field is immediately followed by a comma and a space. There is also a space between the State and PostalCode fields. These elements might be hard to see, but they are present. The label is slightly different from the basic name, address, city, state, ZIP label in that it also includes an attention line. To get the word "Attention:" to appear, type it directly onto the label prototype. "Attention:" will appear on every label.

There might be times when you want to remove a field that has been placed on the label. You can do this by highlighting the desired field and pressing the Delete key, which removes the field from the label but not from the list. The same field can be placed on the label again.

Click the Next > button to move to the fourth step in the Label Wizard. This is where you can decide the sort order of the mailing labels. In Figure 18.5, the PostalCode is selected as the only sort order. This is an excellent feature for companies that use the bulk mailing rates offered by the postal service. A developer can choose one field or multiple fields for the sort order. All the fields selected here will appear on the sort order of the reports' Design view.

FIGURE 18.5.

Select the fields for the sort order of the mailing labels.

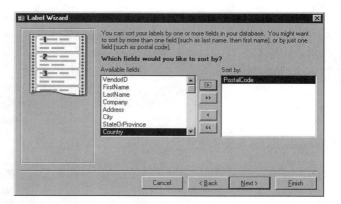

The last of the five steps in the Label Wizard is shown in Figure 18.6. In this dialog box, you can opt to keep the name of the report as it is assigned by the Access Wizard or type a new name. Reports have only two views—Design and Preview. You can choose the view to go into when the Finish button is clicked. When the Yes, help me work with labels box is checked, Access displays additional Help at the time of creation of the new report. This Help file shows how to customize the label report.

FIGURE 18.6.

In the final step, you choose the view.

Click the Finish button to create the label report. If you need to go back to previous dialog boxes to change labels, fields, or options, you can do so by clicking the < Back button. The < Back button enables you to go all the way back to the first dialog box in the wizard if you want to.

Because the Modify Label Design option was checked on the last wizard step, the report is brought up in Design view. In Figure 18.7, the Sorting and Grouping dialog box is on-screen. The PostalCode field has already been placed in the cell. This act was performed by the Access Label Wizard based on the information you entered in the sorting step (Figure 18.5).

FIGURE 18.7.

Grouping and sorting information has already been entered.

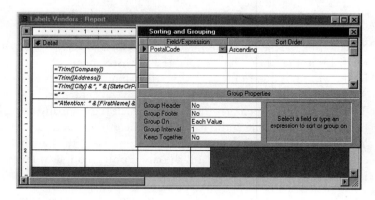

When you're looking at the fields on-screen, you'll see that the first few fields have the word "Trim" before the name of the field. This was added by the wizard; if the same field were pulled down to the report, "Trim" wouldn't appear on the field. In Figure 18.8, the properties sheet for the first field, Company, is visible. On the Control Source for the field, this expression appears:

```
=Trim([Company])
```

FIGURE 18.8.

The fields with the Trim *function associated.*

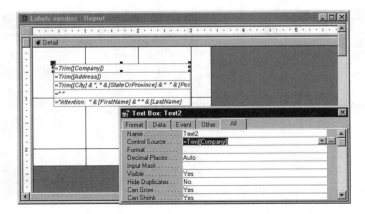

When users enter data into tables and forms, invariably some records will have some fields that have extra spaces. The word "Trim" refers to the Trim function, which removes the leading and trailing spaces found in a field. This action ensures that the label is left-aligned.

> **TIP**
>
> Three Trim functions are available—LTrim, RTrim, and Trim. LTrim removes all the spaces to the left of an expression. RTrim removes all the spaces following an expression. Trim removes all the spaces before and after an expression.

Several things are going on in Figure 18.8. The Trim function is being performed on some of the fields in the label. The FirstName and LastName fields were automatically concatenated by the wizard. A question was raised earlier about records that have two lines of address in the Address field. Notice that the fields have the Can Shrink and Can Grow properties turned on. This capability compensates for fields in which the company name might be longer than the field drawn for it. The entire name would be printed, because the Can Grow property is set to Yes. The same goes for the Address field. Conversely, the City field has the Can Shrink property set to Yes. This means that if the city is only a couple of letters long, the entire field size isn't used.

The Access Label wizard helps developers turn out advanced labels in a short amount of time. Certain functions, properties, and expressions are created based on the answers to a few simple questions. You can view the labels in Print Preview view by pressing the Print Preview button that appears on the toolbar. You can also view the labels by selecting File | Print Preview. It's important to realize that you can create labels based on tables or queries that might not have records. If a label is based on a record source that doesn't contain any records, Access returns an #Error in place of the label data. If this occurs, check the record source of the report to make sure that records are present. The next section covers the printing of the labels.

Printing Mailing Labels

Printing labels is a bit more tricky than simply pressing the Print button from the Print Preview of a report. A couple of issues need to be addressed:

■ What kind of label is being used—sheet or continuous?

■ What kind of printer will be printing the labels?

■ Will the same printer be used every time for these particular labels?

■ How many labels are being printed at one time?

■ Which font is being used?

■ Will this database be distributed to other people—either throughout a company or through mass distribution?

■ What is the default printer?

Start with the first issue. What kind of label is being used? Continuous labels are usually tractor-feed, dot-matrix labels, whereas single-sheet labels can be used in a dot-matrix printer but are usually used in a laser printer.

NOTE

Tractor-feed laser printers also exist. Big government offices, such as the IRS, use these printers, which are priced on the high end. Most companies use regular sheet-fed lasers or dot-matrix printers.

What printer are the labels being printed on? If they are tractor-feed labels, they should go through a dot-matrix printer. Sheet labels, however, can go through a dot matrix printer, a laser printer, an inkjet printer, or a deskjet printer.

How many labels are being printed at one time, and what font is being used for those labels? Some developers like to make their labels artistic. They use larger pitches, TrueType fonts, and sometimes logos. The more artistic the label, the slower the print job. Having very artistic labels is all right for a few labels, but if the number of labels is high, the printer could be tied up for hours. One way to increase the speed of a large print job is to change the font being used on the label.

Three types of fonts are available: TrueType, system, and printer. TrueType fonts are the fancy fonts that have a small TT icon associated with them. System fonts are those that come with Windows. Printer fonts are the fonts contained in the printer itself. System fonts and printer fonts are faster to print than TrueType fonts. How can you tell which font is which? There are a few ways. The first method is to refer to the documentation that comes with the software, computer, and printer being used. That method can be a hassle at times. An easier way is to go to the properties of a field on the label. Go to the Font property, click the drop-down list box, and select a font.

There can be a disadvantage to not using TrueType fonts in your reports, especially when the precision of the output is a concern. Fonts that aren't TrueType fonts might not appear the same on paper as they do on-screen.

TrueType fonts have a small TT icon to the left of the name. The system fonts and printer fonts have the "sheet of paper leaving a printer" icon to the left. Printer fonts, which are the fastest fonts to print, have the word "Printer" following the name of the font. The drawback to using printer fonts is that they aren't as attractive as TrueType fonts. A good rule of thumb is the more labels to be printed, the less attractive they need to be.

With TrueType fonts, the pitch can be as small as 1 point (type 01 in the Font Size box). When you change the font to a printer font, the pitch is usually 8 or 10 points. This change in size will affect the output. Fewer lines per label will fit. When you change the font, be sure to view the label in Print Preview mode before printing.

When developing a database, it's important to know how the database will be used. Will it be installed on local hard drives, or will it be a shared copy on a network? When you're working with a database, you have the ability to save every report to a specific printer by opening the report in Design view, selecting File | Page Setup, and selecting the desired printer from the Page tab. This feature is great for users who have the database stored on their local hard drive. Each user can store the same report to a different printer and not interfere with the other users' reports. For example, user A can store the Vendors report to the HP4 printer, and user B can store the same Vendors report to the Epson LQ 850. When each user runs the Vendors report, one user will print from the HP4 and the other user will print from the Epson LQ 850.

What happens if the database is a shared copy on a network? If user A saves the Vendors report to the HP4 and user B doesn't have access to the HP4, Access displays a dialog box. This dialog box informs user B that the report has been saved to a printer that isn't available and gives user B the option to run the report from her default printer or another printer that is available to user B. If user B accepts the usage of her default printer, the report will be saved to user B's default printer. When user A opens the Vendors report again, it prints from user B's default printer. If user A doesn't have access to user B's default printer, a dialog box appears informing user A that the Vendors report has been saved to another printer. User A then has the option of printing the Vendors report to user A's default printer or choosing another printer.

If the database is being developed for mass distribution or will be used as a runtime application, users won't have access to the Page Setup option for each report. In these cases, reports should be saved to the default printer. The default printer doesn't refer to the developer's default printer but to the default printer of the computer that the application is being installed on. This allows the reports to be printed without requiring the user to interact with the dialog box mentioned in the preceding paragraph.

> **CAUTION**
>
> There might be cases when you develop a report and use fonts that aren't available to the user who executes the report. In these cases, if Windows 95 can't find a font that is used in a report, it defaults to a similar font. When it defaults to another font, the report output might change. In this case, it's necessary to view the report in Print Preview view to make sure that the report prints all of the information.

The default printer can vary from machine to machine. If there are multiple printers, how can you tell which printer is the default printer? Pull up Printers from the Settings icon in the Start menu of Windows 95, or pull up Control Panel for the machine and select Printers.

When you right-click the printer icon, you see the shortcut menu. The Default Printer line has a check to the left, indicating that the HP Laserjet 4 Plus is the default printer for this machine.

Even though initially a report is saved to the default printer, the labels still might need to come out of another printer that isn't the default. When dealing with this situation, it's important to know how the database from which the labels are being printed is being used. As mentioned earlier, a database can be used as a local copy on a machine, as a shared copy on a server, or even as a runtime version of the database.

If the database is being saved on a local hard drive, each user can save the same report to a different specific printer. If the database is being used on a network, each user can change the printer that a report is to be printed from. The user can save this change, and as each user activates the report, the report will try to use the printer that it was last saved to. If the new user doesn't have access to that printer, a dialog box appears when the report is activated (see Figure 18.9).

FIGURE 18.9.

The dialog box that appears when the user doesn't have access to the specified printer to which the report is saved.

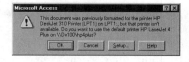

The user then can choose to open the report and use the default printer by clicking OK, not open the report at all by clicking Cancel, or send the report to another specific printer by clicking Setup. If Setup is chosen, the Page Setup dialog box opens and the user can choose any printer under the Page tab. When the report is closed, the new printer that was selected is saved with it. If the report is opened by another user, the dialog box might appear, depending on whether the new user has access to the same printer that the report was saved to.

In the case of a runtime version of the database, if you save the report to the default printer, the default printer for every user will be used to run the report. You might choose to save the report to a common, specific printer. When you do save a report to a specific printer, the entire path to the printer is saved with the report. When your users need to change the printer, you must change the path to match the location of the new printer and then create a new runtime to reflect the printer change.

This method is acceptable if only a few users are using a runtime version of your database, but mass-distribution of your database in runtime is a very different situation. For mass distribution of a runtime application, it might be best to use the `PrtDevMode` property to set the Print Setup dialog box for your reports. The `PrtDevMode` property has 26 different members. They cover all of the items that you see when you look at the Page Setup dialog box. You would need to develop a setup form for your users in which they can choose the printer that each report is suppose to print from. For example, assume that all label reports are to be sent to the Epson LQ 850. When the label report is selected, a macro or event procedure that sets `PrtDevMode` can be executed. The information from the setup form is passed to `PrtDevMode`, and that information sets the printing device mode. Complete documentation of `PrtDevMode` can be found in the Win32 Software Development Kit.

Designing Labels Manually

Designing labels manually isn't as difficult as you might think. One of the reasons developers design labels manually is that the labels being used are not one of the 66 predefined Avery labels. An Access Label Wizard can help here too, by offering a feature that was touched on earlier—the Customize feature. Access can help you create a template for a box of labels that can be used again and again.

> **NOTE**
>
> Before you begin manually designing labels, we should cover a few details about the printer fonts. Printer fonts are printer-specific, meaning that a printer font found on an Epson might not be exactly like one found on a Panasonic. Printer fonts are usually available in a 10-point pitch. Pitch is important when you're determining how many lines there are per page. Sheet printers (such as laser printers) can hold up to 60 lines per page. Continuous printers (such as tractor-feed printers) can hold as many as 66 lines per page.

To create a label manually, follow these steps:

1. Get a sheet of the appropriate labels and a ruler.
2. Go to the Reports tab of the database container.
3. In the Reports module of the database container, click New. Choose the desired table or query on which the new labels will be based. Click the Label Wizard and click OK.
4. The first Label Wizard dialog box is where all the predefined labels are displayed. A button in the center of the form reads Customize. Click that button to bring up the New Label Size dialog box, shown in Figure 18.10.

FIGURE 18.10.

New labels can be customized in the Label Wizard provided by Access 95.

5. Choose the Unit of Measure and Label Type before clicking the New button. You can see the heart of the custom label process in Figure 18.11.

FIGURE 18.11.

The heart of the custom label process.

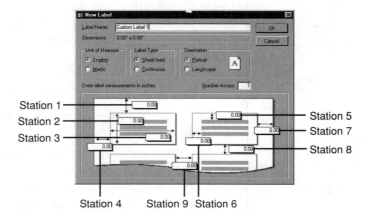

6. Type the desired name of the new label being created.
7. Press the Tab key to confirm the Unit Of Measure being used. Indicate whether the ruler being used is an English measure ruler (inches) or a Metric ruler (centimeters).
8. Press the Tab key to confirm the type of label being used. If the edges of the label paper have small tractor holes, choose Continuous.

9. Press the Tab key to move over to the Orientation of the label. Choose either Portrait or Landscape.

10. Press the Tab key and enter the number of labels that go across the top of the label paper.

NOTE

When you're entering a number for the number of labels field, the number must be an integer from 1 to 20.

11. This is where the ruler comes into play. In Figure 18.11, measurements need to be entered in nine stations to complete the new custom label. To move from station to station for this example, press the Tab key. You also use your mouse to click into the desired station or use Shift-Tab to go backward. Table 18.1 gives the information to be entered in each station.

Table 18.1. Measurements needed to create a custom label.

Station	Information to Enter
Station 1	The number of inches or centimeters from the top of the upper-left label to the top edge of the label paper.
Station 2	The height of the label itself in inches or centimeters.
Station 3	The width of the label itself in inches or centimeters.
Station 4	The number of inches or centimeters from the left edge of the label to the left edge of the label paper.
Station 5	The number of inches or centimeters that should appear as the upper margin of the label itself.
Station 6	The number of inches or centimeters that should appear as the left margin of the label itself.
Station 7	The number of inches or centimeters from the right edge of the rightmost label to the right edge of the label paper.
Station 8	The number of inches or centimeters from the bottom edge of one label to the top edge of the next label (the horizontal gutter).
Station 9	The number of inches or centimeters from the left edge of one label to the right edge of the next label (the vertical gutter).

A label must have a horizontal and vertical dimension set before the wizard can proceed. It's not possible to print on a label on which station 2 and station 3 are not positive numbers.

12. After the new label is finished, click OK. The new custom label now appears in the New Label Size dialog box, shown in Figure 18.12. These labels can be edited, duplicated, or deleted at any time.

FIGURE 18.12.

New custom labels appear here.

13. If the report will be stored on your machine, choose the printer that will be used for the new labels by selecting File | Print. Select the printer name from the drop-down list box if it isn't the default printer, and click OK.

Depending on the custom label type (either sheet or continuous), it will appear as a selection in the Label Wizard dialog box, as long as the Show custom label sizes box is checked (see Figure 18.2). The rest of the Label Wizard dialog boxes pertaining to the prototypes and naming will be the same as if the label had already existed. Remember, the printer saved with this report is the one that will be used when the report is executed again. If this report will be used by other people, it's suggested that the default printer be saved with the report. Each user of the custom report can resave the report to coincide with her specific printer.

When you're creating labels without the help of a wizard, you need to make certain adjustments. This section especially pertains to creating dot-matrix labels. Before creating a label for a dot-matrix printer, you must set the default printer and paper size. You do this by selecting Start | Settings | Printer Settings in Windows. To change a default printer, highlight the desired default printer in the Printers window. Then select File | Set As Default.

After the printer has been set as the default printer, edit the properties for that printer. You can do this by selecting File | Properties or by right-clicking on the printer icon and selecting Properties. On the Paper tab of the properties, select the paper size to be Custom, as shown in Figure 18.13.

FIGURE 18.13.

Select the custom paper size.

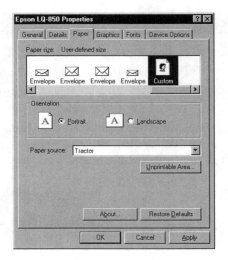

As soon as the Custom icon is selected, Access displays the User-Defined Size dialog box, shown in Figure 18.14. This is where you enter the dimensions (length and width) of the label.

FIGURE 18.14.

Enter the length and width of the label.

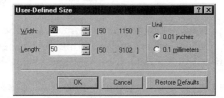

If there is more than one label for this custom label, measure the far-left label's left edge to the far-right label's right edge. This measurement equals the width. The length is measured from the top of the first label to the top of the second label (including the gutter).

Click OK to save any changes. After setting the printer and paper size, you can create the custom label report. Return to Access and the Reports module of the Database window, and create a New blank report. Access brings up the Design view of the report. If the Report Headers/Footers option is checked, uncheck it by selecting View | Report Headers/Footers. Report Headers/Footers is usually turned off because they can throw off the placement of the labels.

Some kinds of labels have a small area at the head and foot of the label page. It's possible to have something print in this area by placing text or a text field in the Page Header/Footer area. However, you should be careful to make sure that this doesn't throw off the spacing for the rest of the labels.

Move the edges of the report so that the Detail section matches the height and width of one label. Open the properties for the report. Change the report's X gridline to read 20 and the Y gridline to read 24 (if they aren't set at that already). This action allows for greater control of the objects that will be placed on the label.

From the Field List, drag the fields that should appear and drop them on the label. Remove the labels that are attached to the fields (unless they're needed for the label). You can create margins for the label by making sure that the fields are two grid point increments from the top and bottom edges of the label.

Concatenate the fields that will appear on the same text line of the label. For example, City, State, and ZIP usually appear on one line in an address label. In Figure 18.15, the City field's properties are visible. The StateOrProvince and PostalCode fields are concatenated with the City field in a new text box.

FIGURE 18.15.

Concatenate any fields that will appear on the same text line of a label in a text box.

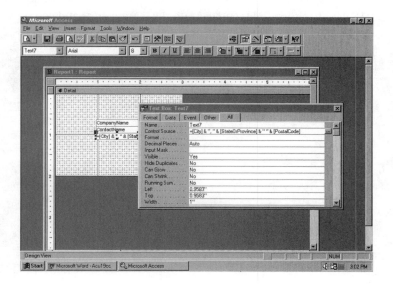

Change all the fields' `Can Shrink` and `Can Grow` properties to Yes. You can do this in one stroke by highlighting all the fields on the label and pulling up the Properties sheet, which represents the properties for all the fields highlighted. Change the `Can Shrink` and `Can Grow` properties to Yes. For the `Can Grow` property to take effect, the fields below it can't be touching it. For example, an address field can have two text lines in it. For the `Can Grow` property to take effect, the top of the City, State, ZIP field can't be touching the bottom of the Address field.

CAUTION

For the `Can Grow` property to be active, the field below can't be *mathematically* touching the Can Grow field. To check the mathematics of each field, pull up the properties of the Can Grow field. Add the value that appears in the Top field to the value that appears in the Height field. Look at the example shown in Figure 18.15. The Address field is also set to Can Grow. The Top value of the Address field is .375". The Height value is .1667". When the two are added together, the result is .5417. The Text7 text box, where the City, StateOrProvince, and PostalCode fields are concatenated, has a Top value of .5417. This means that if a record has an Address field that contains more than one text line (such as a suite number), the address field won't grow to accommodate the second text line.

After you've placed the fields on the custom label, it's time to print the label. Select File | Page Setup. Change all the margins shown in Figure 18.16 to 0.0. Some printers don't allow for a 0.0 margin. When 0.0 is entered into the margin areas and you move to the next field, Access displays the minimum amount of margin that is required.

FIGURE 18.16.

Change all the margins to 0.0.

Move to the Page tab. Select the Default printer. Then move to the Layout tab, shown in Figure 18.17. Enter the number of labels that appear across the top of the label paper. In the Row Spacing box, type the amount of space that appears between the bottom of one label and the top of the next label (the horizontal gutter). In the Column Spacing box, type the amount of space that appears between the right edge of one label and the left edge of the next label (the vertical gutter).

The custom label is now ready for print preview. When you're satisfied with the print preview of the custom label report, the report is ready to be printed. If it isn't satisfactory, return to Design view and make corrections.

Here is a quick review of the custom label process. First, set the desired printer for the custom label as the default printer through the Windows Printer Settings. Customize the paper size of the label through the Windows Printer Settings. Return to Access and create a new, blank report. Turn off the Header and Footer groupings. Change the X and Y grids to be 20 and 24, respectively. Bring the desired fields onto the detail section of the report. Any fields that will appear on the same text line on the label should be concatenated. Turn on the Can Shrink and Can Grow properties for all the fields on the label. Make sure that the fields aren't mathematically touching. Change the margins of the report to zero under File | Page Setup. Finally, change the layout under File | Page Setup.

FIGURE 18.17.

Change the Page Setup options for a custom label report.

Using the Mail Merge Wizard

When you're using the Mail Merge Wizard, it's important to remember that the wizard uses Microsoft Word for the merge. The Mail Merge Wizard uses an OLE automation link to Microsoft Word. This doesn't mean that you can't merge to a WordPerfect document. It means that when the Merge It button is clicked, WordPerfect won't run; only Microsoft Word will run. However, any file that can be run by Microsoft Word can be merged to from Access. This includes not only WordPad and NotePad files, but also Write files, RTF files, WordPerfect files, and Excel files. If, for some reason, you can't read these files, it could have to do with your installation of Microsoft Word. You might need to reinstall Word and do a complete installation, as opposed to a minimum installation.

The Mail Merge Wizard is available from the database container, but it is available only from the Tables and Queries tabs. Even though it is visible from the Forms, Reports, Macros, and Modules tabs, it isn't available. The Mail Merge Wizard can be found as the first item under the Office Links button. The Office Links can also be accessed from the Tools menu.

Using the wizard is a two-step process. After you click the Merge It button, you must decide whether to merge records to an existing document or a new Word document. This is also the reason that Merge It is available only on tables and queries. Forms, reports, macros, and modules don't contain records. Tables and Queries are the only two tabs that actually store records.

After you choose whether the document to be merged to is an existing document or a new document, the second step is to pull the fields onto the document. An additional toolbar—the Merge toolbar—is placed at the top of the screen (see Figure 18.18). The fields that were available in the table or query can be inserted from the Insert Merge Field button, like the one that is displayed.

FIGURE 18.18.

Merged fields are listed under the Insert Merge Field button.

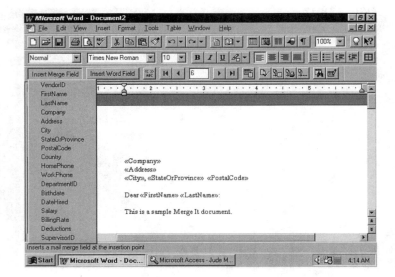

The next button to the right is the Insert Word Field button. By enabling you to set parameters on the incoming data, this button gives you more control over the records being exported by Access. All the options are shown in Figure 18.19.

Nine fields can be inserted. By inserting different fields into the main document, you can control how the data is being merged. The nine fields are described in Table 18.2.

FIGURE 18.19.

The ways in which you can set parameters and conditions on the incoming records.

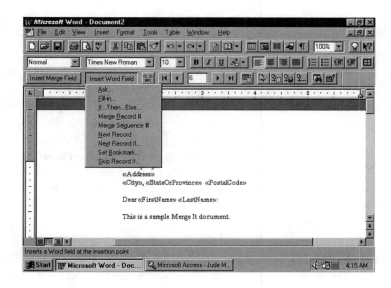

Table 18.2. The Insert Word Field list.

Field	Description
Ask…	Displays a prompt so that the user can add personal notes to individual records. This information can be added to all of the merged records or can be customized on a record-by-record basis.
Fill-in…	Displays the response to the Ask… field when the document is printed. The Fill-in… field is similar to the Ask… field in that questions can be asked on the records being merged. Fill-in… fields display dialog boxes that ask questions of the user, and the information that the user enters is filled into the document.
If…Then…Else…	Prints records only if the condition specified is met. If the condition is true, the condition equals –1. When the condition equals –1, the instruction that follows the word Then is executed. When the condition equals 0 or False, the instruction that follows the word Else is executed. It's possible to have a nested If condition that would read If w Then x ElseIf y Then z. You can have as many ElseIf statements as needed. The ElseIf allows for a second If condition to be contained within the If statement.

continues

Table 18.2. continued

Field	Description
Merge Record #	Displays the sequential order of the data record selected, not the autonumber field. It's the number of each record as it appears in the group of records that are being merged.
Merge Sequence #	Counts the number of records that were successfully merged. This number might be the same number as the Merge Record #, or it might not be the same. The difference between the two is that the Merge Sequence # is a count of the records that are being merged, whereas the Merge Record # is the number of the record as it appears in the possible number of merge records.
Next Record	Places the data records into the current merge document instead of starting a new one. It allows you to insert information from following records into the current record's document.
Next Record If...	Compares two expressions, and if the true part is valid, it merges the next record. It's similar to an If...Then...Else... field, except that you can't have a nested NextIf field. This is helpful in preventing blank lines in merged documents.
Set Bookmark...	Assigns a value to a bookmark or placeholder. This is similar to an electronic sticky note in that you can name a location in a document and move to it quickly. It differs from a sticky note in that a bookmark can insert information or perform calculations.
Skip Record If...	Compares two expressions and, if true, cancels the current record that is being merged into a document and moves to the next record to be merged. With this field, it's possible for you to skip records if a field is greater than a certain date or amount.

The next couple of buttons are the View Merged Data button and the Record Selector button. When you click the View Merged Data button, the records appear on the document, as opposed to the field name placeholders. The following seven buttons are new to Access 95 and the merge capabilities:

- Mail Merge Helper produces form letters and other documents for merging. This button appears on the Mail Merge toolbar that is offered within Microsoft Word but isn't necessarily needed when Word is launched from Access because the OLE link has already been established. This button actually allows a Word user to work backward and extract data from a database through this button. Clicking the Mail Merge Helper button is the same as selecting Tools | Mail Merge in Word, and it can be seen in

Figure 18.20. This button is helpful, except in the case of a merge that was initiated from Access. This confusing situation should be rectified with the next version of Access.

FIGURE 18.20.

The Mail Merge Helper enables users within Word to extract data from a database by giving them a step-by-step process to follow.

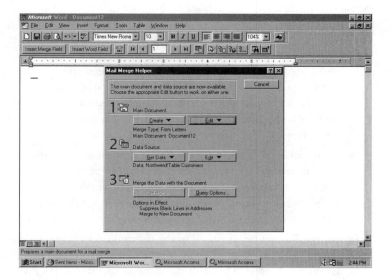

Notice at the bottom of Figure 18.20 that two copies of the same Access database are running. There seems to be some sort of confusion between Access and Word wherein Word automatically launches a second session of Access during a merge. This confusion should be corrected in the next version of Access.

Also, look at the helper in Figure 18.20. Step 2 shows that there is a data source, but you still don't have access to the Merge button in step 3 because the Word document has no Merge fields. If you move to step 3 and click the Query Options button, you are allowed to set criteria on the incoming records. When you click OK, the merge tries to start and you get a `Cannot re-establish a DDE connection` error. This can be confusing, because the DDE connection has already been established from Access. This confusion should be rectified in the next version of Access.

■ Check for Errors checks for errors that might have prevented the merge. This isn't a spell-checker button. It is a button that checks to make sure that the data source is properly set up. Figure 18.21 shows the three methods of reporting the errors that occur during a merge.

FIGURE 18.21.

The Check for Errors button checks the data that is being merged into the document.

The first method simulates the merge and reports all of the errors in a new Word document. The second method actually begins the merge process and notifies you as it encounters errors. The third method completes the merge process and reports all of the errors in a new document. The difference between the first method and the third method is that the third method actually performs the merge, whereas the first method only simulates the merge. If you choose the first method, the merge has yet to take place.

- Merge to New Document takes existing results and moves them to a new document. This allows you to keep an exact replica of the main document and creates a new document that looks exactly like the main document. This enables you to create a different letter based on the main document for different data sources. When the letter is reopened, Word displays the records that were merged into the letter.

- Merge To Printer prints all of the merged documents. Up to this point, the records haven't been merged. To merge all of the documents and print them, click the Merge to Printer button. This isn't the same as selecting File | Print. Selecting Print simply prints the document that is active, rather than all the remaining record documents.

- The Mail Merge button brings up the Merge dialog box and allows you to choose to e-mail this document. When you click this button, you're presented with a dialog box like the one shown in Figure 18.22.

FIGURE 18.22.

The Mail Merge button enables you to send the document electronically.

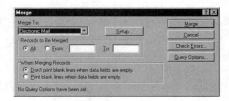

The Merge To combo box is in the upper-left corner of this dialog box. You have three options in this combo box. You can merge to a new document (which is the same as clicking the Merge to New Document button, discussed earlier). You can merge to the printer (which is the same as clicking the Merge to Printer button, discussed earlier). The third option is to e-mail the document. When this option is selected, the Setup button is made available. When you click the Setup button, the dialog box shown in Figure 18.23 appears.

FIGURE 18.23.

The e-mail information is extracted from one of the data fields being merged.

When merging a document to e-mail, you must include a mail or fax address before the merge will take place. You can enter a message on the Message Line, but this isn't necessary in order to send the document. A check box appears at the bottom. This allows each merged document to be sent as an individual Word document. Therefore, if you have a merge of 100 records, 100 individual Word documents will be e-mailed.

■ Find Record helps you find a record in the table or query that is being merged. When you click this button, a Find dialog box appears, as shown in Figure 18.24. You can search for data in a single field by selecting the field from the drop-down box. It's important to make sure that the View Merged Data button is pressed before the Find Record button is selected. If it isn't, your find process goes to the first record that matches the find criteria and stops. Because you can't see the data, you might think that something is wrong with the Find Record process.

FIGURE 18.24.

The Find Record button enables you to check all the records in a data field for a criteria.

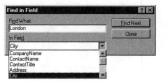

■ Edit Data Source displays the data from Access. It actually opens Access and brings the table or query into Datasheet view so that you can make changes to the data while it is in its database (see Figure 18.25).

FIGURE 18.25.

The Edit Data Source button enables you to make changes to the data while it is in the database.

Even though you're allowed to make changes to the records, you aren't allowed to change the source of the merge. If you want to change the source, you should close the document and return to Access; or you can close Access and use the Mail Merge Helper button from the Mail Merge toolbar in Microsoft Word.

> **TIP**
>
> The Alt-F9 key combination toggles all the field codes. These field codes can be seen in Figure 18.26.

FIGURE 18.26.

You can see the field codes for the merge fields by pressing Alt-F9 to toggle between the views.

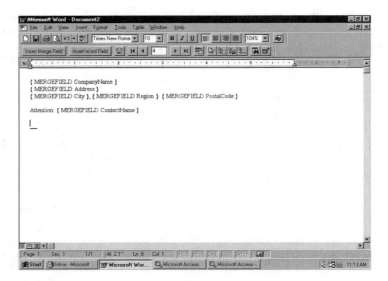

> **TIP**
>
> Access uses the field names from a table or query in its mail merge. Field names that are longer than 20 characters are truncated. Any characters in the field names that aren't letters, numbers, or underscores get converted to underscores.

Exporting Data for Use in Word Processors

Exporting data has become easier with each progression of Access. You can export the data in an Access database in several ways. First, the data in a table can be exported through the File menu. As shown in Figure 18.27, a table can be exported either within the current database or to another database.

FIGURE 18.27.

Export from the File menu.

The next step in exporting a report is choosing the target database. Access displays the Save dialog box, shown in Figure 18.28.

FIGURE 18.28.

Locate the target database for the exported report.

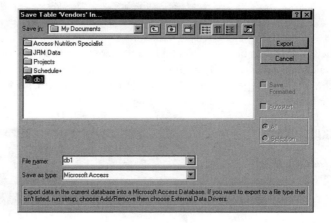

The final step in exporting a report is giving the destination report a name. In the Export dialog box, shown in Figure 18.29, type the name of the report as it should appear in the destination database.

FIGURE 18.29.

Type the desired name of the exported report.

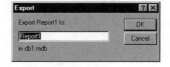

Access offers a couple of methods for exporting data besides those found in the Office Links. You can find them on the toolbar of the database container or by selecting Tools | Office Links. The Office Links button shows three methods for exporting data (see Figure 18.30). The first method in office links is Merge It, which is covered in the next section. The other two office links are Publish It, which invokes Microsoft Word, and Analyze It, which invokes Microsoft Excel.

FIGURE 18.30.

The Office Links button.

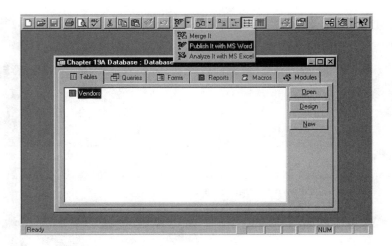

The Office Links button is available anywhere from the Database Container window. Publish It takes the output of the highlighted object (table, query, form, or report) and saves it as a rich text format (.RTF) file. Microsoft Word is automatically loaded, and the output is placed on a blank document, as shown in Figure 18.31.

FIGURE 18.31.

The rich text format output is placed on a Word document.

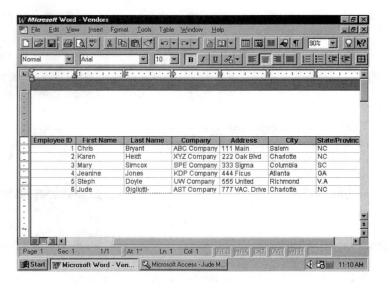

NOTE

Merge It and Publish It are similar in that they both invoke Microsoft Word. They are different in that Merge It allows the individual manipulation of fields, whereas Publish

It brings in the records in a datasheet format. Merge It is available only on tables and queries, whereas Publish It is available on tables, queries, forms, and reports.

The final Office Link object is Analyze It. This operation can be performed on tables, queries, forms, and reports. It takes the records and saves the output as a Microsoft Excel file. When Analyze It is launched, it takes the output of the highlighted object and brings it into an Excel spreadsheet, as shown in Figure 18.32.

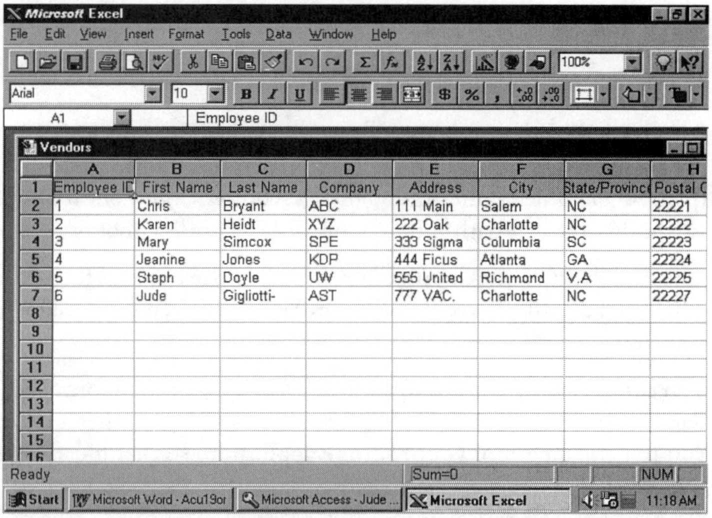

FIGURE 18.32.

The output of the highlighted object is placed in an Excel spreadsheet.

Most of the formatting is preserved during this operation. Now all the records from the Access object can be manipulated using the Excel tools.

It's possible to move data from an Access database into applications other than Microsoft Word and Excel. The data must be located in either a table or a Select query. You can do this easily through the Transfer actions that can be found in macros or through Visual Basic procedures.

If you're developing a database that will become a runtime application, the user won't have access to the database container and might need to export the data into an application other than Word or Excel. This can easily be done through macros. Figure 18.33 shows a macro with an action called TransferText.

The TransferText action enables you to export, as well as import and link data to and from Access. The Transfer Type argument shows that you can export data in a delimited or fixed-width format. Choose the format that best suits the import needs of the application that is receiving the data. The Specification Name argument determines how the file is to be exported, imported, or linked. If you choose one of the Fixed Width Transfer Type arguments, you must fill out the Specification Name argument.

FIGURE 18.33.

Macros can let you export data into applications other than Microsoft Word and Excel.

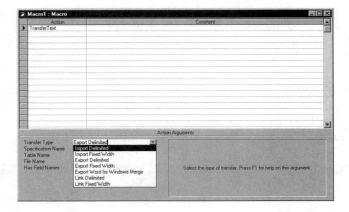

The Table Name argument asks for the name of the Access table to which you are exporting, importing, or linking. This doesn't have to be a table; you can also choose from your Select queries. The File Name argument is a required argument for which you type in the filename (including the full path) of the table or Select query that is being exported.

The Has Field Names argument refers to the first row of the text file that is being transferred. The usual default is No. If you select Yes, the field names are inserted into the first row of the text file.

You can attach this macro to a button that appears on a form. When the button is clicked, the data is transferred into a file that can be accessed by another application. This is an easy way for you to get data out of your runtime application so that it can be used by another application.

> **TIP**
>
> If you use a Select query for your TransferText action, it must not have any parameters set in it. If your Select query contains parameters, you might want to create a Make Table query that builds a table on the data needed. Then you can use the name of the table that is made instead of the query name.

There is another way to make it appear as if you're merging data to a word processor—through a report. You can creatively use the tools available in the toolbox to simulate a word processing document. This is a quick and dirty way to create specific documents. In Figure 18.34, you can see how to make a report look similar to a word processing document.

Your company's logo appears in the Page Header of the report. The return address information is the CompanyName and Address fields pulled onto the report; the City, Region, and PostalCode fields are concatenated to give it that "just-typed-in" look.

FIGURE 18.34.

Reports can be made to look like word processing documents.

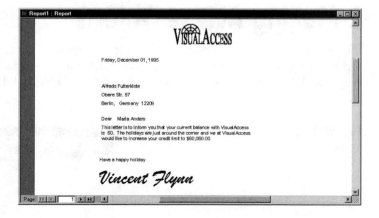

The heart of the document/report is just one text box. The information that appears in Figure 18.35 makes it look like a real word processing document.

FIGURE 18.35.

The heart of the report is just one text box.

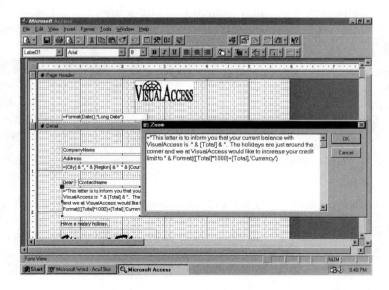

This is a quick and dirty way to create a report that looks like a word processing document, which is acceptable if the document is a short note, as is this one. However, if the document needs to be longer, remember that only 255 characters can fit into the Control Source of the text box. If you want more text on the report, you need to enter another text box. You can use labels instead of text boxes if you aren't performing any concatenations.

424

E-Mailing Access Objects

There is one other way to export data that doesn't appear on the Office Links button: you can e-mail objects from Access to another person. Highlight the desired object that is to be mailed and select File | Send. The sender has a choice of three formats for the output data, as shown in Figure 18.36.

FIGURE 18.36.

Objects can be e-mailed.

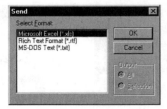

After choosing the format, you must enter the Profile Name. If the method of e-mail is Microsoft Exchange, the Profile Name automatically defaults to that, as shown in Figure 18.37. If another e-mail service is being used, you must enter that Profile Name.

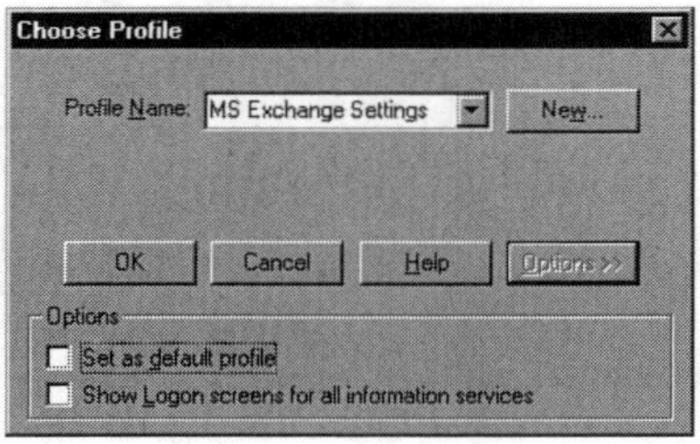

FIGURE 18.37.

Enter the type of e-mail service on the Profile Name line.

After you've entered the Profile Name and clicked OK, the e-mail service is executed. In this example, Microsoft Exchange was launched with the Vendors file icon already in the Note section of the e-mail. The only thing left to do is select the name of the person who is to receive this file. This e-mail note, shown in Figure 18.38, functions like any other e-mail note in that it can be sent to a number of people, it can be carbon-copied, it can have a subject line, and you can add additional text to the note.

The File | Send option performs the same action as the SendObject method. It also takes the datasheet of a form or a report or module and sends it in an e-mail message. Each datasheet being e-mailed can be listed as an Excel icon (.XLS), a Word icon (.RTF), or an MS-DOS icon (.TXT). The SendObject method uses the Microsoft Mail Application Programming Interface, usually referred to as MAPI. If the e-mail service is something other than MAPI, set up a dynamic-link library that converts the MAPI message to the desired protocol.

FIGURE 18.38.

Sending objects through the e-mail service is like sending any other type of note through the e-mail service.

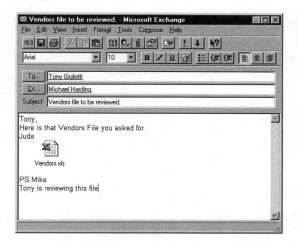

TIP

Report objects that have subreports can be sent, and the subreport will follow. Form objects that have subforms can be sent, but the subform won't follow.

Summary

This chapter covered information on the production of mailings. The mailing process can be broken into two halves. The first half concerns mailing labels. The second half deals with the merging of records with Microsoft Word documents (or documents from any word processor). The operation of creating custom labels from a set of predefined Avery labels was covered, as was the process of creating custom labels (labels that don't appear in the list of 66 predefined Avery labels) from scratch. After labels are printed, the documents need to be produced. The act of merging records into word processing documents was enumerated, and so was the process of merging records into spreadsheets.

PART

VI

Controlling Access and Using Other Applications

Creating
Access Macros

*by Ewan
Grantham*

19

IN THIS CHAPTER

The Basics of Access Macros

Macros in Access are used to automate tasks by building lists of actions. These actions occur in response to events, such as a command button being clicked. The list is built in the order that you want these actions to occur, and it covers virtually all the features available through the menus, as well as some that aren't. By using macros, you can automate the process of importing and exporting data, create buttons that perform complex queries, and perform other useful actions.

In Access 95, three new macro actions have been added to enhance your ability to manipulate objects or the appearance of applications. These new actions are described in Table 19.1.

Table 19.1. New Access macro actions.

Action	Description
Save	Saves the specified database object or the active object if a specific object isn't named.
SetMenuItem	Sets the state of menu items on custom menus (including shortcut and global menus) for the active window. Items can be enabled or disabled and checked or unchecked.
ShowToolbar	Displays or hides a built-in toolbar or a custom toolbar. You can display a built-in toolbar in all Access windows or just the view in which the toolbar is normally displayed.

In the rest of this chapter, you will learn about creating simple and complex macros, working with existing macros, associating macros with various events, calling macros from within macros, and troubleshooting your macros.

Writing Access Macros

Unlike writing a Visual Basic for Applications (VBA) program, where you can be as structured or unstructured as you want, writing macros tends to be very regimented. To get an idea of this, look at Figure 19.1, which shows the initial window for creating a new macro. You'll notice that each line has an Action and a Comment column. The actions you can select from are shown in the drop-down list.

Once you choose a possible action, the arguments for the action appear in the bottom panel, as shown in Figure 19.2, where the default arguments for a TransferDatabase (import or export of data to a supported database) action are already filled in.

FIGURE 19.1.

The opening window for a new macro.

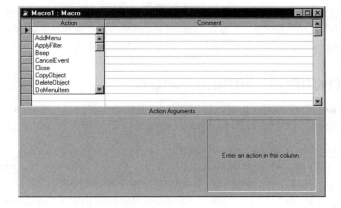

FIGURE 19.2.

Macro arguments for `TransferDatabase`.

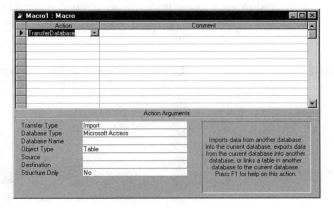

Just as there is a list of supported actions for macros, many of the arguments for an action also have drop-down lists. Figure 19.3 shows that for the previous example you have quite a few choices for a target database.

FIGURE 19.3.

The argument drop-down list.

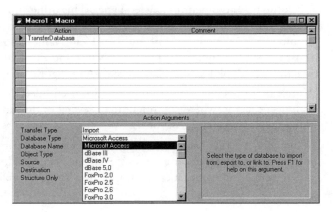

Not all the arguments contain drop-down lists, however, so you still have to be somewhat aware of what you're trying to do. With all these lists, you can see how easy it is to quickly build macros that will make your job easier without being too technical.

Creating a Simple Macro

In order to understand this a little better, create a simple macro to import a text file. This is one way to bring in data from a larger system.

1. Select the Macros tab in the Database window and then click the New button. At this point, your screen should look like the one you saw in Figure 19.1, with an empty column for actions and another for comments.

2. Go into the first action field and click the button on the right side of the field to see the drop-down list. For this macro, select the TransferText option. Your screen should look similar to the one shown in Figure 19.4, which shows the `TransferText` action and the default arguments.

FIGURE 19.4.

The start of a macro using `TransferText`.

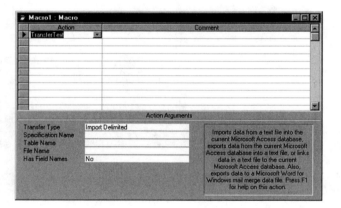

3. Click the first argument (Transfer Type). This brings up a button you can click for another drop-down list—this time, a list of the different possible values for the argument. Specification Name and Has Field Names also have drop-down lists. You must type in the arguments for Table Name and File Name. The final version of this macro might look like the example shown in Figure 19.5.

   Notice that the Comment column has also been filled in. This is especially important in longer macros, where you might have several of the same actions doing the same thing for different tables or forms.

4. When you exit the macro, you are prompted to save your changes and name the macro. Because you can use up to 255 characters (including spaces), you should try to use a meaningful name, such as "Import for Patients Table."

FIGURE 19.5.

The final version of the sample macro.

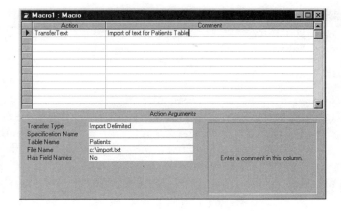

Part of the trick to writing macros is knowing what actions are available. Table 19.2 describes the available macro actions.

Table 19.2. Macro actions.

Action	Arguments	Function
AddMenu	Menu Name Menu Macro Name Status Bar Text	Creates a menu bar containing drop-down menus. The menu bar appears when the form to which AddMenu has been assigned is active.
ApplyFilter	Filter Name Where Condition	Restricts or sorts the data available to a form or report using a filter, query, or SQL WHERE clause on the under-lying table.
Beep	(no arguments)	Produces a beep tone for use in warnings or alerts.
CancelEvent	(no arguments)	Cancels the Access event that caused the macro with this action to run. If a validation macro failed, the update of the database could be canceled.
Close	Object Type Object Name Save	Closes the active window (the default) or a specified win-dow. Lets you specify if the

continues

Table 19.2. continued

Action	Arguments	Function
		object should be saved before being closed.
CopyObject	Destination Database New Name Source Object Type Source Object Name	Duplicates the specified database object in another database or in the original database using a different name.
DeleteObject	Object Type Object Name	Deletes the specified object.
DoMenuItem	Menu Bar Menu Name Command Subcommand	Runs any command on an Access menu bar.
Echo	Echo On Status Bar Text	Turns the screen refresh on or off during macro operation. Hides results until they are complete, and speeds macro operation.
FindNext	(no arguments)	Finds the next record specified by the FindRecord action or the Find command.
FindRecord	Find What Match Match Case Search Search As Formatted Only Current Field Find First	Finds the next record after the current record meeting the specified criteria. Searches through a table, form, or datasheet object.
GoToControl	Control Name	Selects the control named in the argument. Used to select a control or field when a form opens.
GoToPage	Page Number Right Down	Selects the first field on the designated page in a multipage form. The first field is the first field as designated by tab order.

Action	Arguments	Function
GoToRecord	Object Type Object Name Record Offset	Displays the specified record in a table, form, or datasheet object.
Hourglass	Hourglass On	Displays an hourglass in place of the mouse pointer while the macro runs. Use it while long macros run.
Maximize	(no arguments)	Maximizes the active window.
Minimize	(no arguments)	Minimizes the active window to an icon within the Access window.
MoveSize	Right Down Width Height	Moves or changes the size of the active window.
MsgBox	Message Beep Type Title	Displays a warning or informational message box.
OpenForm	Form Name View Filter Name Where Condition Data Mode Window Mode	Opens or activates a form in one of its views. Form can be restricted to data-matching criteria, different modes of editing, and whether the form acts as a modal or pop-up dialog box.
OpenModule	Module Name Procedure Name	Opens the specified module and displays the specified procedure.
OpenQuery	Query Name View Data Mode	Opens or activates a Datasheet or Crosstab query. You can specify the view and data entry mode.
OpenReport	Report Name View Filter Name Where Condition	Opens a report in the view you specify and filters the records before printing.

continues

Table 19.2. continued

Action	Arguments	Function
OpenTable	Table Name View Data Mode	Opens or activates a table in the view you specify. You can specify the data entry or edit mode for tables in Datasheet view.
OutputTo	Object Type Object Name Output Format Output File Auto Start	Copies the data in the specified object to a Microsoft Excel (.XLS), rich text format (.RTF), or DOS text (.TXT) file. Autostart = Yes starts the application with the association to the extension.
PrintOut	Print Range Page From Page To Print Quality Copies Collate Copies	Prints the active datasheet, report, or form.
Quit	Options	Exits from Access and saves unsaved objects according to the command you specify.
Rename	New Name Object Type Old Name	Renames the specified database object.
RepaintObject	Object Type Object Name	Completes recalculations for controls and updates specified or active database objects and/or screens.
Requery	Control Name	Updates the specified control by repeating the query of the control's source.
Restore	(no arguments)	Restores a maximized or minimized window to its previous window.
RunApp	Command Line	Runs a Windows or MS-DOS application.

Action	*Arguments*	*Function*
RunCode	Function Name	Runs a user-defined function written in Access Basic.
RunMacro	Macro Name Repeat Count Repeat Expression	Runs the specified macro.
RunSQL	SQL Statement	Runs an Action query as specified by the SQL statement or a Data-Definition query.
Save	Object Type Object Name	Saves the specified database object, or the active object if a specific object is not named.
SelectObject	Object Type Object Name In Database Window	Selects a specified database object.
SendKeys	Keystrokes Wait	Sends keystrokes to any active Windows application.
SendObject	Object Type Object Name Output Format To Cc Bcc Subject Message Text Edit Message	Sends the specified object as an attachment to a Microsoft Mail 3.x message. You enter the Recipients of the message with the values of the To, Cc, and Bcc arguments. You can specify the subject header for the message, add text to the message, and edit the message in Microsoft Mail.
SetMenuItem	Menu Index Command Index Subcommand Index Flag	Sets the state of menu items on custom menus (including shortcut and global menus) for the active window. Items can be enabled or disabled and checked or unchecked.
SetValue	Item Expression	Changes the value of a field, control, or property.
SetWarnings	Warnings On	Turns warning messages on or off.

continues

Table 19.2. continued

Action	Arguments	Function
ShowAllRecords	(no arguments)	Removes any filters or queries and displays all records in the current table or query.
ShowToolbar	Toolbar Name Show	Displays or hides a built-in toolbar or a custom toolbar. You can display a built-in toolbar in all Access windows or just the view in which the toolbar is normally displayed.
StopAllMacros	(no arguments)	Stops all macros.
StopMacro	(no arguments)	Stops the current macro.
Transfer Database	Transfer Type Database Type Database Name Object Type Source Destination Structure Only	Imports, exports, or attaches to Access and non-Access databases.
Transfer Spreadsheet	Transfer Type Spreadsheet Type Table Name File Name Has Field Names Range	Imports or exports Access data to a worksheet or spreadsheet file.
TransferText	Transfer Type Specification Name Table Name File Name Has Field Names	Imports or exports Access data to a text file.

Using the *SendKeys* Action

One of the more complex actions is SendKeys. By using SendKeys, you can enter information into an open Access dialog box or another active Windows application. An example of when this can be helpful goes back to the import you were using in the sample macro. If you're transferring large amounts of data from one system to another, you probably don't want to keep the data stored uncompressed and take up all that disk space. You can keep the data in a zip file and then use a Windows-based unzip program and the SendKeys action to unpack the import file when you need to use it again.

If you're sending literal text data (such as a name), it needs to be in quotation marks for most arguments.

To send keystrokes that are used for commands or movements, you need to use the special key arguments listed in Table 19.3.

Table 19.3. Special key arguments.

To Get This Key...	Use This Keystroke Argument
Alt	%
Backspace	{BACKSPACE} or {BS} or {BKSP}
Break	{BREAK}
Caps Lock	{CAPSLOCK}
Clear	{CLEAR}
Ctrl	^
Delete	{DELETE} or {DEL}
Down arrow	{DOWN}
End	{END}
Enter	{ENTER} or ~
Esc	{ESCAPE} or {ESC}
Function key	{F*x*} (where *x* is a number from 1 to 16)
Help	{HELP}
Home	{HOME}
Insert	{INSERT}
Left arrow	{LEFT}
Num Lock	{NUMLOCK}
Page Down	{PGDN}
Page Up	{PGUP}
Print Screen	{PRTSC}
Right arrow	{RIGHT}
Shift	+
Scroll Lock	{SCROLLLOCK}

continues

Table 19.3. continued

To Get This Key...	Use This Keystroke Argument
Tab	{TAB}
Up arrow	{UP}
Codes for Reserved Characters	
Braces ({ or })	{{} or {}}
Brackets ([or])	{[} or {]}
Caret (^)	{^}
Percent (%)	{%}
Plus (+)	{+}
Tilde (~)	{~}

When you press two keys in combination, such as Alt-F, specify this action as

%F

To press Alt-F, followed by P (without the Alt), use

%FP

If a key is held down while two or more keys are pressed, enclose the group of following keys in parentheses. The following example is equivalent to Alt-D-V:

%(DV)

When you want to send the same keystroke many times, add a number specifying how many times to repeat. To move up three times, for example, use the following:

{UP 3}

Running Your Macro

There are several ways to run a macro once it's written. The first is to click the Run button that appears when your macro is open for editing. You can also use the Run menu. You will notice that you then have the choice of Start or Single Step. You generally want to use Start.

Similarly, you can run a macro by clicking the Macros tab in the Database window and then double-clicking its icon.

Your macro might depend on having a particular form already open. In this case, you need to open the appropriate form and select Tools | Macro. You then get the Run Macro dialog box, shown in Figure 19.6, where you can type in or select the macro to run.

FIGURE 19.6.

The Run Macro dialog box.

You can also have one macro run another macro using the RunMacro action. This is discussed later in this chapter.

You usually run a macro as a result of a specific event occurring. Events that kick off a macro include the following:

> A button being clicked by the user
>
> Moving between fields
>
> Changes being made in a record
>
> Tables and forms being opened or closed
>
> A shortcut key being pressed
>
> A custom command from a custom menu being clicked

Most macros can be run using any of these methods, although a particular form or record might need to be active in order for it to complete successfully.

Modifying Existing Macros

You often need to make changes to your macros or modify someone else's macro. Therefore, Access provides some of the reusability of an object-oriented development environment. Let's begin by bringing up the macro created earlier, Import for Patients Table.

1. Click the Macros tab in the Database window. You'll see a window like the one shown in Figure 19.7, with the macros for this database listed.

FIGURE 19.7.

A list of macros.

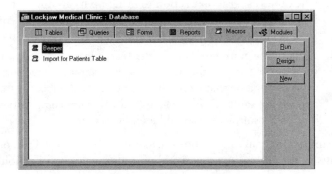

2. Click the icon for the macro and then click the Design button. This brings the macrosheet up. To modify this macro, you add a few steps to make the import process

a little more robust. If you're going to be doing these types of imports regularly (and if you weren't, why would you be writing a macro?), you want to first import the data into a temporary table. That way, any major problems occur there rather than possibly affecting the data in the table that the application uses. Doing it this way also allows for more flexibility in merging the data into the application table.

3. To make this modification, begin by clicking the first action in the Action column.

4. Select Insert | Row (which should be the only available option). You should now have an empty row above the TransferText row.

5. Use the button on the right side of the field for the drop-down list and select OpenQuery. The window should now look like Figure 19.8.

FIGURE 19.8.

The current version of the sample macro.

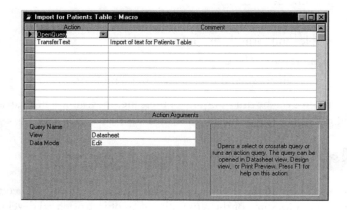

6. Type Empty Temp Patients as the Query Name and then enter an appropriate comment. You can do this to add a number of rows at the top or between other rows in longer macros.

7. Click the TransferText action to bring up its argument table again. Change the Table Name from "Patients" to "Temp Patients." Change the comment to reflect the change in tables as well. Again, this is something that you can do to as many lines as needed.

8. Click in the empty row below the TransferText row. At this point, you can add new steps as needed. For the purpose of this example, one more action is needed—another OpenQuery name that would be used to copy the records from the temp table to the application table. Call it "Move Records from Temp Patients" and add a comment. The end result, which should look like Figure 19.9, is ready to be saved.

To summarize, you can modify a macro by inserting new rows of actions, changing the arguments in the current rows, and adding additional rows of actions. With these tools, you can change the actions of an existing macro, alter a macro to accomplish a similar process, or correct an error in a macro.

FIGURE 19.9.

The final version of the sample macro.

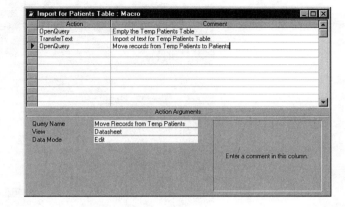

Adding Macros to Events

As mentioned earlier, you usually associate a macro with an event. These events occur throughout an Access database—when a form is opened, for example. Depending on what you're trying to do, you might want a macro in a form, a report, a custom menu, or connected to a shortcut key. All these options are covered in this section.

Adding Macros to Forms

To add a macro to a form, you can either create a control that you associate the macro with or edit the Event properties of the form or field to call the macro. In either case, you must open the form in Design view to allow changes to be made. At the form level, you edit the Event properties by first clicking somewhere in the Form Design window, but not on the form itself. Right-clicking brings up a floating menu with a Properties choice. Selecting it gives you a tabbed property form like the one shown in Figure 19.10, which has all the events that are associated with the overall form.

To associate your macro with one of these events, simply click the drop-down list button, which shows the macros that are currently available (see Figure 19.11), or click the button with the three dots. Then you can choose the Macro Builder option to build your macro directly from this point. At the Form level you can also click the Other tab and associate a macro with the Menu Bar option.

FIGURE 19.10.

*Event properties for
form level.*

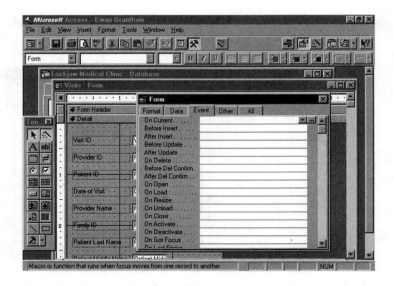

FIGURE 19.11.

*Choosing the macro for
the event.*

Table 19.4 covers the events you will work with the most, as well as how and when to use them.

Table 19.4. Common form-level events.

Event	Description	Use
AfterUpdate	Runs the macro after you leave a record and after changes in the record have been recorded in the database. Also see AfterUpdate for control-level events.	Transmits changed records to other applications or updates other forms using the new data.
BeforeInsert	Runs the macro when you begin entering data in a new record and again just before you add a new record to a table or query.	Displays needed data or a warning when the user begins to enter data, and prompts for confirmation when the user adds data.
BeforeUpdate	Runs the macro after you leave a record but before the record is updated in the database.	Asks the operator for confirmation that the record should be updated.
OnClose	Runs the macro before the form disappears.	Asks the operator to confirm that the form should be closed or transmits data to another application when the form is closed.
OnCurrent	Runs the macro before a record becomes current or is displayed in the form.	Moves the focus to a specific control every time the record is updated.
OnDelete	Runs the macro when you attempt to delete a record but before the record is deleted.	Asks the operator to confirm that the record should be deleted before deleting it.
OnOpen	Runs the macro when the form opens but before displaying a record.	Opens or closes other forms when a form is opened.

Each section of the form (Header, Detail, and Footer) also has its own events. To work with these events, click in the section you want to work with, and then right-click to bring up the floating menu. Select Properties and then click the Events tab. You'll see a group of choices like the ones in Figure 19.12. Notice that fewer options are available at this level.

FIGURE 19.12.

Events for a section of the form.

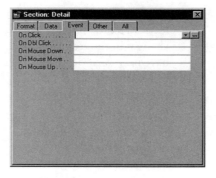

Finally, you can use this process to work with events at the field level. For this, click the field you want to work with, right-click to bring up the floating menu, and select Properties. The options here are shown in Figure 19.13. It's important to remember that these macros are associated only at the level where you defined them. In other words, an `AfterUpdate` defined at the field level isn't activated if you update a different field. If your macro could be used by more than one field, you would want it associated with either a section or a form-level event.

FIGURE 19.13.

Events for fields on the form.

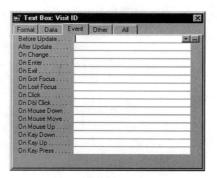

Macros also can be associated with controls on the form. The events vary somewhat, depending on the type of control being worked with. As an example, in Figure 19.14 a command button has been defined, and a macro is being associated with one of its events. The macro could also have been associated with the command button when the button was created by specifying that it was a Run Macro button in the Command Button Wizard.

Just as with forms, controls have certain events you tend to use fairly often. These are described in Table 19.5.

FIGURE 19.14.

Events for a Command button on the form.

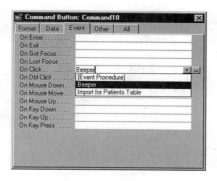

Table 19.5. Common control events.

Event	Description	Use
AfterUpdate	Runs the macro after you leave a control and after the control changes.	Updates other controls depending on the entry in the control that has just changed.
BeforeUpdate	Runs the macro after you leave a control but before the control is changed.	Validates the entry for this control using more extensive validation than is available with control properties.
OnClick	Runs the macro when you click a command button on a form.	Runs any type of macro associated with button operations, such as opening other forms, printing a form, or updating records.
OnDblClick	Runs the macro when you double-click a control or control label.	Displays Help information or forms that help the user with data entry.
OnEnter	Runs the macro when you move the focus to a control but before focus is on the control.	Asks the operator for a password for that field or displays information about how to enter data in the field.

continues

Table 19.5. continued

Event	Description	Use
OnExit	Runs the macro when you attempt to move to another control but before the focus moves away.	Uses the GoToControl action to move the focus to a specific control. Uses conditions to define different controls to go to, depending on the values entered.

Adding Macros to Reports

Reports tend to be another area in which macros can be very useful. Similar to what happens with forms, there are two levels of events for reports. Access 95 adds some additional events to reports. My favorite is the OnNoData event, which enables you to handle empty tables more gracefully.

Figure 19.15 shows the events that are associated with the Report object. To bring up the Report object, click an area of the Report Design window that isn't part of one of the report sections, right-click to pull up a floating menu, and select the Properties option.

FIGURE 19.15.

Events for a report.

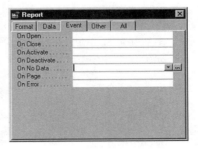

Table 19.6 describes the Report events.

Table 19.6. Report events.

Event	Description
OnActivate	Runs the macro when a report receives the focus and becomes the active window.

Event	Description
OnClose	Runs a macro when the report closes.
OnDeactivate	Runs a macro when the report loses the focus but before the next object gets the focus.
OnError	Runs a macro when an error occurs in the running of a report.
OnNoData	Runs a macro when a report returns no data to be printed.
OnOpen	Runs a macro when the report opens but before printing.
OnPage	Runs a macro when the page is about to be printed.

Within a report there are also sections, and each section can have the events associated with it set up with a corresponding macro. These events are described in Table 19.7.

Table 19.7. Report section events.

Event	Description
OnFormat	Runs a macro after Access has accumulated or calculated the data for the section but before Access formats the section for printing or previewing.
OnPrint	Runs a macro after the data in a section is laid out but before printing.
OnRetreat	Runs a macro when Access returns to a previous report section during report formatting.

Adding Macros to Custom Menus

When you create a custom menu for your application with the Menu Builder, each menu choice activates a macro. The menu bar itself becomes a macro that is called by setting the MenuBar property of the first form your application loads.

The macros are added to the menu as choices when you build the menu. This can be done within the Menu Builder or by building the custom menu from scratch. When you create a custom menu bar from scratch, you first create a macro group that defines each custom menu and its commands. For example, if you wanted eight menus on your menu bar, you would create eight macro groups. To create a macro group, click the New button in the Macros tab in the Database window and click the XYZ button on the toolbar. You then have a window like the one shown in Figure 19.16.

FIGURE 19.16.

Creating a macro group.

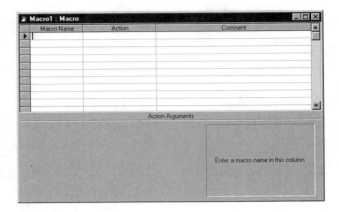

To create the menu bar, follow these steps:

1. Create a macro group for the menu, entering each menu command in the Macro Name column of the Macro window. Commands should be entered in the order they are to be displayed on the menu. Each command is an individual macro in the macro group.

2. In the Action column of the Macro window, enter the actions you want to carry out when each command is selected. Make sure to set the appropriate arguments for each action.

3. When you add the menu you have created to a custom menu bar, enter the name of the macro group in the Menu Macro Name argument of the menu bar macro's AddMenu action.

> **NOTE**
>
> To create a line between two menu commands, type a hyphen (-) in the Macro Name column between the appropriate menu commands.

Of course, macro groups can also be used to store associated macros together. In that case, you create the group as described. Then, when you want to run one of the macros from the group, you specify it as macrogroup.macro using the name of the macro group and the name of the macro. Macros in macro groups can be used anywhere a stand-alone macro can be used.

Adding Shortcut Keys for Macros

If you have macros you use often, you might want to assign a shortcut to them. For example, you could have Ctrl-P run a print macro you've defined. To assign a macro a shortcut key, do the following:

1. Create a macro group.
2. Create the macros that you want shortcuts defined for in the macro group.
3. In the Name column for each macro, type the shortcut key you want to use.
4. Enter the name of this new macro in the Key Assignment Macro field.

The possible shortcut key selections are described in Table 19.8, which also shows how the names must be entered into the Name column.

Table 19.8. Shortcut key codes.

Shortcut Key or Combination	*Code for the Name Column*
Ctrl-*letter*	`^letter`
Ctrl-*number*	`^number`
Function key	`{F1}`, `{F2}`, and so on
Ctrl-*function key*	`^{F1}`, `^{F2}`, and so on
Shift-*function key*	`+{F1}`, `+{F2}`, and so on
Insert or Ins	`{Insert}`
Ctrl-Insert or Ctrl-Ins	`^{Insert}`
Shift-Insert or Shift-Ins	`+{Insert}`
Delete or Del	`{Delete}` or `{Del}`
Ctrl-Delete or Ctrl-Del	`^{Delete}` or `^{Del}`
Shift-Delete or Shift-Del	`+{Delete}` or `+{Del}`

CAUTION

You can assign shortcut key combinations that are predefined in Access, such as Ctrl-C and Ctrl-X, to your own macros. However, your macro replaces the predefined meaning of the shortcut combination. Beware of using Ctrl-C, Ctrl-V, Ctrl-X, and Ctrl-Z for this reason.

Nesting Macros

Not only can you group macros together, but you can also have a macro run another macro. In that case, you have nested macros—macros composed of more than one macro.

The simplest form of this is when a macro calls another macro using the `RunMacro` action. This action is specified within the macrosheet at the point in the macro where the second macro is supposed to run. As an example, create a macro called Beeper with a single action of Beep. Then open the sample macro created earlier, and, after the last OpenQuery action, add a RunMacro action. Specify Beeper in the Macro Name argument, and enter the number of times you want it to beep in the Repeat Count argument. As always, make sure you enter a meaningful comment. This gives you a window similar to the one shown in Figure 19.17.

FIGURE 19.17.

Using RunMacro.

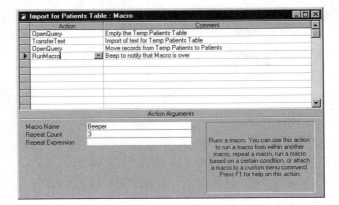

Another common use for a nested macro is for a startup macro for a particular database. In Access 95, you can now specify a startup form directly in the Startup option of the Tools menu. However, you might still want to have the form specified in a startup macro so that it can be altered programmatically, or there might be other options you want to set.

To have a startup macro, create your macro as you normally would, including calls to any other macros you want to run. Then name the macro AutoExec when you save it.

One other consideration when you're nesting macros is whether you always want to run the other macros. For example, if there was a problem with the import, instead of beeping three times, you might want to have the macro action beep only once (or vice versa). To do that, you need to set some conditions for the macro using the Condition column.

By default, the Condition column isn't visible. However, you can make the column visible by clicking the flowchart-looking button on the toolbar, as shown in Figure 19.18, where the sample macro has been loaded.

You then enter a condition using expressions and control names, much the same way as you enter them for queries. To make this work with the sample macro, you would need to use the Dcount function to see how many rows were inserted into the Temp Patients table. Also, because there is no ELSE for macro steps, you need to have two steps: one for a successful macro run and one for when the import fails.

FIGURE 19.18.

Making the Condition column visible.

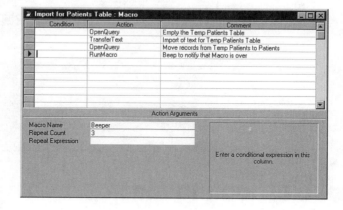

To code the condition, you need to right-click in the Condition field next to the action that occurs when the condition is true and then click Build to bring up the Expression Builder. The evaluation for the successful import should look like Figure 19.19. Be sure to notice the order in which the table and field are specified.

FIGURE 19.19.

Creating the condition to be evaluated.

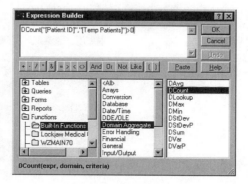

The final version of this macro with the conditions should look like Figure 19.20. You will notice that the final move of records has been moved to a position where it will occur after the check for the successful import. You could add the condition that checks for success here as well so that the Append query runs only when there are records to be appended.

FIGURE 19.20.

The sample macro with conditions.

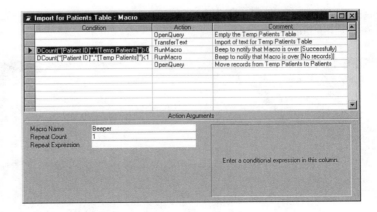

Troubleshooting Macros

Although it's nice to think that every macro you write will run correctly the first time you code it, the reality is that sometimes they won't. Usually you build something simple, test it, get it working, add more complex statements, and so on until you get the final version of your macro.

One way you know your macro isn't working is when you see the Action Failed dialog box, shown in Figure 19.21. This shows you which macro failed, what step it was on when it failed, and the arguments that were being used for that step.

FIGURE 19.21.

The Action Failed dialog box.

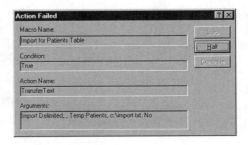

If you get this, you want to jot down not only the macro name and the step, but also any open forms, reports, or queries. Then click the Halt button to close the dialog box. If you don't already have the macrosheet open for the offending macro, open it and see if you can figure out why that step caused the failure. Things to look at include whether what you thought should happen matched what appeared to be happening (particularly a problem with reports), whether the logic in the conditions matches what you thought you coded, and whether there was a condition in the data being analyzed that you didn't expect.

Once you've looked at these items, if there still is no apparent problem, it's time to try stepping through the macro using the Macro Single Step button. Begin by opening the macro and any forms or reports that would normally be open when it runs. Click the Macro Single Step button (to the right of the exclamation point) to start the Single Step process, and then run the macro.

As the macro goes through each step, you get a dialog box similar to the one shown in Figure 19.22, in which the step being executed and the information about that step are displayed.

FIGURE 19.22.

The Single Step dialog box.

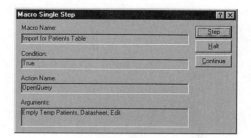

You have three choices at each step. You can click Step (the default) to take you to the next action, Halt to stop execution of the macro, or Continue, which runs the macro from that point on without stopping until it hits the end of the macro or an error.

Something else you can do to troubleshoot is use the MsgBox action to display a message at that point of the macro. Your message could let you know if you've executed an action you didn't think you would (in which case you should check your Condition statement), or it can give you the value of a variable you're working with.

On longer macros where you might have several similar actions, you probably won't want to single-step through the macro. In that case, you should use the StopMacro action to stop the macro after the point where you think the error is occurring. Then, by moving this action back and forth, you can make sure you're working on the correct action.

Finally, you can avoid many errors simply by reusing macro code you know is good. You can do this by using RunMacro to call already debugged macros or by copying code from a good macro into your new macro and making minimal changes.

Once your macro has been debugged, you'll probably want to finish the macro by adding a SetWarnings action to the beginning of it with the argument of Off. That way, system messages, particularly confirmations for queries, don't appear to the end user. Along the same lines, you might want to add an Echo action to turn off screen updates while your macro is running. Doing so has another benefit: if you're switching between several forms or reports, the macro runs much faster.

Summary

In this chapter you learned about macros—not only what they are, but also the basics of coding, modifying, and troubleshooting them. You should also be more comfortable with deciding when to use them and how to make sure they run when you want them to.

Working with Graphs and Graphics

20

by Jeff Morelan

Graphs Explained

Graphs can enhance an Access application by representing data as graphic information. Graphs provide more flexibility for your application by offering a rich set of powerful visual tools not built into Access.

Graphs are OLE objects that become embedded as part of your application. After a graph object or any other OLE object has been embedded, you can size it, move it, and edit it. A graph can be edited by Microsoft Graph 5.0, by its parent application, or through code. These methods are explored further in this chapter.

Creating a Graph

The first step in working with graphs is to create a graph object on a form or report. In Form Design or Report Design view, select Insert | Object. Select Microsoft Graph 5.0 from the list and click OK. Figure 20.1 shows you how to select a Microsoft Graph 5.0 object for the form or report using the Insert Object dialog box.

FIGURE 20.1.

The Insert Object dialog box lets you choose the object type you would like to insert.

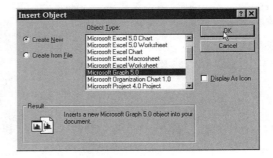

Click OK. Microsoft Graph 5.0 will be displayed. At this point, you can choose from a number of configuration items. See the section "Customizing the Graph" later in this chapter to see the customizing choices and how to change these options at runtime. For now, choose File | Exit & Return to [*your formname*] from Microsoft Graph 5.0.

The graph has now been inserted into the form or report in Design view. Currently, no data is being used to display or draw the graph. To specify the data for this graph, you would use the Row Source and Row Source Type properties. Row Source Type specifies what type of data will be used to display the graph, Row Source specifies what the data is. The Row Source property can be a table, SQL statement, query, or even a list of user-defined values.

Preparing the Data Source for the Graph

Before a graph can be displayed, you must create a data source. The information you would like displayed on your graph(s) will dictate how your data source should be organized.

Data

Decide which table or query will supply the data for the chart. If you're going to use a query, create the query and include these fields:

- The fields containing the data that will be graphed. At least one of these fields must have a number field (Number, Currency, or AutoNumber field data type).
- The fields containing the labels you want to display in the chart.
- The linking fields. If you want the chart to change from record to record, the value in the graph's linking field must match the value in a field in the underlying table or query of the form or report. If the form's underlying query includes the ProjectName field, you will want to include the ProjectName field in your graph's underlying query so you can link that graph's child field to the form's master field.

Titles and Legends

Titles are a valuable component of any graph. Pay attention to titles to get the most out of your graphs. The legend entries will be a reflection of whatever column headings are in your table or query. The query name will likewise appear in the graph's title section. These can be edited in Microsoft Graph. If you double-click on the graph inside the Access form and select View | Datasheet, you can then click on the cell with the title and edit it from there. This method, though, will automatically name the titles/legends for you.

> **NOTE**
>
> To ensure valuable legend entries, use an expression in your graph's underlying query for each column heading, such as `Billed: SumOfAmountBilled` (instead of just selecting SumOfAmountBilled) or `Paid: SumOfPaymentAmount` (instead of just SumOfPaymentAmount). The word Billed will replace SumOfAmountBilled and the word Paid will replace SumOfPaymentAmount in your graph's legend.

Linking Data

If any of the tables that you need in order to create the chart are in another database or application, import or link them to your Access database.

To create a link, follow these steps:

1. In the source document, select the data you want to link to the Graph datasheet. For example, if you're working in an Excel worksheet, select a set of cells.
2. Copy the data using the Copy command.
3. Activate the Graph chart.
4. Display the datasheet by choosing View | Datasheet.
5. Select Edit | Paste Link. Step 1 of 1 of the Chart Wizard will appear.
6. In the Chart Wizard, specify whether the data series should be in rows or columns, and specify how the data in the first row and column should be used in the graph. (See the next section for an explanation of the different types of graphs.)
7. Click the OK button.
8. Close the Microsoft Graph 5.0 Editor. The data set will be reflected in the graph.

Graph Types

Fourteen main graphs are available in Microsoft Graph 5.0 and each has one or more subtypes. The following sections briefly describe each main graph type.

Area Chart

This shows the amount of change over a period of time. The area chart emphasizes the sum of plotted values and the association of individual values to the total rather than to a time and rate of change.

3-D Area Chart

This shows a three-dimensional view of an area chart, which emphasizes the sum of plotted values and separates chart-data series into distinct rows to show differences between the data series.

Line Chart

A line chart shows trends or changes over a given period of time. It's similar to an area chart, but a line chart accentuates the flow of time *and* the rate of change rather than the *amount* of change.

3-D Line Chart

A 3-D line chart shows a three-dimensional view of a line chart, which emphasizes not only compared values over time but also a particular data series.

Pie Chart

Pie charts show the relationship or proportions of parts to the whole. They always contain only one data series, which makes it useful for emphasizing a significant element.

3-D Pie Chart

The three-dimensional pie chart not only shows the relationship or proportions of parts to the whole but also emphasizes a particular data set within that graph.

Doughnut Chart

A doughnut chart shows the relationship or proportions of parts to the whole and can contain more than one data series. The doughnut chart, like the pie chart, shows the proportions of parts to a whole. The main difference is it can show more than one data series.

XY (Scatter) Chart

An XY (scatter) chart either shows the relationship among the numeric values in several data series or plots two groups of numbers as one series of x-y coordinates. It can show clusters of data and is commonly used for scientific data. The points can be open, connected by straight lines, or connected by curved lines.

Column Chart

A column chart could show variations over a period of time or illustrate comparisons between items. Categories are organized horizontally, values vertically, placing emphasis on variation over time.

3-D Column Chart

A 3-D column chart not only shows variation over a period of time but also emphasizes a particular data series, much like the 3-D bar chart.

Bar Chart

A bar chart shows individual figures at a specific time or illustrates comparisons among items. A bar chart is much like a column chart, except that the data is displayed horizontally instead of vertically.

3-D Bar Chart

The 3-D bar chart is much like the bar chart, except it can emphasize a particular data series as well.

Radar Chart

A radar chart shows changes or frequencies of data series relative to a center point and to each another. Each category has its own value axis extending from the center point. Data in the same series are connected by lines.

3-D Surface Area

A 3-D surface-area chart is useful for finding combinations between two sets of data. This chart is especially good for large amounts of data that would otherwise be difficult to view. Colors or patterns show areas that are at the same value, which is different from other chart types.

Customizing the Graph

Customizing the graph is necessary for showing data in a format that will be acceptable for the data presented. Seldom will a graph look perfect when it's first created. You can customize the graph using the Chart Wizard, the Microsoft Graph 5.0 Editor, or Access code.

Using the Chart Wizard

The Chart Wizard is the internal Access tool for creating and customizing a graph.

1. To create a form with a new graph, first create a new form by selecting the Form object type from the Database window and clicking the New button.

2. Select Chart Wizard from the list box and choose a table or query for a record source from the drop-down list. You must select a record source before you continue. Figure 20.2 shows the new form-selection form, which can be a starting point for the Chart Wizard.

FIGURE 20.2.

Selecting the Chart Wizard in the New Form dialog box.

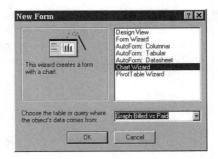

Working with Graphs and Graphics

3. Click the OK button to start the Chart Wizard.

4. Select the fields you wish to use in your graph from the record source. In this example, we will select all of the fields from the query. Figure 20.3 shows the first Chart Wizard dialog.

FIGURE 20.3.

The first step lets you choose fields for the graph.

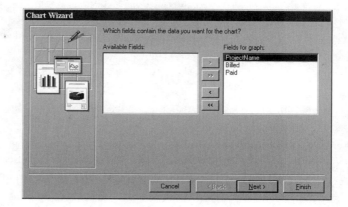

5. Click the Next button to continue. This will bring up the next dialog box of the Chart Wizard, shown in Figure 20.4. Select the graph type you wish to use.

FIGURE 20.4.

The second step lets you choose a graph type.

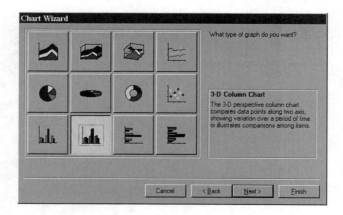

6. For this example, choose 3-D column chart for your graph type and click the Next button to continue. You can choose from several options at this level. These options are shown in Figure 20.5.

7. The Chart Wizard makes some assumptions how the data should be displayed. Billed, for example, has been made into SumOfBilled. To correct this (it has already been summed at the query level), modify the field by following the next steps.

FIGURE 20.5.

The third step lets you modify the presentation.

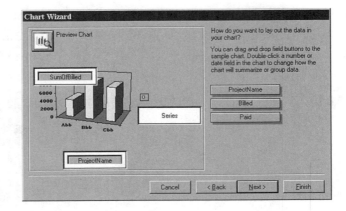

8. Double-click on the SumOfBilled section just above the graph. A summarize dialog will be displayed, wherein the choices of summarizing a field include None, Sum, Average, Min, Max, and Count. Choose None for this example and click the OK button.

9. Click the Paid button on the right side of the Chart Wizard dialog and drag the Paid field to the Chart area. Doing so will add the Paid field to the same section as the Billed field. You will need to change the summary from Sum to None within the summarize dialog, shown in Figure 20.6.

FIGURE 20.6.

The fourth step lets you modify the data field.

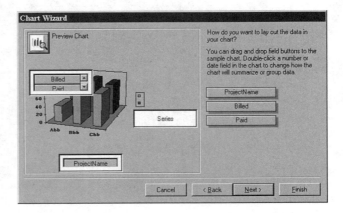

10. Click the Next button to continue. The final Chart Wizard dialog will appear. Here you can change the chart title, choose whether a legend will be displayed, choose to open the form in Design or Form view, and choose whether to show help on graphs.

11. Click the Finish button to continue. The form will be created and displayed on-screen with a graph object already inserted. Right-click on the graph object and choose Properties from the list. Look at the Row Source property. The row source has been

changed to a SQL Select statement. This may or may not be what you want. In this instance, this change isn't what is needed since we created a query already (see the section called "Data"), so a query can be selected as the row source instead. Open the form in Form view to see how the graph appears.

Customizing the Graph Through Microsoft Graph 5.0

Microsoft Graph 5.0 provides full options for changing an existing graph. To invoke the Microsoft Graph 5.0 Editor, double-click on the graph object while in the form's Design view.

At this level, you have a host of options from which to choose. The format options provide flexibility and customization possibilities. Select any part of the graph object you wish to customize and choose the first option from the Format menu. The formatting options you can select are Axis, Plot Area, Chart Title, Data Series, Walls, Legend, and Chart Area. Each option also has one or more subsections.

Format Axis

The Format Axis dialog lets you choose Axis options, Tick-Mark Label options, and Tick-Mark Type options. Figure 20.7 shows the choices from which you can select.

FIGURE 20.7.

The Patterns tab of Microsoft Graph 5.0 Format Axis dialog lets you customize axis options.

The scale can be changed to reflect a different minimum or maximum, and so on. This can maximize or minimize the appearance of change on your graph. Figure 20.8 shows a formatting figure for scale changes.

Fonts can be changed on the axis as well as anywhere on the graph where there is text. Refer to Figure 20.11 for a view of how font styles and sizes can be changed.

You can adjust the way the axis numbers are displayed by using the Number tab in the Format Axis dialog. Figure 20.9 shows the number options. (Refer to Figure 20.12 for text-alignment options.)

FIGURE 20.8.

The Axis tab lets you change the data scale.

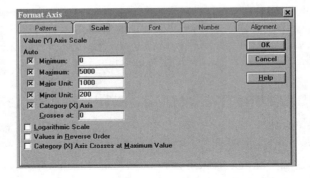

FIGURE 20.9.

The number options that can be used to modify the numbers on the graph's axis.

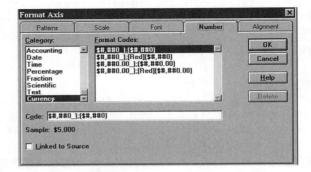

TIP

Use a number format of $#,###_);($#,##0) to change the axis to reflect currency instead of raw numbers.

Plot Area

The plot area is the graph only. To format the plot area, select the chart only and choose Format | Selected Plot Area. The entire plot area's pattern, color, and borders can be formatted in the pattern section. For an example, see Figure 20.10.

Chart Title

To format the graph's chart title, click on the chart title and select Format | Selected Chart Title. For example, you can change the font, as shown in Figure 20.11. You can change the pattern of the chart title as well. (Figure 20.10 shows the customization options of the pattern section.) Figure 20.12 shows text-alignment options.

FIGURE 20.10.

This dialog lets you change pattern options, including the border, color, and pattern of the section you're formatting.

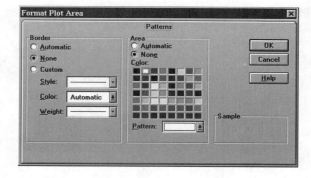

FIGURE 20.11.

The Font subsection of the formatting options.

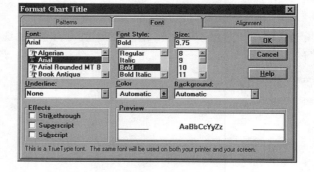

FIGURE 20.12.

The choices available for text alignment.

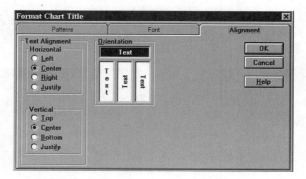

Data Series

The data series is the chart's graph section (for example, a single column in a column chart or a single slice of a pie in a pie chart). Select a data series and choose Format | Selected Data Series. Within this option, you can customize patterns (see Figure 20.10), the axis (see Figure 20.13), y error bars (see Figure 20.14), and data labels (see Figure 20.15).

FIGURE 20.13.

The Axis options let you change on what axis you would like your data graphed.

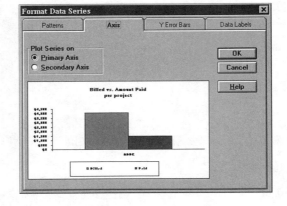

FIGURE 20.14.

The Y Error Bars options let you show variances by amount or by percentages.

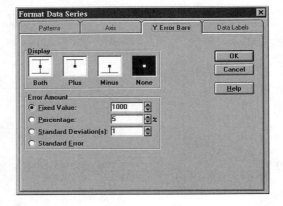

FIGURE 20.15.

You can customize how your data labels will appear.

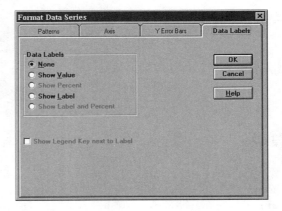

Walls

The walls can be changed with the Pattern options. These changes affect the borders and the graph's background. To adjust the walls, select the border area, choose Format | Selected Walls, and make changes as necessary. See Figure 20.10 for a sample of pattern choices.

Legend

You can customize the legend by selecting it and choosing Format | Selected Legend. Options include changes to legend patterns (see Figure 20.10), fonts (see Figure 20.11), and placement (see Figure 20.16).

FIGURE 20.16.

The Placement choices.

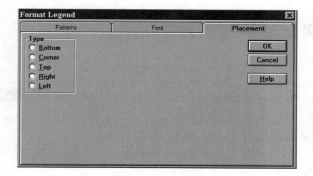

Chart Area

The chart area refers to the chart only, not including the title, legend, and so on. To customize the chart area, select the chart and choose Format | Selected Chart Area. You can change patterns (see Figure 20.10) and fonts (see Figure 20.11).

Explore these options through Microsoft Graph 5.0 to get a better understanding of everything that can be customized.

Customizing the Graph Through Code

This is a programmatic reference on how to customize graphs. Although, the following information will provide a starting point and valuable reference guide, the material is by no means a complete programming reference for Microsoft Graph 5.0. Refer to the Microsoft Office Developer's Kit for more detailed information.

To refer to a graph object, you must refer to *[Form]![Control].Object.[object section or property]*. You can do this by creating pointers to the object in some early stages of a form's creation. To do this, include the following code in the general declarations section of your form's code:

```
Option Compare Database
Option Explicit
'Used to refer to graph OLE Object
Dim objGraph as Object
```

In the `Form_Load` event of the form containing the graph object, set the objMyGraph object to the graph control name and to the `Object` property. This initialization of an object pointer will make referencing the graph object easier and faster:

```
Private Sub Form_Load
    Set objMyGraph = Me!objGraph.Object
End Sub
```

Changing Graph Types

You can change graph types at runtime by referring to the object's `Type` property.

> **WARNING**
>
> Don't change the graph type if it isn't necessary. Changing a type forces a graph redraw, which is memory-intensive.

The following subroutine can be used (in a command button, for example) as a test to examine each one of the possible graph types:

```
Private Sub SetGraphType (iGraphType as Integer)

    'Set OLE graph type to user-selected graph type, if necessary
    If objMyGraph.Type <> iGraphType Then
        objMyGraph.Type = iGraphType
    End If
End Sub
```

Another method would be to do the following:

1. Create a form similar to the one shown in Figure 20.17 to change graph types.

2. Create an option group named GraphTypes.

3. Create a series of toggle buttons inside this option group with the option values for each button set to the corresponding values from Table 20.1. (Some of the buttons have been omitted from the example.)

FIGURE 20.17.

An example of how to change graph types at runtime.

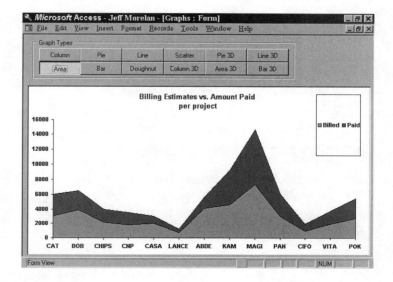

Table 20.1. Each graph type and the value to be used to change to each graph type with its code value.

Graph Type	Option Value (Chart Type)
Area	1
Bar	2
Column	3
Line	4
Pie	5
Doughnut	6
Radar	7
XY Scatter	8
Area—3-Dimensional	9
Bar—3-Dimensional	10
Column—3-Dimensional	11
Line—3-Dimensional	12
Pie—3-Dimensional	13
Surface—3-Dimensional	14

Insert a graph object. Invoke the Microsoft Graph 5.0 Editor by double-clicking on the graph object and select Data | Series in Columns. This will render the data applicable for most of the graphs that are used in this example.

Create the following code in the option group's `After Update` event. This will set the graph's chart type at runtime.

```
Private Sub GraphTypes_AfterUpdate( )
    'Set OLE graph type to user-selected graph type, if necessary
    If objMyGraph.Type <> Int(Me!GraphTypes) Then
        objMyGraph.Type = Int(Me!GraphTypes)
    End If
End Sub
```

Changing the Underlying Data

You can completely change the underlying data by changing the graph's `Row Source` property. As you know, this can be done at design time, but it offers more possibilities at runtime.

To change the underlying data, we can use the previous example with some extra code and more objects added to the form. The user has a number of ways to change the row source to different queries or different Select statements, so let's explore one example.

Create a list box filled with a list of queries that you wish to use. You can do this by creating a table to house the queries that can be used. When a different query is chosen, change the row source with the following code:

```
objMyGraph.RowSource = Me!lstQueries
```

The underlying data set will be changed and the graph will automatically redraw to reflect the new changes. This may change the way the graph ultimately looks, and the formatting for the previous graph might not be adequate for the new data set.

Adding and Removing the Legend

Using code to add or remove a legend is a simple process. Create a control on the form that you wish to use as your legend changer.

This example will use a command button with the `Caption` property set to Add/Remove Legend and the `Name` property set to ChgLegend. Create an event procedure for the button's on-click event with the following code. This will make the legend visible if it wasn't visible and make it not visible if it was visible.

```
Sub ChgLegend_Click( )
    objMyGraph.HasLegend = Not objMyGraph.HasLegend
End Sub
```

Adding and Removing the Title

Create a command button called ChgTitle with the `Caption` property set to Add/Remove Title and the `Name` property set to ChgTitle. Create an event procedure for the button's on-click event with the following code:

```
Private Sub ChgTitle_Click( )
    objMyGraph.HasTitle = Not objMyGraph.HasTitle
    objMyGraph.Title = Me!txtTitle
End Sub
```

Exploding Pie Slices: Rotating and Elevating a 3-D Graph

At runtime, data can be emphasized in a number of ways. You can emphasize a set of data by exploding or pulling out one or more of its slices. The set of data can be rotated around its vertical or horizontal axis.

Create a list box named PieSlices and set the Row Source property to the Payment Method query for this example. Payment Method is a query that gives all the possible payment methods of a time and billing database along with the sum of the amounts paid on each method.

Create a form that has the controls and properties specified in Table 20.2.

Table 20.2. Controls and properties for exploding a graph.

Control	Property	Setting
ListBox	Name	PieSlices
	Row Source	Payment Method
OLE Container	Name	OLEGraph
	Row Source	Payment Method
Command Button	Name	Explode
	Caption	Explode
Command Button	Name	RotateDown
	Caption	RotateDown
Command Button	Name	RotateLeft
	Caption	RotateLeft
Command Button	Name	RotateRight
	Caption	RotateRight
Command Button	Name	RotateUp
	Caption	RotateUp
Command Button	Name	Normal
	Caption	Normal

Create a graph object named OLEGraph with the Row Source property set to Payment Method. Now you have a list of payment methods in the list box and a graph with the slices equal to those payment methods.

Create command buttons for rotating up, down, left, and right. Create a command button for exploding a pie slice and create a command button for setting the graph back to its default. Figure 20.18 shows the form with exploding and rotating options.

FIGURE 20.18.

This form can explode and rotate a pie graph.

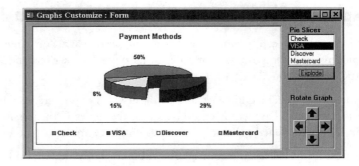

Create the following code to implement exploding and rotating options:

```
'Place this code in the form's General Declaration section
Option Compare Database
Option Explicit
Dim ObjGraph As Object
Const GRAPH_ROTATE_CHANGE = 10
Const GRAPH_EXPLODE_CHANGE = 20

'Place this code in the Form Load event of the form
Private Sub Form_Load( )
    Set ObjGraph = Me!OLEGraph.Object
End Sub

'Place this code in the Explode button click event
Private Sub Explode_Click( )
    Dim iSlice As Integer
    iSlice = Me!lstPieSlices.ListIndex + 1
    ObjGraph.SeriesCollection(1).Points(iSlice).Explosion =
    ➡ObjGraph.SeriesCollection(1).Points(iSlice).Explosion + GRAPH_EXPLODE
    ➡CHANGE
End Sub

'Place this code in the RotateDown button click event
Private Sub RotateDown_Click( )
On Error Resume Next
    ObjGraph.Elevation = ObjGraph.Elevation + GRAPH_ROTATE_CHANGE
End Sub

'Place this code in the RotateLeft button click event
Private Sub RotateLeft_Click( )
On Error Resume Next
    ObjGraph.Rotation = ObjGraph.Rotation - GRAPH_ROTATE_CHANGE
End Sub

'Place this code in the RotateRight button click event
Private Sub RotateRight_Click( )
```

```
On Error Resume Next
    ObjGraph.Rotation = ObjGraph.Rotation + GRAPH_ROTATE_CHANGE
End Sub

'Place this code in the RotateUp button click event
Private Sub RotateUp_Click( )
On Error Resume Next
    ObjGraph.Elevation = ObjGraph.Elevation - GRAPH_ROTATE_CHANGE
End Sub

'Place this code in the Normal button click event
Private Sub Normal_Click( )
On Error Resume Next
    ObjGraph.Elevation = 0
End Sub
```

When the left and right rotate buttons are clicked, the graph will rotate around its vertical axis. When the up and down rotate buttons are clicked, the graph will rotate around its horizontal axis.

When a slice is selected in the list box and the Explode button is clicked, the slice will be pulled away from the center of the pie by 10 points. As the Explode button is clicked more times, the slice will move further and further away from the center of the pie.

These options can all be customized to your satisfaction by adjusting the amount of change and the method in which the form is changed. You can adjust the amount of change by setting new values for the constants, or you can create a very flexible environment by building a configuration form. In such a form, the user can adjust by how many points he would like his objects to rotate, move, and so on.

Sizing the Chart and the Legend

Sizing the chart (plot area) and sizing the legend can be valuable in rounding out the charting capabilities of your application. In the following example, a form was created to size the different sections of the graph and to allow the legend and title to be toggled visible and invisible. Figure 20.19 shows a form that can size objects and turn the legend and title on or off.

FIGURE 20.19.

This form, which an be used to manipulate a 3-D pie chart, provides sizing and titling options.

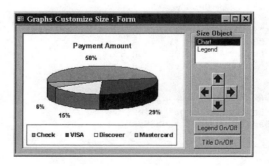

Create a form that has the controls and properties specified in Table 20.3.

Table 20.3. Controls and properties for sizing the chart and legend.

Control	Property	Setting
ListBox	Name	lstObject
	Row Source	Chart, Legend
	Row Source Type	Value List
OLE Container	Name	OLEGraph
	Row Source	Payment Method
Command Button	Name	HeightLarger
	Caption	Larger Height
Command Button	Name	HeightSmaller
	Caption	Smaller Height
Command Button	Name	WidthLarger
	Caption	Larger Width
Command Button	Name	WidthSmaller
	Caption	Smaller Width
Command Button	Name	LegendVisible
	Caption	Legend Visible
Command Button	Name	TitleVisible
	Caption	Title Visible

The following code was used for the form in Figure 20.19:

```
'Place this code in the form's General Declarations section
Option Compare Database
Option Explicit
Dim objGraph As Object
Dim objSection As Object
Const GRAPH_SIZE_CHANGE = 5

'Place this code in the form's Form Load event
Private Sub Form_Load( )
    Set objGraph = Me!OLEGraph.Object
    Call lstObject_AfterUpdate
End Sub

'Place this code in the HeightLarger button click event
Private Sub HeightLarger_Click( )
    objSection.Height = objSection.Height + GRAPH_SIZE_CHANGE
End Sub
```

```
'Place this code in the HeightSmaller button click event
Private Sub HeightSmaller_Click( )
    objSection.Height = objSection.Height - GRAPH_SIZE_CHANGE
End Sub

'Place this code in the LegendVisible button click event
Private Sub LegendVisible_Click( )
    objGraph.HasLegend = Not objGraph.HasLegend
End Sub

'Place this code in the 1stObject AfterUpdate event
Private Sub lstObject_AfterUpdate( )
    Select Case Me!lstObject
        Case "Chart"
            Set objSection = objGraph.PlotArea
        Case "Legend"
            Set objSection = objGraph.Legend
    End Select
End Sub

'Place this code in the TitleVisible button click event
Private Sub TitleVisible_Click( )
    objGraph.HasTitle = Not objGraph.HasTitle
End Sub

'Place this code in the WidthLarger button click event
Private Sub WidthLarger_Click( )
    objSection.Width = objSection.Width + GRAPH_SIZE_CHANGE
End Sub

'Place this code in the WidthSmaller button click event
Private Sub WidthSmaller_Click( )
    objSection.Width = objSection.Width - GRAPH_SIZE_CHANGE
End Sub
```

Sizing the Title

Sizing the title is somewhat different. The chart title doesn't have Width or Height properties.
You can adjust the size of the title only by referencing the ChartTitle.Font.Size property of
the graph object:

```
objGraph.ChartTitle.Font.Size = 12
```

The font can also be changed by referring to the ChartTitle.Font.Name property:

```
objGraph.ChartTitle.Font.Name = "Arial"
```

Moving the Chart, Legend, and Title

Using code to move objects is also an easy task. The plot area, the chart title, and the legend
can all be moved with routines that are similar to those that are used for sizing. Here movement is made by referring to the object's Top and Left properties.

Create a form that has the controls and properties specified in Table 20.4.

Table 20.4. Controls and properties for moving the chart, legend, and title.

Control	Property	Setting
ListBox	Name	lstObject
	Row Source	Chart, Legend, Title
	Row Source Type	Value List
OLE Container	Name	OLEGraph
	Row Source	Payment Method
Command Button	Name	MoveUp
	Caption	Move Up
Command Button	Name	MoveDown
	Caption	Move Down
Command Button	Name	MoveRight
	Caption	Move Right
Command Button	Name	MoveLeft
	Caption	Move Left

Use the following code for a form that manipulates object movement:

```
'Place this code in the form's General Declarations section
Option Compare Database
Option Explicit
Dim objGraph As Object
Dim objSection As Object
Const GRAPH_MOVE_CHANGE = 5

'Place this code in the Form Load event
Private Sub Form_Load( )
    Set objGraph = Me!OLEGraph.Object
    Call lstObject_AfterUpdate
End Sub

'Place this code in the MoveUp button click event
Private Sub MoveUp_Click( )
    objSection.Top = objSection.Top - GRAPH_MOVE_CHANGE
End Sub

'Place this code in the MoveDown button click event
Private Sub MoveDown_Click( )
    objSection.Top = objSection.Top + GRAPH_MOVE_CHANGE
End Sub

'Place this code in the 1stObject AfterUpdate event
Private Sub lstObject_AfterUpdate( )
    Select Case Me!lstObject
        Case "Title"
            Set objSection = objGraph.Title
```

```
        Case "Chart"
             Set objSection = objGraph.PlotArea
        Case "Legend"
             Set objSection = objGraph.Legend
    End Select
End Sub

'Place this code in the MoveRight button click event
Private Sub MoveRight_Click( )
    objSection.Left = objSection.Left + GRAPH_MOVE_CHANGE
End Sub

'Place this code in the MoveLeft button click event
Private Sub MoveLeft_Click( )
    objSection.Left = objSection.Left - GRAPH_MOVE_CHANGE
End Sub
```

Bound Versus Unbound Graphical Objects

Deciding whether to use a bound or an unbound graphical object takes some consideration. First you must know what you wish your graph to accomplish. The information in this section will provide you with information helpful in choosing bound or unbound graphs.

Bound Graphical Objects

Bound graphs are stable; you know what the data should look like. For an application where it's important to see the data the same way every time, a bound graph is the best answer. Of course, the graph can be customized, but a bound graph doesn't provide the flexibility of an unbound graph.

Unbound Graphical Objects

Unbound graphs provide flexibility in changing what the user can see. If your application has a large amount of data to graph and will be changing in the future, it may be best to utilize unbound graphs. With unbound graphs, you don't need to know exactly what the graph must look like; all you need to know is a relative framework. By simply changing the Row Source property, the graph can redraw with a new set of data.

With both bound and unbound graph types, the graph type can be changed. If the graph type is changed at runtime, the data set will most likely not be formatted correctly. To fix this possible problem, it may be necessary to institute a system of defaults.

For more complex scenarios, it's possible to create a system with both flexibility and structure. You can have a list of graphs to choose from in a list box or combo box. Each graph can relate to a record in a table that has information on the row source, the graph type, the sizing of each object, where each section (title, plot area, and legend) will be located, and so on.

When the user selects a graph, the graph will redraw with the new set of data, and all the sections can be moved and sized to their optimum settings; thus, the user wouldn't need to move or size any of the objects. However, you can give the user the option of making modifications as needed and the option of resetting the default values for that graph. Of course, this will take much more code and quite a bit of time.

Changing the Graph While Navigating Through Records

Another powerful feature of a graphed object is the ability to show a new graph with each new record. This is done by linking master and child fields. The Master Field property refers to the parent form field to link on. The Child Field property refers to the graph field to link on. In Figure 20.20, the graph is linked on the field called ProjectName for both child and master fields.

FIGURE 20.20.

The graph on this form changes as you go to new records using the navigation buttons.

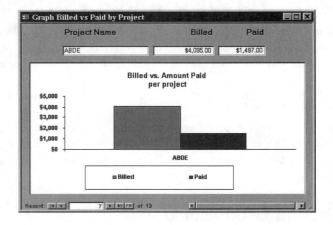

When the navigation button is clicked, not only is information regarding that record displayed on the form, but significant data is also automatically shown on the graph for the linked objects.

The form is bound to the query Graph Billed vs Paid by Project, which includes fields called Project Name, Billed, and Paid. The graph needs to have a row source that has Project Name in it. The graph could show anything significant that can be linked by project name. In this example, the graph's Row Source property is also set to the query Graph Billed vs Paid by Project. This example shows a graphical representation of the information that is shown textually on the form.

This is a powerful use of the graphing possibilities. Graphs can redraw to show specific information about a particular record. This is also simple, because it doesn't require any special coding.

Summary

Experiment with Microsoft Graph 5.0 and Access 95. Their functionality can be intermixed to create powerful decision-support systems and to add polish to any application. Spending time with the graphing functions will pay off in the long run.

Using OLE and OLE Automation

21

by Ricardo Birmele

IN THIS CHAPTER

Because you're reading this book about Access, you're probably already familiar with Windows. You know that you can have more than one Windows-based program running at a time, and that you can use the clipboard to move, say, a Paintbrush picture right into your Word document.

That's pretty convenient—certainly a big usability step up from MS-DOS. It would be even more convenient, however, if you didn't have to "start" another program to be able to use it. For example, if you could paint a picture from within your Access database. Or use Word's spell-checker and grammar-checker while in an Access form.

That's what this chapter is about. The technology is called object linking and embedding, better known as OLE. This chapter will give you an idea of how you can use OLE to work easily and automatically with other programs from within Access, a process known as OLE Automation.

The discussion will begin with some definitions and a look at the concepts underlying OLE Automation. Also, you'll learn a bit about a couple of tools. The first of these is the Windows 95 Registration Database, a kind of replacement for the familiar Windows application .INI files. The second tool is the Access Object Browser, which enables you to see which objects are available. Also in this chapter, you'll create an Access application that will enable you to catalog and pass along some of those clever ideas you might have now and then.

> **NOTE**
>
> You might have noticed that Windows 95 displays icons, known as shortcuts, on its default desktop. What you might not know is that when you click one of these shortcut icons, you are actually using an OLE link between it and the program itself.

A Few Definitions

Before you go any further, you need to have a few definitions to increase your understanding of the subject. The most important definition is covered first.

Objects

In the computer world, an object is anything you can figuratively "touch." For example, in Access you can figuratively touch such objects as a form, a field, and a control button. In Figure 21.1, you "touch" each object using the mouse or the keyboard, or programmatically through instructions you include in Access macros or code modules.

Like real-world objects, one kind of Access object is basically similar to every other like object. Take Access dialog boxes, for example. Each is similar to every other Access dialog box in that it probably has controls on it, each of which is itself an object.

FIGURE 21.1.

Almost everything on a Windows application is an object.

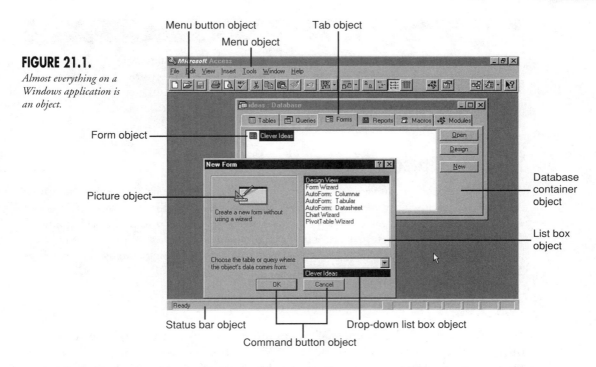

Menu button object

Menu object

Tab object

Form object

Picture object

Database container object

List box object

Status bar object

Drop-down list box object

Command button object

In Access you pretty well know what to expect when you see and manipulate a dialog box. That expectation carries over when you use a dialog box in another Windows-based application. The controls on a Word for Windows or WordPerfect dialog box behave in the same way as do the controls in an Access dialog box.

It's this similarity of behavior among controls from different manufacturers that allows OLE technology to exist.

OLE

OLE is an acronym for object linking and embedding. It is a technology by which different kinds of applications—spreadsheets, word processors, databases, and so on—can work seamlessly together by exposing certain of their objects to each other. It doesn't matter if the applications come from different manufacturers. What does matter is that the applications and their objects behave in predictable ways and that they have certain capabilities built into them that comply with the OLE "standard."

> **NOTE**
>
> It's kind of a misnomer to speak of OLE as having or being a "standard" to which applications using that technology must comply. Nothing is set in stone or formally agreed on yet. Instead, as OLE technology has developed into OLE version 2, more and more software manufacturers have been complying with the standard.

Exposed Objects

To be OLE-capable, a software application must be able to expose its objects to other OLE-capable applications. That means that the application has the capability to share its objects and their manipulations built into it. The program exposing its objects runs in the background—"hidden," so to speak. Because it's running, that program is what's actually controlling its exposed objects. All you—or your program—see are those objects being employed by your application.

OLE Client

An OLE "conversation" between applications involves two participants. For the purposes of this chapter's discussion, the first participant is Microsoft Access. Because Access will be served the objects of the other application much as a client is served by a consultant, the Access database application you're running as you implement OLE is called the OLE client. It is also known as the container application because it comes to "contain" the objects of the other software.

OLE Server

An OLE server is the other participant in an OLE conversation. It exposes its objects to the client, thus providing the client with an object to link or embed. If, for example, you were going to use Word's text-editing capabilities in your Access database, Word would be the OLE server and Access would be the OLE client.

Embedded Objects

An embedded object is one that is copied from the OLE server and becomes part of your OLE client. When you activate it in place, however, it behaves just as if it were still part of the OLE server. Its menus and menu options are the same, and it responds to keystrokes and mouse manipulations in the same way. All the while, however, it is actually a part of the OLE client. After an object has been embedded, a person must be running your same Access database application to be able to modify it. For example, if the object is a Paintbrush picture, then to modify the picture, you must call up the picture object from within your Access application.

Linked Objects

A linked object is one that is merely connected to your application. You can use your Access database application to modify it, of course. But anyone else can modify that object as well. They can do so by also linking it to their own application, or by running its original server application.

With a Paintbrush picture, for example, anyone with access to your computer's hard disk could run PBRUSH.EXE, load your picture into it, and scribble away with abandon, regardless of how long it took you to create the picture or how important it is to your project. Of course, this alteration could present something of a surprise the next time you open your database.

> **TIP**
>
> You can use OLE automation to link a file stored anywhere you have access to it. This could be on your own hard disk, as in the example, or it could be on another computer networked to yours.

> **NOTE**
>
> Clearly, the tradeoffs between linking and embedding objects have to do with how access to the objects needs to be controlled. If it's OK—and more efficient—for anyone to be able to doodle with the object, then link it. On the other hand, the object is more secure if it is embedded.

A Comparison of Linking and Embedding

As you decide whether you want to link or embed a file into your client application, you should keep a couple of things in mind. The first thing is the difference in the potential size of your client application data file; the second is the performance differences between embedding and linking.

When you link a file, it mostly remains separate from the client. The only things the client needs to keep track of internally are pointers to the linked file's location, what kind of file it is, and so on. Obviously, there's not a big size hit there. On the other hand, if you embed an object, all of the object is incorporated into your client. This includes not only the data involved, but also all the information the client needs to find the object's server so that the object can be edited in place. This usually represents a significant size hit. A simple image record, for example, can add hundreds of kilobytes of data to your database.

The performance differences are less easy to qualify. Usually, it's faster to deal with an embedded object. Because everything necessary to edit it is already there in your client, you don't have to worry about network or own-system executable seek/load/run constraints. On the other hand, because of the potentially extreme size (and therefore practical performance) hit, quite often you should link data objects instead.

A Project: Clever Ideas and a Way to Remember Them

The project you'll next tackle is a database application that enables you to easily remember and describe your clever ideas. It stores a picture and a description of an idea in an Access database. It uses OLE and OLE automation to augment Access's limited picture-drawing and description-writing capabilities. When you're done, you'll have an application you can build on to create even more sophisticated solutions.

You'll start with a simple table to store the data. You'll add to that a form to make your data entry easier. And on the form, you'll place controls that will automate your use of OLE.

Creating the Database

The following steps tell you how to create the database:

1. If it's not already running, start Access and open a blank database using the dialog box shown in Figure 21.2. Name the database Clever Ideas.

FIGURE 21.2.

Open a blank database.

2. With the Tables tab selected, click New in the Database window to create a new table. Access displays its Table Design dialog box.

3. Create a table composed of the following four fields, as shown in Figure 21.3.

Field Name	Data Type	Description
Name	Text	A name for my idea
Category	Text	A category for my idea
Picture	OLE Object	A place to sketch my idea
Comments	OLE Object	A place to describe my idea

FIGURE 21.3.

Clever Ideas table design.

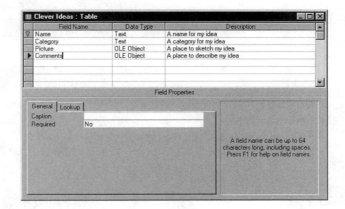

4. Save your table, naming it Clever Ideas.

> **NOTE**
>
> The OLE data type is a bit different from the "normal" data types, such as integer, that represent some actual data in your table and that can be used as a sorting index. Instead, it's more like the memo type in that it too is a pointer—in this case, a pointer to the OLE object that will be embedded or linked to the OLE object field in your table. It is stored in your database field as a 4-byte address.

A Quick OLE

After you've created this table with its OLE object fields, you can use them right away. To do so, follow these steps:

1. Click the Table View button on the far left of your Table Design toolbar. Access displays your table in Datasheet view, as shown in Figure 21.4.

FIGURE 21.4.

You can enter object data by using OLE and Datasheet view.

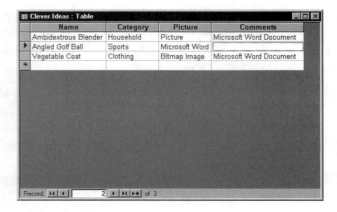

2. Because the Name field is the primary key field in the sample table, you'll always need to enter data into the Name field. Also, because it's a text field, all you must do is move to the field and start typing the name for your idea. Enter a name there now.

3. Move the mouse cursor to the picture column and right-click. (Alternatively, you can select Insert | Object.) As shown in Figure 21.5, Access displays a pop-up menu containing the Insert Object option, which you should select. Access displays the Insert Object dialog box, shown in Figure 21.6.

FIGURE 21.5.

Select Insert Object from the pop-up menu.

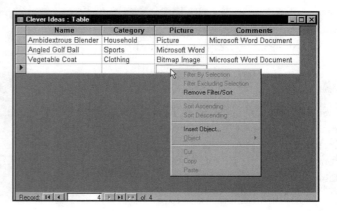

4. Pick one of the graphical objects to insert into your picture field by moving down the Object Type listbox. If you want to use clip art, Microsoft includes a ClipArt Gallery with Word for Windows. If, on the other hand, you want to draw something yourself, choose Paintbrush Picture or Microsoft Draw. For the purposes of this example, work with Paintbrush. Click OK after you've made your decision.

FIGURE 21.6.

Insert a graphic object into the OLE object field.

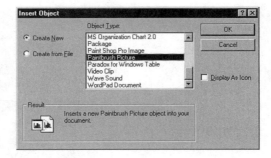

NOTE

Microsoft WordArt is a name that can fool you. It's not a drawing program in the sense that you use lines and circles to create pictures. Instead, it's an application that enables you to graphically manipulate text objects. For example, you can use it to create a fancy word logo.

---

5. In this case, you're using Paintbrush to sketch an idea (see Figure 21.7). After you're done with your sketch, select the File menu. Its Exit option will read something like "Exit & Return to Clever Ideas: Table," as shown in Figure 21.8. This lets you know that while you are using another application, its product will become part of your database's table.

FIGURE 21.7.

A sketch in the making.

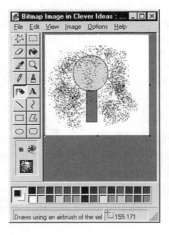

That's about all there is to creating an OLE object and putting it into your table. As shown in Figure 21.9, Access notes the existence of the object within your file with the words Bitmap Image.

FIGURE 21.8.
Exiting this application puts its output right into your table.

Clever Ideas : Table

Name	Category	Picture	Comments
Ambidextrous Blender	Household	Picture	Microsoft Word Document
Angled Golf Ball	Sports	Microsoft Word	
Vegetable Coat	Clothing	Bitmap Image	Microsoft Word Document
Tessla Coil / Fog Generat	Misc	Bitmap Image	

Record: 4 of 4

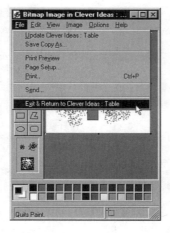

FIGURE 21.9.
OLE objects become part of your table.

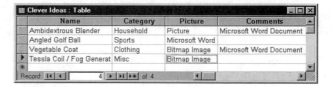

Activating Your Object In-Place

One of the more useful capabilities of OLE objects is that of activating and editing objects "in-place." Although you can't see the objects themselves in your table, you can see what kind of objects they are. After they're in your table, you can treat them just as you would any other kind of data. In other words, you can delete an OLE object, copy it, move it, or edit it.

That's where in-place activation—also known as visual editing—comes into play. To edit an OLE object that already exists in your table, perform the following steps:

1. Display your database table in datasheet form.
2. Pick an OLE object field that contains an OLE object, and right-click it. Access displays a pop-up menu that includes an option regarding the kind of object in that field, as shown in Figure 21.10.
3. Select the Object option (in this case, it's the Bitmap Image Object option). Access displays a submenu that gives you the option of opening, editing, or converting the object.
4. Select the Edit option on the submenu. Access calls up its server application, loads the object into that server application, and then lets Windows display it for you to edit.

After you're done with your edits, you save the newly edited object back to your database by selecting the appropriate Exit option from the object's File menu.

FIGURE 21.10.

Access knows what kind of object is pointed to by the OLE object field, and what kind of manipulations you can perform on it.

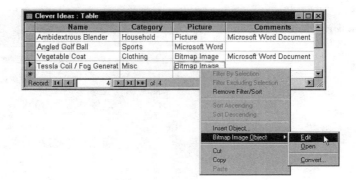

Creating a Form for Your Project

No Access database would be complete without a form to use for entering and viewing data. Because this database is simple—comprising a single table—the form can be simple, too. To create it, perform the following steps:

1. If it's not already running, start Access and call up the Clever Ideas database.
2. In Access's database container, click the Forms tab to make it active.
3. Click the New button to call up the New Form dialog box.
4. In the New Form dialog box, make sure that the name of the Clever Ideas table appears in the drop-down listbox in the lower-right portion of the dialog box. That indicates to Access that Clever Ideas is the table that the form object's data is supposed to come from. Also make sure that Design View is selected in the large listbox at the right side of the dialog box.
5. Click OK and Access creates a blank form, ready for you to put in the fields from the Clever Ideas table.
6. Save the form under the name Clever Ideas.

Placing the Fields on the Form

With the form open in Design view, you are ready to add fields from the Clever Ideas table. To do so, perform the following steps:

1. If it isn't already displayed, display the field list by clicking the Field List button on the Form Design toolbar. Drag field names down from the field list onto the form itself, as shown in Figure 21.11.
2. Add a command button just below the Comments field. Later, you'll attach code to it that will enable you to use OLE automation. For now, under the Format tab in the Properties dialog box, give the button a caption property of &Add Text. Also, under the Other tab, give the button the name property cmdAddText.

FIGURE 21.11.

A suggested form field layout.

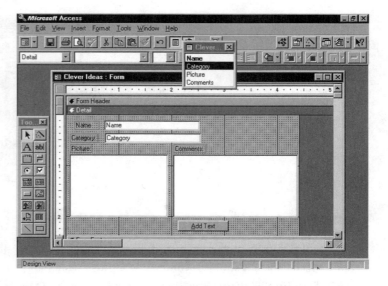

When you use an ampersand (&) in a caption, Access underlines the letter following it. Access also creates an internal link between that letter and an internal command that's invoked by the user pressing that letter and the Alt key. That command automatically runs the code associated with the key's Click event. That means that the user could either press Alt-A or click the command button to cause the task to be performed.

3. If the Properties dialog box isn't active, click the Properties button on the toolbar. Then on the form, select the Picture OLE object field.

4. Returning your attention to the Properties dialog box, select the Format tab. For the Size Mode property at the top of the list, choose Zoom from the drop-down list. With that done, you'll be able to see the entire picture object regardless of its size when it is manipulated in its server application, much like in Figure 21.12.

5. Be sure to save your form once again.

Image objects can be displayed in a number of ways, depending on which Size Mode property you select. I've found that it's usually best to use zoom (which automatically resizes your image) rather than clip (which crops it) or stretch (which distorts it) to display the image.

FIGURE 21.12.

Zooming provides just the right objective view.

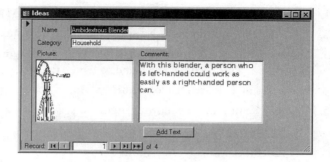

Bound and Unbound Fields

Fields on an Access form can be bound or unbound. Bound fields are connected (bound) to a field in the underlying table. They automatically display the contents of the underlying field. Unbound fields, on the other hand, don't take this same action. They display whatever you programmatically tell them to—the results of a calculation, for example.

Because you dragged the field names down to the form from the Field List, they are automatically bound fields. They will display the text or OLE object contained in the corresponding field in the Clever Ideas table.

Displaying OLE Images

Well, you've got a form now. If you wanted to insert an object into the Picture or Comments fields, it would be as easy as 1-2-3. Here's how:

1. Select either the Picture field or the Comments field.
2. Select Insert | Object or right-click on the field. Access displays the Insert Object dialog box you saw at the beginning of this chapter.
3. Choose an object type from the list in the dialog box and click OK. Access calls up its server application, activates it, and then stores the data in the appropriate OLE object field in your Clever Ideas table.

Automatically Inserting an OLE Object

Earlier in this chapter, you read that you could double-click an OLE object field with the table in Datasheet view, and that Access would automatically call up the Insert Object dialog box. Unfortunately, that's not true with OLE object forms. As a matter of fact, if you were to do so, Access would display an error dialog box prompting you to link or embed an object.

One solution is to create an Access macro that is invoked whenever you double-click an empty OLE object field. To try that for the Picture field in your Clever Ideas database, carry out the following steps:

1. With the Database Container window active, click its Macros tab.

2. Click the New button. Access displays a blank macro sheet.

3. Display the Macro Name column and type the name `AutoInsertObject` in the Macro Name field. This becomes the name by which this macro will be known.

4. In the Action field, select DoMenuItem. Access places it in the Action field.

5. Give DoMenuItem the following arguments, as shown in Figure 21.13:

Argument Name	Argument Parameter
Menu Bar	Form
Menu Name	Insert
Command	Object

FIGURE 21.13.

A macro can comprise a single line.

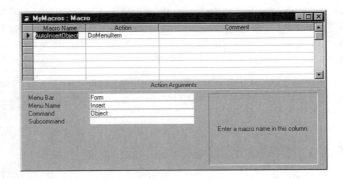

6. Save the macro sheet under the name MyMacros.

Adding the Macro to an Event

With the macro created, all you need to do is add its name to the `On_ Dbl_Click` event in the Clever Ideas form property sheet. To do so, perform the following steps:

1. Call up the Clever Ideas form in Design view.

2. Select the Picture OLE object frame. Access indicates that it is active by displaying a border and sizing handles around it.

3. With the Properties dialog box active, click the Event tab. Access displays the contents of the Event tab.

4. Sliding the mouse cursor down to the `On Dbl Click` event, select MyMacros.AutoInsertObject from the drop-down listbox, as shown in Figure 21.14.

5. Save the form.

Now when you double-click the Picture OLE object field, Access automatically displays its Insert Object dialog box. And as you can with the table in Datasheet view, you can select an object type to insert into your field. And if an object is already in the field, Access will call up the object's server application so that you can edit the object.

FIGURE 21.14.

The On Dbl Click *event is called when a control is double-clicked.*

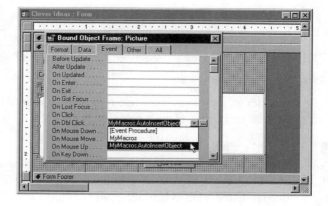

OLE Automation

Sometimes it's easier for your user to click a button and be presented with a specific object type. Access makes this kind of thing easy with OLE Automation. In your Clever Ideas form, you'll add code to the Add Text button. To do so, perform the following steps:

1. With the form in Design view, click the Add Text command button.
2. In the Properties dialog box, select the On Click event on the Event tab.
3. Click the Builder button to the right of the blank field. (It's the one with an ellipsis on it.) Access displays the Choose Builder dialog box.
4. Choose the Code Builder option. Access displays its code builder form, into which you should type the following code:

```
Private Sub cmdAddText_Click()
On Error GoTo AddTextErr
Comments.Class = "Word.Document"
Comments.OLETypeAllowed = acOLEEmbedded
Comments.Action = acOLECreateEmbed
Comments.Action = acOLEActivate
AddTextErr:
    MsgBox Error$ & Chr$(13) & "Unable to embed word document"
    Resume AddText

AddText:

End Sub
```

5. Select Run | Compile All Modules. Access compiles all the code modules in your application, apprising you of any errors.
6. Click the Save button on the toolbar to save your work to disk.

Examining the Code

The following discussion takes a closer look at each line of code to see what it does.

```
Private Sub cmdAddText_Click()
```

This is the necessary first line for the code subroutine. It lets you know that this code is associated with the `cmdAddText` command button and is invoked by that control's `Click` event.

```
On Error GoTo AddTextErr
```

This line provides an out in case the code runs into an error during its execution. The statement points to an embedded routine below.

```
Comments.Class = "Word.Document"
```

This statement sets the property that determines what kind of object is to be embedded into the Comments field. Taken together, it is the object's class name. Its syntax comprises the object's server application name, a period, and the kind of object that server is providing.

If you wanted to, you could add another period and a version number. In this case, the result could be `"Word.Document.6."` If you take this action, however, that version of the server application would have to be loaded on the machine running your Access database application. In this case, this syntax avoids the version number and yields a more general usage. In other words, this way the routine simply looks for Microsoft Word for Windows, in whatever version is installed on your computer.

```
Comments.OLETypeAllowed = acOLEEmbedded
```

The next line indicates whether you want the object to be linked or embedded into the Comments OLE Object field. If you wanted it to be linked instead, you could have used the constant `acOLELinked` in place of `acOLEEmbedded`.

```
Comments.Action = acOLECreateEmbed
```

This statement creates a placeholder in memory for the object to be embedded. This is the last step necessary to prepare for the OLE operation.

```
Comments.Action = acOLEActivate
```

Finally, there's the last statement that actually calls up the OLE server application. The rest, as they say, is automagical.

```
AddTextErr:
    MsgBox Error$ & Chr$(13) & "Unable to embed word document"
    Resume AddText
```

These three lines provide an error-handling routine for this procedure. All they actually do is advise you of the error's occurrence through a message box and then allow the procedure to continue without "bombing out."

AddText:

This line is nothing more than a way of saying "keep on going" to the computer as it works its way through this procedure.

End Sub

Every Access BASIC subroutine must end with this statement.

Access OLE Constants

Access has built into it some intrinsic constants. Many of these are specifically to be used for OLE operations. They all behave just like any other programming constants with which you might be familiar.

OLE Action Constants

When an OLE object "does something," it performs an action. You indicate what action it is to perform by using the syntax

OLE_Object.Action = *foo*

in which *foo* is one of the constants listed in Table 21.1.

Table 21.1. The action constants.

Constant	Description
acOLEActivate	Activates a server application.
acOLEClose	Closes an OLE object.
acOLECopy	Copies an OLE object to the Windows clipboard.
acOLECreateEmbed	Creates a placeholder for an embedded OLE object.
acOLECreateLink	Creates a placeholder for a linked OLE object.
acOLEDelete	Deletes an OLE object.
acOLEFetchVerbs	Obtains the verbs available for an OLE object.
acOLEInsertObjDlg	Calls up the Insert OLE Object dialog box.
acOLEPaste	Pastes an OLE object from the Windows clipboard.
acOLEPasteSpecialDlg	Calls up the Paste Special dialog box.
acOLEUpdate	Updates the contents of an OLE object field.

OLE Application Constants

You can use various constants when manipulating OLE objects. These constants are listed in Table 21.2.

Table 21.2. The application constants.

Constant	Description
acOLEActivateDoubleClick	Activates a server application when the field is double-clicked.
acOLEActivateGetFocus	Activates a server application when the field gets the window's focus.
acOLEActivateManual	Activates a server application only with direct user intervention.
acOLEChanged	Sees whether an OLE object has been changed.
acOLEClosed	Sees whether an OLE object has been closed.
acOLECreateFromFile	Creates an OLE object from a server application file.
acOLECreateNew	Programmatically creates a new OLE object.
acOLEDisplayContent	Shows the contents of an OLE object.
acOLEDisplayIcon	Displays an icon to represent an OLE object.
acOLEEither	Allows the insertion of either a linked or an embedded OLE object.
acOLEEmbedded	Allows the insertion of only an embedded OLE object.
acOLELinked	Allows the insertion of only a linked OLE object.
acOLENone	Sees whether there is no OLE object.
acOLERenamed	Sees whether an OLE object has been renamed.
acOLESaved	Sees whether an OLE object has been saved since it was last modified.
acOLESizeAutoSize	Automatically sets up the size of a field that is to hold an OLE object.
acOLESizeClip	Formats an OLE field so that it clips the display of its OLE object.
acOLESizeStretch	Formats an OLE field so that it stretches the display of its OLE object to fit the field.
acOLESizeZoom	Formats an OLE field so that it zooms the size of the OLE object to fit the field.

Constant	Description
acOLEUpdateAutomatic	Automatically updates the contents of an OLE object field.
acOLEUpdateFrozen	Updates an OLE object without changes.
acOLEUpdateManual	Manually updates an OLE object.

OLE Verb Constants

Verbs are similar to actions in that when you call them, they cause something specific to happen to an OLE object. The difference between the two is that actions are more general calls, whereas verbs are calls that can be used only with OLE objects. These verbs are listed in Table 21.3.

Table 21.3. The OLE verb constants.

Constant	Description
acOLEVerbHide	Hides the server application for an embedded OLE object.
acOLEVerbInPlaceActivate	Activates an embedded OLE object within the OLE object field on your form, without server application menus being available.
acOLEVerbInPlaceUIActivate	Activates an embedded OLE object within the OLE object field on your form, with server application menus being available.
acOLEVerbOpen	Opens a server application window and edits an OLE object.
acOLEVerbPrimary	Obtains the default verb for an OLE object.
acOLEVerbShow	Actually edits an OLE object.

Browsing Objects

With all the applications and objects there are for OLE operations, how can you know which of their properties or methods are available? Access enables you to find out by using its built-in Object Browser. As an example, and remembering that Access itself can be an OLE server, take a look at the objects it exposes to potential Windows clients.

To call up the Object Browser, perform the following steps:

1. The Object Browser is available in Access only in a code module window. From the Database window, click the Modules tab.
2. Click the New button on the Visual Basic toolbar. Access opens a code module window.
3. Click the Object Browser button on the Visual Basic toolbar. Access displays the Object Browser window, shown in Figure 21.15. It shows you what objects and properties can be exposed to client applications.

FIGURE 21.15.

The Object Browser window.

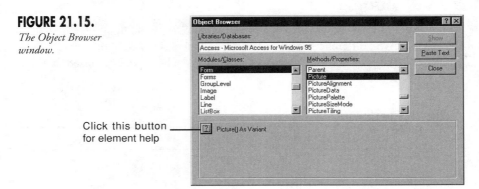

Click this button for element help

4. In the Libraries/Databases drop-down listbox, select Access - Microsoft Access for Windows 95. Access displays its exposible modules in the Modules/Classes listbox.

Take a moment and select a module or two. In Figure 21.15, the Form module has been selected. Notice that its intrinsic methods and properties are displayed in the Methods/Properties listbox to its right.

If you select a method or property, its syntax is displayed at the bottom of the Object Browser window. You can then get help on it, specifically, by clicking the Element Help button to the immediate left of the syntax example.

Finding OLE Objects

It used to be the case that every Windows application used an initialization file (with an extension of .INI) to keep track of various necessary details. These details included the application's operating parameters, where its data files could be located, and so forth. At first that seemed to be a pretty good scheme—until Windows became so popular. Eventually, different applications were using .INI files with the same name.

To solve that problem—one that could only get worse—Microsoft came up with a kind of database that it calls the Windows Registry. Configuration data for hardware and initialization information for software are kept here. Access also stores in this database the information it needs for initialization.

To open the Windows Registry and see its contents, perform the following steps:

1. Click the Start button on the Windows desktop and select Run. Access displays the Run dialog box.

2. Type regedit in the Open drop-down listbox and click OK. Access calls up the Registry Editor.

3. In the left pane of the Registry Editor, you can see several keys beginning with HKEY_ listed under the heading My Computer, as shown in Figure 21.16. These are roughly analogous to the bracketed headings in the (now) old-fashioned .INI files. Click the plus sign to the left of HKEY_LOCAL_MACHINE. Access opens the list of local machine parameters.

FIGURE 21.16.

The Registry Editor gives you access to Windows initialization and configuration settings.

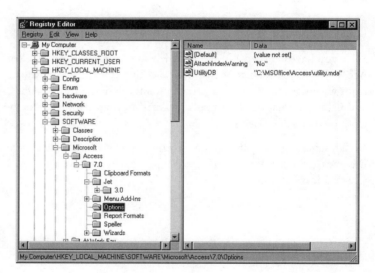

4. Click the plus sign to the left of the SOFTWARE heading. Access reveals headings for initialization parameters for the software installed on your computer.

5. In the same way, successively open the Microsoft, Access, and 7.0 lists.

When you're in the system Registry, you see a number of interesting things. Among these is the name of every application on your machine that can be a server application. To find which ones can be server applications, simply look up the word *server*. When you open a server folder, the Registry Editor displays the path to the server application. The name of the entry at the server's root is the name of the server application's class.

While you're in the Registry Editor, you can change any of the configuration or initialization data by clicking the appropriate field in the right pane of the Registry Editor and then typing the new data. That data becomes active the next time you start Windows.

> **NOTE**
>
> You must be very careful when using the Windows Registry. Any changes you make—inadvertent or not—could be reflected in the behavior of your Windows-based applications. If you're going to experiment, you should first back up the Registry using the Windows File Manager in the normal way. It's comprised of two files whose filenames are SYSTEM.DAT and USER.DAT. You'll find them in your Windows System directory.

Summary

Now you have a taste of OLE and how you can use it in Access. You've learned that objects in Access are very similar to their physical counterparts. As you know, you can manipulate them from within a program. And you can manipulate them from afar, so to speak, by using OLE and OLE automation. You've also learned to divine some of the heretofore mysterious functions of the system Registry.

It's a fascinating and yet-emerging technology. My best advice to you is to experiment, experiment, experiment. If nothing else, this process might give you new clever ideas to store in your Clever Ideas database.

Interacting with Other Microsoft Office Products

22

by Ewan Grantham

IN THIS CHAPTER

The programmers at Microsoft had a number of design goals when they started developing Access 95. One of the major goals was to make it easier to share data between Access and the other Office applications. This was done, in part, by adding several functions to OFFICE.DLL, which has common code used by all Office 95 applications for such things as File Open dialog boxes, Spell Check Wizards, and AutoCorrect. Access 95 has also been made more consistent with the other Office 95 applications by the addition of a Format Painter and an AutoFormat tool.

Changes have also been made to the Office suite itself, particularly with the addition of the Office Binder, that improve transferring data to and from Access, as well as building compound documents. As part of this, the easiest way to move data now is to simply select the region of data you're interested in, copy or cut it, and paste it into the target application. In the case of Excel, Word for Windows, and Access, this data comes across properly formatted without further intervention.

One question that always comes up when you start looking at integrating data and applications is which way the integration should go. In other words, should you bring Excel data into Access or bring the Access data into Excel? With Office 95, there is little difficulty in working with the data either way. However, you can usually figure out the best way to go by thinking about how you work (or how the person you're designing the project for works). If you normally do a lot of data entry or sophisticated queries, you probably want to remain in Access. If you mainly crunch numbers or analyze trends, you would want to stay in Excel. Whatever application you're most comfortable with or work with the most should be your interface.

Another consideration is whether you want to actually move the data or whether you want to create a link to it. In general, if the data is updated often in both applications, you want to create a link. That way, you avoid doing a lot of imports, exports, and reconciliations. If you're just trying to put out some information for a report or are moving the data to a particular platform that will be worked on only from there in the future, moving the data through some form of export and import is probably your best option.

In this chapter, you will discover how to move data between Access 95 and the other Office 95 applications using somewhat more powerful methods than cutting and pasting. By learning about these methods, you will also learn how to more tightly integrate the tools to build custom solutions to your problems.

Working with Word

Access and Word tend to be used together quite a bit in business settings because of the need to track things such as mailing addresses (which Word doesn't do well) and the need to create memos and reports (which Word is much better at). Because of this, several different methods have been made available for sharing data between the two.

Using the Mail Merge Wizard

If you're using Microsoft Word version 6.0 or later, the first way to share data is to use the Microsoft Word Mail Merge Wizard to create a mail merge document in Word. Once this link has been established, you can open your document in Word at any time to print a new batch of form letters or labels using the current data in Access. To set this up, you would open the Database window and click the name of the table or query you want to export. Then select OfficeLinks | Merge It.

Once you have done this, the Mail Merge Wizard is automatically loaded. It enables you to specify an existing document to use or create a new one. Figure 22.1 shows this Wizard in action.

FIGURE 22.1.

Running the Mail Merge Wizard in Access 95.

Creating a Mail Merge Data Source File

Another method of exporting Access data that can be used by version 6 or earlier of Word is to create a mail merge data source file. This can then be used with Word's mail merge feature. Although this is a little more complex, it also provides more flexibility because the resulting file can be sent to remote or networked users. It also enables you to archive who was sent what, if this is an essential part of your business.

To export to a Microsoft Word mail merge data source file from Access 95, do the following:

1. Open the Database window in Access for the database you want to work with.
2. Click the name of the table or query you want to export and select File | Save As/ Export.
3. In the Save As dialog box, shown in Figure 22.2, click To an external File or Database and then click OK.
4. In the Save As Type list box, select Microsoft Word Merge.
5. Click the arrow to the right of the Save In list box and select the drive or folder to export to.
6. In the File name list box, enter the filename or accept the default. At this point, your screen should look like the one shown in Figure 22.3.

FIGURE 22.2.

The Save As dialog box for a table.

FIGURE 22.3.

Ready to export the table to be used by Word.

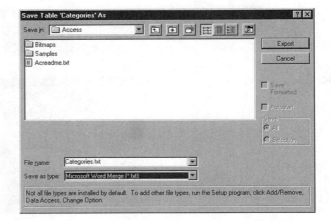

When you click Export, Access creates the data source containing the field names and all the data from your table.

When you create a Word mail merge file, Access uses the field names from the table or query. Because Word has different formatting rules than those for Access, field names longer than 20 characters are truncated, and characters other than letters, numbers, or underscores are converted to underscores.

In a Word mail merge file, the first record in the file contains the field names and is called the *header row.* All the other records are *data rows.* The field names in the header record must match the field names in the main document. If they don't match, edit the field names either in the export file (you can open this in Word for Windows) or in the main document so that they do match.

Creating an .RTF File

This method of sharing data with Word is similar to what was described in the previous section, but it's designed to handle the output of a datasheet, form, or report where you want to carry not only the data, but also the formatting. A rich-text format (.RTF) file preserves formatting, such as fonts, colors, and styles. An .RTF file can be opened with Word (versions 6 and 7) as well as other Windows word processing and desktop publishing programs.

To create an .RTF file from Access 95, do the following:

1. In the Database window, click the name of the object you want to save. To save a section of a datasheet, open the datasheet and select a portion of it before continuing. In Figure 22.4, a section of the Northwind database's Customers table has been selected.

FIGURE 22.4.

A section of customer records from the Northwind database.

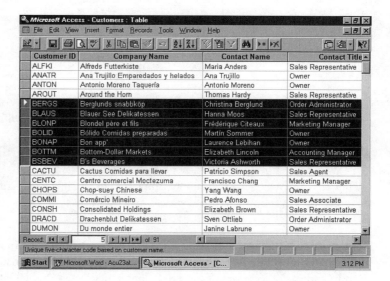

2. Select File | Save As/Export.
3. In the Save As dialog box, click To an external File or Database and then click OK.
4. In the Save As Type list box, click Rich Text Format.
5. Click the arrow to the right of the Save In list box and select the drive or folder to save to.
6. In the Save area at the left of the dialog box, click the Selection button.
7. If you want to start Word and load the resulting .RTF file, check the Autostart check box.
8. In the File Name list box, enter a name for the file (or use the suggested name) and then click Export.

To show you what the final output looks like, Figure 22.5 shows the .RTF file that was output when loaded into Word.

FIGURE 22.5.

How Word sees the .RTF file that Access 95 created.

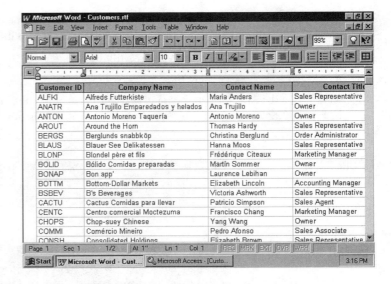

> **TIP**
>
> The filename will automatically be converted to an eight-character name for compatibility with Windows 3.x word processors.

You can also use the OutputTo action in a macro to save an object in another application's file format (such as .RTF). When you use this action, you specify the database object you want to output, and the object doesn't have to be open or selected in the Database window. To learn more about using macros in Access, read Chapter 19, "Creating Access Macros."

Creating an .RTF File and Autoloading Word

By going through the process somewhat differently, you can not only create an .RTF file but also have Word loaded automatically to start working on it. This is particularly useful if you're building an application in which you want to use Word's text-editing capabilities without having user intervention.

The process looks like this:

1. In the Database window, click the name of the table, query, form, or report you want to save and load into Word. To save a section of a datasheet, open the datasheet and select the portion of the datasheet before continuing.

2. Select Tools | OfficeLinks and click Publish It With MS Word. The output is saved as an .RTF file in the folder where Access 95 is installed. Word automatically starts and opens it.

The resulting file looks exactly the same as when you just create an .RTF file.

> **NOTE**
>
> When you use the Save As/Export menu option discussed in the section "Creating an .RTF File," a check box labeled Autostart will start Word after the exported file is created.

Working with Excel

There are a multitude of ways you can use the same data in both Access and Excel. There are two instances when this is most useful:

- You have legacy data in spreadsheet format that you'd like to import and use in Access.
- You have Access data that you would like Excel to analyze or chart for you.

Access is good at organizing and relating information from multiple sources (organized as tables), while Excel is good at data analysis and charting.

Creating an .XLS File

Creating an Excel spreadsheet format (.XLS) file is similar to the technique used for saving Access data from forms, reports, and datasheets to .RTF. Saving output to Excel versions 5.0 or 7.0 file formats preserves most formatting from the original Access form or report, such as fonts and colors. When you save to an Excel file, report group levels are saved as Excel outline levels, whereas a form is saved as a table of data.

The process is as follows:

1. In the Database window, click the name of the object you want to save. To save a section of a datasheet, open the datasheet and select the portion of the datasheet you want to export.
2. Select File | Save As/Export.
3. In the Save As dialog box, click To an external File or Database and then click OK.
4. In the Save As Type list box, select the version of Excel to which you will be exporting.
5. Click the arrow to the right of the Save In list box and select the drive or folder to save to.
6. In the File Name list box, enter a name for the file (or use the suggested name).
7. If you're exporting a table or query and have chosen to export to Excel versions 5

through 7, you can select the Save Formatted check box. This will format the data in the spreadsheet. Columns will be wide enough to display the longest piece of data, and the first row will be formatted to look like column headings and will use the field's Caption property as column heading text. Not using the Save Formatted option will cause Access to export only the data. The column widths won't be optimized, and the first row will contain the field names, not the captions.

8. If you've selected Save Formatted, you can also specify that you want to start Excel with the new file loaded (check the Autostart check box).

9. If you have selected a portion of a table datasheet to export to Excel 5 through 7, you must check the Save Formatted check box and then click Selection in the Save area (below the Save Formatted check box).

10. After you've set all the necessary options, click Export.

Figure 22.6 shows what the Northwind data looks like when it is loaded in Excel 7. Compare this to what it looked like originally and how Word displayed the .RTF version of the same data.

FIGURE 22.6.

How Excel 7 sees the .XLS file that Access 95 created.

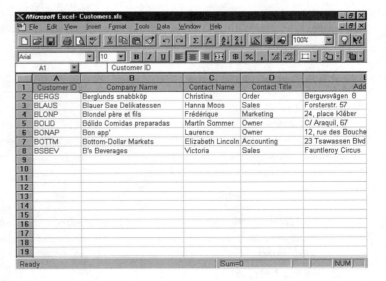

CAUTION

With one exception, if you export to an existing spreadsheet file, Access deletes and replaces the data in that spreadsheet. The exception occurs when you export to an Excel 5.0 or 7.0 workbook (which contain multiple worksheets), in which case the data is copied to the next available worksheet.

Creating an .XLS File and Autoloading Excel

Again, just as Word can be automatically loaded with the information exported to it, you can work with Excel in the same way. The process looks like this:

1. In the Database window, click the name of the table, query, form, or report you want to save and load into Excel. To save a section of a datasheet, open the datasheet and select that portion of the datasheet before continuing.

2. Select Tools | OfficeLinks and then click Analyze It With MS Excel. The output is saved as a Microsoft Excel (.XLS) file in the folder where Access is installed. Excel automatically starts and opens it.

The end result looks the same as if the file had been exported and then loaded. This saves a couple of steps, however, and also makes it easier to integrate Excel into an overall solution, since data can be easily exported to Excel using the OfficeLinks tools. These tools can be accessed from Visual Basic for Applications code to let the developer give the user an easy-to-export Excel function.

Excel, Access, and OLE

As part of the overall philosophy of more tightly integrating the various Office 95 elements, a package called AccessLinks comes with Excel as an add-in (to Excel) to make working directly with Access forms and reports easier. To use AccessLinks, you must have both Access 95 and Excel 7 installed. If the Access Form, Access Report, and Convert To Access commands don't appear on Excel's Data menu, you need to install AccessLinks. From Excel, select Tools | Add-ins. In the Add-ins Available box, select the check box next to the add-in you want to load.

If the add-in you want to load doesn't appear, click Browse and then locate the add-in you want to load. If the add-in isn't installed on your computer, check the Excel User Manual for instructions on how to load the add-in from your original disks or CD-ROM.

In addition to looking at AccessLinks, this chapter looks at other ways to link information between Excel and Access.

These solutions rely on the underlying OLE 2 technology that is part of the Office 95 (and Windows 95) architecture. OLE (Object Linking and Embedding) has been around for a while. The previous version of Access could work with other OLE applications, but the latest version allows Access to be an OLE server. What this means in real terms is that Access 95 has the capability to more closely control what happens with data coming in and going out.

Using Access Forms in Excel

The first step in using Access forms in Excel is to create a new Access form from Excel that is built specifically to take into account the link with the spreadsheet. To do this, follow these steps:

1. From Excel, select Data | Access Forms.
2. The dialog box shown in Figure 22.7 appears. It specifies information about the worksheet and how to link it to Access.

FIGURE 22.7.

A dialog box for specifying which database to put the link and form in.

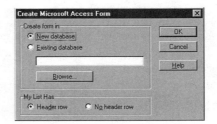

3. Choose to either create a new database or associate this form with an existing database, and then click OK.
4. Access is loaded with a defined link to the spreadsheet.
5. The Access Form Wizard is then loaded, using the linked table with data from the spreadsheet. It guides you through building a data entry form for the Excel list. You can enter additional data into the list by clicking the View Access Form button, which is placed in the worksheet by the Access Form Wizard.

Be aware that a significant amount of time can pass between steps 3 and 4, and again between steps 4 and 5. If it seems that nothing is going on, wait a couple minutes and see what happens before killing the process. Fortunately, Windows 95 is a multitasking operating system that lets you work on other tasks while these steps are taking place.

After you've created a form, you might want to use the existing form again. To do so, simply click one of the cells and then click the Forms button on your worksheet. If Excel can't find the form, the Locate Microsoft Access Form dialog box enables you to browse your folders for the .MDB file that is linked with your worksheet.

Using Access Reports in Excel

Using Access Reports is very similar to using Access Forms. The procedure looks like this:

1. Select Data | Access Reports.
2. A dialog box like the one shown in Figure 22.7 comes up to prompt you for the database to put the link and report in.

3. Choose to either create a new database or associate this report and linked table with an existing database, and then click OK.

4. Access is loaded with a defined link to the spreadsheet.

5. The Access Report Wizard is then loaded, using the linked table with data from the worksheet. It guides you through building a report for the Excel data.

Be aware that a significant amount of time can pass between steps 3 and 4, and again between steps 4 and 5. If it seems that nothing is going on, wait a couple minutes and see what happens before killing the process.

After you've created a report, you might want to use it again. To do so, simply click one of the cells and then click the Report button that was placed on your worksheet. If Excel can't find the report, the Locate Microsoft Access Report dialog box enables you to browse your folders for the .MDB file that is linked with your worksheet.

Linking an Access Table to Excel Data

You may have already worked with linking tables between different Access databases, or between an Access database and an external database such as DB2, Oracle, or Paradox. You can also use this process to link your table to an Excel worksheet. To do this, follow these steps:

1. Open the database you want to create the link in.

2. Select File | Get External Data | Link Tables.

3. You get the Link dialog box, which gives you the default option of linking to another Access database. Instead, use the Files of Type list box to select Microsoft Excel as the file type, and then navigate through the folders to find the Excel worksheet you're interested in. You should end up with something similar to Figure 22.8.

FIGURE 22.8.

Specifying the worksheet to link to.

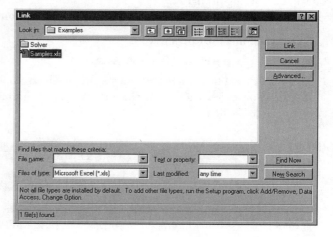

4. Click Link. The Link Spreadsheet Wizard is loaded, and it shows you how it inter-prets what it sees in your worksheet. Figure 22.9 shows you what this looks like.

FIGURE 22.9.

*Working with the Link
Spreadsheet Wizard.*

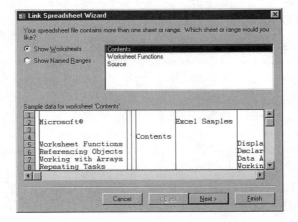

5. Click Next. One more window comes up for giving your linked table a name. Use the default or type in a different name and then click Finish. If you look at a list of the tables in your database, you now see that one of them has a small Excel icon next to it, indicating that it is a linked table—and that it is linked to an Excel spreadsheet.

To remove the link, simply delete the linked table from your database. Although this deletes the link, the original worksheet remains intact.

Creating an Access Table from Excel Data

If you will be working primarily with a set of data from Access, your best option is to create an Access table from your Excel worksheet. The procedure for doing this is as follows:

1. Select a cell in your worksheet list.

2. Select Data | Convert to Microsoft Access.

3. You get a dialog box where you can specify in which database you want to put the new table or to create a new database that contains this table. Figure 22.10 shows you what this looks like.

FIGURE 22.10.

*Specifying a destination for
the new table.*

4. The Access Table Analyzer Wizard is then loaded (along with Access). It guides you through permanently converting your Excel data to an Access table in a database.

Working with PivotTable Dynamic Views

There are times when it would be nice to be able to use the cross-tabulation features of a Pivot-Table on a form—for example, to analyze sales patterns. Cross-tabulation involves summarizing data across different fields. For example, you might want to view total sales by month and product category. A PivotTable is perfect for such a function. With Access 95, you can now create a form that has a PivotTable embedded in it but uses the data from your Access table or query. The process is run through the PivotTable Wizard. To get to this, follow these steps:

1. Open the database that has the table or query your data comes from.

2. Go to the Forms tab and click the New button. You will see a number of choices in a list on the right side, but the one you want for this process is the PivotTable Wizard.

3. Click OK.

4. Click Next to bypass the initial dialog box. You then see a dialog box like the one shown in Figure 22.11, which is the second dialog of the PivotTable Wizard.

FIGURE 22.11.

The second dialog of the PivotTable Wizard in Access 95.

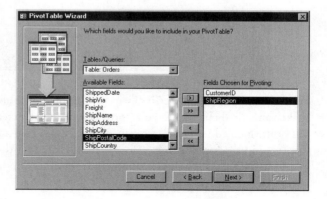

5. You'll notice that the Orders table is being used and that two fields from that table have been selected. Any query or table in Access can supply one or more fields to this form.

6. Click Next to bring up the layout window, shown in Figure 22.12. It contains a diagram of the PivotTable, along with the fields that can be used to build it.

7. Drag the fields to the proper places to provide the answers you're looking for. Press Alt-D to add to the Summary field in the DATA area. In this case, a comparison of Customers to Regions is being created, so the fields would be arranged as shown in Figure 22.13, where Customer ID has been defined as the Row, ShipRegion as the column, and Count of Customer ID as the result.

FIGURE 22.12.

The PivotTable layout window in the PivotTable Wizard.

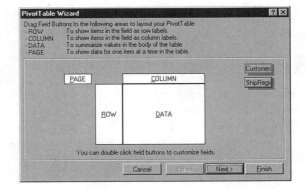

FIGURE 22.13.

The layout window with the fields arranged for the form.

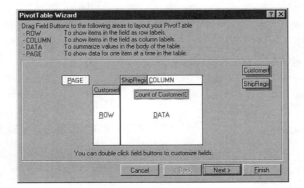

8. Select Next to bring up the final window in the PivotTable Wizard, where you can make some final changes to your form before actually creating it. The default name has been changed (as you can see in Figure 22.14) to better represent what is actually displayed in the form. Using "(Pivot)" to indicate that this is a PivotTable form is a good way to help differentiate this form from others in the database and to let other users know that this form might be a bit slow to load.

FIGURE 22.14.

The final window in the PivotTable Wizard with the recommended changes.

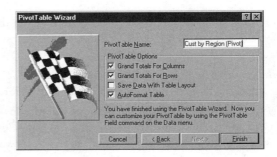

9. Click Finish.

This is a good place (actually, before starting would have been better, but that's not how it always works) to consider whether this will really be a good PivotTable candidate. By using Customer ID and Region, the PivotTable has as many rows as there are customers. What you really want to do is summarize some of this data before comparing it (by dollar amount or type of customer, for example). The summarization could be done in a table (if the base table is large) or through a query (for smaller tables). I bring this up because one of the problems that is often faced when using Access to get data from large corporate databases is the tendency to try to "suck an elephant through a straw."

A better PivotTable example is shown in Figure 22.15, where the PivotTable being edited shows the relationship between who is doing the shipping of products in each region. Already you can see some interesting trends, particularly for the CA region.

FIGURE 22.15.

The PivotTable form showing who is doing how much shipping in each region.

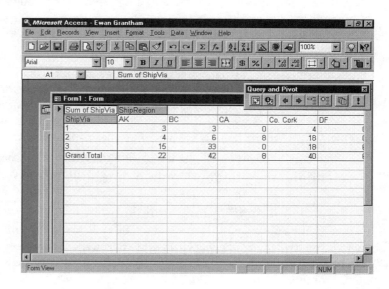

After walking through this example, you should feel comfortable enough to try this feature for yourself. Think of some business questions you're interested in examining, and then try a PivotTable form.

Embedding and Linking Excel Worksheets in Access

The next section has a full walkthrough of the process of embedding and linking Excel worksheets in Access, but the basic steps are as follows:

1. Create a field in the table that holds your data with a type of OLE object.

2. Create a form that includes that field. If you use one of the Access Form Wizards, a Bound Object Frame is automatically created for you. Otherwise, you need to do this yourself.

3. When it's time to enter data into the OLE field, select Insert | Object.

4. Select the type of object you're interested in (most likely an Excel worksheet in this case) and the icon for representing it if you choose to use an icon rather than always showing all the contents.

5. Either create a new worksheet or specify an old one to be embedded or linked.

6. When you're done with the Excel object, be sure to select File | Close and Return to.

Word, Access, and OLE

When it comes to Word and Access, the main forms of sharing data are through exports between the two products (covered earlier in this chapter) and through embedding and linking. As I mentioned earlier, there are times when you want to link and times when you want to embed. As a quick example of when you would want to do one or the other with Word, consider the following:

Link   You have an employee table for a group of computer consultants. You want to be able to search through your database for the ones who have Access experience. Once you find them, you want to be able to print their resumes. The resumes should be linked Word documents so that changes to the resumes are picked up automatically.

Embed   You are an author and have to track changes to chapters that are being written. You want to be able to call up various versions of a chapter to track changes. The chapters should be embedded so that you can lock them from further changes.

So, if you have a document that must always be available and is fairly static, you want to embed it. If you have something that changes often, you should probably link it. The one thing to keep in mind if you choose to link, however, is that if the base file is moved or renamed, the link is broken.

The first step to linking or embedding is to have a field in the table storing the data that shows the type of OLE object. Figure 22.16 shows a table that tracks patient visits to a medical clinic. It also stores the doctor's and nurse's notes for the visit.

Now that a table has been created that can store the data, you must find a way to get the data into the table. In this case, the Form Wizard can help you. Click the Forms tab in the Database window and select New. When the New Form dialog box appears, choose Form Wizard and select the table—in this case, Visits. Click OK. Use the Form Wizard (described in detail in Chapter 13, "Designing and Customizing Forms,") to add all the fields from the table to the form. Choose Columnar in the layout dialog and Colorful 2 in the style dialog. Name the form Visits on the final dialog and click the Open form in data mode button before clicking Finish. The form should appear similar to Figure 22.17. Although some captions need adjusting and there are other spacing problems, the form is fine for now.

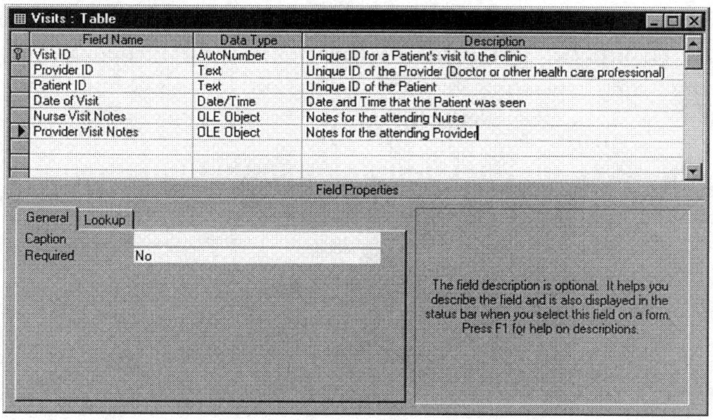

Chapter 22

FIGURE 22.16.

An example of a table used to store some OLE data.

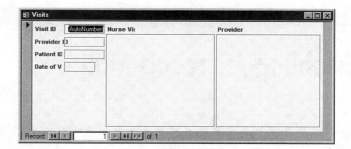

FIGURE 22.17.

The form created for the Visits table.

You can now enter the data for the new record. Enter some data in the text boxes, click inside the bounded area (called a Bound Object Frame in the Access documentation), and either right-click or select Insert | Object. Several different types of objects can be selected, but in this case, select the Word document.

If the Word document is supposed to be linked, you must use the Create from File option. To embed, use the Create New option. If you want to embed an existing object, use Create New and load the document into Word.

You can also change the icon that appears for the document at this point. Each of the Microsoft products has a group of icons. The icon choices are somewhat different for items to be linked than for items to be embedded. To change the icon, click the Display As Icon check box. A Change Icon button will appear in the bottom-right corner of the dialog. Click this button to activate the Change Icon dialog box, where you can select the icon to be displayed as well as change the caption to be displayed with the icon.

For this example, Create New was chosen. Because Access 95 and Word 7 support in-place editing, the OLE container changes to a Word edit window. You can use all of Word's functionality in this edit window, including the toolbars and menus that Access 95 makes available in place of the Access toolbars and menus. When you've finished entering your Word object, click anywhere outside the object container.

Returning to the form, the provider's notes are entered as a linked document (often they are entered after being transcribed, and then they are revised by the provider, so this isn't too far from reality). The final version of the record looks like Figure 22.18. All that remains is to save the information by selecting Records | Save Record or by moving to the next record.

FIGURE 22.18.

A record with embedded and linked data.

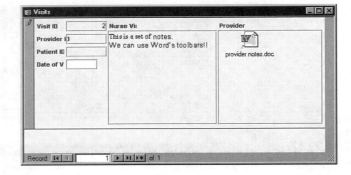

Enabling Microsoft Mail

One other way to share Access data is by sending your data through electronic mail. You can choose the file format to send in the e-mail message. The data can be output as a Microsoft Excel (.XLS), rich-text format (.RTF), or MS-DOS text (.TXT) file. You should choose a format based on which application the recipient will use to view the data. For instance, if the recipient doesn't have Microsoft Excel, don't choose that file format. The procedure for sending data through e-mail is as follows:

1. Open the database that has the object you want to send (if it isn't already open).
2. In the Database window, click the name of the object you will attach.
3. Select File | Send.
4. Click the format you want to use for the attached file, and then click OK.

After you have clicked OK, Access opens a new mail message and attaches the output of the object in the format you selected.

> **NOTE**
>
> If the Send command is grayed out, your e-mail program might not be installed properly. Another possibility is that it might not support MAPI (the Messaging Application Programming Interface). Check your e-mail program's documentation to confirm that it supports MAPI. If it does, try reinstalling the mail application to make the Send command functional.

You can use the `SendObject` action in a macro to attach an output file to an e-mail message. When you use this action, you can specify the database object you want to attach, the file format to be used, and any message information (recipient, subject, and so on). If any necessary information is omitted when you use this action, Access will prompt the user to fill it in. The specified database object doesn't have to be open or selected in the Database window.

An Overview of Data Access Objects

In addition to the various methods I've mentioned so far, you also can use programming languages to get at Access data. Data Access Objects (DAOs) enable you to use a programming language to access and manipulate data in databases, as well as make it possible to manage databases, their objects, and their structure.

You can use Data Access Objects to manipulate databases in either the native MDB format or in other installable ISAM (Indexed Sequential Access Method—originally developed for mainframe systems) database formats. ISAM formats that are already supported include dBASE, Excel, Paradox, and delimited text (among others). You can use the Jet database engine (the database engine for Access) to access Microsoft SQL Server or any other database that can be accessed with an ODBC (Open Database Connectivity) driver.

DAOs are designed to be used by programmers, but they certainly point to where the future of Access might be going—with an open engine that can be attached to and worked with by several other tools.

Summary

This chapter was designed to introduce you to many of the methods available for moving data between Access and other Office 95 tools. You now have a large toolkit of solutions so that you can pick the best one for your particular needs the next time you have to share data with your other applications.

Although drag-and-drop works, it's not nearly as customizable as using the Mail Merge Wizard to move information into Word. And although you can do some good analyses with Excel, you can do even better analyses when you put Excel and Access together using tools such as the PivotTable Wizard.

When you run into a situation where you wish your data were available in a different tool, don't just wish—exchange that data.

IN THIS PART

Programming in Access

Visual Basic
for Applications

_M_
Ala_

Visual Basic for Applications is the programming language used by Access. Visual Basic for Applications code is used when you need to go beyond the scope of macros to tie your application together. In this version of Access, Visual Basic for Applications (VBA) replaces the Access Basic language. VBA is a superset of the language that was used in the previous version of Access; it includes new commands, functions, enhancements, and object-oriented capabilities. VBA is a language that is common to other Microsoft products and allows these products to interact and share data easily.

An Introduction to Visual Basic for Applications Code

Visual Basic for Applications, hereafter referred to as VBA, enables you to develop more complex and robust applications. Typical uses are controlling the user interface, field and record validations, and trapping errors.

When to Use Visual Basic

Without using Visual Basic, you can still write many applications by incorporating macros into your Access application. However, macros lack some of the more complex features that can be found only in Visual Basic.

Here's a partial list of the advantages you gain by using Visual Basic in your Access applications:

- You can use DAOs (Data Access Objects) in your application.
- You can trap the errors that occur in the application.
- You can incorporate OLE into the application.
- You can incorporate DDE into the application.
- You can use Transaction processes.
- You can make calls to Windows API functions.
- You can call DLLs that add or enhance functionality to your application.
- You can include complex decision looping (If...Then...Else, Do...While, Select Case).
- You can create reusable and generic routines.

The Visual Basic Containers

Access supports two types of containers, called *modules,* for Visual Basic code—Class modules and Standard modules. A Standard module is a collection of variable and constant declarations, functions, and procedures. It's a storage container for Visual Basic code. A module is used to store custom subprocedures and functions that you write for an application.

A `Public` procedure defined in a Standard module is available to referencing databases in addition to the current database in which it's defined. These procedures are available in the Object Browser from the referencing database. For more information on how to establish a reference to another database, see Chapter 35, "Add-Ins and Libraries."

> **NOTE**
>
> If a module contains the Option Private Module statement in its Declarations section, its scope rules follow the rules for Class modules. This means that `Public` procedures and variables are available only within the current database, and the procedures don't appear in the Object Browser.

Class modules in Access are either form or report modules. A form or report module is a container that houses code that responds to events as well as other procedures that belong to the form or report. The scope of a form or report module depends on how it's declared. A `Private` procedure (function or subprocedure) is available only in the module in which it's declared. Access automatically declares all event procedures as `Private`. For an example, see Listing 23.1.

Listing 23.1. The `Private` procedure.

```
Private Sub Text1_GotFocus()
End Sub
```

By default, Access declares all nonevent procedures as `Public`. A form or report procedure declared as `Public` is available to any other procedure within the current user database.

> **NOTE**
>
> The `Public` keyword is optional. Any procedure not declared with either the `Private` or the `Static` keyword is a `Public` procedure.

The Module Window

The Module window, shown in Figure 23.1, is where you add and maintain all the code in your application. This is the same window that is used by both Standard modules and code that is stored for objects such as a control on a form.

All the procedures you write can be stored in one module or kept in separate ones. It's best to keep similar procedures in the same module. For example, all the code that is needed to import an ASCII file of daily sales should be kept in one module.

FIGURE 23.1.

The Module window.

Once you're in the Module window, the module toolbar is displayed. This toolbar provides you with shortcuts when working on procedures.

As with all Access toolbars, the buttons change depending on where you are and what you're doing. Figure 23.2 shows the basic toolbar for the Module window. You can modify this toolbar to add, remove, and change the toolbar buttons.

FIGURE 23.2.

The module toolbar.

Naming Requirements

When it comes time to save a module, Access prompts you for a name. Typically, you enter a meaningful and descriptive name that informs you what types of procedures are stored in the module. Access does have some rules about the names you can use for modules. Here are some of the naming requirements for modules:

- The name can't start with a space. If it does, Access removes the space.
- The name can contain only characters and numbers.
- The name can't contain either exclamation points (!) or periods (.). These characters are reserved by Access and are used in referring to objects on forms and reports.
- The name of the module is limited to 64 characters.
- The name can contain spaces for readability.
- The name must be unique within the database (.MDB).
- The name can't be a VBA keyword.

Just as with modules, there are also rules for naming subprocedures and functions. Here are some of the naming requirements:

- The name must start with a character.
- The name can contain numbers.
- The name can't contain any spaces.
- The name can't contain any exclamation points (!) or periods (.). These characters are reserved by Access and are used in referring to objects on forms and reports.
- Names must be unique within the module, form, or report.
- The name can't exceed 200 characters.

When it's time to name your modules and procedures, you not only have to follow these rules but you should also use some sort of naming convention. A naming convention is used to help maintain the application's code. The goal of any naming convention is to help you and other developers work on the application now and in the future. Here are some possible guidelines for naming your procedures and modules:

- Name the module something meaningful. The name should inform you what all the procedures in the module do.
- Assign each module a two- or three-letter unique ID. Add this ID to each procedure that resides in the module. Here is how a procedure that deletes a record in a module with the ID of CF would be named: DeleteCurrentRecord_CF().
- Use descriptive and somewhat short procedure names. It's easier to make typos when typing longer procedure names than it is with shorter ones.

Looping Constructs

The looping construct is one of the fundamentals of Visual Basic code. Looping constructs are used throughout most of the procedures that are written. They enable you to navigate through records in a table and execute blocks of code. The following sections show you basic syntax and how to use each of these looping constructs.

If...Then...Else

The If...Then...Else statement is one of the most basic looping constructs in many programming languages. The If...Then...Else statement is made up of two possible situations—true and false conditions. If the condition is true, certain code is executed. If not, another set of code is executed.

In Visual Basic code this statement can take on several different appearances. The basic syntax for the statement looks like this:

```
IF <condition> Then
   ' A block of code for the condition being true.
ElseIf <condition n> Then
   ' A block of code for the condition n being true.
```

```
Else
    ' A block of code for the condition n being false.
End If
```

The reserved word `Then` is required and must follow every line that contains an `If` or `ElseIf`, such as `If...Then` or `ElseIf...Then`.

As you can see from the preceding example, the `If` statement can have several levels of conditions. Only one block of code can ever be executed in the `If` statement. Once a true condition has been found, it executes that block of code and exits the `If` statement when it encounters an `ElseIf`, `Else`, or `End If`.

Now let's take a look at the different ways in which to use this statement. Here's a very easy example. If a condition is true, a value is stored in a memory variable:

```
If x = 1 Then
    answer = "Yes"
End If
```

In this example, if x is equal to 1, the string `"Yes"` is stored in the memory variable `answer`. You can also write the example like this:

```
If x = 1 Then answer = "Yes"
```

Both of these examples do the same thing. The only problem is that if x isn't equal to 1, the memory variable doesn't have a value stored in it. To do this you need to add the `Else` condition to the `If` statement. The `Else` condition is optional:

```
If x = 1 Then
    answer = "Yes"
Else
    answer = "No"
End If
```

You can also rewrite this line to use the one-line `If` statement version. If you decide to do it this way, it's a good idea to first store a default value in the memory variable. Here's how it would look:

```
answer = "No"
If x = 1 Then answer = "Yes"
```

Select Case

The `Select Case` statement is another type of looping construct. It looks somewhat like the `If...Then...Else` statement. The basic syntax for the `Select Case` statement looks like this:

```
Select Case <testexpression>
Case expressionslist
    'Statement block

Case expressionslistn
    'Statement block n
```

```
Case expressionslistn
    'Statement block n

Case Else
    'None of the other cases were true
End Select
```

To understand how this command works, let's break it down into separate pieces. The first line is where the variable is named that is used for the testing. For example:

```
Select Case tblCustomers!State
```

Here the state ID field in the Customer table is used for the comparison testing.

The `Case expressionslist` lines are where the variable is compared to a value. For example, you might want to see if the state ID field was equal to `"FL"`. To do this, you need this line of code:

```
Case "FL"
```

If the condition is true (state ID = `"FL"`), the next block of code is executed. Once it has executed the code in the block, it exits the `Select Case` statement and executes the first line of code following the statement.

If none of the conditions are true, none of the blocks of code are executed. However, you can add the `Case Else` condition to trap for this event. This condition is run if none of the other conditions are true.

Here's an example of how to use the `Case Else` condition when no match is made:

```
Select Case txtGrade
Case "A"
    grade = "Excellent"

Case "B"
    grade = "Good"

Case "C"
    grade = "Fair"

Case "D"
    grade = "Poor"

Case Else
    grade = "None"
End Select
```

As you can see, the `If...Then...Else` and `Select Case` statements look and act somewhat alike. There are advantages to using one or the other in different situations. It's often simpler and clearer to use `Select Case` when there are many conditions for which the same variable will be tested. The preceding code provides a good example of this situation. On the other hand, `If...Then...Else` is a good choice when the branching decision is based on varying criteria requiring different variables.

IIf() (Immediate If)

The Immediate If (IIf()) is another very powerful programming construct. It's like the one-line If...Then...Else statement, but it returns a value. The syntax for the IIf() is as follows:

```
lvar = IIf(<expression>, <true return value>, <false return value>)
```

The advantage that IIf() has over the If...Then...Else statement is that it can be used in places that the other can't . For example, you can use it as part of the Control Source for an object on a report. If the value of the object is 0 (zero) you might not want to print a zero on the report. To do this you use the IIf() statement in its place:

```
=IIf(DiscountRate = 0), " ",DiscountRate)
```

You can also use it to trap for the dreaded "Divide by Zero" error that always seems to show up on reports. Here's how you use it to trap for this error:

```
=IIf(DiscountRate = 0, 0, (TotalSales / DiscountRate))
```

Now if the value of [DiscountRate] is zero, a zero (0) value is returned.

Do...Loop

The Do...Loop statement is used to repeat a block of code until a condition occurs or until a condition is no longer valid. This statement can be written in two different ways. Here are the two variations:

```
Do While ¦Until [condition]
    <block of code to execute>
    Exit Do
Loop
```

and

```
Do
    <block of code to execute>
    Exit Do
Loop While¦Until [condition]
```

Both sets of code perform the same way. However, the first way is a little easier to read. You can easily lose track of what the Do...Loop statement is doing in a large procedure. It gets even more complicated when you have several nested Do...Loop statements.

To exit a Do...Loop statement at any point, you need to issue the Exit Do command. This terminates the loop and executes the next line of code following the Loop statement.

Here's an example of how to use the Do...Loop statement to skip through the records in a recordset. The Do...Loop statement ends when the first customer that starts with a B is encountered:

```
Dim dbName As Database
Dim tblName As Recordset
```

```
Set dbName = CurrentDb()
Set tblName = dbName.OpenRecordset("Customers")

Do While Left$(tblName!CompanyName, 1) <> "B"
    tblName.MoveNext
Loop
```

You can replace While with Until in the preceding example. However, this has a major effect on the outcome and how the procedure executes.

```
Dim dbName As Database
Dim tblName As Recordset
Set dbName = CurrentDb()
Set tblName = dbName.OpenRecordset("Customers")

Do Until Left$(tblName!CompanyName, 1) <> "B"
    tblName.MoveNext
Loop
```

The preceding code is very similar to the previous code, except that the Until clause was used. Changing the code to use the Until clause causes different results. The While clause causes a code segment to be executed as long as the condition is true. On the other hand, the Until clause causes a code segment to be executed until that condition is met. If the first record in the table starts with an A, the rest of the records aren't processed in the Until loop. To make this code act the same way as the While clause did, you would have to change the condition to the following:

```
Do Until Left$(tblName!CompanyName, 1) = "B"
```

If you modify the Do...Loop statement to have the condition on the loop part, there is a noticeable difference. Take a look at this block of code:

```
Dim numb As Integer

numb = 0
Do
    numb = numb + 1
    MsgBox Str(numb), 0, "First Test"
Loop While numb <> 5

numb = 0
Do
    numb = numb + 1
    MsgBox Str(numb), 0, "Second Test"
Loop Until numb <> 5
```

The result of running this procedure is as follows. The first statement displays the value of numb until it's equal to 5. The second statement shows the value of numb one time and terminates the loop.

While...Wend

The While...Wend statement is very similar to the Do...Loop statement. Both are used to loop through a block of code, executing it until a condition is met. The difference between the two is that the `While...Wend` statement doesn't have an exit point. Access continues to execute the block of code until the condition is no longer true. Here's the syntax for this statement:

```
While <condition is true>
    <code to be executed>
Wend
```

You can nest this statement as many deep as you wish. Try not to have too many, because you might not be able to debug it later.

Here's an example of how you might use this statement in your code:

```
Dim dbName As Database
Dim tblName As Recordset
Set dbName = CurrentDb()
Set tblName = dbName.OpenRecordset("Customers")

tblName.MoveFirst
While Left$(tblName!CompanyName, 1) <> "B"
    MsgBox tblName!CompanyName, 0, "First Test"
    tblName.MoveNext
Wend
```

For...Next

The `For...Next` statement is used to repeat a block of code for a set number of times. The syntax for this statement is as follows:

```
For <counter?> = start To end [Step increment]
    <code to be executed>

    Exit For

Next [counter, counter2]
```

Just as with the `Do...Loop` statement, you can exit the statement from within the loop. The `Exit For` command exits the loop at any point, and Access executes the next line of code after the `Next` command.

Next is an example of how to use the `For...Next` statement. In this example, the value of x is displayed until it reaches 10:

```
For x = 1 To 10
    <block of code to be executed each time>

    MsgBox Str(x), 0, "For...Next"
Next
```

The following example displays the value of x 19 times (1, 1.5, 2, 2.5, and so forth).

```
dim x as single
For x = 1 To 10 Step .5
    MsgBox Str(x), 0, "For...Next"
Next
```

You can modify the Step value so that it never reaches the end. 10 is the ending value of this example, so Access terminates the looping whenever the value of x is greater than 10. For example, the maximum value displayed by the following code segment is 9:

```
Dim x As Single
For x = 1 To 10 Step 4
    MsgBox Str(x), 0, "For...Next"
Next
```

Memory Datatypes

When writing Visual Basic code, you often need to store values temporarily. Memory variables are similar to fields in a table—they both have a datatype. The datatype states the type of value and the size that can be stored in it.

Defining the Memory Variables

Before you can use a memory variable, you must declare it. To do this you use the Dim statement. The Dim statement declares a memory variable and allocates storage space for it. When this is done, you can store a value in it.

The syntax for the Dim statement is as follows:

```
Dim varname[([subscripts])][As [New] type][, varname[([subscripts])][As [New]
➥type]]...
```

The arguments for the Dim statement are shown in Table 23.1.

Table 23.1. The Dim statement arguments.

Argument	Description
varname	The name of the variable to be created.
subscripts	The dimensions of an array variable. You can declare a multidimensional array.
New	A keyword used to indicate that a declared object variable is a new instance of a Visual Basic object or an externally creatable OLE Automation object. For more information on OLE Automation, see Chapter 21, "Using OLE and OLE Automation."
As type	A reserved word that is used to declare the datatype of the variable.

The datatype value can be one of several types, as shown in Table 23.2.

Table 23.2. The datatype values.

Datatype	Description
Integer	A numeric value within the range of –32,768 to 32,767.
Long	A numeric value within the range of –2,147,483,648 to 2,147,483,647.
Single	A numeric value within the ranges of –3.402823E38 to –1.401298E–45 for negative numbers and 1.401298E–45 to 3.402823E38 for positive numbers and 0.
Double	A numeric value within the ranges of –1.79769313486232E308 to –4.94065645841247E–324 for negative numbers and 4.94065645841247E–324 to 1.79769313486232E308 for positive numbers and 0.
Currency	A numeric value within the range of –922,337,203,685,477.5808 to 922,337,203,685,477.5807.
String	0 to around 65,535 bytes of text.
Variant	Any numeric value up to the length of a Double datatype or any character text.

Arrays

Arrays are created in the same way you would create any other memory variable. When defining an array, you not only give it a name, you also set the upper and lower subscripts.

To define an array, you can use one of the following lines of code:

```
Dim aNames(4)
```

or

```
ReDim aNames(4)
```

or

```
Static aNames(4)
```

All three lines of code declare an array called aNames that contains five elements. The first element number is 0 and the last is 4. If you want the first element number to be 1, you can use one of the following lines of code:

```
Dim aNames(1 to 5)
```

or

```
ReDim aNames(1 to 5)
```

or

```
Static aNames(1 to 5)
```

Now the starting element number is 1 and the ending element is 5. For some developers, this makes it a little easier to read, because you don't have to stop and add or subtract 1 from the element number to know its real location in the array.

You can also use negative numbers as the starting and ending element numbers. Here is how you do it:

```
Dim aNames(-5 to -1)
```

or

```
ReDim aNames(-5 to -1)
```

or

```
Static aNames(-5 to -1)
```

The ReDim statement does one other thing. It enables you to resize a dynamic array that has already been declared. The array must have been created using either the ReDim command or the Dim command without specifying any of the elements of the array. For example, let's say you have an array defined as having six elements and you need to add one more element to it. To do this you use the ReDim statement like this:

```
ReDim aItems(1 To 7)
```

This erases all the data that was stored in the six elements of the aItems array. To save the data that was in the array when you resize it, add the keyword Preserve. Now when you resize the array, all its original data is left intact:

```
ReDim Preserve aItems(1 to 7)
```

If you didn't want to declare the number of elements in your array initially and later wanted to store six elements, you could code the following in your Declarations section:

```
dim aItems()
```

Then in a procedure the code would be

```
ReDim aItems(1 To 7)
```

If you need to determine the starting and ending elements in your array, you use the lBound and uBound functions. For example, if you use the preceding ReDim statement, lBound(aItems) would return 1 and uBound(aItems) would return 7.

Variable Scope

When you create memory variables in Visual Basic, they have a set scope or lifetime. Scope refers to where and when you can make references to a memory variable.

Local Scope

Variables declared within a procedure are private to that procedure and can't be made public. Local variables can be referenced only within the procedure that declares them. If a local variable is declared as Static, the variable exists whenever its module is a part of the running program, and it retains its value throughout the life of the application. Nonstatic local variables are created each time the procedure runs and are destroyed when the procedure ends. This means that a nonstatic local variable is reinitialized each time that particular procedure runs.

If you call another procedure, the memory variable declared in the calling procedure can't be referenced by the called procedure. You can use the Dim statement to declare a variable of the same name in the new procedure and even assign a different datatype to it. When you leave that procedure and return to the first procedure, the memory variable still contains its original value. Try these two procedures to see how it works:

```
Sub mvar_Local ()
   Dim txtName As String
   txtName = "Alan McConnell"

   '--   Call another procedure.
   mvar_Local2

   MsgBox txtName, 0, "Back in the main procedure."
End Sub


Sub mvar_Local2 ()
   Dim txtName As Double
   txtName = 100
   MsgBox Str(txtName), 0, "In the called procedure."
End Sub
```

Modular Scope

Variables declared at the module level are, by default, private to the module. This means that the variable can be referenced only from within the module and not by any procedures outside it. To create a modular scope memory variable, you define it in the Declarations section of a module, form, or report.

You can't assign a value to the variable in the Declarations section—you have to do it within a procedure. From that point on, any other procedure in the module has access to it and can also change its value. Module-level variables are essentially static variables and retain their value throughout the life of the application.

Here's an example of how this works:

```
Option Compare Database    'Use database order for string comparisons
Dim mCompany As String

Sub module_Test ()
   mCompany = "Big Ben's Tire Barn"

   '--   Call the other procedure.
   module_Test2

   MsgBox mCompany, 0, "Back in the main procedure."
End Sub


Sub module_Test2 ()
   MsgBox mCompany, 0, "In the called procedure."
   mCompany = "Brian's Auto Shope"
End Sub
```

If you call a procedure that resides within another module, the memory variables don't have any values. You can declare the variables again in the new module, give them new values, and manipulate them with code. When you return back to the calling procedure, they once again have their original values.

Application-Wide Scope

The `Public` statement is used to declare a memory variable that can be referenced by all the procedures in the application. The `Public` syntax is the same as the `Dim` statement. The only difference is that it must be declared in the Declarations section of the module. The correct syntax is as follows:

```
Public varname[([subscripts])][As [New] type][, varname[([subscripts])][As [New]
➡type]]...
```

Before you can have access to the `Public` memory variable and its value, you need to call a procedure in the module that sets a value to it. For this reason, it's best to create one module that defines and stores an initial value for all the `Public` memory variables that are used in an application. This way you don't have to search all over your application looking for where each one was created.

Access Scope

Although `Public` module-level variables can't be viewed through the Object Browser, they're still available to referencing databases. This provides an Access-wide scope to the variable. For example, `myVar` is declared in the module `myMsg`. This module is part of database db2.mdb. The value of `myVar` is then set in the procedure `mySub`. See Listing 23.2.

Listing 23.2. `Public` variables.

```
Option Compare Database
Option Explicit
Public myVar As String

Sub mySub()
    myVar = "Here I am"
    MsgBox myVar
End Sub
```

You can now close the Access database db2.mdb and open db1.mdb. In db1.mdb, you can establish a reference to db2.mdb. Assuming that you have a command button named cmdMsg on a form, you can execute the code that appears in Listing 23.3.

Listing 23.3. Using `Public` variables from another database.

```
Private Sub cmdMsg_Click()
    MsgBox myVar
End Sub
```

Static Memory Variables

A static memory variable is one that doesn't lose its value when you exit the procedure, as local variables do. When you return to the procedure, the variable still contains the value it had before, just like a module-level variable. The difference is that only this procedure has access to the value. No other procedures have access to the variable or its value.

Here's how you declare a static variable. You can declare it only from within a procedure:

```
Static  variablename[([subscripts])] [As type] [, variablename[([subscripts])]
➥[As type] ]...
```

Constants

Constants are memory variables that are assigned a value and can't be changed. After they're assigned a value, you can refer to them by name. Access uses constants to store values in, so you don't have to remember the value—just the name of it. The use of constants makes your code easier to read and maintain because you can avoid the use of hard-coded literals.

The syntax for the Const statement is as follows:

```
[Public ¦ Private] Const constname [As type] = expression
```

Constants follow the same scope rules as variables.

Functions and Subprocedures

Code routines that are written in Visual Basic are in the form of either functions or subprocedures. The code contained in each of them is the same. The only difference is that a function can return a value. The term procedure is used to refer to both functions and subprocedures.

Functions

A function is a Visual Basic routine that is written to perform a specific task and return a value. The task it performs depends on what you want it to do. You can have it return a customer's average order dollar amount or update an employee record with a new address. You can make the function as complex or simple as you like.

To have a function return a value, you simply assign the return value to the name of the function. For example, if the function is called GetSalesRepId(), to return a value you store the value to GetSalesRepId. For example: GetSalesRepId = tblReps!RepId.

The syntax for the Function statement is as follows:

```
[Public ¦ Private] [Static] function name [(arglist)] [As type]
```

Here's an example of a typical function:

```
Function TotalSales (pCustomerId As String) As Double
    '-- code block

    '-- return a value
    TotalSales = 100
End Function
```

Let's break down the components of the Function statement to make it easier to understand. The Function statement has six parts: Static, Private, Public, *function name, arglist,* and As type. They are described here:

- Static: Indicates that all the function's local variables have their values preserved between calls. Any variables that are declared outside the function aren't affected by it.

- Private: Makes the function available only to the procedures within the same module. All other procedures can't access it.

- Public: Makes the function available to all other procedures in all modules.

- *function name:* The name the function is called by. This name must be unique within the form, report, or module. If a procedure with the same name appears in more than one module in an Access application, you can execute the correct procedure by qualifying the procedure name with the module name. For example, to designate the procedure myFunction in module myModule you would specify Sub [myModule].myFunction().

- *arglist:* A list of the parameters that are passed to the function. Each argument contains the name of the variable and its datatype.
- As type: Used to denote the datatype that is returned by the function.

To exit a function at any time, use the Exit Function statement. This exits the function and returns control to where it was called from.

> **NOTE**
>
> When writing a Private procedure, it's a good idea to add some comments at the top of it saying where it's called from. This reminds you and other programmers why this procedure needs to be private.

Subprocedures

A subprocedure works the same way as a function. The only difference is that it can't return a value. This difference doesn't limit what you can do with a subprocedure in any way. It simply means that you can't have it return a value.

The syntax for the Sub statement is

```
[Private ¦ Public] [Static] sub name [(arglist)]
```

Here's an example of a subprocedure:

```
Private Sub TotalSales (pCustomerId As String)
    '-- code block

End Sub
```

The following list breaks down the components of the Sub statement to make it easier to understand:

- Static: Indicates that all the sub's local variables have their values preserved between calls. Any variables that are declared outside the subprocedure aren't affected by it.
- Private: Makes the function available only to the procedures within the module. No other procedures have access to it.
- Public: Makes the subprocedure available to all other procedures in all modules.
- *sub name:* The name the subprocedure is called by. This name must be unique within the form, report, or module. If a procedure with the same name appears in more than one module in an Access application, you can execute the correct procedure by qualifying the procedure name with the module name. For example, to designate the procedure mySub in module myModule you would specify Sub [myModule].mySub.
- *arglist:* A list of the parameters that are passed to the subprocedure. Each argument contains the name of the variable and its datatype.

To exit a subprocedure at any time, use the `Exit Sub` statement. This exits the subprocedure and returns control to where it was called from.

Passing Parameters

For a procedure to accept arguments, you must first pass them to it. The ways you pass parameters or arguments to a subprocedure and function are a little different. Let's look at how to pass parameters to a subprocedure first.

There are two ways to pass a parameter to a subprocedure. How you send the parameter depends on how the subprocedure is called. Here is one example:

```
Dim nCustId as Integer
nCustId = tblCustomer.SalesRepId
GetCustomerSalesRep nCustid
```

Here is another example:

```
Dim nCustId as Integer
nCustId = tblCustomer.SalesRepId
Call GetCustomerSalesRep(nCustid)
```

What makes the second example different is the `Call` statement. The `Call` statement is a reserved word and isn't required when calling a subprocedure. If you do use it, you need to enclose all the parameters in parentheses. If you don't use the reserved word, you must omit the parentheses around the parameter list.

Passing parameters to a function is similar to using the `Call` statement with a subprocedure. The parameters are enclosed in parentheses. The main difference between subprocedures and functions is that a function returns a value. Therefore, you must do something with the value that is returned.

You can store the returned value in a memory variable or a field in a table, display it in a message, use it as an object's property, or whatever you want.

The syntax for passing parameters to a function looks like this:

```
Dim txtSalesRep As String
Dim RepId As Integer
RepId = 1234
txtSalesRep = GetSalesRepName(RepId)
```

Receiving Parameters

After you send the parameters to a procedure, you must receive them. Receiving parameters works the same way for both subprocedures and functions. In both cases you assign a name to the parameter and declare its datatype. Here's an example of how both receive parameters:

```
Sub procedure:
Sub GetRepName (pRepId As Integer)
```

```
Function:
Function GetRepName (pRepId As Integer) As String
```

By default, when you pass a parameter to a procedure, you're passing it by reference. By reference means that you're passing the actual variable to the procedure. When you return to where the procedure was called from, the variable that was passed contains any changes that were made to it. For example, you pass a procedure a variable that contains the name of the company. The procedure converts the company name into uppercase. When you return to the main procedure, the variable that contains the company name is now in uppercase.

Here are two procedures to show how this works:

```
Sub Parameter_Reference ()
    Dim txtMsg As String
    txtMsg = "Test Value"
    '--    Call the procedure.
    Parameter_Reference2 txtMsg

    MsgBox txtMsg, 0, "Back in the main procedure."
End Sub


Sub Parameter_Reference2 (pMsg As String)
    MsgBox pMsg, 0, "Passes by Reference"
    pMsg = "MS Access"
End Sub
```

There is a way to pass parameters to a procedure without having it change the variable's data. To do this, pass the parameter ByVal (by value). Passing a parameter by value is when just the contents of the variable are passed, not the actual variable. Any changes that are made to the variable or value aren't reflected in the variable back in the calling procedure.

Here's some code that shows how do to this:

```
Sub Parameter_ByVal ()
    Dim txtMsg As String
    txtMsg = "Test Value"

    '--    Call the procedure.
    Parameter_ByVal2 txtMsg

    MsgBox txtMsg, 0, "Back in the main procedure."
End Sub

Sub Parameter_ByVal2 (ByVal pMsg As String)
    pMsg = "MS Access"
    MsgBox pMsg, 0, "Passed by Value"
End Sub
```

Required and Optional Parameters

The passing of parameters to a procedure determines whether a routine is developer-friendly. The number of parameters needed to be passed to a routine also determines how easy it is to use. However, the more parameters that can be passed, the more flexible the routine is. So, where do you draw the line on parameters?

Parameters are divided into two groups: required and optional. Required parameters are the ones that must be provided for the routine to work. Optional parameters are the ones the routine can work with or without. If they aren't passed, the routine uses default values in their place.

To make a parameter optional, you must include the keyword `Optional` in the subprocedure or function declaration line. The datatype for the parameter must be `Variant`. If you use the `Optional` keyword for one parameter, all parameters that follow must also be declared as `Optional`. In addition, you can't use the `Optional` keyword if `ParamArray` is used. You can use the `isMissing` function to check for missing parameters. Listing 23.4 provides an example of how to write a function that has an optional parameter.

Listing 23.4. Using optional parameters.

```
Function MyFunction (pCode As String, Optional pRegion As Variant, Optional pId
➥As Variant)
dim myRegion as Variant
if ismissing(pRegion) then
    myRegion = "US"
else
    myRegion = pRegion
end if
End Function
```

Calling this function is done the same as before. If you want to omit all the optional parameters, you would call the function like this:

```
mvar = MyFunction("ABC123")
```

To omit only the second parameter, you would need to use a comma as a placeholder. In this case, you would call the function like this:

```
mvar = MyFunction("ABC123", , 1)
```

When you have several optional parameters, passing and receiving parameters can become complicated. You must get all the comma placeholders correct or your procedure will fail to function properly. One solution to this problem is to group all the optional parameters together into one argument and pass it to the routine. The routine then parses out the optional parameters and assigns a default value to any that are missing. The advantage to this method is that the programmer can choose the parameters to pass in and put them in any order they want. You can do this by using the `ParamArray` keyword.

The `ParamArray` keyword can be used only as the last argument in the parameter list. It's an optional array of `Variant` elements. The `ParamArray` keyword can't be used with the `Optional`, `ByVal`, or `ByRef` keywords.

548

```
Sub ParameterPassing(ParamArray pNameAddress() As Variant)

    Dim Var As Variant

    Debug.Print "Name and Address"
    For Each Var In pNameAddress
        Debug.Print Var
    Next Var

End Sub
```

As you can see from the preceding code example, it's possible to pass just one parameter and parse out the individual components.

Objects and Collections

Although Access enables you to manipulate objects without any need for programming, Visual Basic greatly expands this capability. With Visual Basic, you can create, delete, and modify objects at runtime.

In Access, objects of a specific type are grouped together in collections. For example, the Forms collection consists of all the open forms in the application, and the Controls collection consists of all the controls on a specific form. The objects that are part of the Microsoft Jet engine are called the data access objects (DAOs). These objects are also accessible from your Visual Basic code. For more information about DAOs, see Chapter 25, "Data Access Objects."

Referring to Objects

You can refer to an object that is part of a collection by following one of the ways presented in Table 23.3.

Table 23.3. Referring to objects.

Syntax	*Use*
`identifier![ObjectName]`	Directly name an object as a member of a collection. This syntax is required when referring to an object whose name contains a space or an object whose name is a restricted Visual Basic identifier.
`identifier("ObjectName")`	Directly name an object as a member of a collection or use a string variable to contain the object name.
`identifier(index)`	Refer to an object by its position in the collection. You can use this syntax to loop through all the members of a collection.

For example, the following code shows the three different ways of referring to the form `frmCustomers`. The last method assumes that `frmCustomers` is the first form in the Forms collection:

```
Forms![frmCustomers]
Forms("frmCustomers")
Forms(0)
```

In Visual Basic, you can refer to properties of an object by using the syntax `Object.property`. For example, you can set the `Caption` property of the form `frmCustomers` as follows:

```
Forms![frmCustomers].Caption = "Customers"
```

If you wanted to set the `Caption` property for all the forms in the Forms collection, you could make use of the `Count` property. The `Count` property reflects the total number of objects in a collection. Because it's zero-based, the last or highest object is always one less than the actual `Count` property. An example of this is shown in Listing 23.5.

Listing 23.5. Setting properties for all members of the Forms collection.

```
Sub SetCaption()
    Dim  intCounter as Integer
    For intCounter = 0 to Forms.count -1
        Forms(intCounter).Caption = "Customers"
    Next intCounter
End Sub
```

Declaring and Assigning Object Variables

An object variable is a variable that refers to a specific type of object, such as a form or report. You can declare an object variable using the same syntax as for any other type of variable. Table 23.4 shows the Access objects and which of those objects can be represented by a variable.

Table 23.4. Access objects.

Object	Description	Variable Permitted?
Application	Access	Yes
Control	Control on a form or report	Yes
DoCmd	Macro actions used in VB	No
Debug	Immediate window	No
Form	Forms and subforms	Yes
Report	Reports and subreports	Yes
Module	Form, report, and standard	Yes

continues

Table 23.4. continued

Object	Description	Variable Permitted?
Screen	Screen display	No
Section	Form or report section	No

Before you can use an object variable, you must associate it with an existing object by using the Set statement. The syntax for the Set statement is

```
Set variablename = objectexpression
```

If you use the Set statement to associate more than one variable with a specific object, you're always referring to the same object. This means that changing the properties of one variable also changes the properties of all variables that refer to that object. For example, Listing 23.6 shows how to associate a variable name with an object.

Listing 23.6. Associating a variable name with a specific object.

```
Dim myform1 as form
Dim myform2 as form
set myform1 = Forms![frmCustomers]
set myform2 = Forms![frmCustomers]
myForm1.caption = "Customers"
```

After this code has been run, myForm2.Caption is also set to Customers.

Using the *New* Keyword

The New keyword enables you to create a new instance or version of an existing object. When a new instance is created, it has its own set of properties. Setting the Caption property of a new instance of frmCustomers doesn't affect the Caption property of another instance. For example, Listing 23.7 creates a new instance of frmCustomers.

Listing 23.7. Creating a new instance.

```
Sub NewForm()
Dim myForm As New Form_frmCustomers
myForm.Caption = "Customers -2"
myForm.Visible = True

End Sub
```

Determining the Type of Control

In Access, all variables that represent controls on a form or report are declared generically using the `Control` keyword rather than specifying a specific control type. As a result, you need to use a variation of the `If...Then...Else` statement to determine what type of control your variable is referring to. For example, Listing 23.8 shows how to set the `ForeColor` property of all the textboxes on a form to red.

Listing 23.8. Using the `TypeOf` control.

```
Sub SetColor(myForm As Form)
    Dim myControl As Control
    Dim intCounter As Integer
    Dim intRed As Integer

    intRed = RGB(255, 0, 0)
    For intCounter = 0 To myForm.Count - 1
        Set myControl = myForm(intCounter)
        If TypeOf myControl Is TextBox Then
            myControl.ForeColor = intRed
        End If
    Next intCounter
End Sub
```

The ability to have multiple instances of an object allows for great flexibility in your application. For example, each of the `frmCustomers` instances could represent a different customer from the Customers table. This would enable the users of your application to work with more than one customer at a time.

> **NOTE**
>
> You can't use the `Not` keyword with the `TypeOf` syntax. Instead, code an empty statement block combined with the `Else` clause.

Properties and Methods

Properties describe an object's characteristics. When you change a property setting, you change that particular characteristic. Methods enable you to control how an object behaves. For example, the `SetFocus` method can be used in Visual Basic code to move the focus to a specific control on a form.

Setting and Retrieving Properties

Assigning a property to a variable in Visual Basic enables you to retrieve its value. You can change a property value by setting it to something else. In Listing 23.9, the ForeColor property of txtText1 is obtained via the variable lngColor. Then lngColor is used to set the ForeColor property of txtText2.

Listing 23.9. Setting and retrieving properties.

```
Dim lngColor As Long

    lngColor = txtText1.ForeColor
    txtText2.ForeColor = lngColor
```

Setting Multiple Properties

The With statement provides a way to set multiple properties without specifying the object each time a new property is set. For example, Listing 23.10 shows how several textbox properties can be set using the With...End With construct.

Listing 23.10. Setting properties using the With...End With construct.

```
Private Sub Form_Load()
    With Text1
        .Text = "Text"
        .ForeColor = RGB(255, 0, 0) 'Red
        .BackColor = 0
    End With
End Sub
```

> **CAUTION**
>
> Errors or unpredictable behavior can occur if your code jumps out of a With block and either the With or the End...With statement isn't executed.

Using Methods

Methods are similar to other Visual Basic functions and statements. For example, if a method returns a value, it's like a function and you enclose its arguments in parentheses. However, there is one major difference between methods and other functions and statements: a method acts directly on an object or reflects a predetermined object behavior. In Listing 23.11, you can examine the use of the ItemData method. The ItemData method returns the data in the bound column for the specified row in a list box or combo box. In this case, the ItemData method is used to retrieve the customer ID when the combo box cboCust is clicked.

Listing 23.11. Using the ItemData method.

```
Private Sub cboCust_Click()
    Dim lngCustid As Long

    lngCustid = cboCust.ItemData(cboCust.ListIndex)

End Sub
```

Properties That Represent Objects

With Visual Basic you can refer to whatever object is in a particular state without referring explicitly to that object by using properties. For example, you might want to refer to the form, report, or control that is currently active. Properties that represent objects enable you to work with the properties, methods, and controls of that object. Table 23.5 shows the properties that can be used to represent objects.

Table 23.5. Properties that represent objects.

Property	What It Applies To	What It Refers To
ActiveControl	Screen object, form, or report	Control with the focus.
ActiveForm	Screen object	Form with the focus or the form that contains the control with the focus.
ActiveReport	Screen object	Report with the focus or the report that contains the control with the focus.
Form	Subform control or form	Subform: Form associated with the subform control. Form: The form.
Me	Form or report	Form or report.
Module	Form or report	Module of a form or report.
Parent	Control	Form or report that contains the control.
PreviousControl	Screen object	The control that previously had the focus.

continues

Table 23.5. continued

Property	What It Applies To	What It Refers To
RecordSetClone	Form	Clone of a form's recordset.
Report	Subreport or report	Subreport: Report associated with the subreport control. Report: The report.
Section	Control	Section of a form or report where a control is located.

Screen Properties

The `PreviousControl`, `ActiveControl`, `ActiveForm`, and `ActiveReport` properties refer to the screen object. You can use these properties when your code depends on which form, report, or control has the focus. For example, you might have a `Save` routine that calls different routines depending on which form is active. Listing 23.12 shows how to use `ActiveForm` for this purpose.

Listing 23.12. Using the `ActiveForm` property.

```
Sub SaveData()
    Dim sMyForm As String

    sMyForm = Screen.ActiveForm.Name
    Select Case sMyForm
        Case "frmCustomers"
            SaveCustomers
        Case "frmEmployees"
            SaveEmployees
        Case Else
            MsgBox "Invalid Form"
    End Select
End Sub
```

Form and Report Properties

The `Me`, `Module`, and `RecordSetClone` properties apply to forms or reports. The `RecordSetClone` property is covered further in Chapter 25. The `Module` property can be used to insert a procedure into a module at runtime. You can use the `Me` property to indicate the form or report where code is currently running. For example, Listing 23.13 shows how to use `Me` to pass the form as a parameter to a procedure.

Listing 23.13. Using the Me property.

```
Private Sub cmdSave_Click()
    SaveData Me
End Sub
Sub SaveData(myForm As Form)
    Dim sMyForm As String

    sMyForm = myForm.Name
    Select Case sMyForm
        Case "frmCustomers"
            SaveCustomers
        Case "frmEmployees"
            SaveEmployees
        Case Else
            MsgBox "Invalid Form"
    End Select
End Sub
```

Control Properties

The Form and Report properties refer to subforms and subreports. For example, in the expression Forms![frmCustomers].Form![frmSubCusts], the term Form refers to the subform currently displayed by the subform control. The form that is displayed is controlled by setting the SourceObject property of the subform control on the form frmCustomers. For more information on forms and subforms, refer to Chapters 12 through 14.

The Parent property represents the container for the control. For example, the parent of a textbox is the form it's on. The parent of an option button is the option group it's in. The Parent property is frequently used with subforms and subreports. For example, Listing 23.14 shows how the Parent property is used with a subform.

Listing 23.14. Using the Parent property.

```
Private Sub Form_Load()
    Dim sFormName As String
    sFormName = Form![frmSubCusts].Parent.Name
End Sub
```

The Section property refers to the section of a form or report on which a control is located. For example, a control might be located in a form, header, detail, or footer section. Listing 23.15 shows an example of displaying a message based on whether or not the detail section of a form (referred to as Section(0)) is visible.

```
If Forms![Cust].Section(0).Visible = False Then
    MsgBox "no detail"
Else
    MsgBox "detail"
End If
```

User-Defined Objects

User-defined objects are custom objects developed in a Class module (forms or reports). In the Class module, you can create procedures that are the properties and methods for the custom object. Creating these procedures is accomplished through the use of the `Property Let`, `Property Set`, and `Property Get` statements.

Property Let

The `Property Let` statement assigns a value to a property. The syntax for the `Property Let` statement is as follows:

```
[Public ¦ Private][Static] Property Let name [(arglist)]
```

The components of the `Property Let` statement are shown here:

- `Public`: Indicates that the `Property Let` procedure is accessible to all other procedures in all modules.

- `Private`: Indicates that the `Property Let` procedure is accessible only to other procedures in the module where it's declared.

- `Static`: Indicates that the `Property Let` procedure's local variables are preserved between calls.

- *name*: The name of the `Property Let` procedure. It follows standard variable naming conventions except that the name can be the same as a `Property Get` or `Property Set` procedure in the same module.

- *arglist*: A list of variables representing arguments that are passed to the `Property Let` procedure when it's called. The name and datatype of each argument in a `Property Let` procedure (except the last one) must be the same as the corresponding arguments in a `Property Get` procedure. The last argument is the value assigned to the property on the right side of an expression. The datatype of the last (or sometimes the only) argument must be the same as the return type of the corresponding `Property Get` procedure.

Property Set

The `Property Set` statement sets a reference to an object. The syntax for the `Property Set` statement is as follows:

```
[Public ¦ Private][Static] Property Set name [(arglist)]
```

The components of the `Property Set` statement are shown here:

- `Public`: Indicates that the `Property Set` procedure is accessible to all other procedures in all modules.

- **Private:** Indicates that the Property Set procedure is accessible only to other procedures in the module where it's declared.
- **Static:** Indicates that the Property Set procedure's local variables are preserved between calls.
- *name*: The name of the Property Set procedure. It follows standard variable naming conventions except that the name can be the same as a Property Get or Property Let procedure in the same module.
- *arglist*: A list of variables representing arguments that are passed to the Property Set procedure when it's called.

Property Get

The Property Get statement gets the value of a property. The syntax for the Property Get statement is as follows:

```
[Public ¦ Private][Static] Property Get name [(arglist)]
```

The components of the Property Get statement are as follows:

- **Public:** Indicates that the Property Get procedure is accessible to all other procedures in all modules.
- **Private:** Indicates that the Property Get procedure is accessible only to other procedures in the module where it's declared.
- **Static:** Indicates that the Property Get procedure's local variables are preserved between calls.
- *name*: The name of the Property Get procedure. It follows standard variable naming conventions except that the name can be the same as a Property Let or Property Set procedure in the same module.
- *arglist*: A list of variables representing arguments that are passed to the Property Let procedure when it's called. The name and datatype of each argument in a Property Get procedure must be the same as the corresponding arguments in a Property Let procedure.

Using Property Procedures

If you wanted to open the form frmCustomers to add new customers or edit existing customers, you could use a combination of the Property Get and Property Let procedures. In the Property Let procedure you would set the AllowEdits and AllowAdditions properties of the form. In the Property Get procedure you would retrieve the values that had been set. Listing 23.15 shows an example of how to do this. Notice that you can refer to the custom object EditType just as you would any other property on the form.

Listing 23.15. Designing custom objects with Property Let and Property Get.

```
Option Compare Database
Option Explicit
Public intFormType As Integer
Const TYPE_INSERT = 0
Const TYPE_EDIT = 1

Property Let EditType(intFormType As Integer)

    Select Case intFormType
        Case TYPE_INSERT
            AllowEdits = False
            AllowAdditions = True

        Case TYPE_EDIT
            AllowEdits = True
            AllowAdditions = False
    End Select

End Property

Property Get EditType() As Integer
    EditType = intFormType
End Property
```

If you wanted to use these custom objects from the click events on the buttons in the form shown in Figure 23.3, you would follow the code in Listing 23.16.

FIGURE 23.3.

*Setting properties of
custom objects.*

Listing 23.16. Setting properties of custom objects.

```
Option Compare Database
Option Explicit
Const TYPE_INSERT = 0
Const TYPE_EDIT = 1
Private Sub cmdEdit_Click()
    DoCmd.OpenForm ("frmCustomers")
    Forms![frmCustomers].EditType = TYPE_EDIT
End Sub

Private Sub cmdInsert_Click()
    DoCmd.OpenForm ("frmCustomers")
    Forms![frmCustomers].EditType = TYPE_INSERT
End Sub
```

```
Private Sub Form_Load()

End Sub
```

The Object Browser

You can use the Object Browser to display the types of objects available in Access and other applications. This enables you to find and use objects as well as move through the procedures in your application.

You can open the Object Browser, shown in Figure 23.4, by selecting View | Object Browser or by clicking the Object Browser toolbar button when a Visual Basic module is open.

FIGURE 23.4.

The Object Browser.

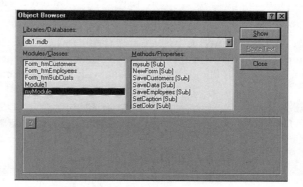

The Object Browser has several parts. At the top is the Libraries/Databases box. This is where you select the libraries or databases to browse. In Figure 23.4, db1.mdb is the selected database. The Modules/Classes box then displays the types of objects available, and the Methods/Properties box shows the related properties and methods. After selecting the property or method, you can use the Paste Text button to add code from the Object Browser into your application.

You can add additional databases and libraries to the Object Browser by establishing references to them. For information on how to establish a reference, see Chapter 35.

Debugging and Error Handling

The next sections discuss debugging and error handling through the use of such things as the Debug window, setting breakpoints, pausing code execution, error trapping, and more.

The Debug Window

The Debug window is used to test Visual Basic subprocedures, functions, and expressions. To test a function or expression, you must preface it with the keyword Print or the ? sign. The returning value is displayed.

To test a subprocedure, enter its name in the Immediate window. Because it can't return a value like a function, Print and ? aren't needed.

To see the value of a memory variable, enter the name of the memory variable and preface it with the keyword Print or the ? sign. Its value is displayed on the line below it.

Setting Breakpoints

A breakpoint is a place in a procedure where you want it to stop running. Setting breakpoints enables you to stop and watch the execution of the procedure.

You set the breakpoints by first selecting the line where you want to stop. You can either click the hand icon on the toolbar or press the F9 key. The line where the pause occurs is now highlighted, as shown in Figure 23.5. The line with the breakpoint isn't executed.

FIGURE 23.5.

A block of code with a breakpoint.

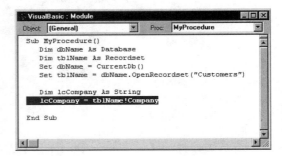

You can have as many breakpoints as you like in a procedure. To remove the breakpoint, select the line of code with the breakpoint and click the hand icon on the toolbar or press the F9 key.

When the procedure has stopped running, you have several options. You can run the rest of the code line by line or resume execution of it. To step through it line by line, you can use either one of these toolbar icons:

The Step Into icon executes the current line of code. If the line of code is a call to another procedure, it displays that code on-screen. You can now walk through each line of this code as well.

The Step Over icon executes the current line of code. If the line of code is a call to another procedure, it executes it without displaying it to you and pausing in it. Once it has completed the procedure, it pauses on the next line of code in the calling procedure.

While the procedure has stopped running, you can use the Watch window to query the values of memory variables. You can also change the values of these memory variables.

To continue executing the procedure, press the F5 key. After you resume the procedure, you don't see the lines of code that are being executed.

Pausing Code Execution

Another way to pause the code is to use the Stop command. The Stop command halts execution of a procedure the same way a breakpoint does.

The difference between the breakpoint and the Stop command is that when you close a module with a breakpoint, it disappears. The breakpoint isn't saved. However, the Stop command is part of the code and remains there. This is helpful when debugging a module in a form or report.

Resuming execution of a procedure with a Stop command is done the same way as a breakpoint.

TIP

When using the Stop command or any other code for debugging, it's a good idea to not indent it with the rest of the code. If it's placed at the far left, it stands out and is easier to remove later.

CAUTION

Be sure to remove all the Stop commands from your application before delivering it.

The Need for Error Trapping

As with all good Visual Basic procedures, there is a need for some sort of error trapping routine. This need is based on the two types of errors: syntax and runtime. Your code should be written so that it can handle these errors without always terminating the application.

Syntax errors are caused by not using a Visual Basic function or keyword correctly. For example, if you enter the line of code If age = 5 in your procedure, an error occurs. The correct syntax for this statement is If age = 5 Then. Most syntax errors are caught by the syntax checker in Access, but not all are.

You can turn the syntax checking on and off by selecting Tools | Options. Select the Module tab, shown in Figure 23.6, and select or deselect Auto Syntax Check.

FIGURE 23.6.

The Module tab of the Options dialog, with syntax checking enabled.

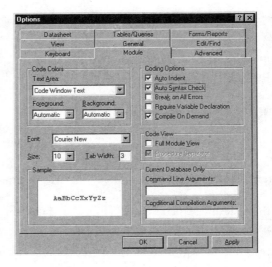

The runtime errors are the hardest to catch because you don't know they're there until you run the code. Not only do you have to run the code, but there might have to be special conditions before the error shows up. These errors are caught only by testing the procedure.

Runtime errors are divided into two different types. One type of error is referred to as recoverable. These are the errors that can be corrected with or without the user's involvement. The following are some examples of these errors.

Before creating a new QueryDef, you should delete it if it already exists. If you delete it and the QueryDef doesn't exist, Access gives you an error. This error should be ignored and the code should continue.

Here's another example of a recoverable error: A report is based on selections that were made on a form. The report's record source is an SQL statement that is made based on these selections. One of the required entries on the form is missing, causing the SQL statement to fail because one of its required parameters is now missing. You can handle the error by displaying a message to the user informing him to enter the information before proceeding.

The other type of runtime error is nonrecoverable. These are the dangerous ones, where there is no escape. When these occur, the application should be terminated, and corrective action should be taken to fix them.

How a runtime error is handled depends on where it occurred. If the error occurred in the Access interface or Jet engine, you should add code to the Error event procedure of the form or report where it occurred. Otherwise, you should add an OnError statement and error handling code to your procedures.

The *Err* Object

Access provides you with several ways to determine which error has occurred. The Err object displays information about runtime errors via its properties. It also provides two methods, Raise and Clear, that enable you to set and clear errors. By using the Err object, you can decide how to handle the errors and what to do next. When you use the Err object, you don't need to create a new instance of it in your code, because it already has global scope.

Err.Number

The Err.Number property returns a Long Integer value of the runtime error code that occurred. The error number range starts at 3. Unused error numbers within the range of 1 to 1000 are reserved for future use by Visual Basic.

The vast majority of these error codes fall into the category of Reserved Errors. As a general rule, these are the errors that occur right before the project deadline.

Err.Description

The Error.Description property returns a string that contains the message for the error code.

Some of the error messages use internal variables to help provide specific information about the error. When the error occurs, Access adds the appropriate text to the error message. If Access can't provide the appropriate text, it displays "Application-defined or object-defined error." For example, this procedure tries to open a form that doesn't exist:

```
Sub OpenCustomerForm ()
    On Error GoTo ErrorTrap
    DoCmd.OpenForm "Customer"
    Exit Sub

ErrorTrap:
    MsgBox err.number
    MsgBox err.description
    Resume Next

End Sub
```

Two different error messages are displayed to the user. The first message box that appears displays the error number, and the second displays the message.

Err.Source

This property is the name of the Visual Basic project where the error occurred.

Err.HelpFile

This is the name of the help file associated with the Visual Basic project.

Err.HelpContext

This property is the help file context ID.

Err.LastDLLError

This property is the system error code for the last DLL call made. For more information on calling DLLs, see Chapter 34, "Working with the Windows API."

Err.Raise

This method generates a runtime error. The syntax for `Err.Raise` is

```
Err.Raise(Number, Source, Description, HelpFile, HelpContext)
```

The arguments for `Err.Raise` are shown in Table 23.6.

Table 23.6. `Err.Raise` **arguments.**

Argument	Description
Number	A Long integer that identifies the error. This argument is required.
Source	A string expression naming the object or application that originally generated the error.
Description	A string expression describing the error.
HelpFile	The fully qualified path to the Microsoft Windows help file in which help on this error can be found.
HelpContext	The context ID identifying a topic within the help file that provides help for the error.

Err.Clear

The `Err.Clear` method is used to clear the `Err` object after an error has been handled. This method provides the same functionality that was included in previous versions of Access by using `Err = 0`. Listing 23.17 provides an example of using `Err` object methods. This case simulates the `Out of memory` error. When the code is run, a message is displayed as though an actual out of memory condition occurred. Figure 23.7 shows how this message is displayed.

Listing 23.17. Using `Err` object methods.

```
ErrorTrap:
    Err.Clear
    Err.Raise (7)
Resume Next
```

FIGURE 23.7.

*Generating an error
condition.*

NOTE

The `Err` and the `Error` statements are still retained for compatibility with prior versions of Access. However, mixing use of the `Err` object and the `Error` statement can lead to unexpected results. For example, even if you fill in the `Err` object's properties, they're reset to their default values when the `Error` statement is run. Although you can use the `Error` statement to generate Visual Basic runtime errors, it's retained principally for compatibility with existing code. You should use the `Err` object and the `Raise` and `Clear` methods for system errors and in new code, especially for OLE Automation objects.

On Error Statements

The `On Error` statement enables you to direct Access where to go when it encounters an error. It's also used to disable an error trapping routine. The `On Error` statement can be used several different ways.

On Error GoTo LabelName/LineNumber

This enables the error handling routine that starts at that line number or line label. From that point on, if any error is encountered, the program control branches to that line or label. If you use the line number, the line number must reside in the same procedure as the `On Error` statement. If it does not, a compile-time error results.

On Error Resume Next

If you use this statement, when an error is encountered the program control goes to the next line of code following the error. Using this statement as the only error trapping isn't a good idea. This could result in a snowball effect resulting in lost or damaged data. It's best used inside an error trapping routine once the error has been dealt with. Then the program can continue working.

On Error GoTo 0

This is used to disable any error trapping routine in the current procedure. If there is no On Error routine, Access displays its own error message. If the application is running in runtime mode, the application terminates.

Error Trapping Routines

Before you begin writing error trapping routines, you need a naming convention. Access doesn't let you have two error routines with the same name in the same module, form, or report.

One possible naming convention is to use the name of the procedure and add _Error to it. For example, if the procedure is called cmdAdd_Click, its error-trapping routine is called cmdAdd_Click_Error. This way, all your error routines have unique names.

Most error trapping routines are made up of two parts. The first is responding to the error, and the other is the action taken as a result of the error.

Responding to the error might involve informing the user or prompting him for a response. For example, if a file can't be opened for import, you might want to inform the user about it and allow him to try it again.

The action that is taken as a result of the error largely depends on the type of error. If a table's index is missing, you might want to exit the procedure. If information is missing on a form, you might want to put the cursor back in that control. If a form, report, or table is missing, exiting the application would be a good idea.

Error trapping routines normally end with one of these statements:

- Resume Next: This returns program control to the next line of code after the one that caused the error.
- Resume: This returns program control back to the line of code that caused the error. Access then reexecutes the line of code that caused the error. Be sure that the error has been fixed; otherwise, you might be trapped in an endless loop.
- Exit Sub or Exit Function: This exits the current procedure and returns program control back to where the procedure was called from.

> **CAUTION**
>
> If you use error trapping in a procedure, be sure to add the statement Exit Sub or Exit Function before the error routine. If you don't, the error routine is executed even if there was no error.

Form and Report Error Trapping

Both forms and reports have a built-in error trapping event (OnError). It's triggered when an error caused by either the Access interface or Microsoft Jet engine occurs on a form or report that is open. You can use a macro or write a procedure for each form and report. You can also write a generic error-handling function for all your forms and reports.

The basic design of an error routine for a form or report is the same as one that is used in a module. In the code for the Error event, the type of error and response are passed into the procedure. The example in Listing 23.18 specifically checks for the duplicate index error number 3022. If it finds this error, it displays a message box and sets Response to acDataErrContinue, which tells the application to continue processing after receiving a data access error.

An easy way to handle these types of errors is to write an OnError routine that looks like Listing 23.18.

Listing 23.18. Handling data access errors.

```
Private Sub Form_Error(DataErr As Integer, Response As Integer)
Const DUPLICATE_INDEX = 3022

    If DataErr = DUPLICATE_INDEX Then
        MsgBox "This is a duplicate customer ID"
        Response = acDataErrContinue
    End If
End Sub
```

You need to expand the Select Case code to handle any other type of error that might occur.

In the procedure Form_Error, two parameters are passed. DataErr and Response both have the datatype of Integer. The DataErr parameter contains the code for the error that has just happened. You can use this error number to trap for any recoverable errors.

The Response parameter contains the value 1. If you assign any value to the parameter, it prevents the Access error message from being displayed. In other words, if you don't give it a value you first see your error message, followed by an Access error message.

> **NOTE**
>
> You can use the `Debug.Print` command to display values in the Immediate window while the procedure is running.

Standard Modules

As stated earlier, standard modules are the procedures you create in the Module window of the database container. These functions and subprocedures are available to the application at all times. They can be called from other procedures, forms, reports, queries, and macros. They're loaded into memory when the application is loaded and stay there until the application terminates.

All the procedures must have a unique name within the module. Because of this you need to assign a naming convention. One possible naming convention is to assign the module a meaningful name and add a two-letter code to the end of it. This two-letter code can then be used as the starting two letters for all its functions and subprocedures.

For example, the module is used by the Customer form. The module might be called `frmCustomer` (`cf`). All the modules start with `cf`. The procedure to add a new customer would be called `cfAdd` or `cf_Add`. The delete procedure would be called `cfDelete` or `cf_Delete`.

This way you're assured that each procedure is given a unique name. The two-letter code also helps in finding where the procedure resides. The function name `cf_YearToDateSales()` tells you that it's in the `[frmCustomer (cf)]` module.

Code Behind Forms (CBF)

Code Behind Forms (CBF) is a term that is used to describe where the procedures for forms and reports are located. In the CBF method, you place the event code procedures inside the form or report. You do this by clicking the Builder button(...), shown in Figure 23.8, to invoke the Choose Builder.

FIGURE 23.8.

The Property window.

Select the Code Builder option in the Choose Builder window. After you make the selection, another window appears. This window is used to enter the code. This is the same window that modules use, and it has all the same functionality as well. When you're finished writing the code, close the window. You'll return to the form or report.

The CBF modules are made up of three sections. The object events, form or report events, and general. The object events section is made up of all the events for that object. The number and type of events differs from object to object based on what it is.

The form or report events are those events that relate only to the form or report itself. Access 95 has 29 form-level events and seven report-level events to choose from.

The general section of the CBF module is where you place the procedures that are common to all objects in the form or report. To move to this section, select the General option from the Object Box on the tool bar.

An example of a General procedure is an audit trailing routine. When the user adds, edits, or deletes a record, an audit trail record is written. Because this same code is used in different places, you should have to write the procedure only once. If you place it in the General section, all the procedures in the form have access to it.

The scope of the CBF modules is only within the form or report. If a form opens another form, the modules in the first form aren't available in the second form.

Any procedure in the form can call another procedure. For example, the form contains a command button named cmdSave. Its OnClick event code can call a procedure in the General section. The code for the Save button would look like this:

```
Function cmdSave_Click ( )
    '--    See if all required entries are there.
    If OkToSave() Then
        Me.Refresh
    Else
        Msgbox "Missing Information.", 16, "Data Entry"
        DoCmd.CancelEvent
    End If
End Function
```

You can also have one command button call the OnClick procedure of another command button. The code to do this is as follows:

```
Function cmdExit_Click  ( )
    '--    See if there were any changes to the current record.
    If Me.Dirty Then
        '--    Save the changes to the record.
        cmdSave_Click()
    End If
    DoCmd.Close
End Function
```

The Purpose of Reusable and Generic Code

The purpose of reusable and generic code is to minimize the amount of code written for an application. The less code there is for an application, the faster it runs and the easier it is to maintain.

It's easier to maintain generic code because you have to make the modifications in only one place. For example, you use a common function to exit all forms. If the client requests that the user be prompted before exiting all forms, you need to make the change in only one place. If your application has 50 forms, think of the time this will save.

The drawback to using generic code is that when you make a change, you need to be concerned about the effect it will have throughout the application.

Design Considerations

Before you start to write your own reusable and generic code, you should be aware of a few design considerations. Following these guidelines should help you write better routines.

The Scope of the Routine

What is the scope of the routine? Will it be used throughout the application or just for a few forms, reports, queries, macros, or modules? Will this routine be used only in this application or will other applications use it as well?

Avoid Direct References to Objects

Avoid making references to objects that are on a form or report. What happens if the form or report that called this routine doesn't have that control? It's better to pass the control's value to the routine as a parameter.

The following is an example of having the `Visible` property change for a `Save` command button.

This is the calling procedure:

```
Sub Button0_Click ()
     SetVisible Me!cmdSave
End Sub
```

This the generic code that changes the `Visible` property:

```
Sub SetVisible (pControl As Control)
     pControl.Visible = Not pControl.Visible
End Sub
```

In the preceding sample code, you can pass in the name of any control and have its `Visible` property changed. Another way to do this is to have a `cmdSave` command button on all the forms that call it.

How Will This Routine Be Called?

Will this routine be called as a subprocedure or a function? Remember that only a function can return a value.

Error Trapping

Just like any other procedure, you need to have an error trapping routine. Without a routine, an error might cause the application to terminate, crash, or cause lost or damaged data.

Documentation and Comments

It's a well-known fact that the one thing all programmers hate doing is documentation of any type. However, it's extremely important that you document and comment your generic routines. Without this, it would be next to impossible for anyone else to use and fix them later.

When it comes time to document your routines, here are some places you should pay particular attention to:

- Procedure header: One or two sentences about what the procedure does. Just enough information to explain its purpose.
- Parameter list: A list of the parameters that are passed in with a description and if they're required or optional parameters. If you're using the parsing method to pass in a parameter that contains several options, you need to show how to pass each one and its default value.
- Calls to other procedures: One line about what that procedure will do. It will look something like this:

```
'--   Get the list order number for this customer.
LastOrder = LastCustOrder(tblCustomer!CustomerId)
```

- Common blocks of code: A comment about what that block of code does. Because this is a common block of code, you might want to spend more time documenting it.

Summary

Using Visual Basic code in your application enables you to go beyond the scope of macros and to tie an application together. Without code, many of today's applications would be impossible or severely limited in what they can do. Learning to write code is a slow and steady process that begins with mastering the fundamentals that were outlined in this chapter.

Working with the Access Event Model

24

by Chris Barnes

Understanding Events in Access

Microsoft Access is a development tool that enables you to create event-driven applications. An event is a recognized action (such as a mouse click, the opening of a form or report, or the pressing of a key) that occurs within an Access application and returns some type of response. That response can be the execution of a macro, the running of some Visual Basic for Applications code (a subprocedure), or a user-built expression that returns a value. You can determine what the response will be through the Event properties of the specified control, form, or report.

> **NOTE**
>
> Another response generated solely by the operating system is the receiving of the focus. The focus occurs when an object on the screen receives, in effect, the attention of the system, and anything that happens at that point is happening to that object. You can also generate user-written responses within the GotFocus and LostFocus events.

Macros, subprocedures, and expressions are initiated in the Event property of an object. These are created and edited through the Properties window of a control, form, or report. Within the Properties window, you just click the Events tab and then click the Build button of the event for which you want a response returned. The Choose Builder dialog box appears, as shown in Figure 24.1, giving you the option of creating an expression, writing a macro, or writing a subprocedure using Visual Basic code.

FIGURE 24.1.

The Choose Builder dialog box.

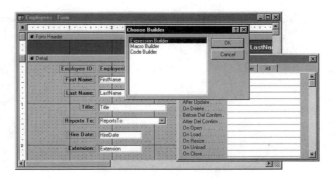

Unlike applications in procedural programming languages, which are written using top-down methodology, Access applications are designed to respond to events from users. The order in which the code is executed depends on which event is invoked by a user action. This is the essence of *event-driven* programming; it puts the user in charge, and your code responds accordingly. This is an important factor to consider when you're designing your own applications. You're required to make some assumptions. For example, you can assume that a text box must be filled in before a command button can be clicked. To code for this assumption, just disable the command button until something has been entered in the text box.

Types of Access Events

Access has many different events to give the application developer several options in responding to some action taken by a user. The different types of events are summarized in the following sections.

Data Events

Data events occur whenever data is added, updated, or deleted from a form or control—for example, when text changes in a text or combo box, or when updates happen to data in a control (in Form view) or a record (in Datasheet view). Another example is when the focus moves from one record to another.

Current

This event occurs when you first open a form or when you move from one record to another. This event also occurs when you refresh or requery a form's underlying table or query.

Delete

This event occurs when the user performs a delete action, such as pressing the Delete key or clicking a command button that performs the delete operation. This event occurs before the record is actually deleted by Microsoft Access. The event procedure for a delete takes one parameter, Cancel, which can be modified. If Cancel is set to True within this procedure, the delete action isn't performed, and the `BeforeDelConfirm`, `AfterDelConfirm`, and `Current` events don't occur. If Cancel isn't set to True any time during the delete, the following events occur in order:

1. `Delete`
2. `Current` (accesses the next available record)
3. `BeforeDelConfirm`
4. A system message box confirming the delete
5. `AfterDelConfirm`

> **CAUTION**
>
> If you have Confirm Record Changes set to Off under Tools | Options | Edit/Find, the `Delete` event will occur, but the `BeforeDelConfirm` event, the system confirmation, and the `AfterDelConfirm` event won't occur.

BeforeDelConfirm

This event occurs after the user deletes one or more records and before a dialog box displays to confirm the deletion. This procedure takes two arguments: Cancel and Response. Setting Cancel to True (any nonzero value), cancels this event and restores the record, and the confirm dialog doesn't appear. If Cancel is set to False, the Response parameter determines whether the confirm dialog box appears. Response can have one of two values: 0 or 1. A setting of 0 tells Microsoft Access to continue deleting without displaying the confirm dialog box. A setting of 1 tells Microsoft Access to display the confirm dialog box. These two values are stored in predefined constant variables: DATA_ERRCONTINUE is set to 0, and DATA_ERRDISPLAY is set to 1.

AfterDelConfirm

This event occurs after the confirmation and/or deletion of the record(s) or when the deletion is canceled. Even if the BeforeDelConfirm event is canceled, this event still occurs. This event procedure carries one argument, Status, which determines whether a record has been deleted. Status can have one of three values: 0, 1, or 2. Zero tells Microsoft Access that the deletion was successful. One tells Microsoft Access that the deletion was canceled within Access. Two tells Microsoft Access the deletion was canceled by the user. These three values are stored in predefined constant variables; DELETE_OK is set to 0, DELETE_CANCEL is set to 1, and DELETE_USER_CANCEL is set to 2.

BeforeInsert

This event occurs when the user types the first character of a new record but before the record is actually inserted into the table. This event allows you to determine whether an insert should be allowed. This event procedure has one argument, Cancel. Setting Cancel to True cancels this event; however, you can't cancel the AfterInsert event.

AfterInsert

This event occurs after a new record is added to a table. This event allows you to requery a recordset each time a record is added in order to keep your users up-to-date.

BeforeUpdate

This event occurs before any data in a control or record is updated in the record. This event procedure has one argument, Cancel. Setting Cancel to True cancels this event and the update action; however, you can't cancel the AfterUpdate event.

AfterUpdate

This event occurs after data in a record or control has been updated. For bound controls, you can use this event along with the OldValue property to cancel an update. The OldValue property keeps the value of the control before it was updated until after this event has occurred. Therefore, it's possible to set the control equal to its OldValue. The following syntax is an example of restoring a control to its previously updated value (your own undo command):

```
FORMS!formname!controlname = FORMS!formname!controlname.OldValue
```

> **TIP**
>
> Changing any data in a control or record using a macro or Visual Basic won't trigger the BeforeUpdate or AfterUpdate events.

Change

This event occurs when the contents of a text box or the text portion of a combo box changes. A change can be any character directly inserted or deleted.

> **CAUTION**
>
> You must be very careful with this event, because if you have two text boxes that affect each other when one is changed, it can cause an infinite loop of change events (known as cascading events).

NotInList

This event occurs only within combo boxes and when the user enters a value in the text portion of the combo box and that value isn't in the list. In order for this event to occur, you must set the LimitToList property, which allows only values that are in the list, to Yes. This event procedure carries two arguments: NewData, the data entered by the user, and Response, which indicates how the event is handled. Response can have one of three values: 0, 1, or 2. Zero tells Microsoft Access to display the default message to the users, telling them that they have entered a value not in the list. One tells Microsoft Access not to display the default message and also not to add the new data to the list. This gives you the opportunity to display a custom-built message. Two tells Microsoft Access not to display a message but to add the new data to the combo box list. Microsoft Access then requeries and refreshes the combo box. These three values are stored in predefined constant variables; DATA_ERRDISPLAY is set to 0, DATA_ERRCONTINUE is set to 1, and DATA_ERRADDED is set to 2.

> **NOTE**
>
> When Response is set to DATA_ERRADDED, you must still add the new data to your
> control source, programmatically, of the combo box. You don't need to refresh the
> combo box.

Updated

This event occurs when an OLE object's data has been modified. This event applies only to
bound and unbound object frames. The event procedure has one argument, Code. This argument indicates how the OLE object was updated. Code can have one of four values: 0, 1, 2, or
3. Zero tells Microsoft Access that the object's data has been changed. One tells Microsoft Access
that the object's data was saved by the application that created the object. Two tells Microsoft
Access that the OLE object file was closed by the application that created it. Three tells Microsoft
Access that the OLE object file has been renamed by the application that created it. These four
values are stored in predefined constant variables. OLE_CHANGED is set to 0, OLE_SAVED is set to 1,
OLE_CLOSED is set to 2, and OLE_RENAMED is set to 3.

> **NOTE**
>
> This event isn't related to the BeforeUpdate and the AfterUpdate events for bound
> and unbound object frames. This event happens when the object's data changes.
> BeforeUpdate and AfterUpdate occur when the object is updated and after the
> Updated event.

Error Events

These events occur when an error is encountered.

Error

This event occurs whenever there is a runtime error within your Microsoft Access application.
This event applies to forms and reports and includes errors that occur using the Microsoft Jet
Database Engine. However, this event won't happen when an error occurs in Visual Basic code
within a function or procedure. This event allows you to trap any Microsoft Access error messages and display your own custom error message to your users. This event procedure has two
arguments: DataErr, which is the error code returned by the Err function that is executed each
time an error occurs, and Response, which determines if a system-default error message should
be displayed. You can use the DataErr argument with the Error$ function to map the error
code to its appropriate message. Response can have one of two values: 0 or 1. Zero tells Microsoft

Access to continue without displaying the default error message. This allows you to display your own message. One tells Microsoft Access to display the default error message. These two values are stored in predefined constant variables. DATA_ERRCONTINUE is set to 0, and DATA_ERRDISPLAY is set to 1.

Timing Events

Timing events occur when you're setting the TimerInterval property on a form.

Timer

This event occurs at regular intervals when specified by the TimerInterval property within a form. When the TimerInterval property is set to 0, this event won't occur; however, when the property is set to any value greater than 0 and less than 65,536, the Timer event will occur as scheduled. This event is best used to keep data synchronized in a multiuser environment.

> **NOTE**
>
> The time setting in the TimerInterval property is expressed in milliseconds.

Focus Events

Focus events occur when any control, form, or report receives or loses focus (or becomes active or inactive).

Enter

This event occurs before a control receives the focus from another control on the same form. Or, when a form is first opened, the Enter event occurs on the first control. This event occurs before the GotFocus event and after the Current event.

Exit

This event occurs just before a control loses the focus to another control on the same form. This event occurs before the LostFocus event.

> **NOTE**
>
> Unlike the GotFocus and LostFocus events, the Enter and Exit events won't occur if the focus leaves a control and goes to another form or report. These events are best used to display messages or instructions before allowing an update of controls, or to change the tab order of the controls on a form.

GotFocus

This event occurs when a form or a control on a form receives the focus. This event won't occur for a form unless all the controls on the form have been disabled. Also, a control can receive the focus only when it is enabled and visible. This event occurs after the Enter event.

LostFocus

This event occurs any time the focus leaves a form or a control on a form. This event occurs after the Exit event, unless the Exit event doesn't happen, which would be the case if the focus went from a control on one form to a control on another form.

Activate

This event occurs when a form or report receives the focus to become the active form. A form or report receives the focus when it is opened, when a control on it is clicked, or when you use the SetFocus method within Visual Basic code. A form or report must be visible for this event to occur.

Deactivate

This event occurs when a form or report loses the focus to another window, such as the Table, Query, Form, Report, Macro, Module, or Database. This event doesn't occur, however, when the focus goes to a dialog box, or another application.

Keyboard Events

Keyboard events occur when a key is pressed or as a result of the SendKeys action or statement.

KeyDown

This event occurs anytime a key is pressed within a control or a form that has the focus.

KeyUp

This event occurs anytime a key is released within a control or in a form that has the focus.

The KeyDown and KeyUp events are best used to distinguish when a user presses a function key, a navigation key (the arrow keys, Home, End, Page Up, and so on), or a combination of keys with Shift, Ctrl, or Alt. However, these events don't occur when you press the Enter or Esc key if there is a command button on the form or report with its Default or Cancel property set to Yes.

These two event procedures have two arguments: KeyCode and Shift. KeyCode is an integer representing the key that was pressed. To prevent a control from receiving a keystroke, you just set KeyCode to 0. Shift is an integer that determines if Shift, Ctrl, or Alt was pressed in combination with another key. The value of Shift is 0 if none of the keys were held down, 1 if the Shift key is down, 2 if the Ctrl key is down, and 4 if the Alt key is down. If any combination of these keys is held down together, the value of Shift is just the sum of the keys' individual values.

KeyPress

This event occurs when the user presses and releases any combination of keys within a control or a form that corresponds to a printable character. This event doesn't occur when you press the function keys, navigation keys, or any of the mask keys (Shift, Alt, and Ctrl). Unlike the KeyDown and KeyUp events, this event distinguishes between uppercase and lowercase. This event procedure has one argument, KeyAscii, which is an integer representing the character pressed. To determine the character pressed, you can use the Chr function.

> **CAUTION**
>
> Although these events are a good way of determining what a user is doing, be careful where and when you use these events, because if a key is held down, the KeyDown and KeyPress events occur repeatedly, which greatly increases the chances of an application locking up (running out of system resources). You may want to consider using the data events that are available, such as Change and Updated.

Mouse Events

Mouse events occur when the mouse performs some action on a form or control.

Click

This event occurs when the mouse is clicked over a control on a form, a section of a form, or the form itself. This event doesn't occur on controls within an option group, but it does occur on the option group. This event also occurs in the following situations when the mouse button isn't clicked:

- An item is selected from a combo box by using the arrow keys and pressing the Enter key to place it in the text property of the combo box.
- The space bar is pressed when a check box, command button, or option button has the focus.
- The Enter key or Esc key is pressed on a form that has a button with the Default property of Yes or the Cancel property of Yes, respectively.
- A command button is accessed using its shortcut key (Alt plus the underlined letter in the caption of the command button).

To determine which mouse button was clicked, refer to the MouseDown and MouseUp events.

DblClick

This event occurs when the mouse is clicked twice in succession over a control on a form, a section of a form, or the form itself. This event doesn't occur on controls within an option group, but it does occur on the option group.

The DblClick event procedure takes one argument, Cancel, which when set to True cancels this event.

For some controls, double-clicking has other responses after the DblClick event. For example, clicking an object that contains an OLE object will cause the object to be opened in the application that created it. However, by using this event effectively, you can change what happens when you double-click an object. For example, when double-clicking an OLE object, you can first send the object to a printer to print, and then set the Cancel argument to True, which will then cancel the event and not start up the application that created the object.

> **TIP**
>
> The Click event occurs when you enter a value and then leave a combo box, even if you don't use your mouse—for example, tabbing to the control, entering a value, and then tabbing to the next control.

MouseMove

This event occurs when the user moves the mouse over a control, a form, or a section of a form. This event is repeated continuously as the mouse is being moved over a control. Even if a form or control is moved using Visual Basic code within a procedure and it passes underneath the mouse pointer, this event will occur. This event is best used when you wish to display a small form whenever a user moves the mouse over a certain control.

This event procedure has four arguments: Button specifies which mouse button was clicked; Shift tells you if the Shift, Ctrl, or Alt key is being held down while clicking; and X and Y give you the coordinates of the current mouse pointer. X and Y are always measured in twips (1/1440 of an inch) rather than pixels.

The Button argument has the following values: Zero indicates that no mouse button is pressed, and one indicates that the left mouse button is pressed and is defined as constant value LEFT_BUTTON. Two indicates that the right mouse button is pressed and is defined as constant value RIGHT_BUTTON. Four indicates that the middle mouse button is pressed and is defined as constant value MIDDLE_BUTTON. A value of 3 indicates that the right and left mouse buttons are pressed, a value of 5 is the left and middle, a value of 6 is the middle and right, and a value of 7 indicates that all three mouse buttons are pressed.

The Shift argument tells Microsoft Access if the Shift, Ctrl, and/or Alt keys are depressed while the event occurs. The value of Shift is 0 if none of the keys are held down. The value is 1, defined as constant value SHIFT_MASK, if the Shift key is down. The value is 2, defined as constant value CTRL_MASK, if the Ctrl key is down. The value is 4, defined as constant value ALT_MASK, if the Alt key is down. If any combination of these keys is held down together, the value of Shift is just the sum of the keys' individual values.

MouseDown and MouseUp

These events occur when a mouse button is pressed and released while over a control, a form, or a section of a form. These events enable you to determine which button (or combination of buttons) was used, which you can't determine in the Click and DblClick events. You can also find out if the user held down any combination of the Shift, Ctrl, and Alt keys.

This event procedure has four arguments: Button specifies which mouse button was clicked; Shift tells you if the Shift, Ctrl, or Alt key is being held down while clicking; X and Y give you the coordinates of the current mouse pointer. X and Y are always measured in twips (1/1440 of an inch) rather than pixels.

The Button argument has the following values: One indicates that the left mouse button is pressed and is defined as constant value LEFT_BUTTON. Two indicates that the right mouse button is pressed and is defined as constant value RIGHT_BUTTON. Four indicates that the middle mouse button is pressed and is defined as constant value MIDDLE_BUTTON.

The Shift argument tells Microsoft Access if the Shift, Ctrl, and/or Alt keys are depressed while the event occurs. The value of Shift is 0 if none of the keys is held down. The value is 1, defined as constant value SHIFT_MASK, if the Shift key is down. The value is 2, defined as constant value CTRL_MASK, if the Ctrl key is down. The value is 4, defined as constant value ALT_MASK, if the Alt key is down. If any combination of these keys is held down together, the value of Shift is just the sum of the keys' individual values.

> **NOTE**
>
> The button argument for the MouseDown and MouseUp events is somewhat different from the MouseMove event. For MouseDown and MouseUp, this argument indicates only one button per event. Therefore, two buttons being clicked would result in two events for both MouseDown and MouseUp. On the other hand, MouseMove would have only one event and would indicate only the current state of all the mouse buttons—in this case, adding up the values of the mouse buttons.

Print Events

Print events occur when a report is being formatted for printing or is actually printed. These events occur for each section of a report.

Format

This event occurs before Microsoft Access actually formats each section of a report but after data has been selected. For the detail section of a report, this event occurs for each record, allowing you to format each record differently if you so desire. In the group headers of a report, this event occurs each time a group by field changes value.

This event procedure has two arguments: Cancel and FormatCount. Cancel, if set to True, will cancel the formatting for the current section and move on to the next section. FormatCount is the number of times the Format event has occurred for the current section. This is so you know if a section spans more than one page.

Retreat

This event occurs when Microsoft Access must return to a previous section of a report while formatting. This event will occur after the Format event but before the Print event. This allows you to change any formatting you may have already done. This can be useful if you want to change any headers when a section spans more than one page or if you want to change the font size of a section to fit on a single page.

Print

This event occurs after the data has been formatted but before anything is displayed or printed. Like the Format event, this event occurs for each section of a report. This event procedure has two arguments: Cancel and PrintCount. Setting Cancel to True won't print the section or the current record on the report but instead will leave a blank space. The PrintCount argument keeps track of the number of times this event has occurred for the current record. This way, you can tell if a record spans more than one page and cancel it if you so desire.

> **NOTE**
>
> The Print event won't let you set any properties for an object on the report.

Window Events

Window events occur when any window (Form or Report) is sized, opened, or closed.

Open

This event occurs whenever a form or report is opened but before the first record is displayed or before a report is previewed or printed. This event occurs before the Load event. This event has one argument, Cancel. When Cancel is set to True, the form or report isn't opened. This event is best used to prompt a user for some criteria that will affect the data which is shown when the form is displayed. For example, if you're displaying a generic form, you can prompt the user to enter a table name and code that name in the record source of a control on the form (after first validating the name, of course). This is also the best place to set the focus to a particular control on the form.

Close

This event occurs whenever a form or report is closed and no longer visible on the screen. This event occurs after the Unload event. This event is usually where you will open another form or display an existing message if the user is leaving the application.

Load

This event occurs whenever a form is opened and records are displayed. This event occurs before the Current event for the first record or control but after the Open event. You can't cancel this event; however, if the Open event is canceled, this event won't occur.

Unload

This event occurs whenever a form is closed but before it's removed from the screen. This event is triggered by the closing action and occurs before the Close event. This event procedure has one argument, Cancel. When Cancel is set to True, the form won't close or unload from the screen.

> **CAUTION**
>
> Be careful when setting Cancel to True in this event. If you do, the form won't close or be removed. Therefore, if you don't set Cancel back to False programmatically, you will never be able to close this form unless you end the application. Also, if the form is modal, you might not have access to any other applications, which could be cause for a reboot.

Resize

This event occurs whenever a form is opened or the size of the form changes in any way. This event allows you to change the size of any controls on the form when it is resized. Also this event is the best place to use the Repaint method, which updates all controls on the form.

The Ordering of Access Events

Each control and form has several events, so it's important to understand the order in which they're executed. The order in which events occur affects how and when your macros and procedures run. For example, if you have more than one procedure that must run in order, you must make sure the events occur in the correct order. This is assuming that the events are triggering a subprocedure.

Event Order for Controls on a Form

When a control receives the focus by the user's clicking on it or tabbing to it, the order of events is as follows:

- Enter
- GotFocus

CAUTION

Though it may seem that these two events occur together, the Enter event doesn't apply to check boxes, option buttons, or toggle buttons within an option group—only to the option group itself. However, the GotFocus event does apply to these individual controls within an option group. This same rule applies for the Exit and LostFocus events.

When you enter or change data in a control and then move the focus to another control, the following events are performed in order:

- KeyDown
- KeyPress
- Change
- KeyUp
- BeforeUpdate
- AfterUpdate
- Exit
- LostFocus

NOTE

The events NotInList and Error occur after a value is entered into a combo box and it isn't in the combo box list. These two events occur after the KeyUp event.

Event Order for Records on a Form

Separate events occur for records when they're displayed on a form. These are different events from those which occur to the controls that hold the data of the fields that make up a record.

When you change a record by moving within the controls on a form and then move to the next record, the following events occur in order:

- Current (form)
- Enter (control)
- GotFocus (control)
- BeforeUpdate (control)
- AfterUpdate (control)
- BeforeUpdate (form)
- AfterUpdate (form)
- Exit (control)
- LostFocus (control)
- Current (form)

NOTE

This example assumes that the focus is on the last control on a form. For other controls that aren't the last, there would be an Enter event and a GotFocus event before the AfterUpdate event for the form would occur.

When you delete a record on a form, the following events occur in order:

- Delete
- BeforeDelConfirm
- AfterDelConfirm

NOTE

In the Delete event subprocedure, you can test to determine if you really want to allow the user to delete the current record. If not, you can set Cancel to True, the delete won't happen and the BeforeDelConfirm and AfterDelConfirm events won't execute. The confirm dialog box won't display, either.

When you move the focus to a new (blank) record, the following events occur in order:

- ■ Current (form)
- ■ Enter (form)
- ■ GotFocus (control)
- ■ BeforeInsert (form)
- ■ AfterInsert (form)

> **NOTE**
>
> The BeforeUpdate and the AfterUpdate events for the controls and records on a form will occur after the BeforeInsert event and before the AfterInsert event.

Event Order for Forms

Events that occur within forms include opening, closing, moving between forms, and working with the data on a form.

The following illustrates the form event occurrences (in order) when you open form1, click a button to open form2, and then move back to form1:

- ■ Open (form1)
- ■ Load (form1)
- ■ Resize (form1)
- ■ Activate (form1)
- ■ Current (form1)
- ■ Open (form2)
- ■ Load (form2)
- ■ Resize (form2)
- ■ Deactivate (form1)
- ■ Activate (form2)
- ■ Current (form2)
- ■ Deactivate (form2)
- ■ Activate (form1)

Each time a form receives the focus, the Activate event occurs; however, if the form is already open, the Open and Load events don't occur. This is true even if a form is called by the OpenForm action.

As you can see from the preceding example, when you open a second form, the `Deactivate` event from the first form doesn't occur until the second form executes its `Open`, `Load`, and `Resize` events. This makes it possible for you to check that the second form opens without any errors. If it does have errors, you can just close the form, and the focus returns to the calling form. (Don't forget about displaying the appropriate error message.)

When working with forms and subforms, the order of events is as follows:

- Events for the subform's controls
- Events for the form's controls
- Events for the form
- Events for the subform

> **NOTE**
>
> Remember, the only events on a subform control are `Enter` and `Exit`. Any events tied to controls within the subform happen when the subform receives the focus or is updated by the result of the Link Master Fields changing.

Event Order for Keystrokes and Mouse Clicks

Keyboard and mouse events occur for forms and controls when they receive the focus.

The order of events for keystrokes is as follows:

- `KeyDown`
- `KeyPress`
- `KeyUp`

The `MouseMove` event occurs when you move the mouse over a control or form. The other mouse events occur in the following order when you press and release a mouse button while pointing at a control on a form:

- `MouseDown`
- `MouseUp`
- `Click`

There is also a `DblClick` event, which occurs after the `Click` event.

Event Order for Reports

Events occur for reports and all the sections of a report when you print, print preview, or close a report.

When you open a report to print or print preview and then close it, the following events occur in order:

- `Open`
- `Activate`
- `Format`
- `Print`
- `Close`
- `Deactivate`

The `Open` event occurs before any underlying query is executed, allowing you to update or add SQL as needed.

The `Format` and `Print` events enable you to run macros or execute procedures. This gives you the opportunity to perform calculations (such as running totals), or change the layout of a report before it's printed.

The `NoData` event occurs if the report doesn't generate any records to print.

The `Retreat` event will occur if Access has to go back to a previous section, because all the data won't fit in a current section. This can allow you to run a macro or subprocedure to reformat your report in some way.

Assigning Code to Events

Once you've decided which events to have some action take place in, you need to assign Visual Basic code to the event procedure. Figure 24.2 shows the Event tab of the Properties window. By clicking the down arrow to the right of any event, you can choose a predefined macro or the event procedure.

FIGURE 24.2.

The Event tab of the Properties window.

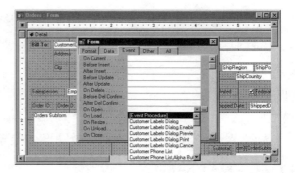

When you assign code to an event, Access automatically sets up the following skeleton subprocedure for you:

```
Sub procedure name ()

End Sub
```

This allows you to customize any process within your Access application—for example, formatting reports, creating and running queries, setting properties to controls, or adding, updating, and deleting database records using recordsets.

Subprocedures and functions both execute code, but subprocedures are executed from events procedures, not functions. However, you can call a function from a subprocedure. Also, subprocedures can't return a value, but functions do return a single value from where they were called.

CAUTION

It's possible to have a recursive subprocedure or function (calling itself), but you run the risk of a stack overflow. Also, you can't nest subprocedures or functions, but you can call other subprocedures from within a subprocedure.

Creating an Event Procedure

To create a subprocedure, which is invoked automatically in response to an event, follow these steps:

1. Open a form or report in Design view. The entire form or report is selected by default, but you may select a single control for which the event procedure is created.
2. Click the Properties button on the toolbar. Microsoft Access displays the property sheet for the form, report, or control.
3. From the list box at the top of the property sheet, select the Event tab.
4. Select the event that will trigger the event procedure.
5. Select [Event Procedure] from the list.
6. Click the Build button to display the Module window.
7. Type the event procedure code between the Sub line and the End Sub line.
8. Click the Compile All Modules button on the toolbar to compile the event procedure.

TIP

A shortcut to this process would be to right-click, click Build Event, and click Code Builder.

> **CAUTION**
>
> If an error message is displayed during a compile, it will be necessary to correct the source of the error and recompile.

9. Save changes to the module.

When the form or report is open, each occurrence of the event will cause the event procedure to be called.

Sample Code for Subprocedures

The following code is an example, from NWIND.MDB, of the Click event on a form running Visual Basic code that opens a report. When you click the Print Invoice button from the Orders form, the following code is executed:

```
Sub PrintInvoice_Click()
' This code is created by Command Button wizard.
On Error GoTo Err_PrintInvoice_Click
Dim DocName As String
Dim strWhere As String      'This line is not needed.
DocName = "Invoice"
' Print Invoice report, using Invoices Filter query to print
' invoice for current order.
DoCmd.OpenReport DocName, acNormal, "Invoices Filter"
Exit_PrintInvoice_Click:
Exit Sub
Err_PrintInvoice_Click:
MsgBox Err.Description
Resume Exit_PrintInvoice_Click
End Sub
```

The name of the subprocedure, PrintInvoice_Click, is automatically created by Access. Notice that the name comprises the name of the control (PrintInvoice), an underscore, and the name of the event (Click). This is how all subprocedures are named. All lines in your code that start with a single quote (') are comment lines, which means that Access doesn't try to evaluate them. Actually, whenever there is a single quote in a line, Access treats the rest of that line—everything to the right of the quote—as a comment. (See line 5 in the preceding code example.)

Line 3 sets the error checking for this procedure. This means that any time this code is executing and any error occurs, processing will go directly to wherever the On Error command tells it to go; in this case, it will go to label Err_PrintInvoice_Click. Also, any time you use the On Error method, you must also have a Resume or Exit also coded, as shown in line 14.

Lines 4 and 5 demonstrate how to declare variables local to the subprocedure. This means as soon as the procedure exits, all local variables are deleted. You can declare variables global to the form or report by placing the declare statements (Dim) in its declaration section.

Line 9 is the actual command that opens the report and prints it immediately. `DoCmd.OpenReport` takes four arguments, the first being the only one required. That first parameter must be a valid report in the current database. The second parameter, *view*, tells Access what to do with the report once it's created. The default value is to send it to the printer; otherwise, you could open it in Design view or Preview view. The third parameter, *filtername*, must be a valid query in the database. If this argument is coded, it will temporarily place the query name in the `RecordSource` property of the report; otherwise, the report will use whatever is already there. If you use the last argument, `where` *condition*, it must be a valid SQL `where` statement, excluding the keyword `Where`. This statement will be temporarily placed at the end of the report's underlying query.

NOTE

You can leave an optional argument blank in the middle of the syntax, but you must include the argument's comma. If you leave one or more trailing arguments blank, don't use a comma following the last argument you specify; otherwise, you will get a syntax error.

CAUTION

Be careful when deleting controls that have code written behind them. Remember that the code isn't deleted with the control—it is just placed in the general object of the form or report. This is also the case when you rename a control, so make sure you cut and paste the code back to the appropriate control. If you forget to do this, the code will stay out there and never execute, but it won't cause any runtime errors. On the other hand, don't forget that when you're pasting a control on a form or report, any code that's behind the control that was cut or copied doesn't get pasted with the new control.

Summary

Understanding how events work is one of the most important steps in developing Access applications. Utilizing the event procedure allows you to easily customize any type of application. Event procedures also give you the flexibility to develop an open system that can be modified quickly and easily to meet the changing needs of any business environment.

Note that this chapter concentrates on using the event procedure and developing Visual Basic code rather than using macros. This is because procedures are much faster, more flexible, and easier to maintain. Visual Basic also allows you to easily trap any errors that might occur in your application. You can supply your own error messages and prevent the application from crashing (utilizing the Error event and the OnError function), which macros can't do. Unfortunately, there are three macro actions that you can't write into code: Autokeys, Autoexec, and Addmenu. These have no Visual Basic equivalent. Hence, you will be forced to use them. However, you can overcome the Autoexec limitation by having the Autoexec macro action be a one-line Runcode macro that calls your Visual Basic Autoexec function. Using Access's new code, Visual Basic for Applications, you can more easily integrate Access with Microsoft's other products that use Visual Basic as their coding language (such as Word and Excel).

Data Access Objects

25

by James Bettone

In previous chapters you've read how to access data through the Access user interface. Data Access Objects, or DAO, provide a set of objects and collections that enable a developer to create and manipulate database components programmatically. Each object or collection has properties and methods that describe and manipulate these database components. These objects and collections form a hierarchy or hierarchical model of the database and its components that you, the developer, totally control.

This chapter will cover data access objects, the DAO hierarchical model, and the different types of objects and collections that compose the hierarchy. The text will discuss the power of DAO, how to programmatically use the same capabilities of the user interface, and many more topics.

DAO Today

Access 95 and Visual Basic 4.0 introduced DAO 3.0. DAO 3.0 is a fully host-independent set of OLE objects that any OLE-compatible client can use. New properties, methods, and objects have been added, and some have been changed.

With the release of Microsoft Access 95, Microsoft Excel 95, and Microsoft Visual Basic 4.0 (32-bit), DAO 3.0 is a shared resource (usually installed in the \Program Files\Common Files\Microsoft Shared\DAO directory). Any OLE-compatible client can use DAO 3.0, including C developers (using dbDAO and its SDK).

> **NOTE**
>
> DAO is 32-bit in Microsoft Access 95. That is, you can create only 32-bit applications with Access and thus can use only DAO 3.0 (which is 32-bit). DAO 2.5 is not supported in Access 95.

What's Different in DAO 3.0

Some major changes have been made to DAO. If you're converting or porting your application to Access 95, you'll probably want to take full advantage of this new functionality. Following are some of the changes made to DAO (for more information, see the later section "DAO Compatibility" or the online Help for DAO):

- DBEngine—IniPath property: Windows 95 and Windows NT no longer support the use of INI files, but instead store INI-type information in the system registry. IniPath now returns the PATH in the system registry. Here's an example:

```
DBEngine.IniPath = "HKEY_CURRENT_USER\Software\VB and VBA Program
➥Settings\MYDBApp"
```

■ Recordset object: Rows from a Recordset object can now be retrieved into an array using the GetRow method. That is, to populate an array with records from a recordset, you would normally have to iterate through the recordset. With the GetRow method, shown in Listing 25.1, you can now retrieve whole blocks of records or smaller blocks.

Listing 25.1. An example of the GetRow method.

```
Public Sub GetRowsSample()
    Dim dbsDatabase As Database, rstSampleRecordSet As Recordset
    Dim varMyRecords As Variant, iCount As Integer

    Set dbsDatabase = CurrentDb()
    ' Place this all on one line
    Set rstSampleRecordSet = dbsDatabase.OpenRecordset("SELECT FirstName, " &
    ➥"LastName, Title FROM Employees", dbOpenSnapshot)

    varMyRecords = rstSampleRecordSet.GetRows(3)

    Debug.Print "First Name", "Last Name", "Title"

    ' The first subscript of the array identifies the Fields
    ' collection (moves horizontally across the record)
    ' Print the first field in the first record
    Debug.Print varMyRecords(0, 0),

    ' Print the second field in the first record
    Debug.Print varMyRecords(1, 0),

    ' Print the third field in the first record
    Debug.Print varMyRecords(2, 0)

    ' The second subscript of the array identifies the record number
    ' (moves vertically through records)
    ' Print the first field in the second record
    Debug.Print varMyRecords(0, 1),

    ' Print the second field in the second record
    Debug.Print varMyRecords(1, 1),

    ' Print the third field in the second record
    Debug.Print varMyRecords(2, 1)

End Sub
```

■ Container/Document object AllPermissions property: This property returns the permissions pertaining to each of the objects (either a Document object or a Container object) that the user or the user's group has access to. AllPermissions differs from Permissions in that it includes the permissions for the group as well as permissions for the user. If the UserName property is set to a group, AllPermissions and Permissions function the same.

- Replication: This is a new feature of Access 95 and DAO that allows for replication of databases. For more information, refer to Chapter 39, "Replication."

- Backward compatibility: Access 95 supports both DAO 3.0 and DAO 2.0 and includes a compatibility layer for older applications. If you're porting your application to Access 95, the DAO 2.5/3.0 Compatibility Library will automatically be selected. You can either use the DAO 2.5/3.0 Compatibility Library for compatibility with older versions of DAO or deselect this reference to use the DAO 3.0 library only. The latter choice removes support for the older objects, properties, and methods.

The DAO Hierarchy

DAO in Access 95 is a set of OLE objects that represent the functionality of the Jet engine. This layer of objects sits between your application and the database you're trying to manipulate. This insulates you, the developer, from the complexities of database programming while providing a high level of flexibility and control.

Each object in the DAO is actually a class. A class is not unlike a data type. You dimension an object as type class just as you dimension a variable as some data type. Here's an example:

```
Dim MyWorkSpace As Workspace
Dim iCount As Integer
```

Because in this chapter most of the discussion is about objects you create and manipulate, the term "object" is used rather than "class" to keep things clear.

Each of the data access objects has its own properties that help define it and methods that manipulate it, and almost every object has its own collections. Collections are simply a means for an object to contain other like objects. In other words, an object can have a collection that contains other objects with collections that contain other objects, and so forth. This is how the hierarchy is implemented—through collections. For more on objects, properties, methods, and collections, see Chapter 23, "Visual Basic for Applications."

DBEngine

The DBEngine object, shown in Figure 25.1, is the top object in the DAO hierarchy. It is a predefined object and it can't be created. The DBEngine object represents and directly manipulates the Jet Database Engine. There is only one instance of the DBEngine object per application. The DBEngine object therefore isn't an element of a collection; it is the object that contains everything else.

> **NOTE**
>
> Before version 3.0, you could have only up to 10 instances of the DBEngine object. In version 3.0 this limitation is removed, and you can run as many instances as you want.

FIGURE 25.1.

The DBEngine object.

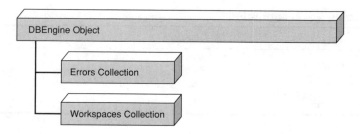

The DBEngine object can be used to compact or repair databases, register ODBC databases, get the Jet version number, and set the login timeout. Errors that occur from DAO actions will be placed into the DBEngine object's Errors collection. Table 25.1 shows the methods, properties, and collections of the DBEngine object.

Table 25.1. Methods, properties, and collections of the DBEngine object.

Methods	Properties	Collections
CompactDatabase	DefaultPassword	Errors
CreateWorkSpace	DefaultUser	Workspaces (default)
Idle	IniPath	Properties
RepairDatabase	Version	
RegisterDatabase	LoginTimeOut	
	SystemDB	

Errors

The Error object, shown in Figure 25.2, receives all errors when an action or activity performed by DAO fails. The collection is cleared, and all errors that occurred are placed into the collection. This action is taken because multiple errors might occur during a given activity or action by DAO. Errors in the Errors collection are ordered by Error number; that is, the Error with the lowest number is the first element, the next higher Error is the next element, and so forth. Error handling for this collection is discussed later in this chapter. Table 25.2 shows the properties and collections of the Error object.

Table 25.2. Properties and collections of the Error object.

Properties	Collection
Description	Properties
HelpContext	

continues

Table 25.2. continued

Properties	*Collection*
HelpFile	
Number	
Source	

FIGURE 25.2.

The Errors collection and the Error object.

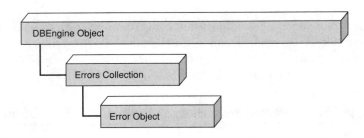

Workspaces

To define a session for the user, use the Workspace object, shown in Figure 25.3. This object contains all open databases for the user and a transaction scope for that user. Transactions within a Workspace object are global across all databases for that Workspace object. Access by default creates a Workspaces(0) object. If there is no security setup for the current database, the Name property is set to #Default Workspace#, and the UserName property is set to Admin. This is commonly referred to as the default Workspace.

FIGURE 25.3.

The Workspaces collection and the Workspace object.

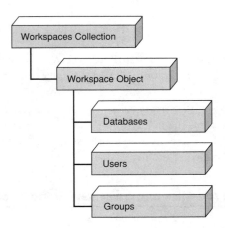

The Workspaces collection is a collection of all Workspace objects. Table 25.3 shows the methods, properties, and collections of the Workspace object.

Table 25.3. Methods, properties, and collections of the Workspace object.

Methods	Properties	Collections
BeginTrans	IsolateODBCTrans	Databases (default)
Close	Name	Groups
CommitTrans	UserName	Properties
CreateDatabase		Users
CreateGroup		
CreateUser		
OpenDatabase		
Rollback		

Databases

The Database object, shown in Figure 25.4, represents a database that has been opened by or created with DAO. If you use the CreateDatabase method of the Workspace object, the database is automatically appended to the Databases collection. Closing the Database object (using the Close method) removes it from the Databases collection.

FIGURE 25.4.

The Databases collection and the Database object.

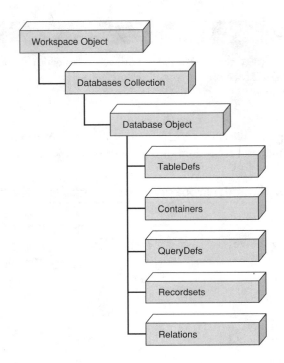

The Database collection is a collection of all the Database objects opened by DAO, including the current database that was opened by Access. It's important to note that the "internal" or hidden databases (wizards, system.mda, and so on) used by Access aren't in this collection and aren't accessible through this collection.

> **NOTE**
>
> Databases(0) is the current database opened by Access every time. You can always use the CurrentDB object, which is the same as DBEngine.Workspaces(0).Databases(0).

Table 25.4 shows the methods, properties, and collections of the Database object.

Table 25.4. Methods, properties, and collections of the Database object.

Methods	Properties	Collections
Close	CollatingOrder	Containers
CreateProperty	Connect	Properties
CreateQueryDef	Name	QueryDefs

Methods	Properties	Collections
CreateRelation	QueryTimeout	Recordsets
CreateTableDef	RecordsAffected	Relations
Execute	Transactions	TableDefs (default)
MakeReplica	Updatable	
OpenRecordset	V1xNullBehavior	
Synchronize	Version	

Users

Each User object represents users that exist in the workgroup database (see Figure 25.5). The User object represents a user account as defined in the workgroup database. For more information on security, see Chapter 30, "Security." Table 25.5 shows the methods, properties, and collections of the User object.

FIGURE 25.5.

The Users collection and the User object.

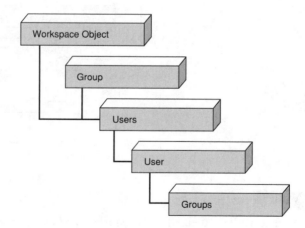

Table 25.5. Methods, properties, and collections of the User object.

Methods	Properties	Collections
CreateGroup	Name	Groups (default)
NewPassword	Password	Properties
	PID	

Groups

Like the User object, the Group object (shown in Figure 25.6) represents groups that have been defined in the workgroup database. A Group object usually represents groups of users and their appropriate security. Each user in a group is represented by a User object in the Users collection of the Group. For more information on security, see Chapter 30. Table 25.6 shows the methods, properties, and collections of the Group object.

Table 25.6. Methods, properties, and collections of the Group object.

Methods	Properties	Collections
CreateUser	Name	Users (default)
	PID	Properties

FIGURE 25.6.

The Groups collection and the Group object.

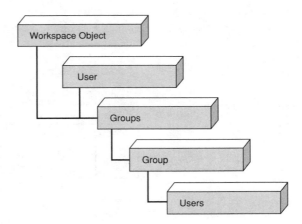

QueryDefs

Each query that has been defined in Access or created using CreateQueryDef is represented by a QueryDef object in the QueryDefs collection (see Figure 25.7). With the QueryDef object, you can create Recordset objects, add your own properties (more on this topic later), pull out the SQL, tell whether it returns records, or just execute it. Because QueryDefs are precompiled SQL statements, they generally run faster than dynamic SQL (Jet doesn't have to compile it on-the-fly). You can create queries with the CreateQueryDef method. Table 25.7 shows the methods, properties, and collections of the QueryDef object.

FIGURE 25.7.

The QueryDefs collection and the QueryDef object.

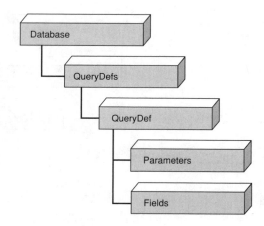

Table 25.7. Methods, properties, and collections of the QueryDef object.

Methods	Properties	Collections
CreateProperty	Connect	Fields
Execute	DateCreated	Parameters (default)
OpenRecordset	LastUpdated	Properties
	LogMessages	
	Name	
	ODBCTimeout	
	RecordsAffected	
	ReturnsRecords	
	SQL	
	Type	
	Updatable	

TableDefs

TableDef objects represent tables or stored table definitions in a given database (see Figure 25.8). The table can be in the current database or in an attached table from an external database. With the TableDef object, you can tell whether the table is attached, its validation rules, whether it is updatable, or the number of records in the table. Table 25.8 shows the methods, properties, and collections of the TableDef object.

FIGURE 25.8.

The TableDefs collection and the TableDef object.

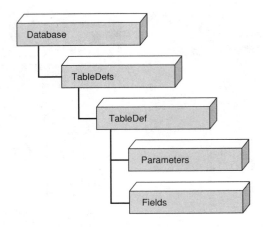

> **NOTE**
>
> When a table is attached, the properties that define its definition are read-only. You must go back to the source database (where the table resides) and make changes there.

Table 25.8. Methods, properties, and collections of the TableDef object.

Methods	Properties	Collections
CreateField	Attributes	Fields (default)
CreateIndex	ConflictTable	Indexes
CreateProperty	Connect	Properties
OpenRecordset	DateCreated	
RefreshLink	LastUpdated	
	Name	
	RecordCount	
	SourceTableName	
	Updatable	
	ValidationRule	
	ValidationText	

Indexes

Indexes of a recordset or tabledef are represented by the Index object, shown in Figure 25.9. This way, the developer can set the index for a table, for instance, just by referring to an index in the Indexes collection. Table 25.9 shows the methods, properties, and collections of the Index object.

FIGURE 25.9.

The Indexes collection and the Index object.

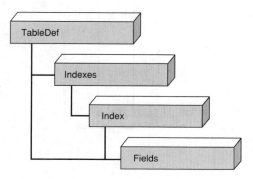

Table 25.9. Methods, properties, and collections of the Index object.

Methods	*Properties*	*Collections*
CreateField	Clustered	Properties
CreateProperty	DistinctCount	Fields (default)
	Foreign	
	IgnoreNulls	
	Name	
	Primary	
	Required	
	Unique	

Fields

Field objects represent common columns of data sharing similar properties and a common data type (see Figure 25.10). Relation, Recordset, TableDef, QueryDef, and Index objects all have a Fields collection. For instance, if you're looking at a table using Access, each column of information is a field and is represented by a field object. The attributes of a field are represented by the different properties (and can be modified) as well as the *value* of the field. Table 25.10 shows the methods, properties, and collections of the Fields object.

FIGURE 25.10.

The Fields collection and the Field object.

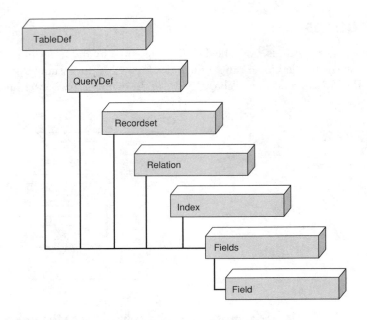

Table 25.10. Methods, properties, and collections of the Field object.

Methods	Properties	Collection
AppendChunk	AllowZeroLength	Properties
CreateProperty	Attributes	
FieldSize	CollatingOrder	
GetChunk	DataUpdatable	
	DefaultValue	
	ForeignName	
	Name	
	OrdinalPosition	
	Required	
	Size	
	SourceField	
	SourceTable	
	Type	
	ValidateOnSet	
	ValidationRule	
	ValidationText	
	Value	

Recordsets

The Recordset object, shown in Figure 25.11, is probably the most used and also the most powerful object DAO provides. With this object, you can programmatically access Jet tables as well as attached tables from SQL Server, Oracle, or an ISAM database. This type of object is somewhat different from the other objects in that it is created each time your application runs and you create recordsets. These objects are never stored on disk—or anywhere, for that matter. They're just temporary.

NOTE

The properties, methods, and collections of a Recordset object vary depending on the *type* of the recordset. See the DAO online Help for a complete listing of properties, methods, and collections for this object.

FIGURE 25.11.

The Recordsets collection and the Recordset object.

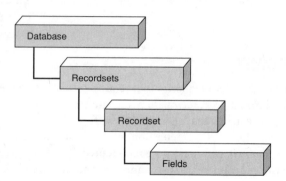

Relations

All relations of an Access database are represented by a Relation object, shown in Figure 25.12. A relation is defined as a relationship between fields in two or more tables. The Relations collection contains all the defined relationships for that Database object. For more information on creating and manipulating relationships from Access 95, see Chapter 6, "Relationships." Table 25.11 shows the methods, properties, and collections of the Relation object.

Table 25.11. Methods, properties, and collections of the Relation object.

Methods	Properties	Collection
CreateField	Attributes	Fields (default)
ForeignTable	Properties	

continues

Table 25.11. continued

Methods	Properties	Collection
	Name	
	Table	

FIGURE 25.12.

The Relations collection and the Relation object.

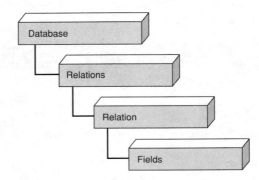

Parameters

In Access, you can define queries that require formal parameters and supply these parameters at runtime. Formal or *explicit* parameters are parameters that have been defined in a query's SQL using the PARAMETERS keyword. These formal parameters are represented in the Parameters collection by the Parameter object, shown in Figure 25.13. It's important to note that *explicit,* not *implicit,* parameters are represented. The Parameter object only provides information on existing parameters. You cannot append or delete objects from the Parameters collection. Table 25.12 shows the properties and collections of the Parameter object.

FIGURE 25.13.

The Parameters collection and the Parameter object.

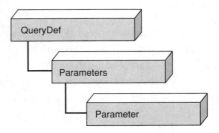

Table 25.12. Properties and collections of the Parameter object.

Properties	Collection
Name	Properties
Type	
Value	

Containers

Using Container objects is one way DAO achieves its application independence (see the "Using DAO" section later in this chapter). The Container object, shown in Figure 25.14, stores such items as Access forms, databases, and modules. This object is generic enough to store these types of objects yet flexible enough to maintain independence from any one application. Table 25.13 shows the properties and collections of the Container object.

Table 25.13. Properties and collections of the Container object.

Properties	Collections
AllPermissions	Documents (default)
Inherit	Properties
Name	
Owner	
Permissions	
UserName	

FIGURE 25.14.

The Containers collection and the Container object.

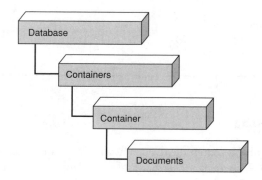

Documents

The Document object, shown in Figure 25.15, represents each *individual* application object (such as forms, modules, or tables). For instance, when you created your database, DAO created a Forms Container that contains a Document object for each form in the database. Table 25.14 shows the properties and collections of the Document object.

FIGURE 25.15.
The Documents collection and the Document object.

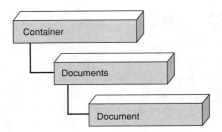

Table 25.14. Properties and collections of the Document object.

Properties	Collection
AllPermissions	Properties
Container	
DateCreated	
KeepLocal	
LastUpdated	
Name	
Owner	
Permissions	
Replicable	
UserName	

Properties

A Property object represents the characteristics of an object (see Figure 25.16). Every object in DAO has a Properties collection, and each Property object can be a built-in or user-defined characteristic. The developer can manipulate these properties at runtime and can even add new properties using the CreateProperty method.

FIGURE 25.16.
The Properties collection and the Property object.

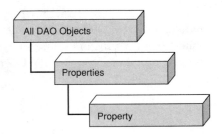

User-defined properties are properties added at runtime to a specific instance of an object. It's important to note that properties added to an object type are for only that instance of that object type. The developer is responsible for setting and changing values in user-defined properties. This is the only type of property that can be deleted from the Properties collection; built-in properties cannot be deleted. Table 25.15 shows the properties and collections of the Property object.

Table 25.15. Properties and collections of the Property object.

Properties	Collection
Inherited	Properties
Name	
Type	
Value	

Using DAO

Now that you understand the hierarchy, you can get down to the basics of using DAO. By now you're comfortable with accessing data through Access 95's user interface or by using the built-in data control of a form. When you use the user interface to manipulate the database (creating queries, adding or creating tables, and so on), Access 95 calls Jet directly; that is, it doesn't hand off the request to DAO. The only time Access 95 uses DAO is in a code module. Refer to Figure 25.17 to see where DAO sits in relation to your application or database.

FIGURE 25.17.

The application object model.

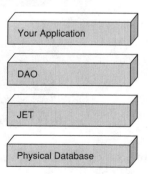

DAO can now be accessed from any OLE-compatible client (Microsoft Visual Basic 4.0 32-bit, Microsoft Excel 95, or Microsoft Access 95), and all the objects, properties, and methods are exposed to the developer as an OLE in-process server.

In-process servers are OLE Automation servers that are compiled as DLLs and share the same process space as the calling (your) application. What is the difference between a DLL and an OLE server? An OLE server exposes all its object, properties, and methods to the developer (just like a DLL), but an OLE server also exposes descriptions and explanations of each object, property, and method in an associated *type library*.

You can browse the type libraries of all the OLE servers in your application during design time by using the Object Browser, shown in Figure 25.18. The Object Browser is available from the Access 95 Toolbar, by pressing F2, or by selecting View | Object Browser. For more help on using the Object Browser, see Chapter 23.

With the Object Browser, you can navigate through the DAO hierarchy and see each property and method for each object in the hierarchy. This feature is useful because it offers Help, an example, and a paste function that enables you to paste the method or property (or collection) into your code.

Objects and Collections

The concept of objects and collections is very important in DAO. In the hierarchy (see the earlier section "The DAO Hierarchy"), most objects have collections which contain that object type's members. For instance, the DBEngine object has a collection of Workspaces that contain individual Workspace objects. Most objects are part of a collection that has objects, which in turn can have collections.

FIGURE 25.18.

The Object Browser.

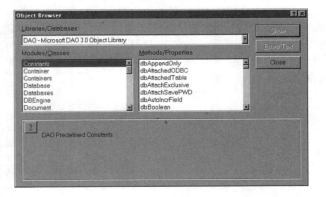

Usually in the OO (object-oriented) world, a collection is the plural of the object type that the collection contains. For example, the Workspaces collection contains Workspace objects. Notice that the collection (Workspaces) is the plural of the object (Workspace) it contains. This information is useful when you don't know the name of an object's collection—if, for example, the DBEngine has a collection of Workspace objects, and you want to use that collection (just make "Workspace" plural and you've got it).

Declaring DAO

To use DAO, you first must declare an object variable of whatever object type you want to use. As mentioned earlier, although DAO is actually a hierarchy of classes, this chapter refers to the classes as objects to avoid confusion. Classes are usually a type of object that you declare something as and can't use directly. For example, I don't have an object called Workspace, but instead have a variable wksMyWorkspace of the Workspace type or class:

```
Dim wksMyWorkspace as Workspace
```

Object Variables

Due to the nature of DAO's hierarchical structure, it could become cumbersome to keep referring to objects through the DAO hierarchy. This is where something called object variables comes in. Object variables are simply a pointers or references to another object. Using an object variable instead of using the hierarchy directly will make your code more readable and easier to type (no more typing those long references!). The downside of using object variables is that dereferencing occurs at runtime, and this timing could cause some rather tricky debugging situations. Overall, the advantages outweigh the negatives, and you should always use object variables if you're referencing a property more than once. Here's an example:

```
Dim rstMyRecordset As Recordset, strName As String, strConnect As String
Dim iCount As Integer, strUpdatable As String, dbsMyDatabase As Database
Set dbsMyDatabase = CurrentDb
' This is the SLOW method (DON'T DO THIS)
' References get resolved through each iteration
For iCount = 1 To 10
    Debug.Print dbsMyDatabase.Name

Next


' This is the FAST method
' References get resolved just once
strName = dbsMyDatabase.Name
For iCount = 1 To 10
    Debug.Print strName

Next

' Use the With when refering to the same object a bunch of times
With dbsMyDatabase
    strUpdatable = .Updatable
    strName = .Name
    strConnect = .Connect

End With
```

DAO Unleashed

DAO is broken down into two parts: Data Definition Language, or DDL, and Data Manipulation Language, or DML. DDL is the part of DAO that *defines* the database, its objects, and its data, whereas DML *manipulates* the database, its objects, and its data. The following discussion covers how to create a database and then manipulate it using DAO.

Creating Databases

Creating databases with DAO is a fairly simple and straightforward process. If you have a good data model driving this process, things will flow that much more smoothly. Too many developers design their data models "on-the-fly," and although this technique might satisfy a deadline, it will probably come back to bite you! The saying "A house is only as good as the foundation" also rings true for databases—a database is only as good as the data model it is designed from (database being a physical database, not a database application). That being said, let the process begin!

> **NOTE**
>
> Access can create only Access Databases (MDBs). ODBC databases must be created in their native environments—Access has the capability only to manipulate these databases, not to create them. For help on creating Access ISAM databases, see the online Help.

Follow these steps to create an Access database using DAO:

1. Declare a database object for the database you want to create:

   ```
   Dim MyNewDatabase as Database
   ```

2. Use the `CreateDatabase` method of the Workspace object to create an empty database and database file:

   ```
   Set MyNewDatabase = WorkSpaces(0).CreateDatabase("MyNewDB")
   ```

3. Define each table in your new database. You should already know which fields and indexes should go into this table (from your data model).

4. Use the `CreateTableDef` method to create each table in the database:

   ```
   Dim tdfNewTable as TableDef

   Set tdfNewTable = MyNewDatabase.CreateTableDef("Employees")
   ```

5. Use the new TableDef object to create fields in the new table by using the `CreateField` method of the Field object. This example creates a number of different fields:

   ```
   Dim fldNewField As Field
   Set fldNewField = tdfNewTable.CreateField("Employee_ID", dbLong)
   fldNewField.Attributes = dbAutoIncrField
   tdfNewTable.Append fldNewField
   ```

```
Set fldNewField = tdfNewTable.CreateField("First_Name", dbText, 25)
fldNewField.Attributes = dbAutoIncrField
tdfNewTable.Append fldNewField

Set fldNewField = tdfNewTable.CreateField("Last_Name", dbText, 25)
fldNewField.Attributes = dbAutoIncrField
tdfNewTable.Append fldNewField
```

6. Now that the Table is defined, append it to the database. This step actually creates the table in your database and appends it to the Database collection. After this step is done, though, you can't make any changes to the appended fields (you can, however, add and delete new ones):

```
MyNewDatabase.Append tdfNewTable
```

7. At this point, you can create one or more indexes using the TableDef object's `CreateIndex` method.

8. Use `CreateIndex` to create an Index object:

```
Dim idxNewIndex As Index

Set idxNewIndex = tdfNewTable.CreateIndex("Employee")
```

9. Use the `CreateField` method of the Index object to create a field object for every indexed field in the Index object and append it to the Index object:

```
Set fldNewField = idxNewIndex.CreateField("Employee_ID")
fldNewField.Primary = True
idxNewIndex.Fields.Append fldNewField
```

10. Now append each Index object to the Indexes collection of the TableDef object using the `Append` method. Your table can have several indexes or no indexes:

```
TdfNewTable.Indexes.Append idxNewIndex
```

You have just created your first database. Using the Access user interface is a much simpler way of accomplishing this task, but it's always good to know how to do it the hard way.

Using the Current Database

Normally, when developing Access applications, you are using the database that was opened from the design environment. DAO has a function called `CurrentDB` that is a pointer to the currently open database. This is a very handy little function to have around—whenever you need to reference the current database, a reference is already established.

`CurrentDB` references the database the same way DBEngine.Workspaces(0).Databases(0) does. You can't close Databases(0) as well as `CurrentDB`. (CurrentDB.Close has no effect and is ignored.) Although the second method is supported in Access 95 and probably will be supported in future versions, it is recommended that you use the `CurrentDB` function instead. Why? The `CurrentDB` function is a lot more friendly in multiuser environments than the older method. `CurrentDB` creates another instance of the open database (similar to using OpenDatabase on the current database) instead of referring to the open instance.

A Special Note on the *Close* Method

The Close method can cause lots of strange problems in an application. Strange problems normally don't pop up until final release of your application. In older version of DAO, the Close method would cause an error if it was used at the wrong time (when you had recordsets open) or if it wasn't used at all (problems were most likely to occur the next time your application was started).

This small section of text is devoted to the Close method because of its new behavior. The discussion starts with some of the new changes for this method. For the most part, the biggest change in this method is what happens when you use it. If you close an open database using the Close method, *all* objects referencing that database will be dereferenced, *any* pending updates or edits will be rolled back, and *all* recordsets against that database will be closed. Any object that falls out of scope will have similar results (if you don't explicitly close the object).

So the gist of the story is that you should always explicitly close your Database, Recordset, TableDef, and Workspace objects.

Handling Errors

Error handling is done with the DBEngine's Errors collection of Error objects. Whenever an error occurs, you can examine the Errors collection for all errors. Basically, the Errors collection holds all errors that occur during an action or transaction, and each error is represented by an Error object. If you're writing a generic error handler, you can examine the Errors collection and report errors (based on an Error table or a basic Select Case statement). Here's an example:

```
On Error Goto ErrorBlock_Err:
Dim dbsMyDatabase as Database, errErrorObject as Error

Set dbsMyDatabase = OpenDatabase("BogusDB.MDB")
dbsMyDatabase.Close
Exit Sub
ErrorBlock_Err:
   For Each errErrorObject in dbsMyDatabase.Errors
        Debug.Print errErrorObject.Description
        Debug.Print errErrorObject.Source
        Debug.Print errErrorObject.Number
   Next
Resume Next
```

DAO Compatibility

With the new improved object model, some of the following objects, methods, and properties are no longer supported in DAO 3.0. Table 25.16 shows the object, method, or property and its corresponding replacement.

Table 25.16. DAO compatibility.

Functionality Not Present in DAO 3.0	Recommended DAO 3.0 Replacement
FreeLocks	Not needed in Access 95
SetDefaultWorkSpace	DBEngine.DefaultUser/DBEngine.DefaultPassword
SetDataAccessOption	DBEngine.IniPath
BeginTrans (Database object)	`BeginTrans` method of the Workspace object
CommitTrans (Database object)	`CommitTrans` method of the Workspace object
RollBack (Database object)	`RollBack` method of the Workspace object
CreateDynaset (Database object)	(Database.)OpenRecordSet of type Dynaset
CreateSnapshot (Database object)	(Database.)OpenRecordSet of type Snapshot
DeleteQueryDef (Database object)	QueryDefs collection's `Delete` method
ExecuteSQL (Database object)	`Execute` method and `RecordsAffected` property of the Database object
ListTables (Database object)	TableDefs collection of the Database object
OpenQueryDef (Database object)	QueryDefs collection of the Database object
OpenTable (Database object)	(Database.)OpenRecordSet of type Table
Table ListIndexes	Indexes collection of the TableDef object
CreateDynaset (QueryDef object)	`OpenRecordset` method of the QueryDef object
CreateSnapshot (QueryDef object)	`OpenRecordset` method of the QueryDef object
ListParameters (QueryDef object)	Parameters collection of the QueryDef object
Dynaset Object	Recordset object of type Dynaset
Snapshot Object	Recordset object of type Snapshot

continues

Table 25.16. continued

Functionality Not Present in DAO 3.0	Recommended DAO 3.0 Replacement
Table Object	Recordset object of type Table
ListFields method (Table, Dynaset, and Snapshot)	Fields collection of the Recordset object
CreateDynaset (QueryDef and Dynaset object)	OpenRecordset method of the object with type Dynaset
CreateSnapshot (QueryDef and Dynaset object)	OpenRecordset method of the object with type Snapshot

If your old project contains some of the older objects, properties, or methods and you just want to convert to Access 95, you can use the Microsoft DAO 2.5/3.0 Compatibility Library. This library provides backward compatibility with older versions of DAO and Jet. To check whether you're using this type library, select Tools | References from a Module window, and look in the References dialog box for the Microsoft DAO 2.5/3.0 Compatibility Library option (see Figure 25.19).

FIGURE 25.19.

The References dialog box.

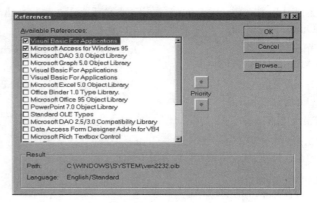

It's important to note that applications or databases converted to Access 95 will automatically reference this type library. Likewise, applications and databases created in Access 95 won't have this reference. If you have an older application and you're not sure whether you're using any of the older objects, deselect the Microsoft DAO 2.5/3.0 Compatibility Library option, and select Run | Compile All Modules while in a Module window. If your application recompiles without errors, you don't have to use the Compatibility Library, shown in Figure 25.20.

FIGURE 25.20.

The Compatibility Library.

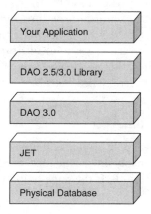

To ensure proper compatibility with future versions of DAO, it is recommended that you convert to DAO 3.0. Your application won't have the additional overhead of another layer, and you won't have to distribute the Compatibility Library with your application.

> **NOTE**
>
> A note on version 2.5 of DAO and Jet: Access 95 won't use DAO 2.5 because it's a fully 32-bit environment. Databases created as 2.5 can be converted to 3.0, or the developer can use the Compatibility Library.

Bang (!) Usage Versus Dot (.) Usage

In the previous version of DAO, you could use either the bang (exclamation point) or the dot (period) separator when referring to members of a collection. In DAO 3.0, most objects don't support the use of the dot separator. Eventually, support for the use of the dot separator will go away (and rolling over to new versions of DAO won't be as easy). Any future applications you develop should therefore use the bang separator only. Here's an example:

```
MyRS!Employee_ID ' This is OK
MyRS.Employee_Name ' This is OK, but not recommended
DBEngine.Workspaces(0) ' No longer supported
DBEngine!Workspaces(0) ' Correct usage
```

Optimizing DAO

The following sections cover some of the actions you can take to improve the performance of your application (strictly related to DAO). It's important to note that although some optimizations might provide a significant performance increase, some or all of the suggestions discussed here might not do anything for your application. Some external factors affect how much you can gain from each suggestion. Identifying key areas of functionality would be a good place to start optimizations—usually, only 10 percent of the code in an application provides 90 percent of the functionality. Start by concentrating on the 10 percent.

Use Object Variables

As stated earlier, whenever your application needs to reference a DAO property, store its value in a variable. This is probably one of the most common mistakes made by Access developers. Here's a simple rule of thumb: If the same object or property is used more than once, use an object variable.

Default Collections

All objects have a default property or collection. This setup might make your code difficult to read (some developers might get confused as to which property you're using if you're referring to the default property or collection). The code will run faster, however, because the compiler doesn't have to resolve an extra reference. For instance, the default collection of the DBEngine object is the Workspaces collection:

```
DBEngine.WorkSpaces(0).Databases(0)
```

You could use this instead:

```
DBEngine(0).Databases or DBEngine(0)(0)
```

The second version refers to the default collection of the DBEngine object. Confusing? Not really, after you learn what the default collections are for each object. After you have done one application using DAO, you get pretty familiar with data access objects.

Refreshing

Avoid refreshing unless you absolutely can't avoid it. Refreshing a collection gives you an up-to-date view of that collection's objects and properties or data, but in a multiuser environment or a speed-critical application, this is a very "expensive" method to use (in other words, it takes a lot of processor time or system resources).

Using Queries

Queries are precompiled SQL stored in Access. When your application uses dynamic SQL (SQL created on-the-fly), Jet still needs to optimize and compile the SQL statement during runtime. If you use queries whenever possible, the optimization and compilation are done beforehand (when the query is created in Access), and you don't suffer the degradation in speed at runtime.

Recordset Snapshots

If your application doesn't need to update data in a recordset, use a snapshot. A snapshot's data is brought locally into your system's memory (except MEMO and OLE fields) and doesn't need the additional overhead for being able to update data. Additionally, if you're ever populating listboxes or combo boxes manually, use the dbForwardOnly option when creating the snapshot. This technique keeps links to only the next record (and realizes more memory savings) and can only go forward through the recordset.

Accessing Remote Databases

Some applications made with Access will be used against a remote database such as SQL Server or Oracle. It's important to note that DAO is optimized for use with Jet and ISAM databases, not remote databases such as SQL Server. If you ever programmatically access a remote database, use RDO rather than DAO (see the next section).

RDO—What It's All About

Probably by now you've heard of a new set of data access objects that support connection to remote data sources such as Microsoft SQL Server or Oracle. In fact, RDO or Remote Data Objects are optimized for manipulation of remote databases and are there for enterprise-wide solutions. RDO is actually an extremely thin layer around the ODBC API and driver manager that exposes all the functionality provided by ODBC, similar to how DAO is implemented.

With RDO, you can take advantage of the powerful, sophisticated query engines of remote databases such as SQL Server and Oracle. The "remote" in "Remote Data Objects" means that queries aren't processed locally and use a minimum of local resources. This means your application can access ODBC data sources without sacrificing performance or flexibility, and even though you can use RDO to access any ODBC data source, it is designed and optimized to take advantage of the sophisticated query engines found in today's remote databases, such as Microsoft and Sybase SQL Server or Oracle.

With RDO you can create simple cursorless or complex cursor result sets, execute different types of stored procedures (procedures that will or will not return result sets, or procedures with or without parameters or return values), and limit the number of rows returned. You have complete control over the executing query because you can watch all the messages and errors generated by the remote database without compromising performance. RDO can do this because it can run either asynchronously or synchronously—that way, your application doesn't have to remain locked while executing large queries. Figure 25.21 shows the RDO and DAO application layers.

FIGURE 25.21.

The RDO and DAO application layers.

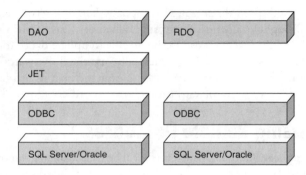

> **NOTE**
>
> Remote Data Controls, or RDC, are not supported in Access 95.

What RDO Means to the Access Developer

As an Access developer, you now have the ability to create enterprise-wide solutions with Access 95 that take advantage of the speed and power of the remote server. Like DAO, RDO is an application-independent set of objects that sits between your application and the database. The hierarchy of RDO is very similar to DAO, making it easy for the Access developer to convert to RDO. Table 25.17 lists the DAO objects and their equivalent objects in RDO.

Table 25.17. DAO objects and their equivalent RDO objects.

DAO Object	RDO Object	Comments
DBEngine	rdoEngine	Top-level object
Workspace	rdoEnvironment	Same functionality as object and collection

DAO Object	RDO Object	Comments
Database	rdoConnection	Same functionality as object and collection
Recordset	rdoResultset	Same functionality as object and collection
Snapshot-type Recordset	Static-type rdoResultset	Same functionality as object and collection
Dynaset-type Recordset	Keyset-type rdoResultset	Same functionality as object and collection
Not implemented	Dynamic-type rdoResultset	No equivalent in DAO
Table-type Recordset	Not implemented	No equivalent in RDO
Not implemented	Forward-only-type rdoResultset	No equivalent in DAO
Forward-only-scrolling	Not implemented type Recordset	No equivalent in RDO
Field	rdoColumn	Same functionality as object and collection
QueryDef	rdoPreparedStatement	Same functionality as object and collection
TableDef	rdoTable	Same functionality as object and collection
Parameter	rdoParameter	Same functionality as object and collection
Error	rdoError	Same functionality as object and collection
Record	row	Terminology
Field	column	Terminology

In most respects, the biggest difference between DAO and RDO objects is in their respective Recordset objects. In DAO a recordset could possibly span a whole table, whereas in RDO this would be impractical. You should always limit your recordsets to what's really needed—RDO enforces this rule in a way by not allowing whole table views. Also, an RDO forward-only result set similar to the DAO forward-only snapshot *can* be updatable, whereas the DAO equivalent cannot.

Because RDO has been implemented in a manner similar to DAO, you can, for the most part, take an existing application using DAO and with minimum changes, morph over to RDO. But *buyer beware:* you need to keep in mind that there are some differences because of the way RDO has been designed and implemented for use with relational databases. Remember, the "remote" in RDO means that processing happens on the remote database's server—in other words, RDO has no query engine but instead relies on the remote database to process all queries and return result sets.

ODBC or RDO?

By now you're probably wondering about using the ODBC API directly and not even messing with RDO. It's important to remember that both RDO and ODBC have the same functionality. The savings come from RDO's being a RAD (Rapid Application Development) tool. Most of the savings from RDO are in development time and code development. RDO has been thoroughly tested and optimized to do its job. Each time you develop an application, you have a fully tested set of objects you can use in your application.

Legal Issues

Unlike DAO, RDO isn't part of Access 95 or any of its components, and thus tricky legal issues are involved in distributing solutions with RDO and Access 95. In fact, to get RDO installed on your machine, you must have Visual Basic 4.0, Enterprise Edition, installed. But having that edition of Visual Basic still doesn't give you the legal right to distribute RDO solutions through Access 95; it only gives you the ability to use them in your application. You can distribute RDO solutions only with the Visual Basic 4.0, Enterprise Edition.

The solution to this dilemma is to create an in-process OLE server with Visual Basic that uses RDO, and then you can call this server from your solution code. If you do this, welcome to the world of three-tier client/server computing!

> **NOTE**
>
> Using an in-process OLE server won't slow down RDO. In-process servers share the same process space as the calling application. When the server is in process, it doesn't have to manage anything (it's managed by the calling application)—it just has to do its thing!

Summary

This chapter discussed the use of RDO and Access 95. Some applications created with Access will be used against a remote database such as SQL Server or Oracle. It's important to note that DAO is optimized for use with Jet and ISAM databases, not remote databases such as SQL Server. If you ever programmatically access a remote database, use RDO rather than DAO.

Menus and Toolbars

26

by Dwayne Gifford

When you're developing an application in Access, you generally work with the default toolbars and menus. It is the goal of this chapter to give you an understanding of how to add or change the menus and toolbars for an Access application.

This chapter focuses on how you can use the Menu Builder and the macro environment to create or modify menus. You will also learn how to modify a toolbar and how to add a new toolbar.

Using the Menu Builder

The Menu Builder, a Wizard that is shipped with Access, is a step-by-step assistant that helps you create and edit menus for your Access applications. If you're creating a menu, the Menu Builder generates the required macros to create the menus when the application runs. In order to edit a menu, you must have a menu macro already in the database.

To start the Menu Builder, select Tools | Add-ins | Menu Builder. A dialog will appear with all the macros that are currently in the database (if there are any).

Adding a New Menu

To add a new menu, click the New button. The dialog box shown in Figure 26.1 will appear.

FIGURE 26.1.

Selecting the type of menu to model.

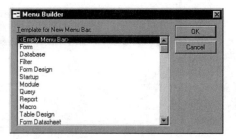

This dialog lets you select a template that the new menu will be based on. There are 16 available templates to select from—15 different Access menu templates and an empty menu bar template (the default). When you select any of the Access menu bar templates, you create a menu system that will function just like the equivalent Access menu. But just because you select one of the Access menu templates doesn't mean you have to use what it comes with. You can add or remove menu items as you wish. Selecting the empty menu option lets you set up an empty menu bar that you can add items to. Figure 26.2 shows you what the Menu Builder dialog looks like when you select Empty Menu Bar as the template.

At the moment, the only option available is the Caption text box. The name you type here will become the first-level menu name and will appear on the far left of the new menu. To start the process, type &File. The & makes the F the shortcut key. The & won't appear on the menu as a character. Instead, it will cause the F in File to be underlined. To have a message appear on the status bar at the bottom of the Access window when the menu item is activated, type the message in the Status Bar Text box. To have the File item appear in the menu list at the bottom of the dialog, click the Next button. Figure 26.3 shows what the dialog looks like after you fill in the information just discussed.

FIGURE 26.2.

The Menu Builder dialog.

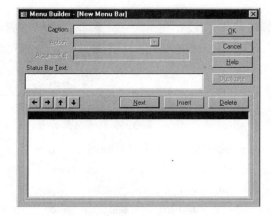

FIGURE 26.3.

The Menu Builder dialog with the file information.

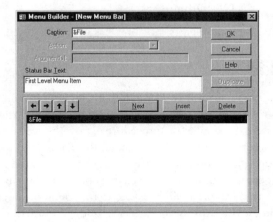

What you have created is a first-level menu item. The next step is to create a second-level menu item. In Access you can create a 10-level menu system. To add the item that will appear below File, click the arrow button that is pointing to the right (directly below the Status Bar Text box). You will see three periods appear under &File, letting you know that you're creating a second-level menu item. Enter the caption for the new second-level menu item in the Caption text box. For this example, type &Open and then press the Tab key to move to the Action combo box. Click the drop-down arrow to see the three choices—DoMenuItem, RunCode, and RunMacro. If you don't select one of the actions and its argument now, the macro for the File menu item will be created, but it will be created as an empty macro.

DoMenuItem

When you select the DoMenuItem option from the Action combo box, you will observe that the Argument(s) text box gets filled in with Form;File;New Database..., which is the first menu item available for Access. In order to change this entry, click on the three dots to the right of the Argument(s) text box. This will take you to the dialog box shown in Figure 26.4.

FIGURE 26.4.

The DoMenuItem Arguments dialog.

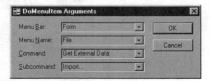

Here you can select any of the menu commands that Access has available. Follow these steps:

1. Select a menu item from the Menu Bar list box.
2. From the Menu Name list box, select the menu that contains the command you want.
3. Select the command you want to run.
4. In the Subcommand list box, select the subcommand for the current command.
5. Click the OK button.

Notice that the Argument(s) box now has your item listed.

RunCode

When you select RunCode from the Action combo box, you will observe that the Argument(s) text box is not filled in and that there is no button with three dots for you to click. Here you are expected to remember the procedure name. A procedure name refers to the name of a function that you have created in VBA code. Also remember that following a procedure name you need to type (). If you're not sure exactly how the name is spelled, simply type any letter. If you don't enter at least one letter for this option, the menu item won't get created. When you type one letter, the entry will be added to the Menu macro, and you will be able to go into the macro and use the Expression Builder to find your function name. Remember that the expression will show you only functions that aren't located in VBA code of a form. But also remember that if the form is the active form when the function is called, a function of the form can be called.

RunMacro

When you select RunMacro from the Action combo box, you will observe that the Argument(s) text box is not filled in and that there is no button with three dots for you to click. Here you are expected to remember the macro name. The macro name could be just the name of a macro object. But if you have macros inside the macro object, you will need to reference it with `MacroName.MacroNames`. For more information on creating macros, refer to Chapter 19, "Creating Access Macros." Again, if you're unsure of the name at this point, type any letter. You will see later how you can go back and change this. If you don't enter at least one letter for this option, the menu item won't get created.

Now, change the action to `DoMenuItem` without changing the Argument(s) box. After you have done this, you should have a first-level menu option of `&File` and a second-level menu option of `&Open`. You will now add one more menu item. Type `&Close` in the Caption box and type `RunMacro` in the Action box. Because you're unsure of the macro name, simply type any letter as the macro name. Now click OK. You will be prompted for the menu bar name. In this case, type `Test` and click OK. You are returned to the Database window, where you will see two new macros named Test and Test_File. When you're creating a menu system for Access, it will create a new macro for each menu level. In this case, you have only one level—File. Let's say you had a two-level menu system and under File was an option called Get External Data that opened another menu. The Menu Builder would build three macros—id Test, Test_File, and Test_File_Get External Data.

Editing a Menu

To edit a menu, open the Menu Builder. This time, instead of clicking the New button, you need to activate the Main Menu macro by clicking on it in the list of macros. Then click the Edit button instead. Because you created Test, you should select the macro named Test, not Test_File. If you select Test_File, you will run into a problem in which you're working on a first-level menu item but the Menu Builder thinks you're adding a new first-level menu item. Figure 26.5 shows what Menu Builder looks like when you're editing a previously built menu.

FIGURE 26.5.

The Menu Builder dialog with a previously built menu.

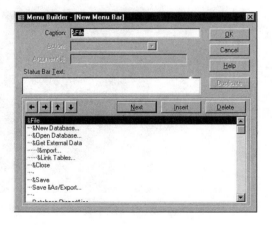

In this figure, I've created a new menu based on the template Form. Notice that it defaults to the first item in the list, and that the menu item list has all the items you would see if you had a form active and you clicked a menu option. When you're working with the Menu Builder dialog, you can edit menu items by clicking on them and changing either their actions or their arguments. You can remove an item by selecting the item you want to remove from the menu and clicking the Delete button. To add a new menu item, select the item that you want the new menu item to appear before, and then click the Insert button to move the selected item down one. This also will default the new item to be the same level as the selected item before you clicked the Insert button.

Modifying Menus Through Macros

Using the macro editor, you will add a first-level option of Edit and a second-level option of Undo. To do this, open the macro named Test by activating the Macro tab in the Database window and then selecting the macro named Test. Click the Design button. Notice that the first item is `Addmenu` and that the menu name at the bottom of the Macro window is `&File`. To add a new level-one option, follow these steps:

1. Click on the line just below the first Addmenu.
2. In the Action field, select Addmenu from the combo box.
3. In the Menu name box at the bottom of the Macro window, type `&Edit`.
4. In the Menu Macro Name box, type `Test_Edit`. Figure 26.6 gives you an idea of what these first four steps would look like.

FIGURE 26.6.

Adding an Edit menu option to the Test macro.

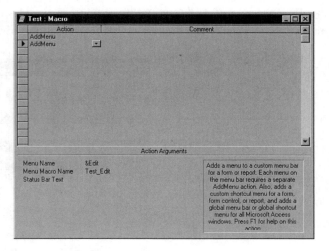

5. Save the macro by selecting File | Save.

6. Close the Macro window by selecting File | Close.

In the Menu Macro Name text box, you typed in a macro that is not yet in the database. If you had already created this macro, you could have selected it from the drop-down combo box. Remember that Menu Builder adds a new menu for each level in the menu system. So, if you're going to add a new level one, you must add a new macro. To add the new level-two option to the level-one item of Edit, you need to add the macro Test_Edit. Follow these steps:

1. Click the Macro tab in the Database window.

2. Click the New button.

3. Select DoMenuItem from the Action combo box.

4. In the Menu Bar field, select Form.

5. In the Menu Macro Name field, select Edit.

6. In the Command box, select Undo.

7. You need to add a macro name for this item. If the Macro Name field isn't visible, click View Macro Name. In this case, you need a macro name of &Undo.

8. Now select File | Save and give the macro the name you typed in earlier—Test_Edit.

9. Close the Macro window by selecting File | Close.

By adding the macro name in the macro of &Undo, you have told Menu edit to use the name Undo as a menu option when Edit is selected.

To change the RunMacro field from a macro that is not in the database to one that is, you need to make the change to the macro Test_File. Because this macro isn't in the database, follow these steps:

1. Click the Macro tab.

2. Click the New button.

3. Select Close from the Action combo box.

4. In this case, leave the Action arguments as they are.

5. Select File | Save and give the macro the name you typed in earlier—Test_File_Close.

6. Close the Macro window by selecting File | Close.

Now that you've added the macro, it's time to edit the Macro_File. This is where you told the MenuItem Close to do a RunMacro and the macro name was saved as a letter. In the Database window, select the Macro tab (if it isn't already active), select the macro named Test_File, and click the Design button. The Macro Names option for this macro is turned off, but you can turn it on either by selecting View | Macro Names or by selecting the action of RunMacro. If the macro name says Change, change it to File_Close.

For details on how to use your menus instead of the Access menus, refer to Chapter 28, "Putting It All Together."

Creating and Modifying Toolbars

Windows usually has three ways of accomplishing any operation—using hot keys, a menu item, or a toolbar. The next sections discuss how to create and modify toolbars.

Creating a Toolbar

To add a new toolbar to the current database, first you must open the Toolbars dialog, shown in Figure 26.7, by selecting View | Toolbars.

FIGURE 26.7.

The Toolbars dialog.

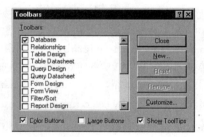

In this dialog you will see all the toolbars that Access comes with, as well as any toolbars that are local to the current database. To add a new toolbar, click the New button. The Name the Toolbar dialog will appear. Type the name you want the new toolbar to have. In this case, call it TestToolbar. After you have typed the name and clicked OK, again you will see the Toolbars dialog, where the new toolbar you just added will be the active item.

Modifying a Toolbar

To add new buttons to a toolbar, click the Customize button in the Toolbars dialog. You will see the dialog shown in Figure 26.8.

For this example, you will add the Test_Undo macro to a button on the new toolbar. Follow these steps:

1. In the Categories list, select All Macros.

2. In the Objects list, select Test_Undo.

3. To add Test_Edit to the new toolbar, left-click on Test_Edit, drag it to the new toolbar, and let go of the mouse button.

FIGURE 26.8.

The Customize Tool-bars dialog.

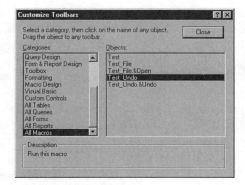

A button will appear on the toolbar. Now that you've added the button, you should give it a more understandable image than the default. Follow these steps:

1. Right-click the new button and select Choose Button Image.

2. Figure 26.9 appears, giving you two choices. You can choose one of the many images available or you can use a word for the image. In this case, use the word Undo on the button face. To do this, type Undo in the text box at the bottom of the dialog.

FIGURE 26.9.

The Choose Button Image dialog.

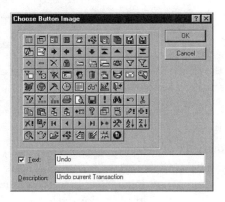

3. If you want a more meaningful tool tip than the default that is assigned, change the current text in the Description box.

There is only one way to have a function run from a toolbar, and that is to create a macro that has an action of `RunCode` and that has the function name entered in the Function Name text box. Here is a sample function that closes the active object:

```
Function FormCloseActive()
    DoCmd.Close
End Function
```

Then, in the File_Close macro, you need to change the action from RunCode to Close, and the procedure name should be FormCloseActive(). In order for the toolbar to call this function, you need to add a button to the TestToolbar by following the steps you saw earlier that showed you how to add a button to the toolbar. But this time, add the File_Close macro instead of Test_Undo. Now, when you click the Close Toolbar button you just added, it will close the active object—not a good move if the active object happens to be the Database window. For the best way to close and open objects, refer to Chapter 28. If you don't remember the name of the macro, click the three dots to the left of the Function Name text box to open the Expression Builder, shown in Figure 26.10.

FIGURE 26.10.

The Expression Builder dialog.

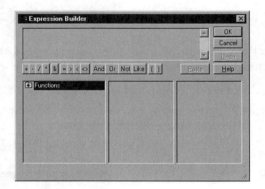

The Expression Builder lets you explore all the built-in Access functions, loaded Wizard functions, and all the functions of the current database. Follow these steps to use the Expression Builder to select the function FormCloseActive:

1. Double-click Functions to expand the list of available databases from which to select functions.

2. Select your current database.

3. In the middle window you will see a list of available modules for the currently selected database, as shown in Figure 26.11. In this example, my function is in the mdlUtil function. To see available functions, select the module where your function is located. If you're not sure, you can click each module. A list of functions will appear for each module in the right window.

4. After you've found the function you want to use, double-click the function name. It will appear in the upper window, followed by ().

5. To make the macro use this function, click OK. This is also how you would change any functions that you added through the Menu Builder earlier.

FIGURE 26.11.

The Expression Builder dialog with a function selected.

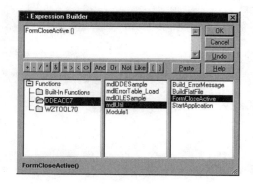

Note that if you select a function from one of the listed Wizard databases, if the database isn't loaded, the call to this function will fail. This doesn't include built-in functions or functions in your current database.

To make the toolbar start when the application starts, refer to Chapter 28.

Summary

This chapter detailed the creation of menus and toolbars that allow the user to extend the Access interface. Commands and macros may be attached to menu options and tools. Macros may utilize Access's extensive macro language and can incorporate complex expressions that create powerful commands. This chapter's information will help you customize Access to meet your needs.

Programming in Reports

27

by
Debbie Barnes

IN THIS CHAPTER

It's often necessary to use programming to produce a desired report. In Chapters 16 and 17 you learned how to create, design, and customize reports. This chapter explains in depth the different properties associated with a report and how to change these properties using Visual Basic.

First we will review the different events that occur when a report is opened, printed, or closed. Understanding when each event occurs will make you aware of the different options the programmer can set up. Then the sorting and grouping properties will be explained. The sorting and grouping properties can greatly change the layout of a report. Each section of a report has different properties that can be changed as the report is formatted or printed. These properties are also explained in detail. Finally, we will use forms to create a report menu and condition forms.

> **NOTE**
>
> This chapter refers to the Northwind database, which is included with Access 95.

Events

Reports, like other objects in Access, can initiate events. Events occur when you load and unload a report and as each report section is prepared to be printed. The programmer can use these events to set the report criteria or determine the format of the report.

Report Events

Report events apply to the overall settings of the report when you're loading and unloading it. Table 27.1 shows the available events within a report and explains when the event would occur. For instance, when a report is opened, the OnOpen and OnActivate events take place in that order.

Table 27.1. Report events.

Event Property	When It Occurs
OnOpen	Before the report become visible or starts printing.
OnClose	After the report is closed.
OnActivate	When the report becomes the active window or after the OnOpen event has occurred.
OnDeactivate	After a new window is activated or after the OnClose event has occurred.
OnNoData	After the OnOpen and OnFormat events.

Event Property	When It Occurs
OnPage	After the OnFormat and OnPrint events.
OnError	After a runtime error has occurred.

OnOpen and OnClose

The OnOpen event occurs before the report is previewed or printed. At this point, the underlying query or SQL hasn't been run. This allows an event procedure to be used in the OnOpen event to collect different parameters from the end user before the report is open. For example, a pop-up form could be constructed to request conditions related to the report. Then an event procedure could be written for the OnOpen event to open the pop-up form for criteria input from the end user.

The OnClose event occurs once the report is closed and before the OnDeactivate event takes place. This event can be used to close the pop-up form just discussed.

The Sales By Year report in the Northwind database uses these events to open a dialog box to collect parameters and then closes the form once the report is closed. Listing 27.1 contains the code associated with the OnOpen and OnClose properties for the Sales By Year report.

Listing 27.1. The OnOpen, OnClose code for the Sales By Year report.

```
OnOpen Event
Private Sub Report_Open(Cancel As Integer)
' Open Sales by Year Dialog form.
' IsLoaded function (defined in Utility Functions module) determines
' if specified form is open.
    Dim strDocName As String
    strDocName = "Sales by Year Dialog"
    ' Set public variable to True so Sales by Year Dialog knows that report is in
    ' the Open event.
    fOpening = True
    ' Open form.
    DoCmd.OpenForm strDocName, , , , , acDialog
    ' If Sales by Year Dialog form isn't loaded, don't preview or print report.
    ' (User clicked Cancel button on form.)
    If Isloaded(strDocName) = False Then
        Cancel = True
    End If
    'Set public variable to False signifying that Open event has completed.
    fOpening = False
End Sub
Close Event
Private Sub Report_Close()
' Close the Sales by Year Dialog form.
    Dim strDocName As String
    strDocName = "Sales by Year Dialog"
    DoCmd.Close acForm, strDocName
End Sub
```

OnActivate and OnDeactivate

The `OnActivate` event occurs after the `OnOpen` event, and the `OnDeactivate` event occurs after the `OnClose` event. These events also occur when the focus is received or lost from the Report window. For example, if two reports were open and Report A receives the focus from Report B, first the `OnDeactivate` event would occur for Report B. Then the `OnActivate` event would be initiated for Report A. `OnActivate` and `OnDeactivate` are used primarily for setting up menus and toolbars associated with the report.

> **NOTE**
>
> The `Deactivate` event doesn't occur if the window that received focus is a dialog box whose `PopUp` property is set to Yes or if the window is another application. Focus occurs when an object on the form or a window receives the system's attention.

OnNoData

The `OnNoData` event occurs when there are no records to display. This event occurs after the `OnOpen` event if no records are found for the report. This event can be used to stop the report from being created and bring the end user back to the dialog form to enter new parameters. The Employee Sales by Country report in the Northwind database uses this event to create a message box telling the end user what date range to use in the Sales by Year Dialog form. The request is then canceled. The code associated the `OnNoData` event is shown in Listing 27.2. Figure 27.1 shows the message box the user would see if the criteria range selected didn't contain any records.

Listing 27.2. The code for the `OnNoData` event.

```
Private Sub Report_NoData(Cancel As Integer)
' Display a message if user enters a date for which there are no records.
    MsgBox "You must enter a date between 1-Jul-93 and 3-May-95.", 0, "No Data
    ➥for Date Range"
    Cancel = True
End Sub
```

FIGURE 27.1.

The message box displayed when no data is found for the Employee Sales by Country report.

OnPage

The OnPage event occurs after the OnNoData, OnFormat, and OnPrint events, but before the report is actually printed. The purpose of this event is to give the user the ability to add graphical elements to the report. For example, the Circle method can be used to add a circle to the report before it's printed.

OnError

The OnError event occurs after a runtime error has occurred. This event includes Microsoft Jet Database Engine errors, but not runtime errors in Visual Basic. This event can be used to intercept a Microsoft Access error message and replace it with a more meaningful message to the end user.

Sections

Section events occur for each section of a report as Access prints each record. These events can affect how each section of the report is formatted and printed. Table 27.2 shows the events a section can initiate and explains when the event would occur.

Table 27.2. Section events.

Event Property	When It Occurs
OnFormat	After Access has selected the data in the section.
OnRetreat	When Access needs to move to a previous section.
OnPrint	After Access has formatted the data, but before it has printed or displays the data.

OnFormat

The OnFormat event occurs for each section. This event takes place before Access has formatted the section. The OnFormat event reviews each section differently. In the detail section, the OnFormat event occurs for each record. For group headers, the OnFormat event occurs for each new group and evaluates both the group header and the first record in the detail section. Group footers respond the same as group headers except the OnFormat event has access to the last record in the detail section.

The Employee Sales by Country report in the Northwind database uses this feature. If the employee's total sales amount is greater than $5,000, the phrase "Exceeded Goal" is displayed on the report. Listing 27.3 shows the code associated with the OnFormat property of the Salesperson header for the Employee Sales by Country report. Figure 27.2 shows the report.

Listing 27.3. The `OnFormat GroupHeader2` code for the Employee Sales by Country report.

```
Private Sub GroupHeader2_Format(Cancel As Integer, FormatCount As Integer)
' Display ExceededGoalLabel and SalespersonLine if salesperson's
' total meets criteria.
If Me!SalespersonTotal > 5000 Then
    Me!ExceededGoalLabel.Visible = True
    Me!SalespersonLine.Visible = True
Else
    Me!ExceededGoalLabel.Visible = False
    Me!SalespersonLine.Visible = False
End If
End Sub
```

FIGURE 27.2.

The Employee Sales by Country report.

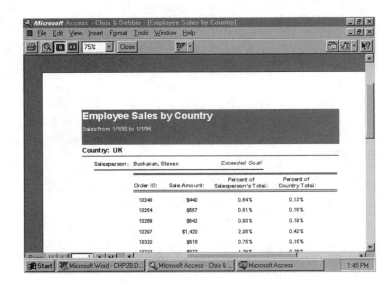

OnRetreat

The OnRetreat event occurs when Microsoft Access returns to a previous report section during report formatting. This event occurs after the OnFormat event but before the OnPrint event. This allows any settings established during the OnFormat event to be reversed. An example of when this might occur is when you have the KeepTogether property set to either Whole Group or First Detail in the group levels, and the data expands beyond the page. When that occurs, you might want the second page of the detail to be formatted differently.

The Sales by Year report in the Northwind database displays how the OnRetreat event works. The KeepTogether property for ShippedDate header must be set to Whole Group or First Detail and the detail box must be selected in the Sales by Year Dialog form in order for the OnRetreat event to work. The OnRetreat event makes the page header section visible on the continued pages of the group. This allows the continued pages of the group to display only the page header and the detail section while the first page of the group will display the ShippedDate header and detail section of the report. Please note that the report header will be on the very first page of the report. Figures 27.3 and 27.4 show the first two pages of the report.

FIGURE 27.3.

The first page of the Sales by Year report.

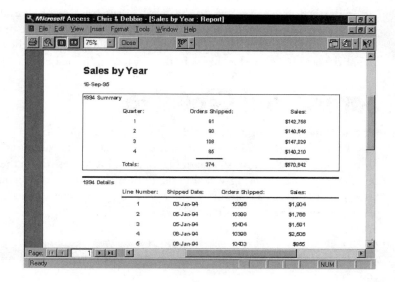

FIGURE 27.4.

The second page of the Sales by Year report.

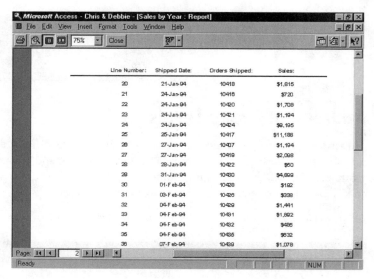

OnPrint

The OnPrint event occurs after the section is formatted for printing, but before the section is printed the OnPrint events reviews the report similar to the OnFormat event. Like the OnFormat event, the OnPrint event occurs for each section. The OnPrint event reacts differently depending on the section of the report. In the detail section, each record is evaluated by the code. For group headers, the OnPrint event occurs for each new group and evaluates both the group header and the first record in the detail section. Group footers respond the same as group headers, except the OnPrint event has access to the last record in the detail section.

Sorting and Grouping

One advantage of using reports is that you can group similar data. For example, a financial report my be more useful if it were grouped by quarter. This option is available through the Sorting and Grouping box, shown in Figure 27.5. Properties within the Sorting and Grouping box can be controlled using Visual Basic. Existing settings can be changed or added to the report using events. By using this feature, the end user will have the ability to print one report sorted and grouped many different ways.

FIGURE 27.5.

The Sorting and Grouping dialog box.

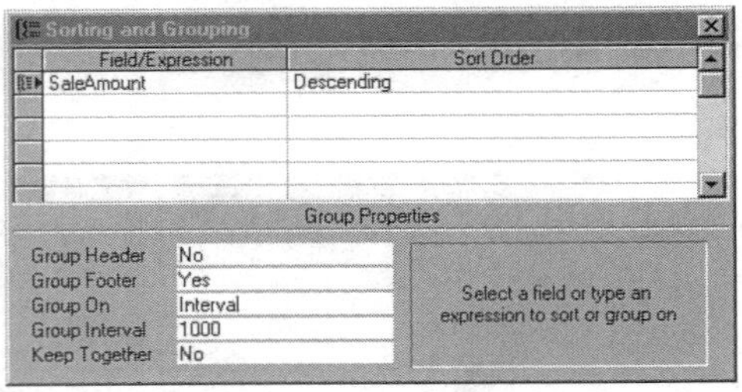

Addressing Group Levels

Properties associated with the Sortings and Grouping box can be added or changed by referring to a group level. The first group level in the Sorting and Grouping box is referred to as grouplevel(0), and the second is grouplevel(1). There can be up to nine levels. The following code shows how to refer to a grouplevel(0):

```
Reports![Sales by Year].GroupLevel(0).SortOrder = True
```

WARNING

You can't refer to group levels by using the expression box. This code will have to be entered manually.

Group Level Properties

You can access all the group-level properties with Visual Basic. The following sections review all the properties within the Sorting and Grouping box and how they may be added or changed using Visual Basic.

The *ControlSource* Property

The ControlSource property refers to the field or expression that is being grouped or sorted. For example, the Alphabetical List of Products report in the Northwind database, currently grouped by product name. An option would be to allow the user to group by Product Name or Category Name. Listing 27.4 contains the code that would allow an end user to change the ControlSource property using a conditions form. Figure 27.6 shows the selection form.

FIGURE 27.6.

The Choose a Group and Sort Order form is used to select the group and sorting properties of the Alphabetical List of Products report.

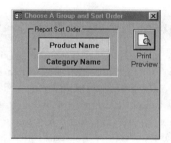

The end user would open the form, select the report sort order option, and click the print preview button to initiate the event. The event opens the form in Design view and changes the grouplevels(0) setting to the report sort order. Then the report is opened in Print Preview mode.

Listing 27.4. Code for changing the ControlSource property.

```
Private Sub cmdPreview_Click()
On Error GoTo Err_cmdPreview_Click
'Declare Variables
    Dim strField As String
    Dim strOrderBy As String
    Dim strRptName As String
    Dim rpt As Report
'Set Values
    strOrderBy = Me![grpSort]
    strRptName = "Alphabetical List of Products"
    If strOrderBy = 1 Then
        strField = "ProductName"
    Else
        strField = "CategoryName"
    End If
```

continues

Listing 27.4. continued

```
'Open Report in Design View and set rpt value
    DoCmd.OpenReport strRptName, A_DESIGN
    Set rpt = Reports![Alphabetical List of Products]
'Set Grouplevel and FirstLetterofName Control
    rpt.GroupLevel(0).ControlSource = strField
    rpt.GroupLevel(1).ControlSource = strField
    rpt![FirstLetterofName].ControlSource = "=Left([" & strField & "], 1)"
'Open Report
    DoCmd.OpenReport strRptName, A_PREVIEW
Exit_cmdPreview_Click:
    Exit Sub
Err_cmdPreview_Click:
    MsgBox Error$
    Resume Exit_cmdPreview_Click
End Sub
```

> **WARNING**
>
> Many properties can only be set in Report Design view. To set these properties using Visual Basic, you must first open the report in Design view, set the properties and then open the report using Print or Print Preview. Therefore, whenever you're changing properties in the Report Design view, it has to take place before the OnOpen event. For example, you can't open a condition form using the OnOpen event if that condition form needs to have the report opened in Design view to change the conditions.
>
> Listing 27.4 shows how this is done by setting the ControlSource properties. The properties that need to be changed in Report Design view include ControlSource, KeepTogether—Groups, PageHeader, PageFooter, GrpKeepTogether, NewRowOrCol, and KeepTogether. These properties are explained later in this chapter.

> **TIP**
>
> Listing 27.4 changes only existing group levels. Use the CreateGroupLevel() function to create a new group level. This function is available only in Report Design view. The arguments the CreateGroupLevel() function requires are the report name, the field or expression to group on, and whether a group header or group footer should be created.

The *SortOrder* Property

The SortOrder property sets the sort order to ascending or descending within the Grouping and Sorting box. This can be done using Visual Basic. This property can be set in Report Design view or in the OnOpen event procedure. The following example shows you how to set the SortOrder property to descending for the ProductName header in the Alphabetical List of Products report:

```
Reports![Alphabetical List of Products].GroupLevel(0).SortOrder = True
```

The *GroupHeader* and *GroupFooter* Properties

The GroupHeader and GroupFooter properties can't be set directly using Visual Basic. However, you can refer to the property to see if a header or footer exist. To prevent the report from printing or displaying the header or footer, set the Visible property to False. The following code shows you how to set a GroupFooter property on the Alphabetical List of Products report to not visible:

```
Reports![Alphabetical List of Products].Section(6).Visible = False
```

The *GroupOn* and *GroupInterval* Properties

The GroupOn property can be used to specify how the data will be grouped. This property can be set in Report Design view or using the OnOpen event. Different options are available depending on the data type. Table 27.3 shows the different options available.

Table 27.3. GroupOn **property options by data type.**

Field Data Type	Setting	Visual Basic Value	Groups Records With
Text	Each Value	0	The same value in the field or expression
	Prefix Characters	1	The same first *n* number of characters in the field or expression
Date/Time	Each Value	0	The same value in the field or expression
	Year	2	Same calendar year
	Qrt	3	Same calendar quarter
	Month	4	Same month
	Week	5	Same week
	Day	6	Same date
	Hour	7	Same hour
	Minutes	8	Same minute
Counter, Currency, Number	Each Value	0	The same value in the field or expression
	Interval	9	Values within an interval

The GroupInterval property works with the GroupOn property to specify how the data will be grouped in reports. For example, if the GroupOn property is set to Months and the GroupInterval property is set to 2, the data will be grouped based on two months of data. Another example is the Alphabetical List of Products report from the Northwind database, shown in Figure 27.7. The GroupOn property for the Product Name group is set to Prefix Character, and the GroupInterval property is set to 1. Therefore, the report is grouped on the first character of the product name. This option can be set in Report Design view and the OnOpen event.

FIGURE 27.7.

Print preview of the Alphabetical List of Products report.

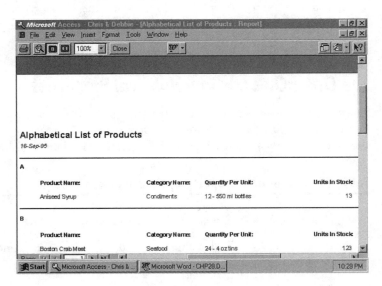

The *KeepTogether* Property—Groups

The KeepTogether property for groups in reports keeps all the parts of the group together on the same page. The parts of the group includes the group header, group footer, and detail. Both the group header and the group footer properties should to be set to Yes for this function to work. Table 27.4 lists the different options available with this property.

The following code would set the KeepTogether property to With First Detail for the ProductName header. The KeepTogether property can be set only in Report Design view:

```
Reports![Alphabetical List of Products].GroupLevel(0).KeepTogether = 2
```

Table 27.4. KeepTogether **property options.**

Setting	Visual Basic Value	Description
No	0	Prints the group without keeping the group header, footer, and detail section on same page.

Setting	Visual Basic Value	Description
Whole Group	1	Prints the group header, footer, and detail sections on the same page.
With First Detail	2	Prints the group header on the page only if it can also print the first detail record.

WARNING

If the KeepTogether property is set to Whole Group and the group is too large to fit on one page, Access will ignore the setting for that group. (More details on this occurrence and possible solutions can be found in the "Events" section of this chapter.)

Report and Section Properties

There are many properties within a report and its sections. These properties control how the report will look when it's printed. For instance, you might want page headers and footers on every page except the one that contains the report header. These properties also control how the data is organized. For example, you might want the report to continue on the next page once it has finished listing all data related to a certain group, even if there is room on the current page to continue with the next group.

Report Properties

Each report has many properties that you can set while you're designing the report. This includes all the properties that affect the overall report. For example, the RecordSource property controls where Access gets the data for the report. All of these properties may also be changed using Visual Basic in an event procedure.

The *RecordSource* Property

The RecordSource property identifies the source of the data from a form or report. The RecordSource property can contain a table, query or an SQL statement. The ability to change the RecordSource property allows the programmer to develop one reusable report that can display different data depending on the value of the RecordSource. The report will automatically requery if its RecordSource property has been changed.

The following is the code for changing the `RecordSource` property. This will change the `RecordSource` property from an SQL statement to the Products table:

```
Reports![Alphabetical List of Products].RecordSource = "Products"
```

> **WARNING**
>
> Changing the `RecordSource` property to the Products table in the Alphabetical List of Products report will result in an error because the field CategoryName is from the Categories table. Make sure when you change the `RecordSource` property that all the fields in the report are part of the new recordsource.

The *PageHeader* and *PageFooter* Properties

The `PageHeader` and `PageFooter` properties identify whether the page header or the page footer will be printed with the report header or report footer. The Catalog report in the Northwind database uses this feature to ensure that the page header and page footer don't print when the report header or report footer is printed. This sets up the first page of the Catalog report to be used as a cover page and the last page of the report as an order form. Table 27.5 lists the available options for the `PageHeader` and `PageFooter` properties.

The following example would set the `PageHeader` property for the Alphabetical List of Products report to not print the page header on the same page as the report header. The `PageHeader` and `PageFooter` properties can be set only in Report Design view.

```
Reports![Alphabetical List of Products].PageHeader = 1
```

Table 27.5. `PageHeader` and `PageFooter` property options.

Setting	Visual Basic Value	Description
All Pages	0	The page header or footer is printed on all pages of the report.
Not With Rpt Hdr	1	The page header or footer is not printed on the same pages as the report header.
Not With Rpt Ftr	2	The page header or page footer isn't printed on the same page as the report footer.
Not With Rpt Hdr/Ftr	3	The page header or page footer isn't printed on a page that has either a report header or report footer.

The *GrpKeepTogether* Property

The GrpKeepTogether property identifies whether the group is kept together by page or column. This property is used only when a report has the KeepTogether—Group property set to Whole Group or With First Detail in the Sorting and Grouping box. Report Products by Category in the Northwind database uses this feature to keep each category grouped together by column. The KeepTogether—Group property is set to First Detail and the GrpKeepTogether property is set to Per Column. Figure 27.8 shows the results of the Products by Category report.

FIGURE 27.8.

Print preview of the Products by Category report.

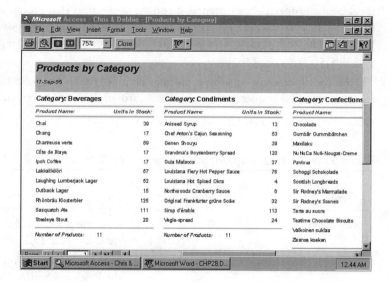

Table 27.6 shows the options available for this property. The following example set this property to Per Column using Visual Basic. This property can be set only in Report Design view.

```
Reports![Products by Category].GrpKeepTogether = 1
```

Table 27.6. GrpKeepTogether **property options.**

Setting	Visual Basic Value	Description
Per Page	0	Groups are kept together by page.
Per Column	1	Groups are kept together by column.

The *DateGrouping* Property

This property determines how the dates are grouped. This property works in conjunction with the GroupOn property. For instance, if you set up a report that groups by week, the report's results may be incorrect if the settings are from Sunday to Sunday but the end user thinks it's from Monday to Monday. Two different options are available for this property. They are listed in Table 27.7.

The following example sets the DateGrouping property for the Sales by Year report to use system settings. This property can be updated through Report Design view and the OnOpen event.

```
Reports![Sales by Year].DateGrouping = 1
```

Table 27.7. DateGrouping **property options.**

Setting	Visual Basic Value	Description
US Defaults	0	Uses the default U.S. settings for first weekday (Sunday) and first week (Jan1).
Use System Settings	1	Uses settings based on the locale selected in the Regional Settings section of the Windows Control Panel.

Section Properties

Each section has many properties that you can set while designing the report. These properties can be set up differently for each section of the report. Most of these properties can be changed using an event procedure and Visual Basic.

The *Section* Property

The Section property can be used to identify a section in a form or report and provide access to the properties of that section. Section properties are referred to by number, as shown in Table

27.8. The group-level headers and footers can continue past 9 if more than two group levels exist. The following code shows how to refer to a section:

```
Reports![Sales by Year].Section(4).Visible = True
```

This would make the page footer (section 5) of the report visible.

Table 27.8. Section settings.

Setting	Description
0	Detail section
1	Form or Report Header section
2	Form or Report Footer section
3	Form or Report Page Header section
4	Form or Report Footer section
5	Report GroupLevel0 Header section
6	Report GroupLevel0 Footer section
7	Report GroupLevel1 Header section
8	Report GroupLevel1 Footer section

The *ForceNewPage* Property

The ForceNewPage property is accessible to all sections except the page header and page footer. This property allows the end user to control the page break for each section. The Employee Sales by Country report in the Northwind database uses this feature to force a page break to occur after the Country footer. Therefore, if the country changes or there is no data left to display, a page break occurs. The different options available through the ForceNewPage properties are listed in Table 27.9.

The ForceNewPage property can be set in all views. The following example shows how to set the Employee Sales by Country report's Country footer to After Section:

```
Reports![Employee Sales by Country].Section(6).ForceNewPage = 1
```

Table 27.9. Property settings for the ForceNewPage property.

Setting	Visual Basic Value	Description
None	0	The current section is printed on the current page.
Before Section	1	The current section is printed at the top of the next page.
After Section	2	The section immediately following the current section is printed at the top of a new page.
Before & After	3	The current section is printed at the top of a new page and the next section is printed at the top of a new page.

The *NewRowOrCol* Property

The NewRowOrCol property applies only to multicolumn reports. This property is used to indicate whether a section is printed in a new row or column. The Products by Category report in the Northwind database uses this option. The CategoryName section's NewRowOrCol property is set to Before Section. This results in a new column every time the category name changes. Table 27.10 lists the available property settings.

The property can be set only in Report Design view. The following code sets the NewRowOrCol property on the CategoryName header to Before Section:

```
Reports![Products by Category].Section(5).NewRowOrCol = 1
```

Table 27.10. Property settings for the NewRowOrCol property.

Setting	Visual Basic Value	Description
None	0	The row or column breaks are determined by the setting in the Print Setup dialog box and the available space on the page.
Before Section	1	Starts printing the current section in a new row or column. It then prints the next section in that same row or column.

Setting	Visual Basic Value	Description
After Sections	2	Starts printing the current section in the current row or column. The following section would print in the next row or column.
Before & After	3	Starts printing the current section in a new row or column and the next section in the next row or column.

NOTE

You access the settings for printing a multicolumn report by choosing File | Page Setup | Layout. The grid settings, item size, and layout options are defined here. The grid settings set the row spacing, column spacing, and the number of items across. The item-size setting includes the width and height of the detail area. The orientation of the report is set in the layout options. This affects how the data will be listed in the detail area. The choices are down and across or across and down.

The *KeepTogether* Property—Section

The KeepTogether property for sections is similar to the KeepTogether property for groups. The KeepTogether property for sections prints an entire section on one page, whereas the KeepTogether property for groups prints an entire group on one page. As with the KeepTogether property for groups, if the section is greater than one page, the section will continue on the next page. The Top Products by Country report in the Northwind database uses this property to keep all the data in the Country header together. The KeepTogether property options for sections are listed in Table 27.11.

The following is an example of setting the KeepTogether property to Yes for the Country header section in the Top Products by Country report. This property can be set only in Report Design view.

```
Reports![Top Products by Country].Section(5).KeepTogether = True
```

Table 27.11. KeepTogether property options.

Setting	Visual Basic Value	Description
Yes	True (–1)	Section starts printing on next page if entire section can't be printed on current page.
No	False (0)	Section will print on current page and continue to next page if necessary.

The *Visible* Property

The Visible property can be set to show or hide a section or control. The Sales by Year report in the Northwind database uses this feature to make some of the controls in the detail section invisible if the detailed check box on the Sales by Year dialog form isn't selected. This is done using the OnFormat event for the ShippedDate header. Table 27.12 lists the available settings for the Visible property.

The following is an example of the code to make the CategoryName header section invisible:

```
Reports![Alphabetical List of Products].Section(5).Visible = False
```

Table 27.12. Visible property options.

Setting	Visual Basic Value	Description
Yes	True (–1)	Makes the control or section visible.
No	False (0)	Makes the control or section invisible.

The *CanShrink* and *CanGrow* Properties

The CanShrink and CanGrow properties determine whether a control or a section can grow or shrink vertically. These properties are useful when printing a memo field or subreport. These properties adjust the size of the field vertically so that all data in that field is displayed on the report. If a control within the section's CanGrow property is set to Yes, the section's CanGrow property will automatically be set to Yes. The Sales by Year report in the Northwind database uses this feature. The ShippedDate header grows to display the available data.

> **WARNING**
>
> Sometimes the CanGrow and CanShrink properties don't do what they're set to do. This can be caused by many things. For example, if the controls are overlapping, they can't grow or shrink. Also, report headers and footers can't grow or shrink. Lastly, if there is a large object in the same horizontal location, the controls that are horizontal to the large object won't shrink.

Table 27.13 lists the available options for the CanGrow and CanShrink properties. The property settings are read-only in Visual Basic.

Table 27.13. CanGrow and CanShrink property options.

Setting	Visual Basic Value	Description
Yes	True (−1)	Section or control can grow or shrink.
No	False (0)	Section or control can't grow or shrink.

The *RepeatSection* Property

The RepeatSection property determines if the group header is repeated on the next page or column. For instance, you might want the group header printed on the following pages if the group requires more than one page. The Employee Sales by Country report in the Northwind database uses this option. The Salesperson header is repeated if the group expands across more than one page. The different options available are listed in Table 27.14.

The following code would set the RepeatSection property in the Employee Sales by Country so that the group header doesn't repeat:

```
Reports![Employee Sales by Country].Section(7).RepeatSection = False
```

Table 27.14. RepeatSection property options.

Setting	Visual Basic Value	Description
Yes	True (−1)	Group header is repeated.
No	False (0)	Group header isn't repeated.

The *WillContinue* and *HasContinued* Properties

Both the WillContinue and HasContinued properties have no settings and are available as read-only. The WillContinue property determines if the current section will continue on the following page, and the HasContinued property determines if part of the section has been printed on the previous page. These properties can be used to determine if a hidden label field such as Continued should be made visible.

Using a Form to Select Reports and Conditions

To fully utilize Access as a programming tool, the Database window shouldn't be visible to the end user. The end user should see only forms, opened reports, and opened queries. The forms should flow together smoothing allowing the end user easy access to the data. Therefore, to created a completed Access product, forms will need to be created for a report menu and for setting report conditions.

Creating a Report Menu

A report menu needs to be created for any application. In Access, the report menu is a form that allows the end user to select the desired report to be printed. The report menu can be as simple as creating an option box listing the available report and a print button to print the reports. Following are the steps of creating a report menu for the Northwind database:

1. Create a new unbound form. (Select the Form tab in the Database window and then click the New button.)
2. Add an option box using the Option Group Wizard in the toolbox.
3. Add the report names as label names. Include Alphabetical List of Products, Products by Category, and Sales by Year, as shown in Figure 27.9.

FIGURE 27.9.

Option Group Wizard label names.

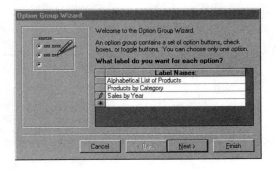

4. Set the Alphabetical List of Products report as the default option.

5. Leave the values assigned to each option as the default. These are the option values that will be assigned to the option buttons and that will be used in the Visual Basic code to determine which option button has been selected.

6. Select Option Buttons for the type of control and Shadowed for the style.

7. Set the caption to Reports for the option group.

8. Rename the option box to grpReport.

9. Add two buttons to the form without using the Command Wizard.

10. Rename the buttons cmdPrintPreview and cmdExit.

11. Change the caption to Print Preview and Exit.

12. Add a form header/footer to the form and type Report Menu in the form header. Then resize the label to size 18.

13. Adjust the height and width of the footer and detail section.

14. Change the form properties as follows:

Property	Setting
BorderStyle	Dialog
Caption	Report Menu Dialog
DefaultView	Single Form
NavigationButtons	No
RecordSelectors	No
ScrollBar	Neither
ViewsAllowed	Form

15. Add code to the OnClick event for both the Print Preview and Exit command buttons.

Listing 27.5 gives the code for the Print Preview button. The case statements are used to determine what report the end user wants to open. Listing 27.6 contains some code to close the form.

Listing 27.5. The code for the Print Preview button.

```
Private Sub cmdPrintPreview_Click()
On Error GoTo Err_cmdPrintPreview_Click
'Declare Variables
    Dim strRpt As String
    Dim strOption As String
'Set Values
    strOption = Forms![Report Menu Dialog]![grpReports]
    Select Case strOption
        Case 1
            strRpt = "Alphabetical List of Products"
```

continues

Listing 27.5. continued

```
        Case 2
            strRpt = "Products by Category"
        Case 3
            strRpt = "Sales by Year"
        Case Else
            GoTo Err_cmdPrintPreview_Click
    End Select
    'Open Selected Report in Print Preview View
    DoCmd.OpenReport strRpt, acPreview
Exit_cmdPrintPreview_Click:
    Exit Sub
Err_cmdPrintPreview_Click:
    MsgBox Err.Description
    Resume Exit_cmdPrintPreview_Click
End Sub
```

Listing 27.6. The code for the Exit button.

```
Private Sub cmdExit_Click()
On Error GoTo Err_cmdExit_Click
'Closes current form
    Docmd Close
Exit_cmdExit_Click:
    Exit Sub
Err_cmdExit_Click:
    MsgBox Err.Description
    Resume Exit_cmdExit_Click
End Sub
```

Your form should look like Figure 27.10.

FIGURE 27.10.

The complete Report Menu dialog form.

Creating a Report Condition Form

To make a report more flexible, it's often helpful to have a condition form open on the OnOpen event of the report to set the criteria of the report. When you include a conditions form with the report, fewer reports will need to be created, and the end user will appreciate the different options. The following steps create a condition form and attach it to a report:

1. Create a new unbound form. (Select the Form tab in the Database window and then click the New button.)

2. Add a list box using the List Box Wizard in the toolbox.

3. Click the option button that states "I want the list box to look up a value in a table or query."

4. Select the Categories table.

5. Add CategoryName to the selected fields to include in the list box.

6. Make the column as wide as it needs to be.

7. Set the label to Category Name for the list box.

8. Rename the list box lstCategoryName.

9. Add two buttons to the form without using the Command Wizard.

10. Rename the buttons to cmdPrintPreview and cmdCancel.

11. Change the caption to Print Preview and Cancel.

12. Add a form header/footer to the form and type `Alphabetical List of Products Condition` in the form header. Then resize the label to size 14.

13. Adjust the height and width of the footer and detail section.

14. Change the form properties as follows:

Property	*Setting*
BorderStyle	Dialog
Caption	Alphabetical List of Products Condition
DefaultView	Single Form
NavigationButtons	No
RecordSelectors	No
ScrollBar	Neither
ViewsAllowed	Form

15. Change the SQL statement in the `RecordSource` property of the Alphabetical List of Products Condition report to the following:

```
SELECT DISTINCTROW Products.*, Categories.CategoryName
FROM Categories INNER JOIN Products ON Categories.CategoryID =
➥Products.CategoryID
WHERE (((Categories.CategoryName)=[Forms]![Alphabetical List of
➥Products Condition]![lstCategoryName]) AND ((Products.Discontinued)=
➥No));
```

Now the report will use the condition selected in the Alphabetical List of Products Condition form.

16. Add code to the necessary event.

Listing 27.7 contains the necessary code for this process. First the `OnOpen` event occurs, which opens the Alphabetical List of Products Condition form. After a category name is selected and the Print Preview button is clicked, the report continues to open, using the Category Name condition set on the form.

Listing 27.7. The code for the Print Preview button.

```
Private Sub Report_Open(Cancel As Integer)
On Error GoTo Err_Report_Open
    Dim strFrm As String
    strFrm = "Alphabetical List of Products Condition"
    DoCmd.OpenForm strFrm, , , , , acDialog
Exit_Report_Open:
    Exit Sub
Err_Report_Open:
    MsgBox Error$
    Resume Exit_Report_Open
End Sub
Private Sub cmdPrintPreview_Click()
On Error GoTo Err_CmdPrintPreview_Click
    Me.Visible = False
Exit_CmdPrintPreview_Click:
    Exit Sub
Err_CmdPrintPreview_Click:
    MsgBox Error$
    Resume Exit_CmdPrintPreview_Click
End Sub
```

Your form should look like Figure 27.11.

FIGURE 27.11.

The complete Alphabetical List of Products Condition form.

Summary

With Access reports, events are used to initiate Visual Basic code. This code may change the different properties associated with reports, including sorting and grouping properties, report properties, and section properties.

A database isn't beneficial unless the user can view the data. The way the data is grouped, sorted, and organized also can make the report more meaningful. By using events and Visual Basic, you can manipulate the report so that the preferred results are obtained. Also, a report can be changed with Visual Basic to provide many views of the same data.

PART

IN THIS PART

Building Access Applications

Putting It All Together

28

*by Dwayne
Gifford*

One of the hardest tasks when developing an Access application is bringing it all together. You must be aware of some very important issues beforehand or they will come back to haunt you at the end of the application. Some of these issues include the actual structure of the application, making sure the data is compatible with other applications that might need to use your data, and making sure you're compliant with them because you might need their data. These are only a few of the issues you will run into when you try to put the application together.

Structuring an Access Application

All applications need to be designed from somewhere. Most Access applications start in one of two places—either from the database up or from the interface down. Note that the following methods are just two of the many that can be used.

Database Up Design

When the analyst begins working on the application, he or she works with the database architect to make sure that all database rules are followed and that the design of the application meets the application's requirements. After the design has been laid out, the database architect starts building the tables and the relationships that are required for the application. When the table layout is finished, the analyst starts building the form layouts for the client to approve. When the forms have been approved, the developers develop the forms. At this point, the analyst starts the layouts for any further requirements by means of reports or other forms.

User Interface Down Design

Starting from the interface makes it a bit more difficult to make sure the database rules and relationships are followed properly. When developing applications with Access, this is the design that is usually followed. This is because most end users are limited in their ability to develop applications in Access. They can continue only until the form doesn't do everything they want it to do, or more users need to use it and they're running into record locks, or it's just too big for them to support. At this point the IS group (Information Systems department) is called in to fix the problem and add enhancements.

In almost all cases, the table structure needs to be rebuilt, making sure that the database relationship is followed and that all the needs of the database are met. In this type of design, the first step is to get an analyst to work with the client to get the layouts for the forms approved. After the forms have been approved, the database architect can work on rebuilding the tables for the database. The last step is for the developers to make any required changes to the forms. This design is very similar in process to the database up design, except that in this design, there is usually already an application to work from.

Standardizing Data and Code

Very few stand-alone applications exist anymore, and if they're still around, they won't be for much longer. Most applications need to share data with more than one application and receive data from more than one application. When designing the application, it's important to get a database architect involved early. He can help in designing the table layouts, and he can also guide the use of other applications' data. He has an understanding of where the new application might benefit from other applications' data. Also, later on, when the architect works on other applications, he can borrow data from this application. Note that it's much more productive to borrow functionality from other applications than to rebuild the functionality each time a new application is built. For example, let's say your order entry system is outdated. A new application will take orders and will need to bill the customers. Instead of rebuilding the billing system for the new application, the new application can share its data in a format that the billing system will understand, and the billing system will bill the customers for the new application.

Creating Common Data Formats

Most companies have a set of data that is used in some way in all applications. This data, referred to as *common data,* often includes information on customers or the products or goods that the company sells. One of the biggest problems facing IS groups these days is trying to get a common format to common data. Usually after an application has been put in place, the IS group finds out that another application actually has some of the data that this application needs for the user to do his job properly. However, the format that the user sets up on the new application isn't the same as the other application, requiring him to type the data in manually. This isn't a big problem when the user is using only one application, but as time passes and cutbacks occur, he needs to use more than one application and no longer has time to update the old application. This application becomes useless in no time because it isn't up to date.

Standardizing Code for Applications

One of the biggest problems facing Access development teams is making sure they set a standard that they will follow when programming the application. This is vital because, for example, if one developer needs the ability to clear the form, he or she develops this piece of code without checking with the other developers. When a second developer needs a new form cleared, this developer programs the same code without checking with anyone. If this continues, soon each form has its own clear form function.

At the outset of the application development, it's important to assign one developer to program all common tasks. These tasks include form handling operations that aren't form-specific, generic control handling, or any generic operations that aren't application-specific.

If another developer needs a form operation function developed, this developer needs to talk with the standard code developer. This way the code becomes portable, which means that the code is generic to any form handling or any control handling. Once it has been coded, it can be used over and over by porting it to other applications.

Naming Conventions

Another important issue about standard code is making sure that the developers are following the same naming conventions. This is necessary so that if a developer leaves and a new developer comes on board, this new developer can ask questions of the other developers and get good foundation questions answered. Many times I have come on board to help develop an application and no one can answer my simple questions about the other developer's code because they haven't been using the same standard. Imagine starting a new job and none of the application's developers are still around, and each form in the application uses a different naming convention. Just think how long it would take you to get an understanding of how the application works.

It's important to set the naming conventions for everything in the application. This means that you follow the same naming convention for naming the controls, forms, reports, macros, queries, and modules, as well as the naming of variables in the VBA code. Numerous naming conventions are used in the marketplace, and technically there are no right or wrong choices as long as the same naming convention is used throughout the application. It's important that the programmers stay consistent with this, even if it's a Friday night and they want to leave early.

Planning for Performance

One of the biggest problems an application runs into is performance. It's important to look at this early in the application's development. One way to plan for this is to make sure that the tables that will be used in queries are indexed. This helps to achieve the best available performance. Also, if at all possible avoid multiple table joins to get at required data. Both of these issues come back to proper database architecture from the start. One of the ways to improve performance is with list boxes. List boxes can be populated in three ways. The first is to use a table and reference the column or columns you wish to have shown. The second is to write the Select statement in the control source, and the third is to create a query and then reference the query from the control source. All three methods work great in their own way. Following is a list of which method to use when populating the list box, depending on how it will be used. These guidelines will help you get the ultimate performance for a form:

- If it's static data coming from one table, use the table itself and reference the columns.
- If it's static data coming from two or more tables, write a query that loads the required data.

■ If it's data coming from one or more tables that need to be queried as other data changes, write the Select statement in the control source.

User Interface Guidelines

One of the biggest problems with applications that get built in Access is that they don't always follow the Windows interface guidelines. Instead of this book giving you a new guideline to follow, it's more important to emphasize the importance of following the Microsoft Windows Interface Guidelines. These guidelines didn't change much from Windows 3.x to Windows NT, but with the release of Windows 95, it's important to learn the new guidelines. The simple and sure method of following the guidelines is to make your application duplicate the look and actions of Access itself.

Running the Application

When you give the user the application, it's important to give him his own taskbar item or shortcut item to use when he wants to open the application. This is because you don't want users searching through folders on their computer trying to remember what you called the application. Also, by doing this you can add any required command-line parameters. For an understanding of how to use command-line parameters, refer to Chapter 32, "Multiuser Programming and Techniques." If the program has been turned into a stand-alone application, it's important to remember to create a setup program for the application. The reason for this setup program is to make sure all files get placed on the user's computer in the correct folder. To turn an application into a runtime Access application, you need to use the Access ADT, a package of wizards and applications that will help you make your applications look more professional.

Startup Options

When a database starts up, users need to be able to get to the starting window or dialog box to work from. Access 95 has two ways to achieve this. The first method is to use the Startup dialog box, and the second is to use the Autoexec macro. Both have their own purposes, and I suggest you use both to your advantage.

The Startup Dialog Box

To open the Startup dialog box, shown in Figure 28.1, select Tools | Startup. This dialog box has 13 items that can be set for the current database. Each item is explained in the following list.

FIGURE 28.1.

The Startup dialog box.

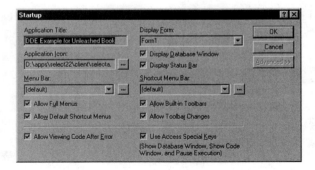

■ Application Title: This item lets you use your title instead of Microsoft Access. To add the title, click the textbox and type your title for the application. This title appears as the caption for the application in the task list instead of Microsoft Access.

■ Application Icon: If you know the icon file name, you can type it in or click the button to the right of the textbox. This button lets you navigate your way to the icon folder. By default it shows you icon files only. To make it also show executable files, type *.exe in the Filename textbox at the bottom and press Enter.

Whatever icon you select becomes the icon for this application, so when the application is minimized, this icon appears instead of the Access icon. Also, if you tab between applications, this is the icon displayed.

■ Menu Bar: This is how you tell the database which menu bar to use as the default menu bar. If you set this, the default menus no longer run, so I suggest not setting this until you're about to release the application to the end users. If you haven't built the menu yet, click the builder button, which is located to the right of the list box. You're placed in the Menu Builder Wizard, where you can build the macro. For details on how to use the Wizard, refer to Chapter 26, "Menus and Toolbars."

■ Allow Full Menus: If you want to limit the menu access to the users, turn this option off.

■ Allow Default Shortcut Menus: To enable the users of the database to use the default shortcut menus, select this option.

■ Display Form: This is the default start form. If you want the users always to start at one form, select that form from the list box. If you haven't created the startup form yet, refer to the section "Defining the Switchboard" later in this chapter.

■ Display Database Window: This is important because you usually don't want the user to be able to view the Database window at startup. If you turn this option off, the Database window isn't displayed at startup. If you want the Database window to be visible at startup, turn this option on.

■ Display Status Bar: This option is covered in the section titled "Keeping the User Informed." I strongly suggest leaving this option on.

- **Shortcut Menu Bar:** To set a shortcut menu bar, select the macro from the list box that you want to run as the default shortcut menu. If you want to use a shortcut menu and haven't set it up, click the button with the three dots to the right of the list box. You're placed in the Menu Builder Wizard. For details on how to use the Wizard, refer to Chapter 26.

- **Allow Built-in Toolbars:** If you don't want the users to be able to see the default toolbars, turn this option off.

- **Allow Toolbar Changes:** If you want the user to be able to modify the toolbars, leave this option on.

The next two options are available when you click the Advanced button.

- **Allow Viewing Code After Error:** By turning this option off, you can make sure that the users won't see the code if an error occurs. This option also turns the Ctrl-Break option off and on when you're running code.

- **Use Access Special Keys:** Selecting this option ensures that all the shortcut keys available in Access are deactivated and no longer usable.

The Autoexec Macro

Previous versions of Access didn't have a Startup dialog box, so you needed to program a macro and name it Autoexec. The other way to run a macro at startup is to use the command-line option. To do this, you need to add /X *macro* after the database name, with *macro* being the name of the macro. To have Access run the macro when the database starts, you name the macro Autoexec. You can also perform other options with a macro that the Startup dialog box can't handle, such as finding out who the current user is.

Defining the Switchboard

One of the most important parts of developing an application is setting up the application's starting and ending points. To help you with this, Access has a wizard called the Switchboard Manager. To open it, select Tools | Add-ins | Switchboard Manager. If the current database doesn't have a switchboard, the dialog box shown in Figure 28.2 appears, asking if you would like to create a switchboard.

FIGURE 28.2.

The switchboard confirmation to create the initial switchboard.

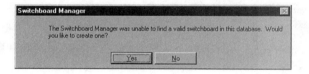

If you click No, you're returned to the Database window. If you click Yes, the wizard creates a new table called Switchboard Items, which is made up of the columns listed in Table 28.1.

Table 28.1. Columns in the Switchboard Items table.

Column Name	Description
SwitchboardID	This ID number tells the Switchboard form which pane of the switchboard the current item belongs to.
ItemNumber	The order in which the item is to appear on the Switchboard form for the current SwitchboardID.
ItemText	The text that will appear in the ItemNumber position.
Command	A number between 0 and 8. For information on available commands, see Table 28.2.
Argument	The form name, report name, macro name, function name, or switchboard number that the command will carry out.

After the table is built, a form named Switchboard is created. After the form has been built, the window shown in Figure 28.3 is opened with the default switchboard of Main switchboard already entered for you.

FIGURE 28.3.

Switchboard Manager with the default switchboard.

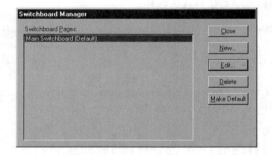

Five options are available:

Close, New, Edit, Delete, and Make Default.

- Close: Ends the current Switchboard Wizard and returns you to the Database window.
- New: Opens the Name New Switchboard dialog, which defaults to New Switchboard Page. To change the name, type in the new name of the switchboard and press Enter. If you don't want to add a new switchboard page, click the Cancel button.
- Delete: Prompts you to confirm the deletion of the currently selected switchboard page.

■ Make Default: Places the word *default* beside the currently selected switchboard page and removes the word *default* from the old default switchboard page. This tells the Switchboard form which page to open first.

■ Edit: Opens the dialog box shown in Figure 28.4, with the switchboard defaulted to the currently selected switchboard page in Figure 28.3.

FIGURE 28.4.

The Edit Switchboard Page dialog.

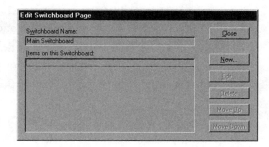

Here you can add, edit, and delete items for the currently selected switchboard page. As you add items, they are placed in the order that you add them. If at any time you want to change the order, click on the item and then click the move down or move up button. These buttons move the current item up one or down one place. If this is the first time in the Edit Switchboard page for the current page, two options are available: Close and New. The Close button returns you to the dialog box shown in Figure 28.4. The New button opens the dialog shown in Figure 28.5.

FIGURE 28.5.

The Edit Switchboard Item dialog.

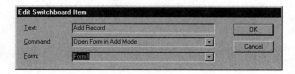

To add a new item, follow these steps:

1. Enter the name of the item in the Text box.

2. Select the command from the Command list box.

3. Depending on the command you select, you might need to select the appropriate third item. The label changes depending on the command selected. If you select Design application or Exit application, you aren't asked for the third item.

The Switchboard Manager limits you to eight command items per switchboard page. The switchboard can run any of the commands shown in Table 28.2.

Table 28.2. Commands available from the switchboard.

ID Number	Command	Description
1	Go to Switchboard	Changes the current switchboard to the switchboard number that is in the argument column.
2	Open Form in Add Mode	Opens the form in the argument column in Add mode.
3	Open Form in Edit Mode	Opens the form in the argument column in Edit mode.
4	Open Report	Opens the report that is in the Argument column.
5	Design Application	Customizes the switchboard.
6	Exit Application	Closes the current application and leaves Access open.
7	Run Macro	Runs the macro that is in the argument column.
8	Run Code	Runs the function that is in the argument column.

When you see a command of 0 in the table, you will notice that it is the starting point for a new switchboard page. This tells the Switchboard form what to change its caption to and where the new page starts.

NOTE

Even though the Switchboard Wizard limits you to eight command buttons, the code is already there for you to add more buttons as needed. To do this, you need to edit the Switchboard form and add a new command button and label just as you did for the other eight items. Make sure that you continue the naming convention for the labels and command buttons. Then go into the Switchboard Items table and add the item manually. For an example of this, see SwitchBoard.MDB on the CD that comes with this book. In the function `FillOptions`, you need to change `Const conNumButtons = 8` to `Const conNumButtons = ?`, depending on how many control buttons you added. After you do this, the switchboard will operate without any problems.

After you have added the items to the switchboard page, you can edit them by selecting the item from the list and clicking the Edit button. This brings you back to the window shown in Figure 28.4, but the currently selected item information is filled in for you to edit. If you want to delete the currently selected item, click the Delete button. A delete item confirmation is displayed. Click OK to delete the item. If you click Cancel, the item won't be deleted, and you will be returned to the window shown in Figure 28.4. If you want to change the name of the currently selected switchboard page, click on the Switchboard Name text box and change the name. When you close the Edit Switchboard page and return to the Switchboard Manager, the currently selected switchboard page name is the one you typed in the Edit Switchboard page.

> **NOTE**
>
> Remember that as you add new switchboard pages, you must add the `goto Switchboard` command to the main page in order to get to the page, and then you must add a command item to get back to the main page. To see an example of this, refer to SwitchBoard.MDB on the CD that comes with this book.

When you click a command button that performs an action of `goto Switchboard`, it changes the filter on the form to use the new page instead of the old page. This in turn forces a reload of the form based on the new information.

The Drill-Down Concept

When you start at the top of a dataset, you see all the available records. The idea of drilling down is to get to the bottom of the dataset, where only one record is available. This process has three steps. The first two take care of the data retrieval and requerying of the data, and the third displays the information retrieved:

1. Prompt the user for information that will help narrow down the number of records available.
2. If more than one record is available, repeat step 1. Otherwise, go to step 3.
3. When only one record is left, display this record in whatever format the user wants to see it in.

This view can be achieved in many ways. Two controls that come with the ADT for Access 95 help you achieve this type of view. They are the Data Outline Control 1.1 and TreeView Control.

The Way to Open a Form

There is only one way to open a form, but you can call the `openform` event two different ways. The first way is through a macro, and the second is from inside VBA code. The best of the two is from VBA code. If you add a button to a form and use the Button Wizard, you will notice that it creates the call in VBA code. As mentioned earlier, it's important to set up a standard code for all generic calls, and opening a form is a generic call. The best way to open a form is to create a standard function that opens the form. This function requires seven arguments: the form name, the type of view, the filter name, the `where` condition, the data mode, the window mode, and opening arguments. These arguments are listed in Table 28.3. The reason for these arguments is that these are the seven arguments that `Docmd.OpenForm` takes. The only mandatory parameter is the form name. The rest are optional parameters.

Table 28.3. Arguments for `Docmd.OpenForm`.

Argument	Description
FormName	A valid string of a form in the current database.
View	Any of the following constants: `acNormal`, `acDesign`, `acPreview`, or `acFormDS`. `acNormal` opens the form in Normal mode. `acDesign` opens the form in Design mode. `acPreview` opens the form in Print Preview. `acFormDS` opens the form in Datasheet mode. If left blank, `acNormal` is assumed.
filtername	A string expression of a valid query name in the current database.
WhereCondition	A string expression made up of a valid SQL `where` clause without the `where`.
Datamode	One of the following constants: `acAdd`, `acEdit`, or `acReadonly`. `acAdd` is used to allow adding new records only. `acEdit` is used for editing and adding new records, and `acReadonly` is used to open the form in read-only mode. The default is `acEdit`.
WindowMode	The following constants are valid: `acNormal`, `acHidden`, `acIcon`, or `acDialog`. `acNormal` opens the form in normal mode; `acHidden` opens the form hidden; `acIcon` opens the form minimized; and `acDialog` opens the form as a dialog box.
openargs	A string expression that is used to set the `OpenArgs` property of the form being opened.

The following example gives you an idea of what a generic open routine looks like. In this example, all parameters that the open form call can take are passed in, and all optional parameters for the open form are also optional for the subroutine.

```
Sub OpenLocalForms(stFormName, formProperty, Optional FormView As Variant,
➥Optional FormFilter As Variant, Optional FormWhere As Variant, Optional
➥formdata As Variant, Optional FormWindow As Variant, Optional formArg As
➥Variant)
    lblTypeofOpen.Caption = formProperty
DoCmd.OpenForm stFormName, FormView, FormFilter, FormWhere, formdata, FormWindow,
➥formArg
End Sub
```

In the `OpenForm` routine for the sample application, I added one extra parameter—`formProperty`. I added this parameter because the forms that I have coded have `Property Get`, `Property Let`, and `Property Set` added. This enables me to open the form with additional options. For more information on the Property methods, refer to Chapter 23, "Visual Basic for Applications." Also notice that I made all parameters except `stFormName` and `formProperty` optional parameters. The following line of code is an example of how to call the `OpenLocalForms` routine:

```
Call OpenLocalForms(stDocName, 1, , , "FilePath = 'Bob'", , 3)
```

This call opens the form that the string `stDocName` is equal to. Property Let is equal to 1, `FormView` is left blank, `FormFilter` is blank, `FormWhere` is set to `"FilePath = 'BOB'"`, `formdata` is left blank, and `FormWindow` is set to 3. This opens the form with only the records that met the filter you passed in. In this case, the filter is only records that have a `FilePath = Bob`. Also, the form is opened as a dialog box. By making one standard `OpenForm` routine, you can make sure that all forms are being opened the same way.

Switching Out Subforms

One of the best examples of how to switch out subforms is included in the Setup Wizard application that is shipped with the Access 95 ADT. The idea of switching out the subforms is that you will have one Main form that can display one subform at a time. When the user opens the Main form, it displays the default subform. When the user wants to move to the next subform, you need to change the `SourceObject` property of the control for the subform. To do this you need to have some code that places the correct string value into the `SourceObject` property. The code would look something like this:

```
Me!subView.SourceObject = FormName
```

The `SourceObject` is set to *FormName*. This value is the name of a form in the current database. When you're doing this, it's important to make sure that all subforms are the same size; otherwise, the Main form looks different each time it changes to a new subform. The idea here is to make sure the user doesn't notice a difference as he scrolls through the subforms. Also, when you set the `SourceObject` equal to the new form, the `Load` event for this new subform is called. Before this event is completed, the `Unload` event of the old form is called if the form has an `Unload` event set up. If you want to look at the Setup Wizard, you need to open WZSTP70.MDA with the Shift key pressed. The form to start with is stp_frmSetup. When the user clicks the Next or Back button, it calls a routine to switch out the subforms. Make sure you don't make any changes to this database. If you do, it isn't guaranteed to function properly and perform the setup of other programs.

Using the Tab Metaphor

In many cases, a form contains so much information that it becomes almost impossible to read, or it doesn't fit on the screen. Usually a form contains information that is important and is referred to as the main or header information. This is the information the user wants to view all the time, and the rest can be grouped together. One of the ways to group information is to use a tab metaphor. To do this, you can use the tab control that comes with the Access 95 ADT or the Sheridan Tab that comes with Visual Basic 4.0. This control gives you the ability to group information together under its own tab. When the user needs to see the information, he can click the tab. Clicking the tab brings the information into focus and causes the other data to be removed from focus. Figure 28.6 shows what a tab control looks like and how it can group the information and still make sure the header information is always visible.

FIGURE 28.6.

A form with a tab control being used.

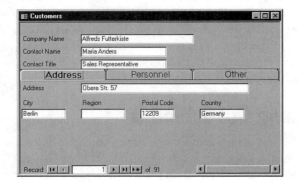

This form includes tabs for Address, Personnel, and Other. Each of these tabs contains information relating to the tab name. For example, if you want to find out personnel information on the customer, you simply click the Personnel tab.

A Generic Form for Printing Reports

One of the most common mistakes in any application is enabling the user to print from the currently active form. This is impossible to support and fix if something goes wrong. The best idea is to have one common place to do all the printing from. This enables you to keep all the code required for printing in one common location. Also, imagine if you needed to fix one of the reports that isn't printing properly. If you had the ability to print from everywhere, you would need to take not only this report out of service but also the form. This definitely isn't a good idea. Figure 28.7 shows an example of a generic form for printing.

When you set up the printing form, it's important to remember to set the following options:

Option	How to Set It
Views Allowed	Set to Form.
Allow Edits	Set to Yes.
Allow Deletions	Set to No.
Allow Additions	Set to No.

Scroll Bars	Set to Neither.
Record Selectors	Set to No.
Navigation Buttons	Set to No.
Auto Center	Set to Yes.
Border style	Set to Thin. This ensures that the user can't adjust the size of the form.
Min Max Buttons	Set to Min Enabled. This ensures again that the user can't make changes to the form.

FIGURE 28.7.

A generic form for printing.

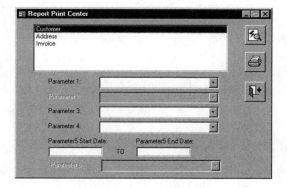

These are only suggestions, but it's important to remember that when you set up a generic form, no user should be able to make changes to the form. Another idea to use when working with generic report printing forms is to use a table that contains a list of parameters used to populate the report form. This table contains a column for report names and one for each available parameter on the report form. These parameter columns are of type Yes/No. For each control or group of controls on the form, there is a matching parameter column in the table. Thus, if you have 20 possible parameters for any given report, there should be 20 parameter columns in the table. Therefore, by having a Report Name column, you can populate the report option list box from this column in the report table. Table 28.4 is a sample table outline for the report table.

Table 28.4. A report table sample.

Column Name	Column Type	Default
Report	Name: String, FieldSize: 35, Description: Name of report to appear in list box	

continues

Table 28.4. continued

Column Name	Column Type	Default
Parameter1	Yes/No	No
Parameter2	Yes/No	No
Parameter3	Yes/No	No
Parameter4	Yes/No	No
Parameter5	Yes/No	No
Parameter6	Yes/No	No

As you can see in Figure 28.7, I have grouped the start date and end date to one parameter (Parameter5), so that if a start date is required an end date is also required. Remember that this is only a suggestion, but it makes support much easier. It also makes the development of reports faster because if you need a new report created you know what parameters are already available.

Referring to Controls from a Query

To have a query use a parameter that is based on a form, you need to create the query and in the Criteria section add something like the following:

```
=forms![Customers]![CompanyName]
```

The form tells the query to look at the form collection. The Customers form provides the form name, and the Company Name form tells it what control to reference. Remember to use the preceding syntax, because if you start using `Screen.Activeform` and not the actual form name, you could run into invalid results because the form you want lost the focus before this call. This means that you're referring to the wrong control. If the form happens to be in design mode when you make the call, Null is assumed. For more information on queries, refer to Chapter 9, "Specialized Queries."

Keeping the User Informed

It's very important to keep users informed about what you're doing. There are two ways to do this: through a macro or through VBA code. To do this through a macro you need to add this line to your macro: `Action set to Echo, Echo On to No`. The text that you want to display is typed in Status Bar Text. In VBA code, the following line would need to be added: `DoCmd.Echo False, "Text to be placed on the Status Bar"`. By adding either of these, you place the text of the message in the Status Bar at the bottom of the screen. In some cases this isn't enough information to be passed on, or it might be something where the user should be able to cancel out of the operation. To accomplish this you need to open a dialog form. This dialog form is similar to a msgbox dialog box, but you need to pass information to it throughout the transaction. Figure 28.8 is a sample dialog box that gives the users information on the operation and gives them the option of canceling the operation by clicking the Cancel button.

FIGURE 28.8.

A generic status form.

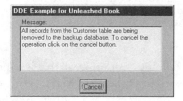

When you set up this form, it's important to remember to set a few of the form options. The following list is in addition to the list setting up the print form:

Option	How to Set It
Allow Edits	Set to No
Auto Modal	Set to Yes
Border style	Set to Dialog
Min Max Buttons	Set to None
Modal	Set to Yes
Control Box	Set to No

These extra options are set to make sure the user is unable to do other work while this critical operation is occurring and to make sure that he can't minimize or close the form while it's still working. The only ways out of this form are to cancel the operation or to let it finish, at which time the Cancel button changes to an OK button and the user knows the task has completed. Figure 28.8 includes a textbox for the information you wish to display to the users, as well as a Cancel button. You could also add a progress indicator bar to this form. However, when you do this, you will find yourself programming this functionality instead of making the application function correctly.

Exiting the Application on the Close of the Main Form

It's important that when the user closes the Main form, the application also closes. It's also important to remember that if the user is running Access and not a runtime version of Access, you shouldn't close Access on the close of the Main form. There are two ways to accomplish this. The first is to create a macro that is called whenever a Close button is selected. The second is to create a VBA function that receives a parameter of *FormName*. Whether the form closes and activates the Main form or closes the application depends on the form. The following is an example of VBA code that closes a form or the application depending on who calls the function:

```
Sub CloseForm(strName As String)
    If strName = "Main" Then
        DoCmd.SelectObject acForm, strName
        CloseCurrentDatabase
    Else
        DoCmd.SelectObject acForm, strName
        DoCmd.Close
        DoCmd.OpenForm "Main"
    End If
End Sub
```

To have the form call this subroutine, all that is required is a `Call closeform(me.name)`. It compares the name passed in to the word Main. If the form that placed the call is Main, the application is closed, leaving Access open. Otherwise, the calling form is closed and the Main form is opened.

One Way to Program in Access

When you start programming Access, in most cases you start looking for the fastest way to get it done. In most cases this is to use the macro language. This is okay as you learn, but it limits your application's capabilities as you start requiring more complicated applications. The next step in development is to use the basic VBA code that is available to you. For more information on VBA code, refer to Chapter 23. After spending some time using VBA code, you will want to start using VBA code to its fullest. The only way to achieve this is to have a full understanding of Jet, Data Access Objects (DAO), and Microsoft Access Objects (MAO). MAO offers the programmer and application developer some very powerful features. If you stay with the macro environment you can still get to these commands, but you're limited. For example, `Runsql` in the macro window lets you use only 256 characters. If you were making the same call `Docmd.RunSQL`, you could use 32,768 characters.

Summary

When you develop an Access application, you should always take your applications to the next level, making them look and feel more professional.

Testing and Debugging Applications

29

by Dwayne Gifford

IN THIS CHAPTER

One of the biggest problems you face when designing and developing applications in Access is debugging your Visual Basic for Applications (VBA) code. The topic of debugging always brings up the question of how to make sure that the code you have written actually does what it's meant to do. You sometimes must walk through your code to confirm that each line is acting as expected. Another problem area is tracking version control on a database application. These areas are covered in this chapter. The information provided in this chapter should help you avoid both of these problems when you design applications in Access.

Using the Access Debugger

The first step in using the Access 95 debugger is to open a new or existing module. You then open the Debug window by selecting View | Debug Window.

> **TIP**
>
> The Debug window was known as the Immediate window in previous versions of Access.

Before you read about how to use the Debug window, you should know a few things that will help make your job and future developers' jobs easier. When you write VBA code, keep the following points in mind:

- It's important to always use comments throughout your code. Most developers think they will later remember what they were using a routine for. Well, three months from now, you probably won't remember a thing about that routine. So when your boss asks you to comment your code so that the next developer or support person will know what each routine in the application is doing, he could be doing you a big favor, if you happen to be that next person.

- Some of the common problems with VBA code occur because you use variables you think are the same, but they are actually named differently. To get around this problem, you can turn on Option Explicit. This will make sure that all variables are defined before they can be referenced. To do this, select Tools | Options, select the Module tab, and make sure that the option Require Variable Declaration is turned on.

> **NOTE**
>
> If you have created any modules before you have turned on the option called Option Explicit, you need to type this line of code yourself at the start of the Module declaration section, for each of the old modules. The line of code would be `Option Explicit`.

The Debug window is composed of two areas or panes:

- The immediate pane: This pane shows the immediate evaluation of statements, methods, and subprocedures. The immediate pane is always visible if the Debug window is open.

- The watch pane: This pane is displayed only if a watch expression has been set. Watch expressions are explained later in this chapter.

You must run the code to analyze it in the Debug window. One method of running the code is to call it from VBA code during normal execution of a module. An example is when the user clicks a button, the function `dosomething()` is called and executed. The second method is to enter the print function, by the function name, into the Debug window. But before you open the form or enter the command into the Debug window, you need to be able to stop the code at a certain point. When code isn't running, the Debug window shows `<Ready>` in its status line at the top of its window, but when code is running, it shows the current procedure name.

Setting Execution Breakpoints

It's often desirable to set a breakpoint that suspends program execution at a certain point in the code. This technique enables the developer to examine the state of the program at that point. There are two ways to set an execution breakpoint. The first method is to set a breakpoint. The second is to set a suspend execution point. In both cases, you must click the line of code where you want the code to be suspended. To set a breakpoint after you have set the active line of code, select Run | Toggle Breakpoint or press the F9 key. To set a suspend execution, move the current line of code down one row, and type the word `stop`. The only problem with using the suspend execution option is that when you're ready to release the code to the end users, you need to remember to either comment out the stop code or remove it. Otherwise, when a user runs the code, it suddenly stops and opens the function or sub where the stop was placed.

> **TIP**
>
> To clear an existing breakpoint, highlight the breakpoint in the code. Then choose Run | Toggle Breakpoint or press F9.

Entering Commands

To start the execution of the code, open the form or enter the `?` statement followed by the function name. An example is `? dosomething()`. The parentheses are optional if no parameters are to be passed into the function. If you want to call a sub, type `call dosomething`. For more information on subs and functions, refer to Chapter 23, "Visual Basic for Applications." Also, after the code has stopped, you can look at variables' values; controls' values on forms, by referencing the control with `form!formname!control`; or just about anything that has a value and is in scope of the database. For example, suppose that you have a control on a form named main, and the name of the control is lblMainType. To refer to the caption of this control, you type ? `forms!Main!lblMainType.Caption`. For details on data access objects and their collections, refer to Chapter 25, "Data Access Objects."

Watch Expressions

Two types of watches are available to you, the Access developer: instant watch and watch expression.

Instant Watch

The instant watch enables you to look at an expression once. To do this, first highlight the expression, and then select Tools | Instant Watch. If you want to then add the expression to the Watch pane of the Debug window, click the Add button. The Add Watch dialog box, shown in Figure 29.1, opens. It walks you through the steps for adding the current expression to the Watch pane. You sometimes can find an expression too hard to interpret, and the instant watch won't be able to display the answer. Or the instant watch won't be able to display the expression because the expression is too large. To get around either of these difficulties, click the Immediate pane of the Debug window and enter a ? expression. The value is displayed for you.

FIGURE 29.1.

The Add Watch dialog box.

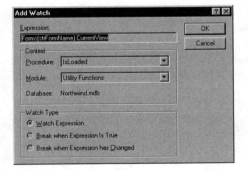

Setting Watch Expressions

You can set a watch expression in two ways, but first you must select the variable you want to watch. You then should select Tools | Add Watch. The Add Watch dialog box is opened with the expression set to the variable you had selected.

In this dialog box are two areas you can fill in: the Context area and the Watch Type area. The Context area enables you to set the scope to one specific procedure of the currently selected module or to all procedures of the currently selected module. From the Module drop-down list, you can select whether to watch the expression at a Module level or a Database level. To set the scope at a Database level, select (All Modules). It's best to select the module first, followed by the procedure. The module defaults to the current module from which the expression was built. The procedure defaults to All Procedures.

> **NOTE**
>
> If you have selected All Modules, All Procedures is the only option in the Procedure drop-down list.

The next area of the Add Watch dialog box is Watch Type. This area gives you three options to choose from: Watch Expression, Break when Expression Is True, and Break when Expression has Changed. The first option, Watch Expression, enables you to view the expression in the Watch pane of the Debug window, and it doesn't pause execution. The second option, Break when Expression Is True, enables you to view the expression in the Watch pane, and it pauses the code when it's set to True. The third option, Break when Expression has Changed, enables you to view the expression in the Watch pane, and it pauses the code when the value changes.

Figure 29.2 shows three expressions listed in the Watch pane. The first is a Watch Expression. Notice that the icon to the left of the expression is a pair of glasses. The second expression is a Break when Expression is True, and its icon is a hand with a sheet of paper. The third expression is Break when Expression has Changed, and it's represented by a hand with a triangle in the palm.

FIGURE 29.2.

The Debug window with the Watch pane and the Immediate pane open.

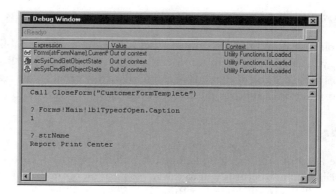

Tracing Program Execution

After you have the code suspended, 10 options are available to you to debug your code: Continue, End, Reset, Step Into, Step Over, Step to Cursor, Toggle Breakpoint, Clear All Breakpoints, Set Next Statement, and Show Next Statement. These options are located on the

Run menu. During this process, if you want to see which procedures have been called up to the current point in code, you can select Tools | Calls, which opens the dialog box shown in Figure 29.3.

FIGURE 29.3.

The Calls dialog box.

This figure shows the chain of calls to this point. The procedures are listed in the order in which they have been called. The first item in the list is the current procedure, and the other procedures are listed next, all the way down to the originator of the calling sequence. If you click a function in the list and then click the Show button, you're placed back in Access with the function you selected as the active function. If instead you want to cancel and return to the current procedure, click Close.

Continue

When you finish stepping through your code to the point were you want it to continue without your help, select Run | Continue. This action tells the code to run as it would normally until it completes the code or until it finds another code break.

End

If you have found the problem and you want to keep all the public variables set as they are so that you can refer to them through the Debug window, select Run | End. This action terminates the execution of the code, clearing all private variables but leaving all public variables set. This selection also leaves the cursor at the current position in the code.

Reset

The Reset option operates just like the End option except that it ends the code and resets all variables. It also returns you to the active position of the cursor upon completing the end-of-code call. To run Reset, select Run | Reset or press Shift-F5.

Step Into

The Step Into option calls each line of code. If it hits a call to a procedure, it steps through this procedure and calls each line of code there. This is the most thorough way to dig into a procedure to find a problem. As you check each step and confirm that each is correct, you should move the breakpoint down, making sure that you aren't wasting your time stepping through code that works. To run Step Into, select Run | Step Into or press F8.

Step Over

Step Over treats each call to a procedure as a line of code, so if you know the procedure is working correctly, you can step over the whole procedure instead of walking through it. To run Step Over, select Run | Step Over or press Shift-F8.

Step to Cursor

The Step to Cursor option continues the code from the currently executing line to the cursor position in the code. The cursor must be in the current procedure; otherwise, it does a continue. To set the cursor position, click a line to make it the active line, and then select Run | Step to Cursor or press Ctrl-F8. I don't know about you, but many times I have moved down to a line of code and then set a new breakpoint so that I could skip the middle code because I knew it worked. This option certainly helps you get around turning so many breakpoints off and on.

Toggle Breakpoint

To set a Breakpoint in the code, select Run | Toggle Breakpoint or press F9. If there is already a breakpoint, this selection turns off that breakpoint for you.

Clear All Breakpoints

If you have found your problem and you want to run the code without being stopped at any breakpoints, select Run | Clear All Breakpoints or press Ctrl-Shift-F9.

> **NOTE**
>
> This option clears only those breakpoints set by Run | Toggle Breakpoint; it doesn't remove stop code calls you have added.

Set Next Statement

The Set Next Statement option enables you to change the flow of the code for the current procedure only. You can step over a piece of code or rerun a piece of code. Also, because you can change code when you have the program suspended, it's best to rerun the piece of code you change, then to reset and rerun the code. You will find with time that this is the most useful option. To use the Set Next Statement option, you first must set your cursor to the part of code you want to run next. Then select Run | Set Next Statement or press Ctrl-F9.

Show Next Statement

When you're looking through the code in debug mode, you will sometimes forget what procedure you were running before you started looking through the code. To get back to this spot, select Run | Show Next Statement, and you're moved back to the next statement to be run.

Displaying Values Dynamically

Sometimes when you run into problems, even after stepping through the code, you can't reproduce the problem. So you still need to find the problem but without stopping the code. To do this, you need to use the debug object that has a method of `Print`. The `Print` method takes an optional parameter of an expression. The expression type is any type you want to pass in. If you leave the parameter blank, `Print` prints a blank line for you. The following code is from the DDE.MDB file on the CD that comes with this book from the routine used in module mdlOLESample. The procedure is OLEMAIN. Notice here that `Debug.Print` was added for each `DoCmd.Echo` call. This way, there would be a copy of the output in the Debug window.

```
DoCmd.Echo False, "Opening file - " & snpInfo("FP") & snpInfo("FN")
Debug.Print "Opening file - " & snpInfo("FP") & snpInfo("FN")
objWord.fileOpen "" & snpInfo("FP") & snpInfo("FN") & ""

DoCmd.Echo False, "Merging Document"
objWord.MailMergeToDoc
Debug.Print "Merging Document"
DoCmd.Echo False, "Printing Document"
objWord.[FilePrint]
Debug.Print "Printing Document"
DoCmd.Echo False, "Closing Documents"
objWord.FileClose 2
objWord.FileClose 2
Debug.Print "Closing Document"
DoCmd.Echo False, "Terminating Object"
Debug.Print "Terminating Object"
Set objWord = Nothing
```

Notice in Figure 29.4 that OLEMAIN was called from the Immediate pane of the Debug window. Then, as the code was called, the debug statements appeared.

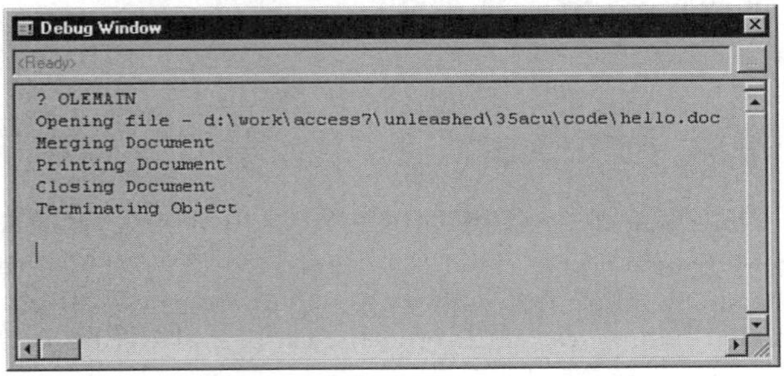

FIGURE 29.4.

The Immediate pane of the Debug window with the debug statements shown.

At times, you will try to do something that causes an error in the code, but when you step through the code, it works. The reason this sometimes happens is that when you walk through the code, the Debug window will actually change which object has focus, and this fixes the problem. So by using Debug.Print, you can print something to the Debug window, and then when you get the error, you can find out were the problem really happened. Also, if you use Debug.Print without the procedure being opened, it still prints the data to the Immediate pane, and when you open the Debug window next, you will see your Debug.Print statements in the Immediate pane.

Using the Performance Analyzer Wizard

The Performance Analyzer Wizard in effect debugs the application from a performance standpoint. To get to the Wizard, select Tools | Analyze Performance. The dialog box shown in Figure 29.5 appears, showing you the Wizard with the defaults set.

FIGURE 29.5.

The Performance Analyzer dialog box.

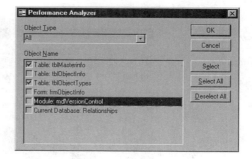

When this dialog box first opens, the default Object Type will be set to the current selected object in the Database window. In the Object Name list, you will see all objects of the type Form, but they won't be selected. To change to a different type of object, click the Object Type drop-down list, and select the type from the list. If you select the Current Database choice, you can analyze the relationships that have been set in the database. If you select any of the other options, you can view all objects that are of the selected type. If you select the All option, you're given a list of all the objects in the database.

After you have chosen what object type you want to analyze, the next step is to select the actual objects you want the Analyzer to analyze. To do this, find the object in the list and select it; then either click the box located to the left of the object name or click the Select button. This action places a check mark beside the item to indicate that the item is selected. If you want to remove an item from the selection, click the object and then either click the check mark or click the Deselect All button. This action removes the check mark from beside the name of the object. If you want to select all items from the list, click the Select All button. If at any time in the process you want to start over, click the Deselect All button. Also, you can select or de-select items from each object type. For example, say that you select an item from the Table object and then you change to the object type of Query; the table you selected previously is still selected. Select All and Deselect All are for the current object type only.

NOTE

Hidden and System Object won't appear in the object list unless they are marked as being visible.

After you have selected the objects you want to analyze, click OK. If the Analyzer has any sug-gestions, recommendations, or ideas, it opens the dialog box shown in Figure 29.6. Otherwise, an acknowledgment dialog box is displayed, informing you that the Analyzer has no recom-mendations, ideas, or suggestions for the objects you selected, and then you're returned to the Database window.

FIGURE 29.6.

The Performance Analyzer with the suggestions dialog box open.

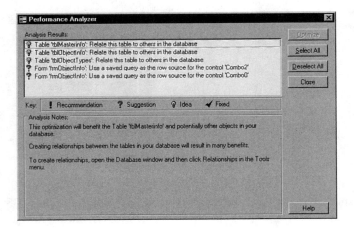

When the dialog box shown in Figure 29.6 is first opened, it displays a list of all the items for which it has a recommendation, suggestion, or idea, with the corresponding icons beside them. If the Analyzer has a recommendation, a blue ! is shown beside the item; if it has a suggestion, a green ? is shown; and if it has an idea, a yellow light bulb is shown. After you have fixed an object, a blue check mark is placed beside it. As you select each object in the list, the notes in the Analysis Notes section will change to reflect reasons why you should follow the suggestion, what should be done, and how to accomplish it. To have the Wizard fix an object, you must follow these steps:

1. Select the object you want to fix.

> **NOTE**
>
> For the Wizard to be able to optimize the object, it must have had a recommendation or a suggestion; otherwise, the Optimize button is disabled.

2. Click the Optimize button.

> **NOTE**
>
> The Analyzer provides a step-by-step procedure for fixing each type of problem. In the sample case, the Analyzer created the queries for you and then changed the row source to reference the queries it just made rather than an SQL statement.

3. Type the name of the query.
4. Click OK.

The Analyzer then creates the query, changes the row source, and puts a blue check mark beside the object in the list.

At any point in the process, you can click the Close button and be returned to the Database window. There is a limit to the number of suggestions the Analyzer can give you; it will be up to you in the future to look for performance suggestions. Always try to remember what the Analyzer suggests or recommends so that as you develop more objects in Access, you're always developing for the best performance available for the application.

Version Control with Access

One of the hardest things to do with Access is to implement a good version-control application. The reason it's so hard is that all objects are contained in one file. Most version-control applications perform version control on the file, not the objects internal to the file. So it's really left up to you, the developer, to implement a version-control system for your application.

Also, when you have an Access application in production, your developers won't be able to work against the production database that the users are using. The developers also need to be able to revert to the version of the object that existed before they started working on the object. One of the best ways to provide this capability is to implement a replication system that doesn't update data but only updates the objects.

But with replication, you can't replicate a table object without replicating the data for the table as well. So if all you want to do is a version-controlled application, you need to implement a system that updates objects and not data as required. First, you need the master database that neither the users nor the developers will work against. Before you create copies of the master, you first get the master set up. It's possible that you won't want to have some of the objects sent out to the other databases. So to keep those objects from being sent, don't enter them into the Object Control table. Also, you will want to handle different types of updates, meaning that for forms, you can just delete the old object and then copy in the new one. But this technique isn't suggested for tables because of the data they contain.

After the master is set up, you need two other databases. This requirement is based on the users all running off of one database. The first database is for the users to make changes to the data, and the second is for the developers to develop on. Then in each database there needs to be a table that contains the object name, the updated date, and the version number. If you want to, you can also have a version date column. For every object in the database, there needs to be an entry in this table with its appropriate version and the date it was updated. As the developers make changes to the objects in their database, they can update the object in the master database and its entry in the object table.

Then, when the user's database detects that a newer version exists, it updates itself to the newest version of the object. The detection can be whenever the first user of the day opens the database or when the last user closes the database. It could be any time you, the system administrator, decide. The thing to remember is that if you update a module when users are still in the application, the object isn't updated for them until the next refresh interval, or until they close the database and then reenter. On the CD-ROM that comes with this book, you'll find a sample Version_Control.MDB database that will help you set up a version control for your Access application.

Summary

This chapter covered testing and debugging applications using the Performance Analyzer Wizard and version control. The information provided here should help you avoid some problems when you start designing Access applications.

Security

30

by Dwayne Gifford

About Access Security

When you start working with Access, one of the first things you will want to know is what kind of security Access has available. Two security methods are available in Access: setting a password on the database, and user-level security. Each method offers a different level of security, and each can be used in its own way. Although this chapter is written primarily for the workgroup user on a local area network (LAN), most security features can be used with a stand-alone Access database.

Security for an Access application is always enabled, even if you don't sign into the application. Most users think that the security is turned off because they didn't need to enter a username and password. In reality, security is on because by default you go into an Access application as the default user. The default user is the Admin user and in turn has full permissions. One of the problems facing you when setting up user-level security for your application is ensuring that the default user doesn't have permissions to the application.

Plan for Security from the Start

When an Access application is started, one of the most forgotten parts of the development is security. It's very important that before you add your first object to the database, you have already started thinking about and planning the security that will be needed for the application. One of the ways to do this is to have a table that will help you map the users to their groups, and then have another table that will help you map your groups to the objects in the database and then to the type of permissions required to the object. As an object is added to the database, you then can map groups to the object, making sure that the users who need access to the object have it. And as a new user is added, you can add the groups to the user as required, making sure that the new user can do the required job in the database.

> **NOTE**
>
> Permissions should be added at a Group level and not at a User level. This way it will be easier to add users because you tell the user to be part of this group, and automatically this user will have the same permissions that the group has. It's easier to remove or add permissions because you remove or add it once for the group and not for each user. This in turn makes the application easier to support.

The Database Password

To add a database password, you select Tools | Security | Set Database Password. As shown in Figure 30.1, the Set Database Password dialog box is opened, prompting you for the password and a verification of the password. If you aren't logged onto the database in exclusive mode and you try to set the database password, an error is displayed, telling you to reopen the database in exclusive mode.

FIGURE 30.1.

Setting the database password.

The level of security offered by a database password is very straightforward—either you know the password and can get into the database, or you don't know it and can't get in. This is the easiest security to implement and is the most likely to have problems. The problem is that one user will tell another user, and then those people tell someone else, and so on, until you have no security left on the database. The other problem comes about when everyone forgets the password. If you do forget the password for the database, there is no way to recover the database. If you're going to use replication, you can't use a database password because the synchronization becomes impossible. The reason is that the calling database has no way to supply the database password. Also, if you try to import or link tables from this database you will be required to enter the database password. The only other time the user will be prompted for the database password on a linked table is if the database password gets changed.

Workgroups and the SYSTEM.MDW File

By default, when you open Access, you're signing in as the Admin user. The Admin user is a member of the Admins group and the Users group. You're also using the default SYSTEM.MDW, which is the workgroup file that gets put on your computer during any type of Access installation. The SYSTEM.MDW file contains all groups and user account information. This is also where each user's preferences will be stored. So before you add a new user to the database or groups, it's important to either create or join a new workgroup. To do this, you must use the Workgroup Administrator application.

Using the Workgroup Administrator

The Workgroup Administrator application will help you join new workgroup files or create workgroup files as needed. The first step in using the Workgroup Administrator is to open the application. There are two ways to do this. The first method is to look for MS Access Workgroup Administrator in the Microsoft Office group, and the second is look in the folder where Access is installed and locate the file named WRKGADM.EXE. With this tool, you can join an already created workgroup or create a new workgroup.

Creating a New Workgroup

To create your own workgroup, carry out the following eight steps:

1. Now that Workgroup Administrator is open, click the Create button. This selection opens the Workgroup Owner Information dialog box. This dialog box is shown in Figure 30.2 with all information entered.

FIGURE 30.2.

The Workgroup Owner Information dialog box.

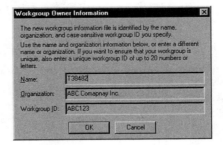

2. The first piece of information required on this dialog box is for the Name text box. Enter your name here. The maximum is 39 alphanumeric characters.

3. The next text box is Organization. Enter the company name in this box. The maximum is 39 alphanumeric characters.

4. Workgroup ID is the last piece of required information. Enter the ID, keeping in mind that the Workgroup ID is case sensitive. The maximum is 20 alphanumeric characters.

5. Click OK.

6. The next prompt is the Workgroup Information File dialog box. Indicate the name to save the workgroup as and where to save it. If you aren't sure of the location, you can click Browse and use the Select Workgroup Information File Locator to locate where you want to have your new workgroup created.

NOTE

The information used here to create the new workgroup file should be saved in a safe place in case you ever need to create a new workgroup file.

WARNING

Don't save the workgroup file with the same name as the application but a different extension, because Access requires the ability to open both the database file and the workgroup file. So if the files have the same name when the application is opened,

Access tries to create a .LDB file for both the Access database and the workgroup file. When it tries to create these files, you receive an Error unable to create file message, and Access can't open the database. For example, say that you have a database called Accounts.MDB, and you name the workgroup file Accounts.MDW. When Access is opened, it creates an Accounts.LDB file. Then when the database Accounts.MDB is opened, Access tries to create another Accounts.LDB. But it can't, because it will have a write conflict when it tries to use Accounts.LDB. The .LDB file is the Lock File that Access creates to keep track of who has what record locked. It defaults the file to *filename*.LDB. When the database is closed, it also removes all .LDB files for you. It's also suggested that you not take the default setting, because it will overwrite the default SYSTEM.MDW that came with Access.

7. After you have entered the new workgroup name or path, click OK.

8. The dialog box shown in Figure 30.3 opens, prompting you to confirm the information you just entered. Click Change if you want to change any information.

FIGURE 30.3.

The Confirm Workgroup Information dialog box.

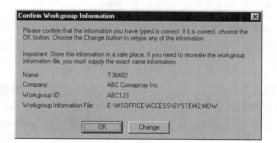

9. Click OK to create the workgroup file. If the file already exists, you're prompted to confirm the overwrite of the existing workgroup file. When the file has been created, a confirmation dialog box is displayed, informing you that the workgroup was created.

Joining an Existing Workgroup

If you have created a workgroup file with security features, the next step is to have the users of the database application join this workgroup. First, open the Workgroup Administrator. Next, click the Join button to display the Workgroup Information File dialog box, shown in Figure 30.4.

FIGURE 30.4.

The Workgroup Information File dialog box.

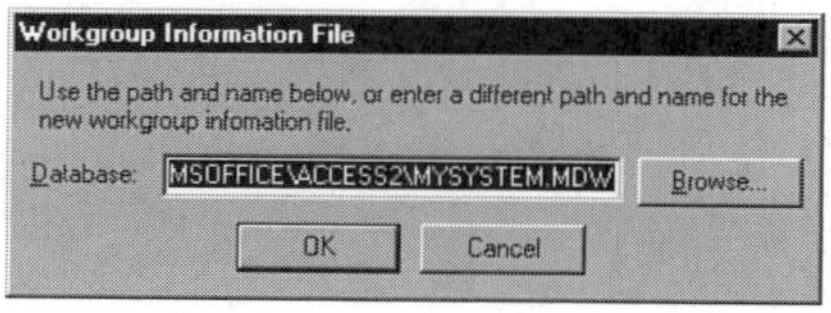

In this dialog box, you can enter the path of the workgroup. This can be a drive letter, folder names, and file name, or it can be a network share name such as *MachineName\ ShareName\Directory\WorkgroupName*.mdw. If you aren't sure of the workgroup name and location, click the Browse button. This selection brings up the File Locator dialog box. This dialog box enables you to navigate your way through drives, folders, and network shares. When you have located your workgroup file, select it and then click OK. If you do use a share name rather than a physical drive or network drive that has been already connected to your machine, it's important to remember that this share name can never change, unless you change each user's workgroup share information to reflect this share-name change.

The Concept of Permissions

The idea behind permissions is to allow or disallow a user access to objects that are in the database or even disallow access to the database itself. Permissions to the database are granted in two ways: to the user or to a group.

User and Group Accounts

To do anything with users or groups, you first must open the User and Group Accounts dialog box, shown in Figure 30.5. To open this dialog box, select Tools | Security | User and Group Accounts.

FIGURE 30.5.

The User and Group Accounts dialog box.

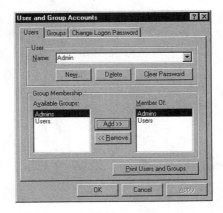

In this dialog box, you can add new users, delete a user, clear a user's password, add new groups, delete a group, change the password for the current user, add a user to a group, or remove a user from a group.

Adding and Deleting Users

To add or delete a user, you must be a member of the Admins group. To add a user, follow these steps:

1. Click the New button.
2. In the dialog box that appears, enter the User Name and Personal ID. If you're on a network, it's suggested that you use the user's login name from the network. Otherwise, make sure that the name is unique for each user of the workgroup. Also be sure to use a unique Personal ID.
3. Click OK.

> **TIP**
>
> Follow common guidelines for creating a secure and unique Personal ID. At minimum, use a mix of alphanumeric characters to create a string that isn't an actual word.

To delete a user, follow these steps:

1. Select the user from the User listbox. To do this, click the drop-down arrow and select the user you want to delete.
2. Click the Delete button.
3. A Confirmation dialog box appears, making sure that you really want to delete the currently selected user.
4. If you're sure, click Yes; otherwise, click No.

You're then returned to the dialog box shown in Figure 30.5.

Adding and Deleting Groups

To add or delete a group, the first step for either process is to activate the Groups tab. To do this, click the Groups tab shown at the top of Figure 30.5. To add a group, follow these steps:

1. Click the New button.
2. Enter the New Group Name and Personal ID for the group.
3. Click OK.

You're returned to the dialog shown in Figure 30.5, and the active group is the group you just entered.

To delete a group, follow these steps:

1. Select the group from the group listbox. To do this, click the drop-down arrow and select the group you want to delete.
2. Click the Delete button.
3. A Confirmation dialog box appears, making sure that you really want to delete the currently selected group.
4. If you're sure, click Yes; otherwise, click No.

You're then returned to the dialog box shown in Figure 30.5.

> **NOTE**
>
> When you're adding a new user or group, the name must be unique between both user and group, meaning that you can't have a group and user with the same name. If you do, a `Microsoft Access Account name already exists` message is displayed, and you're returned to the dialog shown in Figure 30.5 after clicking OK.

Adding or Removing a Group from a User

It's important to remember that not all users will belong to the same groups. So after you have added the groups, it's time to tell the users what group or groups they are members of. First, if you aren't on the Users tab, click the tab labeled Users. To add a group to a user, you then carry out the following steps:

1. Select the user from the User listbox. To do this, click the drop-down arrow and select the user you want to work with.
2. In the Group Membership area, click a group in the Available Groups listbox, and then click the Add >> button. This action adds the currently selected group to the user.

To remove a group from a user, carry out the following steps:

1. Select the user from the User listbox. To do this, click the drop-down arrow and click the user you want work with.
2. In the Group Membership area, click a group in the Member Of listbox, then click the << Remove button. This action removes the currently selected group from the user.

Changing Your Logon Password

To change your password, you need to activate the Change Logon Password tab. To do this, click the tab labeled Change Logon Password. Here you're required to enter the following three pieces of information:

- The old password
- The new password
- A verification of the new password

If the old password doesn't match the current password, you can't change the password. Or if the new password and the verify password don't match, you can't change your password. After you have typed the old, new, and verify passwords, you can click either Apply or OK. The Apply button leaves you at the dialog shown in Figure 30.5, and the OK button returns you to Access.

Clearing a User Password

To clear a user password, the first step is to make sure that you're on the Users tab. Then select the user from the User listbox, and click the Clear Password button. Before clicking the Clear Password button, make sure that you've selected the correct user because there is no confirmation—the password is just reset.

User and Group Permissions

After you have added the users and their groups, it's time to define the permissions that these groups or users will have on the objects in the database. To do this, you must be signed in as a member of the Admins group. After you're into the database, you need to open the dialog box shown in Figure 30.6. To open this dialog box, select Tools | Security | User and Group Permissions. This dialog box has two tabs available: Permissions and Change Owner.

FIGURE 30.6.

The User and Group Permissions dialog box with the Permissions tab active.

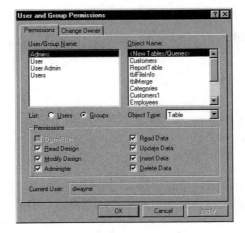

The Permissions Tab

The Permissions tab is the active tab shown in Figure 30.6. This tab has three components. The first element is the User/Group Name area, which contains a list of users or groups, depending on which List option button is active. The second element is an Object Name listbox, which is composed of all objects that match the object type currently selected in the Object Type combo box. The Object Name listbox is a multiselect listbox, meaning that you can select more than one object in the list at a time. To do this, hold down the Shift or Ctrl key while selecting the objects with the mouse. The third area is the Permissions for the currently selected user or group and the selected object.

Here is the step-by-step process for changing the permissions on an object in the database:

1. Select the user or group for the User/Group Name listbox. If you want to change from a user list to a group list, click the List option button named Groups.

2. Select the object from the Object Name listbox. To change the list to a different type of object, click the arrow at the side of the Object Type combo box, and select the object you want to change the permissions for.

3. Based on the type of object selected and the user or group selected, the Permissions check boxes fill in appropriately. To remove a permission or add a permission, click the corresponding Permissions check box.

4. Either click Apply, which applies the permissions without prompting for confirmation, or select a new object. If you select a new object, you're prompted as to whether you want to apply your changes. If you have made a change and you try to close the dialog box or try to select a new object, a Change dialog box appears, asking whether you want to save the permission changes.

Different permissions are available to select from for each object type in the database, depending on the active object type. The following list gives you some notes to remember when trying to turn on or off permissions on a Table object:

■ If you mark any of the data options—Read Data, Update Data, Insert Data, or Delete Data—Read Design is selected by default.

■ If you select any data option other than Read Data, Read Data is selected by default.

■ If you deselect Read Data, all other data options and design options are turned off except Read Design.

■ If you select Modify Design, the Read Data, Update Data, and Delete Data options are selected by default.

■ If you select Administer, all design and data options are selected by default.

The following list gives you some notes to remember when trying to turn on or off permissions on a Queries object:

■ If you mark any of the data options—Read Data, Update Data, Insert Data, or Delete Data—Read Design is selected by default.

■ If you select any data option other than Read Data, Read Data is selected by default.

■ If you deselect Read Data, all other data options and design options are turned off except Read Design.

■ You can select Read Design with all the data options or none of the data options.

■ If you select Administer, all design and data options are selected automatically.

For Form objects, four permissions options are available:

■ If you select Open/Run, the user or group can open and run the form.

■ If you select Read Design, the user or member of a group can view the form design.

■ If you select Modify Design, the user or member of the group can make changes and delete the form.

■ If you select Administrator, all permissions are selected automatically.

For Report objects, four permissions options are available:

■ If you select Open/Run, the user or group can open and run the report.

■ If you select Read Design, the user or member of a group can view the report design.

- If you select Modify Design, the user or member of the group can make changes and delete the report.
- If you select Administrator, all other permissions are selected automatically.

For Macro objects, four permissions options are available:

- If you select Open/Run, the user or group can open and run the macro.
- If you select Read Design, the user or member of a group can view the macro design.
- If you select Modify Design, the user or member of the group can view, make changes, and delete the macros.
- If you select Administrator, all other permissions are selected automatically.

For Module objects, three permissions options are available.

- If you select Read Design, the user or member of a group can view the module design.
- If you select Modify Design, the user or member of the group can make changes and delete the module.
- If you select Administrator, all other permissions are selected automatically.

The last database object you can set permissions on is the database itself. To do this, select Database from the Object Type listbox. Notice that in the list of object names, only one option is available: Current Database. Also, only three permissions options are available:

- If you select Open/Run, the user or member of the group can open and run the database.
- If you select Open Exclusive, the user or member of the group can open the database exclusively. If you want to make sure that no user opens the database exclusively, this is the best way to do it.
- If you select Administrator, all other permissions are selected automatically.

If a group needs to be able to open the database to use forms and run reports, the minimum permissions you need to give this group are as listed here:

- Tables: The group needs Read/Design and Read Data to be selected or else forms and reports won't be able to open.
- Queries: To have the queries operate, the group needs Read Design and Read Data to be selected.
- Forms: For the forms to be opened by the group, Open/Run needs to be selected.
- Reports: For the reports to be run or printed, Open/Run needs to be selected.
- Macros: If any macros will be run by the forms or reports or on open, Open/Run needs to be selected.
- Modules: You need not select anything for the modules to function correctly.

■ Database: The group needs to have Open/Run selected or else the group's users won't be able to open the database.

The Change Owner Tab

Figure 30.7 shows the User and Group Permissions dialog box with the active tab set to Change Owner. The Change Owner tab has three components. The first part is the Object and Current Owner listbox. This area derives its list from the Object Type combo box, whose default is Form. The second part is the New Owner combo box, which is derived from the List item that is selected (either Users or Groups). The last part is the Change Owner button. This button takes the currently selected object and changes the owner to the selected New Owner. If you have permissions to change the owner, the object is updated to the new owner; otherwise, an Error dialog box appears, indicating that you can't change the owner of this object. Three buttons are available to select here: the OK and Cancel buttons, which return you to the dialog shown in Figure 30.5, and the Help button, which opens Help and gives you some information on how to fix the problem. You can change all objects in the database this way except the actual owner of the database.

FIGURE 30.7.

The User and Group Permissions dialog box with the Change Owner tab active.

The following is a five-step process for changing the owner of a database:

1. Start Access using the New Owner, and create a new database.
2. Select File | Get External Data | Import.
3. In this dialog box, first make sure that the File of Type box is set to Microsoft Access. Then navigate through the Folders until you locate the database you want to change the owner for. Select the database and then click OK.
4. Make sure that you select all objects under each of the six tabs.
5. Click OK.

The dialog box changes from the list of objects to the status of the import. For more details on how to import and export data, refer to Chapter 5, "Importing and Exporting Data." When you're finished importing all the objects, you have successfully changed the database owner.

> **NOTE**
>
> When you're assigning ownership of objects, it's possible to assign the ownership to groups. But the database object must be assigned to a user.

The Security Wizard

To run the Security Wizard, select Tools | Security | User-Level Security Wizard. But before you do this, it's important to open Access as the new Admin user. The reason is that the new database will be created using the current user as the owner. After you have signed in as the new Admin user for the database and have opened the Security tool, the dialog box shown in Figure 30.8 is opened, prompting you for which objects you want to secure in the new database.

FIGURE 30.8.

The Security Wizard dialog box.

> **NOTE**
>
> The Security Wizard creates a new database and doesn't affect the current database.

After you have selected the objects you want to be secured, click OK. If you want more information on the process, click the Help button. The Cancel button returns you to the Database window. If you didn't sign in as the new Admin user, but as Admin, the message shown in Figure 30.9 is displayed.

FIGURE 30.9.

The Security Wizard
Admin warning dialog box.

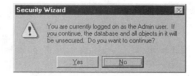

This dialog box is letting you know that the database can't be successfully secured when you're signed in as user Admin. You can carry on, but the database won't be secured the way that the Security Wizard is designed to secure it. It's suggested that you sign out and then sign in again as the new Admin user. Otherwise, the Destination Database dialog box shows up next and wants to know the new name for the secured database. The default name is Secure + *DatabaseName*.MDB. After you have entered the new database name and its new location, click the Save button. If you watch the Status bar, you can see the progress as the database is secured. When the secured database has been created, the dialog box shown in Figure 30.10 is displayed.

FIGURE 30.10.

The Security Wizard
acknowledgment
dialog box.

This dialog box announces that your new database has been created successfully. If you acknowledge the dialog box by clicking OK, you're returned to the Unsecure Database window.

> **NOTE**
>
> First, Security Wizard Tool also encrypts the database for you, making sure that the database is fully secure. Second, it leaves the Admin user as a member of the Admins group, and it leaves the Users group with Open/Run permissions on the database.

Database Encryption

After you have secured the database, you can take one more step to make sure that no user can view its data. That step is to encrypt the database so that the database can't be read by a utility program or a word processor application. To do this, follow these steps:

1. Open Access without any database being open.

2. Open the Encrypt Tool by selecting Tools | Security | Encrypt/Decrypt database.

3. The Encrypt/Decrypt Database Locator dialog box opens. Navigate through folders on your local machine or network share until you locate the database you want to encrypt or decrypt, and select that database.

4. Click OK.

5. The Encrypt Database dialog box appears. Type the new database name and the location in which to save it. I suggest that you not delete the original in case something goes wrong with the new database.

6. Click OK.

> **NOTE**
>
> To encrypt or decrypt the database, you must be able to open the database in Exclusive mode, meaning that no users can be using the database. Also, you must have at least Modify Design permissions on the Table objects.

After the encryption process has finished, you're returned to Access. If you want to decrypt a database, you follow the same steps except that you're prompted for the decrypt database name rather than the encrypt database name in step 5 of the preceding six-step process.

A Walkthrough of Securing a Database

To secure your database to its fullest, follow these steps:

1. Create a new workgroup using the Workgroup Administrator Tool.

2. Open Access, signing in as Admin user.

3. Open the database in question you're securing.

4. Add a new Admin user. It's suggested that you use a name convention such as *Application Name* + Admin.

5. Add the Admins group to the new Admin user.

6. Change the Admin password. This change will force you to sign in the next time you open Access.

7. Change Users Group permissions to be No Run/Open, No Open Exclusive, and No Administer on the Database Object.

WARNING

Any user of a database that has Open/Run permissions can create new tables, queries, forms, reports, macros, or modules. So if you leave the Users group with Open/Run on the database, then by default, the Admin user can open your secured database and create any new object he wants. The creator retains administrator privileges on this new object. So for a secure database, make sure that the Users group has no permissions on the database.

8. Close Access.

9. Reopen Access, this time signing in as the new Admin user.

10. Open the database in question you're securing.

11. Run Security Wizard on the database, making sure that you select all objects in the first dialog box.

12. When the Security Wizard has completed, close Access again.

13. Reopen Access, this time signing in as the new Admin user.

14. Open the database in question you're securing.

15. Remove the Admins group for the Admin user. This action ensures that any user who opens that database without using the correct workgroup file can't see any of the database objects.

16. Add the groups that will be required for the database.

17. Add all users to their correct groups.

18. Assign permissions to the groups as required.

19. As new objects are added, add or remove the permissions as required.

This is a walkthrough of how to set up security on an Access database. You could run into problems if the user needs to run against two different workgroup files. To work around this situation, on the icon for your application, use the command-line parameter of /wrkgrp *workgroupname*. This tells Access when it opens to use this workgroup file rather than its default.

Summary

Security is often neglected as an aspect of database and workgroup administration. This chapter armed the administrator (and user) with information on creating workgroups and adding users to them. Creating users and assigning user permissions and passwords were detailed. And the coverage of the Security Wizard and database encryption showed additional methods for adding security features to Access applications.

Access in a Network Environment

31

by Dwayne Gifford

As more and more people are discovering, Access can be used in a network environment. Most of the time, Access is used as a single-user development tool. However, it isn't limited to just this function. By the end of this chapter, you will have a clear understanding of what is involved in having Access run properly in a network environment.

This chapter looks at the topics of network setup and running Access in shared mode, plus other issues you need to be familiar with in order to have Access function properly in a network environment.

Network Installation

After purchasing a software application such as Access, you would normally install it on each user's local drive using floppies or a CD-ROM. To save you time and effort, Access provides a way to install the software into a network share, or shared folder. Users can then run the Setup program from this shared folder. By performing this type of setup, you have control over who uses Access, because users must have a minimum of read access to the shared folder in order to install Access. Other settings can be set when the folder is created. These are covered accordingly in the following sections.

Installing to a Network Shared Folder

To create a network installation, follow these steps:

1. Run Setup with a parameter of /A.

> **NOTE**
>
> A network installation requires about 59 MB of disk space.

2. The first prompt says "Welcome to Access for Windows 95." Click Continue to carry on with the setup.
3. Next is a warning about network installation. To continue with the setup, click OK.
4. The next prompt is looking for the organization. When a user runs Setup from the shared folder later, he is asked only for his name.
5. The confirmation of the organization gives you a chance to make changes if you like. Click OK to continue.
6. Next is the Product ID acknowledgment dialog.
7. Choose in which folder you would like Access installed.
8. Choose which folder you want the common files placed in. Usually they are placed in the shared Windows Msapps folder. If the folder doesn't exist, you are prompted to create it after clicking OK.

9. The dialog box shown in Figure 31.1 is displayed, prompting you to confirm the Msapps folder, drive letter, and server name, as well as how to connect to the server.

FIGURE 31.1.

The Network Server Confirmation dialog box.

10. Do you want shared files to be loaded to the user's hard drive (the fastest way to run Access), left on the server (which saves user disk space), or let the user choose? If you aren't using a shared installation of Windows, the best choice is Local Hard Drive.

NOTE

Before you make a selection here, you need to be aware of a problem that can arise. If the user isn't running a shared version of Windows and you've selected Server, all the shared options in Access are rendered unusable.

After Access has finished copying the files to the share, the Microsoft Access for Windows 95 success or failure dialog box is displayed. To complete the setup, click the OK button.

Installing from a Network Shared Folder

Follow these steps to install from a network:

1. Enter the username only, because the organization defaults to the organization that was entered when the share was created. Click OK to continue.

2. The Name Confirm dialog box is displayed. If the name is correct, click OK to continue. Otherwise, click Change. You will be returned to the previous dialog.

3. You now see a dialog box that gives you the licensee agreement and your product ID number.

4. You choose where you would like Access to be installed. The default is c:\msoffice. If you want to install to a different folder (or directory), click the Change Directory button. Here you can change to another folder that has already been created. If it hasn't yet been created, in the Path text box type the name of the folder (or directory) into which you want Access installed.

5. If you choose to let the user pick where the common files are to be placed, the dialog box shown in Figure 31.2 appears, enabling the user to make this decision.

FIGURE 31.2.

Choices of placing shared files.

> **NOTE**
>
> Remember that if the user doesn't have a shared version of Windows, it is important that he select Local Hard Drive.

6. After you select the folder, the dialog box shown in Figure 31.3 appears. It gives the user a choice of three types of Access installations: Typical, Compact, and Custom.

FIGURE 31.3.

Choices of installation types.

Be aware that by choosing the Compact installation, you could make some of the wizards unavailable to Access. But this can be a good thing if the user is going to use Access only to run a predeveloped application. Also remember that if the user isn't running a shared version of Windows and the shared files aren't being loaded onto the local hard drive by default, the only way to have all options load correctly is to choose Custom and then click the Select All Button. After Access has finished copying the files to the folder, the Microsoft Access for Windows 95 success dialog box is displayed. Also, if you have a modem and want to register Access 95 online, click the Online Registration button. To complete the setup, click the OK button.

When you're setting up a network shared folder, there are two things to keep in mind. First, all users will require read access if they are to install from this folder. Second, if the network becomes unavailable, so does the capability to set up Access.

Controlling Access in a Network

Normally, when you're running Access in a network environment, multiple users will be using the database. To make sure that Access is set up for this situation, it is essential that you do a couple of things:

- First, you need to set up the user's local copy of Access so that it is using the correct workgroup.
- Second, you need to set some options in Access to ensure that it behaves correctly when a user tries to save a record to the database.

Locating Your Workgroup

To locate your workgroup, go into the Access program group and locate the Workgroup Administrator icon. If it isn't present, select Start | Run. Then type `c:\msoffice\access\wrkgadm.exe`, assuming that Access is installed in the default directory. If it's installed in a different directory, replace `c:\msoffice\access` with the location where you installed Access. After you click OK, the dialog box shown in Figure 31.4 appears.

FIGURE 31.4.

The Workgroup Administrator dialog box.

Two choices are available: create a new workgroup or join an existing workgroup.

Joining an Existing Workgroup

To join an existing workgroup, click the Join button. You are prompted for the location and the filename of the new workgroup. If you know the drive, the folder name, and the name of the file, type them in. Otherwise, click the Browse button, which places you in the File Locator dialog box. Here you can navigate to the workgroup you want to join. After you have located the file and selected it, click Open. Notice that the file you have selected is now displayed in the Database name text box. If you are satisfied with your selection, click OK. If you can join this workgroup, a success dialog box is displayed. Confirm the success dialog box by clicking OK.

> **NOTE**
>
> Location can be a drive and a folder or it can be a network share, as long as the workgroup is located when you click OK (for example, `d:\data\newworkgroup.mda` or `\\mymachine\data\newworkgroup.mda`).

Creating a New Workgroup

To create a new workgroup, click the Create button. The dialog box shown in Figure 31.5 is displayed, requiring you to fill in three text boxes.

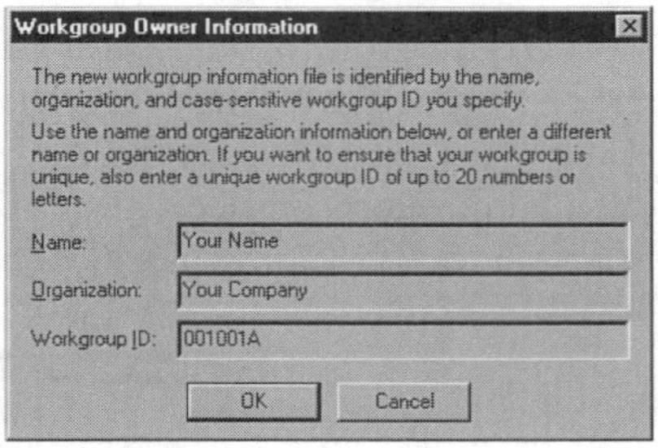

FIGURE 31.5.

The Workgroup Owner Information dialog box.

The Name text box is first, which defaults to the registered owner of Access. Next is the Organization text box, which defaults to the registered organization name. Third is the Workgroup ID text box, which requires a unique ID number. By entering the ID number, you guarantee that the new work workgroup will be unique. The minimum information required is the registered owner, but I strongly recommend that you fill in all three options.

> **WARNING**
>
> Make sure that you keep a copy of the name, organization, and workgroup ID. Always confirm that you have it in the same syntax that it was typed in. If you ever need to re-create the workgroup file, you must supply the same information exactly as you entered it the first time. If you can't do this, you might not be able to regain access to your applications that have been secured based on this workgroup file.

After you fill in the information and click OK, you're prompted for the location and the name to be used for the new workgroup.

> **NOTE**
>
> Location can be a drive and folder or it can be a network share, as long as the workgroup is located when you click OK (for example, `d:\data\newworkgroup.mda` or `\\mymachine\data\newworkgroup.mda`).

You can type the new name and folder, or you can simply click the Browse button and change the folder using the File Locator dialog box. To create the new workgroup, click OK. To stop the creation of the workgroup, click Cancel. If you click Cancel, you're placed back at the Workgroup Owner Information dialog box (shown in Figure 31.5); otherwise, a Please Confirm Information dialog box is displayed. This dialog box shows you the information you have filled in. If the information is correct, click OK. If it isn't, click the Change button. When you click the Change button, you're placed back at the Workgroup Owner Information dialog box with the same information filled in. Otherwise, a success dialog box is displayed, letting you know that the workgroup was created. After you click OK, you're placed back at the Workgroup Administrator dialog box.

Sometimes a user needs to run Access with more than one workgroup. To work this out, you need to read about "command-line options, Startup command-line options" in the online Help for Access. The import topic to read is /WrkGrp. This option wasn't available in Access 2.0. You had to make a copy of the MSACCESS.INI file and then make changes to the `SystemDB` line. Then, on the command line, you placed an `/INI` option after the database name. In Access 95, you need to add a `/WrkGrp` option to have this workgroup used instead of the default Access workgroup. An example of using the command line when opening Access would be

```
E:\Access\MSACCESS.EXE D:\work\Version_Control.mdb /Wrkgrp e:\Access\system.mdw
```

Network Concerns

When you're using Access on a network, it is vital that you go into each user's installation of Access and make some changes to the default options. To do this, you need to open Access with your application database that is up on the network. When you're in the application, open the Options dialog box by selecting Tools | Options. The dialog box shown in Figure 31.6 is displayed. Click the Advanced Tab. Here you need to be concerned with the options at the lower right.

FIGURE 31.6.

Advanced options in Access.

You can set the following four items to help gain a better level of performance when running Access on a network:

- The default for the first of these options, Number of Update Retries, is 2. This number is fine when only two users will be accessing the database. The suggested number of retries, however, is 5. Remember that as the number goes up, so does the response time. Any number between 0 and 10 is a valid choice. In some cases, no matter what number you put here, you will need to add VBA code that will increase the number of retries. For an idea of how to add this type of code, refer to Chapter 32, "Multiuser Programming and Techniques."

- The next option is ODBC Refresh Interval (sec). A value between 1 and 3,600 is valid; the default is 1,500, which is a good refresh interval. If you're running a system that requires the most up-to-date data at all times, a lower refresh number is better. Otherwise, stay with the default. If you aren't using any ODBC connections, don't worry about this option.

■ The next option, Refresh Interval (sec), is used to tell Access how often it should update or refresh records. The default is 60 seconds. A valid value for this option is between 1 and 32,766 seconds. When you're working with multiple user databases, this option is important to make sure that data is kept as current as possible. If you keep the data current at all times, 60 is just fine. Remember that as the transactions go up in number, the refresh takes longer. Therefore, try to keep this number at a level that won't interfere with application performance—perhaps around the 10,000 range.

■ The last option is Update Retry Interval (msec). Here you have an option of 0 through 1000 milliseconds. The default is 250; a good starting number is actually around 750. The reason for using a high number is that you want to give the other user a chance to save the record before trying again.

Using an Access Database Residing on the Network

When you're thinking about using a database residing on the network and Access itself on your local drive, you should be aware of a few things, which are covered in the following sections.

Installing the Database on the Network

To install the database on the network, you simply place the database in a shared folder that all users have read/write access to. After the database is in place, you should create a shortcut or icon that points to this database for the users. But be aware that Access will run much slower from the network than it would if the database were local. Also, it's possible that the database can become unavailable if the network goes down.

Exclusive Mode Versus Shared Mode

When a database is being run on the network, normally more than one user will be using the database. The database therefore needs to be opened in shared, not exclusive, mode. However, at times you will want to open the database in exclusive mode, such as when you want to convert, compact, or repair a database. To run any of these options, you need to open Access while a database is not open. Then, under Tools | Database Utilities, you will see the options Convert a Database, Compact a Database, and Repair a Database. For more information on converting, compacting, or repairing a database, refer to Chapter 3, "Databases."

Database Administration

When dealing with an Access database on the network, the administrator finds that his job becomes a little bit tougher because he or she must worry about many more issues. The following is a list of some of the possible issues about which the administrator should be concerned:

- The administrator must make sure that all users have read/write access to the common database's shared folder.
- The user needs to be added as a user to the database. For more information on how to add a user or new groups to the database, refer to Chapter 30, "Security."
- Run Setup to give the user an Access installation.
- Set up Access so that it runs against the correct workgroup.
- Make sure that the application opens and runs correctly for the user.
- When changes need to be made to the database, all users must close the database. This action gives you the ability to make the necessary changes. If the users don't close the database, it's possible that some of the users will run the incorrect version of an object, which could cause data corruption. More information on updating a database appears in the next section.

Splitting the Database

Many times, having the data in one place and all the code in another place is required. Access offers two ways to split the data from the main application. The first is to use the Database Splitter Wizard, and the second is to manually link the table objects from the table database back into the current database.

The Database Splitter Wizard

Most of the time, you should back up the data being added by the users. One of the ways to do this is to use the database splitter and split the tables objects away from all the other objects of a database. You would have the table object database located on a network share and all other objects' database located on the user's local machine. The Database Splitter Wizard is designed to help you make the move from local tables in the current database to linked tables in a new database. After the splitter has exported the tables to the new database, it links the table objects from the new database back into the original database. To start the database splitter, select Tools | Add-ins | Database Splitter.

1. You are first asked to verify that you want to split the database. If you are sure you want the database split, click the Split Database button.

2. The dialog box in Figure 31.7 is displayed, asking you where you want the new database located.

Chapter 31

FIGURE 31.7.

The location finder for a new database.

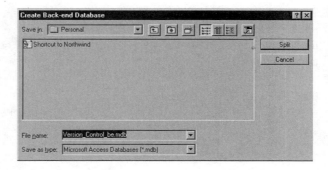

3. To change the drive, click the Save in listbox and click the drive letter desired. After you select the drive letter, a list of folders appears below it. To move down to the next folder, double-click the folder you want to change to. To move up to the next folder above the current folder, click the up-one-level button, located beside the Save in listbox. After you locate the folder for the new database, you need to give it a name. To do this, click the File name listbox and type the name. You don't need to remember the extension because Access transparently adds an .MDB extension.

4. After you have the folder and have added the name to the File name list box, click the Split button.

5. You will see the status bar display the current tables that are being exported and then which table is being linked. On completion of the export and link, a Database Splitter Success or Failure dialog box is presented. Click the OK button to return to the Database window.

Notice that the tables now have a black arrow beside them. This arrow tells you at a glance which tables are linked and which are not.

Issues with Splitting the Database

When you start to split a database, you need to be aware of some possible pitfalls:

■ Linked tables will run slower then nonlinked tables. The performance decrease occurs because when a save is done, it needs to pass the data through to the other database and wait for an acknowledgment that the save has completed successfully.

■ If you will be writing VBA code to work against the linked tables, don't use any open-table calls. Open-table calls can't work against linked tables.

■ With everything but the data residing in another database, you need to have a plan to update any changes that will be made to the nondata database. As any fixes are made to database objects, you need a way to roll these changes out to the users' databases that are residing on local machines. There are two ways to tackle this issue. One is to use replication, and the other is to look at version control. For more information on replication, refer to Chapter 39, "Replication." For more information on version control, see Chapter 29, "Testing and Debugging Applications."

Linking Tables Manually

To link tables manually, follow these next steps:

1. Select Get External Data | Link Tables. This opens the dialog box shown in Figure 31.8.

FIGURE 31.8.

Creating a database link.

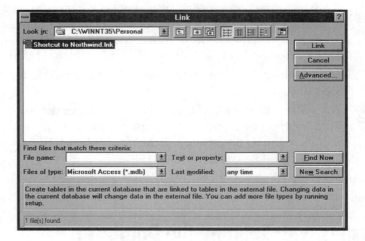

2. Locate the database file that you want to link the tables from.
3. After you have selected the database, click the Link button.
4. The dialog box shown in Figure 31.9 appears, listing the tables that are available for linking from the database you have selected.

FIGURE 31.9.

Tables to be linked.

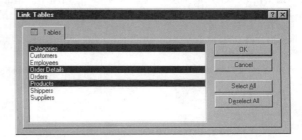

5. In this dialog box you can select the tables that you want to have linked to your current database. You have two possible ways to select the tables. The first is to click the Select All button, which will cause all tables to be marked to be linked. The second is to click on the table name. This will mark it to be linked. If at any time you want to unselect a table, click on the table name again. If at any time you want to start the selection process over, click the Deselect button.

6. After you have marked the table(s) to be linked, click the OK button.

7. Upon completion of the linking, you are returned to the database.

> **NOTE**
>
> If an error occurs while you are trying to link a table, an error message appears, allowing you to acknowledge the error. Then you can carry on with the linking of the other tables.

Maintaining Linked Tables

After you have tables that are linked, you need to manage these links. Sometimes you need to move databases from one folder to another. If this occurs, you need to refresh the link, letting the database know where the tables are now located. To carry out this task, use the add-in called the Linked Table Manager. To open it, select Tools | Add-ins | Linked Table Manager. The dialog box shown in Figure 31.10 appears, listing the tables that are currently linked.

FIGURE 31.10.

The Linked Table Manager.

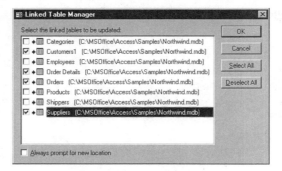

To the right of the table name is the path and database name in parentheses. You can update one table or all the tables in the list. There are two ways to select tables from the list:

■ To select one table at a time, click on the box that is located to the left of the table name.

■ To select all the tables simultaneously, click the Select All button.

There are two ways to deselect tables that have been selected:

- To deselect one table, click on the box that is located to the left of the table name.
- To deselect all currently selected tables, click the Deselect All button.

After you have selected the tables that you want to refresh, click the OK button. If any tables can't be refreshed or you've clicked the Always prompt for new location check box, the Link dialog box appears, prompting you for the location and name of the database to refresh the tables with. After you have selected the database, click Find Now. If the Linked Table Manager is successful in locating the table objects you have selected, it will give you a Microsoft Access dialog acknowledgment that the selected tables were successfully refreshed. Then you are returned to the Linked Table Manager dialog box. Otherwise, if the table objects couldn't be located, you receive a Linked Table Manager error. If you click OK, you're placed back in the Linked Table Manager dialog box, and the tables that could not be refreshed are still selected.

If you want to view where the database is getting its data from, you can go into design mode of the table and select View | Properties. Under Description, you will see something like DATABASE=D:\test.mdb;TABLE=Ship. You can't make any changes to the Description field, but at least you can view it without going into the Linked Table Manager.

Summary

When you're dealing with a network, many issues can arise, and it's important to look at them from the start of application development. Always remember that you will face performance problems when running databases from the network, because you have added a new piece to the application and it must get the data from your machine to the database on the network.

IN THIS PART

PART

Advanced Programming

Multiuser Programming and Techniques

by Rob Newman

32

IN THIS CHAPTER

An Overview of Locking

With the rapidly increasing popularity of shared information systems and groupware-enabled applications, providing methods for ensuring secure, stable, centrally accessible databases is a high priority in any Relational Database Management System (RDBMS). Without these methods, the usability of your database, data integrity, and performance will begin to degrade the moment the database is used by more than one person. Fortunately, Access has provided various means of controlling the availability of records, objects, and even the entire database that give the developer tools for creating a sensible approach to designing and maintaining a multiuser application.

Locking Methods Used by Access

Unlike other desktop RDBMSs that implement a fixed-length record structure and use true single record locking, Access, because of its variable-length record structure, employs the page locking method to provide multiuser access to an Access database. This locked page is a static (it can't be changed) 2 KB (2048-byte) chunk of data that contains your record and any other surrounding records that Access needs to fill the 2 KB page. So, for example, if you have a record that is 1200 bytes long, to fill the 2 KB page buffer, Access locks the surrounding records when a lock is activated.

Because of this type of locking, it's important to know how and when to enforce the various methods of locking and when to be aware of certain actions that cause Access to enforce its own locks. There is nothing worse than an arcane record-locking-violation message abruptly interrupting your application. (See the section "Handling Multiuser Locking Errors" later in this chapter.)

Access uses the following types of locking in a multiuser setting (see the later section titled "Optimistic Locking Versus Pessimistic Locking" for more information on locking):

- Optimistic: This method locks the record only while the record is being updated. This is the default locking method used by Access.
- Pessimistic: This method locks the record when editing begins and releases it when the record is updated.
- Full or Exclusive: This method locks the entire recordset. This is a very restrictive lock and is generally used only when batch updates are being performed or when changes are being made to database objects.

> **NOTE**
>
> When you edit data in a linked SQL database table using ODBC, Microsoft Access doesn't lock records; instead, the rules of that SQL database govern the locking.

Differences in Locking Behavior Between Jet 2.x and Jet 3.0

With Access 95, several changes were made to the locking behavior used in version 3.0 of the Jet database engine. These changes, which include support for multithreading and implicit transactions, were added to improve performance in a multiuser application mainly by reducing the number of read/write and locking operations performed on the database. In Jet version 2.x, data was written immediately after each Recordset.Update method. With Jet version 3.0, the locks remain, and edits are cached and written when the cache is full or until two seconds pass.

In most situations, this would be a desired improvement, but this new locking behavior has a side effect. Because locks can be in place for longer periods, the number of concurrent users who have access to the locked records can be reduced. In some situations, you might want to mimic the locking behavior in Jet 2.x by modifying your code to use explicit transactions. (See the section titled "Transactions" later in this chapter.) Or you can use queries that employ Data Manipulation Language (DML) commands such as UPDATE, INSERT, and DELETE (which aren't affected by the new locking behavior).

The *RecordLocks* Property

The RecordLocks property is used to determine how records are locked when Access queries, forms, or report objects are being used. You can set this property individually for each object by using the object's property sheet, a macro, or Visual Basic.

> **NOTE**
>
> You can set the default RecordLocks setting by selecting Tools | Options | Advanced. This setting affects the RecordLocks setting for most Access objects that have this property.

The .LDB File

The .LDB file is a special file used by Access to maintain control of the locking for shared databases. Access automatically creates the file for every database whenever you open the database in a shared environment. The .LDB file is named with the same name as the database file but with the .LDB extension. For example, MyDatabase.mdb would have a file called MyDatabase.ldb. This file is kept in the same folder (directory) as the parent .MDB file.

In previous versions of the Jet engine, after Access created the .LDB file, the file was permanent (unless deleted by the user). With Jet 3.0, this file is now temporary. Access automatically deletes the .LDB file when the last user closes the database, and re-creates it when the database is reopened. This is done primarily to handle database replication and improve performance-managing locks on the database.

> **CAUTION**
>
> If you intend to use an Access database on a NetWare 3.11 file server (later versions of NetWare have solved this problem), you need to be aware of a bug that limits the amount of data that Access can lock to 1 MB. The problem lies with the default in NetWare that limits the number of locks on a single workstation to 500; when this limit is reached, it can bring down the entire server. If you're using NetWare 3.11, you can use a patch to resolve this error. The file 311PTD.ZIP is located in the libraries of the NOVFILES forum on CompuServe. The patch is in the form of a NetWare Loadable Module that needs to be loaded on your server.
>
> In addition to the patch, you can also increase the server's `maximum record locks` parameters to their maximum limits. In the file server's AUTOEXEC.NCF file, enter the following commands:
>
> ```
> set maximum record locks per connection = 10000
> set maximum record locks = 20000
> ```

Optimistic Locking Versus Pessimistic Locking

In any well-designed multiuser application, it's critical to have a good, solid understanding of record locking. This section looks at two methods of record locking—optimistic and pessimistic—to help you decide which strategy might work best for your application.

Optimistic Locking

Optimistic locking is the default locking method used by Access. It's easy to implement and is the preferable method when many users will be editing or adding records. With this type of lock, the edited record is locked only for an instant when the record is being updated, such as when Access is moving to a previous or next record, closing the recordset, or specifically updating the recordset. This locking method significantly reduces the problems and locking conflicts that result from concurrent editing of the same record. An optimistic lock is also less likely to prevent other users from editing the same record or even adding a new record than is a pessimistic lock. When Access is using optimistic locking, a good error handler is needed to handle any conflicts that might arise when updating the recordset. For example, the Write Conflict dialog box, which can be confusing to the user, can be replaced by a custom dialog and a procedure created to save the data temporarily and reattempt the update at a later time.

Pessimistic Locking

When pessimistic locking is enforced, the record (or page) is locked when the user begins to edit it. This type of locking is similar to the record locking used by other RDBMSs; consequently, your users might be more accustomed to having this type of control while editing. And with this type of locking, you can avoid having to deal with the Write Conflict dialog box. You should, however, be aware of some problems with using pessimistic locking in Access.

As explained previously, when Access locks a record, it grabs any records near the one you're editing, up to the 2 KB limit. Thus, it usually locks multiple records and can even prevent the user from adding new records if the locked record is at or near the bottom of the recordset. Another problem is that if the user begins to edit a record and is delayed from updating it for some reason, a record (or multiple records) can be locked for a long time. For these reasons, pessimistic locking should generally be avoided, particularly if you have many concurrent users, because there will likely be a large number of locking conflicts.

Handling Multiuser Locking Errors

Record-locking conflicts are the inevitable consequence of having users concurrently editing the same set of records in a multiuser application. Fortunately, Access has provided some options for preventing and handling these conflicts when they arise.

> **TIP**
>
> Access 95 includes two new Data Access Objects (DAOs) for handling errors. The `Error` and `Err` objects contain details about data access errors, each of which pertains to a single operation involving data access objects. (See Chapter 23, "Visual Basic for Applications," for more information.)

Access's Data-Locking Settings

Access enables you to specify certain default settings to help you avoid record-locking conflicts between users in a multiuser environment. These settings are located under Tools | Options | Advanced, as shown in Figure 32.1.

- Number of Update Retries: This setting controls the number of times Access attempts to save a changed record when it encounters a lock. Valid settings are 0 to 10.

- ODBC Refresh Interval: This setting specifies the interval for automatically refreshing records in an ODBC database. Valid settings are 1 to 3,600.

- Refresh Interval: This setting specifies the number of seconds for refreshing records in Datasheet or Form view. Valid settings are 1 to 32,766.

■ Update Retry Interval: This setting specifies the number of milliseconds for Access to attempt to save a changed record that is locked by another user. Valid settings are 0 to 1,000.

FIGURE 32.1.

Access data-locking settings.

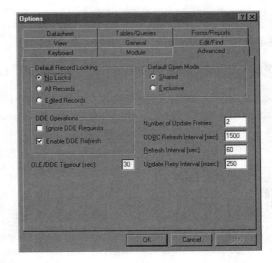

Although these settings can be used to prevent or at least delay some of the locking conflicts you will encounter, your application still needs to be able to handle the errors in a graceful manner that will prevent confusion and create a stable multiuser environment. (See the later section "A Generic Form Error Handler" for sample code to handle these errors.) Two of the more common locking errors your application will need to handle are the Write Conflict error and the Locked Record error.

The Write Conflict Error

The Write Conflict error appears when optimistic locking is used and the user attempts to update changes to a record that has been changed by another user. This error dialog box, shown in Figure 32.2, can be confusing to your users, particularly if they've had experience using other RDBMSs that use individual record locking or if they are new to an Access multiuser application.

FIGURE 32.2.

The Write Conflict dialog box.

The Locked Record Error (Error 3260)

The Locked Record error happens when you try to update data located on a page that is currently locked. For example, if one user is using pessimistic locking on a set of records and another user edits the same records using optimistic locking and attempts to update the records, this error will occur.

The *FormError* Event

Microsoft added the OnError event to forms in Access 2.0. This event is triggered by the Error event and was added to help the developer trap for standard data errors. For some reason, however, the Error event didn't pass locking or write conflict errors to the OnError event. This situation created difficulties for Access developers when they were deciding whether to use bound forms in a multiuser application because of the lack of programmatic control of locking errors.

With Access 95, this oversight has finally been fixed. The developer now has an extra measure of control when designing an application using bound forms and reports. Using this event, you can replace a default, often confusing, error message with an error message of your own.

> **NOTE**
>
> When using bound forms, you're still limited in dealing with certain errors—in particular, the Write Conflict error. Although you can trap for this error, your only options are to allow Access to display its normal Write Conflict dialog box or to just ignore it, in which case the user loses his changes. For this reason, using unbound forms might in some cases still be the better option.

The structure of the Form Error procedure looks like this:

```
Private Sub Form_Error(DataErr As Integer, Response As Integer)
```

The Error event procedure uses the following arguments:

- ■ DataErr: The error code that is returned by the Err object when an error occurs.
- ■ Response: A constant value used to specify whether an error message is displayed. The response choices are

    acDataErrContinue: Ignore the error and continue code execution. This allows you to display a custom error message.

    acDataErrDisplay: Display the default error message.

A Generic Form Error Handler

This section shows you some ways to handle record-locking errors that can be called by all your data access forms. By taking advantage of these techniques, you can give your users an application capable of handling most of the common data-locking conflicts gracefully. Some of the more common multiuser errors are shown in Table 32.1.

Table 32.1. Some common multiuser errors.

Error Number	Error Message
3006	Database `<Item>` is exclusively locked.
3186	Couldn't save; currently locked by *username* on *machine name*.
3188	Couldn't update; currently locked by another session on this machine.
3197	Data has changed; operation stopped.
3260	Couldn't update; currently locked by *username* on *machine name*.

A Generic Error Procedure for Use with Bound Forms

The following code example shows some of the techniques possible for handling errors when using bound forms in Access. Although the more common errors are trapped for in this procedure, it could be enhanced to include specific error trapping for many different situations.

```
Private Sub Form_Error(DataErr As Integer, Response As Integer)

' a generic form level error handler
' traps for the common record locking errors and displays
' a custom error message

' use constants for error codes because they can change between versions
Const conDatabaseLocked = 3006
Const conFileInUse = 3045
Const conLockedByAnotherSession = 3188
Const conDataHasChanged = 3197
Const conTooManyUsers = 3239
Const conLockedByUser = 3260

Dim strMsg As String

Select Case DataErr

    Case conDatabaseLocked   ' 3006 Database <Item> is exclusively locked.
        Response = acDataErrContinue
        strMsg = "The database is currently locked by another user" & Chr(13)
        strMsg = strMsg & "and is unavailable at this time. Please try running
        ➥application later"
```

```
        MsgBox strMsg, vbExclamation
        End

    Case conFileInUse  ' 3045 Couldn't use <Item>; file already in use.
        Response = acDataErrContinue
        strMsg = "The database is currently locked by another user" & Chr(13)
        strMsg = strMsg & "Please try running application later"
        MsgBox strMsg, vbExclamation
        End

    Case conLockedByAnotherSession ' 3188 Couldn't update; currently locked by
                                   ' another session on this machine.
        Response = acDataErrContinue
        strMsg = "This record is currently locked by another user" & Chr(13)
        strMsg = strMsg & "Please try updating it later"
        MsgBox strMsg, vbExclamation

    Case conDataHasChanged  ' 3197 Data has changed; operation stopped.
        Response = acDataErrDisplay

    Case conTooManyUsers  ' 3239 Too many active users.
        strMsg = "The database is opened by the maximum number of users (255)"
        ➥& Chr(13)
        strMsg = strMsg & "Please try running application later"
        MsgBox strMsg, vbExclamation
        End

    Case conLockedByUser  ' 3260 Couldn't update; currently locked by
                          ' user 'Item2' on machine 'Item1'.
        Response = acDataErrContinue
        strMsg = "This record is currently locked by another user" & Chr(13)
        strMsg = strMsg & "Please try updating it later"
        MsgBox strMsg, vbExclamation

    Case Else
        Response = acDataErrDisplay

End Select

End Sub
```

Figures 32.3 and 32.4 illustrate how you can use your own custom messages to reduce confusion and control what the user sees (you wouldn't want him to "debug" your code, would you?).

FIGURE 32.3.

Error 3260: Access's standard error dialog box.

FIGURE 32.4.

Error 3260: A custom error dialog box.

Transactions

Transaction processing is a method of performing batch updates and modifications to a database in a single operation. It's an excellent choice for use in a multiuser database application and should be used in your applications whenever possible. By using transactions, you have greater control over when locks are placed on the data and, to an extent, greater control when dealing with locking conflicts. Transactions can also improve performance in your application because it's much more economical in terms of computing resources to update data in batches rather than performing the same updates using code or bound forms.

Data integrity is better maintained using transactions as well. Because you can abort, or roll back, your transaction if one or more updates fail, you can ensure referential integrity rules more easily when using transaction processing. For example, if you've started a transaction session and an error occurs or some data validation rules fail, you can cancel any records created that might be incomplete by simply issuing a RollBack statement without violating any entity relationships that are in place. This would very difficult or impossible to duplicate using implicit transaction methods.

Following is the transaction syntax:

```
workspace.BeginTrans ¦ CommitTrans ¦ Rollback
```

Table 32.2 describes the three transactions methods.

Table 32.2. Transaction methods.

Method	Description
BeginTrans	Begins a new transaction.
CommitTrans	Ends or commits the current transaction and saves the changes.
Rollback	Cancels the current transaction and restores the data to the condition it was in when the current transaction began.

The basic form of a transaction session looks like this:

```
Sub SomeProcedure()
On Error GoTo Err_SomeProcedure

    Dim wspTrans As Workspace
    Set wspTrans = DBEngine.Workspaces(0)

    wspTrans.BeginTrans      ' Start of transaction.
    'Code to edit dynaset

    wspTrans.CommitTrans     ' Commit changes.
```

```
Err_SomeProcedure:
    wspTrans.Rollback      ' In case of error, cancel changes.

End Sub
```

The *BeginTrans* Method

The BeginTrans method is used to start a new transaction. After the transaction process begins, all the additions, changes, and deletions are retained by Access until you issue the CommitTrans method or the operation is canceled with the Rollback method.

The *CommitTrans* Method

The CommitTrans method commits the current transaction and saves the changes to the database. When you issue CommitTrans, appropriate record locks will be implemented and all updates will be made (unless errors are encountered). You must issue a CommitTrans for each level of BeginTrans that was started.

The *Rollback* Method

The RollBack method is used to cancel the changes made during the editing session and return the data to the state it was in before the BeginTrans was issued. The RollBack method is usually called when errors have occurred during the CommitTrans method.

Here are some things you should be aware of when using transaction processing:

- You can nest transactions up to five levels deep. You must resolve your transactions from the lowest back to the highest level.

- If you close a Workspace object without using the CommitTrans or RollBack methods, the transactions are automatically rolled back, releasing any changes to the data.

- Using CommitTrans or Rollback methods without first using the BeginTrans method creates an error. Remember to always resolve each level of transactions just as you would with nested If...End If or Select Case...End Select constructs.

- Some databases don't support transactions (Paradox, for example). To make sure that the database you're using supports transactions, you should first check whether the value of the Transactions property of the Database object is set to True before using the BeginTrans method.

- When using external ODBC SQL databases, you can issue only one transaction at a time. You can't nest transactions.

Command-Line Options

Access has a wide selection of command-line options that enable you to start an Access session with specific parameters you supply. You can create a shortcut on your desktop (search Windows Help for "shortcuts") or add them to your Windows Start menu. One good use for these shortcuts is in developing and testing an Access application. You can have several shortcuts on your desktop—each one with a different user or workgroup, for example—for testing database concurrency and locking issues. Table 32.3 shows some of the command-line options that can be useful in a multiuser database.

Table 32.3. Access startup command-line options.

Option	Description
/Excl	Use this option to open a database exclusively. If the database is currently open by another user, this will generate an error dialog.
/User *username*	This option starts Access by using the specified username.
/Pwd *password*	Use this option with the /User switch. It's useful only if your database is using Access security.
/Wrkgrp *Information File*	Starts Access with the specified Workgroup Information File. See Chapter 30, "Security," to learn how to set up workgroups.

Summary

This chapter has looked at some of the issues facing a developer of a multiuser application using Access 95. It's estimated that by the year 2000, 90 percent of all desktop computers will be networked and running shared applications. The importance of developing a good strategy for designing multiuser applications will continue to increase as the requirement for shared systems grows. It should therefore be the goal of every designer of multiuser applications to diligently address these issues.

Programming with OLE and DDE

33

by Dwayne Gifford

IN THIS CHAPTER

It is the goal of this chapter to give you a clear understanding of the differences between Object Linking and Embedding (OLE) and Dynamic Data Exchange (DDE) when they're used from Visual Basic for Applications (VBA) code. You will need to rely on DDE when you're working with the many applications that don't support OLE. (Microsoft Excel and Microsoft Word support both OLE and DDE.) To demonstrate the ability of OLE and DDE, a sample Word MailMerge is supplied on the CD that comes with this book. This sample will give you an idea of just how easy it is to use OLE and DDE. The way to look at OLE and DDE is, why reinvent the wheel? What I mean is that, if you have a document that is merged with customer data, for instance, why not borrow this functionality from Word and let it do the work for you?

This chapter looks at the differences between OLE and DDE, the basics of DDE, how to make Access a DDE or OLE server, and how to use OLE objects from VBA.

The Differences Between OLE and DDE

When you look at OLE and DDE, you will notice that they are very similar. However, there are a few differences:

- DDE requires the server application to be open during communication. With OLE, you don't need to open the server application first.
- DDE requires you to use the server application's environment to view the document. With OLE, you can view the document in the current application.
- OLE temporarily passes control to the other application. With DDE, the application that started the communication maintains control.
- DDE posts error messages from the client application. With OLE, you receive the error that the server application posts.

The Basics of DDE

DDE is similar to sending a fax: The calling application has control. In other words, one application calls and the other application answers. The first application tells the second application what it needs to do. Then, when it has completed the task, the second application either returns a success or does not respond. A lack of a response causes the calling application to time out. After all tasks have been completed and a success has been passed back, the calling application hangs up.

Initiating Communication

The very first thing that is required in all DDE transactions is to start the communication. To do this, you need to call the DDEInitiate function, which in turn will return a channel value. This value is how your program will identify what program it's communicating with.

To open a communication line between the applications, call DDEInitiate. This function has the following syntax:

```
Channel = DDEInitiate(Application Name, Topic)
```

To have the DDEInitiate call work correctly, you need to dimension *Channel* to be a variant data type. The *Application Name* argument is the same as the actual application name without its extension, and the *Topic* is usually System. For a full list of topics that an application will support, refer to that application's manual or Help file.

To initiate communication, start the application by executing the Shell command with the following *CommandString* and *WindowStyle* arguments:

```
intReturn = Shell(PathName[, WindowStyle])
```

To call Shell correctly, you need to define intReturn as an integer data type. This in turn will be set to the ID of the started program if successfully executed. *CommandString* can be as simple as Winword.EXE if the location of Winword.EXE is in the path. Otherwise, you will need to include the path with Winword.EXE. *WindowStyle* can be set to any of the values in Table 33.1 or left blank. If you leave *WindowStyle* blank, it will default to option 2 in Table 33.1.

Table 33.1. Available Windows styles.

WindowStyle *ID*	*Description*
0	The application is opened hidden, and focus is passed to the application.
1	The application is opened in its original size and location, and it has focus.
2	The application is opened minimized, and it has focus.
3	The application is opened maximized, and it has focus.
4	The application is opened to its normal size and location, but without focus.
6	The application is opened minimized, but without focus.

NOTE

If an attempted communication returns the error 282, the application is not currently running, or the Shell command failed.

In most cases, you will want to use option 4, which is to open normally without focus. The reason for this is that I have seen some calls fail when the application is minimized. Also, since your application has control over the other application, why show the other application to the users?

Communicating with Other Applications

After the communication channel has been opened, three types of communication are available:

- `DDERequest` lets you receive information from the other application. Its parameters are *Channel* and *Item*. *Channel* is the channel that is set when `DDEInitiate` is called. *Item* is the information that you want to receive. `DDERequest` will return the information as a string if the request was successful.

- `DDEPoke` lets you pass data to the other application. The parameters for `DDEPoke` are *Channel*, *Item*, and *Data*. *Channel* is the channel that is set when `DDEInitiate` is called. *Item* is a `String` expression that the other application will understand. *Data* is a value that you want to place in the other application.

- `DDEExecute` has the parameters *Channel* and *Command*. *Channel* is the channel that is set when `DDEInitiate` is called. *Command* is the action that you want the other application to perform. To find out what actions are available for the other application, you need to go into the other application and use its object browser. Figure 33.1 shows the object browser that comes with Excel.

FIGURE 33.1.

Excel's object browser.

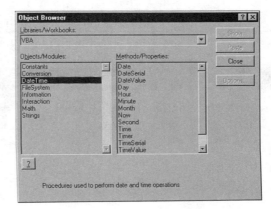

The object browser allows you to view all available Visual Basic objects for the application. If the other application doesn't have an object browser, you can always go into the application and record the function you wish to perform from DDE. After you have recorded the operation, you can borrow the code and place it in the command location.

The following steps open a Word for Windows document:

1. Open Word for Windows and select Tools | Macro | Record.
2. Click OK to accept the defaults in the Macro Name dialog.
3. Select File | Open, select a document to open, and click OK.
4. Select Tools | Macro | Stop Recording.
5. Select Tools | Macro, and then select the macro you just recorded.
6. Click Edit to view the command string.

Notice that Word has recorded the macro as `FileOpen .name = "name.doc"`. To call this command from your application, you need to run `DDEExecute`. Here is the syntax:

```
DDEExecute Channel, "[FileOpen(""name.doc"")]"
```

The square brackets (`[]`) are a convention that Excel and Word use to tell them that it is a macro that is being called. The use of two pairs of quotation marks, which both Excel and Word require, ensures that quotes will be embedded into the string.

Terminating the Conversation

Two different commands can be used to terminate the communication:

- `DDETerminate` terminates the channel that was set by the `DDEInitiate` command. The only argument is `Channel`, which is set by `DDEInitiate`.

- `DDETerminateAll` terminates all open channels. There are no required parameters.

TIP

The best approach is to terminate each channel at the point where it is no longer needed for communication. This frees program resources and eliminates a possible source of program conflict.

Handling DDE Errors

When dealing with DDE errors, it is important to understand that there is really only one error that you can do anything about—error 282. This error tells you that the other application isn't open, so before continuing, you should try to open the application in question. But remember to try only once, or you could get stuck in a unending loop. This unending loop could occur if the user's computer doesn't have the application that you're trying to open. When you receive an error working with DDE, normally it will be error 286—a DDE response timeout. This is the most common error because DDE has no way to show you what error the other application ran into. To see the error, you need to change focus to the other application, where you will see the Error dialog. It is vital that you have the user pass this error back to the database administrator when the user is reporting errors. This will help you or the database administrator figure out why the problem occurred and also help you find a resolution.

Table 33.2 shows possible errors that you could run into when using DDE in Access.

Table 33.2. DDE errors.

ErrorID	ErrorText
280	DDE channel not fully closed; awaiting response from other application.
281	No more DDE channels are available.
282	Can't open DDE channel; Microsoft Access couldn't find the specified application and topic.
283	Can't open DDE channel; more than one application responded.
284	DDE channel is locked.
285	The other application won't perform the DDE method or operation you attempted.
286	Timeout while waiting for DDE response.
289	Data not provided when requested in DDE operation.
290	Data supplied in a DDE conversation is in the wrong format.
292	DDE conversation closed or changed.
293	DDE method invoked with no channel open.
295	Message queue filled; DDE message lost.
298	DDE transaction failed. Check to ensure you have the correct version of DDEML.DLL.

If you would like a list of all the errors that Access uses, go into DDE.MDB (which is on the CD that comes with this book) and open the report named rptError. This will run the macro LoadErrors if the table tblError is not yet built. The LoadErrors macro is set up to do a runcode, which in turn takes a parameter of a valid function name. In this case, the runcode is using the LoadTable function, located in the module mdlErrorTable_Load. After you run this function, you will have a new table called tblErrors. This table will contain all the errors from 1 to 32767, excluding reserved and user-defined errors. Errors after 7951 are reserved or user-defined and will not be displayed.

A DDE Example

The following code is a quick application to show you how to use DDE to open, print, and close a Word file. For an example of how to do a mail merge using DDE, simply take a look at DDE.MDB.

```
Function DDEMain ()
    On Error Resume Next
    Dim intError As Integer, intChan As Integer
    Dim strAppname As String, strDDEName As String
    strAppname = "c:\msoffice\winword\winword.exe"
    strDDEName = "winword"
    intChan = DDEInitiate(strDDEName, "System")    ' Try to start communicating
                                                   ' with the application
    If Err <> 0 Then    ' If an error occurs, try to open the application
    Err = 0
        intError = Shell(strAppname)
        If Err <> 0 Then    ' If the application was started successfully,
                            ' try to initiate again
            MsgBox ("The application - " & strAppname & " cannot be located.")
            Exit Function
        End If
        intChan = DDEInitiate(strDDEName, "System")
        If Err <> 0 Then    ' If there is an error again, end the function
            Exit Function
        End If
    End If
    DDEExecute intChan, "[FileOpen(""c:\name.doc"")]"
    DDEExecute intChan, "[FilePrint]"
    DDEExecute intChan, "[FileClose]"
    DDETerminate Chan
End Function
```

Other Uses of DDE

Usually you use DDE from inside a VBA module. Nevertheless, you can use DDE in text boxes in forms and reports. Once you have placed the text box on the form, you can go into the ControlSource property and set it to one of two choices. The first is DDE, which has the required parameters *Application*, *Topic*, and *Item*:

```
DDE(Application, Topic, Item)
```

Application, just like in DDEInitiate, will most likely be the application's executable name without the extension. *Topic* is a string expression recognized by the application—Sheet1 for Excel, for example. *Item* is a string expression recognized by the application—R1C1 for Excel, for example.

The second choice is DDESend, which will send data from the current application to the other application like DDEPoke. The parameters for DDESend are *Application*, *Topic*, *Item*, and *Data*.

```
DDESend(Application, Topic, Item, Data)
```

Application, just like DDE, will likely be the application executable name without the extension. *Topic* is a string expression recognized by the application—Sheet1 for Excel, for example. *Item* is a string expression recognized by the application—R1C1 for Excel, for example. *Data* is the information you want to place in the other application.

For an example of how to use DDE and DDESend, see the form named frmDDE in sample database DDE.MDB that is on the CD-ROM. If you don't have Excel open when you open this form, the form will try to open Excel for you. If it can't open Excel, you will see #Error in both the DDESend and DDE text boxes. To see this form work correctly, open Excel, leave book1 open, and reopen the form frmDDE. In DDESend you will see nothing, and in DDE you will see 1000. Also, if you go back to Excel, you will see that it now has 1000 in cell A1.

Programming Using OLE Objects

When you start an OLE automation, you need to set the object to the type of object you want to access. In the OLE sample in DDE.MDB, you will see that it performs the same way as the DDE example but doesn't require you to make sure that the application is running. The sample OLE function is called mdOLEsample. To see it run, run the OLE macro.

Opening an OLE Object

To start a conversation with an OLE object, you need to do a CreateObject call in a function or sub. CreateObject takes a parameter of *Class*, which is made up of two pieces of information. The first is the application name or object name, and the second is the object type or the class of the object that you wish to create. To actually use this function call, you need to type something like the following:

```
set variable = CreateObject("object.string")
```

The nice part about using OLE is that if the object isn't open, OLE will open it. Also, if an instance of the object is already open, it will piggyback onto this object and not create a new instance. For example, if you wanted to open Microsoft Word, you would use Word as the application name and Basic as the object type. If an OLE instance is already open for Word, you can use the GetObject function instead of CreateObject. This call takes two parameters. The first is *Pathname*, which would have the path and filename. The second is the *Class* parameter, which is the same parameter that CreateObject took.

Communicating with the Other Application

To communicate with the OLE object, you need to invoke methods that the object will understand. To do this, you first need to reference the object. We will use the variable that we set with CreateObject, and then we will place a method or function that the object will understand. An example of this would be

```
Object.Bold = True
```

The object would make all text bold if it understood bold as a method or a function call. To find out which functions or methods an application will understand, use the object browser for that object. (Figure 33.1 shows Excel's object browser.)

Closing an OLE Object

There are two ways to close an OLE object:

- Issue an *object*.[Quit] command
- Issue a set *object* = nothing command

You must put square brackets around Quit so that VBA knows that you are referring to the object method and not a VBA method. Also, if your call to CreateObject actually started the object, the close call will close the object. But if you didn't start the application, only the communication channel is closed, not the actual object.

An OLE Example

The following is a very simple application that opens a word document and then prints it. After it has printed the document, it closes not only the file but also Word if it was opened by your OLE call. You will notice that this example performs the same task as DDE did but uses 50 percent less code. Also, the OLE example will close Word if it opened it, but the DDE example does not. Also remember that the DDE example has error handling but the OLE example does not. For a mail merge example just like the DDE mail merge, refer to the DDE.MDB file on the CD-ROM and run the macro called OLE. For the DDE example, run the macro called DDE.

```
Function OLEMain ()
Dim objWord As Object

' Set the object to a Word object
Set objWord = CreateObject("Word.Basic")

' Open the word file
objWord.FileOpen " c:\name.doc"

objWord.FilePrint
' Print document
objWord.FileClose 2
Set objWord = Nothing
End Function
```

A Final Note on Using DDE and OLE

One of the most frustrating things you will run into when using either OLE or DDE is which commands the other application will accept. The fast way is to use the other application's object browser. But not every application has an object browser. I have found that one of the fastest ways to get around this is to go into that application's macro language and get the command to work first there. Then use the same code in Access, but either placed in quotation marks or referenced after the period. Note that this won't work in all cases. An example would be WordObject.MailMergeToDoc for OLE or DDEExecute channel, "[MailMergeToDoc]" for DDE. If the command still won't work, you will have to play with the syntax until it functions the way you want it to. Also, when you're designing an application with either OLE or DDE, always keep in mind that when a new version of the application comes out, it's possible that some of the methods or functions will have changed. This makes it possible that this application might always need maintenance, whereas if you didn't use OLE or DDE, it wouldn't.

Making Access a DDE or OLE Server

One thing that is important to remember is that now you can have Access function as an OLE server as well as a DDE server. To have Access function as a DDE server, you must make sure that Ignore DDE Requests is not selected, as shown in Figure 33.2. To open this dialog, select Tools | Options | Advanced. Also be sure that Enable DDE Refresh is checked and that OLE/ DDE Timeout is set to a number between 0 and 300. What you will set this number to depends on the computer your user will be running the application on. It's best to test it on each computer as you set up the application. When you set the DDE refresh, it will rely on the timeout setting.

FIGURE 33.2.

Advanced options.

Now that everything is set up, you can go into the other application and run Access from there using either DDE or OLE. The things to be aware of when running Access from the other application are the same things you need to be aware of when you run other applications from

Access. If you need to know which methods or functions you can call for the other application, you could start by using the Access object browser.

To open the Access object browser, open a module and press F2. You can navigate through the different methods and functions that are available for Access.

The following example shows you how to use Access as a DDE server and gives you an idea of how to use DDE from Word 6.0. This example makes a connection to Access and then opens the database called DDE.MDB. After the database is open, Word will get Access to open the report called `rptError`. This report will print the error table. If the table doesn't exist when the report is opened, the report will create the table for you. After Access has opened the report, Word will get Access to print the report. Then Word will close the database and the communication channel to Access.

```
Sub MAIN

    intChan = DDEInitiate("MSAccess", "System")
    DDEExecute intChan, "[Opendatabase A:\DDE.MDB]"
    DDEExecute intChan, "[OpenReport rptError]"
    DDEExecute intChan, "[Print]"
    DDEExecute intChan, "[closedatabase]"
End Sub
```

Notice that there is no error checking and that the routine assumes that Access is either open or in the path and can be opened. Also, to get this code to run on your machine, you will need to replace the drive letter A with the drive plus the path where the sample DDE.MDB is located.

Summary

This chapter detailed both Object Linking and Embedding (OLE) and Dynamic Data Exchange (DDE). Command and code examples showed practical ways to open communications channels that allow applications to exchange data. This chapter also showed you how to allow text boxes on forms or reports to use DDE, as well as how to turn Access into a DDE server.

Working with the Windows API

34

by Michael Murphy

Microsoft Access provides a great deal of flexibility and control for your Access application. Using macros and Visual Basic for Applications (VBA), you can develop sophisticated applications that can satisfy even the most demanding user. However, there might be times when you want more control of your application or want to do something that isn't directly supported by Access. By using dynamic-link libraries (DLLs), you can open a whole new set of functionality that is available to you by calling procedures contained in DLLs.

This chapter gives you an overview of the Windows Applications Programming Interface (API), tells you reasons you might want to use the Windows API, shows you how to use the Windows API, and offers you some examples of how easy it is to include this functionality into your database application.

An Overview of the Windows API

Dynamic-link libraries are files that contain a function or set of functions that can be called from your Access database application (or other Windows programs). DLLs are libraries of procedures that are dynamically linked to your application and loaded into memory when an application uses the DLL and then unloaded when the application is closed.

Microsoft Windows' operating system contains several DLLs that make up what is called the *Windows API.* In fact, all Windows applications use the Windows API to perform tasks such as creating windows, changing window size, reading and writing files, and so on. DLLs have several advantages:

- Functions can be reused and shared among many applications.
- You need only one copy of the DLL (not one for each of your applications).
- You can modify the DLL without modifying your application (assuming that you don't change the `Declare` statement).
- DLLs are usually written in the C/C++ programming language. These DLLs tend to be faster because they're linked and compiled into a stand-alone executable, unlike VBA code, which must first be translated.

The Windows 3.x API is made up of three main DLLs: GDI.DLL, KERNEL.DLL, and USER.DLL. These DLLs were replaced in Windows 95 and Windows NT by the following 32-bit versions: GDI32.DLL, KERNEL32.DLL, and USER32.DLL. If you have an earlier version that contains API calls, refer to the section "Converting Code That Calls a DLL" in the Access 95 Help file for information on converting your API calls. In addition to these DLLs, several other DLLs now make up the Windows 95 and Windows NT API. These 32-bit DLLs contain system-related procedures that include functions, data structures, data types, messages, and statements that you can take advantage of while developing applications to run under Windows 95 and Windows NT.

For more information on using 32-bit Windows APIs, you can refer to the Microsoft Access Developer's Toolkit, which contains the Windows API Viewer. This includes Visual Basic syntax for all 32-bit declarations, data types, and constants.

Making Access Aware of Your API Routines

In order to use the Windows API or other DLLs, you must first *declare* the function you want to use. By declaring the function, you give Access VBA the information it needs in order to make the appropriate call to the external procedure. Once you've used the `Declare` statement, you can call the function just like any other procedure. The declaration of the function contains the following information:

- The name of the function you want to call
- The name of the DLL you're calling
- The number of arguments and their datatypes to be passed to the DLL
- The datatype of the returning value if the procedure is a function

There are two basic steps to making a call to an external procedure:

1. Use the `Declare` statement to tell VBA which procedure to call and the arguments it expects.
2. Make the call to the procedure.

The Structure of API Routines

The `Declare` statement is used to declare a reference to an external procedure. You can declare the external procedure at the module level of a standard module, which is public by default. You can also declare an external procedure at the form or report module level by placing the `Private` keyword before the `Declare`. The syntax for the `Declare` statement is

```
[Public ¦ Private ] Declare Sub name [CDecl] Lib "libname" [Alias "aliasname" ]
➡[([arglist])]
```

or

```
[Public ¦ Private ] Declare Function name [CDecl] Lib "libname" [Alias
➡"aliasname" ] [([arglist])][As type]
```

If the external procedure doesn't return a value, it will be declared as a `Sub` procedure. For example:

```
Declare Sub FreeSid Lib "advapi32.dll" Alias "FreeSid" (pSid As Any)
```

If the external procedure does return a value, it will be declared as a Function procedure. For example:

```
Declare Function GetDriveType Lib "kernel32" Alias "GetDriveTypeA" (ByVal nDrive
➥As String) As Long
```

> **NOTE**
>
> It is very important that you declare the procedure correctly. The best way to do that is to copy and paste the declaration from a source such as the Windows API view that is included in the Access Developer's Toolkit. Also note that functions in the 32-bit Windows API are case-sensitive and that functions in the 16-bit Windows API are not.

The Lib clause in the Declare statement specifies the name of the DLL you're calling and can also specify the exact location of the file. The following example specifies KERNEL32.DLL in the \WINDOWS\SYSTEM directory:

```
Declare Function GetDriveType Lib "c:\windows\system\kernel32.dll" Alias
➥"GetDriveTypeA" (ByVal nDrive As String) As Long
```

Most external procedure calls don't contain the fully qualified path of the DLL. Instead, the name of the DLL is given without the path and the .DLL extension. If the path and extension aren't included in the Lib section, VBA assumes a .DLL extension and will look for the DLL in the following order:

1. The application's directory
2. The current directory
3. The Windows 32-bit system directory (in Windows NT)
4. The Windows system directory
5. The Windows directory
6. The PATH environment

The Alias section and passing arguments to the external procedure are discussed in the following sections.

Aliasing API Calls

The optional keyword Alias is often used in the declaration of an external procedure. There are several occasions when you need to use the Alias clause when declaring a procedure:

- When the external procedure name is the same as a keyword in Access
- When the external procedure has the same name as a public variable, constant, or any other procedure within the same scope

■ When the external procedure name isn't allowed by the DLL naming convention in Access

■ When the external procedure doesn't contain the name of the procedure and you must specify the *ordinal number* of the procedure

If you find that an external procedure name is the same as a keyword in Access or the procedure name is already a public variable, constant, or other procedure within the same scope, you must alias the procedure. You might find this useful if, for example, you write a great deal of code and you later add external procedure calls and find that the name of the procedure has already been used as a variable. Instead of going back and replacing all occurrences of the variable, you can simply alias the procedure to give VBA the unique name it needs to make the appropriate procedure call.

The following two sections describe the third and fourth bulleted points just listed.

When the External Procedure Name Is Not Allowed by the DLL Naming Convention in Access

You need to alias any external procedure that contains characters that aren't allowed by VBA. The procedure name must contain alphanumeric characters or the underscore (_) character. However, the first character of the procedure must be a letter. The following is an example of a function call that uses the Alias clause because the function contains an underscore as the first character:

```
Declare Function lclose Lib "kernel32" Alias "_lclose" (ByVal hFile As Long)
➥As Long
```

When the External Procedure Does Not Contain the Name of the Procedure

Each procedure in a DLL is assigned a number called the *ordinal number*. You can call the procedure by its name (if it exists) or by the ordinal number. The ordinal number is another way of referencing the procedure you're calling. In fact, some DLLs don't contain the name of the procedure—only the ordinal number.

> **TIP**
>
> Although calling the procedure by the ordinal number is slightly faster than calling it by its name, I recommend that you call the procedure by name because the name of the procedure is usually much more descriptive than the ordinal number. Therefore, calling the procedure by name is easier to read, and it's less likely that you will call the wrong procedure by mistake.

If you call a procedure by ordinal, you must first find out the number that you want to call by referring to the documentation for the DLL you're calling. You then alias the procedure by inserting the number sign (#) and the ordinal number you're calling. The following is an example of a fictitious external procedure call using the ordinal number instead of the name:

```
Declare Function MyRemoveSpaces Lib "MyDLL" Alias "#100" (ByVal lpszMyArgument As
➡String) As Long
```

Here is the same procedure call using the name:

```
Declare Function MyRemoveSpaces Lib "MyDLL" Alias "RemoveSpaces" (ByVal
➡lpszMyArgument As String) As Long
```

Passing Parameters

When you pass parameters to a DLL, you must be sure to pass arguments that the DLL expects, both in terms of the order in which they're passed as well as the datatype of the argument. Additionally, you must specify how the argument is passed. Making sure you pass the right argument(s) is the most difficult part of making DLL calls. If you pass the wrong datatype to an external procedure, for example, you can cause a Windows General Protection Fault (GPF), which can cause Access to crash. Be sure to save your work before running your application if you use external procedure calls.

By default, VBA passes all arguments ByRef (by reference). Passing an argument ByRef means that you're passing a memory address, not the actual value, to the procedure of the variable. When passing ByRef, you give the calling procedure the ability to change the actual value of the variable rather than simply changing a copy of the variable, as with passing the variable ByVal (by value). Most DLLs expect arguments ByVal, which means that a copy of the actual value is passed to the procedure. As you can probably deduce, passing ByRef is more efficient than passing ByVal, because you're probably passing less to the procedure.

Of course, there is an exception to every rule. The exception to this rule occurs when you use ByVal with the string datatype. VBA handles string datatypes a little differently. In order to compensate for the differences and to be able to pass the string in a format that the external procedure can use, passing a string ByVal is slightly different than other datatypes. Passing a string ByVal actually means that you're passing the memory address of the first data byte in the string (kind of like what ByRef does). The first data byte in the string gives the calling procedure the information it needs to access the variable. Passing a string ByRef actually means that you're passing the memory address where another address is located, in which that address points to the first data byte of the string.

The Registry and .INI Files

Under Windows 3.x, the standard way of storing configuration information such as the hardware configuration, installed software applications, user preferences, and other settings was in the form of initialization (.INI) files. These .INI files normally reside in the Windows directory, and there are often dozens of .INI files on each PC. In order to organize and consolidate these settings, Microsoft released the Registry in Windows 95 and Windows NT, a system-defined database that contains all system settings. To view entries in the Registry, simply run the regedit application in Windows 95 and the regedit32 application in Windows NT. For additional information on the Windows Registry, refer to the documentation provided by Microsoft Windows.

For example, earlier versions of Access used .INI files to save Access's settings. Figure 34.1 is an example of MSACC20.INI.

FIGURE 34.1.

The MSACC20.INI file for Access 2.0.

Access 95 uses the Registry to save its settings. As you can see from Figure 34.2, settings that used to be in .INI files are now contained in the Registry database in HKEY_LOCAL_MACHINE\SOFTWARE\Microsoft\Access\7.0.

FIGURE 34.2.
The Registry for Access 95.

Interacting with the Registry and .INI Files

You might want to save configuration information or store user preferences for your Access application. The Windows Registry is a good place to save those settings. The following examples of saving user preferences include saving settings to .INI files as well as saving to the Windows Registry. The following examples show you how to read and write to .INI files and also how to read and write to the Windows Registry. They are intended to show you the differences between the two methods and also to give you some real examples of API calls.

> **TIP**
>
> Although writing to .INI files is still supported, the preferred method of saving settings is saving them to the Windows Registry.

Writing to .INI Files

As I mentioned earlier, when using the Windows API, you must first declare the function you're calling. The WriteProfileString API function call opens the WIN.INI file; writes the section, key name, and setting provided in the argument list; and closes the file. The following is an example of writing a user preference in the Myapp application, which saves the default location for exporting data:

```
Declare Function WriteProfileString Lib "kernel32" Alias "WriteProfileStringA"
➥(ByVal lpszSection As String, ByVal lpszKeyName As String, ByVal
➥lpszString As String) As Long
Sub WriteSettings
    Dim vReturnValue as Long
    vReturnValue& = WriteProfileString("MyApp", "Default Export", "c:\data\")
End Sub
```

Reading from .INI Files

Now that you've saved the user preference to WIN.INI, you need to be able to read that setting. You can do this by using the GetProfileString API call. The following is an example of how to read the setting that was written in the preceding example:

```
Declare Function GetProfileString Lib "kernel32" Alias "GetProfileStringA" (ByVal
➥lpAppName As String, ByVal lpKeyName As String, ByVal lpDefault As
➥String, ByVal lpReturnedString As String, ByVal nSize As Long) As Long
Sub ReadSettings()
    Dim vReturnValue As Long, vReturnString As String * 255
    vReturnValue& = GetProfileString("MyApp", "Default Export", "c:\",
    ➥vReturnString$, 255)
    vReturnString$ = Left$(vReturnString$, vReturnValue&)
End Sub
```

Writing to the Registry

Since the SaveSetting statement is already a part of the functionality of Access VBA, you don't need to declare it as you would with the API call to WriteProfileString. The following is the syntax for the SaveSetting statement:

```
SaveSetting(appname, section, key, setting)
```

Writing to the Registry then becomes quite easy. The following is an example that writes to the Windows Registry:

```
Call SaveSetting("MyApp", "User Preference", "Default Export", "c:\data\")
```

As you can see from Figure 34.3, using the SaveSetting statement in VBA writes to the Registry database in HKEY_CURRENT_USER\Software\VB and VBA Program Settings.

FIGURE 34.3.

A display of the Registry.

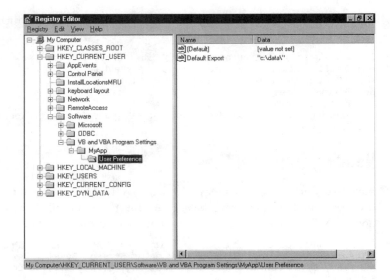

Reading from the Registry

Similar to the SaveSetting statement, the GetSetting function is also a part of Access VBA and doesn't need to be declared as an API call. Note that because GetSetting returns a value, it is a function. The following is the syntax for the GetSetting function:

```
GetSetting(appname, section, key[, default])
```

The following example returns the setting written in the preceding example into the variable vReturnValue:

```
Dim vReturnValue As Variant
vReturnValue = GetSetting("MyApp", "User Preference", "Default Export")
```

Summary

This chapter gave the Access 95 programmer a foundation for understanding and using the Windows Applications Programming Interface (API). Calls to dynamic link libraries (DLL) and API routines were covered, aliasing was detailed, and the developer was shown methods for passing parameters. Programming techniques were presented for reading and writing to the Registry and .INI files.

Add-Ins and Libraries

35

by Merrill Mayer

This chapter focuses on developing and implementing Access add-ins and libraries. First, add-ins are explained, followed by a discussion of libraries. An add-in is a tool that enables the Access user to automate a complex process, extend functionality, or make repetitive tasks easier. Because add-ins are written within the Access environment, no additional programming languages or tools are needed to develop them.

Types of Add-Ins

Access supports three types of add-ins: wizards, builders, and menus. An add-in to create a new table, query, form, or report is a wizard or builder add-in. An add-in that is not context-specific is a menu add-in.

Wizards

A wizard add-in handles complex operations such as creating a form or report. It normally consists of a series of dialog boxes that provide an interface that guides the user through the process of creating an object. Forms, graphics, and text take the user step-by-step through the design process while hiding the behind-the-scenes details of creating an object. The following types of wizards are provided by Access:

- Table and query wizards
- Form and report wizards
- Property wizards
- Control wizards

User-defined wizards enhance existing functionality by providing tools that can be used throughout any Access database. A typical user-defined wizard might generate a specific type of form or report or add controls with certain properties already set. For example, you might consider the following wizard types:

- A form wizard that creates a dialog box and has a text box and command button already on the form when you first open it.
- A report wizard that prompts you for a report title. The wizard then sets the report title you specify as the Caption property of a label it creates and then sets the Forecolor property of that label to Red.
- A control wizard that takes you through setting the caption for a label, its Forecolor property, and its font size.
- A control wizard that creates OK and Cancel buttons. This wizard would automatically set a command button's caption to OK and its Default property to true to create an OK button. This same control wizard might be used to set a command button's caption to Cancel and its Cancel property to true, thereby creating a Cancel button.
- A property wizard that enables you to set the width of a form to a size you pick from a list.

> **NOTE**
>
> User-defined wizards are made available in the same way as built-in Access wizards. If you create a wizard to design a specific type of form, your wizard will be added to the list of existing form wizards after it has been properly installed.

Builders

A builder is a relatively simple tool that guides the user through implementing a data element or an expression. It typically consists of a single dialog box or form, or it might place code directly into a form, report, or module.

When you install a builder you have created, it is added to the list of existing Access builders. You usually invoke a builder for the object that has the focus by selecting Build or Build Event from the shortcut menu or by clicking the Build button. The following types of builders are included with Access:

- Property builders
- Control builders
- Expression builders

User-defined builders provide enhancements to Access by providing a simple tool to handle repetitive tasks. A typical user-defined builder might enable you to set a property by selecting values from a predefined list or place predefined code in a form, report, or module. Following are some examples of user-defined builders:

- A property builder to select among only specific colors rather than the full-color palette when the Build button is clicked and a color property such as Forecolor or Backcolor has the focus on the property sheet.
- A code builder that places code to close the active form in the Click event of a command button when Build is selected from the shortcut menu while a form is open in Design mode.
- A control builder that prompts the user for a command button's caption when Build is selected from the shortcut menu when the command button has the focus.

Menu Add-Ins

A menu add-in is a menu item that the user selects to carry out a specific command. An example of a built-in menu add-in is the Database Splitter or Menu Builder. Unlike builders and wizards, a menu add-in is not context-specific. In other words, a menu add-in operates on different types of objects or on the Access application itself.

When your menu add-in is installed, it is available through the Tools | Add-ins option. This means that you can select the menu item and launch your menu add-in in the usual way you enter menu commands (clicking, shortcut keys, and so on). Menu add-ins are always available to the user when the Tools menu is available—you don't have to rely on a specific context such as designing a new form. In other words, if you can select Tools | Add-ins, you can run your menu add-in. This is an important fact to remember when designing a menu add-in because you must make the add-in generic enough not to cause problems in different situations. For example, the Menu Builder always enables you to design a menu even when you have a table or report open in Design mode. Menu add-ins are also available in every Access database on your system, so their design should not be database-specific. For coverage of menu add-ins, see Chapter 26, "Menus and Toolbars."

Development Guidelines

Following is a general set of guidelines to help you design, code, and test your add-in application. The goal of the guidelines is to ensure that your add-in runs efficiently and is easy to use. For more information on program optimization and efficiency, refer to Chapter 23, "Visual Basic for Applications."

General Design

A good design practice is to model your add-in's user interface on the Access built-in add-ins. This technique provides a consistent look and feel with the Access application.

Referencing Objects

An add-in database is the collection of objects that make up your add-in. The add-in database can contain any type of valid Access object. These objects can be forms, reports, tables, queries, modules, or macros. Because add-in databases are normally used to provide functionality to other Access databases, it's important to know when objects in the user database or add-in database are used. In add-in databases, object references follow the rules described next.

Referencing Data Sources

The add-in's forms and reports are bound to the data sources in the add-in. If Access can't find the table or query for the data source, an error occurs. This means that even if a table or query exists in the current user database, the add-in won't find it.

Referencing Macros

Macros are searched first in the add-in database and then in the current user database. This means that your add-in code can run macros in the add-in database or the current user database.

Referencing Domain Aggregate Functions

Domain aggregate functions such as DAvg, DSum, and DCount always reference the current database. These functions don't reference the add-in data. You can use domain aggregate functions in your add-in if you reference the user database. Listing 35.1 shows how you could use DCount to determine the number of records in the first table of the user database by counting the occurrences of the first field in that table.

Listing 35.1. Using domain aggregate functions in an add-in.

```
Private Sub Form_Load()

    Dim iCounter
    Dim db As Database
    Dim tb As TableDef
    Dim fd As Field

    Set db = CurrentDb()
    Set tb = db.TableDefs(0)
    Set fd = tb.Fields(0)

    iCounter = DCount(fd.Name, tb.Name)

End Sub
```

Referencing Toolbars in an Add-In

Access first searches the add-in for custom toolbars. If the custom toolbar isn't found in the add-in, the current database is searched. You can't reference a toolbar that doesn't exist in either database.

Multiuser Considerations

Multiple users can use the objects in your add-in without conflicts. Other aspects of the multiuser environment, however, must be considered. The most important multiuser issue occurs if your add-in needs to write information back to the add-in database. In this situation, you need to handle locking to avoid conflicts in record updating. This means that you allow only one user at a time to change data on a specific record. You can find more information about the multiuser environment in Chapter 32, "Multiuser Programming and Techniques."

Checking and Modifying the Access Environment

Because users have the ability to configure the Access database environment, it's important that any add-in check its environment when it is loaded. Otherwise, the add-in might fail to function properly.

> **WARNING**
>
> Changing the environment within your add-in is generally not recommended unless performance considerations require you to do so.

One particularly troublesome area for the add-in developer is the use of the SendKeys action or statement. SendKeys causes problems when the user has modified the Access environment by reassigning key functions using an AutoKeys macro or has used the Options dialog box to change the behavior of the arrow keys. An example of this would be reassigning Ctrl-X to open a form rather than cut text.

Obviously, you can avoid this situation entirely by not using SendKeys in your add-in. As an alternative, you can check for key reassignment in the AutoKeys macro by using searching through the Scripts document collection. For more information on collections, refer to Chapter 25, "Data Access Objects."

Writing Your Add-In

After you've decided on the type and purpose of the add-in you're designing, it's time to actually begin writing it. When developing an add-in, follow the same techniques you would use for any other Access application. Begin by creating a new database; then add the objects you will need, write the code behind the objects, and test the application. The following section discusses how to proceed with add-in development.

Creating the Add-In Database

Your add-in database should have a unique name that doesn't conflict with other add-in names. It's useful to give your add-in a meaningful name that indicates something about the purpose of the add-in. The naming convention for add-ins uses a file extension of .MDA rather than the .MDB extension used for Access databases. This convention aids in distinguishing an add-in from another type of Access database but doesn't affect the functionality of the add-in.

Creating the Add-In Objects

Now that you have a new add-in database, you're ready to define the objects it will contain. If your add-in uses tables, you should create them in your add-in database. Don't link external tables into your database because this can cause problems if the user moves the database to another folder. In addition, it takes more time to retrieve information from linked tables than to retrieve them from tables defined directly in your database. Add-ins usually have an entry point defined in a module. This is where your add-in first begins execution. When designing forms, follow the general guidelines presented earlier in this chapter. In addition, you should break up complex operations into separate forms. Put as much of the code as possible into the form-level modules, and begin execution with the form's OnOpen or OnLoad events. This method makes your add-in easier to maintain because the code associated with the form is right there with it.

Designing a Wizard

When you're designing a wizard, the look and feel of the user interface is important. As stated earlier, anyone using your add-in will find the process more intuitive if you follow the general design of Access's built-in wizards. To achieve this result, you should follow the form-design guidelines specified next.

Managing the Form's Appearance

Start by designing each of the forms as a modal dialog box. This technique keeps the user from moving to a subsequent form before the information on the current form is complete and ensures that all the relevant information has been gathered by the wizard. For example, the Access built-in single-column form wizard forces you to pick the fields to display on the form before picking a style to customize the form's appearance. Although the use of a modal dialog box forces all essential data to be entered, it doesn't provide any method of validation. You still have to validate any data entered by the user within the context of your particular add-in.

You should also center your forms on the user's desktop by setting each form's AutoCenter property to Yes. In addition, turn off record selectors, scroll bars, and navigation buttons. Modal dialog boxes typically don't use scroll bars, and the need for scroll bars implies that your form is too complex and should be broken down into more than one form. Record selectors and navigation buttons are used to move to different records when a form has an underlying record source. Because the forms used in wizards are present to help design Access objects rather than data manipulation, they usually wouldn't have a record source, so record selectors and navigation buttons would serve no purpose. Even if a record source is present, record selectors and navigation buttons aren't used on modal dialog boxes.

Design your add-in forms to fit a 640 × 480 display with a 16-color palette. Designing for a higher resolution might result in a form that doesn't fit on a user's screen. Also keep in mind that some colors don't display well on monochrome monitors or video systems that have a limited palette.

TIP

Using the Windows 95 default colors will give your add-in a look consistent with other applications designed for Windows 95.

If your wizard has more than one form, use a consistent design when placing controls on the forms. This means that the same type of control that performs a similar function on multiple forms should appear in the same location on each of those forms.

A Form Wizard Example

The following example shows how to create a simple form wizard that generates a modal dialog box. This wizard, named Dialog, can be created as part of any add-in database that you have defined. This wizard opens a dialog box containing a single text box and command button. The form is opened in Design mode to enable the user to customize it. This wizard is similar to the built-in Access wizard that is used to design a new form. The only differences are the form's property settings and the addition of a few controls.

To begin, design a new form and name it Dialog. For more information on creating a form in Access, see Chapter 12, "Creating and Using Simple Forms." Next, set the properties on the forms as shown in Table 35.1.

Table 35.1. Property settings for the Dialog wizard form.

Property	Setting	Description
Default View	Single Form	Show only one record at a time on the form. You don't need to show multiple records on a modal dialog box.
Views Allowed	Form	Allow the form to be viewed only in Form mode and not in Datasheet mode. Because this form is a dialog box, a Datasheet view isn't relevant.
Scroll Bars	Neither	Don't show scroll bars. Scroll bars are not normally part of a modal dialog box.
Record Selectors	No	Don't show record selectors. Record selectors enable you to select specific records from an underlying table or query on the form and are not normally part of a modal dialog box.
Navigation Buttons	No	Don't show navigation buttons. Navigation buttons enable you to move forward and backward among records of a form's table or query. This feature is normally not part of a modal dialog.
Dividing Lines	No	Turn off dividing lines that separate different sections on a form.

Property	Setting	Description
Auto Resize	Yes	Automatically size the Form window to display a complete record.
Auto Center	Yes	Center the form on the user's desktop.
Pop Up	Yes	Cause a pop-up form to prevent access to toolbars and menus as well as other windows until the form is closed.
Modal	Yes	Cause a modal form to remain the active window in an application until that form is closed. All other windows are effectively disabled.
Border Style	Dialog	Create a nonsizable dialog box border.
Min Max Buttons	None	Min and Max buttons allow a window to be minimized or maximized and aren't present on modal dialog boxes.

When you've finished designing your form, save it as Dialog.

After the form is saved, you can add a new module containing a function called `DlgForm_Open()`. This function serves as the entry point for your add-in, the place where your add-in begins executing. The purpose of the `DlgForm_Open()` function is to open a new form in Design mode using the Dialog form as a model. The `DlgForm_Open()` function also sets form-level properties, adds controls, and sets control-level properties. After you've finished designing the module, save it as modDialog. The code for the `DlgForm_Open()` function is shown in Listing 35.2.

Listing 35.2. The `DlgForm_Open()` function.

```
Function dlgForm_Open(mydatasource As String)

    Dim dbWizard As Database
    Dim frm As Form
    Dim ctlText As Control
    Dim ctlButton As Control
    Dim intLeft As Integer
    Dim intTop As Integer
    Dim intHeight As Integer
    Dim intWidth As Integer

    Set dbWizard = CodeDb()
    Set frm = CreateForm(dbWizard.Name, "Dialog")
    frm.RecordSource = mydatasource

    intLeft = 200
    intTop = 200
    intHeight = 1500
```

continues

Listing 35.2. continued

```
intWidth = 6500
Set ctlText = CreateControl(frm.Name, acTextBox, acDetail, "", "", _
  intLeft, intTop, intWidth, intHeight)

intLeft = 2500
intTop = 2000
intWidth = 750
Set ctlButton = CreateControl(frm.Name, acCommandButton, acDetail, "", "", _
  intLeft, intTop, intWidth)
ctlButton.Caption = "OK"
ctlButton.Default = True

DoCmd.SelectObject acForm, "Form1"
DoCmd.Restore


End Function
```

The code in the preceding function creates a modal dialog box in the current user database that contains a command button and a text box. To begin, you declare the function specifying a record source name as the only parameter passed into the function. You must always declare record source name as a parameter for the initial function that executes in a form wizard even if your wizard never uses a record source. If you do not, your wizard will fail to function, and an error will occur when you try to open a form using the wizard.

Next, the DlgForm_Open() function sets the dbWizard variable to the database where the code is actually running—your add-in database. You do this by using the CodeDB() function. You then use this database name along with the form Dialog you just created as parameters for the CreateForm() function. The CreateForm() function opens a form in Design mode in the user database by using the specified form as a template for the new form. You can't simply use the OpenForm method of the DoCmd and open your form in Design mode because this method enables you to save your form in only the add-in database and not the current user database. You can then set any additional form properties. In this case, you set the RecordSource property of the form to the parameter passed into the DlgForm_Open() function. After you've created your form, you're ready to add controls to it.

Forms opened with CreateForm() don't have any controls even if you add them directly to the template. As a result, you must use the CreateControl() function to add controls to your form automatically. In the code for DlgForm_Open(), you use CreateControl() to add a text box and command button to the form specifying the respective controls' size and location. After adding the controls, you can set additional properties such as the Default and Caption properties for the command button. The resulting form would look like the one shown in Figure 35.1.

FIGURE 35.1.

The Dialog form in Design mode.

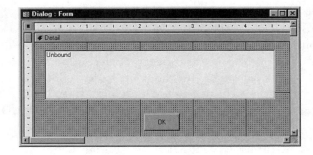

You now have a simple user-defined form wizard that you can use in any Access database!

Designing a Builder

Builders might or might not have a user interface. If the builder you design does have one, you should follow the design guidelines that were specified for creating wizards. Otherwise, you just need to concentrate on designing the code that makes your builder function. In the builder example for this chapter, you will see how to design a code builder that requires no user interface design.

A Code Wizard Example

The following text shows how to design a simple code builder that closes the currently active form when a command button is clicked. You could use this builder to add the code to the dialog box form you created with the Dialog form wizard.

As with the form wizard, you use a function as the entry point to your builder. The code for the function is shown in Listing 35.3.

Listing 35.3. The `Build_Form_Close()` function.

```
Function Build_Form_Close(strCurrentModule As String, strCurentProc As String,
➥strSelection As String)

    Dim strFormName As String
    Dim strEventType As String

    If Left$(strCurrentModule, 4) = "Form" Then
        If UCase$(Right$(strCurentProc, 6)) = "_CLICK" Then
            strFormName = Mid(strCurrentModule, 6, Len(strCurrentModule) - 5)
            Build_Form_Close = "docmd.close acForm, " & Chr$(34) & strFormName &
            ➥Chr$(34) & Chr$(13) & Chr$(10)
        End If
    End If

End Function
```

All the parameters in the Build_Form_Close() function are required for a code builder. If you leave out any of the parameters, you will get an error message when you try to use the builder in your code. The strCurrentModule parameter contains the current module name, and strCurrentProc contains the current procedure name. Because the module name is always preceded by its type, you can use this prefix to determine whether you're in a form module and then remove the prefix to get the correct form name. You can also use the procedure name to determine which procedure you're in. In this case, the code checks for _Click in an attempt to associate the builder with a click event in a form module.

The last parameter passed to Build_Form_Close() is strSelection. Although you don't need to reference the strSelection parameter in this simple code builder, keep in mind that it contains any code you will have selected (highlighted) and that this code will be replaced by the code generated with the builder. To invoke your builder, open the procedure where you would like the builder to place your code and select Build from the shortcut menu. Assuming that you have a form module, Form1, and are currently in the code for the cmdBtn_Click event, the code generated by the builder would look like that shown in Listing 35.4.

Listing 35.4. Code generated by the form close builder.

```
Private Sub cmdBtn_Click()

    DoCmd.Close acForm, "Form1"

End Sub
```

Error Handling

In addition to the code that makes your add-in work, you should include error-handling routines in your application. Without proper error handling, your add-in might generate confusing messages. A runtime error might generate a message like this: A runtime error occurred in database: <name>. You do not have permission to view modules in your database.

This type of message results from the fact that your add-in is stored in a separate database. How to implement error handling is discussed in Chapter 23.

As part of the general debugging and cleanup process, you should also delete any unnecessary objects from your database and then compact it. Unnecessary objects could be forms, reports, or tables you created during the development process that aren't referenced anywhere in your add-in. This method ensures that your database is as small and efficient as possible.

Online Help can also be included with your add-in. Online Help makes your add-in easier to use and document. It's especially useful when an add-in has a complex user interface such as in a multiform wizard that poses many questions to the user. You can create Online Help for objects in your add-in in the same way you would for objects in any other type of Access database. For example, you can set the `ControlTipText` property of the controls on your form to create a pop-up tool tip, or you can use the Microsoft Help Compiler to create the Online Help file for your add-in application. If you create an Online Help file using the Microsoft Help Compiler, you must specify the name of the help file in the `HelpFile` property of your form. For more information on how to implement Online Help in your add-in, see Chapter 38, "Developing Online Help."

After designing your database and adding all necessary objects and code, you're ready to test and debug your add-in. Access has many helpful features for testing and debugging applications. Naturally, you should compile your add-in code and remove any compile-time errors. Then try to weed out any runtime errors, such as divide by zero, and finally make sure that your add-in produces the correct results. You can set breakpoints, step through code, and view results in the Immediate pane to help you with the debug process. For more information about testing and debugging aids, see Chapter 29, "Testing and Debugging Applications."

Installing Your Add-In

You can install your completed add-in using the Add-in Manager. Before installation, however, you must set certain database properties and register your add-in.

Setting Database Properties

Database properties provide general information about your add-in. You must set these properties before installing your add-in. The following steps guide you through setting the necessary database properties:

1. From the Database window, select File | Database Properties.
2. Click the Summary tab.
3. Enter the appropriate information about your add-in database in the Title, Company, and Comments boxes. The title you enter will appear in the list of available add-ins in the Add-in Manager dialog box. Information in the Comments box will appear as the description when your add-in is selected from the Add-in Manager dialog box.
4. Click OK to save your changes and close the Database Properties dialog box.

Registering Your Add-In

All add-ins must be registered in the system Registry. Access uses the USysRegInfo table to facilitate the registration process. You should create the USysRegInfo table in the same database that contains your add-in. You can't use your add-in if it isn't properly registered.

Tables that begin with USys or MSys are not normally displayed in the Database window. These tables are system objects, not standard user database objects you create and manipulate in Access. Access automatically creates the MSys tables it needs when you create a new database.

Follow these steps to override the default setting and view the Access system objects:

1. Select Tools | Options.
2. In the Options dialog box, click the View tab.
3. Select the System Objects option. Your selection should look like Figure 35.2.

FIGURE 35.2.

Selecting the system objects.

4. Close the Options dialog box.

All USys and MSys tables will now appear in the Database window. The ability to view Access system objects has no effect on other aspects of your database. You need not change back to the default of not being able to view these objects.

An easy way to set up your USysRegInfo table is to import a copy of it from another database. Importing the USysRegInfo table requires the following steps:

1. Select File | Get External Data | Import. The Import dialog box appears, as shown in Figure 35.3.
2. Make sure that your Access folder appears in the Look In text box. This is the folder where you have installed Access.
3. In the File Name box type *.MDA and click the Find Now button.
4. Select Wztool70 and click Import. The Import Objects dialog box, shown in Figure 35.4, is displayed.

FIGURE 35.3.

The Import dialog box.

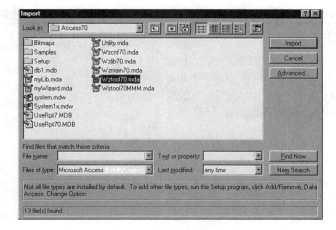

FIGURE 35.4.

The Import Objects dialog box.

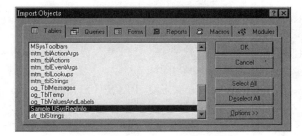

5. On the Tables tab of the Import Objects dialog box, select Sample USysRegInfo and click OK. The Sample USysRegInfo table is imported into your add-in database.

6. Rename Sample USysRegInfo to USysRegInfo.

Modifying the USysRegInfo table means supplying the necessary information to register your new add-in. The USysRegInfo table contains the name of the registry key in the SubKey field and one or more additional values in other fields. Table 35.2 shows the values entered to register the Dialog wizard as a new form wizard and to register the code wizard. Table 35.3 shows the definitions for Type, ValName, and Value given in Table 35.2. You can find more information on the specifics of the values in USysRegInfo by searching Access Online Help.

WARNING

Unless you're familiar with the inner workings of the registry, make no entries or modifications other than the ones shown in Tables 35.2 and 35.3. Incorrect entries can cause significant problems.

Table 35.2. The USysRegInfo table to register your add-in.

Subkey	Type	ValName	Value
HKEY_CURRENT_ACCESS_PROFILE\ Wizards\Form Wizards\Dialog	0		
HKEY_CURRENT_ACCESS_PROFILE\ Wizards\Form Wizards\Dialog	1	Bitmap	C:\MSOffice\ Access70\ Bitmaps\ Newobj\ f-dlg.bmp
HKEY_CURRENT_ACCESS_PROFILE\ Wizards\Form Wizards\Dialog	4	Datasource Required	0
HKEY_CURRENT_ACCESS_PROFILE\ Wizards\Form Wizards\Dialog	1	Description	Build a dialog box
HKEY_CURRENT_ACCESS_PROFILE\ Wizards\Form Wizards\Dialog	1	Function	dlgForm_Open
HKEY_CURRENT_ACCESS_PROFILE\ Wizards\Form Wizards\Dialog	4	Index	7
HKEY_CURRENT_ACCESS_PROFILE\ Wizards\Form Wizards\Dialog	4	Can Edit	0
HKEY_CURRENT_ACCESS_PROFILE\ Wizards\Form Wizards\Dialog	1	Library	\ACCDIR\ myWizard.mda;1
HKEY_CURRENT_ACCESS_PROFILE\ Wizards\Property Wizards\Module\ Close Form Builder	0		
HKEY_CURRENT_ACCESS_PROFILE\ Wizards\Property Wizards\Module\ Close Form Builder	1	Description	Close Form Builder
HKEY_CURRENT_ACCESS_PROFILE\ Wizards\Property Wizards\Module\ Close Form Builder	4	Can Edit	1
HKEY_CURRENT_ACCESS_PROFILE\ Wizards\Property Wizards\Module\ Close Form Builder	1	Library	\ACCDIR\ myWizard.mda
HKEY_CURRENT_ACCESS_PROFILE\ Wizards\Property Wizards\Module\ Close Form Builder	1	Function	Build_Form_Close

Table 35.3. The definitions for Type, ValName, and Value.

Type	ValName	Value
1	Bitmap	Defines the path to the bitmap (.BMP) that is displayed above the description on the left side of the New Form dialog box when the Dialog wizard is selected.
4	Datasource Required	Determines whether a datasource is required. 1=Yes, 0=No. For the Dialog wizard, you don't need a datasource, so 0 is entered.
1	Description	User-defined. Defines the text displayed on the left side of the New Form dialog box when the Dialog wizard is selected.
1	Function	The function used to start the Dialog wizard.
4	Index	Defines the order in which the Dialog wizard is displayed in the list in the New Form dialog box. The first item is 0, so the Dialog wizard is the eighth entry.
4	Can Edit	Determines whether the wizard can be edited. 1=Yes, 0=No.
1	Library	Defines the path and name of the add-in for the Dialog wizard database: \ACCDIR\MyAddInDb.mda. The first part is always the same. The Add-in Manager substitutes the path to the folder where Access is installed.

Using the Add-In Manager

The Add-in Manager is used make your add-in available to other Access databases. When you install an add-in with the Add-in Manager, you add the information about the add-in to the Registry. The Add-in Manager uses the details you specified in the USysRegInfo table to store this information in the Registry.

TIP

If you uninstall your add-in by using the Add-in Manager, the Registry entries are removed.

To install your add-in using the Add-in Manager, follow these steps:

1. Open the database where you plan to use the add-in.
2. Select Tools | Add-ins | Add-in Manger.
3. If your add-in doesn't appear in the list of add-ins, click the Add New button. The File Open dialog box is displayed. Select your add-in and click OK.
4. In the Available Add-ins box, select the add-in to be installed, and then click the Install button (see Figure 35.5).

FIGURE 35.5.

The Add-in Manager dialog box.

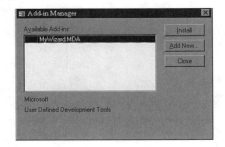

5. Click the Close button when the installation is complete.

Using Your Add-In

Because you installed the Dialog wizard as a new form wizard, it appears as an option in the New Form dialog box. It can now be used as a starting point for a new dialog box. Figure 35.6 shows the New Form dialog box with the Dialog wizard ready for use in your database.

FIGURE 35.6.

The New Form dialog box.

Creating Add-In Libraries for Common Code

A library database provides a mechanism for sharing code across different Access applications. It enables you to store common code that doesn't have to be rewritten each time you develop a new application.

Why You Should Use an Add-In Library

Because an add-in library consists of reusable code, it can speed development time by eliminating the need to rewrite common routines for every new database. In addition, it should help error-proof your application by incorporating code that has already been debugged and tested.

An example of the type of common code appropriate for storing in an add-in library is code that doesn't contain any hardcoded references to specific Access objects. In other words, the code is generic in function. Following is a list of some good candidates for inclusion in a library database:

- Data entry validation, such as making sure that only numeric values are entered
- Conversion utilities to convert between different formats or data types
- Display of messages
- Display of common dialog boxes
- Determination of whether a particular form is currently loaded
- Determination of whether something in a listbox or combo box has been selected
- A library of API declarations and calls

Creating Library Databases

Creating a library database for common code follows the same procedures as creating an add-in library for builders and wizards. You first create a new library database and then add the necessary objects. Follow the steps outlined in the sections "Creating the Add-In Database" and "Creating the Add-In Objects" earlier in this chapter. Be sure to test and debug your library database and include error-handling routines.

Referencing Library Databases

Common code from library databases can be used in a user database application only after a reference to it has been established. This means that a type of link is created from the user database to the library database.

To create the reference, follow these steps:

1. Open your database (not the library database).
2. Open either an existing or a new Visual Basic module.
3. Select Tools | References.
4. If your library database doesn't appear in the Available References box, click the Browse button to select additional libraries, as shown in Figure 35.7.

FIGURE 35.7.

The References dialog box.

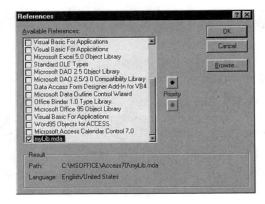

5. Click the check box next the your database library.
6. Click OK to add your library as a reference into the currently open database.

> **WARNING**
>
> When a reference is created, the full path to that library database is stored with the reference. If you move the library database to a different folder, you must reestablish the reference to prevent an error. The code in your current database that references the add-in function won't compile. Instead, the References dialog box will appear, enabling you to reestablish your reference to the library database.

Using Library Databases

After a reference to a library database has been established, you can use the routines stored in the database.

Assume that you have a library database, myLib.mda, to which you've established a reference. myLib.mda contains a function, CheckNum(), which checks for a numeric value whenever the user presses a key. If the key pressed isn't a number, the value entered is discarded, making it seem as if no key has been pressed.

To begin developing your library, first add the following constants in the Declarations section of your module:

```
Const KEY_BACKSPACE = 8
Const KEY_NOKEY = 0
```

Now you can add the code given in Listing 35.5.

Listing 35.5. The `CheckNum()` function.

```
Function CheckNum(ByVal ikey As Integer) As Integer
If ikey = KEY_BACKSPACE Then
        CheckNum = ikey
    ElseIf ikey >= 48 And ikey <= 57 Then
        CheckNum = ikey
    Else
        CheckNum = KEY_NOKEY
    End If
End Function
```

You can now call this procedure in your database the same way you would call any other Access procedure. Access checks for your procedure in any referenced add-in database if it doesn't find it in the current user database. If a procedure in the add-in database and one in the current user database have the same name, the procedure in the current database is executed.

For example, you can use the `CheckNum` procedure in the `KeyPress` event of the Text1 text box to test the keystrokes entered by the user. (If you need more information on Access forms and events, see Chapter 24, "Working with the Access Event Model.") To call the `CheckNum()` function from the `KeyPress` event, write the following code:

```
Private Sub Text1_KeyPress(KeyAscii As Integer)
    KeyAscii = CheckNum(KeyAscii)
End Sub
```

Summary

Add-in libraries, builders, and wizards share many common attributes. All of these tools are kept in an Access library database that is separate from the user database. As a result, they all provide reusable features, in the form of either code or objects. Add-in libraries, builders, and wizards simplify the development process and extend the built-in functionality of Access.

Access 95 and Programming in SQL

36

by Rob Newman

IN THIS CHAPTER

SQL Defined

Structured Query Language or SQL (usually pronounced "sequel") is the most popular relational database query language in use today. It was developed at IBM laboratories in the early 1970s to implement the relational model introduced by Dr. Edgar F. Codd in 1970.

Although it's certainly a query language, SQL is much more, because of its powerful data-definition and data-access capabilities. SQL is known as a transform-oriented language. The user inputs English-like requests for data using a defined structure—hence the word "structured" in the language's name. The requests are then transformed by the RDBMS into the requested output.

Some of the data access commands of SQL are SELECT, UPDATE, INSERT, and DELETE. The SELECT command forms the basis for retrieving data from a database. UPDATE, INSERT, and DELETE allow you to modify the data according to the parameters you supply. These commands are self-explanatory. An UPDATE command updates records in the database. INSERT inserts or creates a new record in the database, and DELETE deletes a record from the database.

The Access 95 SQL Language

Access 95 SQL is a mixture containing elements of both the ANSI SQL-89 and SQL-92 language standards, although it doesn't completely implement either standard. In addition, Access 95 SQL enhances ANSI SQL with additional commands not found in the ANSI SQL standard. Some of the major differences are described in the following sections.

The *BETWEEN...AND* Construct

One difference between Access 95 SQL and ANSI SQL is how Access 95 SQL treats the BETWEEN...AND construct. This construct is used to specify a range of values *between* two values; it has the following syntax:

```
expression1 [NOT] BETWEEN expression2 AND expression3
```

The difference is that in Access 95 SQL, `expression1` can be greater than `expression2`; in ANSI SQL, `expression2` must be equal to or less than `expression3`. This is to your advantage if you're using Access 95 SQL, but you need to beware when using this construct with other SQL databases.

For example, using Access 95 SQL, the following two queries would return the same number of records from the Invoices table. (Notice the dates are reversed in the second query.) Using ANSI SQL would return either an error or an empty recordset, depending on the database you're requesting data from.

Query 1

```
SELECT DISTINCTROW Invoices.*
FROM Invoices
WHERE (((Invoices.[Order Date]) Between #1/1/93# And #1/31/93#));
```

Query 2

```
SELECT DISTINCTROW Invoices.*
FROM Invoices
WHERE (((Invoices.[Order Date]) Between #1/31/93# And #1/1/93#));
```

Access 95 uses different wildcard characters than ANSI SQL. Table 36.1 shows the differences.

Table 36.1. Access 95 SQL wildcard characters.

Access 95 SQL	ANSI SQL	Description
?	_(underscore)	Matches any single character
*	%	Matches zero or more characters

Enhanced Features of Access 95 SQL

Many of the SQL databases in use today contain a mixture of ANSI SQL and proprietary commands that are specific to their product. This helps to build a loyal following of customers for their product and allows software designers to improve the features that they or their users feel are important to enhance.

As mentioned earlier, Access 95 SQL contains commands and features of ANSI SQL-89 and SQL-92 as well as some features that are proprietary to Access 95. Some enhancements that aren't found in ANSI SQL include the following. (See the section titled "Writing Queries with SQL" for examples and more details on these.)

■ The TRANSFORM statement
■ The PARAMETERS declaration

ANSI SQL Features Not Supported in Access 95 SQL

In addition to the enhancements in Access 95 SQL, over 200 ANSI SQL keywords are *not* supported by Access 95 SQL. Because of the large number, it's beyond the scope of this chapter to detail all of these keywords, but here are a few of the more noteworthy features of ANSI SQL that you won't find in Access 95 SQL:

■ Data-definition language (DDL) statements (other than Jet database's)
■ Database security statements, such as COMMIT, GRANT, and LOCK
■ DISTINCT aggregate function references

Why Use Access 95 SQL?

With Access 95, Microsoft has introduced many time-saving features that enhance and simplify management of a relational database management system (RDBMS). Access 95 has new
and improved wizards and builders that make it much easier to create quite large and complex
queries. However, there are limits to these tools, and as excellent as they are, there are still things
that can't be done with them or that simply won't work outside a native Access 95 environment (for example, using SQL pass-through to query data on a SQL database server).

One of the most common implementations of SQL in Access is to use an SQL SELECT statement as the source of records for forms, reports, and controls. You could create a standard query
to use as the record source, but by using a SQL string as the record source, there is one less
object that you must create and maintain in your database. For example, you might have a
form that contains a combo box. For the Row Source property for the combo box, you could
enter a SQL string such as the following:

```
SELECT DISTINCTROW CustomerID, CompanyName
FROM Customers;
```

This would display a list of all the company names when the combo box down arrow is selected. List boxes and combo boxes based on SQL statements are slower than list boxes and
combo boxes based on saved queries, however, so you should weigh this against the benefit of
having fewer query objects in your database.

Some types of queries can be run only using SQL statements (as opposed to using the Query
Designer). Following is a list of SQL-specific queries that are possible only using Access 95
SQL. (These will be explained in more detail later in this chapter.)

- Union queries combine fields from tables or queries into one field.
- Data-definition queries are used to create new or modify existing data objects.
- Pass-through queries are used to communicate with external (ODBC) database
  sources.

Writing Queries with SQL

There are two methods of writing SQL queries in Access 95. The first is by embedding SQL
statements directly in your applications code. This method is often used when working with
ODBC databases. (See the section "SQL Pass-Through" for more details on using this method.)

Secondly, you can write SQL by selecting the View/SQL option while in Query Design view.
This brings up a text window that displays your query in SQL language. (See Figure 36.1.) All
of the examples in this chapter were written using this method.

SQL Conventions

SQL is rigid about certain aspects of your query, such as the order of statements, when you can and can't use particular clauses, and so on. For the most part, however, the appearance of your code is pretty much left up to you. You can, for example, enter a statement such as the following:

```
select distinct [first name],[last name] from employees where [hire date] >1/1/93
```

The following alternative makes the code much easier to read and understand:

```
SELECT DISTINCT [first name],[last name]
FROM employees
WHERE [hire date] > 1/1/93
```

Using uppercase for the SQL keywords and lowercase for the names of the data elements, and entering each command on a separate line, will make it easier for you and for others who may be required to use or maintain your code later.

The SQL examples in this chapter use the following conventions.

Square brackets ([ ]) indicate optional items:

```
SELECT [predicate]
```

Curly braces ({}) combined with vertical bars (¦) indicate a choice:

```
{ * ¦ table.* ¦ [table.]field1 [, [table.]field2.[, ...]]}
```

An ellipsis (. . .) indicates a repeating sequence:

```
FROM tableexpression [, ...]
```

The *SELECT* Command

The SELECT statement is the most commonly used statement in SQL. With its powerful options, there are many ways to retrieve your data and to perform complex data calculations. Access 95 SQL SELECT queries select rows of data and return them as a dynaset (an updateable) recordset.

The basic form of a SELECT query is as follows:

```
SELECT [predicate] { * ¦ table.* ¦ [table.]field1 [, [table.]field2.[, ...]]}
[AS alias1 [, alias2 [, ...]]]
FROM tableexpression [, ...] [IN externaldatabase]
[WHERE... ]
[GROUP BY... ]
[HAVING... ]
[ORDER BY... ]
```

A simple SELECT query might look like this:

```
SELECT *
FROM customers
WHERE City = 'Seattle';
```

Figure 36.1 shows the results of this query.

FIGURE 36.1.

A simple Select *query.*

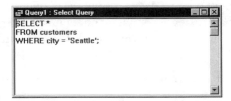

The SELECT command in this query followed by an asterisk (*) indicates that all columns from the selected table(s) are to be returned. This is a quick and easy way to specify all columns without having to enter them all in. The columns are returned in the same order that they were created in the table and the column names are displayed as headings.

The FROM command tells the query engine which tables or queries to select the records from.

The WHERE command allows you to specify which records you wish to return based on the criteria you enter; in this case, all columns from the customers table will be returned where the city matches Seattle.

As another example, what if you wanted to see only the contact name, phone number, and postal code of those customers who live in Seattle in the 98101 ZIP code area? (See Figure 36.2.)

```
SELECT ContactName, Phone, PostalCode
FROM customers
WHERE City='Seattle' AND PostalCode = '98101'
```

FIGURE 36.2.

A query result showing specific fields.

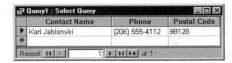

This time you get only the three columns you specified—contact name, phone, and postal code—from the customers table where the city matches Seattle and the postal code matches 98101.

The Predicate Options

You can use four options immediately following the SELECT statement to restrict the number of records returned either for unique values or records or to get the top values or percentages of the records returned. These four predicates are described in the following sections.

ALL

This is the default for a SELECT query. You would use it to return an unrestricted recordset. The following two queries produce the same results and return all the records from the Customers table.

```
SELECT ALL *
FROM Customers;

SELECT *
FROM Customers;
```

DISTINCT

DISTINCT is used when you want to restrict the output to *unique* records (those for which there are no duplicates).

> **NOTE**
>
> When using the DISTINCT predicate, the recordset that is returned is nonupdatable and doesn't reflect subsequent changes made by other users.

For example, to return only unique last names from the Employees table, use the following (see Figure 36.3):

```
SELECT DISTINCT [LastName]
FROM Employees;
```

FIGURE 36.3.

An example of using the DISTINCT clause.

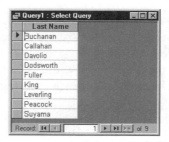

This will return one record for each unique last name. If there are two employees named Jones, only one will be returned.

> **WARNING**
>
> By using the DISTINCT clause, you're omitting records that you may have expected to be included. Keep in mind that by using this predicate, you're specifying that the values for each field listed in the SELECT statement are to be unique.

If your query includes more than one field, the combination of all fields must be unique to be considered a DISTINCT record. For this reason, the more fields you include, the fewer unique records will be returned.

> **TIP**
>
> When you're querying large databases, try to limit the number of fields in your SELECT string. Having too many fields returned can dramatically affect the performance of the query, particularly if the database is networked.

If you had two employees named Bob Jones and one employee named Brenda Jones and you entered this query:

```
SELECT DISTINCT [LastName], [FirstName]
FROM Employees;
```

the result would return only the first Bob Jones and the employee named Brenda Jones.

> **NOTE**
>
> Using the DISTINCT predicate in an SQL query is equivalent to setting the Unique Records property to Yes in the query property sheet in a query's Design view.

DISTINCTROW

You use DISTINCTROW when you want to restrict data to unique records when doing a multitable query. For example, the Customers table contains one unique record for every customer; each Customer, however, can have many records in the Orders table (an example of a "1-M" or "one-to-many" relationship). If you wanted a list of unique names of customers that have placed an order, you would enter a query such as this (see Figure 36.4):

```
SELECT DISTINCTROW [CompanyName]
FROM Customers INNER JOIN Orders
ON Customers.[CustomerID] = Orders.[CustomerID]
ORDER BY [CompanyName]
```

> **NOTE**
>
> Using the DISTINCTROW predicate in an SQL query is equivalent to setting the Unique Records property to Yes in the query property sheet when in a query's Design view.

FIGURE 36.4.

The result of using the DISTINCTROW clause.

TOP

The TOP predicate is used when you want to restrict the output to a certain number or percentage of records. It takes the following form:

```
SELECT TOP nn [PERCENT]
```

Suppose you wanted to see the top 20 most expensive products in your products table (see Figure 36.5):

```
SELECT DISTINCTROW TOP 20 Products.[ProductName], Products.[UnitPrice]
FROM Products
ORDER BY Products.[UnitPrice] DESC;
```

FIGURE 36.5.

A query result using the TOP clause.

This returns a list of the top 20 most expensive products, with the list sorted in descending order from highest to lowest.

NOTE

Note the use of `ORDER BY Products.[Unit Price] DESC`. This tells Access that you want to output a descending sort (highest to lowest) by unit price. If you don't indicate this, an ambiguous set of records will be returned.

To reverse this query and get the top 20 *least expensive*, just remove the `DESC` clause at the end of the `ORDER BY` statement.

What if instead of the top 20 most expensive products, you wanted a list of the top ten percent of products, sorted by the quantity of units in stock? This is how you would do it (see Figure 36.6):

```
SELECT DISTINCTROW TOP 10 PERCENT ProductName, UnitsInStock
FROM Products
ORDER BY UnitsInStock DESC;
```

FIGURE 36.6.
A query result using the `TOP nn PERCENT` *clause.*

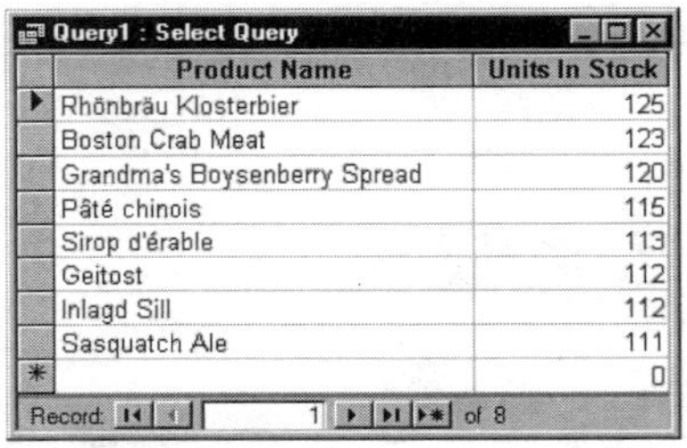
Query1 : Select Query
Product Name
Units In Stock
Rhönbräu Klosterbier 125
Boston Crab Meat 123
Grandma's Boysenberry Spread 120
Pâté chinois 115
Sirop d'érable 113
Geitost 112
Inlagd Sill 112
Sasquatch Ale 111
0
Record: 1 of 8

TIP

The `TOP` command is equivalent to setting the `Top Values` property in the query property sheet in a query's Design view. Using the `PERCENT` clause with the `TOP` command is equivalent to using the percent sign (%) with the `Top Values` property.

The *SELECT...AS* Option

The `SELECT...AS` option enables you to change the name of the output column in your query. This can be used to shorten a long name or to create a calculated or compound column. For example, to create a single employee-name column that is a combination of first name and last name, you would use this (see Figure 36.7):

```
SELECT DISTINCTROW LastName & ", " & FirstName AS Employee
FROM Employees;
```

FIGURE 36.7.
Using the SELECT...AS
option.

If your query includes more than one table or query that contains fields with same name, you must enter the entire table and field name so the query engine knows which fields you want to work with. For example, to indicate the EmployeeID field in tblEmployee, you would enter the following:

```
SELECT tblEmployee.[EmployeeID]
```

The *FROM* Command

The format for using the FROM command is

```
FROM tableexpression [IN externaldatabase]
```

The FROM command indicates the tables or queries you wish to select records from. If more than one table or query is specified, you must also include a JOIN command that joins the tables or queries on specific fields. (See the section "Structuring SQL-92" for more information on using joins.)

> **NOTE**
>
> Access 95 uses the SQL-92 method of applying joins for multitable queries in the FROM clause. This differs from ANSI SQL, where you specify joins in the WHERE clause.

The *WHERE* Command

The syntax for the WHERE command is

```
WHERE criteria
```

The WHERE command is the heart of any good SQL query. It is the means by which you can create simple or complex criteria that identifies which specific records you want returned. The WHERE command must include an operator and two operands. For example (see Figure 36.8):

```
SELECT ShipName, ShipCountry
FROM Orders
WHERE ShipCountry="USA";
```

FIGURE 36.8.

A query using the WHERE command.

This will give you a list of all customers within the United States who have placed orders. If you wish to return all customers EXCEPT the ones in the U.S., simply add the NOT clause before the criteria for Orders.[Ship Country]. Your query now looks like this (see Figure 36.9):

```
SELECT ShipName, ShipCountry
FROM Orders
WHERE NOT ShipCountry="USA";
```

FIGURE 36.9.

The same WHERE query using the NOT option.

Using Wildcard Characters

Any query language would be incomplete without special characters that functions as place-holders for unknown characters. As mentioned earlier, Access 95 SQL uses a ? to match any single character and an * to match zero or more characters.

Suppose you wanted to find all customers whose names start with Paul. You would use the asterisk as follows:

```
SELECT DISTINCTROW Customers.[Contact Name]
FROM Customers
WHERE ((Customers.[Contact Name] Like "Paul*"));
```

This following query returns all customers who live in a city that begins with the letters Ber and is followed with any three other characters:

```
SELECT DISTINCTROW Customers.City
FROM Customers
WHERE ((Customers.City Like "Ber???"));
```

SQL Aggregate Functions

Using SQL aggregate functions, you can perform statistical calculations on your data. These queries can range from simple count or sum queries to complex variance and standard-deviation queries.

The SQL aggregate functions are

- `Avg`: Used to calculate an average of a specified field.
- `Count`: Used to calculate the number of records.
- `Min`, `Max`: Used to calculate minimum or maximum.
- `StDev`, `StDevP`: Estimates the standard deviation.
- `Sum`: Calculates the sum of a given field.
- `Var`, `VarP`: Used to estimate the variance.

The following example produces a count of all orders that have a Required Date between March 1 and March 31 (see Figure 36.10):

FIGURE 36.10.

Using the Count *function.*

```
SELECT Count(OrderID) AS CountOfOrderID
FROM Orders
HAVING RequiredDate Between #3/1/94# And #3/31/94#;
```

This following query produces a list of all customers who have orders placed, as well as the total dollar amount of their orders (see Figure 36.11):

```
SELECT DISTINCTROW Customers.[CompanyName],
Sum(Products.[UnitPrice]) AS [SumOfUnitPrice]
FROM (Customers INNER JOIN Orders ON Customers.[CustomerID]
=Orders.[CustomerID]) INNER JOIN (Products INNER JOIN [Order Details]
ON Products.[ProductID] = [Order Details].[ProductID]) ON
Orders.[OrderID] = [Order Details].[OrderID]
GROUP BY Customers.[CompanyName];
```

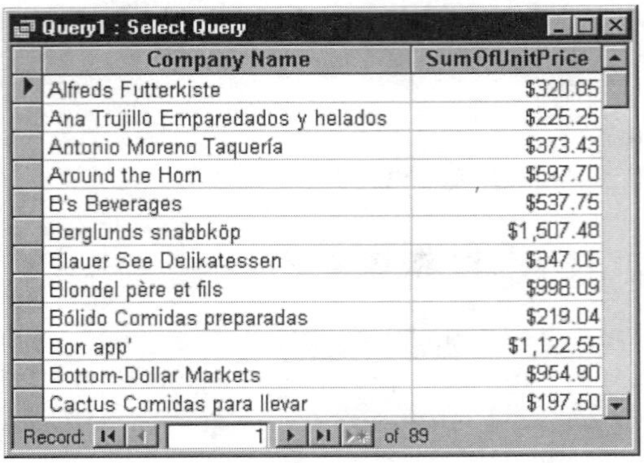
Query1 : Select Query

	Company Name	SumOfUnitPrice
▶	Alfreds Futterkiste	$320.85
	Ana Trujillo Emparedados y helados	$225.25
	Antonio Moreno Taquería	$373.43
	Around the Horn	$597.70
	B's Beverages	$537.75
	Berglunds snabbköp	$1,507.48
	Blauer See Delikatessen	$347.05
	Blondel père et fils	$998.09
	Bólido Comidas preparadas	$219.04
	Bon app'	$1,122.55
	Bottom-Dollar Markets	$954.90
	Cactus Comidas para llevar	$197.50

Record: 1 of 89

FIGURE 36.11.
Using the `Sum` *function.*

Structuring SQL-92

As explained at the beginning of this chapter, Access contains elements of the SQL-92 language. This section looks at some of the SQL-92 commands and demonstrates some ways to use this robust dialect.

The *INNER JOIN* Command

The syntax for the `INNER JOIN` command is

```
FROM table1 INNER JOIN table2 ON table1.field1 = table2.field2
```

In Access 95 SQL, the `INNER JOIN` (also know as an *equi-join*) command is used after the `FROM` command in a multitable query. It's used to specify how and where Access 95 should attempt to join tables on a common field or fields. The query returns a record wherever the fields match in the indicated tables. The fields don't need to have the same name, but they do need to be of the same data type; for example, a field that has a data type of `Text` can join only with another text field. It can't join with a field that has a data type of `Number`.

The following query selects all combinations of Categories and Products records that `JOIN` on `Category ID` (see Figure 36.12):

```
SELECT DISTINCTROW CategoryName, ProductName
FROM Categories INNER JOIN Products ON Categories.[CategoryID]
= Products.[CategoryID];
```

FIGURE 36.12.

A query showing the use of
INNER JOIN.

The *LEFT JOIN* and *RIGHT JOIN* Commands

Two other types of joins are LEFT JOIN and RIGHT JOIN. These types of joins result in what is called an *outer join*. For example, if you wanted to return all records from Categories even if there is no match with the Products table, you would enter the following:

```
SELECT DISTINCTROW Categories.[Category Name], Products.[Product Name]
FROM Categories LEFT JOIN Products ON Categories.[Category ID] =
➥Products.[Category ID];
```

If you wanted the opposite—that is, to return all the records from Products, even if there is no match with the Categories table—you would use a RIGHT JOIN, as follows:

```
SELECT DISTINCTROW Categories.[Category Name], Products.[Product Name]
FROM Categories RIGHT JOIN Products ON Categories.[Category ID] =
➥Products.[Category ID];
```

Using Expressions

The ability to use expressions in your SQL statements is a very powerful feature that enables you to perform analysis and calculations within the statement itself.

The syntax of the statement and the placement of the expressions varies with the type of expression or the calculation you're trying to do.

The following example returns the company name and dollar amount of items ordered where the sum is greater than $1,000 (see Figure 36.13):

```
SELECT CompanyName, Sum([UnitPrice]*[Quantity]) AS OrderAmount
FROM Customers
INNER JOIN (Orders INNER JOIN [Order Details] ON Orders.OrderID =
➥[Order Details].OrderID)
ON Customers.CustomerID = Orders.CustomerID
GROUP BY Customers.CompanyName
HAVING (((Sum([UnitPrice]*[Quantity]))>1000));
```

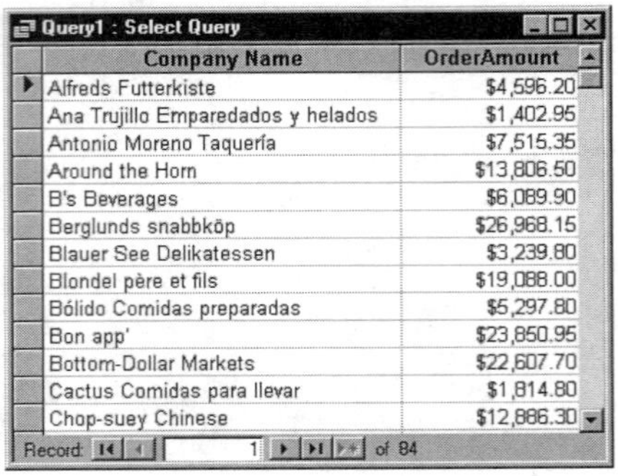

FIGURE 36.13.

A query result using expressions in an SQL statement.

Company Name	OrderAmount
Alfreds Futterkiste	$4,596.20
Ana Trujillo Emparedados y helados	$1,402.95
Antonio Moreno Taquería	$7,515.35
Around the Horn	$13,806.50
B's Beverages	$6,089.90
Berglunds snabbköp	$26,968.15
Blauer See Delikatessen	$3,239.80
Blondel père et fils	$19,088.00
Bólido Comidas preparadas	$5,297.80
Bon app'	$23,850.95
Bottom-Dollar Markets	$22,607.70
Cactus Comidas para llevar	$1,814.80
Chop-suey Chinese	$12,886.30

The *TRANSFORM* Statement

The TRANSFORM statement is used to create Crosstab queries. It's a very effective tool for summarizing data that compacts and groups your records in a spreadsheet-style format.

The syntax for the TRANSFORM statement is

```
TRANSFORM aggfunction
selectstatement
PIVOT pivotfield [IN (value1[, value2[, ...]])]
```

The TRANSFORM command must be the first statement in your SQL string. The TRANSFORM statement is followed by an aggregate function, such as Avg, Count, Sum, and so on. Next is the SELECT statement, which can be any standard SELECT statement, with optional WHERE and GROUP BY clauses. Following the SELECT statement is the PIVOT statement. The *pivotfield* value is where you specify a field to be used for creating column headings used in the returning recordset. If, for example, you wanted a Crosstab showing a sum of all employees' sales for the year summed by quarter, you would pivot on the order-date field, which would create four columns, one column for each quarter. If you wanted to show a sales sum for only those employees hired in a specific month or two, you can do so by restricting the *pivotfield* value to create headings from fixed values (*value1*, *value2*) listed in the optional IN clause.

The following query shows quarterly sales for each employee, with a column totaling all sales by employee (see Figure 36.14):

```
TRANSFORM Sum([Order Details].[UnitPrice]*[Quantity]) AS [The Value]
SELECT Employees.LastName, Sum([Order Details].[UnitPrice]*[Quantity])
AS [Total For Year]
FROM (Employees INNER JOIN Orders ON Employees.EmployeeID = Orders.EmployeeID)
INNER JOIN [Order Details] ON Orders.OrderID = [Order Details].OrderID
GROUP BY Employees.LastName
PIVOT "Qtr " & Format([OrderDate],"q");
```

FIGURE 36.14.

A Crosstab query result using the TRANSFORM statement.

Last Name	Total For Year	Qtr 1	Qtr 2	Qtr 3	Qtr 4
Buchanan	$75,567.75	$21,579.90	$8,462.40	$15,881.00	$29,644.45
Callahan	$133,301.03	$51,456.55	$22,821.81	$27,332.20	$31,690.47
Davolio	$202,143.71	$57,680.58	$32,867.33	$49,460.50	$62,135.30
Dodsworth	$82,964.00	$35,498.55	$14,041.80	$17,295.70	$16,127.95
Fuller	$177,749.26	$55,139.71	$58,501.05	$32,205.35	$31,903.15
King	$141,295.99	$48,385.20	$43,411.55	$30,695.84	$18,803.40
Leverling	$213,051.30	$98,564.54	$47,933.70	$19,047.85	$47,505.21
Peacock	$250,187.45	$87,127.04	$40,395.96	$55,621.72	$67,042.73
Suyama	$78,198.10	$14,505.80	$18,749.74	$15,603.50	$29,339.06

Record: ◄◄ ◄ 1 ► ►► ►* of 9

The *PARAMETERS* Declaration

The PARAMETERS declaration makes a query more reusable by allowing the user to enter parameter values for certain fields in the query. This can dramatically reduce the number of queries the developer needs to create and maintain.

The syntax for the PARAMETERS declaration is

```
PARAMETERS name datatype [, name datatype [, ...]]
```

Like the TRANSFORM command, the PARAMETERS declaration must be the first statement in your SQL string. Following the declaration, enter a unique but meaningful name variable and a data type, such as Text or DateTime. You can specify additional parameters by using a comma between them.

For example, if you have queries that are used to create mailing lists of customers, but you want to specify what city the customers live in, instead of creating a query for every city (even if you knew them all), you could create a single PARAMETERS query like this (see Figure 36.15):

```
PARAMETERS [Enter City] Text;
SELECT *
FROM  Employees
WHERE City=[Enter City];
```

FIGURE 36.15.

A PARAMETERS query result.

Now each time this query is run, a parameter will be inserted, either from within your code or by a parameter-input dialog, and the recordset returned will include only those records that you specified.

The Union Query

Union queries combine fields from tables or queries into one field. This is actually an operation rather than a command and is performed on two or more tables or queries. The combined tables or queries must contain an equal number of fields. (They can be of different data types, however.)

The syntax for a Union query is

```
[TABLE] query1 UNION [ALL] [TABLE] query2 [UNION [ALL] [TABLE] queryn [ ... ]]
```

> **TIP**
>
> Union queries, by default, return unique records only. (This is similar to using DISTINCTROW in a SELECT query.) If you want your query to include *all* records, you must include the ALL predicate.

If you wanted to create a list of name and phone numbers, including the type of contact, for all companies in the Shippers and Suppliers tables, you would enter the following statements (see Figure 36.16):

```
SELECT CompanyName, Phone, "Shipper" AS [Contact Type]
FROM Shippers
UNION SELECT CompanyName, Phone, "Suppliers"
FROM Suppliers
ORDER BY CompanyName;
```

FIGURE 36.16.

A Union query result.

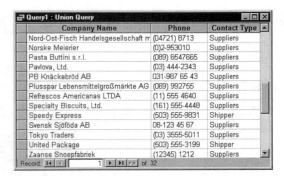

Data-Definition Queries

Data-definition language (or DDL) queries are used to create new data objects or to modify existing ones. With the various DDL commands, you can create new tables and indexes or change (ALTER) an existing table by adding fields. You can also delete (DROP) tables and indexes.

How to Write a DDL Query

Writing a DDL query is a little different from writing a normal Select query and requires a couple of extra steps.

1. Open a new query by clicking the Queries tab in the Database window, and then click New.
2. In the New Query dialog box, click Design View, and then click OK.
3. Click Close in the Show Table dialog box. (Don't add any tables or queries).
4. Select Query | SQL Specific | Data Definition.
5. Now enter the SQL statement for your data-definition query.
6. When you've finished, run the query by clicking the Run (!) button on the toolbar. (You can't use Datasheet view when using a DDL query; doing so will produce an error dialog.)

Here is an example of using the DDL statement to create a table:

```
CREATE TABLE UnleashedDemo
(Field1 TEXT,
Field2 TEXT,
Field3 INTEGER
CONSTRAINT PrimaryKey
PRIMARY KEY);
```

SQL Pass-Through

A SQL Pass-through query is used to communicate with external (ODBC) database sources such as Microsoft SQL Server or Oracle. With Pass-through queries, you work directly with the tables on the server instead of attaching them. Pass-through queries are used to execute SQL queries to perform data-definition functions such as creating and updating tables and other objects or to retrieve records. In the case of a query that returns records, they're always returned in a snapshot which is a nonupdateable (read-only) recordset.

> **CAUTION**
>
> You can't convert a Pass-through query to another type of query, such as a Select query. Doing so will wipe out the SQL statement that you entered.

A popular use for Pass-through queries is to run stored procedures on an ODBC server. Stored procedures are a powerful tool that can be utilized in an Access 95 application by executing them via a Pass-through query.

How to Write a Pass-Through Query

As with DDL queries, writing a Pass-through query involves some extra steps.

1. Open a new query by clicking the Queries tab in the Database window, and then click New.
2. In the New Query dialog box, click Design View, and then click OK.
3. Click Close in the Show Table dialog box. (Don't add any tables or queries.)
4. Select Query | SQL Specific | SQL Passthrough.
5. Set your ODBC connection parameters by clicking the Properties button to display the query property sheet.
6. In the query property sheet, enter information for the ODBC Connect Str property for the database you want to connect to. (Click the Build button to use the ODBC Connect String Builder.)

> **NOTE**
>
> If you leave the ODBC Connect Str property blank or set to the default of ODBC, users will be prompted to enter their connection information each time the query is run. This can be an annoyance—or it can be useful if you want the query to be run using the user's own connection information. (See Figure 36.17.)

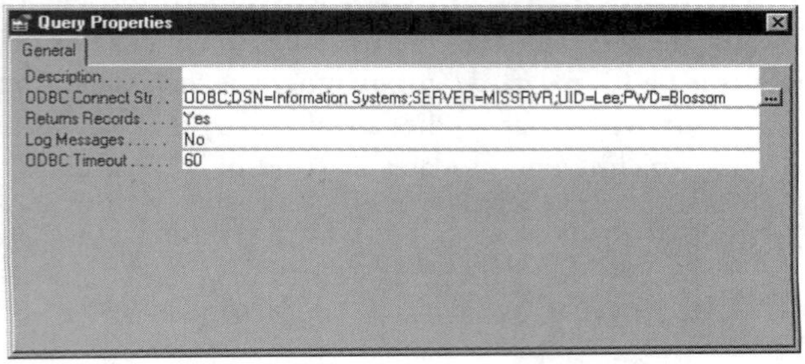

FIGURE 36.17.

Setting the ODBC
Connect Str property.

Query Properties	
General	
Description	
ODBC Connect Str . .	ODBC;DSN=Information Systems;SERVER=MISSRVR;UID=Lee;PWD=Blossom
Returns Records	Yes
Log Messages	No
ODBC Timeout	60

7. Set the `ReturnsRecords` property to No if the query isn't the type that returns records.

8. Enter your Pass-through query.

9. To run the query, click the Run (!) button on the toolbar.

With a SQL Pass-through query, you send the commands using the syntax required by the particular server. Because each database server modifies or enhances its version of SQL, a Pass-through query designed for Sybase might not run correctly on Oracle.

Summary

This chapter has given you a glimpse of the power and possibilities available to you using Access 95 SQL. In deciding how to make the best use of Access 95 SQL, the bottom line is this: If you're creating SQL Pass-through queries to an ODBC database, or queries that might be transferred to another SQL database, you will have to limit your queries to ANSI SQL. However, if you're writing queries that will remain entirely in Access 95, the power and flexibility of Access 95 SQL with its enhanced SQL-92 features makes it an excellent choice.

Connectivity

Using Access in the Client-Server Model

This chapter explains the client-server model for database applications and how to use Access as part of a client-server database solution. It contains hints on designing the application and optimizing its performance, as well as special considerations for working with particular database servers.

Client-Server Defined

Client-server architecture, illustrated in Figure 37.1, is a form of distributed processing in which one process (the client) initiates a transaction by sending a message to another process (the server). Client-server architecture is the basis of many modern operating systems and software applications. In operating systems such as Windows 95, Windows NT, and UNIX, separate processes are assigned to system services. When a program needs a service, such as when it's printing a document, a message is sent from one program to another. This architecture isolates services from one another and simplifies application development by sharing common services among programs. This is why you need not concern yourself with setting up Access 95 when a new printer is installed. When the printer is installed in Windows, it's automatically available to Access (and to all other Windows programs).

FIGURE 37.1.

Client-server architecture.

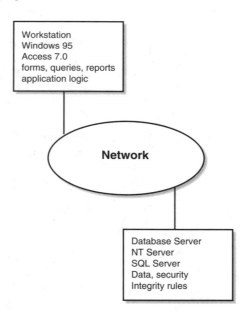

Microsoft Exchange is an example of a client-server application for electronic mail and group communications. The client portion is the exchange inbox that resides on each workstation. It enables users to read their mail, compose new messages, and move their messages among folders even if they aren't connected to other users on a network. The server portion is the exchange server or another mail server (for example, Microsoft Mail). When a workstation connects to the network (through either a local area network connection or dial-up networking), the client communicates with the server and transmits and receives new messages. Schedule+ works in a similar fashion as a client-server application.

In a client-server database, the client (also called the front end) is the program that runs on a user's workstation. The server (sometimes called the database engine or back end), which might be running on another computer on the network, stores data and processes requests for information sent by clients. For instance, Access might be used as a front end to incorporate data in a Microsoft SQL Server database running on a DEC Alpha or other computer.

Using Access as a client-server front end is different from running Access on a file server. The file server merely makes a database file available to several workstations so that they can share data. When a user needs the data, the file is read from the file server hard disk and is sent to the workstation across the network. The workstation must perform all the processing to select rows from the table or join multiple tables. The file server doesn't really help with the processing. In a client-server database, on the other hand, the workstation submits a request for information in the form of an SQL query. The database server processes the query and returns only the rows that the user requested. The database server assists with processing and greatly reduces the network traffic and the work that the workstation must do. After the data reaches the workstation, Access simply formats the data and displays it for the user.

You could even argue that Access is inherently client-server, in that front-end functions are separated from data-management functions handled by the Jet engine. The Jet engine is essentially the native database server for Access. Fortunately, Access can also connect to other database engines. For the purpose of this chapter, I will address only the use of Access as a front end to a database engine.

If this is your first client-server project, you might want additional sources for general information on client-server architecture. You will find much more information on client-server concepts in *Client/Server Computing*, Second Edition (Sams Publishing, 1994). Also, many magazines cover client-server databases, including *DBMS, Data Based Advisor, Database Programming and Design, Software Magazine,* and *Client-Server.*

When to Use a Client-Server Database

Why would you want to use Access as a front end? When would you need to go to client-server architecture for a database application? Several requirements might force you to go client-server.

The most common situation for switching from Access stand-alone or on a LAN to client-server is when you have large data requirements or large numbers of concurrent users. Although Access performs well with a few hundred or a few thousand records in a table, it tends to bog down with hundreds of thousands or millions of records. Imagine, if you will, a database containing the income-tax returns of all U.S. residents for the past 10 years. This database wouldn't fit well on the laptop computer I'm using to write this chapter, or even on a high-performance file server. Client-server solves this problem because I can run the database server on any computer, not just on a PC. I could have terabytes of storage and dozens of processors on a mainframe or even a supercomputer. Client-server architecture allows enterprise-wide access to your database.

A related reason to switch to client-server architecture is to improve the speed of searches and other database transactions. Database server software is highly optimized and can provide much faster processing than the Jet engine, which is suitable for small and medium-sized databases.

Database engines such as Microsoft SQL Server, Sybase SQL Server, Informix, CA-Ingres, and DB/2 provide better security and reliability than Access alone can offer. Some of these products have special support for multiprocessor servers, whereas others have highly efficient optimization algorithms, and often they offer special functions Access is lacking.

Client-server architecture is useful in a heterogeneous computing environment. Imagine that your organization has 500 people with PCs, 75 with UNIX workstations, and 25 with Macintoshes. Access isn't available for UNIX or the Mac, but client-server offers you a way out of this problem. Other UNIX and Mac packages can access data on the database server. You therefore can have all the computer users in the company sharing the same corporate data, reducing redundant data entry.

A final reason to switch to client-server is to provide friendlier, more responsive tools to look at data in mainframe systems. The increased productivity of Windows applications compared to their terminal-based predecessors, combined with the prospect of cost savings, is driving the trend toward downsizing mainframe applications (legacy systems). A legacy system is a system that was built long ago, and the people who built it might not even be at your organization any longer. Still, the data in the system is valuable, and you can't give up the old system overnight. With Access, you can allow users to read and write legacy data, and potentially move the application to a larger or smaller database server as needed.

Access as a Front End

Access 95 works as a front end in a client-server database by means of linked tables. These were called "attached" tables in Access 1.0 and 2.0. Data in a linked table isn't actually stored in the Access database. Instead, the Access table contains a pointer to the location where the information is physically stored, such as a dBASE file or an Oracle database table. See Table 37.1.

Table 37.1. Layers in an Access client-server application.

Layer	Function
Access User Interface (Database windows)	Displays on user workstation; interacts with user.
Jet Engine	Fetches data requested by Access; enforces referential integrity and validation rules.

Layer	Function
ODBC Driver Manager	Links from Access to all ODBC data sources.
ODBC Driver (SQL Server, Oracle, other)	Links from ODBC Driver Manager to a particular data source; may be provided by a third party.
Network Library (NetLib, SQL*Net)	Network communications software that allows data to be exchanged between client and server.
Database Server (SQL Server, Oracle, Informix)	Software that processes requests for data and sends resulting rows or messages to client.

Built-In and ODBC Drivers

Access can link to other database formats through either built-in drivers or Open Database Connectivity (ODBC). Built-in drivers are provided for other Microsoft Access databases; FoxPro files (versions 2.0, 2.5, 2.6, and 3.0); Paradox files (3.x, 4.x, and 5.0); dBASE III, IV, and 5 files; Microsoft Excel files; Lotus 1-2-3 files; fixed-length text; and variable-length text. Access can also export to Word for Windows mail merge, although there is no driver for Access to read Word files directly. The built-in drivers enable you to import, export, and link to these foreign data files.

The typical Access installation doesn't include all the drivers for linking data, not even the ODBC drivers. To include the drivers, run the Setup utility and choose Add/Remove. (Or, when you first install Access, choose Custom installation and select all the drivers.) The dialog box shown in Figure 37.2 appears. Select Data Access and then click the Change Option button. The Data Access options are displayed, as shown in Figure 37.3.

FIGURE 37.2.

Selecting the Data Access option.

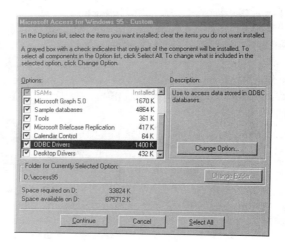

FIGURE 37.3.

The Data Access options.

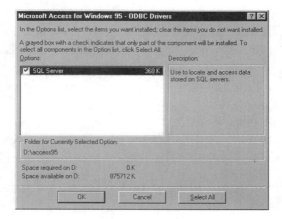

ODBC as a Translator

In addition to the built-in drivers, the standard that makes it easy to link Access to SQL and other data sources is Open Database Connectivity (ODBC). This is the most popular standard for sharing data files in Windows. ODBC can connect an ODBC client to both relational and nonrelational data sources.

Access can act as an ODBC client or an ODBC server. The focus in this chapter is on Access as an ODBC client, but other applications (such as Excel and Crystal Reports) can serve as front ends to Access databases.

ODBC needs a driver for each data source. ODBC drivers are usually provided by the vendor of the server. The driver must be 32-bit and compliant with ODBC 1.0.

ODBC doesn't include its own networking capability, so you need a network library in addition to the ODBC driver for your server. For instance, you might use the Oracle SQL*Net, Named Pipe Net-Libraries, DECNET, or FTP 2.2 with Net-Library. If you encounter problems with your net library, you should search Microsoft TechNet for your net library. You might need patches or upgrades to the net library to work with Access 95. Microsoft TechNet is a great source of technical information on all Microsoft products, especially for advanced topics. TechNet members receive a monthly CD-ROM with the latest information and several other benefits. To enroll, call Microsoft at (800) 344-2121, extension 115.

Working with ODBC Connections

In most cases, Access hides the complexity of the ODBC connection from the user and the developer. This section discusses how to create and manipulate ODBC connections through the Access user interface and with Access Basic code.

ODBC Connection String

Access databases can connect to ODBC data sources through tables or queries. When linked, the tables and queries behave just as a native Access table would behave, and they can serve as the row source for a query, report, or form. The ODBC connection string is stored in the `Description` property of a table. It's created automatically by Access if you attach a table from the Access menu. It can also be created or modified programmatically in Access Basic.

Here is an ODBC connection string for an attached Access table:

```
DATABASE=D:\msoffice\access95\Samples\Northwind.mdb;TABLE=Customers
```

This connection string is simple in that it only needs to identify the Access database filename and the table name.

Here is an ODBC connection string to attach to an SQL Server table:

```
ODBC;DSN=Pubs;APP=Microsoft Access;WSID=D5;DATABASE=pubs;TABLE=dbo.titles
```

If the connection string reads `"ODBC;"` or is blank, Access prompts you for the connection information at runtime. This isn't usually a convenient way to manage your ODBC connections.

You can also create and update ODBC connections with Access Basic. The following lines show the syntax for creating an attached table:

```
Dim tdf As TableDef, fldComments As Field
Dim dbs As Database
Set dbs = DBEngine.Workspaces(0).OpenDatabase("NWIND.mdb")
' Create new TableDef.
Set tdf = dbs.CreateTableDef("Transactions")
' Add field to tdf.
Set fld = tdf.CreateField("TransactionComments",dbMemo)
tdf.Fields.Append fldComments
' Save TableDef definition by appending it to TableDefs collection.
dbs.TableDefs.Append tdf
```

Creating SQL Pass-Through Queries

Pass-through queries are a powerful feature introduced in Access 2.0. They enable you to send SQL statements to the server just as you enter them, without being parsed or generated by Access. With pass-through SQL, you can take advantage of server-specific features such as SQL extensions or stored procedures.

Access Pass-through queries don't use the graphical design features of the Query window. This means that you receive no help from Access in formulating the query or checking its syntax. You therefore might save time and reduce errors by following these steps instead:

1. Write the query in whatever interactive query tool your server provides. The query tool will check the query syntax and perhaps assist with table and field names.

2. Fully test the query in its native environment.

3. Copy the query into an Access Pass-through query or an Access module using cut and paste.

Creating an SQL Pass-Through Query

Here are the steps in Access to create a Pass-through query:

1. Click the Queries tab in the Database window, and then click New.

2. Click New Query. There is no Query Wizard for SQL Pass-through queries, so choose Design View.

3. Close the Show Table dialog box without choosing a table or query.

4. Choose Query | SQL Specific | Pass-Through.

5. The Query Properties sheet, shown in Figure 37.4, is normally displayed at this point. If you don't see the Query Properties sheet, display it by choosing View | Properties or clicking the View Properties tool on the toolbar.

FIGURE 37.4.

The Properties window in an SQL Pass-through query.

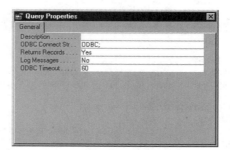

6. Enter the ODBC connection string in the ODBC Connect Str property.

Be careful not to switch the query type of a Pass-through query, because you will lose the SQL you have been typing.

Pass-Through Query Properties

The properties of Pass-through queries are different from those of Access Select queries:

Property	Description
Returns Records	Set to yes if the query will return rows; set to no for other queries.
Log Messages	Set to yes to create a table to store messages returned by the server.
ODBC Timeout	Set the time in seconds before the query times out.

ODBC Connection String Builder

In SQL Pass-through queries, Access provides help for constructing an ODBC connection string so that you don't have to write it from scratch.

The ODBC connection string builder is available only in Pass-through queries; it's not available in the `Source Connect Str` property in the Query Properties window. Note that the ODBC connection string builder isn't installed as a standard option. You must run Setup, choose Add/Remove, and then check the Developer Tools option.

Click the button with the three dots next to the `ODBC Connect Str` property. Access then assists you with building a connection string. A dialog box appears with a list of the installed ODBC data sources, as shown in Figure 37.5. For this example, I am using the Pubs database that comes with Microsoft SQL Server.

FIGURE 37.5.

The ODBC connection string builder.

After you specify the data source, you might be prompted for a username and password (see Figure 37.6). If you wish, you can store the password in the connection string so that you won't be prompted for it again when you run the query (see Figure 37.7).

FIGURE 37.6.

The username and password dialog for the ODBC connection string builder.

FIGURE 37.7.

Choosing whether to store the password in the connection string.

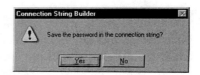

Now that you have answered all the questions posed by the ODBC connection string builder, a finished ODBC connection string is entered in the connection string property (see Figure 37.8).

FIGURE 37.8.

The completed ODBC connection string.

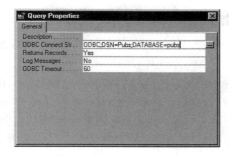

To see whether your connection is working, write a simple query in SQL. For instance, a query of SELECT * FROM AUTHORS will yield the result shown in Figure 37.9. This proves that the ODBC connection is working and that you are retrieving rows from the server.

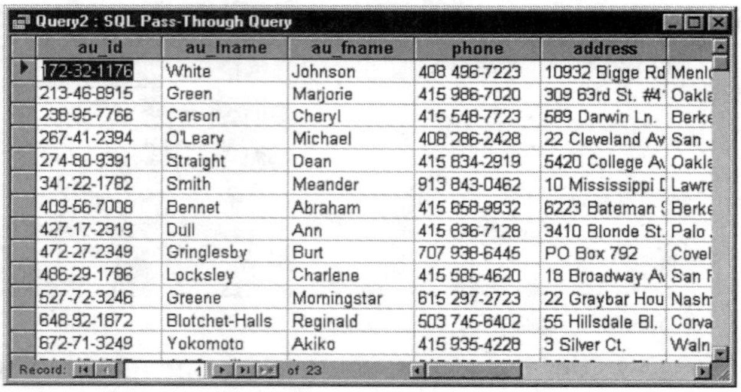

FIGURE 37.9.

*The result of SELECT * FROM AUTHORS.*

If you don't enter an ODBC connection string when you write the query and you don't use the ODBC connection string builder, you will be prompted to choose a data source each time you run the query.

Saving the Results of a Pass-Through Query

You might want to store the results of a Pass-through query in an Access table for later use. A simple way to accomplish this task is to create a Make Table query based on the Pass-through query, including all the fields you want to store in the local table. Each time you run the Make Table query, it will create a new table that stores the results of the Pass-through query. If you don't want to continue duplicating this data in new tables, you can use an Update query instead or delete the table before the Make Table query is run.

For this example, you'll run a stored procedure called SP_HELP that is included with SQL Server. This procedure returns a list of objects that are contained in the database.

1. Start by defining a Pass-through query, as described earlier. In the SQL window, type SP_HELP.

2. Run the query to see which rows are returned. The result should look something like Figure 37.10. You will be prompted to choose the data source and enter your name and password.

FIGURE 37.10.

The results of running the SP_HELP stored procedure.

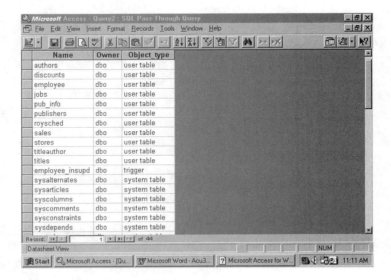

3. Close the query and save it as qrySP_HELP.

4. Create a new query and choose qrySP_HELP as the input for the query in the Show Table dialog.

5. Change the query type to make it a Make Table query.

6. In the Make Table dialog, enter tblSP_HELP as the table name and click OK.

7. Double-click the asterisk (*) in the qrySP_HELP data model to select all the fields from the query. The query will look like Figure 37.11.

8. Run the query.

9. Go to the Database window. Access has created two new tables—tblSP_HELP and tblSP_HELP1. The first table contains the rows produced by the stored procedure, and the second contains an entry for each field definition in that table, as shown in Figure 37.12.

You can create a Pass-through query in Access Basic as well. Follow these steps:

1. In the Database window, choose Modules and then New.

2. Create a new subprocedure by clicking the Insert Procedure button on the toolbar.

3. Make the procedure a sub rather than a function and enter CreatePassThroughSQL as the subprocedure name.

FIGURE 37.11.

A Make Table query based on the SP_HELP stored procedure.

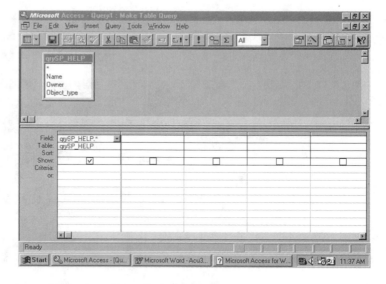

FIGURE 37.12.

Tables produced based on the SP_HELP stored procedure.

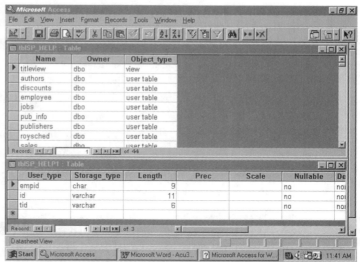

4. Enter the following in this procedure:

```
Public Sub CreatePassThroughSQL()
    Dim dbs As DATABASE, qdf As QueryDef, strSQL As String
    Set dbs = CurrentDb
    strSQL = "SELECT au_lname , au_fname * FROM Authors ORDER BY au_lname"
    Set qdf = dbs.CreateQueryDef("qrySelectAuthors", strSQL)
    DoCmd.OpenQuery qdf.Name

End Sub
```

Next, test the procedure by going to the Debug window. Click the Debug Window tool on the toolbar, press Ctrl-G, or select View | Debug Window.

Using the SQL *IN* Clause

Another way to retrieve data from outside the Access database is to use an IN clause in an SQL query. An outside table can be used as either the source or the destination for a query. The IN clause specifies the database where the foreign table is stored. In xBASE products, the filename and table name are identical, as in the following instance:

```
SELECT CompID FROM Companies
IN "C:\DBASE\DATA\COMP" "dBASE IV;"
WHERE City = "New York";
```

An alternative syntax is also supported. This syntax combines the database type and path in the second argument for IN:

```
SELECT CompID FROM Companies
IN "" "dBASE IV; [DATABASE=C:\DBASE\DATA\COMP;]
WHERE City = "New York";
```

The same syntax is used with INSERT INTO and SELECT INTO statements.

Optimizing the Performance of a Client-Server Application

It isn't enough to build your client-server application as you would build any other Access database but just attach the tables to a database server. Although this technique might work, it would be unlikely to perform well.

Client-server architecture provides you with many options for improving the performance of an application. Unfortunately, the sheer number of parameters you can tune might make client-server development confusing at first. Many optimization techniques are also trade-offs between different types of performance, or between performance and some other factor, such as the portability of the application. The following sections give you general guidelines for getting the most out of your client-server application.

Make the Server Do the Work

In general, the goal of client-server database design is to divide the work between the workstation and the server to take advantage of the strengths of each and avoid their respective weaknesses.

The workstation is best suited for these activities:

- Presenting an attractive and useful user interface

- Formulating queries based on user input and submitting them to the server
- Formatting data on the screen
- Formatting data in a report
- Performing calculations based on retrieved data

The server is best suited for these activities:

- Storing large data sets
- Retrieving, sorting, and manipulating shared data
- Optimizing queries
- Enforcing data integrity rules that apply to all applications

Therefore, it follows that the server should do as much as possible to sift through all the data and return only the rows that the user wants to view or process on the workstation.

Avoid Local Joins and Selects

When you join tables in a query, a database evaluates rows from each table to find which records in one table are related to which records in the other. In client-server architecture, this join operation can be performed on the server or on the client. If a join is performed on the server, only the selected rows (the final result of the join) are transmitted across the network to the workstation. To perform a join locally, rows from both tables to be joined must be sent to the workstation before the join can be carried out. In most cases, particularly when large numbers of records are involved, it's more efficient to perform the join on the server than on the client.

In addition to avoiding local joins, you should steer clear of functions that aren't supported by the server and therefore must be performed by the client.

Joins from Tables from Different Servers

Access enables users to join tables from different servers, even servers that are different types (such as Sybase and Oracle). Unfortunately, the join can be performed on neither of the servers because they don't have distributed join support for each other. The join will therefore be performed on the workstation.

Operations That Can't Be Processed on the Server

Like many other database products, Access adds special features that go beyond the ANSI and ISO standards. The extensions listed next force local query processing because they can't be handled by the server.

The following are the extensions to SQL that are offered by Access but aren't available in most database servers:

- Top *n* or Top *n* Percent
- TRANSFORM (crosstab)
- IN (remote database connection)
- DISTINCTROW (allow duplicates)
- WITH OWNERACCESS (allow query without table rights)

Similarly, user-defined functions can't be processed on the server, forcing the rows to be processed on the workstation. If a user-defined function is frequently used in a client-server application, it will pay to convert it into a stored procedure on the server.

You should also avoid the following items:

- Joining queries that contain aggregation or the DISTINCT SQL keyword: Joins that require calculations for each row of the sets to be joined will force your server to do a significant amount of hard work. If you frequently need to perform these types of queries, you might want to store the results of the aggregation for this purpose.

- ORDER BY expressions not supported by the server: Performance suffers if the workstation must sort a large data set. All the rows would have to be sent to the workstation for processing.

- Multiple levels of GROUP BY: Consider the impact of grouping and sorting operations. You might find that sorting beyond one or two levels has no benefit for presenting data and hurts performance. If you sort customers by last name and first name, you probably don't also need to sort them by postal code and phone number in that query.

- Crosstab queries with more than one aggregate: Most servers can't handle crosstab-style aggregation and therefore end up sending all the detail rows to the workstation.

- Operations with more than one SQL statement, such as nested SELECT: Retrieving with criteria expressed as constants is nearly always faster than using the result of a subquery.

- Access extensions to SQL: All these special Access functions force rows to be returned to the workstation rather than processed on the server:
    - Special Access operators and functions (for example, financial functions)
    - User-defined functions in Access Basic that use remote fields
    - Mixing data types without explicit type conversion
    - Heterogeneous joins between local and remote tables or multiple ODBC sources
    - Functions supported by some but not all servers
    - Outer joins
    - Numeric, string, and date functions
    - Data conversion functions

Make the Criteria Match the Server Data Structure as Much as Possible

Assume that shipping methods are stored as integers but entered by the user as a full name in the combo box of a data-entry form. The following is an example of a bad query:

```
SELECT * FROM Orders WHERE [What Shipping Method?] = IIF (Shipping Method = 1 ,
"Federal Express" , IIF (Shipping Method = 2 , "UPS" , "US Mail" ))
```

The following example selects based on the value in the field rather than evaluating the value and determining whether the immediate IF applies. This query yields better performance:

```
SELECT * FROM Orders WHERE [Shipping Method] = IIF (What Shipping Method? =
"Federal Express" , 1 , IIF ([What Shipping Method?] = "UPS" , 2 , 3 ))
```

Use Stored Procedures If They Are Supported by Your Server

Stored procedures are precompiled SQL programs that can be invoked from the workstation. They run much faster than ad hoc SQL statements that must be compiled at runtime. Many servers, such as Microsoft SQL Server, Sybase SQL Server, and Oracle, offer this feature.

Minimize Unnecessary Calls for Server Data

The less often you have to fetch data from the server, the faster your application will run. The following suggestions will reduce the frequency at which you go to the server.

Open Forms Without Retrieving Data

By default, when opening a form, Access opens the recordset underlying the form, retrieves all rows, and displays the first record from the recordset. This method would be inefficient at best in a client-server environment. For instance, if you opened a Customer form that contained millions of records, it would consume significant server and network resources to open the recordset and send a page of records to the workstation. Moreover, the likelihood that the user would even need to edit that particular record becomes increasingly small as the number of records grows larger.

Place a button on the form to allow the user to search for records based on criteria furnished by the user. In a Customer form, the user might enter a Customer ID or a last name. When the button is clicked, the workstation sends the query to the server, and a small number of rows is returned to the workstation and displayed.

Ask Only for What You Need

As your parents might have taught you, there is virtue in taking only what you can use right now. This lesson is as true in client-server database implementation as it was in kindergarten.

Only fetch rows and columns that the user needs. When you use the asterisk (*) rather than listing the fields from a table by name, the database will retrieve all the fields from the table. Don't select fields with * unless you really need all the fields.

Download Reference Tables

You can significantly improve response time by storing reference tables on the workstation rather than the server. The more frequently these tables are consulted, the more they should be located on the server. If the tables are static, they will be easy to update. Otherwise, you should consider a provision for synchronizing workstation copies with a master copy on the network.

The following code updates a local department reference table from a server-based reference table. You could allow users to run the procedure by clicking a button or include the code in an Autoexec function that runs each time the application is opened.

```
Sub UpdateDeptRecords()
    Dim dbs As DATABASE

    ' Return Database variable pointing to current database.
    Set dbs = CurrentDb
    dbs.Execute "delete * from tbldepts"
    dbs.Execute "INSERT INTO tbldepts SELECT * FROM tblRemoteDepts"

End Sub
```

Create Temporary Local Tables for Users to Manipulate Server Data

In some applications users need to retrieve data from the server and then perform analysis on this data, such as what-if calculations, statistics, or graphs. If this user performs a number of queries on the same data, it might be worthwhile to create a temporary local (or file server) table where this data can reside. This technique reduces the server workload and network traffic and provides better response time for the user. For instance, a business analyst might request sales totals by product type and location for a specified period. Without a local table, if graphs were generated showing this data broken down in several dimensions, the database would be requeried for each form or report as it was run.

Create Views on the Server and Link Them

Views are a powerful feature for controlling access to specified rows and columns and joining tables on the server. If your server supports the technique, you can link the view instead of linking the tables and creating the view in Access.

Avoid Operations That Move the Cursor Through Recordsets

Moving the cursor to the last of 100,000 records is time-consuming, because the server must handle all the records between the record 1 and record 100,000. Relational databases aren't optimized for navigational operations, and in most cases simply moving to a record based on its location in a recordset isn't necessary for a business function. Relational databases are designed to find records based on the values in their fields rather than their relative locations.

Transactions on Attached Tables

Transactions enable you to group several actions together and ensure that they aren't left partially completed. Remember that attached tables must be opened as dynasets rather than tables.

Also, create and close the dynaset on the attached SQL Server table outside the transaction itself, as shown in the following examples:

Incorrect:

```
Dim MyDyna As Dynaset
BeginTrans
    MyDyna = CreateDynaset("Table1")
    'Inserts/Updates/Deletes here
    MyDyna.Close
    CommitTrans/Rollback
```

Correct:

```
Dim MyDyna As Dynaset
MyDyna = CreateDynaset("Table1")
BeginTrans
    'Inserts/Updates/Deletes here
CommitTrans/Rollback
MyDyna.close
```

Use Attached Tables Whenever Possible

Although it's possible to open tables directly in code, attached tables are faster, more convenient, and more powerful. Attached tables are visible as objects in the Database window, and users can access them for queries, forms, and reports.

Use *ForwardOnly* Snapshots If You Do Not Need to Update or Scroll Backward

By default, Access lets you scroll both forward and backward in snapshot recordsets. If you don't need this capability, use the dbForwardOnly flag to specify a recordset that allows only forward scrolling. The recordset will be placed in a buffer area and could perform faster than a default snapshot.

Using Remote Data Caching

Access automatically handles caches for remote data behind datasheets and forms, but you can improve the performance of dynasets by explicitly managing the CacheStart and CacheSize properties to set the number of records that will be cached. You can force the cache to be filled with the FillCache method, as shown in Listing 37.1.

Listing 37.1. Using the FillCache method to fill a range of data.

```
Dim MyRecordset As Recordset, MyDatabase As Database
Set MyDatabase = CurrentDB.OpenDatabase("",0,0,_
"ODBC;DATABASE=MySqlDb;DSN=
 orpSQL;UID=Guest;PWD=")
' Open ODBC database.
Set MyRecordset = MyDatabase.OpenRecordset("OrderDetail",DB_OPEN_DYNASET)
    ' Open local recordset.
MyRecordset.FindFirst "CustID = 1001"
MyRecordset.CacheStart = MyRecordset.Bookmark
 ' Start caching records at Customer ID 1001.
MyRecordset.CacheSize = 12     ' Set cache size to 12 records.
MyRecordset.FillCache     ' Fill cache.
...' Display rows.
```

Do Not Use Combo Boxes Based on Large Numbers of Records

Although it might make sense to have a combo box that enables the user to choose a state when entering an address, it makes less sense to have a combo box to choose a customer in an Orders form if you have millions of customers. In a case like this, replace the combo box with a dialog box. The user would enter criteria in the top of the dialog box and click a button to see matching records. The user would then select the desired record and click a Done button to return to the main form.

Use Snapshot Recordset Objects to Populate Combo Boxes

Because the content of combo boxes is often static and the recordsets for combo boxes are often small, you can get extra speed from using snapshots rather than dynasets to populate combo boxes. On the other hand, you should use dynasets if the user will be allowed to add new values to the combo box list.

Use Background Population to Take Advantage of Idle Time

During idle time, Access retrieves rows from the server by creating a server table called MSysConf. You can change the settings for background population to reduce the network traffic by increasing the interval between each retrieval or reducing the number of rows that are retrieved at a time.

First, you must create a table called MSysConf on the server. It should have the following columns:

Column Name	Data Type	Allows Null?
Config	A data type that corresponds to a 2-byte integer	No
chValue	VARCHAR(255)	Yes
nValue	A data type that corresponds to a 4-byte integer	Yes
Comments	VARCHAR(255)	Yes

Next, add up to three records to the MSysConf table as follows:

Config	nValue	Meaning
101	0	Doesn't allow local storage of the login ID and password in attachments.
101	1	(Default) Allows local storage of the login ID and password in attachments.
102	D	D is the delay, in seconds, between each retrieval (default: 10 seconds).
103	N	N is the number of rows retrieved (default: 100 rows).

Using Access with Specific Products

To get the best results with Access as a front end, you should understand the behavior of the particular database server product you're using. You must be aware of special features the engine offers (or lacks) and of how to tune it for optimum performance. Although most of the popular database engines conform to the SQL 92 standard, they also offer their own, proprietary extensions to SQL.

Field types aren't the same for all database products. You therefore must consider how your Access field types will map to the database server or vice versa. For instance, some databases don't have counter fields, OLE fields, or even time fields.

Field and table names have different formats in Access and server databases. For instance, Access allows spaces in field names, but spaces are prohibited in SQL Server. Many server products allow periods in table names, but periods aren't permitted in Access. Access automatically allows for this restriction and renames tables as it attaches them, substituting an underscore for the period. Another interesting naming convention is that Access appends the table name to the owner name of an attached table. If you attach to a table called Customers on Watcom SQL, for instance, your Access table name will be admin_Customers if you use the default user account. This means that SQL, using the original table name of Customers, will no longer work with the attached table. You can rename the attached table and remove the username portion to solve this problem.

Access 95 offers declarative referential integrity, a feature that isn't yet supported by all server vendors. Declarative referential integrity means that the developer need only define the relationship and specify the rules for enforcing referential integrity for them to be universally enforced. Microsoft SQL Server 6.0 offers declarative referential integrity as well. In some products, such as SQL Server 4.x, triggers are in place of declarative referential integrity. A trigger is an SQL procedure that is run automatically when a certain event occurs (in this case, an INSERT, UPDATE, or DELETE).

Access fields have the Required property to make a value in a field mandatory before the record can be saved. Some servers lack this feature. You can work around this difficulty by using NOT NULL as the default value for a required field.

In general, you should reoptimize your queries after they have been migrated to the server. The optimization schemes used by servers are quite different and might even differ from one server version to the next.

Security schemes on the server are likely to differ from the Access security model. You can opt to redefine all your security rules on the server or to enforce them both at the application level and on the server. Ultimately, server security is more important than application security, because it's the last line of defense for your data. If you have security at both levels, maintaining usernames, passwords, and privileges will be more complicated.

Microsoft SQL Server 6.0

Of all the servers, Access is best integrated with Microsoft SQL Server. This should be no surprise because Microsoft produces both products. Their features therefore are coordinated, and special interoperability is provided.

The Upsizing Wizard has been written for Microsoft SQL Server to automate moving from Access to SQL Server.

Sybase SQL Server

Access is also compatible with Sybase, because Microsoft SQL Server is a descendant of Sybase SQL Server. Migrating from Microsoft SQL Server to Sybase SQL Server is therefore relatively painless. The field types are the same, and both products use the same SQL extensions in Transact-SQL.

In the future, there is no guarantee that this interoperability will continue as the feature sets of Microsoft SQL Server and Sybase SQL Server diverge.

Oracle 7.x

Although Oracle offers many of the same features as SQL Server, these features are implemented differently. For instance, Oracle uses a different language (PL/SQL) for stored procedures than SQL Server (Transact-SQL) uses.

Oracle enables the developer to choose whether a trigger is executed before or after the action on the table takes place. In SQL Server, the trigger always runs after the action.

Oracle field types are different from Access or SQL Server field types. For instance, Oracle uses a special field type ROWID in place of the timestamp used by SQL Server. Oracle indexes also include two options, hash and sequence indexes, not found in SQL Server.

Some extensions of SQL exist in Oracle that aren't supported in SQL Server, and vice versa. For instance, there is no SQL Server equivalent for the ON CASCADE of Oracle; a trigger must be written to provide the same functionality.

If you're migrating an Oracle application to SQL Server, you can import the tables into Access, create the relationships in Access, and then use the Upsizing Wizard to transfer the data model to the SQL Server.

Exporting Tables to a Client-Server Database

After you have chosen a server, you need to figure out how to move your data in the server to your application in Access.

It's often easier to develop the application in Access and then move the data to the server. This is because the developer can work stand-alone or on a file server without being concerned about server features or performance.

You can even use Access as an intermediary when transferring tables from one server to another. If you have sufficient disk space on your workstation or the file server, you can import tables from the old server into Access and then export them to the new server. You can also attach tables from both servers and use Append queries to move the data from one server to the other.

Exporting tables to a server database is nearly as easy as exporting them to another format such as dBASE or Lotus. It also uses the same menu options. Follow these steps to export a table to a client-server database:

1. Select the table to be exported in the Database window. Choose File | Save As | Export.
2. Choose To An External File Or Database in the Save As dialog box and then click OK.
3. Choose ODBC Databases for the Save As Type (it's the last item on the list) and then click Export.
4. Choose the ODBC data destination or click New to define a new data source.
5. If prompted, enter the username and password for the destination database.

You can also create tables with DLL Pass-through queries. For instance, the following are examples of queries that create tables.

This query creates a new table called This Table with two Text fields:

```
CREATE TABLE [This Table] ([First Name] TEXT, [Last Name] TEXT);
```

This query creates a new table called MyTable with two Text fields, a Date/Time field, and a unique index composed of all three fields:

```
CREATE TABLE MyTable ([First Name] TEXT, [Last Name] TEXT,
[Date of Birth] DATETIME, CONSTRAINT
MyTableConstraint UNIQUE ([First Name], [Last Name], [Date of Birth]));
```

This query creates a new table with two Text fields and an Integer field. The SSN field is the primary key:

```
CREATE TABLE People ([First_Name] TEXT, [Last_Name] TEXT,
SSN INTEGER CONSTRAINT MyFieldConstraint
 PRIMARY KEY)
```

Creating Indexes on New Tables

After you create the table, you should define the indexes. Servers such as SQL Server won't automatically create indexes on tables you export from Access. You can use the tools provided by your server vendor, or you can write a Pass-through query in Access, such as the following one. This query creates an index consisting of the fields Home Phone and Extension in the Employees table:

```
CREATE INDEX NewIndex ON Employees ([Home Phone], Extension);
```

This query creates an index on the Employees table using the Social Security Number field. No two records can have the same data in the SSN field, and no Null values are allowed:

```
CREATE UNIQUE INDEX MyIndex ON Employees (SSN) WITH DISALLOW NULL;
```

This query creates an index on an attached table. The table's remote database is unaware of and unaffected by the new index:

```
CREATE UNIQUE INDEX MailID ON MailList ([Client No.])
```

Using the Upsizing Wizard

Microsoft provides a special tool to simplify migrating an application from stand-alone Access to client-server with Microsoft SQL Server as the database engine. This software, called the Upsizing Tool, can be ordered from Microsoft. The Upsizing Tool wasn't available for Access 95 at the time of this writing. It was scheduled for shipment in early 1996. This version of the Upsizing Tool works with Access 95 and SQL Server 6.0.

Here's how the Upsizing Wizard works:

1. Starting from an Access database with native Access tables, the Wizard creates a table on the server for each Access table. The fields are mapped from Access field types to the corresponding SQL Server field types. If necessary, fields are renamed to remove internal spaces and to conform with SQL Server field-naming rules.

2. Primary keys in Access become primary keys in SQL Server. For compound primary keys, clustered indexes are automatically created.

3. Indexes are created for all fields indexed in Access.

4. Referential integrity rules in Access are translated into declarative referential integrity (SQL Server 6.0) or triggers (SQL Server 4.x).

5. Data is transferred from Access to the server.

6. The Access table is renamed.

7. A query is created in Access for each table on the server. This is called an *aliasing query*, because it renames any fields to their original Access names. The query has the same name as the original Access table. Because Access queries are updatable, this query can serve as the row source for all the other Access objects that originally used the table, such as forms, other queries, and reports.

The Upsizing Wizard gives you a great start on migrating your application to a new server, but there is still work for you to do. To get optimum performance, you must rewrite some portions of the application to take advantage of special server features.

Initialization Settings

In most cases, the default settings Access uses for a standard installation work best, but in some cases you might want to change the behavior of the program by using special settings. Table 37.2 shows the initialization settings for Access that relate to operation in client-server architecture.

Table 37.2. Access initialization settings for client-server.

Setting	Default	Description
DisableAsync	0	When set to 1, forces synchronous query execution.
LoginTimeout	20	Specifies the number of seconds a login attempt can continue before timing out.
QueryTimeout	60	Specifies the number of seconds a query can run before timing out.
TraceODBCAPI	0	Shows whether ODBC API calls are traced in ODBCAPI.TXT. Default is 0 for No. 1 is for Yes.
ConnectionTimeout	600	Specifies the number of seconds that a cached connection can remain idle before timing out.
AsyncRetryInterval	500	For asynchronous processing, this shows the number of milliseconds between polls to the server.
AttachCaseSensitive	0	Indicates whether table name matching is case-sensitive. Defaults to 0 for No.
TraceSQLMode		When set to 1, inspects SQL statements sent to the server.
SnapshotOnly	0	When set to 0 (the default), this forces all recordsets to be returned as snapshots.
AttachableObjects		Contains a list of object types that can be attached (such as tables, views, and so on).
TryJetAuth		When set to 0, prevents Access from attempting login with the default Admin account.

continues

Table 37.2. continued

Setting	Default	Description
PreparedInsert	0	When set to 1, this is used to insert values in all columns.
PreparedUpdate	0	Similar to PreparedInsert, this setting determines whether all columns will be affected by an update, or only the columns that have been changed in the updated record. PreparedUpdate can fire a trigger on a column that wasn't changed.
FastQuery		When set to 1, speeds requerying by using more connections.
SQLTraceMode		Takes the same action as TraceSQLMode.

Summary

Access can be used to develop stand-alone and LAN applications, but it can also serve as a powerful and flexible front end for client-server applications. This means that you can upsize applications for dozens or hundreds of users or use Access as a data analysis tool for report writing, queries, and business graphics.

As this chapter has shown, Microsoft has included many special Access features specifically for client-server operations. The most important of these is probably the Pass-through query, which allows you to take advantage of stored procedures and other server features. You can expect even tighter integration of Access and database engines in the future.

In order to develop an efficient client-server application, you must master not only Access but also your database server software. You face many trade-offs in striving for the best performance from the application. There are few fixed rules here; many things can be determined only by trial and error. Still, the rewards of using Access with client-server architecture are worth the effort.

Finishing an Access Application

PART

Developing Online Help

38

by Rich Freeman

No matter how skillfully you design an Access application, or how intuitively the application functions, your users will still have questions from time to time. At such moments, nothing will please them more than the availability of clear, concise, and thoughtfully organized online Help. Providing Help for your Access applications takes a little extra time, but in the long run it will not only endear you to your users but also greatly reduce the number of technical support calls you receive.

Like most Windows 95 programs, Access 95 has been designed to support the Windows 95 Help system. Using word processing software such as Microsoft Word for Windows or a Help authoring tool such as RoboHELP, Access developers can create their own Windows 95 Help files, complete with hypertext hotspots and colorful graphics. What's more, Access enables you to equip a database with several kinds of *context-sensitive* Help, enabling users to get Help immediately for the form, report, or control they are using.

In this chapter, you will learn how to plan, design, and create a Windows 95 Help file, as well as how to provide context-sensitive Help for the objects and controls in an Access database. You will also learn more about some of the Help authoring tools currently available.

Understanding Windows 95 Help

This section introduces you to the basic elements of Windows 95 Help. For Windows 95, Microsoft has added new features to Help and modified previously existing ones, so it's a good idea to read this section even if you're familiar with prior versions of Windows Help.

Elements of Windows 95 Help

At its most basic, the Windows 95 Help system (commonly referred to as WinHelp) consists of a program named WINHLP32.EXE that serves as a standard Help interface for Windows software. The text and graphics that WinHelp displays are stored in a Help file. When you view Help for a Windows program, WINHLP32.EXE loads and displays the Help file for that program.

By convention, Help files have the extension .HLP. The main Access 95 Help file, for example, is named MSACCESS.HLP. Material within a Help file is divided into *Help topics*. Using WinHelp, you view one Help topic at a time.

Under Windows 3.x, users could usually get Help by opening a Help menu and then choosing either the Contents command or the Search command. In most Windows 95 programs, these commands have been replaced with a single new command called Help Topics. When you choose the Help Topics command, WinHelp displays the Help Topics dialog box, shown in Figure 38.1, which you can use to find Help about a particular subject. By choosing tabs in the Help Topics dialog box, users can switch among its various pages.

FIGURE 38.1.

Use the Help Topics dialog box to view the contents of a Help file and to search for Help.

The Contents tab displays a Help file's table of contents in an expandable/collapsible format. The Find tab enables users to search the text in a Help file for a particular word or phrase. The Index tab (which replaces the Search dialog box that came with the Windows 3.x version of WinHelp) enables users to search for Help topics using keywords. In the text box at the top of the Index tab, you type the subject for which you are searching; as you type, WinHelp displays the most similar keywords in the keyword list. When you double-click a keyword, WinHelp displays the Help topic associated with that keyword. If more than one Help topic is associated with the keyword you double-clicked, WinHelp lists the topics in the Topics Found dialog box, shown in Figure 38.2. You can move to the Help topic you want by double-clicking it.

FIGURE 38.2.

The Topics Found dialog box lists Help topics that match the keyword you chose on the Index tab.

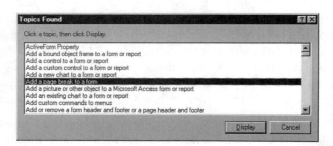

The Help Topics dialog box can integrate several Help files and present them to the user as a single Help system. For example, the Contents tab can send you to topics in multiple Help files, and the Index tab can include keywords from multiple Help files.

WinHelp displays most Help topics in two kinds of window: the *main Help window* and *secondary windows*. In a typical Windows 95 Help file, you view overview information about an application in the main Help window, and step-by-step instructions for specific tasks in a secondary window. A typical secondary window is shown in Figure 38.3.

FIGURE 38.3.

Secondary windows often display instructions for carrying out a task.

Unlike secondary windows, the main Help window features a menu bar with commands you can use to print Help, mark particular topics for future reference, and perform other tasks.

Both the main Help window and secondary windows usually come with button bars you can use to navigate Help and carry out other essential tasks. These button bars can be customized. For example, some button bars come with *browse buttons* (labeled << and >>) that enable you to move to the next or previous Help topic. (For information about customizing a button bar, see "Creating and Customizing Help Windows" later in this chapter).

In many Help topics, portions of the text are underlined and printed in green. These underlined words, phrases, and sentences are called *hotspots*. When you point the mouse at a hotspot, the pointer turns into a small hand. If you then click the mouse, WinHelp performs an action. When you click a hotspot underlined with a solid line, WinHelp either moves you to a different topic or runs a macro, depending on how the hotspot has been configured. When you click a hotspot underlined with a dotted line, WinHelp displays a topic in a special pop-up window that appears above the current Help window. The pop-up window disappears when you click your mouse again.

Some Help files include pictures that have been set up to function like hotspots. Such pictures are called *hypergraphics*. They can be formatted to perform one hotspot action or can contain multiple hotspot regions, each of which performs a different action.

Within the text of some Help topics are *authorable buttons* that execute commands when you click them. Figure 38.4 shows sample authorable buttons.

When you view a Help topic in the main Help window, a line usually appears under the topic title. As you scroll through the topic, the text above the line doesn't scroll out of view. The portion of a Help topic that always stays visible is called the topic's *nonscrolling region*. The nonscrolling region usually contains just the topic title, but sometimes it contains hotspots or buttons that display examples or a list of related topics.

FIGURE 38.4.

Authorable buttons enable users to carry out actions.

Authorable button ——

The Help Project

Every Help file is based on a series of *source files*. Collectively, these source files are referred to as a *Help project*. To create a Help file, you compile the Help project using the Microsoft Help Workshop. When you compile a Help project, Help Workshop combines and compresses the source files into a new file with an .HLP extension that WinHelp can load and display.

Unlike previous versions of the Windows Help compiler, Help Workshop does more than just compile Help files. It comes with a graphical user interface that lets you create and edit important source files. It also comes with a detailed online Help file called the Help Author's Guide. To use Help Workshop, you need three files: HCW.EXE, HCRTF.EXE, and HWDLL.DLL. To use the Help Author's Guide, you need two additional files: HCW.HLP and HCW.CNT. These files are available on the Microsoft Access 7.0 Application Developer Toolkit (ADT), the Windows System Development Kit (SDK), and the Microsoft Developer Network level 2 CD-ROM.

Every Help project must include the following source files:

■ A Help Project file: This is an ASCII text file that defines the Help project. It specifies the other source files that belong to the Help project, the windows you use to display Help topics, and various option settings. Help Project files usually have an .HPJ extension. For more information, see "Creating the Help Project File" later in this chapter.

■ One or more Topic files: These are rich-text format (RTF) documents that contain the Help file's text and formatting codes. Every Help project must include at least one Topic file, but can include more. Topic files generally have .RTF extensions. For more information, see "Creating a Topic File" later in this chapter.

In addition to the files already listed, a Help project can also include the following source files:

■ A Contents file: This is an ASCII text file that defines the table of contents in the Help Topics dialog box's Contents tab. Unlike most other source files, the Contents file must be shipped separately with your Help file. In other words, whenever you distribute a copy of your Help file to users, you must also distribute a copy of the Contents file. Use of Contents files is optional but highly recommended. Contents files generally have a .CNT extension. For more information, see "Creating a Contents File" later in this chapter.

■ One or more Map files: These are ASCII text files that associate each Help topic in the Topic files with a unique number. You use these numbers in your Access database to provide context-sensitive Help for objects and controls. For more information about Map files, see "Creating Map Files" later in this chapter.

■ Any number of graphics files: These are the bitmaps, metafiles, and other graphics that appear as illustrations in the Help file. For more information, see "Adding Graphics" later in this chapter.

■ A full-text search file: This is the file WinHelp uses when you conduct full-text searches with the Find tab in the Help Topics dialog box. You can instruct Help Workshop to create this file automatically during the compile process. If you do, you must distribute a separate copy of the full-text search file with each copy of your Help file that you ship to users. If you don't ship a full-text search file, WinHelp creates one automatically when needed. Full-text search files usually have an .FTS extension. For more information, see "Creating a Full-Text Search File During the Compile" later in this chapter.

Planning a Help File

A well-designed Help file is not only more effective at getting users the Help they need, but easier to write as well. Before you begin creating your Help file, spend some time thinking about the kind of information you want it to include, and how you want to present that information. This section discusses strategies for planning and organizing a Help file.

Deciding What Information to Include

Help files are divided into Help topics, which users view one at a time. Topic files, then, must be divided into Help topics as well. Before you begin writing your Help file, you must decide which topics you want it to cover. If you will be providing context-sensitive Help, you will want to include topics that describe the forms, reports, and possibly controls in your application. You might also, however, want to include overview topics that describe your application in general terms, and reference topics that define key terms and concepts.

Depending on the nature of your application and the types of people who will be using it, consider including some combination of the following topics in your Help file:

- An introductory or "About" topic that describes what the application does.

- Topics that describe forms and reports. It's generally best to devote one topic to each form and report in your application. You can use these topics to provide context-sensitive Help. If you will also be including topics about the controls on forms (see the following bulleted entry), the topics about the forms themselves can be quite brief.

- Topics that describe the function of a control on a form. These, too, should be used as context-sensitive Help. Creating a separate topic for every control on every form takes time but is the most complete way to document an application online.

- Topics that provide step-by-step instructions for carrying out a task. Unlike topics that discuss an individual form or control, these topics describe how to use forms and controls in sequence to accomplish a particular task. Keep these topics as short as possible. If there is more than one way to perform a task, describe only the quickest method.

- Topics that define important terms and concepts, especially those most likely to be unfamiliar to users.

- Topics that provide general information about using your application, such as how to open and close it, and how to log in. In a user manual, this kind of information is often included in a "Getting Started" chapter.

- Topics that describe custom menus and toolbars. You can create one Help topic per custom menu and toolbar, or you can give each menu command and toolbar button a Help topic of its own.

TIP

Hypergraphics are a nice way to provide Help for a custom toolbar. Create a bitmap of the toolbar, and then define a separate hotspot region for each button. When someone viewing your Help file points at a button and clicks their mouse, Help for the button is displayed. For information about creating hypergraphics with multiple hotspot regions, see "Creating Shed Graphics" later in this chapter.

- Topics that describe basic Windows 95 and Access skills. These are especially helpful if some of your users will be new to either system.

NOTE

As you plan the contents of your Help file, remember that the size of your Help file can have a variety of implications. You will, of course, want the information in your

Help file to be complete. However, if you include too much information, your Help file might become so large that it's hard to maintain. Large Help files take longer to compile and require more memory to compile. In addition, large Help files consume more space on distribution disks and user hard drives and operate more slowly. One common reason that Help files get too big is the inclusion of too many graphics, especially large bitmaps. If you feel your Help file has become unwieldy, consider removing a graphic or two rather than eliminating text or whole Help topics.

Presenting Help Topics to Users

You can use the main Help window, a secondary window, or a pop-up window to display Help topics to users. Microsoft has developed a set of conventions regarding the use of windows in Windows 95 Help files; if you want your Help file to resemble other Windows 95 Help files, try to follow these conventions:

- Topics that provide overview information about an application or one of its features should be displayed in the main Help window. In general, use the main window to display longer topics that describe a subject at length and that are likely to require scrolling.

- Topics that provide step-by-step instructions should be displayed in a secondary window. When designing the secondary window you will use to display such topics, set its initial position to a corner of the user's screen so that the user can use the application and read your instructions at the same time.

- Topics that provide reference information about terms and concepts should be displayed in a pop-up window that appears when the user clicks a hotspot. You can't scroll through pop-up windows, so they are a poor means of displaying lengthy topics. They are, however, a great way to give users a quick look at information related to the topic being viewed without exiting that topic altogether.

Tips for Writing Help

As you write Help, keep these guidelines in mind:

- Write for your most likely audience. If most of your readers will be Access novices, don't assume familiarity with even the most elemental terms and techniques. For instance, most readers new to relational databases won't know what a record is or what it means to sort records. On the other hand, if your audience is largely composed of system administrators or other developers, you can employ a more complex vocabulary and need not define common terms and concepts.

- Express yourself clearly and directly. Fewer words are always better than more, and small words are always better than long ones.

■ Be as brief as you can without leaving out vital information. In a step-by-step procedure, describe the simplest and shortest way to accomplish the task. In an overview, don't waste space on information that won't benefit the user (such as which procedures or macros run behind the scenes when a form is loaded).

■ Be consistent, especially in your terminology. If you use the expression "click the button" in one place, don't use "press the button" elsewhere. Similarly, don't call a form a "form" in one place and a "window" or "dialog" in another.

■ Refer to forms and reports by the name that appears in the title bar (as specified in the Caption property), not by their Access name. The name in the title bar is the one users see when they use your application. Say, for example, that your application includes a form whose Access name is `Sales_Order_Form`, and whose Caption property is set to Sales Order Entry. In your Help file, you should refer to the form as "the Sales Order Entry form," not "the `Sales_Order_Form`."

Creating a Help File

In this section, you will learn how to create a Windows 95 Help file without the assistance of a Help authoring tool. It's worthwhile to spend some time with the material in this section even if you intend ultimately to use a Help authoring tool, because a solid grounding in the structure of the Help project source files will help you get the most from such products.

> **NOTE**
>
> The examples in this section show you how to perform various tasks using Microsoft Word for Windows 6.0. You can, however, use Microsoft Word for Windows 7.0 or a different program as long as it can save files in rich-text format (RTF).

Creating a Topic File

A Topic file is a rich-text format document that contains the text users read when they view your Help file. You must use a text editor or word-processing program that can save files in rich-text format to write a Topic file.

To create a new Topic file, simply start a new document and save it in rich-text format.

> **TIP**
>
> You can base a Topic file on any existing template in Word or another word processing program. To standardize the look and feel of your Help files, consider creating a Help template and using it as the basis for all of your Topic files.

Creating and Saving a Sample Topic File

Follow these steps to create a sample Topic file and save it in rich-text format:

1. Open Word for Windows and choose File | New.
2. In the New dialog box, select a template, and then click OK or press Enter.
3. Choose File | Save.
4. In the Save dialog box, type a filename and select a drive and directory.
5. In the list for the Save File As Type box, select Rich Text Format.
6. Click OK or press Enter.

Adding Help Topics

To start a new Help topic, perform the following steps:

1. Insert a hard page break.

> **NOTE**
>
> The first Help topic in a Topic file need not be preceded by a hard page break.

2. Immediately after the hard page break (that is, in the same paragraph), insert a special series of footnotes (as described in the following sections). Each footnote defines a different attribute of the Help topic, and each must be marked with a particular character.
3. Immediately after the footnotes (still in the same paragraph), type the Help topic title as you want it to appear on-screen.

Figure 38.5 shows a typical completed Help topic.

The Asterisk (*) Footnote

The Asterisk footnote specifies the *build tags* with which the Help topic is associated. Build tags enable you to create several versions of a Help file from the same set of Topic files. Each version of the Help file can contain a different combination of Help topics, based on their build tags. For more information, see "Specifying the Build Tags to Include in the Help File" later in this chapter.

The Asterisk footnote is optional and is often omitted. If you choose to include it, it must precede all other footnotes in the Help topic. Use the asterisk character (*) as the footnote mark. In the footnote text, type one or more build-tag names, separated by semicolons.

Following are some examples:

```
* USER
* WORKSTATION;SERVER
* SHAREWARE;COMPLETE;ADMIN
```

FIGURE 38.5.

A typical completed Help topic with footnote codes.

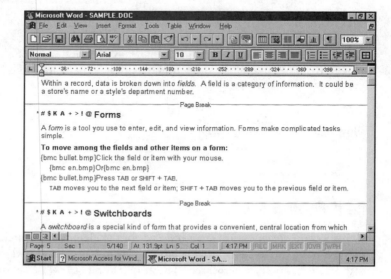

The Pound Sign (#) Footnote

The Pound Sign footnote specifies the Help topic's unique *topic ID*. The topic ID is the name by which WinHelp identifies the topic internally. No two Help topics anywhere in a given Help project, even if they are in different Topic files, can have the same topic ID. This footnote is required for every Help topic.

Use the pound-sign character (#) as the footnote mark. In the footnote text, type a name for the Help topic. Topic IDs can include spaces, but you should try to avoid using leading and trailing spaces. The topic ID and title of a Help topic can be different, but it's helpful to make them as similar as possible.

Following are some examples:

```
# Reference
# Saving Purchase Orders
# Using_the_Main_Switchboard
```

The Dollar Sign ($) Footnote

The Dollar Sign footnote specifies the Help topic's title as it appears in the Topics Found dialog box, the Bookmark dialog box, and the History window.

Use the dollar-sign character ($) as the footnote mark, and type the title in the footnote text. Like topic IDs, titles can include spaces.

> **TIP**
>
> To avoid confusing your users, be sure that the title you type in the Dollar Sign footnote matches the title that appears on-screen when the topic is displayed. If a user selects "Entering Employee Data" in the Topics Found dialog box, for example, they might be disoriented if the title of the Help topic they move to is something other than "Entering Employee Data."

Following are some examples:

```
$ Glossary
$ Exiting the Application
$ Printing a Report
```

The K Footnote

The K footnote specifies the *search keywords* for the Help topic. Search keywords appear in the Index tab of the Help Topics dialog box and are also used in KLink() macros (for more information about KLink() macros, see "The ALink() and KLink() Macros" later in this chapter). Use of the K footnote is optional, but users won't be able to find a Help topic with the Index tab if it lacks a K footnote.

Use a capital K as the mark for this footnote. In the footnote text, type the Help topic's search keywords, separated by semicolons.

Unlike Windows 3.x Help, Windows 95 Help enables you to create second-level keywords. Second-level keywords are like subcategories of a first-level keyword. In the Index tab, they are indented directly under the first-level keyword with which they are associated. Figure 38.6 shows typical second-level keywords.

To create a second-level keyword, type a first-level keyword followed by a semicolon. (See Figure 38.6.) Then type the first-level keyword again, followed by a comma or colon, and the desired second-level keyword. You can include a space after the comma or colon, if desired. For example, to associate a Help topic about invoices with the second-level keywords "Creating" and "Deleting," you would include the following entry in the text for the topic's K footnote:

```
Invoices;Invoices, Creating;Invoices, Deleting
```

Following are some examples:

```
K Users Form;Adding a User;Deleting a User;Users;Users, Adding;Users, Deleting
K Sales Orders;Sales Orders,Editing;Editing;Editing, Sales Orders
K Main Switchboard;Switchboards;Switchboards, Main;Reports Button;Exit Button
```

FIGURE 38.6.

Second-level keywords are indented for easier viewing.

Consistency is important when you assign keywords to Help topics. If you use the keyword "invoice" with some Help topics but "invoices" with others, it will look awkward in your Help file's Index tab. To assure consistent use of keywords, you might want to assign keywords to topics when you plan your Help file, before you actually begin writing.

Also, when assigning keywords to a Help topic, try to cover as many of the synonyms for the topic as possible. For instance, a user who needs Help about closing an application might search for Help about "closing," "exiting," or "logging out." The topic in your Help file that describes exiting the application should include all three of these terms as keywords in its K footnote.

The A Footnote

Use the optional A footnote to specify the keywords searched by `ALink()` macros (for more information about `ALink()` macros, see "The `ALink()` and `KLink()` Macros" later in this chapter). Whereas keywords in the K footnote are visible to the user (in the Index tab), keywords in the A footnote never are. This means that you can use any desired code or notational scheme in the A footnote, and that A footnote keywords need not be changed if you translate your Help file into a foreign language.

The footnote mark must be a capital A; keywords, separated by semicolons, should appear in the footnote text.

Following are some examples:

```
A Backend;maintenance;admin
A Chap. 1;Appendix A
A Controls;text boxes;buttons
```

The Plus Sign (+) Footnote

The Plus Sign footnote identifies the name of the *browse sequence* to which the Help topic belongs. Browse sequences enable you to control the order in which users move through the topics in your Help file when they click the browse buttons. If you will be equipping any of your Help windows with browse buttons, you must include this footnote in every Help topic you want the user to be able to browse to. If you won't be using browse buttons, or if you're creating a Help topic you don't want users to browse to, you can leave out this footnote.

> **NOTE**
>
> For information about adding browse buttons to the main or a secondary Help window, see "Creating and Customizing Help Windows" later in this chapter.

You can create a single browse sequence for an entire Help file, or create multiple browse sequences that correspond to the different components of your Access application or the different sections of your Help file. If your Help file has multiple browse sequences, users won't be able to move from one to another with the browse buttons.

The footnote mark must be a plus-sign character (+). In the footnote text, type a browse sequence code in the format

```
browse-sequence[:sequence-number]
```

in which `browse-sequence` is the browse sequence name (which can't include spaces). Type a colon and the `sequence-number` after the `browse-sequence` only if you want to assign the Help topic a specific, numbered position in the browse sequence. Use of `sequence-number`s is generally worth avoiding. If you don't include `sequence-number`s in your Plus Sign footnotes, the browse buttons automatically send you to the next or previous sequential topic in the same browse sequence. The simplest way to determine the sequence in which users browse through topics, then, is to arrange the topics in the desired sequence in your Topic files.

> **TIP**
>
> If you will be creating only one browse sequence, use "auto" as the footnote text in all Plus Sign footnotes. When you compile the Help file, Help Workshop will automatically create a browse sequence that mimics the order in which topics appear in your Topic files.

Following are some examples:

```
+ Browse_String
+ GettingStarted
+ INTRO_STRING:005
```

> **CAUTION**
>
> When assigning browse sequence numbers to Help topics, be sure to include leading zeros. Use 050 or 0050 instead of 50, for example. Help Workshop sorts sequence numbers in ANSI order rather than numerical order.

The Greater Than (>) Footnote

The optional Greater Than footnote enables you to specify the window in which the Help topic is displayed when a user reaches it from the Index tab, the Find tab, or a macro. The Greater Than footnote can be useful if you've specially formatted a topic to be displayed in a particular secondary window.

Use the greater-than symbol (>) as the footnote mark, and type a window name in the footnote text. The name of the main Help window is always "main"; the names of secondary windows are up to you (for more information, see "Creating and Customizing Help Windows" later in this chapter).

Following are some examples:

```
> Main
> Task
> Wnd2
```

The Exclamation Point (!) Footnote

This optional footnote indicates the names of the *entry macros* you want WinHelp to run whenever this Help topic is displayed. Entry macros can be used to open a secondary window, add a button to a button bar, or perform other tasks. For more information, see "Using Macros" later in this chapter.

Use an exclamation point (!) as the footnote mark, and type one or more macro names, separated by semicolons, as the footnote text.

Following are some examples:

```
! FocusWindow(main)
! CloseSecondarys();CreateButton("HelpOnHelp","&Help on Help","HelpOn()")
```

The "At" Sign (@) Footnote

Use this optional footnote to record comments about the Help topic for reference purposes.

Use the "at" sign (@) as the footnote mark, and type the comments in the footnote text.

> **TIP**
>
> "At" Sign footnotes are a good way to document a Help project that other people will be supporting.

Following are some examples:

```
@ Context-sensitive Help topic for the View Invoice form.
@ Do not use this topic with pop-up hotspots.
@ The entry macro for this topic adds an Index button to the button bar.
```

Adding a Sample Help Topic to a Topic File

The following steps show how to add a typical Help topic to a Topic file. To simplify the example, we will exclude the Asterisk, A, Plus Sign, Greater Than, Exclamation Point, and "At" Sign footnotes (which are all optional).

1. Open a Topic file, and then insert a hard page break by pressing Ctrl-Enter.
2. Choose Insert | Footnote.
3. In the Footnote dialog box, select the Footnote option and the Custom Mark option.
4. In the box next to the Custom Mark option, type #, and then click OK or press Enter.
5. In the lower window pane, type a topic ID (such as `Printing_a_Sales_Order`).
6. Click the end of the paragraph in the upper window pane (or press F6), and then repeat steps 2 and 3.
7. In the box next to the Custom Mark option, type $, and then click OK or press Enter.
8. In the lower window pane, type a title (such as `Printing a Sales Order`).
9. Click the end of the paragraph in the upper window pane (or press F6), and then repeat steps 2 and 3.
10. In the box next to the Custom Mark option, type K, and then click OK or press Enter.
11. In the lower window pane, type search keywords, separated by semicolons. For example, you might type `Printing;Printing, Sales Orders;Sales Orders;Sales Orders, Printing`.
12. Click the end of the paragraph in the upper window pane (or press F6), and then type the Help topic's title as you want it to appear on-screen.

13. Type the Help topic's content.
14. To begin the next Help topic, repeat steps 1 through 13.

TIP

Windows 95 Help can display up to 255 different fonts, so you can use any combination of fonts in your Help file. However, when you write Help topics, try to use the same fonts that appear in your Access application. This integrates your Help file with your application, providing a consistent look and feel.

Adding Nonscrolling Regions to Help Topics

The nonscrolling region is the portion of a Help topic that remains visible when a user scrolls through the topic. Use of nonscrolling regions is optional and is recommended only for Help topics that will be displayed in the main Help window.

Typically, you use nonscrolling regions to keep topic titles in view at all times, but you can include other information in a nonscrolling region as well. For example, you could include a hotspot that reads "See Also" in every nonscrolling region; when the user clicks the hotspot, a list of related topics is displayed.

Two basic rules apply to nonscrolling regions:

- There can be only one nonscrolling region per Help topic.
- A nonscrolling region must include the first paragraph of a Help topic (the one with the footnotes). You can include any number of additional paragraphs as well, but nonscrolling regions generally look and work best when kept as small as possible.

CAUTION

Don't add a nonscrolling region to Help topics you intend to display in a pop-up window. When a topic that has a nonscrolling region is displayed in a pop-up window, only the text in the nonscrolling region is visible; any other text in the topic isn't displayed.

To create a nonscrolling region for a Help topic, simply mark the paragraphs you want to include in the region as Keep With Next. To conduct this process with Word for Windows 6.0, perform the following steps:

1. Select the paragraphs you want to include in the nonscrolling region.
2. Choose Format | Paragraph.

3. In the Paragraph dialog box, choose the Text Flow tab.

4. Select the Keep With Next check box.

5. Click OK or press Enter.

> **NOTE**
>
> The default background color of the nonscrolling region is gray. You can, however, change the background color as it appears in the main Help window or any secondary window. For more information, see "Creating and Customizing Help Windows" later in this chapter.

Adding Hotspots

There are three kinds of hotspots:

- Jumps send the user from the current Help topic to a different one.

- Pop-ups display a Help topic in a pop-up window that appears over the current Help window.

- Macro hotspots run a WinHelp macro. Macros are routines that enable you to carry out tasks such as printing a Help topic, adding a button to a button bar, or closing a Help window. For more information about macros, see "Using Macros" later in this chapter.

The topic that a jump or pop-up displays can be either part of the same Help project as the hotspot itself or a topic from another Help file altogether.

Wherever possible, follow these guidelines regarding hotspots:

- Use jumps to help users navigate your Help file. If your Help file includes an overview topic about creating reports, for example, you might want to include a jump that sends the user to a topic that provides step-by-step instructions.

- Use pop-ups to display definitions of important terms and names. For example, pop-ups are a great way to let novice users take a quick look at Help topics that explain basic Access concepts and terminology.

- Use hotspots sparingly. Too many hotspots in a Help topic can overwhelm a user. You can reduce the number of pop-ups in a Help topic by creating one for the first occurrence only of each unfamiliar term in the topic text.

NOTE

You will find it easier to follow along with the next procedures if you configure your word processing software to display hidden text. In Word for Windows 6.0, you can do this by choosing Tools | Options | View and then selecting the Hidden Text checkbox.

To create a jump hotspot, perform the following steps:

1. Type the hotspot text, followed immediately by the topic ID of the Help topic you want the jump to display. Don't insert a space between the hotspot text and the topic ID. Here's an example:

   ```
   Jump TextTopic_ID
   ```

2. If the Help topic that the jump displays is in another Help file, append @ and the relevant Help file's name. Here's an example:

   ```
   Jump TextTopic_ID@OTHER.HLP
   ```

3. To display the topic in a specific window, append > and a window name. Here's an example:

   ```
   Jump TextTopic_ID>second
   ```

4. Select the hotspot text, and then *double*-underline it. Here's an example:

   ```
   Jump TextTopic ID
   ```

5. Select the topic ID (and the Help file's name and window's name, if relevant), and then mark it as hidden text. Here's an example:

   ```
   Jump TextTopic ID
   ```

To create a macro hotspot, follow the steps in the preceding procedure, substituting an exclamation point and a macro name for the topic ID. For example, the following hotspot runs the `CloseWindow()` macro when clicked:

```
Close Help!CloseWindow(main)
```

To create a pop-up hotspot, perform the following steps:

1. Type the hotspot text, followed immediately by the topic ID of the Help topic you want the hotspot to display in a pop-up window. Don't insert a space between the hotspot text and the topic ID. Here's an example:

   ```
   Popup TextTopic_ID
   ```

2. If the Help topic that the pop-up hotspot displays is in another Help file, append @ and the relevant Help file's name. Here's an example:

   ```
   Popup TextTopic_ID@OTHER.HLP
   ```

3. Select the hotspot text, and then *single*-underline it. Here's an example:

   ```
   Popup TextTopic ID
   ```

4. Select the topic ID (and the Help file's name, if relevant), and then mark it as hidden text. Here's an example:

   ```
   Popup TextTopic ID
   ```

> **NOTE**
>
> By default, WinHelp displays hotspot text underlined and in green, regardless of how the text is colored or formatted in the underlying Topic file. To display hotspot text as underlined but in a color other than green, you must insert an asterisk (*) character before the topic ID. Here is an example:
>
> ```
> Hotspot Text*Topic ID
> ```
>
> To display hotspot text in a color other than green and *not* underlined, insert a percent-sign character (%) before the topic ID. Here is an example:
>
> ```
> Hotspot Text%Topic ID
> ```

Creating a Sample Jump

For the next example, carry out the following steps to create a jump hotspot that reads "Using the Main Switchboard." When you click this hotspot, a Help topic of the same name is displayed in a secondary window.

1. Open a Topic file, and then insert a new paragraph in a Help topic.
2. Type `Using the Main Switchboard`.
3. Type `Using_the_Main_Switchboard` (the topic ID of the topic that the jump will display).
4. Type `>task` (`task` is the name of a secondary window).
5. Select the hotspot text ("Using the Main Switchboard"), and then double-underline it by pressing Ctrl-Shift-D.
6. Select the topic ID (`Using_the_Main_Switchboard`) and secondary window name (`>task`), and then mark them as hidden text by pressing Ctrl-Shift-H. The jump is now finished and should look like this:

<u>Using the Main Switchboard</u>`Using the Main Switchboard>task`

Adding Graphics

WinHelp supports four kinds of graphics files:

■ Device-independent bitmaps. These files usually have either .BMP or .DIB extensions.

■ Windows metafiles. These files usually have .WMF extensions.

■ Shed graphics. These are bitmaps that contain multiple hotspot regions. They usually have .SHG extensions.

■ Multiresolution bitmaps. These are special bitmaps formatted to support multiple screen resolutions, and they usually have .MRB extensions. You use the Microsoft Multi-Resolution Bitmap Compiler to create multiresolution bitmaps (for more information, see the Help file for the Microsoft Help Workshop).

If you want to use a graphic saved in another format (such as a .GIF file) in your Help file, you first must convert the graphic into one of the previously listed formats. A number of commercial and shareware products can convert graphics from other formats into bitmaps or metafiles. (For more information, see "Graphics Conversion Utilities" later in this chapter.)

Graphics can be embedded directly in a Topic file but generally should not be. Bitmaps are often quite large, and a Topic file that contains even a few embedded images might become so big that your computer won't have enough memory to compile it. Instead of embedding a graphic directly, you should use the preferred technique of inserting a graphic by reference. The reference indicates the name of a graphics file stored separately. During the compile process, Help Workshop locates the file you referenced and includes it in the Help file.

To insert a graphic by reference, you insert the following statement where you want the graphic to appear in a Help topic:

```
{bmx[t] filename}
```

filename is the name of the graphics file you're inserting. You can set the *x* parameter to any of three letters: c, l, or r. If you use c, WinHelp treats the graphic as if it were a character, so it flows with any text that shares the same paragraph. If you use l, WinHelp displays the graphic as if it were in a left-justified frame. If you use r, WinHelp displays the graphic as if it were in a right-justified frame. In either of the last two cases, text in the same paragraph as the graphic flows around the picture. Adding the optional t parameter causes WinHelp to replace the background color in the graphic with the background color of the Help topic that contains the graphic.

Following are some examples:

```
{bmc BITMAP.BMP}
{bmrt SHED.SHG}
{bml METAFILE.WMF}
```

Figure 38.7 shows how graphics inserted with the various reference statements look in a finished Help file.

FIGURE 38.7.

A graphic inserted with the {bmc} statement flows with the surrounding text; text flows around a graphic inserted with the {bml} or {bmr} statement.

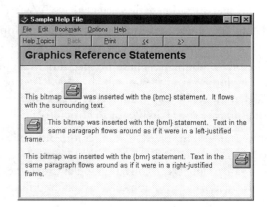

Help Workshop comes with several built-in bitmaps, listed in Table 38.1. If you insert a reference to one of these bitmaps in a Topic file, Help Workshop will include it in your Help file even if there is no corresponding graphics file in your Help project.

NOTE

If one of the graphics files in your Help project has the same name as a built-in bitmap, Help Workshop uses your bitmap rather than the built-in one.

Table 38.1. Built-in Windows 95 bitmaps.

Bitmap Name	Bitmap
BULLET.BMP	■
EMDASH.BMP	—
SHORTCUT.BMP	🔲
ONESTEP.BMP	▶
OPEN.BMP	📖
CLOSED.BMP	📕
DOCUMENT.BMP	📄
DO-IT.BMP	▶
CHICLET.BMP	»
PRCARROW.BMP	▶
CSHELP.BMP	?

TIP

WinHelp doesn't support many symbol characters, such as the bullet marks used by most word-processing programs. To include bulleted lists in your Topic files, insert a reference to the built-in BULLET.BMP bitmap at every position where you want a bullet mark to appear. Here's an example:

```
{bmc BULLET.BMP}     First line of the bulleted list
{bmc BULLET.BMP}     Second line of the bulleted list
{bmc BULLET.BMP}     Third line of the bulleted list
```

Adding Hypergraphics

A hypergraphic is a picture that functions like a hotspot. In fact, to add a hypergraphic to a Help topic, you create a hotspot in which one of the graphic reference statements described previously is substituted for the hotspot text. For example, the following pop-up hotspot displays the Using_the_Print_Button topic when the user clicks a bitmap of the Print button:

```
{bmc PRINT.BMP}Using the Print Button
```

You can also create hypergraphics called *Shed graphics* that contain multiple hotspot regions. For more information about Shed graphics, see "Creating Shed Graphics" later in this chapter.

Graphics Conversion Utilities

As mentioned earlier, WinHelp supports a limited number of graphics formats. However, many commercial and shareware products can convert graphics into a format that WinHelp supports. The following are some of these products:

HiJaak:

>   Inset Systems, Inc.
>   71 Commerce Drive
>   Brookfield, CT 06804
>   Phone: (203) 740-2400
>   Fax: (203) 775-5634

Collage Image Manager:

>   Inner Media, Inc.
>   60 Plain Road
>   Hollis, NH 03049
>   Phone: (603) 465-3216
>   Fax: (603) 465-7195

Paint Shop Pro:

>   JASC, Inc.
>   P.O. Box 44997
>   Eden Prairie, MN 55344
>   Phone: (800) 622-2793
>   Fax: (612) 930-9172

For additional information about graphics conversion utilities, consult CompuServe's Graphics Vendor forums (GO GRAPHAVEN, GO GRAPHBVEN, and GO GRAPHCVEN) or the Desktop Publishing forum (GO DTPFORUM).

Creating Map Files

In a Map file, you associate Help topics with *context numbers*. As you will see later, you use these context numbers to provide context-sensitive Help for the forms, reports, and controls in an Access database. Use of Map files is optional but is recommended for all but the smallest Help projects. If you prefer, however, you can map Help topics to context numbers directly in the Help Project file. For more information, see "Specifying the Map Files in Your Help Project" later in this chapter.

Map files are written in ASCII text, so you can use Notepad or any other ASCII text editor to create them. If you use a word processing program to edit a Map file, be sure to save the file as type MS-DOS Text. For convenience, give Map files an .MAP extension.

Each paragraph of a Map file should employ the syntax

```
#define topic-ID context-number
```

in which *topic-ID* is the topic ID of a Help topic, and *context-number* is the unique context number you want to associate the topic with.

Following are some examples:

```
#define Using_the_Main_Switchboard 100
#define Creating_a_Sales_Order 150
#define Printing_a_Sales_Order 200
#define Deleting_a_Sales_Order 250
```

You will find working with Map files easier if you follow these guidelines:

- Create a corresponding Map file for each Topic file in your Help project. For instance, if your Help project includes Topic files named USER.RTF and ADMIN.RTF, create Map files named USER.MAP and ADMIN.MAP.

- Leave room between context numbers for new topics. For example, if the first two topics in a Topic file are Getting_Started and Logging_In, assign them context numbers such as 100 and 200, rather than 1 and 2. That way, if you later add a new topic between the first two topics, you can keep your Map file in sequence.

- Avoid changing context numbers after you've used them in your Access database. Tracking down and updating every occurrence in an Access application of a context number that has changed is a time-consuming and difficult process. You can avoid it altogether by "freezing" the context numbers in your Map files after you have linked objects and controls to them.

> **TIP**
>
> During the compile process, Help Workshop confirms that every topic whose topic ID begins with IDH_ has been mapped to a context number. To take advantage of this feature, be sure to start the topic ID of every context-sensitive Help topic in your Help file with the IDH_ characters.

Creating a Contents File

The table of contents that appears in the Contents tab of the Help Topics dialog box is defined in a Contents file. Contents files should be given .CNT extensions. You must distribute a copy of your Contents file with each copy of your Help file that you ship to users. In other words, whenever you ship an .HLP file, you must also ship the corresponding .CNT file. Like Map files, Contents files are saved as ASCII text, so you can use Notepad or another ASCII text editor to create them.

> **NOTE**
>
> You can also use Help Workshop to create and edit Contents files. For more information, see the Help file for Help Workshop.

The first paragraph of a Contents file should always contain the `:Base` statement. The `:Base` statement specifies the name of the compiled Help file with which the Contents file is associated. For example, if you're creating a Contents file for a Help file named SAMPLE.HLP, this would be the first line of your Contents file:

```
:Base SAMPLE.HLP
```

You can also specify a default window for your Help file in the `:Base` statement by appending > and a window name. Help topics displayed via the Index and Find tabs, an `ALink()` or `KLink()` macro, or the Contents tab will appear by default in the window you specify, unless a different window is specified in the topic's Greater Than footnote. If you don't specify a default window, WinHelp simply treats the main Help window as the default window.

In addition to the `:Base` statement, a Contents file can also include any combination of these optional statements:

- The `:Title` statement: This specifies the name that appears in the title bar of the Help Topics dialog box (as well as the default name that appears in the title bar of Help windows). For example, to have the title "Help for My Application" appear in the title bar of the Help Topics dialog box, you would include the following paragraph in your Contents file:

  ```
  :Title Help for My Application
  ```

- The `:Index` statement: This identifies a Help file whose keywords you want to include in the Index tab. First you type a name by which the Index tab can identify the Help file to the user, and then an equal sign and the name of the relevant Help file itself. Including other Help files' keywords in your Index tab gives users access to the topics in those external Help files. For example, you could let users search for Help in the Access Help file as well as your own by including the following paragraph in your Contents file:

  ```
  :Index Access 95 Help=MSACCESS.HLP
  ```

  To include multiple Help files in your Help file's keyword list, simply insert multiple `:Index` statements in your Contents file.

■ The :Link statement: This identifies a Help file whose keywords you want to include in ALink() and KLink() macros. To have ALink() and KLink() macros search the keywords in NOTEPAD.HLP, for example, you would insert the following paragraph in your Contents file:

```
:Link NOTEPAD.HLP
```

To include multiple Help files in ALink() and KLink() macros, insert multiple :Link statements in your Contents file.

After the :Base and other opening statements, you define the table of contents itself. Figure 38.8 shows a typical Contents tab. As you can see, it's divided into *headings* (marked with a book icon) and *topics* (marked with a page icon). A heading is a category of Help topics; when you double-click a heading, WinHelp displays an indented list of subheadings and topics. A topic corresponds to a specific Help topic; when you double-click a topic, Help displays the corresponding Help topic in your Help file.

FIGURE 38.8.

The Contents tab breaks a Help file's contents into headings and topics.

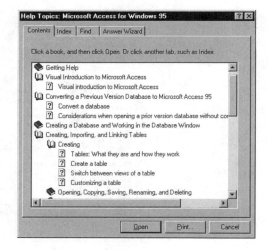

In your Contents file, each heading and topic must have its own paragraph. Each heading paragraph must be followed by paragraphs for the topics and subheadings that belong to the heading (the topics and headings that the Contents tab displays when a user expands the heading). If you will be nesting headings (that is, displaying subheadings under headings), you must precede each heading and topic paragraph with a number that indicates its indentation level. Use 1 for first-level headings and topics, use 2 for second-level headings and topics, and so on.

To create a heading paragraph, type a number (if necessary) and then the heading name as you want it to appear in the Contents tab. Here's an example:

```
1 Getting Started
```

868

To create a topic paragraph, type a number (if necessary) and the topic name as it should appear in the Contents tab, followed by an equal sign and the topic ID of the Help topic to display. Here's an example:

```
2 Logging In=logging_in
```

When creating topic paragraphs, keep the following points in mind:

- If the topic you want to display is in another Help file, append @ and the other Help file's name to the topic ID.
- If you want to display the topic in a window other than the default window (as specified in the :Base statement), append > and a window name.
- To have a topic in the Contents tab run a macro rather than display a Help topic, type ! and a macro (or multiple macros, separated by colons) after the equal sign.

A sample Contents file appears in Figure 38.9.

FIGURE 38.9.

*A sample Contents file,
with opening statements,
headings, and topics.*

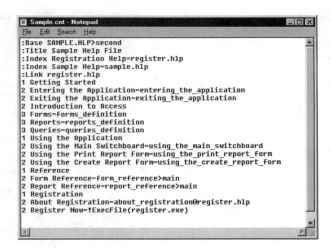

```
:Base SAMPLE.HLP>second
:Title Sample Help File
:Index Registration Help=register.hlp
:Index Sample Help=sample.hlp
:Link register.hlp
1 Getting Started
2 Entering the Application=entering_the_application
2 Exiting the Application=exiting_the_application
2 Introduction to Access
3 Forms=forms_definition
3 Reports=reports_definition
3 Queries=queries_definition
1 Using the Application
2 Using the Main Switchboard=using_the_main_switchboard
2 Using the Print Report Form=using_the_print_report_form
2 Using the Create Report Form=using_the_create_report_form
1 Reference
2 Form Reference=form_reference>main
2 Report Reference=report_reference>main
1 Registration
2 About Registration=about_registration@register.hlp
2 Register Now=!ExecFile(register.exe)
```

In the finished Help file, the Contents file in Figure 38.9 would produce the Contents tab shown in Figure 38.10.

Using the :include statement, you can include another Contents file within your own. The syntax for this statement is

```
:include contents-file
```

in which `contents-file` is the name of the Contents file you are including. Type the :include statement, in its own paragraph, at the position in your table of contents where you want the external table of contents to appear. For example, to include the Access table of contents as the last heading in your Help file's table of contents, add a paragraph to the end of your Contents file and type this:

```
:include msaccess.cnt
```

FIGURE 38.10.

This Contents tab includes three levels of indentation.

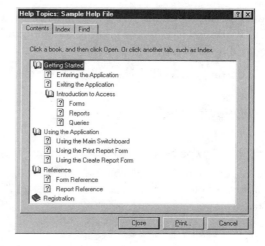

> **NOTE**
>
> If, when opening your Help file, WinHelp can't find the Contents file mentioned in an :include statement or the Help file mentioned in a topic paragraph, it omits the included file or topic paragraph without displaying an error message. Similarly, if WinHelp can't find the Help file mentioned in an :Index or a :Link statement, it leaves the keywords out of the Help file but doesn't display an error message. This means that in a Contents file you can safely refer to other Contents files and Help files even if you don't know for sure that all users have those files on their computers. For example, you can refer to a Help file that belongs to a modular component of your Access application that the user might not have installed.

Creating the Help Project File

The Help Project file contains essential reference information about a Help project. When you compile a Help project, Help Workshop looks in the Help Project file for the following information:

- A list of the Topic files in the project
- A list of the Map files in the project
- The name of the Contents file for the project

■ The path to the folder (or folders) in which graphics files can be found, or a list of the graphics files themselves

■ Definitions of the main and secondary windows in the project

■ The title of the Help file, as you want it to appear in the title bar of Help windows

In addition, you can set various options in the Help Project file. These determine how stringently Help Workshop reports errors during compiling, what level of compression it uses when compiling, and other details of operation.

Use Help Workshop, shown in Figure 38.11, to create the Help Project file by following these steps:

1. Open Help Workshop (HCW.EXE).

2. Choose File | New.

3. In the New dialog box, select Help Project and then click OK.

4. In the Project File Name dialog box, select the folder in which you want to store the Help Project file, and then type a name (with an .HPJ extension) in the File Name box.

5. Click the Save button.

FIGURE 38.11.

Use the Microsoft Help Workshop to create and edit Help Project files.

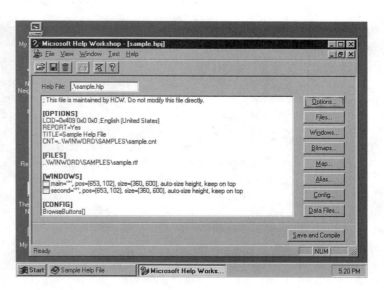

Specifying the Topic Files in Your Help Project

To specify the Topic files in your Help project, follow these steps:

1. In Help Workshop, open the Help Project file.

2. Click the Files button.

3. In the Topic Files dialog box, click the Add button.

4. In the Open dialog box, click the first (or only) Topic file in the Help project, and then click the Open button.

5. To add more Topic files, repeat steps 3 and 4.

6. When you've finished adding Topic files, click OK in the Topic Files dialog box.

Specifying the Map Files in Your Help Project

To specify the Map files in your Help project, follow these steps:

1. In Help Workshop, open the Help Project file.

2. Click the Map button.

3. In the Map dialog box, click the Include button.

4. In the Include File dialog box, type the name of the first (or only) Map file in the Help project, and then click OK.

5. To add more Map files, repeat steps 3 and 4.

6. When you've finished adding Map files, click OK in the Map dialog box.

> **NOTE**
>
> To map Help topics to context numbers in the Help Project file itself, rather than in Map files, click the Add button in the Map dialog box, and then specify a topic ID and context number in the Add Map Entry dialog box. Repeat this procedure for each topic you want to map.

Specifying the Location of Graphics Files

When you compile a Help project, Help Workshop looks for graphics files by default in the folder that contains the Help Project file and the folder that contains the Topic file in which a graphic appears. You can, however, instruct Help Workshop to look in additional folders for graphics files as well. To do so, follow these steps:

1. In Help Workshop, open the Help Project file.

2. Click the Bitmaps button.

3. In the Bitmap Folders dialog box, click the Add button.

4. In the Browse For Folder dialog box, select a folder and then click OK.

5. To add more folders, repeat steps 3 and 4.

6. When you've finished adding folders, click OK in the Bitmap Folders dialog box.

Creating and Customizing Help Windows

Every Help file comes with a main Help window by default; you must create secondary windows yourself. A Help project can contain up to 255 secondary windows; in actual practice, you will probably need only a few. At the very least, following the Windows 95 convention requires that you create a secondary window in which to display step-by-step procedures. To create a secondary window, follow these steps:

1. In Help Workshop, open the Help Project file.
2. Click the Windows button.
3. In the Window Properties dialog box, choose the General tab.
4. Click the Add button.
5. In the Add A New Window Type dialog box, type a name for the window, and then click OK.

NOTE

You can't name a secondary window "main"; WinHelp reserves this name for the main Help window.

6. In the Title Bar Text box, type the text you want displayed in the new window's title bar.
7. To have WinHelp automatically size the height of this window to fit the Help topic it's displaying, select the Auto-Size Height check box.
8. To have WinHelp keep this window visible even when users switch to another window or application, select the Keep Help Window On Top check box.
9. Click OK.

NOTE

If you want to customize the main Help window in any of the manners described in the following text, you must first follow the steps in the preceding procedure, typing the name "main" in step 5.

Using Help Workshop, you can specify where you want WinHelp to position a window when it opens. To specify the position of a window, follow these steps:

1. In Help Workshop, open the Help Project file, and then click the Windows button.
2. In the Window Properties dialog box, select the window you want to position from the list for the Window type box.

3. Choose the Position tab, and then click the Auto-Sizer button.

4. Position and size the Help Window Auto-Sizer window, shown in Figure 38.12, and then click OK in that window.

FIGURE 38.12.

To set the initial position of a window, position the Help Window Auto-Sizer on your screen.

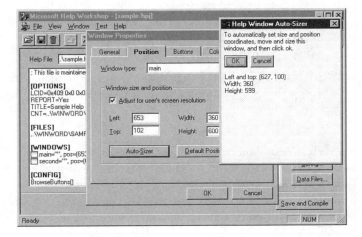

5. To have WinHelp automatically proportion the new window so that it retains its size relative to the screen regardless of the user's screen resolution, select the Adjust for user's screen resolution check box.

6. Click OK.

By default, Help Workshop sets the background color of a window to yellow and sets the background color of the nonscrolling region to gray. You can change either or both of these settings by following these steps:

1. In Help Workshop, open the Help Project file, and then click the Windows button.

2. In the Window Properties dialog box, select the window whose background colors you want to change from the list for the Window type box.

3. Choose the Color tab.

4. To change the background color of the nonscrolling region, click the Change button next to the sample nonscrolling region, and then select a color in the Color dialog box.

5. To change the background color of the topic text area, click the Change button next to the sample topic text area, and then select a color in the Color dialog box.

6. Click OK.

You can customize a window's button bar. When you create a new secondary window, Help Workshop automatically places the Help Topics, Back, and Options buttons on the button bar. This is the recommended minimum set of buttons that every secondary window's button bar should include. You can, however, remove any of these buttons or add more buttons by following these steps:

1. In Help Workshop, open the Help Project file, and then click the Windows button.
2. In the Window Properties dialog box, select the window whose button bar you want to customize from the list for the Window type box.
3. Choose the Buttons tab.
4. Select the check box of each button you want to include on this window's button bar. To include browse buttons on the button bar, for example, select the Browse check box.
5. Click OK.

For each window you create, you can define entry macros for WinHelp to run whenever the window opens. If you want to add a button not included among the choices in the Buttons tab (such as a "See Also" button, for example) to a window's button bar, you can define an entry macro that creates the desired button. You can also use entry macros to perform other functions. For more information about WinHelp macros, see "Using Macros" later in this chapter. To define entry macros for a window, follow these steps:

1. In Help Workshop, open the Help Project file, and then click the Windows button.
2. In the Window Properties dialog box, select the window for which you want to define entry macros from the list for the Window type box.
3. Choose the Macros tab.
4. Click the Add button.
5. In the Add Macro dialog box, type the first (or only) entry macro for this window, and then click OK.
6. To add more entry macros, repeat steps 4 and 5. When this window opens, WinHelp will run entry macros in the order in which they are listed in the Macros tab.
7. Click OK.

Specifying Help Project Options

Among the options you can specify for a Help Project are the title that appears in the main Help window's title bar, the name of the Contents file that belongs to the Help project, and the level of compression you want to use when compiling the Help project. To specify options for your Help project, follow these steps:

1. In Help Workshop, open the Help Project file.
2. Click the Options button.
3. In the Options dialog box, choose the General tab.

4. To specify the title of the Help file as you want it displayed in the main Help window's title bar, type a title in the Help Title box.

5. Choose the Compression tab, and then select a compression option. The greater the compression level selected, the longer it takes to compile the Help file, but the smaller the Help file will be. Smaller Help files take up less space on distribution disks and user hard drives, and they also load more quickly and operate somewhat faster. Before compiling the final version of your Help file, select the Maximum compression option so that your Help file will be as small as possible.

6. Choose the Files tab, and then type the name of the Contents file for the Help project in the Contents File box.

7. Click OK.

NOTE

The preceding procedure tells you how to specify all of the most important options, but you can specify many other options as well. For more information about Help project options, see the Help file for Help Workshop.

Creating a Full-Text Search File During the Compile

When you conduct a full-text search using the Find tab in the Help Topics dialog box, WinHelp draws on the contents of an index stored in a full-text search (.FTS) file. WinHelp creates the .FTS file itself automatically if none exists when it's needed, so you need not deliver one with your Help files. The process of building an .FTS file can take a while, however, especially if the Help file being indexed is large. To save your users time, you can build an .FTS file in advance when you compile your Help file, and then ship the .FTS file with your Access application. Because .FTS files can be quite large, including one with an application you intend to distribute on floppy disks might affect the number of disks required. If you will be distributing your application on CD-ROM, however, including an .FTS file is highly recommended.

To create an .FTS file automatically during the compile process, perform the following steps. The .FTS file created will have the same name as your Help file, but with an .FTS extension.

1. In Help Workshop, open the Help Project file.

2. Click the Options button.

3. Choose the FTS tab.

4. Select the Generate Full Text Search Index check box.

5. Select other options as desired.

6. Click OK.

Creating an Alias for a Help Topic

Using Help Workshop, you can create an alias for a topic ID. During the compile, Help Workshop substitutes the alias for the original topic ID whenever it encounters the original topic ID in a hotspot definition or Map file.

This feature can be useful when you replace a topic with a new one or change a topic ID. For example, say that you delete the Opening_Forms and Closing_Forms topics and replace them with a new topic called Using_Forms. Rather than search your Topic files for every reference to the invalid Opening_Forms and Closing_Forms topic IDs, you can make Using_Forms an alias for both Opening_Forms and Closing_Forms. Whenever the user clicks a hotspot linked to either of the deleted topics, WinHelp displays the Using_Forms topic instead. Similarly, if you change a topic ID from Printing_a_Report to Printing_Reports, you can avoid searching for the old topic ID by making Printing_Reports an alias for Printing_a_Report.

To create an alias for a Help topic, follow these steps:

1. In Help Workshop, open the Help Project file.
2. Click the Alias button.
3. In the Topic ID Alias dialog box, click the Add button.
4. In the Add Alias dialog box, fill in the text boxes as appropriate, and then click OK.
5. To add more aliases, repeat steps 3 and 4.
6. In the Topic ID Alias dialog box, click OK.

Specifying the Build Tags to Include in the Help File

Using the Asterisk footnote (see "The Asterisk (*) Footnote" earlier in this chapter), you can assign one or more build tags to a Help topic. In the Help Project file, you can then specify which build tags to include in the compiled Help file. The Help file will contain only Help topics that include the build tags you specified and Help topics that haven't been assigned any build tags.

WinHelp's build tag feature enables you to create several versions of a Help file based on the same set of Topic files. For example, in addition to the standard version of your Help file, you could create a smaller version to ship with the demo build of your application, and a larger version for system administrators that contains information you don't want to make available to ordinary users. This would entail assigning footnotes such as DEMO, USER, and ADMIN to Help topics using the Asterisk footnote. Before compiling the demo version of the Help file, you would specify in the Help Project file that you want to include only topics which have been assigned the DEMO build tag (or no tag). Then you could modify this setting before producing the administrator's version of the Help file, and recompile.

To specify the build tags to include in your Help file, follow these steps:

1. In Help Workshop, open the Help Project file.
2. Click the Options button.
3. Choose the Build Tags tab.
4. To include topics with a particular build tag, click the Add button below the upper text box.
5. In the Add Build Tag dialog box, type the build tag name to include in the Build Footnote Text box, and then click OK.
6. To include additional build tags, repeat steps 4 and 5.
7. To exclude topics with a particular build tag, click the Add button below the lower text box.
8. In the Add Build Tag dialog box, type the build tag name to exclude in the Build Footnote Text box, and then click OK.
9. To exclude additional build tags, repeat steps 7 and 8.
10. In the Options dialog box, click OK.

Compiling the Help Project

To compile a Help project, follow these steps:

1. Open Help Workshop (HCW.EXE).
2. Choose File | Compile.
3. In the Project File box, type or select the name of the Help Project file for the project you want to compile.
4. Click the Compile button.

TIP

If you want to compile the Help project whose Help Project file you're currently editing in Help Workshop, click the Save And Compile button at the bottom of the Help Workshop window.

When the compile is complete, you will find a Help file in the same folder as the Help Project file. The Help file will have the same name as the Help Project file, but with an .HLP extension.

Tips for Designing Help Topics

You can display a Help topic in the main Help window, in a secondary window, or in a pop-up window. Generally speaking, you should design each Help topic to appear in only one of these window types. When creating Help topics, try to follow these guidelines:

- Help topics that will appear in the main Help window should be given a nonscrolling region and should always include a K footnote so that the topic is accessible from the Index tab and KLink() macros. If you will be including browse buttons with your Help file, be sure to also include the Plus Sign footnote with these Help topics.

- Help topics that will appear in a secondary window can be given a nonscrolling region, but shouldn't be if you want to follow Microsoft's design conventions. Most topics displayed in secondary windows are short enough to not require scrolling. As with topics that appear in the main Help window, always include a K footnote with these topics.

- Help topics that will appear in a pop-up window should never be given a nonscrolling region, nor should they include a Dollar Sign footnote, a K footnote, an A footnote, or a Plus Sign footnote. This rule is especially true of context-sensitive topics that describe Access controls. Topics displayed in pop-up windows are generally most helpful when read in context. By excluding the footnotes previously mentioned, you prevent users from accessing the topic out of context via the Index or Find tabs, a KLink() or ALink() macro, or the browse buttons.

Adding Advanced Help Features

In the preceding section of this chapter, you learned how to create a fully equipped Windows 95 Help file, utilizing the most essential components of WinHelp. In this section, you will learn how to use advanced features—such as macros, Shed graphics, and authorable buttons—to create even more useful and powerful Help files.

Using Macros

WinHelp comes with various built-in macros you can call from your Help files. You can use macros to add new buttons to a window's button bar, to display a Help topic, to open or close a Help window, or even to run an external program or application.

You can run a macro from a Help file in five ways:

- Create a macro hotspot that runs the macro. For more information about macro hotspots, see "Adding Hotspots" earlier in this chapter.

- Create a hotspot region on a Shed graphic that runs the macro. For more information about Shed graphics, see "Creating Shed Graphics" later in this chapter.

- Create an authorable button that runs the macro. For more information about authorable buttons, see "Creating Authorable Buttons" later in this chapter.

- Add a topic to a Contents file that runs the macro. For more information, see "Creating a Contents File" earlier in this chapter.

- Specify the macro as an entry macro for a Help topic, a Help window, or the Help file itself. You specify entry macros for a Help topic in the Exclamation Point footnote (for more information, see "The Exclamation Point (!) Footnote" earlier in this chapter). You specify entry macros for a Help window in the Help Project file (for more information, see "Creating and Customizing Help Windows" earlier in this chapter). To specify entry macros for a Help file, open the Help Project file in Help Workshop, and then click the Config button. For more information, see the Help file for Help Workshop.

Several dozen macros are available. A few of the most useful are described next. For more complete information about macros, see the Help file for Help Workshop.

The *ALink()* and *KLink()* Macros

`ALink()` and `KLink()` macros search your Help file's A and K footnotes, respectively, for one or more specified keywords, and then display a list of the Help topics that include any of the keywords in the Topics Found dialog box. For example, say that you create a `KLink()` macro that searches for the "Printing Reports" and "Reports, Printing" keywords. When the macro runs, WinHelp lists in the Topics Found dialog box every topic whose K footnote includes either (or both) of these keywords. (For more information about A and K footnotes, see "The A Footnote" and "The K Footnote" earlier in this chapter.)

`ALink()` and `KLink()` macros make including "See Also" or "Related Topics" hotspots in your Help file simple, provided that you are thorough and consistent in assigning A and K footnote keywords. To return to the given example, say that you want to include a "See Also" hotspot in your Help file's "Printing Reports" topic. You can configure the "See Also" hotspot to run an `ALink()` macro or a `KLink()` macro that searches A or K footnotes for the keywords "Printing Reports" and "Reports, Printing" (or other similar keywords). Such a hotspot might look like this:

```
See Also!KLink("Printing Reports;Reports, Printing")
```

When a user clicks the hotspot, WinHelp automatically finds related topics and displays them in the Topics Found dialog box. Thanks to `ALink()` and `KLink()` macros, you need not create or maintain a separate "See Also" topic for every "See Also" hotspot in your Help file.

The syntax for `ALink()` and `KLink()` macros is

```
ALink("keyword[;keyword]"[,type[,"topic-ID"[,window]]])
KLink("keyword[;keyword]"[,type[,"topic-ID"[,window]]])
```

in which the parameters have the following meanings:

- *keyword* denotes the keyword you want to search for. Separate multiple keywords with semicolons. If a keyword includes a comma, you must enclose this parameter in quotation marks.

- *type* specifies how you want WinHelp to respond when it finds topics that contain a keyword. By default, WinHelp displays the topics in the Topics Found dialog box and doesn't indicate the Help file from which each topic came. If you set this parameter to JUMP, however, WinHelp jumps directly to a topic if it finds only one with a matching keyword. If you set this parameter to TITLE, WinHelp displays in the Topics Found dialog box the name (as indicated in the Contents file) of the Help file in which it found each topic. The TITLE setting is relevant only if you have included other Help files in the keyword list using the `:Link` statement (for more information about the `:Link` statement, see "Creating a Contents File" earlier in this chapter). You can set the *type* parameter to either or both of these values; if you use both, you must separate them with a space (as in JUMP TITLE).

- *topic-ID* denotes the topic ID of the topic to display (in a pop-up window) if no topics with matching keywords are found. This topic should contain a custom message explaining that no matches were found and perhaps telling the user how to proceed. If the topic is in a different Help file, append @ and the Help file's name to the topic ID (as in no_match_msg@OTHER.HLP). If you don't specify a topic in this parameter, WinHelp displays a standard message box to inform users that no matches were found.

- *window* denotes the name of the window in which you want WinHelp to display the topic that the user chooses in the Topics Found dialog box. If you don't specify a window, WinHelp uses the window in the topic's Greater Than (>) footnote (if any), the default window for the Help file (again, if any), or the current window.

The following example shows an `ALink()` macro that searches A footnotes for the keywords "Getting Started" and "Reference":

```
ALink(Getting Started;Reference)
```

In the next example, the `KLink()` macro searches K footnotes for the "Invoices" and "Deleting Invoices" keywords. If only one matching topic is found, WinHelp jumps to that topic directly. If no matching topics are found, WinHelp displays the standard Windows message box. Topics that the user views via this macro are displayed in the win2 window:

```
KLink(Invoices;Deleting Invoices,JUMP,"",win2)
```

The *CloseSecondarys()* Macro

The `CloseSecondarys()` macro closes all secondary windows but the current one. This macro has no parameters.

The *CloseWindow()* Macro

This macro closes a Help window. The syntax for the `CloseWindow()` macro is

`CloseWindow(window)`

in which *window* is the name of the window to be closed. The following example closes a window named `howto`:

`CloseWindow(howto)`

The *CreateButton()* Macro

Use this macro to add a button to a Help window button bar. The syntax for the `CreateButton()` macro is

`CreateButton(button-ID,name,macro)`

in which *button-ID* is the name by which WinHelp identifies the button internally, *name* is the text that appears on the button, and *macro* is the macro that WinHelp runs when a user clicks the button.

> **TIP**
>
> To specify a keyboard shortcut for a button you create with the `CreateButton()` macro, insert an ampersand character (&) before a letter in the *name* parameter. For example, if you set the *name* parameter to `Close &Window`, the user can choose the Close Window button by pressing Alt-W.

The following example creates a button labeled "Print" that prints the current topic. Because there is an ampersand before the P in "Print," the user can press Alt-P to choose the Print button.

`CreateButton(PrintButton,&Print,Print())`

The *ExecFile()* Macro

Use this macro to run a program or to open a file. You can use the `ExecFile()` macro to display a file (such as a README.TXT file) in Notepad, to execute a batch file, or even to open an Access database. This is the syntax for the `ExecFile()` macro:

`ExecFile(program[,arguments[,display-state[,topic-ID]]])`

program is the name of the program to run or file to open (if you specify a file, WinHelp will open the file that has the program that the file is associated with). *arguments* specifies any command-line arguments for the program. *display-state* is a value indicating how the program's window should be displayed. *topic-ID* is the ID of the Help topic you want WinHelp to display if the specified program or file can't be opened (if this topic is in another Help file, append @ and the Help file's name, as in not_found@OTHER.HLP).

There are 10 values for the *display-state* parameter, including SW_SHOW (activate the window in its default size and position), SW_SHOWMAXIMIZED (activate the window maximized), and SW_SHOWMINIMIZED (activate the window minimized). For a complete list of *display-state* values, see the Help file for Help Workshop.

The following example opens Notepad, maximized:

```
ExecFile(NOTEPAD.EXE,,SW_SHOWMAXIMIZED)
```

The *Exit()* Macro

The Exit() macro closes the Help file. This macro has no parameters.

The *Print()* Macro

This macro prints the current Help topic. This macro has no parameters.

The *Search()* Macro

The Search() macro displays the Index tab in the Help Topics dialog box. This macro has no parameters.

Creating Shed Graphics

A Shed graphic is a hypergraphic that has multiple hotspot regions. These hotspot regions can be configured to function like a jump or pop-up, or to run a macro. Using Shed graphics, you can add interactive illustrations to a Help file. For example, you could define pop-up hotspot regions on a bitmap of an Access form. Whenever a user points at a control on the bitmap and clicks her mouse, Help for the control appears in a pop-up window. Similarly, you could create a Shed graphic that shows a menu from your Access application and enables users to get Help for a menu command by pointing to the command and clicking.

To create Shed graphics, you use the Microsoft Hotspot Editor (SHED.EXE). You can acquire a copy of the Hotspot Editor from the same place as the Help Workshop (see "The Help Project" earlier in this chapter for more information). The Hotspot Editor enables you to open an existing bitmap or Windows metafile, define hotspot regions, and then save the graphic in Shed format. Shed graphics are usually given an .SHG extension.

> **CAUTION**
>
> Always save a Shed graphic under a different name than the original bitmap or metafile on which it is based. Otherwise, the Hotspot Editor simply converts the original graphic into a Shed graphic, which you can't open or modify as you would a standard bitmap or metafile.

To create a Shed graphic, perform the following steps:

1. Open the Hotspot Editor (SHED.EXE).
2. Choose File | Open. Choose and then open an existing bitmap or Windows metafile.
3. Drag the mouse pointer over the portion of the graphic you want to define as a hotspot region. A rectangular border surrounds the area you specify.
4. Choose Edit | Attributes (or double-click anywhere inside the hotspot region).
5. In the Attributes dialog box, select the type of hotspot you want to define from the list for the Type box.
6. If you selected Jump or Popup in the Type box, type the topic ID of the Help topic you want the hotspot region to display in the Context String box. If you selected Macro in the Type box, type the name of the macro you want the hotspot region to run in the Macro box.
7. If you want the borders of the hotspot region to be visible to the user, select Visible from the list for the Attribute box. If you want the borders of the hotspot region to be invisible, select Invisible instead.
8. Click OK or press Enter. The hotspot region is now defined.
9. To define additional hotspot regions, repeat steps 3 through 8. You can include any combination of jump, pop-up, and macro regions on a Shed graphic.
10. When you've finished defining hotspot regions, choose File | Save As and then save the graphic as a new file with an .SHG extension.

Creating Authorable Buttons

WinHelp enables you to add *authorable buttons* to a Help file. Authorable buttons run macros, so you can use an authorable button to do anything a macro can. For example, you might create a "See Also" authorable button that runs an ALink() or a KLink() macro.

To insert an authorable button in a Help topic, you use the {button} statement. The syntax for this statement is

```
{button [label],macro1[:macro2:macro3...]}
```

in which *label* is the text you want printed on the button, and the *macro* values denote the macros you want Help to run when the user chooses the button. You can specify one *macro* or a series of *macros* separated by colons. If you don't specify a *label* for the button, Help displays it as a small blank square.

The following two sample {button} statements create the two authorable buttons displayed in Figure 38.13. The first statement creates a See Also button that displays a list of topics about reports; the second statement creates a blank button that closes all secondary windows and then jumps to the Registration topic:

```
{button See Also,KLink(Reports)}
{button ,CloseSecondarys():JumpId(Registration)}
```

FIGURE 38.13.

Two authorable buttons, one with a label and one without.

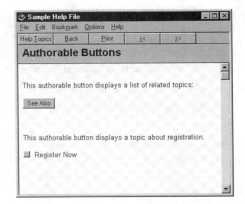

Providing Help for an Access Database

You can give users Help for an Access database in several ways. You can write tips that Access displays in a pop-up window whenever a user points at a control with the mouse. To assist users in searching for Help, you can create a custom Help menu from which users can open the Help Topics dialog box. You can also provide context-sensitive Help, which users can get either by pressing F1 or by clicking the What's This button (marked with a question mark) on the title bar of a form and then clicking a control.

In this section, you will learn how to provide each of these kinds of Help.

> **NOTE**
>
> For information about creating a custom Help Menu, see Chapter 26, "Menus and Toolbars."

Creating Control Tips

Access 95 lets you add *control tips* to your databases. These are much like the ToolTips that come with most Windows programs. A *control tip* is a description of a control that appears in a pop-up window when the user points at the control with the mouse. You can provide control tips only for the controls on a form.

To create a control tip, perform the following steps:

1. Open a form in Design view.
2. To display a control's property sheet, double-click the control.
3. Select the Other tab, and then type the text of the control tip in the ControlTipText box. This text can be up to 255 characters long.

Providing Context-Sensitive Help

You can provide context-sensitive Help for reports, forms, and controls on forms. Providing context-sensitive Help involves establishing a link between a form, report, or control and a specific Help topic in a Help file.

Before you can establish these links, you must assign a unique context number to each Help topic in your Help file. For more information, see "Creating Map Files" earlier in this chapter.

To link a form or report to a Help topic, you set its HelpFile property to the name of a Help file and its HelpContextID property to the context number of a topic within that Help file. To link a control on a form to a Help topic, you set its HelpContextID property to the context number of a Help topic in the Help file you specified in the form's HelpFile property.

For example, say that you want to display a Help topic named Using_the_Main_Switchboard whenever a user requests Help for your application's Main Switchboard form. This topic is in a Help file named DATABASE.HLP, and you mapped it to context number 550. You would set the HelpFile property for the Main Switchboard form to DATABASE.HLP and the HelpContextID property to 550. You can then link the controls on the Main Switchboard form to different Help topics in the DATABASE.HLP Help file by setting each control's HelpContextID property to another context number.

> **TIP**
>
> If you don't specify a path in the HelpFile property, Access looks for the Help file in the folder that contains your application. It's a good idea to place your Help file in the same folder as your application and omit a path in the HelpFile property. That way your HelpFile properties will always be correctly set regardless of where your users install your application.

If a user requests Help for a control you didn't link to a Help topic, Access opens the Help file to the topic for the form that contains the control. If the form hasn't been linked to a Help topic, Access displays the Microsoft Access Help Topics dialog box.

> **TIP**
>
> If your Help file contains one Help topic that describes every control on a form, as opposed to separate Help topics for each control, you can provide context-sensitive Help for the form and all of its controls simply by setting the form's HelpFile and HelpContextID properties.

You can display context-sensitive Help to users in two ways:

- Open the Help file for your application and display the context-sensitive Help topic in the main or a secondary Help window.
- Display the context-sensitive Help topic in a pop-up window. Figure 38.14 shows how Help looks when it's displayed this way.

FIGURE 38.14.

You can display context-sensitive Help topics to users in pop-up windows.

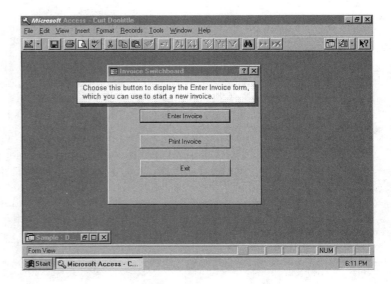

The procedure for linking forms, reports, and controls to Help topics varies depending on which way you want to display context-sensitive Help. Both procedures are discussed in the following text.

Displaying Context-Sensitive Help in a Help Window

To have Access open your Help file and display context-sensitive Help in a Help window, perform the following steps:

1. Open a form or report in Design view.
2. To display the property sheet for the form or report, choose View | Properties.
3. Select the Other tab, and then type the name of your Help file in the HelpFile box.
4. In the HelpContextID box, type the context number of a Help topic. Access displays the topic you specified if the control that has the focus when the user presses F1 hasn't been linked to a Help topic, or if the control to which the user pointed with the What's This button hasn't been linked to a Help topic.
5. To provide Help for a control on a form, click the control.
6. In the HelpContextID box, type a context number.

Displaying Context-Sensitive Help in a Pop-Up Window

To have Access display context-sensitive Help in a pop-up window, perform the following steps:

1. Open a form or report in Design view.
2. To display the property sheet for the form or report, choose View | Properties.
3. Select the Other tab, and then type the name of your Help file in the HelpFile box.
4. In the HelpContextID box, type a minus sign (–) and then the context number of a Help topic. Access displays the topic you specified if the control that has the focus when the user presses F1 hasn't been linked to a Help topic, or if the control to which the user pointed with the What's This button hasn't been linked to a Help topic.
5. To provide Help for a control on a form, click the control.
6. In the HelpContextID box for the control, type a minus sign and then a context number.

Adding the What's This Button to Forms

For users to get Help for a control on a form by clicking the What's This button and then clicking the control, you must add the What's This button to the title bar of your forms by following these steps:

1. Open the form in Design view.
2. Choose View | Properties.
3. Select the Format tab, and then select Yes in the list for the WhatsThisButton box.

Using Help Authoring Tools

Inserting Help topic footnotes and formatting hotspots are repetitive and time-consuming tasks. Fortunately, various Help authoring tools are available that simplify these and other processes. Help authoring tools make creating Help topics, adding hotspots, and inserting graphics faster and easier. They also create and maintain Help Project files and Map files for you automatically. The more sophisticated authoring tools (such as Doc-To-Help and RoboHELP) can even convert user manuals into Help files, enabling you to develop both printed and online documentation in less time than it would take you to create each separately.

Currently, none of the major Help authoring tools provides complete support for the Windows 95 version of WinHelp, so if you want to make use of new features (such as the A and Greater Than footnotes, authorable buttons, and ALink() and KLink() macros), you will still have to edit source files manually sometimes. If, however, you expect to be developing Help files on a regular basis, a Help authoring tool still makes an excellent investment.

This section discusses two of the more popular Help authoring tools.

Doc-To-Help

Doc-To-Help, from WexTech Systems, adds a wide range of powerful Help authoring features to your existing installation of Word for Windows, enabling you to create both a printed manual and an online Help file based on the same set of Word for Windows source documents. The newest release of Doc-To-Help, version 1.6, is compatible with versions 2.x and 6.x of Word for Windows. If you will be delivering both a user manual and a Help file with your application, Doc-To-Help can prevent a lot of duplicated work.

Creating a Help file with Doc-To-Help is far more intuitive than conducting the process by hand. The system comes with a set of Microsoft Word for Windows templates that add buttons and menu commands to the standard Word toolbar and menus. Working entirely within Word, you create a source document, inserting pictures, cross-references, index entries, and glossary definitions where desired. You use this source file to create both your hard-copy user manual and your Help file. When you give the command to create a Help file, Doc-To-Help carries out the following actions:

- Builds a Help Project file and Topic file(s)
- Turns sections marked with headings into Help topics (complete with the appropriate footnotes)
- Converts cross-references into jumps
- Turns glossary definitions into pop-ups
- Turns index entries into keywords

When the compile process is complete, you have a fully equipped Windows Help file that mirrors your printed documentation in content and organization.

NOTE

The current version of Doc-To-Help builds Windows 3.x Help files. The Windows 95 version of WinHelp will run a Windows 3.x Help file, but it won't look or function precisely like a "native" Windows 95 Help file. To convert a Windows 3.x Help file into a Windows 95 Help file, open the Help Project file in Help Workshop, make any desired changes, and then recompile the Help project. The Help Topics dialog box for a Windows 3.x Help file won't have a Contents tab. You can add one, however, by creating a Contents file. For more information, see "Creating a Contents File" earlier in this chapter.

In addition to the Word templates, Doc-To-Help 1.6 includes an additional set of utilities called the Hyperformance Tools. The Doc-To-Help Navigator enables you to view and navigate a Help file by expanding and collapsing branches, much like the Contents tab on the Help Topics dialog box. You can also use the Navigator to print multiple topics in a Help file. Using the Help topic remapping utility, Help authors can replace Doc-To-Help's automatically generated context numbers with different ones without leaving Word for Windows.

For more information about Doc-To-Help, contact WexTech Systems:

WexTech Systems, Inc.
310 Madison Ave., Suite 905
New York, NY 10017
Phone: (212) 949-9595
Fax: (212) 949-4007

RoboHELP

Like Doc-To-Help, RoboHELP, from Blue Sky Software, enables you to conduct the entire Help creation process from within Word for Windows. RoboHELP 3, the newest version, supports versions 2.x and 6.x of Word for Windows. The RoboHELP templates add toolbars, menu commands, and intuitive dialog boxes to Word, enabling you to create Help topics, add hotspots, and insert graphics by pointing and clicking instead of typing footnotes, reference codes, or specially formatted text. To create a jump, for example, you simply click a button on RoboHELP's floating toolbar, type the hotspot text, and then click a topic ID. RoboHELP inserts the jump in your Topic file, fully formatted. You can then test the new hotspot, or preview the entire Help topic that contains it, without first compiling your Help project. Figure 38.15 shows the dialog box you use to create a jump.

FIGURE 38.15.

RoboHELP's intuitive dialog boxes and floating toolbar simplify Help authoring.

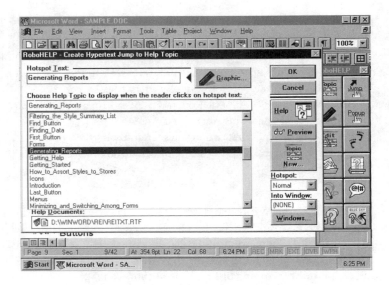

RoboHELP also creates and maintains the Help Project file and Map files automatically, and it comes with conversion features that can turn regular Word documents into Topic files and vice versa. Additionally, RoboHELP includes a simple screen-capture tool you can use to take screen shots of an application, and an image editor you can use to create and edit bitmaps and other graphics files. Compared with Doc-To-Help, RoboHELP provides a somewhat more flexible and comprehensive set of Help authoring features.

RoboHELP is the core product in Blue Sky Software's WinHelp Office suite of Help utilities. Among the handy tools in WinHelp Office is one you can use to convert Windows 3.x Help projects into Windows 95 Help projects, as well as to create Contents files with the help of a graphical point-and-click interface. Other utilities enable you to "decompile" a Windows 3.x Help file (that is, create a rich-text format Topic file based on a compiled Help file), view basic reference information about a Help file (such as a list of the topics it contains and the search keywords for those topics), and add multimedia elements such as sound and video to a Help file.

For more information about RoboHELP, contact Blue Sky Software:

> Blue Sky Software Corporation
> 7486 La Jolla Blvd., Suite 3
> La Jolla, CA 92037
> Phone: (619) 459-6365
> Fax: (619) 459-6366

Other Help Authoring Tools

Although Doc-To-Help and RoboHELP are two of the most popular Help authoring tools, others are available as well. The following are a few additional Help authoring tools:

ForeHelp:

> ForeFront, Inc.
> 5171 Eldorado Springs Dr.
> Boulder, CO 80303
> Phone: (800) 357-8507
> Fax: (303) 494-5446
> CompuServe: 74777,2132

HelpBreeze:

> SolutionSoft
> 370 Altair Way, Suite 200
> Sunnyvale, CA 94086
> Phone: (408) 736-1431
> Fax: (408) 736-4013
> CompuServe: 75210,2214

HDK:

> Virtual Media Technology Pty Ltd.
> DEK Software International
> 1843 The Woods II
> Cherry Hill, NJ 08003
> Phone: (609) 424-6565
> Fax: (609) 424-0785
> CompuServe: 75143,3631

Summary

In this chapter, you learned how to create Windows 95 Help files and how to provide context-sensitive Help for an Access database. Thorough planning is the key to developing Help files that will get your users the Help they need. If you will be creating Help files regularly, consider investing in a Help authoring tool. Help authoring tools greatly reduce the time you spend performing chores such as inserting footnotes, formatting hotspots, and maintaining Map files, thus enabling you to focus on your writing.

The Power to Reproduce

Replication

One of the larger problems facing corporate IS teams today is the timely distribution of business information. As corporations become more dependent on information, centrally maintained databases no longer can keep up with the high volume of user requests for data. More and more systems are becoming decentralized or distributed. However, this raises the issue of how to manage the distribution and synchronization of data to these satellite systems in a timely and accurate manner.

Replication, in general, came about as designers of large distributed database systems found that there was too much time lag, and a certain level of fragility, in making systems rely on two-phased commits for making changes to databases. (A two-phase commit means that both the originating and the target database agree that the proposed change is valid and accepted by both, meaning that the transaction must wait for both databases to allow it to be completed.) To get around this bottleneck, the idea was developed to put the data closer to the end user by replicating the database.

This chapter covers how to create a replicable database. There are several ways to create replicated databases, including the Tools menu, VBA code, and the Briefcase. Each of these methods will be covered in this chapter. After learning how to replicate the databases, you'll read about how to synchronize the databases. And finally, you'll learn how to troubleshoot possible conflicts and get some ideas on how to replicate a database set without causing too much trouble for the database administrator to support.

When to Use Replication

In some cases, replication is ideal; in others, it is not. Using replication creates advantages in the following three types of situations:

First, all databases have some kind of reports that need to be run. When an Access database has a report running, the performance is hit very hard because the report usually causes record locks. Therefore, to keep the performance at its maximum, it's best to create a report database that's updated by replication. Consequently, all reports then run from this new database.

Second, when users are located in different offices and are required to run across the Wide Area Network (WAN), they operate at a slower rating than local users would. To give these users the same performance as the local users, you need to set up a replicated database at each site, enabling the users to run from the new database.

Third, when a database is required 24 hours a day, it becomes impossible to do a backup. In most cases when a database is required 24 hours a day, the data is vital. So to ensure that a backup is being run without the database being taken down, you can use a read-only replica database that will be updated at regular times. Then a backup is done on this new replica database.

Replication shouldn't be used in the following situations:

The first situation is when large numbers of transactions are occurring in a replication set. When the transaction numbers start to increase, so do the data conflicts. When the conflicts increase, it's likely that while the database administrator is trying to fix conflicts, the next synchronization will need to be run, making it impossible for the conflicts to be resolved. Also, the synchronization could take a long time to process all the transactions, causing a lot of network congestion or a synchronization call that never ends. In this type of situation, you should consider keeping all data local to the site and then on a daily, weekly, or even monthly basis, running a batch job that updates the master database with remote databases' records. After the updates have occurred, instead of exporting the data back out to the remote database, copying the master database would be a fast answer.

The second case is when it's absolutely crucial that data be consistent and up-to-date at all times. In these cases, it's unwise to use replication because you can't do transactions between databases, which would guarantee that the data is accurate and consistent.

Making a Database Replicable

The first step in making a database replicable is to create the Master replication database. To do this, you must open the database you want to convert. You then have two ways to change the database to be replicable: by using the Access tool located in the Tools menu and by writing code to convert the database for you.

Using the Access Interface

To convert the database using the tool that comes with Access, simply click Tools | Replication | Create Replica. The dialog box shown in Figure 39.1 opens.

FIGURE 39.1.

The replication prompt to continue with the replication.

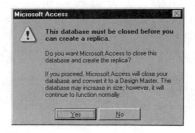

Before the tool can create the Design Master database, it must close the database. You then are asked whether you want a backup of the database before it's converted. I strongly recommend that you have the tool create a backup. The default name is the original filename plus an extension of .BAK. After the Design Master has been built, the dialog box shown in Figure 39.2 appears, prompting you for the name of the first replica database.

FIGURE 39.2.

The Location of New Replica dialog box.

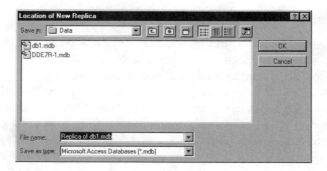

The replica database name defaults to "Replica of" plus the database name. You can change this by clicking the File name text box and typing the new name. It's suggested that you keep some form of the Design Master's name to make the file easier to identify as a replicated database. After you choose to create or not create the database, a confirmation dialog box is displayed for you to acknowledge.

Using VBA

To set the database to be a replica using VBA code, you must set its `Replicable` property to T. If the `Replicable` property already is in the database and you try to append this property to the database, an error will occur. For an example of how to do this, look in the Access Help file under "replication in DAO, converting databases for."

Changes to the Databases

When a database goes through the process of changing from a nonreplicated database to a replicated database, several changes are made to it. First, new system tables are added. Following is a list of system tables that are added to the database. These tables can't be changed by users or developers. It's a plus to know that they're there, but don't worry about them. These aren't all the tables that can be added to the database.

> MSysErrors
> MSysExchangeLog
> MSysGenHistory
> MSysOtherHistroy
> MSysRepInfo
> MSysReplicas
> MsysRepLock
> MSysSchChange
> MSysSchedule
> MSysTableGuids
> MSysTombStone
> MSysTranspAddress

If these tables aren't visible when you open the database, select Tools | Options, and on the View tab, click the Hidden Objects and System Objects check box.

The second change is that new system fields are added to each of your tables. Table 39.1 lists the fields and how they're used.

Table 39.1. The new system fields that are added.

Name	Description
s_Generation	A field that stores information about groups of changes.
s_GUID	A new AutoNumber field that uniquely identifies the record.
s_Lineage	A binary field that contains information about changes.

Also, for every OLE or memo field in the table, an additional system field is added. This field, named GEN_FieldName, is an AutoNumber field used to identify the object. Also, be aware that when you convert a table that has an AutoNumber in it, the field is changed from incremental to random. This change causes any of your reports that were sorting on this field to now not be able to do so. It has been suggested in the Access manual to reference the s_GUID column. The problem is, however, that if the column isn't visible, it's impossible to reference. If you don't plan around this situation before you convert the database, it's something that could come back to bite you. If you add a new AutoNumber field after the conversion to the database, you will be able to select Incremental. So to get around the conversion that occurs, add all ID fields after you've done the conversion of the database.

Last, three new properties are added to the database: `Replicable`, `ReplicableID`, and `DesignMasterID`. The `Replicable` property is used to tell whether the database is replicated. After this field is set, there is no going back, which is why it's strongly suggested that you make a backup. The `ReplicableID` property is a unique ID generated for each replicated database. The `DesignMasterID` property is used to identify the Design Master database. To change the Design Master, you set this value on. Remember that you don't want two Design Masters in a set—that could cause data loss or data corruption.

You can calculate the total number of bytes available in a record in a replicable table using this formula:

```
2048 bytes
    - (16 byte GUID value)
    - (4 bytes * the number of long value fields)
    - (4 bytes for the generation)
    - (4 bytes * the number of replicas that have ever made changes to the record)
```

Access allows a maximum of 255 fields in a table, of which at least three fields are used by replication. You can calculate the total number of fields now available in a replicable table with this formula:

```
255 fields
   - (3 system fields)
   - (the number of long value fields)
```

Few applications will use all the available fields in a table or characters in a record. If, however, you have many memo fields or OLE objects in your table, you need to be aware of your remaining resources.

In addition to decreasing the available number of characters and fields, Access also imposes a limitation on the number of nested transactions allowed under replication. Whereas a nonreplicable database can have a maximum of seven nested transactions, a replicable database can have a maximum of six nested transactions.

Making Objects Local or Replicable

When you start working with replicated databases, you will want to make changes to objects without the objects being replicated out to the replica databases. To accomplish this task, you need to set the property of the object to Keep Local. To change this property, select the object and then right-click on the object. This action brings up a menu, at the bottom of which are the properties options. Click the Keep Local option. The dialog box shown in Figure 39.3 opens.

FIGURE 39.3.

The Properties dialog box for Access objects.

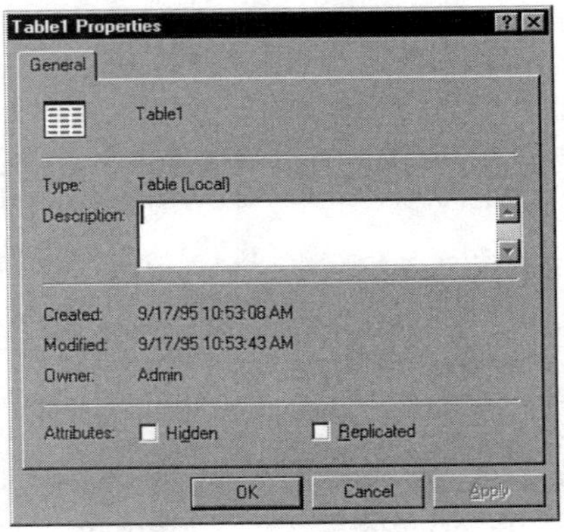

You're interested only in the attribute Replicated, located at the bottom of the dialog box. If a check mark appears in the check box, it's a replicated object; otherwise, it's a local object. To change the setting, click the check box. By default, all new objects are added as local objects. If this option is grayed out without a check mark in the box, the database isn't a replicated database. If it's grayed out with a check mark, it isn't the Design Master database.

What Can Be Replicated

System objects can't be replicated because they are unique to each Access database. All other objects of Access—tables, queries, forms, reports, macros, and modules—can be replicated. Also, because you're using replication, it can be a good idea to use hidden objects. In this way, you still can replicate the objects while ensuring that the objects are out of sight of the users.

Database Security

When you've created a replicated database, security becomes an issue because you won't want just anyone to get into the database. For information on how to create and set permissions on a database, refer to Chapter 30, "Security." The same rules for security apply to replicated databases as to nonreplicated databases. So when you're setting up a replicated database, you also need to copy out a system database, or you need to make sure that the users have access to the share where the shared system databases are located. It's recommended that you use the second option, having all users who need access to the database share the system database, if at all possible. The reason for using this option is that for the database administrator to add a new user to the application, he would need to add the new user to all the system databases that are being used in the remote locations. For users who don't have access to the share, you need a way to replicate the system database out to them. The only effect the users will run into is a slower login process. Another security issue the database administrator needs to be aware of is how to stop users from making a database replicated. There are two ways to do this. First is to set a database password. Second is to make sure that users are signing in through a system database that they don't have administrator privileges on.

WARNING

Be aware that if you set a database password on a replicated database, it's impossible for other databases to synchronize with the databases.

Creating Additional Databases

After you have the Design Master created, you need to create additional replicas of this database. Don't use the original to create replica databases, because what you're doing is creating new Design Masters. To create a replica database of the Design Master, use the tool supplied with Access, or write VBA code that creates new replica databases.

Using the Access Tool

To use the access tool, select Tools | Replication | Create Replica. The dialog box shown in Figure 39.2 appears, prompting you for the name of the new replica database. After you've set the location and named the new database, click OK. When the database has been created, the message shown in Figure 39.4 is displayed.

FIGURE 39.4.

The replica confirmation dialog box.

This dialog box confirms that the database has been created, and it shows you the name and the path where it was created. After you've confirmed the dialog box by clicking OK, you're placed back in the Database window.

> **WARNING**
>
> One problem here is that when you create the replication database through the Access tool, you can't make a read-only replica database, which you would require for a report database or a backup database. The only way to create a read-only database presently is to use VBA code.

Using the VBA

Writing code that enables you to create a replica database is quick and simple. First, you need to open a connection to the database. Second, you must make a call to the MakeReplica function. This function needs to follow the database name, and it takes the following parameters. The first option is the new Replica Database name. The second option is the description that will be placed in the MSysReplicas system table under the description column. The last option is optional, but if you want to create a backup database or a report database, the constant to use is dbRepMakeReadOnly. To make an additional replica database, you must call the MakeReplica method. Here is its syntax:

```
database.MakeReplica replica, description[,dbRepMakeReadonly]
```

Set *database* to the master database of the replica set. *replica* is the name to be used for the new replica database. *description* is any valid string expression. dbRepMakeReadOnly is optional. Here is an example of code that would make a database replica:

```
Function MakeReplicaDatbase()

    Dim dbMaster As DATABASE
    Set dbMaster = DBEEngine (0).OpenDatabase("DDE.MDB")
    dbMaster.MakeReplica "First replica of DDE.MDB", "First replica of DDE.MDB"
    dbMaster.Close
End Function
```

Synchronizing Replicated Databases

After all the databases are in place and on the users' machines or servers, you need to be able to synchronize the data. To get the data synchronized, use the tool that comes with Access, or write VBA code that synchronizes the database either at a certain time or after a certain number of records have been added. This choice depends on how important the data is for the users.

Using the Access Tool

To open the Access tool, select Tools | Replication | Synchronize Now. The dialog box shown in Figure 39.5 opens, prompting you for the Synchronize Database name.

FIGURE 39.5.

The Synchronize Database prompt.

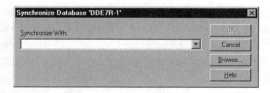

If you have synchronized the database before, the name defaults to the last database it synchronized with. Also, if you click the arrow at the right of the listbox, you're shown a list of previously used synchronized database names. If the database you want to use isn't in the list, you can type the path plus name into the listbox. The synchronization process is capable of using the network path plus database name, which saves you from having to have the share connected at all times. Also, if you don't remember the path and database name, simply click Browse. This action opens the file locator dialog box. This dialog box enables you to navigate through all connected drives as well as any network share. To change drives, click the Look in listbox, and it displays a list of drives that are connected. To see a nonconnected share, click the File name listbox, and type the share name. To change to a folder that is below the current folder, double-click the folder name. To change to a folder one level up, click the one-level-up button, located to the right of the Look in listbox. After you've located the database, activate it and then click OK. This action places you back on the previous dialog box with the path plus filename you selected in the locator dialog box. If this is the file you want to synchronize with, click the OK button. A progress dialog box appears, showing the status of the update. After the synchronization has completed, the message shown in Figure 39.6 appears, explaining that the updates won't be effective until you close the database and reopen it.

FIGURE 39.6.

The confirmation of synchronization.

If you select Yes, the database is closed and reopened. If you choose No, you're returned to the database, where you can continue with your work.

Remember, if you plan to use this method to keep the databases in synch, you must make sure that two tasks are completed. Make sure that the users have access to Tools | Replication | Synchronize Now. And after you've determined that they have access to the tool, teach them how to use the tool.

Using VBA Code

To write VBA code to synchronize the database, you first need to have a list of all the database names and their locations. You can pull this list from MSysReplicas, but this method isn't recommended because this information was created when the replicas were first generated. In the master database, you should have a table that contains all the databases that are part of this set. This way, the replicas aren't doing the work to synchronize. Now that you have a table set up with the names and paths, the next step is to run the Synchronize function. This function requires a database variable preceding it and then two parameters. The first parameter is mandatory, and the second is optional. The mandatory parameter is the database name including the path you want to synchronize with. The optional parameter can be any of the items listed in Table 39.2.

Table 39.2. Optional parameters for the Synchronize function.

Parameter	Description
dbRepImpExpChanges	Imports the data first, followed by the export of the local data that has changed.
dbRepImportChanges	Imports the changes.
dbRepExportChanges	Exports the changes.

The following code uses a table that holds the database names plus the path. First, it sets up a variable that points to the database set. It then sets up a loop to go through this record set, importing the data from each database from the record set. It next resets the record set to the first record. Then it calls the export function of Synchronize. Upon completion of the export, it closes down the snapshot and the database.

```
Function SynchronizeDB()
  Dim db As Database, snpRepDB As Snapshot

  Set db = DBEngine(0).OpenDatabase("A:\CODE\DDEACC7.MDB")

  Set snpRepDB = db.CreateSnapshot("Select DBName from ReplicatedDBs;")
  snpRepDB.MoveFirst
  Do While Not snpRepDB.EOF
    db.Synchronize snpRepDB("DBName"), dbRepImportChanges
    snpRepDB.MoveNext
  Loop
snpRepDB.MoveFirst
  Do While Not snpRepDB.EOF
    db.Synchronize snpRepDB("DBName"), dbRepExportChanges
    snpRepDB.MoveNext
  Loop
  snpRepDB.Close
  db.Close
End Function
```

The reason to first import and then export is to ensure that all the database is current. If you don't do this, the only database that is up-to-date is the last database called. If you have only one database to worry about, making the call to synchronize with a parameter of dbRepImpExpChanges will work just fine. For more ideas on how to implement replication databases, refer to the section "A Better Way to Make Use of Replication." When the code is done, you can view the data changes right away, not after a restart, which makes this a more effective alternative. Also, when this type of code is implemented, no teaching of the synchronization tool is necessary.

Troubleshooting Replicated Databases

When you start working on three or more databases, and users are adding, editing, or deleting records from different databases, there will always be data conflicts. With the replication capability of Access, when it has a conflict, it keeps the record with the most changes done to it. After the decision has been made, a new table is created, named *table*_Conflict, in the database that had the conflict data. The *table* part of the name is the name of the table that had the conflict. For example, say that you had a table named Employee, and when it was synchronized, it had a conflict—the new table would be named Employee_conflict. The contents of this table would be identical to the original, but it would contain only the conflicting data. Access provides two ways to resolve conflicts: by using the Access tool that is supplied and by using code.

Using the Access Tool

If you don't have the database open and there has been a problem with the synchronization, a warning message appears, asking whether you want to resolve the conflict before you proceed. If you answer Yes at this prompt, the dialog box shown in Figure 39.7 is displayed.

FIGURE 39.7.

*The Resolve Replication
Conflicts dialog box.*

Here you are given a list of tables that had conflicts with the last synchronization. If you click Close, you're returned to the database without any conflicts being resolved. If there were any errors with Design, the View Design Error button is enabled. To resolve the conflict, click the Resolve Conflict button. This action opens the dialog box shown in Figure 39.8.

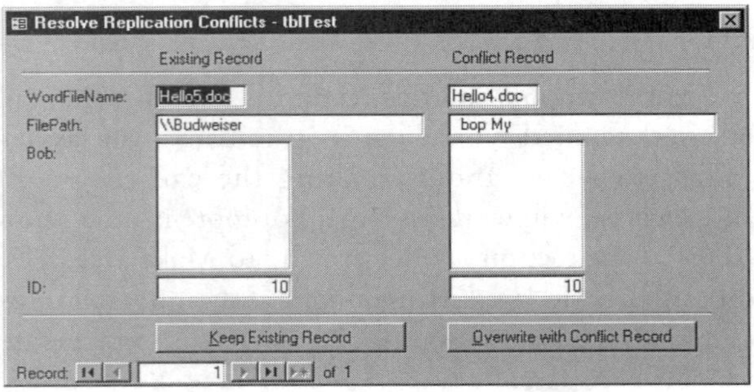

FIGURE 39.8.

*The Resolve Replication
Conflicts dialog box.*

On the right side of this dialog box is the data that Access has decided is the correct data. On the left side is the data you entered that was determined to be the less likely valid data. At the bottom of the dialog box, you're given the choice of whether to keep the existing record or overwrite it with the conflicting data. If you aren't sure which choice to make or if there is more than one record of conflict, you can navigate through each record, making this choice for each record. After you've fixed all the records that had conflicts, you are placed back at the dialog box shown in Figure 39.7.

If you had a data error, the View Data Error button is enabled. When you click this button, the dialog box shown in Figure 39.9 is displayed.

In this case, the error that was received happened to be caused by the addition of an OLE object, and the database was unable to replicate it out to the other database. The Replication Data Error dialog will give you some ideas of how to repair the problem. Furthermore, if there is more than one problem, this dialog enables you to use the record navigation buttons located at the bottom of the dialog box to scroll through the other problems.

FIGURE 39.9.

The Replication Data Errors dialog box.

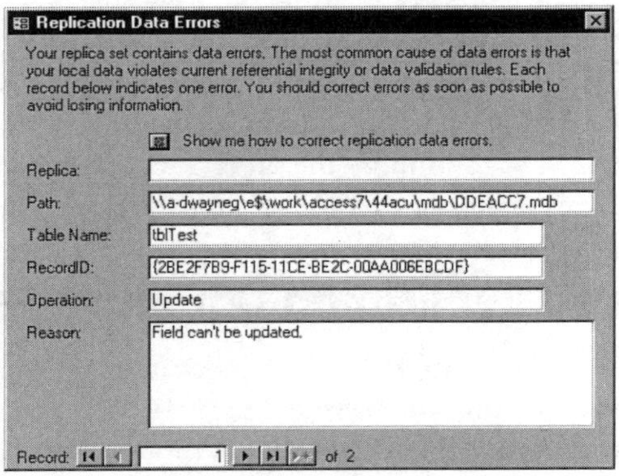

Using VBA Code

First, you need to check to see whether any tables have a conflict table. If there is a conflict, create a record set to the nonconflict table; then create a second record set to the conflict table. Before you can either fix the conflict or delete the conflict, you need to have a method in place to decide how to resolve conflicts. After you've fixed all conflicts using the conflict resolution method, you need to delete the conflict table.

Briefcase Replication

Another unique way to implement database replication is by using the Briefcase. As part of the usability studies that went into the design of Windows 95, Microsoft discovered that many people were copying their files to take them home to work on them. The problem was that there could then be problems when the files came back and the information had to be returned to the original machine. People would forget to update files, or copy the original file over the modified one, or even clobber the changes someone else had made to a shared file.

For all these reasons, Microsoft designed the Briefcase as a tool for handling the distribution and updating of files. Even Access 95 was designed to take advantage of this capability with replicated databases.

Briefcase replication in Access 95 is used to make special copies—called replicas—of an Access database. By doing this, users at different sites can all work on their own copies of the database at the same time, just as was proposed. Replication is different from simple copying because replicated databases can be synchronized with each other. This means that the changes made at each site can be brought back to the central database, and Access can take those changes and apply them to the original database. New replicas can then be made to distribute the changes to all the users.

Two common situations call for the use of replication. In the first case, you might want to replicate a database so that you can take your work home with you and easily update your system when you get back to work. In the second case, you might have a database application that is shared by a number of remote users (such as a sales force that wants to track customer orders), and you want to simplify the process of distributing changes between the users and the master database, as well as among the users.

Creating a Replication Database with Briefcase

Because Access relies on the Briefcase in Windows 95 to create replicated databases, the first step is to make sure that your system was set up with the Briefcase. Figure 39.10 shows a desktop with the Briefcase (in the lower left of the screen, just above the Start menu), as well as the default window shown when the Briefcase opens.

FIGURE 39.10.

A look at the Briefcase and its default window.

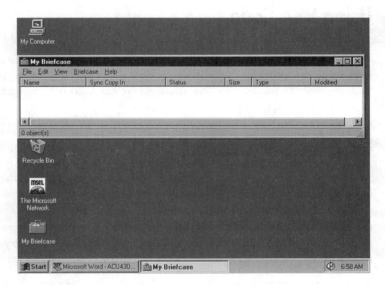

If you discover that Briefcase wasn't installed, select Start | Settings | Control Panel | Add/Remove Programs | Windows Setup, and then follow the on-screen instructions. You need to have your Windows 95 disks or CD-ROM available.

After Briefcase is installed on your system, make sure that the database that will be replicated isn't protected by a database password. If it is, you must remove the password protection before replicating it.

You then need to open an Explorer window and find the .MDB file for the database. It's best to use a previously replicated database file if one exists; otherwise, use the Design Master database. In the following section, you will see figures and examples of previously replicated databases. Double-click the My Briefcase icon, which should be visible on your desktop. This action opens a window for the Briefcase similar to the one shown in Figure 39.10.

Next you simply click the .MDB file and drag the icon to the Briefcase window. After you've done this, you're presented with a dialog that looks somewhat like the one shown in Figure 39.11. This dialog box basically gives you a chance to abort in case you didn't mean to replicate this database.

FIGURE 39.11.

A verification dialog for Briefcase replication.

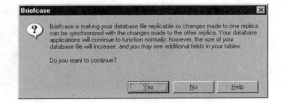

Assuming that you decide to continue, the next dialog (shown in Figure 39.12) gives you the option of creating a backup of the database. If you have the disk space, this is probably a good idea. If you do make a backup, be sure to move it to a different directory to reduce the chance of confusing it with the current database.

FIGURE 39.12.

The backup verification dialog.

Either way, you'll end up spending time watching the screen while sheets are flying in both directions between the Briefcase and the folder.

You then are asked which database should be allowed to have design changes made to it. Although both the original and the replica database can have data inserted, updated, or deleted, only one of them can be allowed to accept changes to the structure of tables. Usually, you will want the original database to be the one that controls changes to the structure of the database. The exception would be if you created a database but are having someone program changes to it, in which case the replica you give the other person needs to be able to have the changes made. The dialog involved is shown in Figure 39.13.

Finally, you end up with the process completed, and a replica of the database in the Briefcase. Figure 39.14 shows what is then displayed.

FIGURE 39.13.

Briefcase's dialog box verification for an editable database.

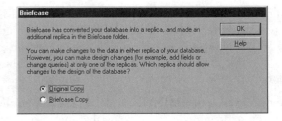

FIGURE 39.14.

The result: a database in both places.

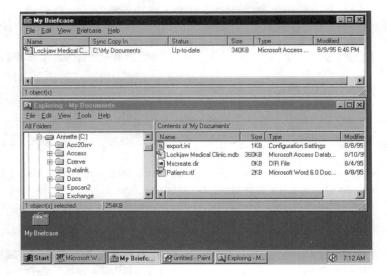

When you reopen the original database in Access, you'll notice that the title for the database has changed. As shown in Figure 39.15, the open master (original) database is displayed.

FIGURE 39.15.

How the original (master) database looks after replication.

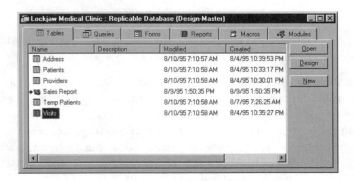

On the other hand, the open replica shows a somewhat different title, as shown in Figure 39.16. Even though the titles are different, you'll notice that everything else (even the linked table) looks the same.

FIGURE 39.16.

The replica version of the same database.

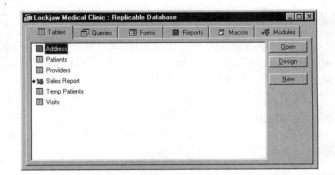

A note about that linked table: Unless you copy over that .XLS file and place it along the same path on the other machine, when you (or whoever you've given the replica to) try to use that table, it will crash. Worse, because that file isn't an integral part of the database, even if you do copy it, updating will be a nightmare.

So to use a linked table, you need to replicate the original .XLS file by placing it into the Brief-case as well, and then also make a copy of the file on the other machine *from the Briefcase*. In other words, the other machine will have both the .XLS file in the Briefcase and a copy of the file dragged from the Briefcase and placed in the correct path.

This is one of those cases in which it probably will be a lot less hassle to simply exchange data between the applications (in this case, Access and Excel) than to try to maintain the link with the data.

After you've converted a database into a replicable database, you can't convert it back to a nonreplicable database. The conversion process works in only one direction, nonreplicable to replicable. You can create a new, nonreplicable database that contains all the objects and data of your replicable database without the additional system fields, tables, and properties associated with replication. This process requires the following steps:

1. Identify the replica that contains the objects and data you want to be in the new, nonreplicable database.

2. On the View tab of the Access 95 Tools | Options command, set the System Objects option to off (unchecked).

3. Create a new database and open it.

4. Import all the objects from the replica into the new database.

5. On the View tab of the Tools | Options command, set the System Objects option to on (checked).

6. Open each table in the new database, and delete the fields labeled s_GUID, s_Lineage, and s_Generation.

7. Save your new database.

Taking It Home with You

The whole purpose of creating the replica is to enable you to take the database with you or distribute it to other people. After the replica has been created, the process of distributing it can be carried out either by using disks (or other removable media that Windows 95 can recognize) or through a direct connection (such as a network).

In the case of a direct connection, you make sure that the other computer is connected and then drag the Briefcase to the target machine. If you're using a disk, you simply drag the Briefcase to the disk window in Explorer.

> **NOTE**
>
> If the Briefcase won't fit on a single floppy, you have a problem, because it doesn't know how to span disks. In that case, you must create a direct connection via a network or through a dial-up RAS connection.

In either case, the Briefcase disappears from your desktop and resides on the new target. Figure 39.17 shows an example of moving the Briefcase to a floppy.

FIGURE 39.17.

The Briefcase has been moved to a floppy disk in drive A.

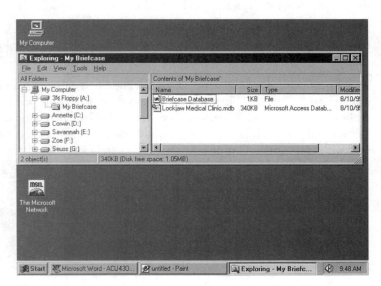

If you want to provide replicas to several people, right-click on the desktop, select New from the floating menu, and then select Briefcase from the drop-down list. By default, this Briefcase is called New Briefcase. After you create a new Briefcase, you need to create another replica of your original database. Remember that every time you replicate the original database, those three fields are added to allow for tracking the changes in each replica of the database. Even if you eventually delete one of the replicas, the tracking information remains on the original database.

Work on the replicated database should be done with it remaining in the Briefcase. In other words, start Access and open the replica file where it is in the Briefcase. If you copy it to the other machine from the Briefcase, you're essentially making a replica of a replica, and then you will have to update the version in the Briefcase before you can bring it back and update the original version.

Bringing It Back and Synchronizing

When you are reattached to the computer that has the original copy of the database, or have the floppy disk in the drive of that computer, open the Briefcase window and click the database file. In the Briefcase window, select Briefcase | Update Selection.

This is what replication is all about. You no longer need to remember what you changed, just that you made a change. The Briefcase will make the necessary changes for you, because it remembers what you have changed. This is referred to as the power of replication. After you have the database set up, keeping it synchronized is very simple. If you have multiple replicas out, they go through this process as each of them is attached to the machine again (or as the floppies come in).

An administrator still needs to be selected to monitor the four tables that were mentioned earlier for any errors that occur if more than two people are using the database. Along the same lines, a process should be developed ahead of time to handle any data disputes so that friction between people can be minimized when someone has to change her database because of a change made by someone else.

A Better Way to Make Use of Replication

Some of the biggest problems with replication in Access occur when a replica database set is poorly implemented. Following are some issues you should be aware of when thinking about using replication:

    The need to make backups of the Design Master.

    Resolving data conflicts without affecting the users of the database.

    Being able to synchronize the databases without causing poor performance for the users.

    The need to make backups without taking the database down and causing downtime for the users.

    Being able to resolve data conflicts without causing downtime for the users.

    Having users run reports off the database without causing performance problems for other users.

Any of these issues can cause a database administrator many headaches, and all of them can cause the database administrator to lose sleep. The hierarchy depicted in Figure 39.18 is a way to help you implement a replica database set to try to make the database administrator's job that much easier.

FIGURE 39.18.

Replication hierarchy.

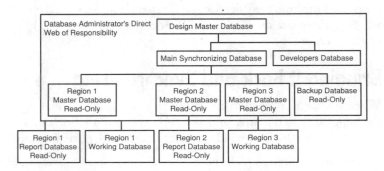

At the top of the hierarchy is the Design Master. Make sure that when you create a Design Master, a backup of the original is created before conversion. Also make sure that no user has the ability to open or work on the Design Master.

The next level is the main synchronize database and the developer's database. The main synchronize database should be the only database that can actually add data to the Design Master, and the developer's database should be the only database that can change the structure of the Design Master.

The next level should be all read-only to ensure that no user can add data directly to these databases. The read-only status also ensures that most data conflicts will occur at this level. The main synchronize database imports the data from here, and then it exports data changes and any structure changes that need to be passed along. The main synchronize database and each main region database fall under the web of the database administrator, and of course, the database administrator is responsible for the Design Master. The backup database is on this level because this database shouldn't directly access the Design Master. This database will be updated after the main synchronize database has been updated with the latest changes from the regions. Only three databases will need to get backed up: the backup database, the Design Master, just in case, and the developer's database. The other databases can quickly be rebuilt from the main synchronize database if something goes wrong. So far the text has concentrated on the database administrator's web and the developer's area. The reason for this is that you want to make sure that this area is clean and easy for the administrator to administrate without much difficulty.

In the hierarchy, there are three regions; this discussion looks only at region 1. This region has a report database and a database that users can update. It's possible that in any region you could find a report database and no user-updated database, as well as the reverse. What you find depends on the demand of the region. The reason for using a report database rather than just the update database is to keep performance at its best. The working database updates the regional master, and then the regional master database updates the main synchronizing database. The regional master database then imports all data changes that the MSD has for it. After the updates have occurred, it then updates the working database, followed by the reporting database.

When and how often the databases are being updated is up to the database administrator. But you don't want to copy large numbers of records across the WAN if you can help it, and you don't want to call the synchronize routine too often if there is no data to be passed on. Also, you need to be able to control the updates to make sure that the database administrator has enough time to fix any data conflicts, thus ensuring that the conflict doesn't ripple its way down the hierarchy.

Summary

In this chapter, you learned what replication is, when you might want to use it, and how to use it. You also read about some potential pitfalls and got some ideas for avoiding them. With this knowledge, you should be ready to identify situations in which replication is the right answer, and you should be able to design and implement the solution.

IN THIS PART

Converting Access Databases

Converting Access 2.0 to Access 95

IN THIS CHAPTER

Although Access 95 has new features, it's compatible with and will easily run older Access databases. It's therefore important to decide early on whether to convert existing Access 1.x and 2.0 applications to Access 95 or whether to use them in their present format.

This chapter deals with converting Access 1.x and 2.0 databases to Access 95. Although throughout this chapter I will refer to conversion from Access 2.0, in most cases the information will apply to Access version 1.x as well. The areas that will be discussed include recommended methods for importing database files from other formats, effective ways to deal with error messages during data conversion, and implementation of code changes.

Planning the Conversion

One of the first decisions you need to make when converting Access 2.0 databases to Access 95 is whether to keep version 2.0 format or convert to Access 95 format. This decision should be based on whether all the users of the database will be upgrading to Access 95. One point to bear in mind is that after the databases have been converted to the new format, they can't be opened with Access 2.0, nor can they be converted back to the Access 2.0 format.

> **TIP**
>
> Even if an Access 2.0 database is converted to Access 95 format, the tables can be exported in a format that can be imported again by Access 2.0.

Using Unconverted Access 2.0 Databases

Access databases created with Access 2.0 can be read from Access 95 without being converted; however, the unconverted databases won't be able to incorporate the new Access 95 features. To maintain an unconverted database that is shared by people who haven't made the upgrade to Access 95 yet, make all modifications to the unconverted database with the Access 2.0 application. Access 95 shouldn't be used to modify or create objects in an unconverted 2.0 database.

> **WARNING**
>
> Access 2.0 uses Access Basic language, whereas Access 95 uses Visual Basic for Applications. This change was made so that Access can be more compatible with other Windows applications. Visual Basic for Applications incorporates new features that can't be executed by the older Access Basic.

Tables in Access 95 that are linked to a database in version 2.0 can be used only when the database is opened from Access 95.

New Features

Improved programming language features can't be used with unconverted Access 2.0 databases. The following are some examples of features unavailable to unconverted 2.0 databases:

- Object-oriented language framework. Procedures and variables can now be declared as Public in form and report modules. This means that they can be made available to other application modules.

- Object-creation syntax. For creating new objects, such as forms or reports, Visual Basic adds the New keyword. This feature is useful because it enables more than one instance of the same form to be open at a time.

- Flexible parameters for procedures. For example, included is the capability to specify parameters by name when calling a procedure. It's now possible to use the Optional keyword, a procedure that can be declared with optional parameters. Also, the ParamArray keyword works with a variable number of parameters.

- Expanded conditional compilation. Code can be specified with the #If...Then and #EndIf statements.

- New data types and statements. Visual Basic includes two new data types: Boolean and Byte. Visual Basic also has more powerful user-defined types, which can include objects.

Converting

After a decision is made to convert the old databases to the new format, the first step is to compile them from Access 2.0.

Compiling Before Conversion

Before you perform the conversion, you must compile Access 2.0 code, including form and report modules, in Access 2.0. To compile Access 2.0 code, follow these steps:

1. Make a backup of the old database.
2. In Access 2.0, open the database to be converted.
3. Open all forms and reports in Design view.
4. Open all modules.
5. Select Run | Compile Loaded Modules.
6. Select File | Save All Modules.

Figure 40.1 shows the Access 2.0 database loaded and ready for compiling.

FIGURE 40.1.

The old database in Access 2.0, loaded and ready for compiling.

TIP

The easy way to start the compile is by clicking the Compile All Modules button on the toolbar.

WARNING

Access displays an error message if it can't compile a database or if further changes are needed. If code errors exist, use Visual Basic debugging tools to examine the values of expressions and variables and trace procedure calls.

Converting the Database

Converting Access 2.0 to Access 95 could very well be an easy task. Some databases, however, won't convert so easily. As a rule of thumb, if the old database doesn't convert, it might be faster to create a new database than to fix the old one.

NOTE

Before converting a file on a network, be sure that you're using the original network account that was used to create the database. This account must have the appropriate security level to perform the conversion.

Convert the database using the following procedure:

1. If the data to convert has linked tables, make sure that the tables are in the directory defined in the link.

2. If the database to be converted is shared, make sure that it isn't opened by other users.

3. Close the old database to be converted if it's open.

4. Select Tools | Database Utilities | Convert Database.

5. The Convert utility prompts the user to select the database to be converted.

6. Select the database and click Convert.

7. Enter a new filename for the converted database and click Save.

8. If the database incorporates security features, convert the workgroup information file as well.

In most cases, the converted database is ready to use now. See the following sections for additional information.

> **TIP**
>
> When an Access 2.0 database is opened from Access 95, a dialog box informs the user that an old database has been loaded. Instructions on how to convert the database are displayed.

Converting Secured Workgroups

Secured workgroup databases require a manual procedure to convert. Follow these steps to convert them:

1. Make sure that Access workgroup users have exited.

2. Start Access without opening a database. Select Tools | Database Utilities | Convert Database.

3. In the Files of Type box, select Add-ins and enter the workgroup information file to convert. These are the files with an .MDA extension.

4. Click Convert. The Database To Convert From dialog box is displayed.

5. In the Convert Database Into dialog box, type a new name for the Microsoft Access 95 workgroup information file, or select a different location if you want to keep the same name.

6. Click Save.

To save the converted file using the new .MDW extension, in the File Name text box, enter the filename with the extension, and in the Save as Type box, select Add-ins before saving the converted file.

One problem with the conversion just described is that users of the older Access workgroup information file that was converted using this procedure won't be able to use a new Access 95 feature, Print User and Group Information, unless they are logged on as members of the Administrator group.

To solve this problem, add the converted workgroup information file from the Access Workgroup Administrator.

> **NOTE**
>
> If it's desirable that all users in the workgroup be able to print the user and workgroup information file, you must create a new workgroup information file. To re-create the original user accounts and groups, reenter the exact names and personal identification.

Potential Conversion Problems

When a version 2.0 (or 1.x) database is converted to Access 95 format, Access converts all the objects in the database, including macros and modules. It automatically changes objects, macros, and procedures to make them compatible with Access 95. In some cases, there might be some problems during conversion. New features might conflict with existing objects and code. The following sections detail some common errors and how to handle them.

Cannot Compile Code

If any code doesn't successfully compile from Access Basic to Visual Basic, one of the following error messages appears:

```
There were compilation errors during the conversion or enabling of this database.
```

```
This database has not been saved in a compiled state. The performance of this
database will be impaired because Microsoft Access will need to recompile the
database for each session.
```

A solution to this problem is to open a module in Design view. Select Run | Compile All Modules. As Access compiles the code, it stops at any line that contains an error. You can then edit the code to correct the error.

When the compilation is complete, check for possible conversion omissions. The conversion utility might fail to convert some syntax. For example, it might fail to modify a `DoCmd` statement, such as the following one, into a `DoCmd` method:

```
DoCmd OpenForm "MyForm"
```

Debug the code or search and replace the faulty entry.

A compile error message might also be received if Access 2.0 modules contain syntax errors. You can avoid this situation by compiling the code under Access 2.0 before converting.

Slow Conversion

If the database is large, the conversion process might take too long to complete. To avoid this problem, use the Import command rather than the Convert Database command:

1. Select File | New Database to create a new Access 95 database.
2. Select File | Get External Data | Import.
3. In the Import dialog box, in the Files of Type box, select Microsoft Access.
4. Click the Look In box to select the drive and folder where the files can be found and then double-click the filename.
5. Click about 20 objects to import.
6. Click OK to import the selected objects.
7. Repeat steps 2 through 6 until all the objects are imported into the new database. Access converts the objects to the new Access 95 format as they are imported.

A drawback is that because the new Access 95 code is more potent, it's bulkier. Importing database objects can therefore increase the size of the database. When the import is complete, compact the database to reduce the size as much as possible. Save the compacted database under a different name to avoid replacing the original database.

Cannot Convert 16-Bit API Calls

If the modules contain 16-bit API calls, you might receive the following error message when converting the database to Access 95:

```
There are calls to 16-bit dynamic-link libraries (.DLL) in modules in this
database. These won't work under Microsoft Windows 95 or Microsoft Windows NT.
```

To resolve this error, change the API `Declare` statements in the converted database to their 32-bit equivalents.

Custom Controls Do Not Convert

When converting a database containing an OLE custom control, you might receive the following error message:

```
One or more forms or reports contains a 16-bit OLE Custom Control with no 32-bit
equivalent. These controls will not function properly under Microsoft Windows 95
or Microsoft Windows NT.
```

This message is displayed when no 32-bit version is found in the computer. Access 2.0 supports 16-bit OLE custom controls, whereas Access 95 supports 32-bit OLE custom controls. When a database is converted to Access 95, the conversion utility can automatically update the control to 32-bit version only if a 32-bit version exists and is registered on the computer.

Table Exceeds Limit of 32 Indexes

The Microsoft Jet database engine version 3.0 has a limit of 32 indexes per table. When a relationship is created and referential integrity is enforced, an index is created for the foreign key table. If the number of relationships exceeds 32, the number of indexes on the foreign key side also exceeds 32.

You might receive the following error message when converting to Access 95 if the database contains a table with 32 or more indexes and relationships:

```
Operation failed. There are too many indexes on table '<table name>'. Delete some
of the indexes on the table and try the operation again.
```

To resolve this error, open the database in version 2.0, and modify the table design to reduce the number of relationships for the primary key table. If possible, remove some indexes from the foreign key table. Try again to convert the database to Access 95.

Name Conflict Stops Conversion

The following error message appears if a module has the same name as a type library, such as DAO, VBA, or Access. The conversion process stops, and Access displays this message:

```
Name conflicts with existing module, project, or object library.
```

To solve this problem, open the database in Access version 2.0, and rename the object.

When a version 2.0 (or 1.x) database is converted to Access 95 format, Access converts all the objects in the database, including macros and modules. Objects, macros, and procedures are automatically changed to make them compatible with Access 95. The conversion utility changes Access Basic to Visual Basic for Applications, used by Access 95.

Access 95 handles most of the issues with the Convert command. Some manual changes might be required, however; for instance:

- Sometimes DoCmd lines aren't converted to the new DoCmd. (dot) syntax. Search and replace the entries.
- All the 16-bit DLL calls will have to be changed to their 32-bit equivalents. They aren't converted automatically. See the later section "Other Conversion Issues."
- To take advantage of the new VBA and DAO syntax, at least part of the application might need to be recoded.
- The exclamation point rather than the dot operator syntax is now used when referencing DAO objects. Search for and change the dot references.

  If you prefer, you can keep the dot references by establishing a reference to the Microsoft DAO 2.5/3.0 Compatibility Library. With the module in Design view, select Tools | References to bring up the References dialog box and enter the dot references.

■ Access 95 might alter the function of some database objects.

Calculating the Time It Takes to Convert

How long the conversion takes depends on several factors, such as how many resources are available and how large the database is. It's advisable to close all open files and programs and to make sure that resources are optimized. The easiest way to do this is to restart Windows to ensure that no application is hovering in the background using resources. The following example demonstrates the time required for conversion:

On a 486DX2-66 machine with 24 MB of RAM, a file with the following objects should take about five minutes to convert:

46 tables
52 queries
17 forms
16 reports
1 macro (2 lines only)
5 modules (more than 5,000 lines)

Changes in the Code Affecting Conversion

When you're converting Access 2.0 databases to Access 95, you might have to make some additional changes manually. The following are some of the problems that might occur.

If errors are reported during conversion, check the data for errors. For example, the old data might contain data in the wrong format, such as if numbers were entered in a text field, or if too many digits were entered in a space-limited field.

■ It's possible that Access conversion didn't assign the correct data type for this field. Edit the text file or spreadsheet to correct errors, and import again. As an alternative, try to complete the conversion by importing the old database again, this time specifying the right data type.

■ It could be that some rows in a data field contain more fields than the number contained in the first row. For example, the second row in a field might have an extra field delimiter character followed by a value that Access can't fit into the new table.

■ When an error message is caused by an error that might result in lost values, Access 95 displays a message indicating that errors occurred during conversion before it actually saves the changes. If this happens, click the Cancel button to avoid the changes, and then click OK to continue and save the changes anyway. No changes will be made.

To fix this error, edit the data from Access 2.0 so that each row has the same number of fields, as shown here:

1. From the Table Design view, click the Data Type column of the field you want to change, click the arrow, and select the new data type.

2. Click Save File to Disk on the toolbar.

3. Attempt the conversion again.

Figure 40.2 shows a typical conversion problem.

FIGURE 40.2.

Error messages typically offer a solution to the problem.

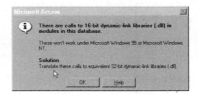

Other Conversion Issues

Programs using the Windows Application Program Interface (API) run differently nowadays. Windows now uses 32-bit rather than 16-bit API calls. The Windows API is a set of dynamic-link libraries (DLLs) containing system-related procedures that include functions, messages, data structures, data types, and statements used in creating applications that run under Windows 95.

For compatibility with Windows 95 applications, Access 95 now uses Visual Basic for Applications and needs to be compatible with 32-bit applications. All these changes make it necessary to alter the old code.

Access conversion will carry out most of the conversions; however, some manual changes will be required to successfully complete some conversions. The following is a list of the required changes:

- Before API is called from Visual Basic, the DLLs first must be declared with a `Declare` statement. After this, they can be called as with any other procedure.

- `Declare` statements need to refer to the correct DLLs. To ensure the referral to the correct DLL files, search and change `Declare` statements. The following table lists the DLL files required for the 16-bit and 32-bit API calls:

16-Bit Windows DLL	32-Bit Windows DLL
User.dll	User32.dll
Kernel.dll	Kernel32.dll
GDI.dll	GDI32.dll

General Conversion Rules

Before converting, check the code using these general guidelines:

- Ensure that any Declare statements refer only to the correct dynamic-link libraries (DLLs). Some library names have been changed. See the preceding information on API calls, and search and change them.

- Bear in mind that functions in the 32-bit Windows API are now case-sensitive, and the names of some functions in the Windows API have changed. Search for and change them.

- Use the CurrentDb rather than DBEngine(0)(0) function to return a Database object variable that points to the current database. You can use DBEngine(0)(0), but it limits the capacity to one variable, whereas the CurrentDb function allows many more variables.

- The code for the DBEngine(0)(0) syntax is still supported, so the Access conversion utility doesn't change it. It would be safer, however, to convert it to avoid potential conflicts later.

- The CurDir function behaves differently than it did in version 2.0 due to the way in which applications interact with Windows 95.

With Access 2.0, CurDir could accomplish several tasks; now, it can only return the current path. The reason for this is that Windows has changed the way it interacts with applications. No action is required for this change, but you just need to be aware of the modification.

Changes to OLE Objects

Visual Basic supplies a Byte data type and new byte functions such as LeftB and RightB. In Access 95, binary data is stored in an array of bytes rather than in a string variable as it was in Access 2.0. The byte functions should be used to manipulate that data. When OLE objects are manipulated in the code, an array of bytes is used to store binary data.

Converting an OLE Object to a Later Version

OLE objects should be converted to take advantage of the features in the current OLE version. Use the following steps:

1. If the objects are unbound, click the object in Form or Report while in Design view, and open the form in Form Datasheet view. If the object is bound, open the form in Form view, find the record to be changed, and click the object.

2. From the Edit menu, point to the corresponding Object command. For example, for a Microsoft Excel object, point to the Worksheet Object and click Convert.

3. In the Convert dialog box, click the type of object to convert the object to. For example, using this method, you could convert a Graph 3.0 object to a Graph 5.0 object.

Working with Variables

You must modify code that creates variables of Integer type to store the channel number and declaration statements. If the `DDEInitiate` function is used to open a `DDE` channel, use the variable that stores the channel number, which is a Long value, as either a Variant or a Long value. In previous versions of Access, the channel number was an Integer value. A solution is to change the code to accept a Long value.

Access 95 can't convert validation rules from Access 2.0 if they contain any of the following elements:

- User-defined functions—functions written in Visual Basic for applications.
- Access domain aggregate functions.
- Total aggregate functions such as these:
  ```
  DAvg function
  DCount function
  DLookup function
  DMin, DMax function
  DStDev, DStDevP function
  DSum function
  DVar, DVarP function
  ```
- References to forms, queries, or tables.
- References to other fields in field validation—user-defined functions.
- References to fields in the current table for record validation can be included in Access domain aggregate functions.

Error Tables

When the Access 95 conversion utility encounters invalid validation rules while converting older Access databases, a table called ConvertErrors is created in the converted database. This table, shown in Table 40.1, contains information to help fix the validation rules.

Table 40.1. The ConvertErrors table.

Field Name	Description
Error	Brief description of the error
Field	Field in the table where the error occurred
Property	Table property where the error occurred

Field Name	Description
Table	Name of the table where the error occurred
Unconvertible Value	Property value that caused the problem

After viewing the table for validation rules that weren't converted, add validation rules as necessary to conform to the following new restrictions:

- To compare the values in two fields, the rule added must be assigned to a record and not to a table field.

- A validation rule can be used for a record to make sure that a field's value is always greater than other values in the same record.

- To add a rule that includes control or user-defined function references, set the rule for a control on a form, not for a field in a table.

Conversion Errors for Numeric Data

Sometimes conversion problems occur when you attempt to convert an Access 2.0 database containing poorly written code. For example, strings containing a percent sign that are assigned to a variable or a field that has a numeric data type won't convert. The database needs to be rewritten for Access 95, and all the percent signs must be searched for and removed. For example, this can be used:

```
intX = "07"
```

But this results in an error message:

```
intX = "7%"
```

A solution for this problem is to search the code for suspected problems and correct them. This isn't an ideal solution, however, so try to avoid the problem by planning ahead when writing code. Whatever code you create today will have to be converted in the near future. Therefore, when you write code, try not to deviate from the expected norm.

Object Macro Changes

To carry out macro actions, Access 95 uses the DoCmd object and its methods rather than the DoCmd statement that was used in Access 2.0 to carry out a macro action. Access 95 automatically converts any DoCmd statements and the actions that they carry out.

The following actions have changed:

- The CopyObject Action: If you specify the current database as the Destination Database argument for the CopyObject action, the copied object doesn't show up in the database immediately. To view or use the copied object, the database must be closed and reopened.

- The TransferSpreadsheet Action: Access 95 can't import Microsoft Excel version 2.0 spreadsheets or Lotus 1-2-3 version 1.0 spreadsheets. If the converted database contained this macro, converting the database changes the Spreadsheet Type action argument to Microsoft Excel version 3.0.

Integer Versus Property Changes

When you're converting code from version 2.0 to Access 95, the code must be changed to accept a Long value. In previous versions of Access, the hWnd property of a form or report was an Integer value, whereas in Access 95, the hWnd property is a Long value. For example:

```
If Not IsZoomed(Screen.ActiveForm.hWnd) Then
    DoCmd.Maximize
EndIf
```

The CLng*(expression)* should now be used instead of Val. This is done to provide conversions from other data types to a Long. In this way, different decimal separators can be recognized.

Changes to Property Objects

Because Access 95 uses Visual Basic for Applications instead of Access Basic, some code functions have been changed. The following examples of code must be searched for and rewritten in Access 95:

- In Access 2.0, object variables in the code used to refer to a Category property object. In Access 95, the Category property for Form, Report, and Control objects isn't supported. Search the code and change or remove old code as required.

> **NOTE**
>
> Think ahead before investing the time to correct converted code. In some cases, it might be much easier to rewrite the code. The rule of thumb is, if the code looks complicated and time-consuming, it's better to rewrite it.

- In forms or reports, Access 95 returns the Form or Report object that contains the control when the Parent property in code control or in an expression is done. There are two exceptions to this rule:

    In attached labels, Access 95 returns the Parent property label that the control is attached to.

    In an option group, the option group controls are sent.

Converting Add-Ins and Libraries

Before you use add-ins or library databases created with Access 2.0, you need to convert them to Access 95 format. The Access 95 conversion utility will convert them automatically, but add-ins might require some manual changes. For example, to use the objects that the add-ins sometimes contain in addition to Visual Basic, a Windows Registry key set must be created. This is required because information that was previously stored in an .INI file is now stored in the Registry.

Referencing Library Databases

Applications using add-ins and library databases need to have links or references to each library database in the Windows Registry. It isn't necessary to create a Registry key set for library databases, but you must create a reference from each application that uses the library database.

To add references to library databases, perform the following actions:

1. Open a Visual Basic module.
2. Select Tools | References.
3. In the References dialog box, check all appropriate references.
4. Click the up- and down-arrow buttons to prioritize the references.
5. Click OK to continue.

Figure 40.3 shows how to create references to library databases.

FIGURE 40.3.

References to one or two library databases can be created.

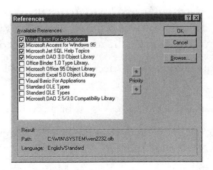

Circular References

Circular references between libraries could be implemented in Access 2.0. For instance, previously it was possible for procedures in library A to call procedures in library B, and procedures in library B could call procedures in library A.

The problem is that Visual Basic for Applications doesn't support circular references. This means that an error will result if you attempt to create a reference from B to A after using references from A to B in the References dialog box. Don't use circular references for Access 95.

Existing circular references in an Access 2.0 database must be removed before conversion. Search the database for circular references, and remove them.

Custom Add-Ins Menus

When custom Add-ins menus are converted, the Add-ins submenu is moved from the File menu to the Tools menu. The reason for this is that Access 95 has the submenu in this new location.

Converting Large Databases

Access 95 code is considerably larger, and requires more storage space, than Access 2.0 code. This means that the 64 KB barrier is reached much faster in Access 95 than in Access 2.0. If the Access 2.0 applications are very large, an Out of Memory error message is displayed while an attempt is being made to convert a large database. The only solution at the moment is to break large modules into multiple smaller modules. In addition, it might help to avoid loading Wizards when loading large modules. The modules should be divided from Access 2.0 into several modules before conversion. Unfortunately, Access 2.0 doesn't have Access 95's built-in capability to split the code. It takes an unrealistic amount of time to perform this task manually.

Converting Macros

When you're converting Access 2.0 to Access 95, you should also convert macros on forms or reports to Visual Basic format in order to take full advantage of the Access 95 format. After the database is converted, convert the macros as described next.

In form or report Design view, select Tools | Macros | Convert <Form or Report>'s Macros to Visual Basic.

To convert a particular macro to Visual Basic code, follow these steps:

1. Open the database containing the macro. For example, open the converted 2.0 database Northwind.mdb.
2. In the Database window, click the Macros tab and select a macro.
3. Select File | Save As | Export.
4. In the Save As dialog box, click Save as Visual Basic Module. Click OK.
5. In the Convert macro dialog box, select the Add error handling/trapping to generated functions option and the Include macro comments option. Click Convert.

Figures 40.4 and 40.5 show some available macro conversion options.

FIGURE 40.4.

The available macro conversion options.

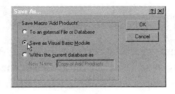

FIGURE 40.5.

The final options before conversion.

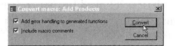

These are the changes the Macro Conversion Wizard performs to convert a single macro to Visual Basic code:

- The macro conversion utility creates a new procedures module. The same names that existed in the original Macro Names are kept.
- Macro actions are converted to appropriate DoCmd methods in Visual Basic.
- If a macro action doesn't have a DoCmd equivalent, the Macro Conversion Wizard takes the following actions:

Command	Action
AddMenu	Comments out these lines in the code. A message is displayed to notify you of this.
MsgBox	Uses the MsgBox function.
RunApp	Uses the Shell function to run other applications.
RunCode	Uses the Call statement and runs the function in Visual Basic.
SendKeys	Uses the SendKeys statement.
SetValue	Sets the value in Visual Basic.
StopAllMacros	Uses the End statement.
StopMacro	Uses the Exit Function statement.

If...Then statements are used rather than expressions contained in the macro's Condition column.

> **NOTE**
>
> How a macro is converted depends on the contents. If the Condition column contains a full reference to a control in a form or report, such as is the case with Forms!MyForm![LastName], Access uses If...Then statements. If the reference refers to a control name such as [LastName], Access uses a With...End With or a CodeContextObject statement.

Summary

This chapter discussed techniques for converting Access 2.0 to Access 95. Clearly, the decision of whether to convert or leave the databases in the original format must be based on the available resources. It's important to bear in mind, however, that eventually the databases in the older format will need to be converted. If you decide to convert, it's reassuring to know that although some databases will need further code manipulation, after they have been compiled by Access 2.0, many databases will easily convert to Access 95.

INDEX

SYMBOLS

A

X-Y-Z

Add to Your Sams Library Today with the Best Books for Programming, Operating Systems, and New Technologies

The easiest way to order is to pick up the phone and call

1-800-428-5331

between 9:00 a.m. and 5:00 p.m. EST.
For faster service please have your credit card available.

ISBN	Quantity	Description of Item	Unit Cost	Total Cost
0-672-30837-1		Visual Basic 4 Unleashed (book/CD)	$45.00	
0-672-30779-0		Real-World Programming with Visual Basic 4, Second Edition (book/CD)	$49.99	
0-672-30743-X		Gurewich OLE Controls for Visual Basic 4 (book/CD)	$39.99	
0-672-30796-0		Visual Basic 4 Performance Tuning and Optimization (book/CD)	$49.99	
0-672-30789-8		Developing Client/Server Applications with Visual Basic 4 (book/CD)	$49.99	
0-672-30797-9		Microsoft SQL Server DBA Survival Guide (book/CD)	$49.99	
0-672-30706-5		Programming Microsoft Office (book/disk)	$39.99	
0-672-30739-1		Excel for Windows 95 Unleashed (book/CD)	$39.99	
0-672-30474-0		Windows 95 Unleashed (book/CD)	$35.00	
1-57521-041-X		The Internet Unleashed 1996 (book/CD)	$49.99	
1-57521-040-1		World Wide Web Unleashed 1996 (book/CD)	$49.99	
1-57521-066-5		Navigating the Internet with Windows 95, Deluxe Edition (book/CD)	$39.99	
❏ 3 ½" Disk		Shipping and Handling: See information below.		
❏ 5 ¼" Disk		TOTAL		

Shipping and Handling: $4.00 for the first book, and $1.75 for each additional book. Floppy disk: add $1.75 for shipping and handling. If you need to have it NOW, we can ship product to you in 24 hours for an additional charge of approximately $18.00, and you will receive your item overnight or in two days. Overseas shipping and handling adds $2.00 per book and $8.00 for up to three disks. Prices subject to change. Call for availability and pricing information on latest editions.

201 W. 103rd Street, Indianapolis, Indiana 46290

1-800-428-5331 — Orders   1-800-835-3202 — FAX   1-800-858-7674 — Customer Service

PLUG YOURSELF INTO...

THE MACMILLAN INFORMATION SUPERLIBRARY™

Free information and vast computer resources from the world's leading computer book publisher—online!

FIND THE BOOKS THAT ARE RIGHT FOR YOU!

A complete online catalog, plus sample chapters and tables of contents give you an in-depth look at *all* of our books, including hard-to-find titles. It's the best way to find the books you need!

- STAY INFORMED with the latest computer industry news through our online newsletter, press releases, and customized Information SuperLibrary Reports.

- GET FAST ANSWERS to your questions about MCP books and software.

- VISIT our online bookstore for the latest information and editions!

- COMMUNICATE with our expert authors through e-mail and conferences.

- DOWNLOAD SOFTWARE from the immense MCP library:
  - Source code and files from MCP books
  - The best shareware, freeware, and demos

- DISCOVER HOT SPOTS on other parts of the Internet.

- WIN BOOKS in ongoing contests and giveaways!

TO PLUG INTO MCP: → WORLD WIDE WEB: **http://www.mcp.com**

GOPHER: gopher.mcp.com

FTP: ftp.mcp.com

Home Page   What's New   Bookstore   Reference Desk   Software Library   Macmillan Overview   Talk to Us

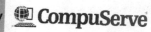

Installing the CD-ROM

The companion CD-ROM contains sample databases developed by the authors, plus an assortment of third-party tools and product demos. The disc is designed to be explored using a browser program. Using Sams' Guide to the CD-ROM browser, you can view information concerning products and companies and install programs with a single click of the mouse. Follow the next steps to install the browser.

Windows 3.1 Installation Instructions

1. Insert the CD-ROM into your CD-ROM drive.
2. From File Manager or Program Manager, choose File | Run.
3. Type `<drive>`setup and press Enter. `<drive>` corresponds to the drive letter of your CD-ROM. For example, if your CD-ROM is drive D:, type `d:\setup` and press Enter.
4. The installation creates a Program Manager group named Access 95 Unleashed. To browse the CD-ROM, double-click the Guide to the CD-ROM icon inside this Program Manager group.

Windows 95 Installation Instructions

1. Insert the CD-ROM into your CD-ROM drive. If the AutoPlay feature of your Windows 95 system is enabled, the setup program will start automatically.
2. If the setup program doesn't start automatically, double-click the My Computer icon.
3. Double-click the icon representing your CD-ROM drive.
4. Double-click the Setup.exe icon to run the installation program. Follow the on-screen instructions that appear. When the setup ends, the Guide to the CD-ROM program starts so that you can begin browsing immediately.

Following the installation, you can restart the Guide to the CD-ROM program. Press the Start button and select Programs | Access 95 Unleashed | Guide to the CD-ROM.

> **NOTE**
>
> The Guide to the CD-ROM program requires at least 256 colors. For best results, set your monitor to display between 256 and 64,000 colors. A screen resolution of 640 × 480 pixels is also recommended. If necessary, adjust your monitor settings before using the CD-ROM.